THE SOCIETY FOR
POST-MEDIEVAL ARCHAEOLOGY
MONOGRAPH 10

FACING OTHERNESS
IN EARLY MODERN SWEDEN

FACING OTHERNESS
IN EARLY MODERN SWEDEN

TRAVEL, MIGRATION
AND MATERIAL TRANSFORMATIONS
1500–1800

Edited by

MAGDALENA NAUM and FREDRIK EKENGREN

THE BOYDELL PRESS

Details of previously published titles are available from the Society

First published 2018
The Boydell Press, Woodbridge

ISBN 978 1 78327 294 5

The Boydell Press is an imprint of Boydell & Brewer Ltd
PO Box 9, Woodbridge, Suffolk IP12 3DF, UK
and of Boydell & Brewer Inc.
668 Mt Hope Avenue, Rochester, NY 14620–2731, USA
website: www.boydellandbrewer.com

The publisher has no responsibility for the continued existence or accuracy
of URLs for external or third-party internet websites referred to in this book,
and does not guarantee that any content on such websites is,
or will remain, accurate or appropriate

A CIP catalogue record for this book is available
from the British Library

This publication is printed on acid-free paper

Printed and bound in Great Britain by
TJ International Ltd, Padstow, Cornwall

FSC
www.fsc.org

MIX
Paper from
responsible sources
FSC® C013056

CONTENTS

ILLUSTRATIONS

FIGURES

TABLES

The editors, contributors and publishers are grateful to all the institutions and persons listed for permission to reproduce the materials in which they hold copyright. Every effort has been made to trace the copyright holders; apologies are offered for any omission, and the publishers will be pleased to add any necessary acknowledgement in subsequent editions.

LIST OF CONTRIBUTORS

Per Cornell   Department of Historical Studies, University of Gothenburg, Sweden

Christina Dalhede   Department of Economy and Society, Unit for Economic History, University of Gothenburg, Sweden

Lu Ann De Cunzo   Department of Anthropology, University of Delaware, USA

Fredrik Ekengren   Department of Archaeology and Ancient History, Lund University, Sweden

Magnus Elfwendahl   Municipality of Uppsala, Uppsala, Sweden

Matti Enbuske   Department of History, University of Oulu, Finland

Adam Grimshaw   School of History, University of St Andrews, UK

Jens Heimdahl   The Archaeologists, The National Historical Museums, Hägersten, Sweden

Lisa Hellman   Department of History and Cultural Studies, Freie Universität Berlin, Germany

Kimmo Katajala   Department of Geographical and Historical Studies, University of Eastern Finland, Joensuu, Finland

Magdalena Naum   Department of Archaeology and Heritage Studies, Aarhus University, Denmark

Jonas M. Nordin   The Swedish History Museum, Stockholm/Department of Archaeology and Ancient History, Uppsala University, Sweden

Risto Nurmi   Faculty of Humanities, Program of Archaeology, University of Oulu, Finland

Kenneth Nyberg   Department of Historical Studies, University of Gothenburg, Sweden

Carl-Gösta Ojala   Department of Archaeology and Ancient History, Uppsala University, Sweden

Joachim Östlund   Department of History, Lund University, Sweden

Claes B. Pettersson   Sydsvensk Arkeologi, Sweden

Christina Rosén   The Archaeologists, The National Swedish Museums, Mölndal, Sweden

Anna-Kaisa Salmi   Faculty of Humanities, Program of Archaeology, University of Oulu, Finland

Göran Tagesson   The Archaeologists, The National Swedish Museums, Linköping, Sweden

Annemari Tranberg   Faculty of Humanities, Program of Archaeology, University of Oulu, Finland

PREFACE

The majority of papers in this book emerged from a conference "Encountering the 'Other' – Understanding Oneself: Colonialism, Ethnic Diversity and Everyday Life in Early Modern Sweden and New Sweden" organized at Lund University in 2013 within the "GlobArch" network and with the support of the Craoford Foundation, the Swedish Research Council and Elisabeth Rausing Memorial Foundation. The conference created an interdisciplinary and international forum to discuss social and cultural developments in early modern Sweden, especially its multifaceted involvement in colonial expansion – as a country having colonies of its own, procuring, exchanging and consuming colonial goods and sharing ideologies of European supremacy. The main theme of the conference was the reaction to the broadly understood newness brought about by the expansion and rise of intercontinental connections as well as the construction (ideological and material) of otherness and sameness in early modern Sweden, New Sweden and other colonies.

The conference and this collection appear at an exciting time, when the traditional national framework of research and focus on political and economic history of the Swedish "Era of Greatness" shifts towards transnational history writing, scrutinizing Sweden's entanglement with the European and global world. This shift is coupled with a greater interest in materiality within the field of history. It is also accompanied by a rapid development of post-medieval archaeology in Sweden and Finland, which offers new perspectives on a range of interesting questions, such as the characteristics of early modern culture, multiculturalism, self-fashioning through material objects, the selective nature of consumption, the rise of modernity and material engagements with novelties and imports. The collection reflects the wide-ranging research directions taken in the fields of history and historical archaeology, and their potential to rewrite the history of early modern Sweden. Our goal is to present, with an international audience in mind, a picture of early modern Sweden that is rarely considered in the available general English-language works on the kingdom: an image of an early modern Swedish society and culture deeply affected by cultural transformations, mobility and connections with the increasingly global world of the 17th and 18th centuries; a country, society and culture not left on the margins of Europe, disengaged from contemporary currents, but rather drawn into and developing dialogical relationships with the rest of Europe and the known world. Set in the socio-political context of a rapidly growing and changing early modern Sweden, the essays in this book consider the character of contemporary encounters with novel ideas, commodities and people within and beyond of Sweden's borders, and their impact on identities and both popular and learned culture in Sweden. They discuss how these intercultural meetings, transformations and novel material culture were perceived and mediated in everyday life and how they impacted on discourses of the familiar and the foreign, the same and the other. The subjects of the essays range from the state's ideology and technology of control to appropriation of classical architecture and urban planning; from interactions in colonial New Sweden and Sápmi to cultural encounters in Africa, South America and Asia; from the appropriation of imports and foreign culture in urban environments to engagement with novel fashions in aristocratic circles; from the translocal connections of Dutch, British and German merchants residing in Sweden to the experiences of peasants moving within the kingdom's borders. By taking this broad and interdisciplinary approach and by departing from traditional themes of political and social history, the collection offers a different and progressive view of early modern Sweden.

This anthology would not be possible without the generous support of the Society of Post-Medieval Archaeology and Boydell & Brewer. We are particularly grateful to Audrey Horning and Francis Eaves for their insightful commentary and copy editing and to Rohais Haughton for making production of this book such a smooth process.

Magdalena Naum, Aarhus University
Fredrik Ekengren, Lund University

ABBREVIATIONS

GLA	Landsarkivet i Göteborg, Gothenburg
GUB	Gothenburg University Library, Gothenburg
HB	Hagströmer Medico-Historical Library, Stockholm
KVA BBS	Bergianska brevsamlingen, Royal Swedish Academy of Sciences, Stockholm
LAV	Landsarkivet i Vadstena, Vadstena
LSL LC	Linnaean Correspondence, Linnaean Society of London, London
LUB	Lund University Library, Lund
RA	Riksarkivet, The National Archives of Sweden, Stockholm
RADK	Rigsarkivet, The Danish National Archives, Copenhagen
RJB	Archivo del Real Jardín Botánico, Madrid
RR RA	Riksregistraturet, The National Archives of Sweden, Stockholm
SSA	Stockholms Stadsarkiv, Stockholm
TKUA	Tyske Kancellis Udenlandske Avdelning, The Danish National Archives, Copenhagen
TNA	The National Archives, London
ULA	Landsarkivet i Uppsala, Uppsala
UUB	Uppsala University Library, Uppsala

I
Material Transformations

Introduction

MAGDALENA NAUM AND FREDRIK EKENGREN

The first chapters of this book focus on material transformations in early modern Sweden. Ideological and cultural currents, such as Lutheranism, Classicism and the Enlightenment; the political and economic currents of European colonial expansion, in which Sweden played an active part; the growth of intercontinental trade and Sweden's ambition to shed the image of a backwater: all these factors had implications for consumption and the engagement with material culture. Between the beginning of the 16th and the end of the 18th century, the material world, practices and habits of Swedish citizens underwent considerable shifts, though the dynamics and effects of these changes were not even. The court and aristocratic circles were quick to embrace and adopt diverse European fashions and ideas. One of these was the passion for furnishing private museums, collecting and displaying souvenirs, specimens of flora, fauna and curiosa from the near and far corners of the world. Colonial expansion and growing participation in trans-oceanic travel provided eager collectors with ever-growing supplies of marvellous objects for their collections. As argued by Jonas M. Nordin, these cabinets of curiosities were not innocent sites. Displaying one's own interests, knowledge and erudition through the coveted material culture of the world signalled, in symbolic and literal terms, one's own power and supremacy. The fashion for collecting exotic objects reflected and expressed in visible form the hegemonic European aristocratic worldview, which distinguished between the "self" and the "other".

It was not only collectables that the colonies supplied, however. An array of colonial and exotic commodities, such as tobacco, sugar and porcelain, made their way into Swedish households. These and other novelties established a visible presence in large towns located at the intersections of international trade, while their reception was often slower and more selective at locations further from commercial and cultural centres.

The material transformations experienced in early modern Sweden were reflections of the increasing connections with the culture and markets of continental Europe stimulated by the kingdom's rise on the political stage. This, in turn, required a certain level of cultural openness and a promotion of foreign influences. However, the adoption of novel materials and ideas depended on a willingness and desire among different groups in society to embrace the new. One can call this process a negotiated response to newness, which included acceptance, manipulation and reworking of new objects to fit established practices. Some of these complex engagements are described by Anna-Kaisa Salmi, Annemari Tranberg and Risto Nurmi in their chapter on foodways in Tornio. The inhabitants of this northern town, which was established in the 17th century, responded to the new material culture and cultural impulses by selective acceptance, appropriation and improvisation, creating an urban culture that was a hybrid and dynamic mix of different traditions. A range of different attitudes to traditional and foreign foods is also discussed by Jens Heimdahl. The methods of beer brewing investigated by the author remained relatively stable and conservative in the countryside, but might have been less so in the urban centres, which were more open to foreign influences and hosted sometimes sizable migrant communities.

The new commodities and changing relation to material culture affected not only the sphere of consumption. Material practices proved to be viable ways to intervene in the lives of ordinary citizens, to instil ideologies and new values, by the state apparatus. Through the 17th and 18th centuries, numerous novelties were introduced to facilitate the processes of ordering, overseeing and controlling the population of the kingdom. By the mid-18th century, all citizens were annotated in the appropriate statistical column; their property was measured, mapped and valued; their taxes calculated; their social position and obligations fitted into a strict hierarchical structure. The state imposed a commodifying, mechanical and objectifying view of people and nature and tried to disentangle their former relationships. The advances of modern state bureaucracy, redesigning of landscapes, experiments in social engineering and processes of rationalization are described by Per Cornell, Christina Rosén and Göran Tagesson. Maps and town plans are examples of material artefacts that visualized landscape (and people in it). These two-dimensional representations of space, produced in abundance throughout the early modern period, were reductive: they projected ideas of order and rationality, abstracting away people's intimate relationships with places and obscuring deep emotional and cultural connections to them. Göran Tagesson, taking the example of the town of Kalmar, illustrates how a Lutheran ideology of hierarchically structured society, and contemporary ideals of order and symmetry, influenced town planning, division of urban space and town architecture. The ideal sketch of the town plan and its materialization emphasized a social ideal – a society in equilibrium, where everything was put in its proper place in order to achieve balance and harmony.

The two themes that unify these chapters are the connections between material culture and identity, and transfigurations of material objects and the ideas they represented. Physical artefacts, whether buildings, house furnishings, everyday objects or drawings and maps, were actively used to project self-images, to negotiate values and tastes. They were also manipulated; fitted into existing practices, traditions and norms.

Tracing *Other* in 17th-Century Sweden

Per Cornell and Christina Rosén

No single concept can convincingly describe 17th-century Sweden. We suggest an approach with focus on variability to get a better grip on the socio-economic processes, and search for new kinds of connections and relations, in which we address the other; the socially defined otherness; the ascribed otherness. But we also search for Other, alterity and difference as such, in the frame of the Swedish "heartland". We focus mainly on the large variability in settlements, on ways of transforming settlements, on the making of new settlements and the ways of representing settlements.

Addressing the 17th century is no easy task. There are so many different kinds of society, of human (and, we must add, non-human) lives. The roles of European superpowers in this period were not straightforward, nor are they easy to comprehend. There has been and still is a tendency towards Eurocentric history writing, which makes us think from a European perspective. The violent history of the colonies in the Americas is a tragedy, and this traumatic experience is, most certainly, first and foremost the result of European expansion. But life in the Americas cannot, and this is important, be *reduced* to the European. The history of the Americas is far more complex and intricate, and we are only starting to grasp this interesting theme.[1] Africa was violently tapped into via the slave trade during the same century, which also had a wide range of long-lasting effects. The 17th century is also marked by the fall, in 1644, of the Ming dynasty, a dynasty which had been powerful and influential far beyond the borders of China. The Moghuls still dominated much of south Asia. And along the eastern and southern borders of Europe this was a period in which the Ottoman Empire, although weakened, continued to play an important role. It was the time of the horrors of the Thirty Years' War in which Europe became the scene of a destructive, partially anarchic and protracted era of violent conflict. This era of horror ended with the peace treaty at Westphalia, which established new political rules of lasting importance. The 17th century was also an era of technical developments, socio-economic change and fervent religious activities.

It is against this background we must address developments in the Swedish realm, a sparsely-populated kingdom in the far north. In traditional Swedish history writing, this era is often called the Age of Greatness. As can be seen from a map from this period (Fig. 1.1), the borders of the country were quite different from those of today. In terms of general politics, Sweden tried to play a role in the larger conflicts on the European continent, not least during the Thirty Years' War. Sweden also developed a particular interest in expansion eastwards, which is a salient feature of the kingdom. The end of the Thirty Years' War was not the end of the Swedish wars, which were a recurrent feature throughout the 17th century.

Much could be said about the Swedish possessions in the Baltic, in the northern parts of today's Poland and Germany, and the small colonies in *Other* parts of the world. The activities of the Swedish army, in different parts of Europe, is an important topic, and much research on the subject is still to be done. Recently, the importance of women in the military campaigns has been discussed in an interesting way.[2] But in this short contribution we wish to address questions related to the perception and construction of landscape in what could be construed as the heartland of the Swedish realm at the time. The intention is, above all, to point to some potential areas for future research and to suggest some possible lines of investigation.

THE QUESTION OF *OTHER* AND THE SWEDISH REALM IN THE 17TH CENTURY

Was there *other* or *Other* in 17th century Sweden? What actually is *Other*? These questions are not easy to address, still less to answer. The intricacy of the term *other* and its highly varied uses make it necessary to consider certain theoretical and methodological issues. Tzvetan Todorov,[3] for example, used the term *Other* in relation to Columbus's arrival in the Caribbean and in relation to the conquest of the Americas in general. One of his arguments has to do with Cortez and the conquest of the allied states in the Mexican highland, and the tremendous Aztec city of Tenochtitlán. In this case, the Europeans were initially greatly impressed and inspired by this huge and highly regulated city, which was illuminated all through the night. Later on, the conquerors were more inclined to downplay this grandeur. In a sense, the initial positive surprise related to the experience of profound difference, as the Aztec world was unlike the familiar sights of Spain or Europe in general. It was, at the same time, something to which it was possible to relate, with its grid-plan cities, agrarian-based economies and unequal societies with an advanced political form. There were points in common between the worlds apart. With the process of conquest, large segments of the elite among the conquerors developed a rhetorical form whereby the conquered were regarded as not only different, but also distinctly inferior. Cortez, argues Todorov, was astute, in the sense that he understood the importance of learning local habits and customs, which turned out to be helpful in the process of conquest. The Cortez family became an important component of Spanish colonial power in the region, and the family held on to seigneurial power in Oaxaca up to the Mexican revolution in the 20th century. Todorov argues that the capacity to understand difference, what he terms *the other*, is a powerful tool, which can be used to be benign and friendly, but can equally facilitate a bloody conquest.

The term *other* has been much in use in certain brands of social theory during recent decades. It frequents postcolonial debate, but is not limited to that field of scholarship. In some schools of philosophy, psychology and psychoanalysis, *other* (French *autre*) was used to denominate what is common: "normality". Such a use can be identified, for example, in the works of Lacan in the 1950s.[4] The *I* develops and grows, according to this famous structuralist and psychoanalyst, in relation to *the other*, which is, in this case, the "normality" (e.g. language, structural patterns) within a given "Symbolic

Fig. 1.1 Sweden, Denmark and Norway in 1645 (map by Joan Blaeu).

Order". In later debates there was a conceptual shift, and *the other* became what is distinctly *not* normal, in relation to a certain "population".[5] This significant shift in the use of the concept is important and should be kept in mind.

The French philosopher Emmanuel Levinas played an important role in redefining the concept of *Other*. Levinas initially showed an enthusiastic interest in German scholars such as Martin Heidegger and Hans-Georg Gadamer. Inspired by this reading, he developed an argument about the infinite difference, to which we return below. However, he also became increasingly sceptical of, and avoided to a certain extent, the way of thinking espoused by these scholars; he considered it "Greek" thinking (which, in the case of these philosophers, according to Levinas, includes the Biblical tradition). Instead, Levinas looked to the Hebrew tradition.[6] He questioned the attention given to Ulysses and the subject of eternal home return in European tradition. While Gadamer talked of *Heimatlosigkeit* (lack of *Heimat*, of homeland),[7] Levinas favoured a discussion of Abraham (the Abraham of the Hebrew tradition), who set out on a journey searching for a new land, never to return to the point of origin, never to *hope* for a return. The land of Canaan is the hope for humanity, to Levinas's way of thinking. Here lies the difference between Gadamer/Heidegger on the one hand, and Levinas, on the other: while the former celebrate belonging to a known, age-old traditional intentional space, Levinas celebrates the creation of a new land. And, of course, we must add, this new land is, actually, the *colony*. Both themes – of the importance of homeland and the importance of the colony – can, of course, be found already incipient in early modern Europe. The period saw a considerable increase in European colonies across the world. There is also an interesting link between homeland and colony, whereby the colony is, in a sense, transformed into a new homeland.

There is, however, a theme common to Gadamer and Heidegger and to Levinas: the quest for a kind of "absolute" sameness. The particularity in Levinas is the introduction of *Other* as the unknown. Levinas's argument can be roughly summarized as follows. There is an Ego which is the same, in identity with itself;[8] that is, entirely coherent with itself. But there is also *Other*, which is the Infinite difference. The advent of a dialogue, a positive relation, a relation between same and *Other* which has no disdain, disregard, no possession, is, according to Levinas, an extremely rare occurrence: it is "metaphysics", in his terms.

Levinas's general argument inspired the French philosopher Jacques Derrida, who worked extensively on questions of the infinite Other.[9] Derrida criticized the idea of Ego as the absolute same, and as a coherent *one*. He looked at this problem as yet another example of philosophy of the absolute presence. Like so many western philosophers, Levinas saw speech and sight as prime senses. They are pure, and non-destructive, almost as if they were outside of history. In looking into each Other's faces and listening, there is a possibility for the metaphysical, according to Levinas. For Derrida, there is no time/space outside "history", and thus no horizon for an "un-polluted" same or an "un-polluted" other, no origin of meaning "before history".[10] Further, this history must always, for Derrida, be contextual; it cannot be completely lifted from its teleological or eschatological horizon.[11] Thus, *if* the term "metaphysics" should be used in this context, contrary to Levinas's pure metaphysics, it would imply an economy and the possibility of the existence of violence.[12] It is in this economy, by its opening, that an access to the other and Other will be determined.[13] This general economy, in Derrida's terms, is *différance*.[14]

Derrida's arguments have played an important role in postcolonial debate and find echoes in the works of Homi Bhabha and Gayatri Chakravorty Spivak's. Spivak stressed the "impossibility" of communication between the colonizer and the colonized, while Bhabha suggested the existence of a "Third Space of Enunciation", a short-lived opening for a kind of communication, which often implied using cultural elements from the others as a tool or even a weapon against them. The use of the third space is not limited to the colonizers, argues Bhabha; it can also be used by the colonized against the colonizer.[15]

Derrida made also a crucial distinction between *autre* and *autrui*, which has been translated from French as *the other* and *Other*. The difference is fundamental, *the other* being what is defined as different, what is considered to be the difference in a particular social setting; the ascribed otherness. This ascribed otherness may, in certain cases, affect the social setting and transform social relations and conditions. *Other*, on the other hand, signifies alterity, what is truly unknown. Given the idea of difference in Derrida's philosophy, the same is never pure. From this it follows that alterity can be found also within our own society, and at times in ourselves. All of us have some *Other* in us, of which we are little or not at all aware. *Radical alterity can thus already be in place, residing in ourselves; it does not only arrive from the "outside".*

Bhabha has pointed, in his discussion of the Third Space of Enunciation, to the existence of an in-between field. At this point, we might recall Lacan's argument about the *Other* as the norm, and Levinas's distinction between sameness and *otherness*; us and them. In both cases, the social is understood as made up of two elements. But, as has been stressed by several scholars, ranging from Peirce to Marx, society requires three constituents. And, as discussed by Derrida in his work on dissemination,[16] there are always more than three elements (the fourth is paramount to him); there is simply a wide field of social, economic, political, and cultural variability and similarity.

Another relevant point is the question of what could be other and *Other*. The human encounter must, of course, be the focus of our attention. But the appearance of hitherto unknown phenomena can often precede the human encounter. In the case of the Americas, what the indigenous population first met of "Europe" was often an animal or an object, or a particular disease, rather than an actual human being. But we must not exaggerate the role of materiality in a *social* sense. The material culture in general may have several immediate effects, and human constructions may also carry certain human social traces. But it is mainly through the wider encounter, beyond the individual, beyond the *two*, that a deeper social effect is produced.

Let us be explicit. Insisting on the importance of complexity, of looking closer, of going into details at times, is not to state that there is nothing general, or that broader views are irrelevant. Quite the opposite. By paying more attention to details, by means of a critical perspective, by looking closer at variability, we will certainly find not only distinct differences but also more evidence of similarities, and new assemblages, which were previously difficult to observe.[17] It is such an approach we would suggest for studying 17th-century Sweden. But it is an early beginning, a search, an effort, almost a prelude to a fascinating field of study.

SWEDEN DURING THE 17TH CENTURY

It is difficult to describe Sweden during the 17th century. The country did not rely upon just one but upon several sources of power. Simple models looking at the state as the only source of control, complete totalitarian rule, do not work at all. Furthermore, there were differences over time in the relative power of the state, and state institutions became more developed towards the end of the century than they were at its beginning. The parliament convened more frequently as the century progressed; and although it was dominated by the elite, it included representatives of other sections of society, among them certain categories of peasant (excluding, however, the landless).

During long periods of war, the state depended on the nobility, compensated for its support and financial credits by landed estates. Peasants who owned their own land and who were not subordinated to a given landlord constituted a large group and had a relatively strong position in Sweden. Protracted warfare meant however that they were under constant pressure of conscription, and a large number of peasants opted to give up their independence and become subject to a landlord, which lowered the threat of being drafted. As a result, the strength of the nobility increased further. The state finally reacted and embarked upon a complex process of power reduction, confiscating the land of certain noble families.[18] The role and power of the state thus varied considerably and was affected too by conflicts within the royal family, within the nobility and between the royal family and the aristocracy. The clergy and the Church in general were central to elite control over vast resources. This group was not homogeneous. While some clergymen were exceedingly wealthy, others had only marginally better living conditions than the peasants.

Special production activities – for example mining, wood processing and metallurgy – played an economic role, and were dominated by particular rich families[19] or the state. Certain mercantilist manufacturing activities also existed, initiated both by the state and by private entrepreneurs.[20] These activities were reliant upon the work of unskilled labourers and skilled artisans, who were semi-autonomous, recruited and employed at various projects. A minority of Swedish society consisted of traders and merchants of different kinds living in the rapidly developing urban centres. At the other end of the urban spectrum were the poor, whose lives were ridden by insecurity. The majority of the population lived in the countryside. The social and economic position of peasants varied significantly, ranging from formally free peasants (paying taxes to the king), to peasants subject to landlords, to landless labourers and helpers.

Sweden was not uniform in terms of culture and ethnicity. It encompassed numerous ethnic minorities, immigrants (with varying degrees of wealth) and other groups, including Sami populations. Treaties and colonial advance extended the borders of the realm, adding to its cultural complexity. Expansion northwards is sometimes described as colonial in intent and execution, and the silver mining projects in those parts of the country are occasionally compared to colonial exploitation in the Americas, particularly the Caribbean.[21] Finally, it must be stressed that regional differences within Sweden were considerable, even in terms of basic demographics.[22]

THE DANNIKE WOMAN – AN OTHER WOMAN, AN OTHER LANDSCAPE?

Human-made landscape plays an important role in creating boundaries and can reinforce exclusion of the predetermined other. But the landscape also plays a role in relation to the unknown, and may make Other almost invisible; or, in the case of an actual encounter with Other, an unknown landscape may be of key importance. The early modern landscape in Sweden was far from homogeneous. There was, as should be evident from the examples in this chapter, a wide range of different settlement and landscape forms, and space was physically and mentally categorized. The core was visualized as a built-up area, plots with farm buildings, common spaces, cabbage patches and small pasture areas. It was surrounded by the infield area with fields, meadows and some pasture. The outland (*utmark*) was furthest away from the settlement, but still played an important role in the economy. It was an area for pasture and for the extraction of various resources, such as iron, timber and peat, but it was also connected with the supernatural, with dangers in the forms of imaginary beings. People were not supposed to settle in the outland, with the exception of the very poor and landless and outcasts. This is a part of the landscape that can be considered an *other* area.

This is not where you would expect to find a burial from the early modern period. But in a peat bog in the parish of Dannike, in the province of Västergötland, an interesting discovery was made in 1942. A coffin with the remains of a woman in her twenties, dead from unknown causes and buried at some point between 1680 and 1720, was uncovered. She was physically handicapped and must have walked with a limp. The woman was wrapped in a man's jacket, clad in a pair of woollen stockings and a pair of shoes specially constructed to compensate for her limp. Her head was severed from the body, but it is unclear whether this happened when the body was found or at an earlier stage.[23] In the coffin a few objects were also found – a clay pipe and four Swedish copper coins of low denominations.

This woman was evidently denied a burial in the churchyard. In this respect at least she was outside official society; she was evidently *the other,* in the most negative sense. She was placed in an*other* landscape; she was removed from the parish and put to rest out of sight in the *utmark.* The Dannike woman might have been considered a witch or a criminal. She might have been killed and the body hidden in the bog. However, no record has been found of her death, nor of any trial. And the burial itself raises many questions. Whatever her status she was nonetheless considered a member of society in some sense, insofar as she was given a burial in a coffin, resembling a proper churchyard burial.

The most important question to ask is whether or not this is a singular event. Could there be more cases of similar exclusion, of which we are not aware? We cannot answer these questions here. But this case clearly illustrates the exclusion and the other, and also, perhaps, provides a hint of *Other* in this woman.

17TH-CENTURY LANDSCAPES AND MAPPING

Moving from this particular case to a larger perspective, let us address map-making and landscape change. In certain approaches to (colonial) landscape production and map-making, it is argued that the change of a landscape made by a colonizer entirely destroys any prior elements. Such is the argument in a famous study by John Noyes on the German colonies in South-West Africa (today Namibia) in 1884–1915. He illustrates how the inhabitants of the region at the beginning of the German colonial project were considered as "without cultural space" (*Raum*), and how the colonizers worked hard to define, or rather create, tribal territories.[24] Noyes also gives examples of German rhetoric in conquering new territories: the space had to be mapped, "written" in German blood.[25] The making of grave-fields for Germans was also part of the strategy of taking possession of the land.[26] This aspect of the newness and the lack of communication with or respect for the existing landscape and its meanings is an important aspect of many colonial endeavours. Noyes, inspired by the French philosopher Deleuze, pushes his argument to an extreme, insisting that the German mapping project created an entirely new landscape. To some extent World System models like that of Immanuel Wallerstein similarly tended to describe the new World System as a new form, which entirely obliterated any prior elements.[27] Perhaps this kind of argument goes too far. Generally, the reorganization and reconceptualization of landscapes is not total; there are certain traces of prior forms, and of parallel developments, rests or "cinder" as it is termed by Derrida. Thus, when discussing 17th-century landscape and map-making, we must see the new, the change, but we should not forget to look for the traces of *Other*. One important aspect here is that *Other* does not always relate to age-old traditions, but can also be *Other* kinds of newness, innovations introduced parallel to those planted by a colonizer.[28]

The *Lantmäteriet* (the Swedish mapping, cadastral and land registration authority) was founded in 1628, during the reign of Gustavus Adolphus. Between 1630 and 1655 more than 12,000 cadastral maps were produced, with detailed descriptions of farms, hamlets, villages and towns. These early maps were mainly used as an inventory of the assets of the Swedish realm, a kind of illustrated cadastral register. In the later 17th century, maps were produced mainly for taxation purposes. They were also made when land was sold or otherwise transferred to new owners. These maps give us a unique insight into certain aspects of the cultivated and inhabited landscape and its organization during the 17th century and subsequently.[29] The surveyors were instructed to register in great detail the arable land, meadows, pasture, woods and forests, fishing waters, mills and other resources as well as boundaries and to record all these features on the maps. The selection of what was relevant to include was mainly (though not entirely) related to the particular interests of the individual map maker. One can note that different kinds of settlement are drawn in the same way: a small town is recorded in a fashion similar to that used for a hamlet or village. The Falköping/Kungslena example (see below) illustrates this.

Map-making introduced a new way of looking at and using landscapes. The maps were part of the collections of books, exotic objects and various paraphernalia that were "must-haves" for the ruling classes. They also served particular systems of control, related to taxation, for example. But their production and use also had other immediate implications. Knowledge of the landscape and how to work it, and the rights to fields and to commons, were all deeply embedded in daily practices and rooted in tradition.[30] Well into the 18th century we can see that, in conflicts over boundaries and access, the oldest men in a village played an important role in explaining how it "had always been done", according to their memories.

Drawing a standardized image of a landscape meant taking out the feel, look and smell of it, transforming it into a piece of paper, looking at it from above. What was lost in the process was the connection between the landscape and the people that lived on and in it. On the ground, there were inscribed not only clearly visible features like fields and pasture but also less evident elements, socially significant boundaries, tales and stories of the past, aspects that were not of major interest to surveyors. By disconnecting parts of the landscape in its transformation into a two-dimensional image, a path was cleared for later re-makings, like large-scale enclosure and the subsequent alienation of the peasant from the land.

The map itself, the artefact, can then, in a sense, be viewed as "other" in relation to the actual landscape. But we should also remember to look closely at the maps for traces of *Other*, for the things present in them that may be overlooked yet in some way carry an alterity. There are certain unexpected features, which have been registered by certain surveyors, and these are, of course, highly relevant. This particular field of study has hitherto been little explored. What has been addressed are mainly references to a distant past, in the form of indications of particular kinds of monuments which aroused interest among members of the elite.

ENCLOSURES AND NEW LANDSCAPES

Enclosures and other new elements, such as a town or a palace introduced in a landscape, enforced several changes in the existing relationship to places. New buildings and other arrangements were sited "on top" of existing structures, which were then demolished or incorporated into the new structures. These older layers could be viewed as obsolete and taken out completely, or put to new use (with some rearrangements), but they could also be used as a bridge between the old and the new: older forms might be iterated to form a connection between already accepted structures and the new ones.

Putting new structures into a landscape can also result in the disconnecting of previously linked nodes within it. Cutting off roads, fencing in gardens or hunting grounds, digging a town dike, building a toll fence around a new town, consolidating arable land: all these force people to choose new ways of moving around the landscape. New patterns are formed. A landscape, then, can be viewed as a palimpsest where the activities of previous generations can be discerned under the traces of later activities. The arrival of other scrapes some of the older "text" off the landscape, but does not wipe it out completely.

Large scale enclosure did not happen in Sweden until the later 18th century. However, in the 17th century some newly-formed estates or old ones given as fiefs to new owners were enclosed, the peasants being forced to move out and new agricultural practices implemented. The case of Sperlingsholm in the province of Halland is a good example of how otherness was imposed on territories coming under Swedish rule in the 1650s. The estate was formed around 1650 when the medieval hamlet of Klockerup with seven farms was acquired by the first Swedish governor in Halland, Baron Caspar Otto Sperling. Sperling (1596–1655) was born in Mecklenburg and arrived in Sweden in 1612 to serve in the army. As governor in Halland he was responsible for enforcing Swedish rule in the recently acquired province. He wiped out the hamlet with its farms, and enclosed the land to form a single estate. A manor house was erected with a formal garden. Traces of the farmland of the former hamlet can still be seen in the landscape in the form of strip parcelled fields (*bandparceller)* underlying the 17th-century enclosure.[31]

HAMLETS, VILLAGES AND TOWNS

When addressing settlements, it is important to avoid rigid concepts and models in the first step of analysis. When looking at the distribution of settlements based on certain selected variables, repeated patterns will be detected which can then be regarded as major elements of that particular cultural landscape. Not only houses or living quarters will be discussed, but other kinds of uses of the landscape as well. The choice of variables we study is of course of major importance, and will depend on certain general theoretical concerns. Among relevant variables we might mention settlement size, settlement density, and repeated spatial patterning in the distribution of different elements, like houses of different kinds. Working this way, certain traditional concepts – hamlet, village, town – will often turn out to be problematic. In the case of 17th-century Sweden, there were large differences between regions and subregions, and these differences are not irrelevant details, but rather key points, even if we attempt to construct a broader general perspective. It is indeed through the study of such variation, and through detecting similarities and differences on a micro-scale, that it becomes possible to make general observations. In Sweden, the base for agricultural activities was an individual small farming unit, but in general more than one family could operate in the same location, in a particular hamlet. A unit that was termed a "farm" in cadastral registers was not infrequently inhabited by several adult individuals, often organized in different households, often with separate housing arrangements and collectively responsible for the paying of rents. Our knowledge of the spatial arrangements in such farms and small hamlets is still limited, and more archaeological fieldwork at such locations would help to elucidate our understanding of everyday life and work. The early modern Swedish landscape was also dotted with larger villages, some quite substantial in size and population. Many contemporary towns consisted of fewer than 50 households: these have been termed "micro-towns" by historian Sven Lilja.[32] There were also other kinds of settlements, such as sites oriented towards a manufacturing activity or special production (*bruk*), for example metallurgical works. These settlements were in some cases comparable to smaller towns in terms of area, population size and built structure. Landed estates of various sizes may also be mentioned, like the large Läckö castle in Västergötland.

Looking more closely at these different forms of settlement one can notice that villages or towns, and even other settlements such as mining sites, were in several cases fairly similar as regards spatial organization. The two maps in Fig. 1.2 show the settlements

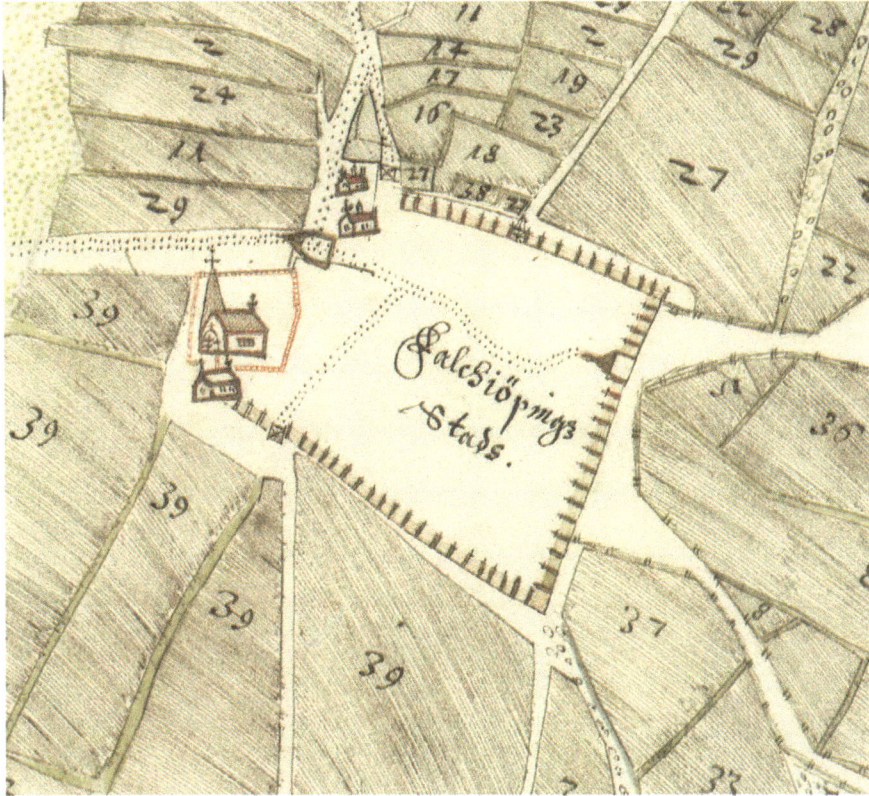

Fig. 1.2 Falköping in 1645 and Kungslena in 1650 (maps courtesy of Lantmäteriet, corrected and redrawn by Christina Rosén).

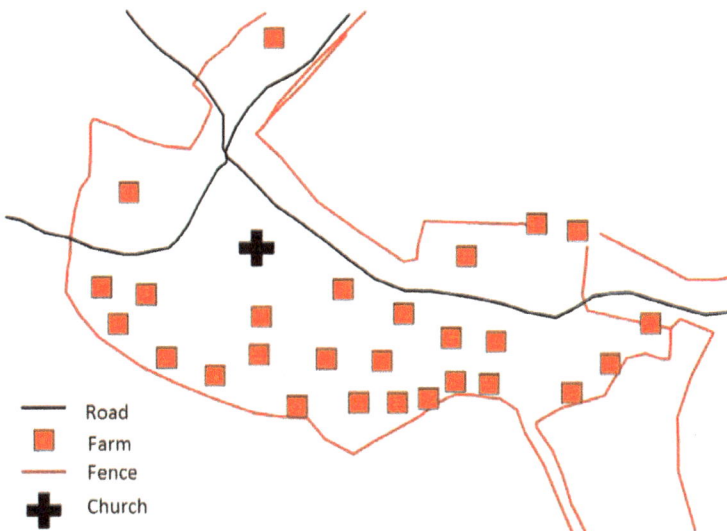

— Road
■ Farm
— Fence
✚ Church

of Falköping in 1645 and Kungslena about 1650, both in the province of Västergötland and around 60 km apart. At this time Falköping had about 40 plots, Kungslena over 30 plus some crofts. In both cases we see a single, enclosed settlement area with gates. The church has a prominent location and the buildings are surrounded by fields and meadows. We see two settlements, topographically and in terms of spatial layout similar in many ways, but which represented two distinct phenomena in a formal administrative and judicial sense: Falköping was a town, Kungslena a village. One major difference between these settlements was legislative, regarding the specific rights in terms of trade and taxation in force in the two locations.

Archaeological investigations in the smallest towns often reveal very few traces of buildings, objects and other aspects of material culture. Various reasons for this have been cited, including sparse populations, large unbuilt areas within towns, and taphonomic conditions.[33] From one point of view these "micro-towns" can be seen as not distinctly different from agrarian hamlets or villages. Many inhabitants farmed to a great extent and had farming as their main source of income. But from another point of view we can see that an urban setting often incorporated certain differences as to the details concerning the construction of dwelling houses, foodways, cooking and eating utensils and gardening. Both inventories and archaeological findings show that some types of object were found almost exclusively in urban environments. A general picture emerging from probate inventories is that kitchenware and cookware were more varied in urban environments, which might be associated with more differentiated food consumption in towns; this has not been systematically investigated, but deserves further study.[34] The role of trade is certainly a possible key factor here, but we should perhaps take into consideration and include in systematic studies other variables such as individual wealth and occupation. Above all, more fieldwork is necessary, not least in larger villages. The extent of general distribution of particular material elements in smaller "towns" is still not entirely known, as is the material variation at "village" sites. Further, regional differences must be addressed in more detail. The variations between regions in general terms, irrespective of settlement type, may well be far greater than the differences between two settlement types in one region.

It is not thus always entirely obvious whether a given location should be defined as urban or rural. Several very small towns lost their town rights for various reasons: at times formal factors (population decline, for example), at times for more political reasons such as competition between towns regarding trade.[35] There are also examples of towns being moved to new locations, sometimes permanently, but in at least one case returning to the old site after a while: Nya Lödöse moved to another location in 1547 and was then re-established at its former site around 1570. What where the consequences of such relocations for the people who lived in these places? Did they continue to live as before, or did something change – and if so, what? Would it be possible to discern changes in such items as material culture, cultivation and food habits? How did older structures survive and change when a place changed its (formal) function? These questions need to be further investigated.

Beyond these issues, we could ask whether the pre-defined ideas of "village" and "town" are, in some ways, obstacles to research. It could well be that these traditional concepts are of no or of low operative value, and that we actually lack a serviceable basic terminology. The term "micro-town" is hardly an ideal choice, for example. We probably need new categories. Starting afresh might help us to find new kinds of patterning, allowing us to develop a somewhat more nuanced knowledge of 17th-century Sweden, and perhaps introduce some unknown *Other*.

WHO ACTUALLY TRADED? PEASANT TRADESMEN IN NORTHERN BOHUSLÄN

To make things even more complex, formal regulations concerning trade were not always followed and exceptions were allowed. Trade and non-agrarian manufacture were normally confined to urban environments, but some trading, which could be on a considerable scale, took place outside the towns. During the 17th century, contacts between the Netherlands and the Norwegian-Swedish coastal province of Bohuslän were intense. Sailors from North Bohuslän served in the Dutch East and West India companies and Dutch merchants shipped large quantities of wood and timber from the forested areas around the present-day border between Norway and Sweden. Between 1616 and 1619, foreign ships visited harbours in North Bohuslän 67 times, to cite one example.[36] Sailors brought back continental goods to their homes in North Bohuslän, including ceramics, shoes, cloth, salt and herrings. Excavations have produced several kinds of pottery such as Dutch faiance and whitewares, which are normally not found in agrarian settings, and early 17th century clay pipes of Dutch and English origin.[37]

Close contacts between Holland and North Bohuslän are documented at least since the early 1600s. There were several small harbours in the North Bohuslän area but no town before 1676, when Strömstad was founded at one of these harbours. According to Swedish law only a few towns and cities were allowed to engage in foreign trade, and after Bohuslän came under Swedish rule in 1658 the trade with Dutch skippers was prohibited. The prohibitions seem to have been quite effective, since there are very few post-1658 Dutch finds in the archaeological material. Probate inventories on the other hand show that Dutch objects stayed in households for several generations.[38] These can be viewed as non-human *other*, in the form of faïence plates and fancy clothing, coming from abroad but given a role and a meaning in the rural households of North Bohuslän.

Other examples from the archaeological record indicate instances in which certain rules and regulations were not always respected. There were strict regulations in the 17th century as to slaughtering, which was prohibited in towns outside specially designated areas. However, the archaeological evidence from the town of Jönköping demonstrates fairly clearly that this general rule was not adhered to, and that slaughtering was conducted in several individual homes.[39] Similarly, evidence from written sources and archaeological evidence from the town of Nya Lödöse demonstrate that hazelnuts (a product in high demand especially in the Netherlands) were illegally traded with neighbouring peasants.[40]

OPEN RESISTANCE

Non-compliance with official rules could lead to forms of open resistance against the elite and the state. The territories conquered from Denmark developed something like guerrilla warfare against the Swedes. But resistance also occurred in the traditional domains of the Swedish king, occasionally manifesting itself as armed rebellion, but in general taking the more peaceable form of failing to fulfil taxation demands. This resistance has been addressed in Swedish historiography employing a variety of rhetorical formats.[41] In 1980, Silvén-Garnert and Söderlind entitled their book on the topic *Another Sweden*. Linde has produced a study on Dalarna, one of the regions with high levels of resistance,[42] which, as demonstrated by Lars Ersgård,[43] saw major changes in settlement organization in the 17th century. This was an area with strong and independent peasant groups, which had developed new strategies for dealing with changes imposed from outside. It was not a question of it being a "backward" area; rather it was a highly developed region that resisted certain forms of state directive, such as the organization of settlement for taxation purposes, and enclosure.

NEW KINDS OF SETTLEMENT

The period from *c.* 1050 until the end of the 13th century was marked by a significant trend involving the development of new kinds of site and increased urbanization. Most Swedish towns of the historical era (i.e. since *c.* 1000 AD) were established during this period, mainly in the south. But we must not forget that the years from 1500 to 1700 also saw many new towns being founded, mainly in the western and northern parts of the realm, including Finland (which was part of Sweden until 1809). The number of towns increased from 69 in the 1570s to 102 in the 1650s. Even more towns were added after 1650; in several cases older towns were relocated to new sites, and some existing towns were restructured according to new grid plans.[44]

The *intention* behind establishing and reorganizing early modern towns was often economic and/or military control. Locating a new town in a landscape meant introducing other in the form of officers, state officials and new regulations. But the individual cases were all different. Much can be said about the way in which a new town or town plan was received and how the people affected by the change acted and reacted: for example, the loud protests of the wealthy burghers in Halmstad when the town was reconfigured in 1619 after a fire and the reorganization meant the loss of their former prestigious plots near the square. Other inhabitants did not have the means to protest, but we can see that they rebuilt their houses on their old plots shortly after the fire despite explicitly being told to wait for the king's engineer to mark out the new grid plan.[45] In other places, the building of a new town meant rearranging an existing agricultural landscape to make way for the town, and ensuring that the townspeople received enough farmland to provide for their own needs.

GOTHENBURG AND BORÅS: CONTRASTING SETTLEMENTS

Gothenburg in 1644 (Fig. 1.3) was a young city, founded around 1620, designed to be a fortress, a harbour and a place for commerce. It was built on the shore of the Göta River, on marshland that was drained by means of Dutch technology. The city combined the functions of the earlier towns in the area as well as the older Älvsborg fortress, twice conquered by the Danes (1563 and 1611) and returned to Sweden in exchange for a very large ransom. The plan was drawn by military experts and the image and idea of the city are what we could call – for want of a better word – "modern". We may note that the map shows only the city itself and we are told nothing about its surroundings. It looks like an island in the middle of nowhere.[46]

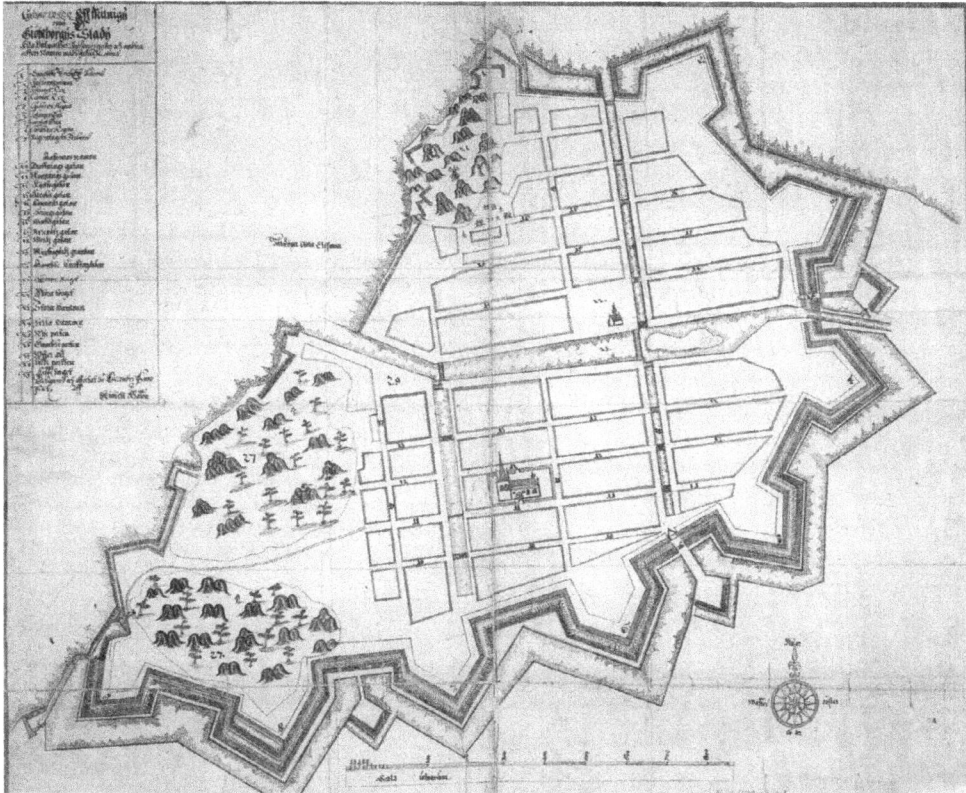

Fig. 1.3 Gothenburg in 1644 (map courtesy of Gothenburg City Museum, after Bramstång and Nilsson Schönborg 2006, Fig. 19).

Approximately 60 km to the east of Gothenburg, Borås was also founded in 1620. This town was not designed for military purposes, but to control the thriving commerce in the area. Here, a flourishing trade in iron objects, textiles and turned wooden objects took place at least from the 16th century, carried out by peasants who travelled over large areas of Sweden (and sometimes Norway, when prices were better). Conflicts between peasants and authorities are documented, as well as complaints from the Swedish mining area of Bergslagen when peasants chose to take their commodities instead to Norway.[47] This type of trade was in fact forbidden, but commonplace nonetheless. Protests from nearby towns, especially the small town of Bogesund, in the middle of this area, increased from the late 16th and early 17th century, however. The towns wanted the neglected regulations to be upheld and the peasants' trade stopped. At the same time a growing Swedish administration needed money. By building a town and imposing strict regulations on the rural trade, the Crown would gain income as well as greater control in the area.[48]

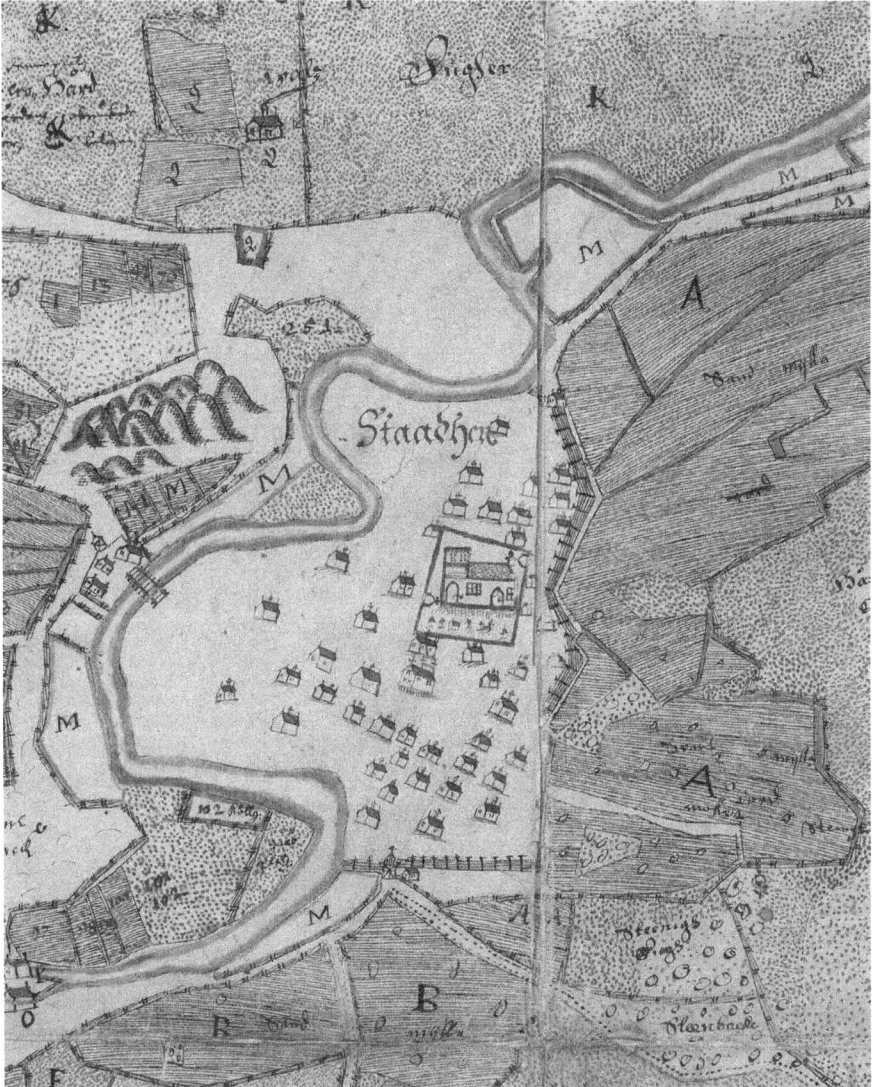

Fig. 1.4 Borås in 1646–7 (map courtesy of Lantmäteriet).

The 1646 map of Borås is not in any way similar to the 1644 Gothenburg map (Fig. 1.4). It lacks a clearly visible town plan, although some kind of order is suggested in the way the house symbols are placed. No streets are marked, no square; only houses and a church. The town is surrounded by an irregularly-shaped fence, marking off the town area from its surrounding fields. The fields, however, are only partially fenced against those of nearby hamlets and it is clear that the townspeople in Borås cultivated their land and grazed their animals in close cooperation with neighbouring peasants. One reason for this close contact is that the town was built on already occupied land. The hamlet Torpa was situated here and its land became the agricultural basis for the new

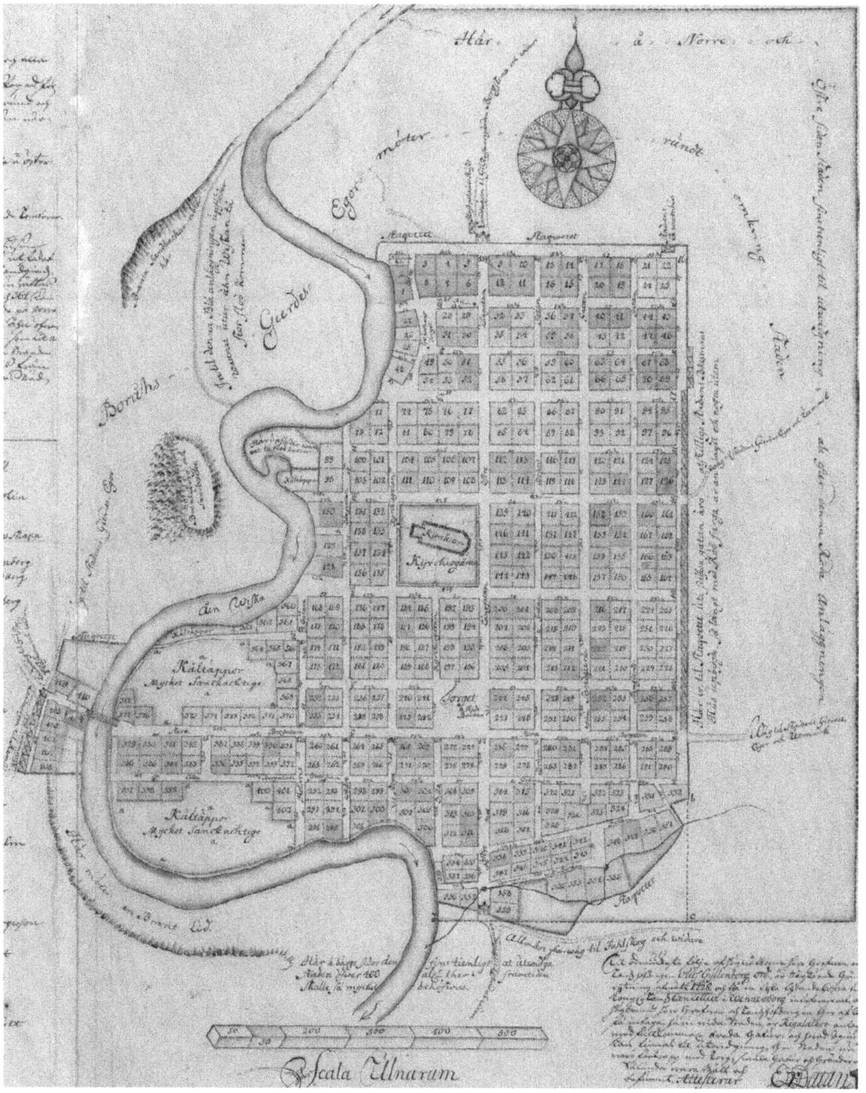

Fig. 1.5 Borås in 1728 (map courtesy of Lantmäteriet).

town. In short, the town of Borås is depicted as was Falköping/Kungslena. If the accompanying text did not designate Borås as a town, its status would not be at all obvious.

In these maps we can discern two distinctly different ways of mapping towns and cities. One is rooted in the view of the town as part of the agricultural landscape, not much different from hamlets and villages around it. The other is rooted in military and engineering/fortification traditions, in which other aspects of the city were stressed. The 1728 map of Borås (made after a devastating fire in 1727) gives us a different picture (Fig. 1.5). Streets are now laid out on a grid plan with plots of mainly the same size, and the former irregular fence has been replaced with a straight one. Fields around the town are not marked. Here, the town is depicted as something quite separate from its surrounding countryside. Certainly the maps were made for somewhat different purposes; but the differences are still striking.

CONCLUSIONS

We have demonstrated the importance of looking at variability, not as an end in itself, but in order to gain a better understanding of the complex socio-economic processes operating within 17th-century Sweden. If such lines of investigation are pursued further, we are convinced *Other* will emerge in the evidence. There is a need to look further at basic concepts, introduce new ones, and revise others. No single concept can convincingly describe 17th-century Sweden. In *Das Kapital*, Karl Marx observed that the 16th and the 17th centuries saw a large number of simultaneous modes of production. Discussing Europe and its colonies, he listed feudalism, slavery, mercantilism, semi-autonomous peasants, and semi-free artisans. Marx stressed also the importance of merchants, adding to this already complex picture. It is not possible here to further examine this analysis; but it could be argued that there were even more modes of production and types of economic engagement than those considered by Marx. He talked too little about the role of the state as an institution, and also missed other factors in his study of the emerging modern economic systems. Future studies should consider expanding on Marx's perspective. Finally, we suggest a greater emphasis upon addressing and exploring variability, and searching for new kinds of connection and relations, to support a new understanding of 17th-century Sweden in which the *other* and *Other* are no longer entirely invisible.

NOTES

1   See Cornell 2015.
2   Sjöberg 2008.
3   Todorov 1982.
4   See e.g. Cornell 2000.
5   Derrida 2000.
6   Levinas 1967.
7   Gadamer 1985, 59.
8   Levinas 1961.
9   Derrida 1967b; 2000.
10 Derrida 1967a; 1967b.
11 Derrida 1967b.
12 Derrida 1967c.
13 Derrida 1967c.
14 Derrida 1967a.
15 Bhabha 1994; Spivak 1999; see Cornell & Galle 2004; Cornell 2007.
16 Derrida 1972.
17 See Hjertman & Cornell 2015.
18 Strindberg 1937; Herlitz 1974.
19 E.g. Per Nilsson Höök and the experiments in ironworks at Engelsberg; cf. Högberg 1975, 60–3.
20 Pettersson 2014.
21 Awebro 1983; Lönn 2004.
22 Palm 2001, 86-92.
23 Ljunge 2007.
24 Noyes 1992, 263–75.
25 Noyes 1992, 252–8.
26 Noyes 1992, 260–1.
27 Wallerstein 1974–80.
28 Cornell 2015.
29 Tollin 1991.
30 Johnson 1996, 114.
31 Connelid & Mascher 1992.
32 Lilja 1996, 54.
33 Rosén 2013.
34 Rosén 2013.
35 Broberg 1981, 10; Klackenberg 1983, 10.
36 Framme 1986, 35.
37 Rosén 2010
38 Framme 1986, 35; Rosén 2010.
39 Bramstång Plura *et al.* 2012; Vretemark 2012.
40 Paring & Forsblom Ljungdahl 2014.
41 See for discussion Silvén-Garnert & Söderlind 1980; Linde 2009.
42 Linde 2009.
43 Ersgård 1997.
44 Ersgård 2013a.
45 Rosén 1999.
46 Bramstång & Nilsson Schönborg 2006.
47 Palm 2005, 20.
48 Palm 2005, 27.

BIBLIOGRAPHY

Awebro, K. 1983. *Luleå silververk: ett norrländskt silververks historia.* Luleå: Norrbottens museum.

Bhabha, H. 1994. *The Location of Culture.* London: Routledge.

Bramstång, C. (ed.) 2006. *Fästningen Göteborg: samlingar till stadens arkeologi.* Mölndal: Avdelningen för arkeologiska undersökningar, Riksantikvarieämbetet.

Bramstång, C. & Nilsson Schönborg, G. 2006. 'Kartmaterial och verklighet', in Bramstång 2006, 35–170.

Bramstång Plura, C., Carlsson, K. & Rosén, C. 2012. 'Arkeologisk undersökning. Nio tomter i Jönköping. Småland, Jönköpings stad, kvarteret Dovhjorten (Druvan), RAÄ 50'. UV Rapport 2012:119. Stockholm: Riksantikvarieämbetet.

Broberg, B. 1981. *Kungsbacka – Gåsekil.* Medeltidsstaden, rapport 25. Stockholm: Riksantikvarieämbetet och Statens historiska museum.

Carrer, F. & Gheller, V. (eds) 2015. *Invisible Cultures: Historical and Archaeological Perspectives.* Newcastle: Cambridge Scholars Publishing.

Cipolla, C. N. & Hayes, K. H. (eds) 2015. *Rethinking Colonialism: Comparative Archaeological Approaches.* Gainesville: University Press of Florida.

Clark, P. (ed.) 1995. *Small Towns in Early Modern Europe.* Cambridge: Cambridge University Press.

Connelid, P. & Mascher, C. 1992. 'Medeltida åkrar vid Sperlingsholm', *Utskrift* 2, 19–26.

Cornell, P. 2000. 'Identidad, proyección y género en los textos producidos por americanistas suecos en la primera mitad del siglo XX', in Medina 2000, 99–117.

Cornell, P. 2007. 'Unhomely space: Confronting Badiou and Bhabha', in Cornell & Fahlander 2007, 100–22.

Cornell, P. 2015. 'Colonial encounters, time and social innovation', in Cipolla & Hayes 2015, 99–120.

Cornell, P. & Fahlander, F. (eds) 2007. *Encounters, Materialities, Confrontations: Archaeologies of Social Space and Interaction*. Newcastle: Cambridge Scholars Press.

Cornell, P. & Galle, H. 2004. 'El fenómeno Inka y su articulación local: Reflexiones desde el sitio de El Pichao, Valle de Santa María (Tucumán)', in Cornell & Stenborg 2004, 211–17.

Cornell, P. & Stenborg, P. (eds) 2004. *Local, regional, global: Prehistoria, protohistoria e historia en los Valles Calchaquies*. Anales N.E. 6. Gothenburg: Instituto Iberoamericano, Göteborgs universitet.

Derrida, J. 1967a. *De la grammatologie*. Paris: Les Éditions de Minuit.

Derrida, J. 1967b. *L'ecriture et la différence*. Paris: Seuil.

Derrida, J. 1972. *La dissémination*. Paris: Seuil.

Derrida, J. 2000. *Le toucher, Jean-Luc Nancy*. Paris: Galilée.

Ersgård, L. 1997. 'Det starka landskapet: en arkeologisk studie av Leksandsbygden i Dalarna från yngre järnålder till nyare tid'. Riksantikvarieämbetet Arkeologiska Undersökningar skrifter 21. Stockholm: Riksantikvarieämbetet.

Ersgård, L. 2013a. 'Tidigmoderna städer i Sverige', in Ersgård 2013b, 30–54.

Ersgård, L. (ed.) 2013b. *Visioner och verklighet: arkeologiska texter om den tidigmoderna staden*. GOTARC Series C, Arkeologiska skrifter 76. The Early Modern Town 1. Gothenburg: Institutionen för historiska studier, Göteborgs universitet.

Framme, G. 1986. *Vätte härad: ur gångna tiders historia*. Skrifter utgivna av Bohusläns museum och Bohusläns hembygdsförbund 25. Uddevalla: Bohusläns museum.

Gadamer, H-G. 1985. *Das Erbe Europas*. Frankfurt: Suhrkamp.

Herlitz, L. 1974. *Jordegendom och ränta: omfördelningen av jordbrukets merprodukt i Skaraborgs län under frihetstiden*. Gothenburg: Institutionen för Ekonomisk historia, Göteborgs universitet.

Hjertman, M. & Cornell, P. 2015. 'Urban marginality: Other, iteration and materiality. Archaeologies of urban life and death in an Argentinian setting (Villa Muñecas, San Miguel de Tucumán)', in Carrer & Gheller 2015, 75–90.

Högberg, S. 1975. 'Engelsberg 1399–1869', in Holtze *et al.* 1975, 39–108.

Holtze, B., Nisbeth, Å., Adamson, R. & Nisser, M. (eds) 1975. *Swedish Industrial Archaeology: Engelsberg Ironworks. A Pilot Project*. Jernkontorets bergshistoriska skriftserie 18. Stockholm: Jernkontoret.

Johnson, M. 1996. *An Archaeology of Capitalism*. Oxford: Blackwell.

Klackenberg, H. 1983. *Bogesund*. Medeltidsstaden, rapport 42, Stockholm: Riksantikvarieämbetet och Statens historiska museum.

Levinas, E. 1961. *Totalité et infini: Essai sur l'extériorité*. La Haye: M. Nijhoff.

Levinas, E. 1967. *En découvrant l'existence avec Husserl et Heidegger*. Paris: Vrin.

Lihammer, A. & Nordin, J. (eds) 2010. *Modernitetens materialitet: arkeologiska perspektiv på det moderna samhällets framväxt*. The Museum of National Antiquities Studies 17, Stockholm: Statens historiska museum.

Lilja, S. 1995. 'Small towns in the periphery: Population and economy of small towns in Sweden and Finland during the early modern period', in Clark 1995, 50–76.

Linde, M. 2009. *I fädrens spår?: bönder och överhet i Dalarna under 1700-talet*. Hedemora: Gidlund.

Ljunge, M. 2007. 'Dannikekvinnan – ett unikt mossfynd', *Fässingen: från Borås och de sju häradena* 50: 173–6.

Lönn, B. 2004. *I skuggan av ett silververk: människor under stormaktstiden*. Stockholm: Svenska förlag.

Medina, M. C. (ed.) 2000. *Mujeres en poder de la palabra*. Serie Haina 2. Gothenburg: Instituto Iberoamericano, Göteborgs univeristet.

Nordman, A.-M., Nordström, M. & Pettersson, C. (eds) 2014. *Stormaktsstaden Jönköping: 1614 och framåt*. Jönköping: Jönköpings läns museum.

Noyes, J. K. 1992. *Colonial Space: Spatiality in the Discourse of German South West Africa 1884–1915*. Chur: Harwood Academic Publishers.

Palm, L. Andersson, 2001. *Livet, kärleken och döden: fyra uppsatser om svensk befolkningsutveckling 1300-1850*. Gothenburg: L. Palm.

Palm, L. Andersson, 2005. *Borås stads historia, 1. Stad och omland fram till 1800-talets mitt*. Lund: Historiska Media.

Paring, M. & Forsblom Ljungdahl, V. 2014. *Hasselnötter – en exportvara*, http://www.staden-nyalodose.se/artiklar/2014-09-25/hasselnotter-en-exportvara/ [accessed 1 December 2014].

Pettersson, C. 2014. 'Jönköpings båda faktorier – en fråga om vapen och ylletyg', in Nordman *et al.* 2014, 153–75.

Rosén, C. 1999. *Föremål och social status i Halmstad ca 1550–1750*. GOTARC Series C, Arkeologiska skrifter 26. Gothenburg: Institutionen för arkeologi, Göteborgs universitet.

Rosén, C. 2010. 'Modernitet och globalisering i norra Bohuslän', in Lihammer & Nordin 2010, 71–88.

Rosén, C. 2013. 'Småstäders urbanitet. Materiell kultur och urban identitet i västsvenska småstäder ca 1640–1750', in Ersgård 2013b, 92–126.

Silvén-Garnert, E. & Söderlind, I. (eds) 1980. *Ett annat Sverige: dokument om folkets kamp 1200–1720*. Stockholm: LT.

Sjöberg, M. 2008. *Kvinnor i fält: 1550–1850*. Möklinta: Gidlunds.

Spivak, G. C. 1999. *A Critique of Postcolonial Reason: Toward a History of a Vanishing Present*. Cambridge, MA: Harvard University Press.

Strindberg, A. 1937. *Bondenöd och stormaktsdröm: studier över skedet 1630–1718*. Stockholm: Bonnier.

Todorov, T. 1982. *La Conquête de l'Amérique: La Question de l'autre*. Paris: Seuil.

Tollin, C. 1991. *Ättebackar och ödegärden: de äldre lantmäterikartorna i kulturmiljövården*. Stockholm: Riksantikvarieämbetet.

Vretemark, M. 2012. 'Bilaga 4. Osteologisk analys av djurben från kvarteret Dovhjorten i Jönköping, Småland', in Bramstång Plura *et al.* 2012, Appendix 4.

Wallerstein, I. 1974–89. *The Modern World System*. 3 vols. New York: Academic Press.

2

Houses of Wood, Houses of Stone:
On Constructing a Modern Town in
Early Modern Kalmar

GÖRAN TAGESSON

The town of Kalmar was moved in the mid-17th century and rebuilt according to contemporary ideals using a modern regulated town plan. Recent archaeological excavations confirm previous hypotheses of a socially divided and hierarchically constructed town with two different housing cultures. Their existence is discussed here in terms of being part of a general effort to produce a structured and hierarchical society. The varied and contradictory currents underlying social processes in 17th-century Sweden, an openness to new global impulses, and at the same time an obsession with structuring people and space are inherent in the case of constructing the new town of Kalmar.

SOCIETY IN CHANGE – A WIDENING HORIZON?

In the period 1600–1718 Sweden was undergoing rapid change, and various aspects of the country, such as the economy, the military, administration and urban development underwent modernization. As a result the kingdom became centralized and its people hierarchically classified.[1] Research on early modern Sweden and its transformation from a medieval society on the northern fringes of Catholic Europe to a nation with grand political ambitions is very extensive. Political history is today somewhat relegated to the background and the more specifically social aspects of society, along with Sweden's participation in globalized networks, are at the forefront of scholarly interest.[2]

In the 17th century, the small and old-fashioned Swedish towns were in the front line of regulatory efforts. Partially, this endeavour stemmed from an awareness of a lack of the sophistication and development characteristic of other aspiring European countries, such as France and the German states. When planning for the funeral of the king Gustavus Adolphus in Stockholm, the government hesitated to invite foreign guests, since "when their ambassadors come, they will see our poverty...".[3] An urban policy, including regulation of the old towns, foundations of new towns, and relocation of some of the most important towns, was intended to act as a driving force for the rest of society. The massive campaign of modernizing and regulating towns on the Swedish mainland, as well as in the provinces on the Baltic Sea, has recently been studied through a large body of preserved town plans.[4] Additionally, recent urban

archaeological research makes possible very close analyses of buildings and plot structure. Large-scale excavations have taken place during the past decade in moved and in
totally renewed towns, including Jönköping, Kalmar and Gothenburg.[5]

The medieval town of Kalmar, situated next to the important castle, was moved in
the middle of the 17th century to the adjacent island of Kvarnholmen. Contemporary
maps show a fortified town, with straight streets, rectangular blocks and symmetrical
arrangements (Fig. 2.1). The overall picture seems to indicate a very firm and rigid structure, the plots being laid out simultaneously and with the same size in a standardized
manner. The desire for uniformity is reflected in the contemporary comments of the
most influential State Councillor Axel Oxenstierna, saying of Kalmar that "it would
have been better if all the houses looked the same".[6]

In reality, the town plan of Kalmar seems to have been mentally and structurally
divided into a southern and a northern part, as an idealized structure mirroring a hierarchical society. To the south, next to the important harbour, the plots were distributed
to the local nobility, administrators, and wealthy burghers. Numerous stone houses were
constructed here as early as the 1650s and 1660s. In the northern and eastern part of the
town, the plots were smaller and narrower, and seem to have been intended for people
less well off, such as craftsmen and labourers.[7]

Similar emphasis on hierarchy is evident in other contemporary towns, especially in
the newly planned and moved towns, which created better settings for introducing new
urban ideals.[8] It may be possible to understand this process as a way of realizing ideology
on the ground, based on the Lutheran theology expressed in the *Haustafel*. The perfect
society portrayed in this ideology is a society in equilibrium, where the different societal
levels, the estates, are distinguished and kept separate and in their proper places.[9] At
the same time, however, the international harbour of Kalmar was in those days a place
for encountering new styles, modes and modernities, reflected in an abundant material
culture in the archaeological source material. The town was also an international arena,
with a mixture of ethnic groups, including immigrants and newcomers – military officials, architects and merchants – many coming from the countries around the Baltic
Sea and taking their place in the upper social strata. They were followed by artisans and
craftsmen, master builders, masons and carpenters.[10]

Such contradictory processes, where new ideals and impulses that widened horizons
and fostered inclusiveness existed side by side with a hierarchical and rigid structure
that enhanced segregation and otherness in different urban zones, were inherent in
17th-century Swedish society. When widening the horizons and encountering otherness,
it is important to know oneself, and define borders in society. The construction of the
town of Kalmar must be seen as a deliberate process, a way of constructing an ideal
town plan, reflecting an ideal society, a society in equilibrium, where everything was
put in its proper place in order to achieve balance and harmony.

TWO ROOMS AND A KITCHEN IN FISKAREGATAN

In recent years, a series of excavations has been carried out in the northern zone of
Kalmar, which may be interpreted as the "back end" of the town. The narrower plots
were laid out already from the beginning of the planning of the town, and plots were

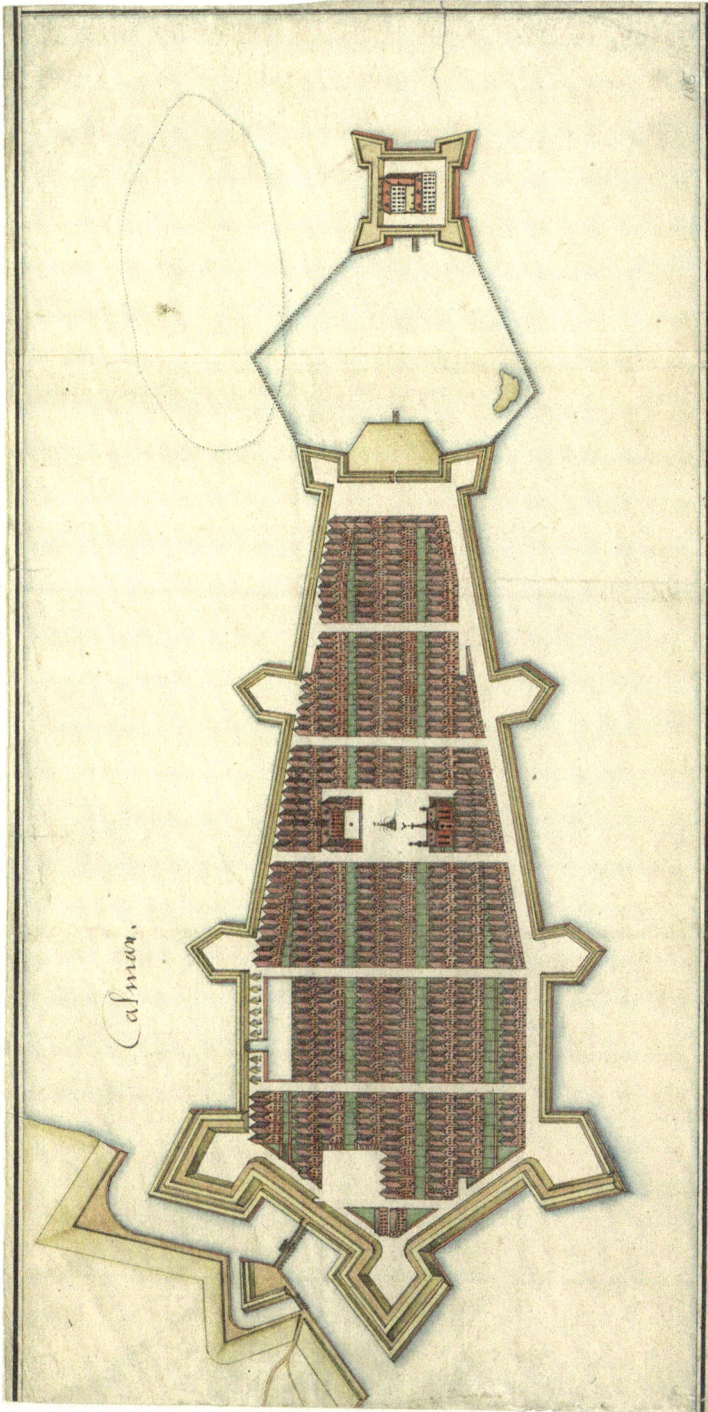

Fig. 2.1 The new town plan of Kalmar drawn in 1648 (Krigsarkivet, sfp Kalmar nr. 53b).

inhabited and houses built as early as the 1650s and 1660s. One of the largest excavations, in 2011–12, comprised no fewer than twelve plots in the most remote block,
including houses dating to the period from 1660 to the beginning of the 19th century.[11]
An overall picture of the plots gives a vivid impression of an extremely densely built
settlement with regular plots and rectangular buildings with their gable-ends fronting
the street. When studying the houses documented so far, one may have an initial general
impression of a fairly homogeneous architecture, which seems to fit perfectly into the
overall picture of a hierarchically-constructed town, with everything in its proper place.
But when one scrutinizes the documentation and looks for the details, a somewhat
more complicated picture emerges. When studying the layouts of the houses, a variety
of applied structural solutions is discernible. There are houses with one or two rooms,
but without stoves, which have been interpreted as outhouses. There are multi-room
buildings with heating facilities that may be interpreted as residential buildings. These
houses are found in many different morphological combinations, such as two- or three-
room buildings, with one or two foundations for stoves. The placing of the stoves is also
found in a variety of combinations: for example, one stove in each room, or one stove
shared by two adjacent rooms.

The different house types identified in the excavations in Kalmar may be compared
to the buildings recognized in traditional Swedish research on vernacular buildings, a
grammar presented by the professor of ethnology Sigurd Erixon in the late 1940s.[12] For
the Kalmar region, the architectural historian Manne Hofrén published a major study
on building culture in 1937, focusing mostly on manors and upper-class buildings, but
also including examples of vernacular buildings.[13] He stated that the most widespread
main dwelling type among the general population during the 17th century was the
three-room house (*parstuga*), with one central entrance, a common living-room and
a guest-room on the other side of the entrance. This was a standard building type for
farmers and for priests, and poorer manors also took this form. The two-room building
(*enkelstuga*) included a living-room, an entrance and a small chamber, and represented a
standard building type for crofters and poorer farmers. One-room buildings did sometimes appear, but seem to have been rather unusual, and were found solely in the
simplest settings. At the other end of the social scale, we find dwellings with extra
chambers added to both two- and three-room houses types (*framkammarstuga*).

Hofrén, as well as Erixon, has suggested that differences in social and economic status
were expressed in these different house types. This is also apparent in the model plans
for different military officials drawn by Erik Dahlberg in 1687. A model house-plan
for low-ranking officers, as well as an ordinary vicarage, seems to show an *enkelstuga*
combined with extra chambers, and a house-plan for high-ranking officers seems to be
a *parstuga* with extra chambers (i.e. *framkammarstuga*).

When analysing the houses in the Gesällen block, it becomes apparent that they
represent differing house types. One example only is a one-room dwelling, a simple type
of accommodation traditionally seen as unusual for this period. Most common in the
material is the two-room building, and the majority of these may be interpreted as variations on the *enkelstuga*, with a bigger living-room and smaller entrance and chamber. In
some cases the living-room had a combined function as kitchen, living-room and place
for domestic work. In most cases, however, the kitchen functions were separated from

the living area, and enacted in the small chamber behind the entrance. There were also two-room buildings with the entrance leading directly into the combined living-room and kitchen, and a chamber in the form of a smaller side-room.

Some of the three-room buildings identified represent the traditional *parstuga* with separate kitchens in the chamber behind the entrance, the third room being interpreted as an extra room for domestic work or storage.[14] The majority seem however to have a somewhat different layout from the similar buildings recorded in rural settings. The third room was smaller than the guest-room in the traditional *parstuga*, and was sometimes equipped with an extra stove. In the written records this room is referred to as a box-room (*kontor*), but the presence of a stove indicates a special function, perhaps for washing or cooking (*bryggstuga* or *grovkök*). In some cases this extra room was very small, measuring just the half of the usual width. These solutions might signal a special urban phenomenon and reflect a necessity to combine various domestic functions (relocated in rural settings to different buildings) in a confined space. Absent from the house remains identified in the Gesällen block is the *framkammarstuga* that combined two- and three-room buildings with extra chambers. This house type is traditionally interpreted as a solution adopted by families that were better off, and its absence (apart from one uncertain example) may indicate the limited social and economic condition of the block's residents.

The remains of small foundations found in the rooms next to the heated chambers in six, possibly seven, houses in the Gesällen and Mästaren blocks, along with extensive stove-tile finds in the context of these foundations, seems to indicate the existence of additional tiled stoves. This is a finding of clear significance, affording precise information as to the presence of secondary heated, smoke-free rooms in the houses in Kalmar. The dating of these additional tiled stoves is somewhat ambiguous; there seem to be at least four or five examples dating to the end of the 17th century or to the decades around the year 1700.[15] Thus these early tiled stoves seemed not to have been constructed from the very beginning, but installed during a refurbishing phase at the end of the 17th century. It is interesting to note that these installations of tiled stoves with black and moulded baroque tiles would appear to be contemporary with the construction of tiled stoves in the new Kalmar courthouse that took place in the 1680s. Written records indicate that black tiles were still in production at that time suggesting that the same tiled stoves were installed not only in the municipal buildings but also in dwellings on the urban fringe.[16]

The function of the buildings recorded in the archaeological excavation has been the subject of meticulous micro-botanical studies, indicating solely food preparation and handling of vegetables.[17] Except for the presence of a smithy on one of the plots dated to the mid-18th century, there are no signs of handicraft or other specialized production activities. This indicates that the plots and the buildings served purely residential purposes, with small gardens and outhouses, and did not combine residential and industrial functions. This may be interpretable as showing a division between home and labour, a trend towards functional separation in the townscape; but this interesting proposition requires more research.

A close study of the written sources has yielded a very detailed picture of the people living on and owning the plots.[18] One of the most important issues is to understand

the chronological and contextual relationship between social structure and built environment. The households consisted of artisans and lower officials, as well as retired
persons and widows, both families and single persons. The size and structure of the
households are extremely important for understanding the changes documented in the
archaeological archive. Generally speaking, households were small during the first half
of the 18th century, but after the mid-1700s the number of persons per household grew,
and included servants, several apprentices and also extra families. To understand the
import of these changes in relation to the built environment is one of the major tasks
for research in the near future.[19]

Variations in planning and organization within the block studied also become
obvious when analysing other aspects of the plots, such as the different ways in which
they were rebuilt and reshaped. Two adjacent units may serve as an illustration of this
phenomenon. Plot no. 290 has a rather complicated history, comprising four different
houses built consecutively one on top of the other, extending from the 1650s up to the
20th century (Fig. 2.2).[20] The earliest was a two-room building, with one fireplace for
both of the rooms. The house was soon extended by a third room to the north. In the
second phase, the new building was based on a three room plan, with a bigger fireplace
in the middle room and a new fireplace in the northern room. This rebuilding phase
was probably initiated by staff sergeant Håkan Klenstedt. A generation later this house
was pulled down, and a new one erected, with a new, smaller fireplace in the middle
room and an old-fashioned tile stove installed in the southern room. This new home

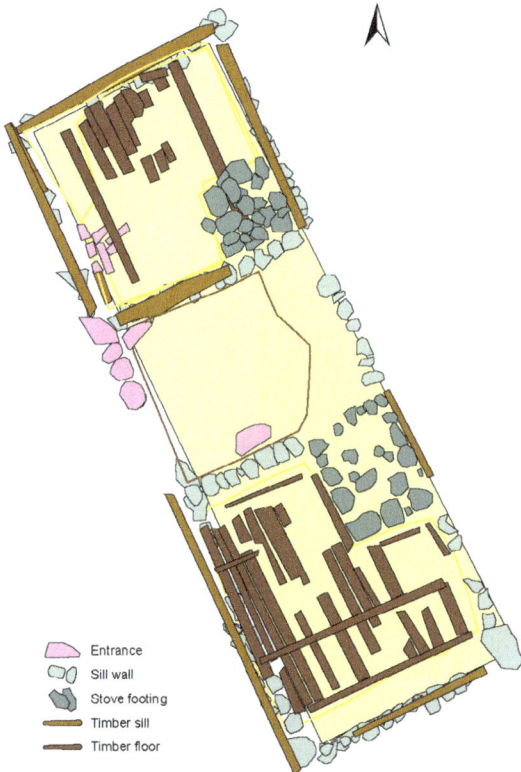

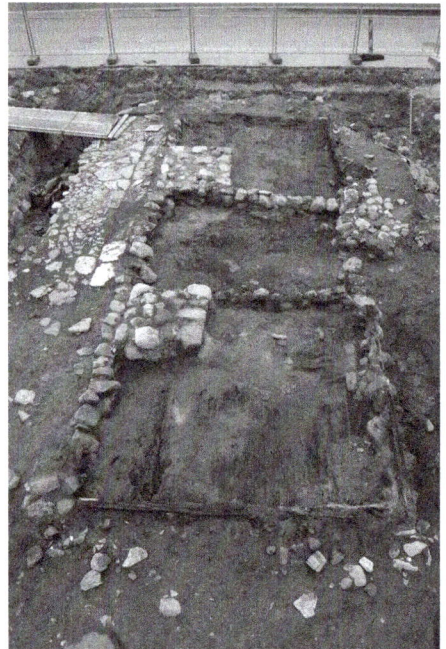

Entrance
Sill wall
Stove footing
Timber sill
Timber floor

Fig. 2.2 Plan and photograph of house
283 on plot 290 (courtesy of National
Heritage Board, Sweden).

was probably built by the customs inspector Anders Kullberg and his family. After a very short period, maybe only 20 years, even this third house was taken down, the old-fashioned tiled stove dismantled, and a fourth-generation house erected.

It is illuminating to compare this complex building history to the neighbouring plot no. 289, where already at the end of the 1660s a three-room building with fireplaces in all of the rooms was erected. The house was renovated many times but the actual building and its interior plan stayed intact for a longer period. At last, in the 1730s, the house was pulled down and re-erected, but following the same layout.[21]

The overall layout and organization of the plots and the buildings in the Gesällen excavation give an impression of designed and structured character of town planning. On a general level, one may discern a pattern: the homogeneity of plot boundaries and sizes, rectangular buildings orientated north–south, multi-spaced houses with two or three rooms, sturdy sills as foundations for log cabins, as well as supports for stoves. On the other hand, looking at the details, we find variations in planning and construction, and there appears to be no pattern in the distribution of the different types of building over the twelve plots.

The excavated houses provide early examples of modern tiled stoves, although homes with these facilities are in a minority – only two out of twelve plots in the Gesällen block had them. Certain other features also indicate that the residents followed new fashions and were interested in acquiring fine household articles such as imported faïence and glassware. The opportunity to study the range of building practices employed, as shown for the two adjacent plots of nos. 290 and 289, meanwhile reveals individual differences and choices in (re)building processes and the houses' varying biographies (Fig. 2.3).

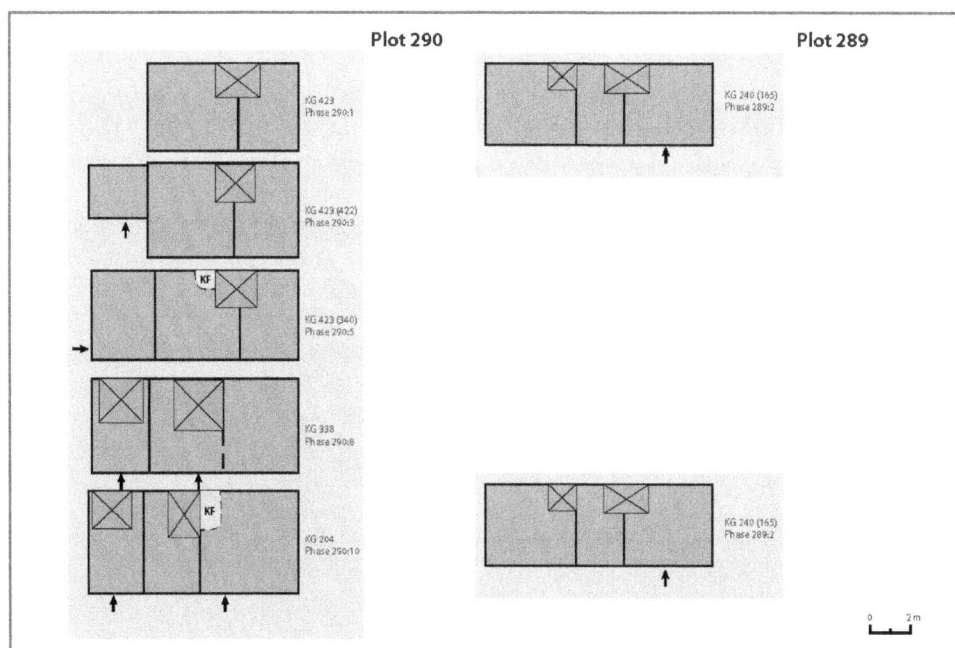

Fig. 2.3 Houses on plots 290 and 289 (drawing: Lars Östlin, National Heritage Board, Sweden).

The documented houses in the Gesällen block on the northern fringe of the town give clear indications of great variation in early modern house types, as well as the presence of types that can be associated with, in social terms, a "middling sort". The diversity of forms calls into question, however, the very utility of the concept "house type". Instead, it might be more productive to think of houses in terms of morphology, as a combination of space units – living-room, entrance room, chamber, kitchen etc. – that can be combined in many different ways. There are interesting examples of a successive (re)construction of houses, from two-room to three-room (e.g. plot no. 290), as well as long continuities. Most of the plots are characterized by a clear discontinuity when it comes to house morphology, but there are also examples of the opposite, with the same kind of layout being maintained over much longer periods.

Another important outcome of the study is the observation that the house types used in the town may also be found in the countryside, which corroborates conclusions of traditional and well-established research on vernacular buildings.[22] The great variety of house plans revealed was not expected, however. These diverse plans were interpreted in earlier research as mirroring different local traditions, as well as different social settings and chronological periods; but in the present case they are confirmed as being both chronologically and geographically contemporary. Whether this degree of variety is also characteristic of the countryside, though hitherto unobserved, or is rather a manifestation of a typically urban phenomenon, is as yet unclear, due to lack of a basis for comparison.

IN ANOTHER PART OF THE TOWN

The well-preserved body of stone houses in Kalmar forms a splendid piece of cultural heritage associated with early modern period. These houses are situated solely in the southern part of the town, next to the important harbour, and constitute its "front end". We can easily identify a pattern involving the siting these buildings along the major streets, especially the north–south arteries leading from the harbour through the main gates in the walls encircling the town, and towards its centre. Many of these houses are also situated at the corners of blocks, or exposed towards open spaces and squares (Fig. 2.4).[23]

The Kaggensgatan, for instance, seemed to form the sort of "grand vista" common and popular in Baroque planning, and used as an eye-catcher to enhance and order perception while moving through the town. The stone buildings were deliberately sited along the street, at the corners of the transverse east–west streets. The deployment of such a grand vista may be understood against the background of the final placement of the cathedral at the rear end of the centrally constructed market place. The centrally planned church, built in 1660–1700, may be interpreted as a focal point for the whole town, visitors thus being firmly conducted from the harbour, along the grand vistas of Kaggensgatan, to the final goal in the very centre.

The stone houses of early modern Kalmar have been studied by Manne Hofrén.[24] Today, about 17 stone buildings are known to have existed, including the cathedral, the town hall and the governor's residence. During the first constructional phase of the new town in the 1640s, townspeople had to sign up for plots, and the mayor Erik Rosenlund's house on Södra Långgatan is reckoned to be the very first stone building in the town, built in the period 1654–8. This was soon followed during the 1650s and

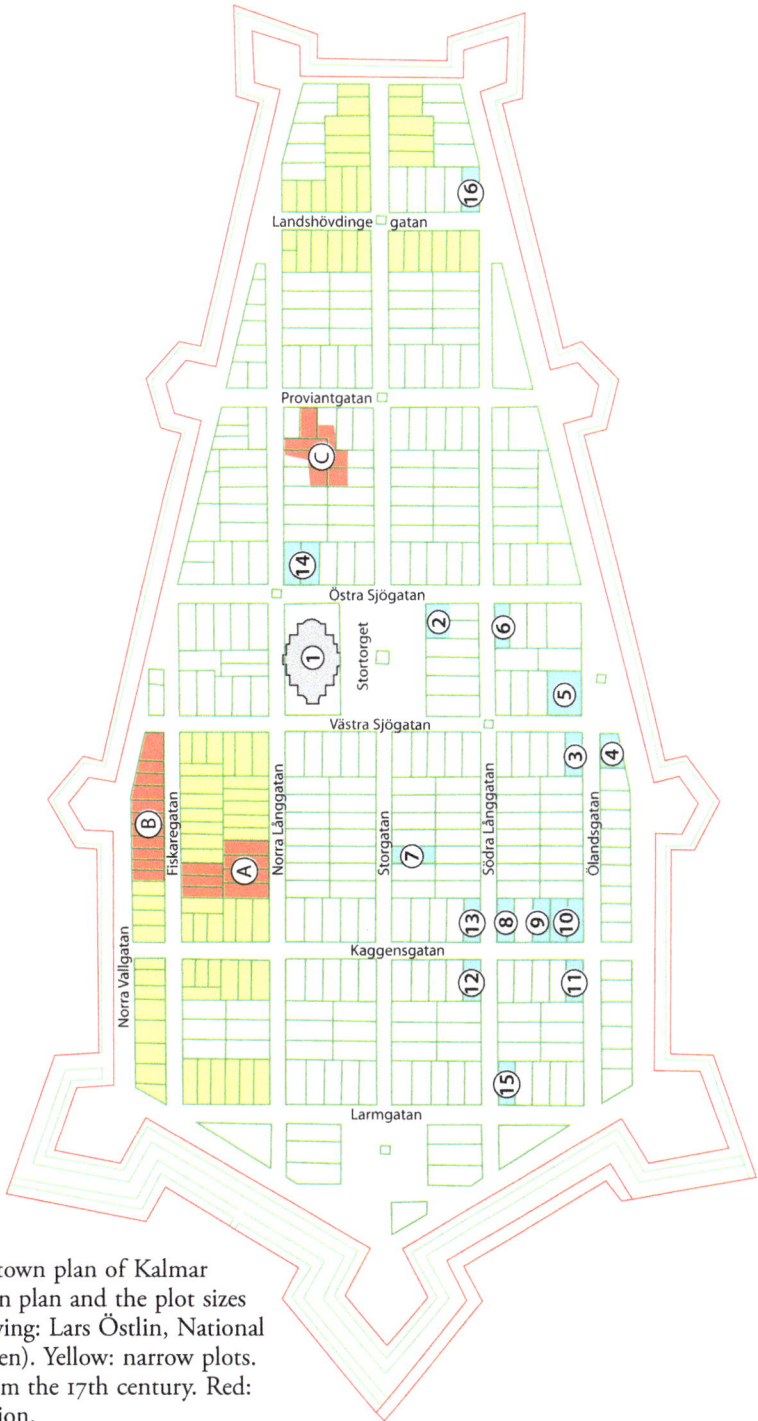

Fig. 2.4 Hierarchical town plan of Kalmar based on the 1651 town plan and the plot sizes of the 1658 map (drawing: Lars Östlin, National Heritage Board, Sweden). Yellow: narrow plots. Blue: stone houses from the 17th century. Red: archaeological excavation.

1660s by the construction of almost all of the other stone buildings. By the time the town hall was completed in 1690, the stone construction boom had come to an end.

The national government constantly presented the stone houses as a prescribed ideal, but it was economically impossible for anybody other than the nobility and the most wealthy burghers and urban officials to afford buildings in stone. The rest of the towns-people protested, and the officials had to accept economic shortcuts, admitting excep-tions to the stone-building programme. There are, however, instructions to the effect that houses, although built in wood, should be attractive, gable-ended towards the street, two-storeyed and provided with good foundations.[25] The stone houses are not identical, but have certain common characteristics. They are cubic in form, two-sto-reyed, and with five or sometimes seven window bays. The rather narrow and tower-like appearance of these buildings may be due to the symmetrical and rather narrow plots in the town. However, when placed on the street corners, the cubic form is apparent. This typical form is also apparent in contemporary wooden buildings in this urban zone, an interesting resource that needs more research, but which lies beyond the scope of this chapter.

The building material was the local limestone, the exteriors being dominated by white plaster, and house-corners lined with limestone ashlars; the houses were referred to in contemporary sources as "white houses". Early photographs show exterior flights of steps as a very common feature; these have since been removed. The portals were cut from limestone, individually shaped, and especially popular in the latter part of the 17th century. The roofs were often hipped, notably high and steep and covered by roofing tiles.[26]

2.5 (above and opposite) Lilla torget and the so-called Dahmska huset, 1650s–60s (photograph: Gunnar Menander; plan after Hofrén 1970).

The interior was often designed in an almost old-fashioned style, with a central corridor leading from the street to the inner yard, sometimes combined with another angular corridor. The partitioning of the houses could be compared to the partitioning of the most common type of vernacular building, the *parstuga*, with a common living room, chamber and kitchen on the one side, and hall and guest-room on the other. This is particularly apparent in the long building of Sahlsteen, and has also been observed in contemporary examples in the town of Vadstena.[27] In most cases, however, a narrower and more quadrangular form prevails, and thus packs the entrance and the central corridor more closely together, with a hall at the street-front, and pairs of chambers, sometimes including a kitchen, on the other side of the corridor. The normal plan is therefore less regular, less integrative, and divides internal space into two-room sections, which is very evident in the stone houses from the 1650s and 60s, but also in the town hall.

These house plans are somewhat irregular and old-fashioned; at the same time the plans do not seem to have a counterpart in the countryside in the houses built by the nobility, clerics, or the richer farmers. Hofrén has interpreted these plans as an expression of a typical urban style, "a local manifestation of the Swedish-German-Baltic fortification towns, with the fortification engineers as architects".[28] Some of the town architects, master builders, masons and carpenters came from northern Germany, from the towns of Danzig and Stralsund among others. The head engineer in Kalmar, Anders Olofsson Bergh, who led the construction of the new town, most certainly constructed his own house there (today known as the "Dahmska huset") (Fig. 2.5). His son-in-law, Magnus Gabriel Craelius, with almost the same background, designed the town hall.[29]

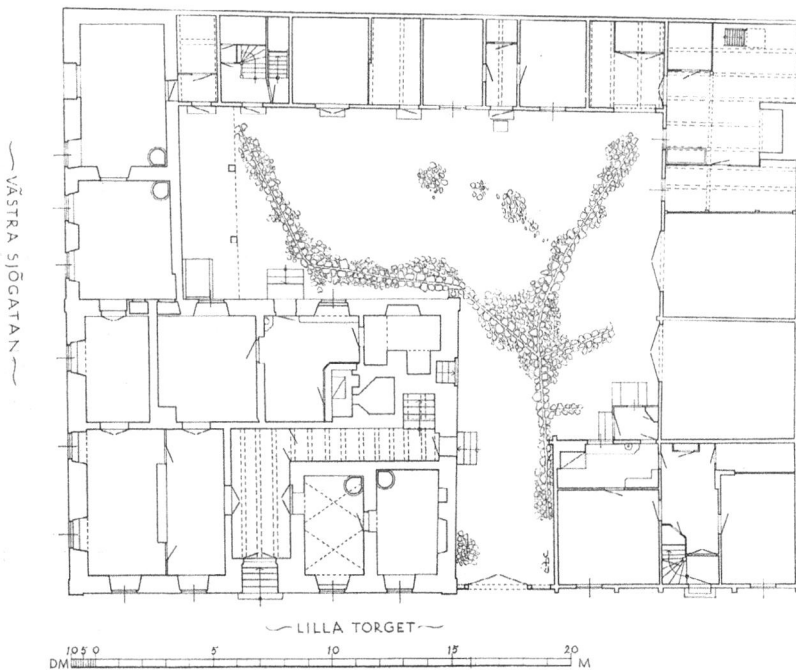

At this time the more modern French six-partitioned plan with a central hall was being introduced in manors and palaces in Sweden, but in the town of Kalmar there are just a few examples of this kind of plan being implemented. The very first stone building, the Rosenlund house, built in the 1650s, has a broader entrance, and a hall in the centre of the building, and on each side are two chambers (Fig. 2.6). The same modern plan is also found in the governor's new residence, which was re-fashioned in the 1690s. This new and contemporary style was introduced in Sweden from *c.* 1650 and promoted by the distinguished architects Nicodemus Tessin the elder and Jean de la Vallé after their grand tour of the continent. In the Kalmar region, the new French style was introduced in the manors, especially during the 1680s and 1690s. In the governor's urban residence on the Lilla torget we find a typical plan including symmetrical construction with partitioning in the master's and mistress's rooms. There are other features too in this governor's residence – for instance rather modern white and blue tiled stoves – displaying a more up-to-date fashion.

Fig. 2.6 (above and opposite) The Rosenlund house, built in the 1650s by the mayor Erik Rosenlund (photograph: Gunnar Menander; plan after Hofrén 1970). The plan on the ground floor shows a fairly early example of the modern French-inspired six-partitioned house plan, with entrance and hall in the centre and two chambers on each side.

ORDERING SOCIETY

The stone houses of Kalmar form a group of astonishingly well-preserved and impressive buildings associated with the constructional phase of the new town and reflecting the social class of wealthy burghers, urban administrators and military officials; not, however, the highest rank of the nobility. The overall impression is that the houses constitute a uniform body of built environment, forming a counterpart to the wooden buildings of the lower classes in the northern part of the town. These two different housing cultures reflect the intended visual and spatial division of the town into distinctive zones inhabited by socially different groups of residents, and a way of constructing an ideal townscape and a hierarchical society.

The two different housing cultures do reflect different attitudes towards building culture during the second half of the 17th century. The wooden buildings for the less affluent in the northern part of the town express a vernacular building tradition with two- or three-room plans (*enkelstuga* and *parstuga*). The mixture and variation in the individual house plans is however an intriguing aspect of the urban housing. It is not at all clear if this derives from a specific local urban context, or was a feature of a rural and/or general context as well. The latter would imply that the traditional image of rather static house plans is greatly oversimplified.

The presence of separate kitchens among the documented urban wooden houses, as well as the presence of tiled stoves and a fairly rich material culture, including Dutch faïence as well as imported fruits and spices, present also in the less affluent part of the town, suggests urban culture of a surprising standard, especially when compared to contemporary towns such as Linköping. The house types, even for the less affluent at the back end of the new town, seem more up-to-date, and reflect a coherent housing culture for common people.

The siting of the wooden houses in the northern part of the town on the southeast plot-corners, with their gables towards the street and the street-front screened by a plank, formed a rather repetitive pattern along the frontage. Such types of building are still preserved in the outskirt blocks of Kvarnholmen, suggesting that they may have been rather common, especially on the fringes of the townscape. This indicates a rather homogeneous pattern, but it is unclear if its repetitiveness was due simply to the preferred house type and narrow plots, or if it was the product of a deliberate intention to construct a strict and visually ordered townscape.

The stone houses in the town centre form a specific urban expression shared by the towns located around the Baltic Sea. The stone houses in Kalmar are all individual creations, probably constructed by local skilled fortification engineers but not the most prominent architects, like the celebrated Nicodemus Tessin the elder, architect of the cathedral, who were busy instead with castles, manors and churches. The plans of these buildings do reflect a contemporary upper-class housing culture of the mid-17th century. The prominent change towards the new French style, promoting a six-partitioned house plan, was being carried through in the manors in the Kalmar region, especially during the 1680s and 1690s, but was applied to only two of the stone houses in the town itself.

The two different building traditions in Kalmar seem to reflect two sides of the housing culture of the newly constructed town. The differences are clear: wood/stone; one storey/two storeys; traditional vernacular plan/international urban plan; uniform/individual. Differences are also evident when one comes to analyse the access to the houses from the street. The wooden houses line the street, gable-ended, with the entrance concealed behind a plank and a porch. The stone houses also line the street, but with the facade and the entrance on to it, enhanced by a richly-adorned porch, often bearing the emblems and the initials of the person who had the house built and his/her family. The main interior hall is oriented towards the street, and inner family life is thus exposed to the public, which also seems to be a specifically urban phenomenon. The contrasts between these two types of building thus consist in the enhancement and exaggeration of differences, making distinctions in class and estate clear for everyone to see.

The two different housing cultures only display uniformity from a "bird's-eye" perspective, however. When we scrutinize them more closely, they no longer appear as homogeneous. None of the houses, neither the wooden ones in the north nor the stone ones in the south, is a replica of another. Instead, we may interpret the body of buildings as sharing a sort of building grammar with a great variety of differences in, for example, number and arrangement of rooms. It is important to state moreover that the two housing cultures also have some features in common: for instance, widespread use of tile-stoves as well as the use of more complex two- or three-partitioned plans, and the combination of two heated rooms with the stove mounted in the joined wall.

In this way, the wooden houses to the north and the stone houses to the south do share a common urban style, in spite of their outer differences.

THE HIERARCHICAL TOWN AND THE LUTHERAN *HAUSTAFEL*

The organization and appearance of houses and urban plots in early modern Kalmar which have been analysed underline the contradictory processes taking place in the town and within Swedish society. The differences between the two urban zones appear to have been very deliberate and may even have been purposefully exaggerated. At the same time, it would seem too that the residential area on the urban fringe had fairly agreeable living standards. The houses are a good illustration of a contemporary desire to build well and practically.

The spatial structure of the town seems to have been initially intended to impose separation and discipline: a system for constructing and enhancing power relations. The same pattern and organizing principle may also be studied in a variety of contemporary contexts: colonial plantations as well as ironworks in central Sweden. This main structuring principle was also obvious in the church, where the pews and the available places for graves were socially graded.[30] Indeed, during the period under study, several authors published works discussing how to build properly according to one's social level. In his *Oeconomia*, from the 1660s, the Swedish nobleman Schering Rosenhane states the importance of building according to one's rank and estate: "A man of estate and fortune has to adapt his building, so posterity may see and estimate his condition."[31] This equates to a sort of visual grammar, according to which the buildings reflect and participate in the construction of a person or a group of individuals as social beings. It is important to see this structure from the point of view of ideology. Of profound importance for understanding mentality and ideology in the 17th century is the Lutheran concept of the *Haustafel*. This doctrine envisions society as divided into three categories or estates (*stånd* in Swedish; broadly, state government, households and Church – *politia*, *œconomia*, *ecclesia*).[32] Its ideological backbone derives from a theological philosophy licensing a hierarchical worldview, God being seen as the supreme creator and ruler of the world, and the king as his legitimate representative on earth. Religion permeated all parts of society and was too the very foundation of the state.[33]

This ideology provided guidelines for social organization. Everyone was assigned a precise place in the social structure, and conditioned according to an ideologically-motivated perception of the specific position of each man and woman in society. However strictly hierarchical, nevertheless, it is important to stress that the three *Haustafel* categories were interrelated and interdependent, forming a relational social order with superior and inferior roles within each estate. Society was seen as an organism where the three estates had their own carefully balanced tasks and roles.[34]

Scholars tend to emphasize the extent to which early modern Swedish society was based on privilege. The status of the individual, as well as his/her rights and duties, was founded on belonging to a certain group; and often these differences are erroneously perceived in purely socio-economic terms. Against a background of ideology, however, it is possible to deepen and problematize the picture: the Lutheran *Haustafel* provided for an ideologically-motivated social order, a way of constructing society through subordination to a divinely-sanctioned scheme. Harmony was a pervasive and fundamental way of understanding society in the 17th century. To question or oppose the hierarchy and obligations implied by one's social standing was not just to upset the balance of power relations in society, but to offend against the order established by God. The relation between the authorities and the commoners has been explained as both hierarchical and at the same time permeated by mutual obligations.[35]

Ideology may be understood as the "given, the obvious, and our ideas about things taken to be natural";[36] and considering the Lutheran *Haustafel* as an important expression of and background to a central ideology in early modern Sweden – an ideology based on the Bible, embracing a strict hierarchical order and permeating all parts of society – provides one way to understand the construction of social order during the period of Sweden's "Age of Greatness". Given which, the highly regulated and symbolic town space exemplified at Kalmar, as regards both the ideal images of the town plans with their centrally-located cathedral and town hall and the above-mentioned existence of the different housing cultures, becomes interpretable at a more complex level. On the one hand, we observe built-in power relations on the ground; on the other, the structuring of the town must be viewed as a way of constructing what was perceived as the "Good Society" – where everyone and everything had its clear position in a divinely-constructed hierarchy. Understood in this way, the ordering and distinguishing principle in the new town plans may be interpreted as a means towards the creation of harmony, order and social balance.

Close analysis of the wooden and stone houses of early modern Kalmar presents us with a degree of complexity, however. Dissimilarities in building morphology, including such factors as building materials, dimensions and orientation towards the street front, seem to express a deliberate physical construction of a social hierarchy on the ground; whilst similarities in style, and in what can be deduced of mentalities and a general attitude towards contemporary currents, seem to form the basis for positing a specific urban culture, distinct from that of the surrounding countryside. The great variety of house types and construction within the different urban zones, meanwhile, suggests that the possibility and/or intention to regulate the housing culture down to the last details was limited or lacking, or that this was not desired. It is crucial, in order fully to understand these differences, to investigate the roles of the inhabitants and the builders as competent actors within a societal structure.[37]

CONCLUSIONS

When scrutinizing the different plans for the new town of Kalmar within a hierarchical, ideological framework, it becomes obvious that the plans were drawn up in the light of contemporary ideals promoting regularity and harmony. As early as the 1640s the town seems to have been construed in accordance with the principles of a hierarchical social topography, as reflected in the differentiated plot sizes, choices of building materials and outward appearance of the house facades. In the northern and eastern parts of the town, the plots are narrower than elsewhere, designed to house the lower classes of artisans and workers. At the same time, the southern blocks were reserved for the elite, and it was in this zone that the intentions embodied in representative stone houses could be fulfilled.

In certain places, especially along the Kaggensgatan, the stone houses were assigned a conspicuous position on the street corners, and acted as iterated elements, directing movement and sight towards the urban focal point in the town's square consisting of the cathedral and town hall.

The houses in the two different urban zones are on the one hand quite different as regards building materials, size, house plans and approach from the street. On the other hand they exhibit some similarities, being divided into several rooms for different functions, showing individual traits, and adopting some novelties such as separate kitchens and tiled stoves. There seem to be indications that both the wooden houses and the stone houses were expressions of a specific urban attitude and living conditions.

The houses of wood and houses of stone may be interpreted as corresponding to two contrasting ideals: the equalized and symmetrical town-plan on maps and images, and the differentiated plot system on the ground. Together they might be taken to summarize two different aspects of the regulated early modern Swedish town: a plan of perfect symmetry, and tendencies to separation. The new plan of Kalmar thus represented an ideologically-founded sample of the ideal town, a materialization of the principles of the Lutheran *Haustafel* on the ground.

ACKNOWLEDGEMENT

I would like to thank Norman Davies, Linköping, for his help with the English-language text of this chapter.

NOTES

1 Villstrand 2011.
2 E.g. Lindström 2006; Naum & Nordin 2013.
3 Råberg 1987, 78. Translation by the author.
4 Ahlberg 2005.
5 Stibéus 2014; Nordman *et al.* 2014; Tagesson & Carelli 2016.
6 Olsson 1965, 97. Translation by the author.
7 Hofrén 1962; Tagesson 2013.
8 Tagesson 2013; Tagesson in print.
9 Pleijel 1970; Stadin 2004.
10 Hofrén 1970, 181.
11 Tagesson 2014.
12 Erixon 1947.
13 Hofrén 1937.
14 In the traditional *parstuga* the third room is interpreted as an extra space for feasts, guests and storage.
15 Tagesson 2014, 280–5; Tagesson & Jeppsson 2015.
16 Hofrén 1970, 41; Tagesson & Jeppsson 2015.
17 Heimdahl 2014.
18 Lindström 2014.

19 Lindström & Tagesson 2015.
20 Tagesson 2014, 34.
21 Tagesson 2014, 44.
22 Erixon 1947.
23 Hofrén 1970; Tagesson 2013; Tagesson in print.
24 Hofrén 1970.
25 Hofrén 1970, 156.
26 Hofrén 1970, 161–4.
27 Söderström 2000, 492–4.
28 Hofrén 1970, 181.
29 Hofrén 1970, 183; Holmgren 2011.
30 Leone 2005; Rosell & Bennet 1989.
31 Cited in Noldus 2005, 22; Bedoire 2001, 133.
32 Pleijel 1970, 258–60; Montgomery 2002, 101; Stadin 2004, 17.
33 Villstrand 2011, 327–30.
34 Pleijel 1970; Stadin 2004; Villstrand 2011.
35 Pleijel 1970, 254; Stadin 2004, 26; Villstrand 2011, 245.
36 Leone 2005, 24.
37 Lindström & Tagesson 2015.

BIBLIOGRAPHY

Ahlberg, N. 2005. *Stadsgrundningar och planförändringar. Svensk stadsplanering 1521–1721.* Uppsala: Sveriges Lantbruksuniversitet.

Arnell, K.-H. (ed.) 2011. *Byggda minnen. Berättelser från Öland och östra Småland.* Kalmar: Länsstyrelsen Kalmar län.

Bedoire, F. 2001. *Guldålder. Slott och politik i 1600-talets Sverige.* Stockholm: Bonnier.

Cornell, P. (ed.) in press. *City, Culture and Social Encounters.* Gothenburg: Göteborgs universitet.

Erixon, S. 1947. *Svensk byggnadskultur. Studier och skildringar belysande den svenska byggnadskulturens historia.* Stockholm: Bokverk.

Ersgård, L. (ed.) 2013. *Visioner och verklighet – arkeologiska texter om den tidigmoderna staden.* GOTARC Series C, Arkeologiska skrifter 76. Gothenburg: Göteborgs universitet.

Heimdahl, J. 2014. 'Odling och växthantering i kv. Gesällen, Kalmar. Teknisk rapport av kvartärgeologiska och arkeobotaniska analyser', in Tagesson 2014, Appendix 2.

Hofrén, M. 1937. *Herrgårdar och boställen. En översikt över byggnadskultur och heminredning på Kalmar läns herrgårdar 1650–1850.* Nordiska Museets Handlingar 6. Stockholm: Nordiska Museet.

Hofrén, M. 1962. *Kvarnholmen i Kalmar. Utredning verkställd av Manne Hofrén 1950–59.* Kalmar: Drätselkammaren.

Hofrén, M. 1970. *Kalmar: karolinska borgarhus i sten.* Nordiska Museets Handlingar 74. Stockholm: Nordiska Museet.

Holmgren, E.-L. 2011. 'Släktband, status och ståtliga stenhus', in Arnell 2011, 121–30.

Larsson, S. (ed.) 2006. *Nya stadsarkeologiska horisonter.* Stockholm: Riksantikvarieämbetet.

Leone, M. P. 2005. *The Archaeology of Liberty in an American Capital: Excavations in Annapolis.* Berkeley: University of California Press.

Lindström, D. 2006. 'Människor och vardagsliv', in Larsson 2006, 89–133.

Lindström, D. 2014. 'Kvarteret Gesällen, Kvarnholmen, Kalmar. Rekonstruktioner av ägarförhållanden, ägoskiften, hushåll och boende för tomterna med nummer 280–90', in Tagesson 2014, Appendix 3.

Lindström, D. & Tagesson, G. 2015. 'On spatializing history – the household as spatial unit in Early Modern Swedish towns', *META Historisk-arkeologisk tidskrift* 2015: 47–60.

Montgomery, I. 2002. *Sveriges kyrkohistoria. 4. Enhetskyrkans tid.* Stockholm: Verbum.

Naum, M. & Nordin, J. M. (eds) 2013. *Scandinavian Colonialism and the Rise of Modernity: Small Time Agents in a Global Arena.* New York: Springer.

Noldus, B. 2005. *Trade in Good Taste: Relations in Architecture and Culture between the Dutch Republic and the Baltic World in the Seventeenth Century.* Turnhout: Brepols.

Nordman, A-M, Nordström, M. & Pettersson, C. (eds) 2014. *Stormaktsstaden* Jönköping: *1614 och framåt.* Jönköping: Jönköpings läns museum.

Olsson, M. 1965. *Kalmar slotts historia. 3. Tiden från 1613 till 1941.* Stockholm: Almqvist & Wiksell International.

Pleijel, H. 1970. *Hustavlans värld. Kyrkligt folkliv i äldre tiders Sverige.* Stockholm: Verbum.

Råberg, M. 1987. *Visioner och verklighet. 1. En studie kring Stockholms 1600-talsstadsplan.* Stockholm: Komm. för Stockholmsforskning.

Rosell, I. & Bennet, F. 1989. *Kalmar domkyrka. Sveriges kyrkor 209. Småland band III:4.* Stockholm: Almqvist & Wiksell International.

Söderström, G. (ed.) 2000. *600 år i Vadstena. Vadstena stads historia från äldsta tider till år 2000.* Stockholm: Stockholmia.

Stadin, K. 2004. *Stånd och genus i stormaktstidens Sverige.* Lund: Nordic Academic Press.

Stibéus, M. (ed.) 2014. *Slaktarens kaj, apotekarens trädgård och fällberedarens gård. Arkeologi på tre gårdar i 1600- och 1700-talens Jönköping.* Stockholm: Riksantikvarieämbetet.

Tagesson, G. 2013. 'Vore bäst alle huus vore lijka – makt, ideologi och modernitet i den tidig-moderna staden', in Ersgård 2013, 127–49.

Tagesson, G. (ed.) 2014. 'Kvarteret Gesällen 4 och 25. Särskild arkeologisk undersökning. Kalmar stad och kommun. Kalmar län. Riksantikvarieämbetet, arkeologiska uppdragsverksamheten. Rapport 2014:93'. Archaeological report. Stockholm: Riksantikvarieämbetet.

Tagesson, G. In press. '"Would be better if all the houses looked all the same…". The early modern town as power, ideology and modernity', in Cornell in press.

Tagesson, G. & Carelli, P. 2016. *Kalmar mellan dröm och verklighet. Konstruktionen av den tidigmoderna staden.*

Tagesson, G. & Jeppsson, A. 2015. 'Varmt och skönt – och iögonfallande modernt. Kakelugnar som social konsumtion i det tidigmoderna Sverige', *Fornvännen* 2015(2): 121–35.

Tagesson, G. & Nordström, A. 2012. 'Kvarteret Mästaren, Kalmar stad och kommun: särskild arkeologisk undersökning 2009. Riksantikvarieämbetet, arkeologiska uppdragsverksamheten, UV Öst. Rapport 2012:104'. Archaeological report. Stockholm: Riksantikvarieämbetet.

Villstrand, N. E. 2011. *Sveriges historia: 1600–1721.* Stockholm: Norstedts.

3

Indigeneity, Locality, Modernity: Encounters and their Effects on Foodways in Early Modern Tornio

Anna-Kaisa Salmi, Annemari Tranberg and Risto Nurmi

Cultural encounters can have a profound effect on everyday practices such as foodways. This certainly was the case in the 17th- and 18th-century town of Tornio in Northern Finland, where people of different ethnic origins came together, forming a new urban community and new hybrid food culture. Three archaeological case studies demonstrate that the food culture of Tornio was dynamic and a mixture of local indigenous and rural traditions and international fashions. In this chapter we use the transformation of foodways in Tornio as a springboard to examine the effects of cultural encounters on everyday practices and material culture, and the roles foodways can play in these encounters.

In the late medieval and early modern periods, the northern part of Finland, at that time part of the Swedish kingdom, became a veritable melting pot of different cultures and ethnicities. The northern parts of Fennoscandia were largely populated by the indigenous Sami people when the first colonial expansion of the Swedish kingdom began during the 14th century. Then the first peasant villages on the northern river estuaries were founded, based on the Crown's centrally-organized relocation of peasant families from the more southern part of the kingdom.[1] Relations between Sweden and the Sami are best described within the framework of colonialism. "Colonialism" refers to a situation of unequal power relations between peoples: Wolfgang Reinhard, for instance, defines it as "the control of one people by another, culturally different one, an unequal relationship which exploits differences of economic, political, and ideological development between the two".[2] Sometimes too the term "internal colonialism" is suggested to describe the relationship between the Sami and the Swedes, especially during the early modern period when the northern areas were already formally a part of the Swedish kingdom.[3]

The intensification of the Swedish Crown's economic and political interests in the north began in the medieval period. The Crown aimed to strengthen its power in the north by taxation of the native population and by encouraging the establishment of agrarian settlement.[4] Moreover, Christianity was promoted as the Catholic Church began to expand into the area and new parishes were founded.[5] An expansion with clearer colonial agendas and ideologies took place from 17th century onwards. The Crown wanted to strengthen its control over trade and resources by establishing mines,

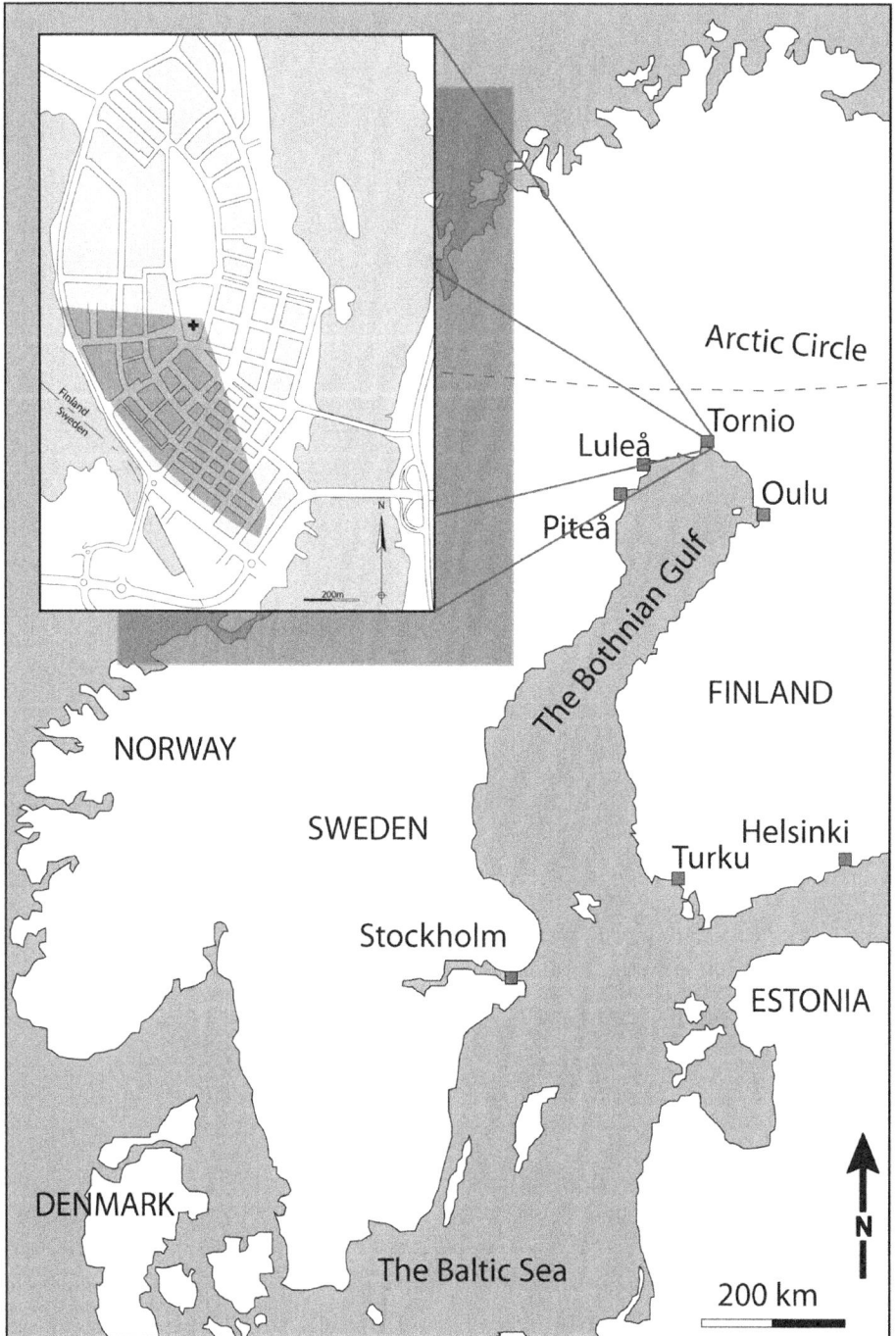

Fig. 3.1 Map of Tornio. The shaded area in the smaller map is Tornio according to a 1698 map (drawing: Risto Nurmi).

production sites, market places and towns through which all the trade was supposed to take place, following the principles of a mercantilist economic system.[6] Swedish attitudes towards the Sami and their culture hardened as well. A sedentary agrarian lifestyle was canonized as the proper Swedish way to live, and assimilation of the Sami to Swedish culture became the ideal promoted by the Crown.[7]

The town of Tornio, the subject of this chapter, was founded in 1621 as a part of a series of new towns established as a means to control the trade taking place in northern Finland. The town was founded in the location of a former marketplace at the mouth of the river Tornio (Fig. 3.1). Its population was recruited from various parts of Finland and Sweden. Some of the local farmers also moved to the new town.[8] It is possible that there were also people of Karelian/Russian origin, and also Sami, whose presence in Tornio seems plausible as the local agrarian community included numerous families of Sami origin.[9] Tornio, like Bothnian towns in general, was essentially a trading post in a domestic market network. In 1766, Tornio was granted privileges to trade directly with foreign ports, which boosted trade and increased international influence and trends in the town[10]. The population in Tornio was a typically colonial society, with people from different origins coming together, negotiating a new culture in a web of complex economic and political power relationships.

In colonial societies such encounters – of different cultures and ethnicities in complex webs of power relationships – produce hybrid cultural forms. Hybridization implies that all participants in the colonial encounter contribute to and co-create the resulting colonial cultural practices.[11] In this process, a third space is created between the cultures: a space of discourse, retranslation, instability, and cultural change.[12] Hybridization occurs in all areas of the culture, from its ideological, religious and political aspects to the details of everyday life. Material culture is also changed and hybridized in colonial settings, and so are everyday practices such as foodways.[13]

In this chapter, we focus on the hybridization of foodways as a result of the cultural and colonial encounters that happened in Tornio during the first two centuries of the town's existence, in 1621–1800. We use three minor archaeological case studies to illustrate how material culture and foodways were hybridized in the encounters of different cultural traditions. First, we will discuss the influence of Sami foodways on urban food culture, especially through observations of the faunal assemblage from Tornio. Secondly, we focus on the preservation of local foodways, especially in regard to the use of cutlery, despite the influx of European fashions and merchandise into the town. Our third example is the hybridization of local traditions and international fashions in the use of vegetable foods, and especially the development of garden culture during the 18th century. Case studies are used to discuss the effects of cultural contacts on foodways in early modern Tornio; case studies which moreover illustrate the complex power relationships that develop in colonial societies, and the roles material culture can play in encounters between different cultures.

ARCHAEOLOGICAL MATERIAL AND METHODS

Tornio was small and agrarian in character, which was typical of early modern Sweden, where small towns had usually only a few hundred inhabitants. It was surrounded by an agrarian landscape and featured agrarian characteristics such as vegetable gardens, animal shelters and livestock.[14] A new urban lifestyle and identity emerged in Tornio in the 18th century. During the late 17th and 18th centuries urban space was reorganized as a new grid plan was introduced and plots were enclosed after the European fashion, and the local domestic material culture became increasingly shaped by modernization.[15] By "modernization" we mean the effects of emerging capitalism, industrialization, rationalization, colonialism, growing urbanization, and the constant change that are understood to be at the core of modernity.[16] The material we rely on in this study derives from several different excavations, and dates to the 17th and 18th centuries. A more detailed overview of the material, as well as a description of the overall changes in foodways in the town during the early modern period can be found in Salmi *et al.* (2014).

The faunal remains used as an archaeological source derive from the Keskikatu, Westring and Välikatu excavations. The material originates from different types of archaeological context: earth fill layers, refuse pits, and underfloor deposits. The material consists of 12,271 bone fragments weighing *c.* 150 kg. The faunal assemblage was dominated by domestic animals as regards number of identified specimens (NISP) counts, but the percentage of wild animal bones was also significant – *c.* 30% in the early 17th-century assemblage. The faunal assemblage suggests an economy based on dairy cattle husbandry, supported by sheep, pig and reindeer husbandry and hunting of game, water birds, arctic hares and seals.[17]

The plant remains were collected at the 12 excavations in Keskikatu.[18] The households studied represent the late 17th century and 18th century. Altogether 18 soil samples weighing 200–2,000 g were taken from different deposits. The sampled deposits consisted of compost heaps, ditches and building remains. In addition to macrofossil analysis, pollen and insect fossil analyses were conducted.[19] The analysis of plant remains revealed that wild plants were widely used in Tornio, especially as medicines and infusions. The use of vegetables in the diet, as well as vegetable cultivation, increased in the 18th century.[20]

Table setting and food storage and preparation were examined by analysing the remains of ceramic and glass vessels and cutlery. Here, we focus solely on the cutlery finds. Overall, the analysis of the material remains of food serving and preparation vessels indicated that the latest European fashions were available to the inhabitants of Tornio, but their adoption and use patterns were influenced by local traditions and preferences.[21]

INDIGENEITY: SAMI FOODWAYS IN TORNIO

The first archaeological example we discuss is the influence of Sami foodways on food culture in Tornio. This is especially apparent in the animal bone assemblage, particularly in the consumption of reindeer meat and marrow from the bones. In the faunal assemblage from Tornio, *c.* 5% of the bones identified to species or genus belonged to reindeer. Multivariate analysis of the osteometric measurements suggests that most of these bones belong to the domesticated reindeer (*Rangifer tarandus tarandus*), with a few fragments from wild forest reindeer (*R.t. fennicus*).[22] Consumption of domesticated reindeer meat suggests Sami influence on local foodways, as reindeer herding was an integral part of

Sami subsistence in the early modern period, and reindeer meat the most important food in many Sami communities.[23] In Tornio, the wealthiest merchants owned small herds of reindeer. They were used for pulling sledges on trade journeys to the northern marketplaces where the merchants traded with the Sami in wintertime. During the summer months, the animals were placed in the care of Sami reindeer keepers.[24] Reindeer herding was and still is practised also by non-Sami people in northern Finland. It was practised too by the Finnish- and Swedish-speaking agrarian population colonizing the area at least from the latter half of the 17th century onwards, and *c.* 1400–1600 many owned reindeer for transportation purposes.[25] The differing skeletal elements of reindeer represented in the animal bone assemblage from Tornio also suggests that the merchants bought reindeer meat cuts from the Sami during winter trading trips – the under-representation of reindeer humeri in the animal bone assemblages from the marketplaces, along with the over-representation of the same skeletal element in the assemblage from Tornio, indicates that the Sami may have sold the better meat cuts to merchants visiting the marketplaces.[26]

Another Sami influence observable in the foodways in Tornio is the consumption of marrow from the lower limb bones of reindeer and cattle. Most fragments of reindeer and cattle metatarsal and metacarpal bones, as well as many radii and tibiae, were broken craniocaudally (i.e. along the head-to-tail axis), or by removing a length of bone from both ends, to obtain the marrow (Fig. 3.2). This manner of breaking lower limb bones of reindeer is ethnographically and archaeologically documented among the Sami.[27] The zooarchaeological evidence from both urban and agrarian settlements indicates that this custom was practised regardless of ethnic affiliation in late medieval and early modern northern Finland.[28] It was probably a Sami influence on local foodways, judging from the fact that it was such an important characteristic of Sami foodways from the medieval period onwards, and, furthermore, has not been documented among the more southern urban and rural communities in Finland and Sweden.

Fig. 3.2 A broken reindeer metacarpal bone from the Tornio Keskikatu excavations (photograph: Anna-Kaisa Salmi).

LOCALITY: TABLE KNIVES AND *PUUKKO* KNIVES

The use of knives provides a valuable example of the persistence and transformation of local foodways. Iron knives are common finds in the archaeological record from Tornio. The knives can be divided into two main types: table knives and *puukko* knives. The *puukko* knife is a traditional thick-bladed single-edged knife, and served as a personal multi-purpose tool carried on the belt (Fig. 3.3).[29] The table knives are mostly small and simple mass-produced cutlery from central Europe and represent one of the oldest imported commodities adopted at the northern Swedish table. They are common on medieval rural sites throughout the north, and their use spans all social classes.[30]

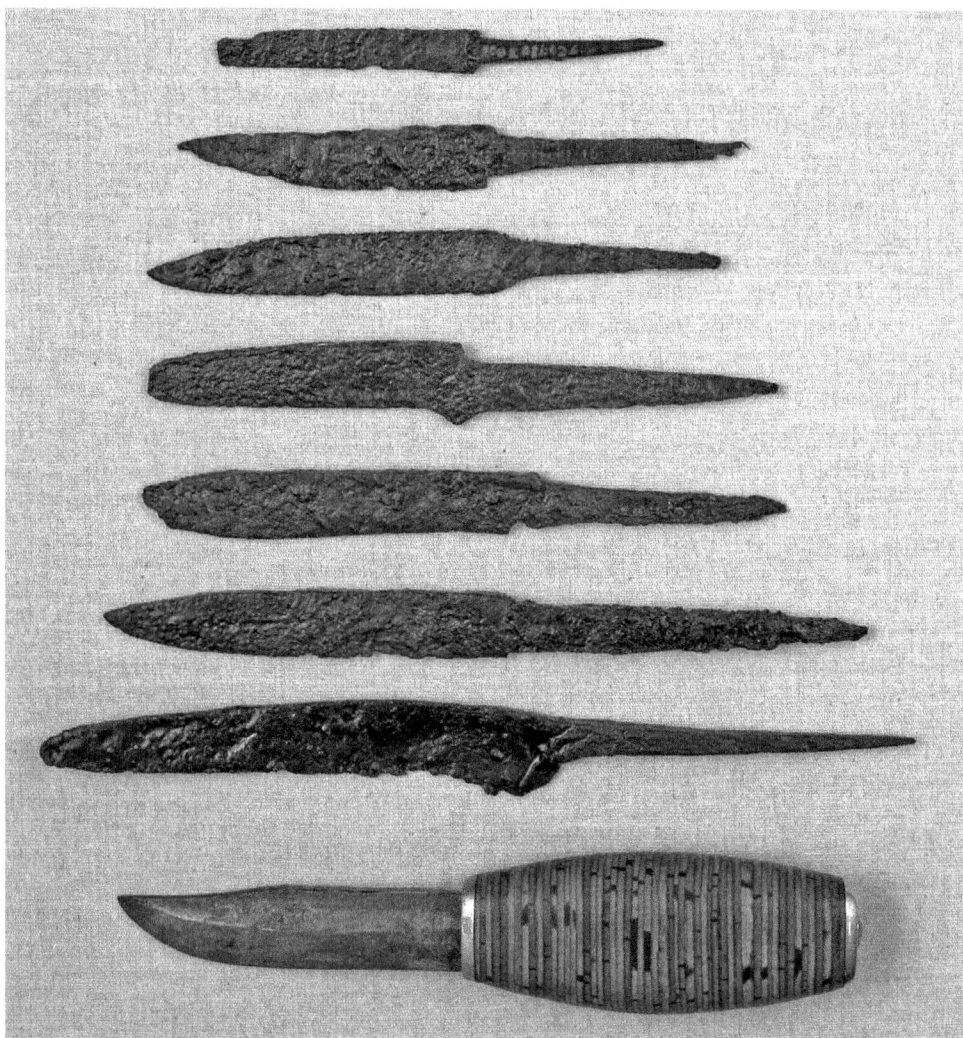

Fig. 3.3 Blades of *puukko* knives from Tornio and a modern hand-made example (photograph: I. Pietilä).

Puukko knives and table knives are quite evenly represented in the assemblages, suggesting that the use of the traditional type of knife continued despite the introduction and adoption of the new table knife. Table knives were specifically designed for eating, and represented modern European ways of dining. The role and meaning of *puukko* knives was much more versatile. They were tools and individual might use for anything from personal hygiene and everyday work to social representation and resolving personal feuds. Thus the introduction of table knives did not supersede *puukko* in the local everyday material culture, not necessarily even in dining practices, although the use of *puukko* at the table may have been seen as vulgar or old-fashioned manners in some social contexts.

Another related example of the persistence of local traditions despite the introduction of new commodities is the lack of interest in the use of forks in Tornio. Unlike the use of table knives, that of forks was uncommon there. It seems that the fork reached Tornio early in the 17th century, but remained a curiosity, despite it becoming a fixture at urban tables during the 17th century in many parts of the western world.[31] The archaeological assemblage includes two forks, one of which is a simple two-pronged instrument which probably had a wooden handle. The other is an apparently luxurious piece with an ivory handle in the shape of a female figure. Despite being known to the people of Tornio from the early 17th century, the fork does not seem to have been popular on local tables, judging from the archaeological data. It should be noted, however, that the increasing use of valuable silver may in part explain the lack of forks (and spoons) in the archaeological assemblage – the silver would have been recycled when the forks wore out.

MODERNITY: GARDEN CULTURE

Our third archaeological snapshot of the transformation of foodways in early modern Tornio regards the adoption of international fashions of gardening and increasing vegetable consumption. Documentary records and archaeological evidence of plant and insect remains indicate that gardening and vegetable cultivation were not commonly practised in early 17th-century Tornio. Wild plants were collected for spicing spirits or beer and for medicinal purposes, and wild berries were picked to enrich the diet. Vegetables seem to have been relatively uncommon.

The historical records indicate that vegetable consumption patterns changed towards the 18th century with the emergence of garden cultivation and an increasing variety of vegetables available.[32] Already in the 1730s, mayor Petter Pipping had a garden, on his farm outside the town, visible in Outhier's map.[33] In the town, wealthy merchants started cultivating gardens on empty town plots, introducing such crops as potato, lettuce, beetroot, parsnip and cucumber, hemp, and several species of herb.[34] Macrofossil research indicates the use of local wild plants, such as wild strawberry (*Fragaria vesca*), *Alchemilla*, juniper (*Juniperus communis*) and raspberry (*Rubus idaeus*), as food, medicine and spice, but there is only limited evidence of cultivated vegetables.[35] This pattern supports the idea of traditional food-plant use remaining common at least until the early 18th century in Tornio. The archaeological plant remains from the later part of 18th century include turnips (*Brassica rapa*), which were probably cultivated on cabbage patches outside the toll fence.[36] Evidence of imported foods, such as figs (*Ficus carica*)

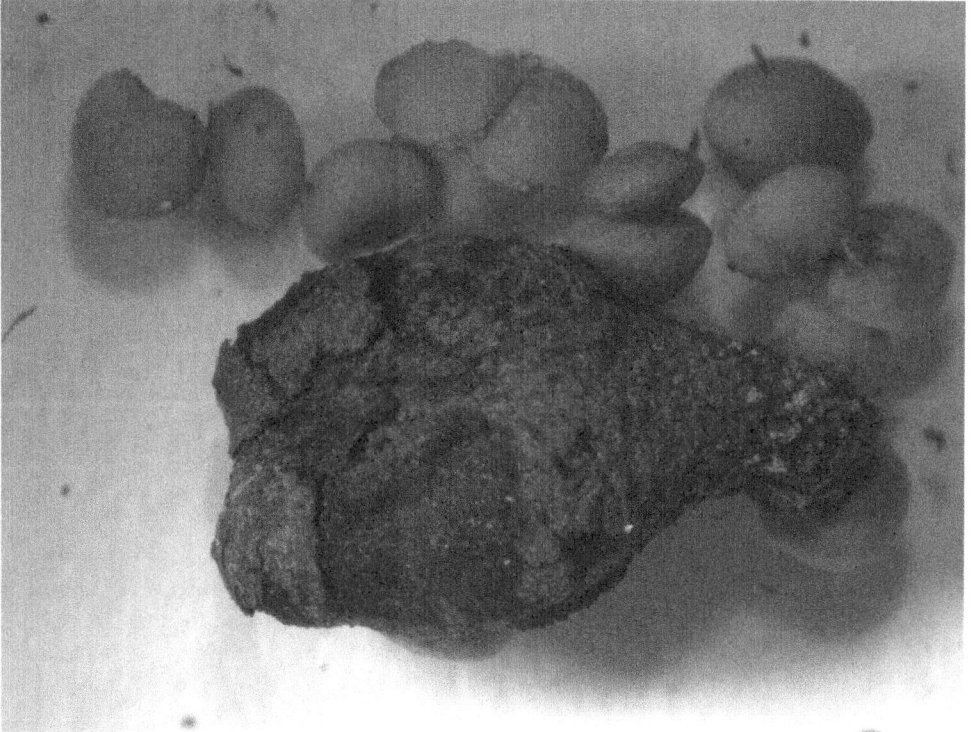

Fig. 3.4 Remains of imported food from a late 18th-century household: common grape (*Vitis vinifera*) and common fig (*Ficus carica*) (photograph: Annemari Tranberg).

and grapes (*Vinis vitifera*), was discovered within late 18th-century deposits (Fig. 3.4).[37] Figs and grapes were commonly imported fruits at that time.[38] According to historical records, in 1782 there were at least two orchards in the town, with apple and pear trees.[39] Moreover, the macrofossil and fossil insect records indicate the possibility of herb (e.g. *Mentha* and *Alchemilla*) cultivation in the Murberg/Wipo plot in the mid- or late 18th century.[40] Not all of the newly introduced plants – for instance hemp and many of the herbs – were successful in the northern climate, but many other novelties soon became a part of the local cuisine. The northern climate, and especially frost, destroyed some new crops introduced in the latter half of the century. Suitable species, like potato, succeeded, but other more exotic species, such as apple and pear, did not.

FOODWAYS IN CULTURAL CONTACT

The material evidence of foodways in Tornio shows multiple strategies for dealing with other cultures in a colonial society. Our archaeological snapshot case studies show that local traditions, such as the use of *puukko* knives, were maintained and mixed with new habits. On the other hand, foodways were also influenced by contacts with the Sami, as well as international trends infiltrating the town by way of its lively trade connections.

The material culture of everyday practices often reflects the creation of identities, lifeways, and worldviews in colonial societies. We have little information on the ethnic identities people held in Tornio – whether with their different geographic and ethnic affiliations they felt connected to their origins, and whether they acquired a new urban identity, or both. Several comparative studies of archaeological remains from northern Finland have failed to identify clear material expressions of class, ethnic, or other identities.[41] It thus seems that manifesting identity in material terms was not important in the small communities where everybody knew each other, and where the availability of goods may have restricted the more salient expressions of identity.[42] Moreover, it seems that although class identity, for instance, was important to the people in northern Finland, expression of this in material terms was confined mostly to special circumstances, and everyday material culture seems to have been remarkably similar among different groups.[43] With regard to Sami identity, there are no clear archaeological indications of Sami families in the archaeological record from Tornio, despite the fact that families of Sami origin may have been present in the town.[44] The prevalence of Sami foodways in Tornio, and also in the countryside of northern Finland, can be taken as an indication of the presence of Sami families in the community, the adoption of Sami foodways by the agrarian and urban communities, or more probably, both.

It has been argued elsewhere that a new urban and modern identity emerged in Tornio, and in northern parts of Finland and Sweden in general, in the 18th century.[45] A new urban lifestyle and identity were reflected, for instance, in the reorganization of urban space, increasing amounts of contemporary furniture and painted house exteriors, a reduction in agricultural activities within the town, and the decreasing role of wild resources in the diet.[46] There was also a developing interest in gardening and vegetable consumption. This new concern, as well as the decrease in hunting, was related to the changing human–environmental relationships of the Age of Enlightenment – a period characterized by an growing interest in efforts to dominate and improve the environment by means of, for instance, agricultural improvement, garden cultivation, and natural science. Gardening and experimentation with new varieties of vegetables in northern Finland therefore partook in the creation of new urban and modern identities.

We feel, however, that instead of concentrating on finding solid ethnic, class-related or, indeed, "modern" identities manifested in the material remains of foodways in Tornio, it is more fruitful to focus on the shifting, dynamic and hybrid nature of the food culture. In postcolonial archaeology, the focus is often placed on practices rather than upon solid cultures – this enables archaeologists to examine the community as fragmented according to, for instance, sex, age, or social standing, and investigate the negotiation strategies of these different groups in colonial societies.[47] Along the same lines, foodways in Tornio can best be described as a hybrid of different practices and choices. This is a typical outcome in colonial settings, as colonial societies usually do not maintain separateness, but become integrated totalities where all parties are affected.[48] It might be said that colonial contacts result in localized cultural forms.[49] Thus another word to describe the mixing of cultural features in colonial contact is "hybridization". The concepts of hybridization and third space are apt to describe many kinds of interaction in colonial and frontier societies.[50] Hybridization means that all participants in the colonial encounter can bring something to the resulting colonial cultural practices.

In such a manner, foodways in Tornio were a hybrid set of practices influenced by local agrarian culture, the Sami culture, and European fashions.

Cultural change in colonial situations has been often simplified into dualities such as "domination and resistance", whereas in reality a wide variety of strategies and processes have taken place when indigenous peoples have negotiated their relationships with their colonizers.[51] Colonial encounters happened on multiple levels, engendering countless interactions and transactions, and taking form from a mix of "consent & contestation, appropriation & accommodation, refusal & refiguration, ethnicization & hybridization".[52] There were many reasons for people in colonial societies to adopt, manipulate and create new cultural forms: for instance, to access new social and political affiliations, to realize hopes for upward social mobility, and to create new identities and social networks. Homi Bhabha (1994, 110) emphasizes especially the ambivalent and often contradictory nature of cultural hybridization in the colonial encounter. According to Ella Shohat (1992), agency is a problematic issue in colonial and neo-colonial hybridization, which may result from, among other things, forced assimilation, social conformism, and cultural mimicry. Hybrid syntheses may become uncontested and reproduced as normal parts of the cultural practice. Still, they contain the "sedimentation of historical experience".[53]

The hybridity of food-cultural practices in Tornio can be seen as a reflection of the multiple strategies people employed to negotiate their standing in a multicultural colonial society of that type. Moving to the town, acting as a merchant, and adopting the ingredients of the urban food culture were surely means to achieve upward social and economic mobility for the farmers and, possibly, the Sami who decided to take such steps. Still, the "sedimentation of historical experience" – the incompatibility of the Sami identity and traditional way of life with the nationalistic project of Swedish state-making – was present in the choices people made and in the material culture they utilized.

ACKNOWLEDGEMENTS

We are grateful for financial support from the Academy of Finland through the projects "Food and Identity in Medieval and Early Modern Urban Communities" and "Town, Border, and Material Culture", as well as from the National Graduate School in Archaeology.

NOTES

1 Wallerström 1995, 146.
2 Reinhard 2001, 2240.
3 Nurmi 2009; see Lindmark 2013 for critique.
4 Vahtola 1991; Wallerström 1995; Nurmi 2009; Kylli 2012; Lindmark 2013.
5 Kylli 2012, 14–15. Eastern Orthodox Christianity was earlier endorsed by the local peasant communities: see Ylimaunu *et al.* 2014.
6 Wallerström 2000; Nurmi 2009; Lindmark 2013.
7 Nurmi 2009.
8 Mäntylä 1971, 33.
9 Vahtola 1991; Nurmi 2009.
10 Mäntylä 1971.
11 Bhabha 1994; Gosden 2001; 2004.
12 Bhabha 2004, 55–6.
13 E.g. Comaroff & Comaroff 1997, 23; deFrance 2003; Amundsen 2011; Pavao-Zuckerman & Loren 2012.
14 Lilja 1995, 50–1; Herva *et al.* 2012.
15 Mäntylä 1971; Ylimaunu 2007.
16 Orser 1996, 86–7; Thomas 2004, 3
17 Salmi *et al.* 2014.
18 Hyttinen 2011.
19 Alenius 2011; Tranberg 2011.
20 Salmi *et al.* 2014.
21 Salmi *et al.* 2014.
22 Puputti & Niskanen 2009.
23 E.g. Itkonen 1921; Wallerström 2000; Lahti 2006; Hansen & Olsen 2007.
24 Mäntylä 1971, 109.
25 Kortesalmi 2008, 108–9.
26 Lahti 2006; Puputti 2010.
27 Itkonen 1921, 10; 1948, 257–8; Hambleton &

Rowley-Conwy 1997, 62; Soppela 2000, 92; Lahti, 2006, 290; Harlin 2009.
28 Salmi 2011.
29 Sirelius 1921, 17; Pälsi 1955; Hyytinen 1999.
30 Koivunen 1991, 147–8; Wallerstöm 1995, 54.
31 Leone & Schackel 1987, 50.
32 Mäntylä 1971, 412.
33 Outhier 1975, 52.
34 Clarke 1838; Mäntylä 1971, 412.
35 Tranberg 2014ab.
36 Mäntylä 1971, 203.
37 Tranberg 2014ab.
38 Mäntylä 1971.
39 Mäntylä 1971, 411–12.
40 Alenius 2011; Tranberg 2011.
41 Herva & Ylimaunu 2005; Herva & Nurmi 2009; Salmi 2011; Salmi & Kuokkanen 2014.
42 Rosén 2004; Herva & Ylimaunu 2005; Herva & Nurmi 2009; Salmi & Kuokkanen 2014.
43 Salmi & Kuokkanen 2014.
44 Vahtola 1991; Nurmi 2009.
45 Ylimaunu 2007; Salmi *et al.* 2014.
46 Mäntylä 1971, 264; Vuorela 1975, 421; Ylimaunu 2007; Puputti 2010.
47 E.g. Silliman 2005.
48 Comaroff & Comaroff 1997; Gosden 2001; 2004; Johnson 2006.
49 Comaroff & Comaroff, 1997, 23.
50 Naum 2010.
51 Lightfoot & Martinez 1995; Lindenfelt & Richardson 2010.
52 Comaroff & Comaroff 1997, 22.
53 Shohat 1992.

BIBLIOGRAPHY

Alenius, T. 2011. 'Siitepölyraportti, Tornio Suensaari, YIT:n tontti (II/2/4), Keskikatu 12. Kaupunkiarkeologiset koekaivaukset 24.5.–4.6.2010 ja kaivaukset 7.6.–6.7.2010'. Pollen report.

Amundsen, C. 2011. 'The zoo-archaeology of multi-room houses', in Olsen *et al.* 2011, 241–64.

Äikäs, T. (ed.) 2009. *Máttut – máddagat. The Roots of Saami Ethnicities, Societies and Spaces/ Places.* Oulu: Giellagas Institute at the University of Oulu.

Clark, P. (ed.) 1995. *Small Towns in Early Modern Europe.* Cambridge: Cambridge University Press.

Clarke, E. D. 1838. *Travels in Various Countries of Scandinavia including Denmark, Sweden, Norway, Lapland and Finland*, vol. 1. London: E. Cadell.

Comaroff, J. L. & Comaroff, J. 1997. *Of Revelation and Revolution.* Vol 2: *The Dialectics of Modernity on a South African Frontier.* Chicago: Chicago University Press.

deFrance, S. D. 2003. 'Diet and provisioning in the High Andes: A Spanish colonial settlement on the outskirts of Potosí, Bolivia', *International Journal of Historical Archaeology* 7(2): 99–125.

Gosden, C. 2001. 'Postcolonial archaeology. Issues of culture, identity, and knowledge', in Hodder 2001, 241–61.

Gosden, C. 2004. *Archaeology and Colonialism. Cultural Contact from 5000 BC to the Present.* Cambridge: Cambridge University Press.

Hall, M. & Silliman, S. W. (eds) 2006. *Historical Archaeology.* Malden: Blackwell.

Halinen, P., Lavento, M. & Suhonen, M. (eds) 2009. *Recent Perspectives on Sami Archaeology in Fennoscandia and North-West Russia.* Helsinki: Museovirasto.

Hambleton, E. & Rowley-Conwy, P. 1997. 'The medieval reindeer economy at Gæccevaj'njar'ga 244 B in the Varanger Fjord, North Norway', *Norwegian Archaeological Review* 30(1): 55–70.

Hansen, L. I. & Olsen, B. 2007. *Samenes historie fram til 1750.* Oslo: Cappelen Damm.

Harlin, E. 2009. 'The possibilities of osteology in historical Sami archaeology: Life and livelihood at the 18th century Ohcejohka Sami market site', in Halinen *et al.* 2009, 121–32.

Hederyd, O., Alamäki, Y. & Kenttä, M. (eds) 1991. *Tornionlaakson historia I, jääkaudelta 1600-luvulle*, vol. 1. Tornio: Torniolaakson kuntien historiakirjatoimikunta.

Herva, V-P. (ed.) 2006. *People, Material Culture and Environment in the North. Proceedings of the 22nd Nordic Archaeological Conference.* Oulu: University of Oulu.

Herva, V.-P. & Nurmi, R. 2009. 'Beyond consumption: Functionality, artifact biography, and early modernity in a European periphery', *International Journal of Historical Archaeology* 13(2): 158–82.

Herva, V.-P. & Ylimaunu, T. 2005. 'Posliiniastiat, varallisuus ja kuluttajakäyttäytyminen 1700-luvun Torniossa', *Suomen Museo* 112: 79–89.

Herva, V.-P., Ylimaunu, T. & Symonds, J. 2012. 'The urban landscape and iconography of Early Modern Tornio', *Fennoscandia Archaeologica* 29: 73–91.

Hodder , I. (ed.) 2001. *Archaeological Theory Today.* Cambridge: Polity Press.

Hyttinen, M. 2011. 'Tornio Suensaari, YIT:n tontti (II/2/4), Keskikatu 12. kaupunkiarkeologiset koekaivaukset 24.5.–4.6.2010 ja kaivaukset 7.6.–6.7.2010'. Excavation report.

Hyytinen, T. 1999. *Puukko: käsikirja.* Jyväskylä: Arma Fennica.

Ikäheimo, J., Nurmi, R. & Satokangas, R. (eds) 2011. *Harmaata näkyvissä, Kirsti Paavolan juhlakirja.* Oulu: University of Oulu.

Ingersoll, D. W. & Bronitsky, G. (eds) 1987. *Mirror and Metaphor. Material and Social Constructions of Reality.* Lanham: University Press of America.

Itkonen, T. I. 1921. *Lappalaisten ruokatalous.* Helsinki: Suomalais-Ugrilainen Seura.

Itkonen, T. I. 1948. *Suomen lappalaiset vuoteen 1945.* Helsinki: Söderström.

Johnson, M. 2006. 'The tide reversed: Prospects and potentials for a postcolonial archaeology of Europe', in Hall & Silliman 2006, 313–31.

Koivunen, P. 1991. 'Suomen Tornionlaakson esihistoriaa', in Hederyd *et al.* 1991, 101–59.

Kortesalmi. J.J. 2008. *Poronhoidon synty ja kehitys Suomessa.* Helsinki: Suomalaisen Kirjallisuuden Seura.

Kylli, R. 2012. *Saamelaisten kaksi kääntymystä. Uskonnon muuttuminen Utsjoen ja Enontekiön lapinmailla 1602–1905.* Helsinki: Suomalaisen Kirjallisuuden Seura.

Lahti, E. 2006. 'Bones from Sápmi: Reconstruction of the everyday life of two ancient Saami households', in Herva 2006, 284–95.

Leone, M. P. & Shackel, P. A. 1987. 'Forks, clocks and power', in Ingersoll & Bronitsky 1987, 45–62.

Lightfoot, K. & Martinez, A. 1995. 'Frontiers and boundaries in archaeological perspective', *Annual Review of Anthropology* 24: 471–92.

Lilja, S. 1995. 'Small towns in the periphery: Population and economy of small towns in Sweden during the early modern period', in Clark 1995, 50–76.

Lindenfeld, D. & Richardson, M. 2010. 'Introduction. Beyond conversion and syncretism', in Lindenfeld & Richardson 2010, 1–23.

Lindenfeld, D. F. & Richardson, M. (eds) 2010. *Beyond Conversion and Syncretism: Indigenous Encounters With Missionary Christianity, 1800–2000.* New York: Berghahn Books.

Lindmark, D. 2013. 'Colonial encounter in the early modern Sápmi', in Naum & Nordin 2013, 131–46.

Mäntylä, I. 1971. *Tornion kaupungin historia. 1. osa. 1620–1809.* Tornio: Tornion kaupunki.

Naum, M. 2010. 'Re-emerging frontiers: Postcolonial theory and historical archaeology of the borderlands', *Journal of Archaeological Method and Theory* 17: 101–31.

Naum, M. & Nordin, J. M. (eds) 2013. *Scandinavian Colonialism and the Rise of Modernity: Small Time Agents in a Global Arena.* New York: Springer.

Nurmi, R. 2009. 'The others among us? Saami artefacts in a 17th-century urban context in the town of Tornio, northern Finland', in Äikäs 2009, 68–87.

Olsen, B., Urbańczyk, P. & Amundsen, C. (eds) 2011. *Hybrid Spaces. Medieval Finnmark and the Archaeology of Multi-Room Houses.* Oslo: Novus.

Orser, C. E. jr 1996. *A Historical Archaeology of the Modern World.* New York: Plenum.

Outhier, R. 1975 (translated by M. Itkonen-Kaila). *Matka pohjan perille.* Helsinki: Otava.

Pavao-Zuckerman, B. & Di Paolo Loren, D. 2012. 'Presentation is everything: Foodways, table-wares, and colonial identity at Presidio Los Adaes', *International Journal of Historical Archaeology* 16(1): 199–226.

Pälsi, S. 1955. *Puukko.* Helsinki: Otava.

Pennanen, J. & Näkkäläjärvi, K. (eds) 2000. *Siiddastallan. Siidoista kyliin.* Oulu: Pohjoinen.

Puputti, A. 2010. *Living with Animals: A Zooarchaeological Analysis of Urban Human–Animal Relationships in Early Modern Tornio, 1621–1800.* BAR International Series 2100. Oxford: Archaeopress.

Puputti, A. & Niskanen, M. 2009. 'Identification of semi-domesticated reindeer (*Rangifer tarandus tarandus*, Linnaeus 1758) and wild forest reindeer (*R.t. fennicus*, Lönnberg 1909) from postcranial skeletal measurements', *Mammalian Biology* 74(1): 49–58.

Reinhard, W. 2001. 'Colonization and Colonialism, History of', in Smelser & Baltes 2001, 2240–5.

Rosén, C. 2004. *Stadsbor och bönder – materiell kultur och social status i Halland från medeltid till 1700-tal.* Mölndal: Riksantikvarieämbetet.

Salmi, A. 2011. 'Riistaa, kalaa ja konttiluita – Pohjois-Suomen ruokakulttuurista n. 1400–1700 AD', in Ikäheimo *et al.* 2011, 221–36.

Salmi, A. & Kuokkanen, T. 2014. 'Bones, buttons and buckles: Negotiating class and bodily practices in early modern Oulu', *Post-Medieval Archaeology* 48(1): 182–206.

Salmi, A., Tranberg, A., Pääkkönen, M. & Nurmi, R. 2014. 'Becoming modern: Hybrid foodways in early modern Tornio, northern Finland', *International Journal of Historical Archaeology* 18(3): 489–512.

Shaw, R. & Steward, C. 2005. 'Introduction: Problematizing syncretism', in Steward & Shaw 2005, 1–24.

Shohat, E. 1992. 'Notes on the "Post-Colonial"', *Social Text* 31/32: 99–113

Silliman, S. W. 2005. 'Culture contact or colonialism? Challenges in the archaeology of native North America', *American Antiquity* 70(1): 55–74.

Sirelius, U. T. 1921. *Suomen kansanomaista kulttuuria II, esineellisen kansantieteen tuloksia.* Helsinki: Otava.

Smelser, N. J. & Baltes, P. B. (eds) 2001. *International Encyclopedia of the Social and Behavioral Sciences.* Amsterdam: Elsevier.

Soppela, P. 2000. 'Poro ravinnonlähteenä', in Pennanen & Näkkäläjärvi 2000, 92–5.
Steward, C. & Shaw, R. (eds) 2005. *Syncretism/Anti-Syncretism: The Politics of Religious Synthesis*. London: Routledge.
Thomas, J. 2004. *Archaeology and Modernity*. London: Routledge.
Tranberg, A. 2011. 'Makrofossiiliraportti, Tornio Suensaari, YIT:n tontti (II/2/4), Keskikatu 12. kaupunkiarkeologiset koekaivaukset 24.5.–4.6.2010 ja kaivaukset 7.6.–6.7.2010'. Microfossil report.
Tranberg, A. 2014a. 'Makrofossiiliraportti, TANK/RYNKS -02, Kaupunkiarkeologinen pelastus-kaivaus, Tornio, Keskikatu 29-35'. Macrofossil report.
Tranberg, A. 2014b. 'Makrofossiiliraportti, TANK -08, Kaupunkiarkeologinen opetuskaivaus, Tornio, Keskikatu 29'. Macrofossil report.
Vahtola, J. 1991. 'Kansojen moninaisuus', in Hederyd *et al.* 1991, 179–217
Vuorela, T. 1975. *Suomalainen kansankulttuuri*. Porvoo: Söderström
Wallerström, T. 1995. *Norrbotten, Sverige och medeltiden: problem kring makt och bosättning i en europeisk periferi*. Stockholm: Almqvist & Wiksell.
Wallerström, T. 2000. 'The Saami between east and west in the Middle Ages: An archaeological contribution to the history of reindeer breeding', *Acta Borealia* 17(1): 3–39.
Ylimaunu, T. 2007. *Aittakylästä kaupungiksi. Arkeologinen tutkimus Tornion kaupungistumisesta 18. vuosisadan loppuun mennessä*. Studia archaeologica septentrionalia 4. Rovaniemi: Pohjois-Suomen historiallinen yhdistys.
Ylimaunu, T., Lakomäki, S., Kallio-Seppä, T., Mullins, R., Nurmi, R. & Kuorilehto, M. 2014. 'Borderlands as spaces: Creating third spaces and fractured landscapes in medieval Northern Finland', *Journal of Social Archaeology* 14(2): 244–67.

4

Brewing an Ethnic Identity: Local and Foreign Beer Brewing Traditions in 15th- to 17th-Century Sweden – an Example from Nya Lödöse

JENS HEIMDAHL

During medieval and early modern times regional variations in beer culture may have been connected to ethnicity. The use of herbal beer additives – hops (Humulus lupulus L.) and gruit – predominantly sweet gale (Myrica gale L.) is reflected in the archaeobotanical record and reveals the Swedish west coast, then belonging to Denmark, as a part of the western European sweet gale belt. The region of Svealand was a hop beer area, and in eastern Götaland mixed beer types were common. Brewing remnants from the west coast town of Nya Lödöse (1480–1540) may indicate multi-ethnic influences within the town and individual households.

BEER AND IDENTITY

In medieval and early modern northern Europe the tradition of brewing and drinking beer was deeply rooted in all levels of society; it worked then (and indeed perhaps works nowadays) as a social glue. However, brewing traditions and culinary preferences varied between geographical regions and social groups, making it plausible to link beer types to the question of the identity and perhaps the ethnicity of its producers and consumers. When referring to identity and ethnicity, the basic model used here is that described by Richard Jenkins (2004) as a process of "being" or "becoming".[1] Thus "identity" is used as a broad term referring to any social identity – such as ethnicity, age, class, gender, profession etc. However, the term "ethnicity" is here used in a much more limited and simplified way, referring to a self-identification by specific ethnic groups. This chapter discusses the possibility of linking certain regional variations in beer culture to ethnicity and regional identity in northern Europe during the 15th to 17th centuries. The main aim is to expose the complexity of the question at hand, and to try to identify possibilities and limitations of the task. It is also to provide an overview of regional variations in beer culture from 1450 to 1800, and to give some background as to how and why these variations may be linked to the identity and ethnicity of the consumers. Central to the discussion is a case study from a town plot in Nya Lödöse in western Sweden, where the archaeobotanical record provides evidence for a brewery on the plot in the period *c.* 1480–1612.

During the period 1450–1800 brewing was carried out in almost every Swedish and other northern European household. Parallel to baking and cooking, it was considered a part of regular household production. Household brewing during the early modern period was rooted in older traditions that can be traced back to the late Iron Age, when housewives supervising brewing held key positions within the religious communion rites of the pre-Christian cult.[2] Although beer lost its role as the communion link between deities and people, in favour of wine, it retained its strong position as a crucial element in maintaining and fostering social relations in the context of dining culture. Aspects of household status, particularly of the housewife, were dependent upon the quality of beer produced and served.

Even though the role of brewing and consumption of beer is well described in the extensive documentary evidence available, the technical aspects of brewing and the nature of the beer itself remain, to a substantial degree, as yet unclear.[3] When it comes to the quality of beer we can observe several modes of description: more technical descriptions related to origin, colour and flavouring; and more subjective comment on aspects of its quality linked to its market price and the social status of the appropriate consumer (it may be described for instance as a "dark hopped beer from Lübeck", or as a "beer aimed at common people"). The focus here is on one of those parameters, easily recognizable in the archaeobotanical record: namely preservative additives and spices in the form of hops (*Humulus lupulus* L.) and/or gruit/grut – in which sweet gale, also known as bog myrtle (*Myrica gale* L.), was the predominant ingredient. In Scandinavia sweet gale (Danish *porse*/Swedish *pors*) was never called a *gruit*, and henceforth it is referred to as sweet gale in its Scandinavian context. The term *gruit* is used in the Dutch/German context.

Finds of hops and sweet gale on archaeological sites generally indicate brewing on the site, and these plants are very common in urban medieval and early modern environments in northern Europe, appearing in most well-preserved contexts with household waste.[4] So far, the impression from the archaeobotanical record confirms the picture that brewing was performed in almost every Swedish household before 1800. Although archaeobotanical analyses have only become common in the last decade, the record is growing.[5] The finds henceforth referred to are almost exclusively from urban archaeological contexts; evidence from rural environments is sparse due to poor preservation and limited investigation, and will not be further discussed in this chapter.

In describing the dynamics of hop and sweet gale beer traditions, it is important to recognize a critical change in practice that is underscored by written records. Late medieval competition between the merchants of different beer additives ended with a total victory for hopped beer. There were a number of reasons for this – an aggressive campaign on the part of Hanseatic hop traders, and not least the superior preservation qualities of hops allowing for a greater export range for hopped beer; its supposed better taste, repeated in many older (and some recent) sources,[6] was not a decisive factor. However, the question of taste was probably important in this development, nevertheless, and factors such as experience, personal preferences and surrounding social and cultural factors also played a part. Moreover, while it has been argued that hops were a new additive in medieval Scandinavia, and that it gradually replaced sweet gale, considered an additive of choice for the poorer population[7] modern palaeoecological studies and archaeobotany have made it clear that hops have grown wild in Sweden since Preboreal times, and seems to have been in use as a brewing additive for as long as in central Europe – that is, from about the 7th or 8th century.[8]

There is also a critical gender aspect to the question of beer culture. The written records concentrate on issues of the beer trade and include information about exporters and production centres, prices of beer and hops, and volumes of beer shipped and in stock, as well as laws concerning cultivation of hops in order to reduce dependence upon imports. Working with written sources, it is essential to remember that the beer trade was predominantly controlled by men; also that the traded beer itself, manufactured in large breweries, was the product of a male craft. Furthermore, the written records were themselves created predominantly by men, and thereby express male perspectives, within which the work and influence of women were generally neglected. On the other hand, the urban archaeological record of brewing reflects the small-scale local traditions directly connected to the individual household, a craft performed and controlled by women, generally the individual housewives. Thus, the written sources and the archaeological records reflect different aspects of beer and brewing culture, and should be approached with these factors in mind (Fig. 4.1).

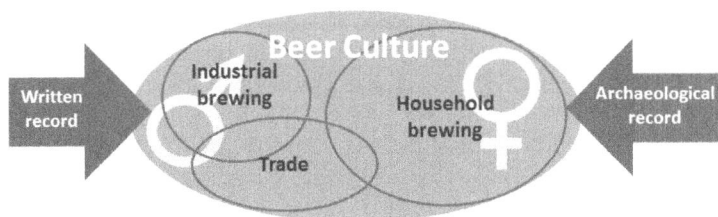

Fig. 4.1 Beer culture according to the written and archaeological records (drawing: Jens Heimdahl). The two types of record tend to reflect different aspects of beer culture in the past. While the written sources record industrial brewing, trade, customs, laws – fields generally controlled by men, the archaeological record captures household production – a domain traditionally controlled by women.

REGIONAL DYNAMICS OF BEER FLAVOURING

During medieval times the beer traditions of northern Europe became polarized into what could be described as the west coast "gruit belt", and the hop area of the northern European inland. This polarity developed due to the natural distribution of sweet gale (the predominant gruit ingredient) along the coastal zone. The regional pattern was old. The use of sweet gale in the western coastal area dates back to the pre-Roman Iron Age and perhaps even the Bronze Age.[9] The origins of the use of hops as a beer additive would seem to precede the earliest finds dated to the 7th century, since these are distributed over vast distances in central Europe and Scandinavia.[10]

In the 13th century, the gruit belt included the coastal area of the Netherlands, north-west Germany, Denmark (including the present Swedish west coast), and Norway (Fig. 4.2). The hop area, on the other hand, covered most of the German territory,[11]

and included Polish (and former Prussian) towns such as Kołobrzeg/Kolberg, Gdańsk/
Danzig and Elbląg,[12] and Estonian/Latvian/Livonian towns such as Pärnu, Tallinn,
Tartu/Dorpat and Viljandi/Fellin.[13] Hops also grew in the gruit belt, and was used in
parallel and in combination with sweet gale. Sweet gale/gruit, on the other hand, was
less common in the European inland, although it did exist, and will be discussed later.

Fig. 4.2 Map of archaeobotanical finds of hops and sweet gale in Sweden dated between 1000
and 1800 (drawing: Jens Heimdahl). Sites 1–24 are presented in Table 4.1. Areas of sweet gale
beer culture are marked by dots, and of hop beer culture by lines; mixed beer culture is marked
by both lines and dots. In Dutch and Danish areas the sweet gale belt as illustrated on the map
existed until about the mid-14th century, to be replaced by hopped beer; the sweet gale tradition
prevailed along the Swedish west coast and in Norway.

Table 4.1 (opposite and following pages) Sites with archaeobotanical brewing remains in Sweden:
hop (black dot) and sweet gale (white dot).

KEY

●	Hop
○	Sweet gale
1 dot	1-10
2 dots	11-100
3 dots	>100

Town	Site	Century								Reference
		11th	12th	13th	14th	15th	16th	17th	18th	
1: Enköping	Fältskären			●●○						Heimdahl 2012c
2: Falun	Västra Falun							●●	●	Heimdahl forthcoming b
3: Karlstad	Stigaren 1						●			Heimdahl 2015a
	Druvan								●	Heimdahl 2005b
	Järnvägsgatan							●—		Heimdahl 2009e
	Örnen								●●	Heimdahl 2006
4: Nora	Ekorren							●●		Heimdahl 2013d
5: Nyköping	Föreningen 18					●				Påhlsson 1989
	Åkroken	○○●	○○○○●●	○○○●●	○○●●●	●				Nordström & Lindeblad 2016
6: Sigtuna	Trädgårdsmästaren	●	●							Engelmark 2002
7: Stockholm	Gråbrödraklostret				—	●—	—			Heimdahl 2013g
	Helgeandsholmen				●●●	●—	●●	●●		Griffin 1983
	Kvasten							●●●		Heimdahl 2008
	Riddarholmen							●●		Heimdahl 2012f
	Äggelunda bytomt					●				Heimdahl 2013f
8: Uppsala	Akademigatan				—	○●—				Påhlsson 1990
	Bryggaren			●		●●				Pälsson 1991
	Svalan		●●	●●○	●○					Påhlsson 1983
9: Jönköping	Diplomaten							●●	●●●	Heimdahl 2009a
	Dovhjorten							●●○	●	Heimdahl 2012e
	Västra kajen				●●○○					Heimdahl 2012a

Town	Site	Century									Reference
		11th	12th	13th	14th	15th	16th	17th	18th		
10: Kalmar	Gesällen							●●●○	●●●		Heimdahl 2014d
	Kalmar slott		○	●					●		Heimdahl 2015d
	Mästaren							●●	●●		Heimdahl 2012b
11: Linköping	Bokbindaren							●			Heimdahl 2013a
	Guldsmedsgränd			●							Heimdahl 2011a
12: Norrköping	Konstantinopel				●●●○		●●○				Heimdahl 2005a
	Lyckan								●		Nordström & Heimdahl 2012
	Mjölnaren						○				Heimdahl 2011b
	Ruddammen							●	●●		Heimdahl 2012d
13: Skänninge	Dyhagen			○	●●	●●○	●	●			Heimdahl 2009c
	Fjärrvärmes-chakt			—	─○─	—					Heimdahl 2014b
	Fogden		●○	●●							Heimdahl 2013e
	Linköpingsgatan			○●	●●						Heimdahl 2014c
	Motalagatan			—	─●○─						Heimdahl 2009d
	S:t Olofs konvent			○		●					Heimdahl 2009b
14: Söderköping	Von Platen			—	─●●○─	—					Magnusson pers. comm.
15: Västervik	Slottsholmen						●●○				Heimdahl 2013h
16: Växjö	Karolinerhuset				●				●		Balic et al. 2015
	Stora torget				○○				●		Heimdahl 2013i
17	Askeby kloster				—	○○●●					Heimdahl 2014a

Town	Site	Century								Reference
		11th	12th	13th	14th	15th	16th	17th	18th	
18: Göteborg	Bastionen								○○●●●	Heimdahl forthcoming a
	Gamla teatern								●	Larsson 1985
	Göta kanal							●		Larsson 1985
	Kronobageriet							●	●	Larsson 1985
	Slusskvarnen							●	●	Larsson 1985
19: Halmstad	Broktorp						○○			Bjuggner & Heimdahl 2009
	Dr Kristina					○○○●●●				Heimdahl forthcoming c
	Fjärrkyla				●	○○○●	○○●●●			Heimdahl 2013b
20: Kungsbacka	Stortorget								●	Heimdahl 2013c
21: Uddevalla	Trappan								●	Heimdahl 2015b
22	Vinberg sn	○○○								Viklund 2011
23: Lund	Adelgatan		○○							Heimdahl 2015 c
	Kattesund				—○○○●●●	—				Hjelmqvist 1991
	Paradiset	○○○●								Heimdahl forthcoming d
	Saluhallen	○○								Heimdahl 2010a
	Saluhallen II		○○○●	●●○						Heimdahl 2013j
	S:t Botulf	○○○●	○○○○●●●							Hjelmqvist 1991
24	Södra Valläkra	—	—○—●—	—						Heimdahl 2007

The main historical interest in the medieval gruit/hop situation resides in the fact that the polarized traditions gave rise to a trade conflict which lasted for two centuries. During the 13th century, the eastern coast of the Baltic Sea was dominated by Hanseatic traders. In the Dutch area the gruit trade was traditionally regulated by the *Gruitrecht* – granting privileges to specific gruit traders. The beer trade gradually increased in the 13th century, and during the 14th to 16th centuries there was fierce competition between Hanseatic traders and Dutch merchants that escalated into a trade war (including armed conflicts between the Hanse and the Netherlands). The conflict partly concerned the beer trade, in which the Hanse tried to capture market share from the gruit beer merchants who had gradually expanded into German territory. The superior preservation quality of hopped beer gave Hanseatic traders an advantage, and they eventually gained the upper hand: in the German archaeobotanical records there is a lack of traces of sweet gale in samples from the 15th to 16th centuries, with exception of the north-easternmost towns of Oldenburg and Bremen – formerly part of the gruit belt. Traces of the plant totally disappear from the samples dated to the 17th century.[14] In order to prevent the gruit trade in the Hanseatic areas, rumours were spread concerning gruit beer. It was said to be an unhealthy brew, causing headache, madness, blindness and diarrhoea. To support the hop merchants, laws like the *Bayerisches Reinheitsgebot* (1516), a decree of purity, were written in order to prevent beer brewers from using other ingredients.

With this history as a background it may be of interest to take a look at areas surrounding the conflict zone. How were local beer traditions affected by this trade conflict and its results? Denmark was a part of the sweet gale belt, and here the situation seems to have been similar to that in north-western Germany. Finds of sweet gale were common in urban contexts from the 13th to 15th centuries, and the plant dominated over hops in the early part of this period. However, from the 16th century onwards hopped beer took over in Denmark.[15] There are apparently no Danish finds of sweet gale from brewing sites dating from after the 15th century. There were, however, regional variations. Evidence of hops is absent in northern and central Jutland.[16] Possibly sweet gale flavoured beer was preferred in this area, with traditions analogous to those of the Dutch areas and (as we shall see) the Swedish west coast. There also appears to be a difference between the beer cultures in rural and urban areas, with the population of the countryside adopting hopped beer later than in towns. It should also be noted that hops and sweet gale are seldom found in the same archaeological contexts in Denmark. Of 41 examples of assemblages from different sites dating from 11th to 19th centuries, only one contains both hops and sweet gale.[17] This probably reflects a tradition whereby either hopped beer or sweet gale beer was preferred, and where combinations seldom occurred.

Local brewing cultures in medieval Sweden were both part of and separate from continental traditions. There were also regional differences, probably due to older traditions, which may be observed in the archaeobotanical record (see Table 4.1 above). The central region of Svealand (including the countryside surrounding Lake Mälaren, Dalecarlia and Värmland) seems to have a long and continuous tradition of hopped beer, generally without sweet gale flavouring. Hopped beer spiced with sweet gale existed,[18] but was not so common: this tradition predates the influence of the Hanse and the hops and beer trade of the 13th to 15th centuries, when Stockholm became an important centre for German traders and boasted a large German population.

The exception to this pattern can be found in the town of Nyköping, where a mixed beer culture existed. In Nyköping, purely hop or sweet gale brewing seems to have been rare, and instead lightly hopped sweet gale beers or fifty/fifty mixtures were favoured. Nyköping is on the northern border of the area of eastern Götaland (here Östergötland, Småland and Blekinge) dominated by mixtures of hopped and sweet gale beers (where hops prevail to a small extent over sweet gale). If we exclude the sites with fewer finds than eleven (<11) of beer additives dated to 1300–1600, we have nine sites and assemblages of which seven include mixed additives, one is a pure hops find (Skänninge, 14th century), and one a pure sweet gale find (Växjö, 14th century). Including Nyköping in this picture strengthens the image of this region as an area of hybrid beers. The mixed beers of eastern Götaland seem moreover to fall back on older traditions, different from the mixed beers of the Dutch and German area, which developed during a transitional phase before the wide adoption of hopped beer.[19]

In contrast to the east coast and the region of Eastern Götaland, the west coast of Sweden (Halland, Västergötland and Bohuslän) and Scania adhered to sweet gale traditions, with a less significant use of hops. The west coast/Scania and the Svealand region act as opposites and in both regions there are signs of longevity of their respective traditions. Finds from Lund and Vinberg indicate a pure sweet gale brewing tradition from the 10th and 11th centuries, with only insignificant use of hops. This region was then a part of Denmark but, in contrast to the material from Jutland and Sjaelland, there are indications that mixed beer types were more common here (although pure sweet gale beer dominates). Another difference is that the sweet gale tradition seems to have survived here longer than in Denmark. In Halmstad, sweet gale still dominated over hops in the 16th century, the shift occurring in the 17th – but with a surviving tradition of putting a smaller amount of sweet gale in the hopped beer, similar to the custom in eastern Sweden.

Finland was the easternmost part of the former Swedish kingdom, and the archaeobotanical record indicates that southern Finland clearly belonged to the hops area. Finds of sweet gale are less common than on the Scandinavian peninsula. Of 15 Finnish medieval sites studied, hops were found at seven, and sweet gale at two sites near Turku/Åbo.[20]

The use of sweet gale survived into the 18th century both on the west coast and in eastern Götaland. There was a clear decrease in the use of this additive from the 17th century onwards, and the evidence from this period indicates that it was added to hopped beer. The tradition of sweet gale brewing has also been noted in the historical record for the 18th and 19th centuries – described as something anachronistic: "the traditions of the old ones".[21] The interior parts of Småland seem to have been the last stronghold of sweet gale brewing in Europe.

The sweet gale beer culture in Sweden shows longevity in comparison with other parts of northern Europe – as an alternative to hops sweet gale survived at least a century longer than on the continent, and as an additive spice for about three centuries. In order to interpret this phenomenon it is essential to take into account how the traditions were influenced by local availability and trade control of hops and sweet gale. The north-western European gruit-trade monopoly was formed on the basis of control of the source: the *gruitrecht* regulated the right to use the wild populations of sweet gale growing exclusively along the coastal wetlands. In Scandinavia on the other hand, sweet gale was also common in the wetlands and lakeshores in the sparsely populated inland forests, making it an uncontrollable resource outside the more densely populated arable plains and coastal areas. Although there are some traces of regulated access to and harvest of sweet gale in Sweden, as in the laws of the 13th and 14th centuries, these seem to apply to limited areas with few lakes and bogs.[22] This situation meant Sweden was little affected by the continental trade conflict between gruit and hop merchants. Even if the gruit trade was inhibited, there was still easy access to domestic sources of sweet gale. Another difference between Sweden and the continent that sustained the old brewing traditions was the earlier specialization, centralization and commercial-scale brewing on the continent during the medieval period, which did not occur in Sweden until the 19th century.[23]

BEER AND ETHNICITY

In the literature surrounding the history of using hops and sweet gale in beer, it is sometimes stated that the original and main reason for these additives was their role as preservatives.[24] This may be the case, but the assertion remains a guess – we will never know the original reason, and this unitary explanation risks oversimplifying a more complex phenomenon. Both plants undoubtedly have qualities as spices, giving the beer significantly different tastes and characters. This is important to bear in mind in interpreting the patterns of regional difference in beer culture. Even if the superior quality of hops as a preservative is the main explanation of its eventual "victory" in the trade war, the properties of the additives as flavourings and their availability should be considered in explaining the regional distribution of the different beer cultures. Apart from floral distribution of additives, traditions of taste may be a crucial factor behind the regional patterns. Different beer types were preferred in different regions.

Taste preferences are closely linked to identity and ethnicity, but they are not fixed or absolute – new experiences may of course alter the preferences of individuals and groups. Generally acquired tastes of groups seem to resist rapid change and require time to be modified. An illustrative example comes from Amsterdam. It took several decades during the 14th century for hopped beer to win approval over gruit beer and to dominate the market.[25] Time was needed, and perhaps also a generational shift, for the people of Amsterdam to begin to appreciate the taste of hopped beer.

When linking specific tastes to specific identities, there is a risk of misinterpreting variations of taste that are linked to other factors, such as personal preferences, sub-regional (local) variations and class. Partly, these are unavoidable sources of error; in archaeology the factors of personal preference and smaller local variation are extremely hard (if not impossible) to identify. Class, on the other hand, may be visible through other types of material culture. In the case of beer flavouring, there is also information contained in the historical record. As pointed out earlier, there has been a tendency in Sweden to interpret hopped beer as a new innovation from the continent and to see its use as an upper-class phenomenon, in contrast to sweet gale beer which has been interpreted as the local beer of the commoners. This idea derives from written records – banquet menus and bills of fare which clearly assign different beers to different classes.

Also, during the 16th century, many Swedish written sources indicated that German beer was generally considered superior to domestic beer. The explanation is not clear, but probably this assumption and preference stemmed from technical differences in brewing or storage,[26] and it stimulated sizable imports of German beer and malt to Sweden.[27] This fact has been applied somewhat uncritically to the question concerning hops versus sweet gale – assuming that taste is something absolute and objective, it has been argued that the German beer was considered better because it was hopped beer, and hops tasted better.[28] Nevertheless, the good quality of hopped beer did certainly boost its popularity, and in Holland, due to the higher prices of hopped beer, gruit beer actually developed into a drink of the poor towards the end of the 14th century.[29] No clear link between additive and class in Sweden is supported, however, by either the written or the archaeobotanical records. Probably both hopped beer and sweet gale beer were of varying quality and aimed towards different classes. This allows us to consider ethnicity/identity as a candidate factor linked to the preference of different beer additives. If we postulate this link, thereby explaining the regional pattern described above as (partly) reflecting ethnicity/regional identity, it should be possible to interpret some certain anomalies as a reflection of diasporas and their associated particular tastes. Isolated signs of a different beer culture in an area could be connected with the presence of immigrants.

Anomalies in beer culture have already been identified as possible ethnic markers in some places, through both the written and the archaeological records. In Norway, which was the northern part of the gruit/sweet gale belt, sweet gale was the predominant additive found in domestic brewing in Bergen, Oslo and Trondheim. However, written sources from the 16th century confirm large imports of hops by the Hanseatic traders of Bryggen – the Hanseatic area of Bergen. Clearly, the German population of this ethnic enclave wanted to brew and drink the kind of beer they were used to consuming. In the Hanseatic documents from Bryggen, the use of sweet gale in brewing is described as "a Nordic practice".[30] This is interesting, since the Hanseatic traders linked the use of sweet gale to something "Nordic" in general, and not to the gruit area of the Netherlands. Is this the simply incidental result of describing this practice as local, or did the Hanseatic traders differentiate between the Nordic use of sweet gale and the Dutch gruit traditions? Is it possible that the regional traditions of sweet gale use in the Netherlands and Norway were two separate phenomena?

Interpretations of archaeobotanical traces of brewing with anomalous additives as ethnic markers of immigrants have been made in the cases of the former Prussian towns of Kołobrzeg/Kolberg (13th century) and Gdańsk/Danzig (11th to 12th centuries). Here, in a strongly hop-dominated area, single finds of sweet gale have been interpreted as possible imports brought by Scandinavian inhabitants of those towns.[31] There are furthermore examples of finds of sweet gale from Tartu/Dorpat in Estonia/Livonia, where hopped beer strongly dominated. These have been interpreted as imports from western Estonia, where sweet gale grows.[32] The sweet gale may also be regarded as an import from other, western European, areas, and a possible trace of a (most likely) Scandinavian or other western diaspora in the town.

Similar interpretations have been made of sweet gale finds from hop-dominated Finland, and these studies have focused on the question of whether sweet gale grows locally or not, or whether it should be considered as an import from other Finnish areas.[33] No attempt to connect the finds to the question of ethnicity has been made. The ethnic situation in Finland during medieval and early modern times was complicated and has not yet been fully investigated. Finland belonged to the Swedish kingdom, and the Swedish-speaking population constituted the bulk of the governing class. It is however not clear to what degree the Swedish speakers were immigrants from the Swedish mainland, or whether they considered themselves as ethnic Swedes with stronger links to the western part of the kingdom than to the Finnish-speaking population. However, in comparison to the Swedish mainland, the pattern of beer culture in Finland reflects more closely the beer culture in the region of Svealand than the mixed beer culture of eastern Götaland.

What then were the reasons for differences between the three regions of the Swedish mainland? We have already stated that the sweet gale beer culture of the west coast and Scania is similar to that of the Danish and Norwegian sphere (which can be explained by this area belonging to the territory of Denmark and Norway). The differences between the central province of Svealand and eastern Götaland may also be due to cultural factors, since these areas were populated by different groups during the period from the 10th to 14th centuries – the Svear (Swedes) and the Götar (Geates), a division significant also during the 15th and 16th centuries. If this ethnic division played a role in how beers were brewed, it would explain both the age of this difference, and perhaps the longevity of the tradition. Perhaps it could also explain the similarities between the hopped beer cultures in southern Finland and Svealand, since these regions are believed to have had stronger cultural connections than did eastern Götaland and Finland.

MULTI-ETHNIC BREWERY IN NYA LÖDÖSE?

The town of Nya (New) Lödöse existed from 1473 until 1624 as the only Swedish port located on the west coast (the rest of the west coast belonged at that time to Denmark and Norway), and boasted a population of approximately 1,500 inhabitants. The town held a key strategic position. Its location along the Göta älv river and connection with the interior, as well as its orientation towards the Atlantic, made it the fourth most important town in Sweden. This location also exposed it to enemy attacks (Fig. 4.3a). Nya Lödöse was preceded by Gamla (Old) Lödöse, positioned about 50 km upstream on the the Göta älv, and it came to be a forerunner to Gothenburg, which was founded 2 km to the south in 1621 (Fig 4.3b). Many of the original burgesses in Nya Lödöse had moved from Gamla Lödöse, and in 1624 they were ordered to move to Gothenburg.[34]

According to the sparse written records, mainly from the early 16th century, Nya Lödöse was inhabited by people of several ethnicities, including Danes, Dutch and Germans, apart from the native Swedish population. A similar situation characterized the town's forerunner, and this was fairly typical for many trading ports in northern Europe. It is not known how these different ethnic groups living in Nya Lödöse were distributed within the town itself. In Gamla Lödöse, German traders made up the most prominent part of the population, inhabiting the central part of the town, but it is unknown whether this pattern was transferred to Nya Lödöse. Nor is there any existing map of the town from which any clues as to settlement patterning can be found. However, many other contemporary towns had ethnic neighbourhoods: for example the

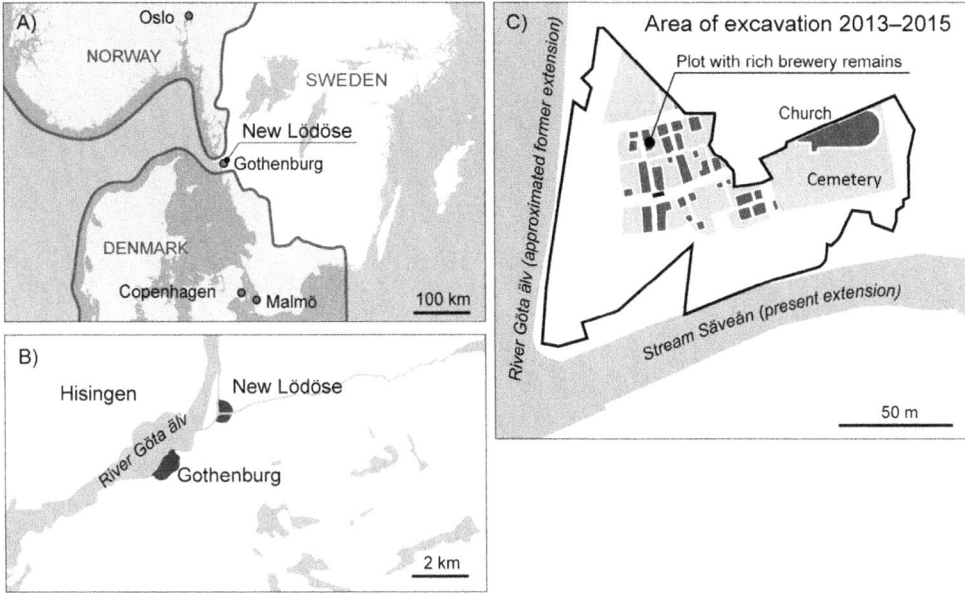

Fig. 4.3a Location of the Swedish town of Nya Lödöse at the boundary between Norway and Denmark.

Fig. 4.3b Location of Nya Lödöse (1473–1624) and Gothenburg (from 1621 onwards) in relation to the Göta älv river.

Fig. 4.3c Town structures of Nya Lödöse as revealed by excavation in 2013–14. The plot with remains of a brewery is marked on the map. (Drawings: Jens Heimdahl)

Danish towns of Aalborg and Helsingør, or Swedish Jönköping or Stockholm, where Dutch and German merchants and/or craftspeople lived in specific districts.[35]

The written records indicate that Nya Lödöse together with Stockholm and Kalmar were the three major urban beer importers in Sweden. The international beer trade seems to have been regulated through these harbours, reducing the beer imports in other Swedish ports. In Nya Lödöse during the five years between 1572 and 1607 average imports amounted to 1,370 barrels of beer a year. This imported beer was dominated by *Sundiskt öl* – beer from Stralsund, the closest German town – making up 80%.[36] However, it is not possible to tell how much of this beer was consumed within the town and how much of it was re-exported. It is, however, evident that a considerable amount of hopped beer of good quality was available in the town.

The imported hopped beer was in line with the contemporary beer traditions of German and Dutch inhabitants. The trade war between hopped and gruit beer merchants was over, and the representatives of the richer urban classes in Holland had already adopted hopped beer for two to three generations. On the other hand, the imported hopped beer contrasted with the local beer tradition at the beginning of the 16th century – the chronological frame of the archaeological records from the town –

Dominating beer culture

German   Dutch   Swedish west coast

1600   Written record

Nya Lödöse 1473–1524

1500   Archaeological record

1400

Hop beer

Sweet gale/Gruit beer

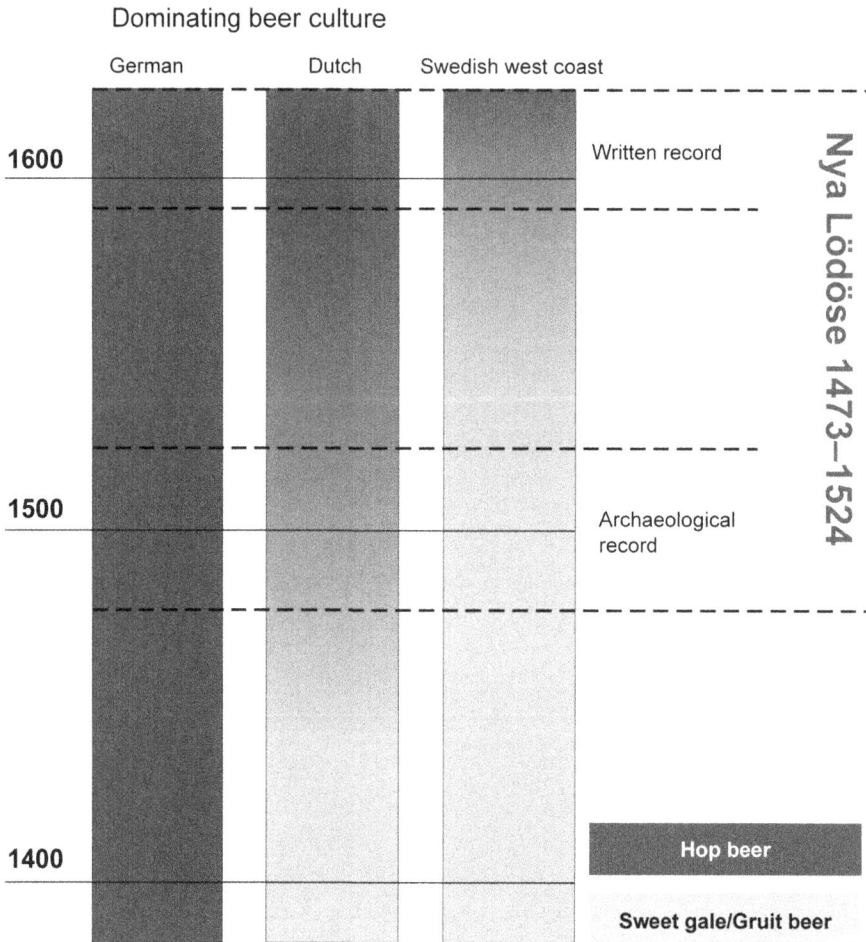

Fig. 4.4 The dominant beer culture among three major ethnic groups living in Nya Lödöse, based on the situation in their areas of origin (drawing: Jens Heimdahl). For several decades in the middle of the 16th century, Nya Lödöse was evacuated to the fortress of Älvsborg, which explains the lack of sources from this period.

but was more like the drink consumed a hundred years later – when most of the relevant written records were composed (Fig. 4.4).

Brewery remains from Nya Lödöse were found during rescue excavations in 2013 – the most extensive archaeological investigations to be performed in the town.[37] The brewery remains contained two distinctive archaeobotanical assemblages: first, one of hops and one of sweet gale, in the earliest and latest phases on precisely the same town plot (see map at Fig. 4.3c above, and Fig. 4.5); and second, what could be called "the local brewery noise" – consisting of minor finds of hops and sweet gale scattered within the excavated area. In its oldest phase (dating approximately to 1473–1500) the plot in question also contained a larger amount of pottery in total and also a larger amount of foreign pottery (of German, Dutch and French origin) than the surrounding plots.[38] The large amounts of pottery waste on this plot, together with the fact that most of the buildings were dwelling-houses, were reasons to interpret the remains as possibly those of a tavern.[39]

The oldest collection of samples came from a barrel filled with pig dung, dated to *c.* 1480. The dung probably originated from pigs held on the plot and fed with brewery waste from the household, and it may have been intended as fertilizer. It consisted of two components: plants collected for pig-feed, and brewing waste consisting of fragmented barley and 2,103 hop fruits. The plants used in the brewing process are somewhat out of context in the pig dung, but probably signify the existence of a local brewery on the town plot.

The samples with younger brewery remains consisted of 2,816 carbonized fruitlets of sweet gale, found on a floor layer in a burned-down building interpreted as a brewery. The destruction of the building dates to a fire in the latest phase of the town, possibly connected to an event during the Kalmar War in 1612. The find has direct parallels in similar remains found on floor layers (not however burned) in Halmstad, dated to different periods between 14th and 16th centuries,[40] and from a floor plank in the abbey of Askeby, probably from the 14th to 15th century,[41] which have been interpreted as traces of brewing *in situ*. Together with sweet gale, three hop fruits and a small amount of barley were found. The material collected from the floor layer indicates that the additive was applied after the sieving of the malt.

The local hops and sweet gale noise (single finds of brewery waste in different contexts) consisted of 99 hop fruits and 14 sweet gale nutlets, mostly found in stables and thus interpreted as originating from pig dung. Almost all the finds of sweet gale were made together with hops: in two of the samples in about an equal proportion, and in one case in a smaller quantity than the hops.

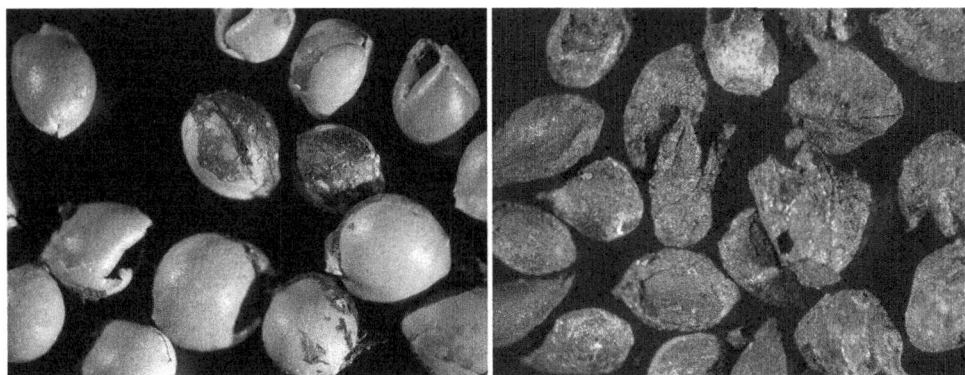

Fig. 4.5 Hop (*Humulus lupulus* L.) dated to 1473–1500 (left) and carbonized nutlets of sweet gale (*Myrica gale* L.) dated to 1600–30 (right) from Nya Lödöse (photograph: Jens Heimdahl). The fruitlets and nutlets measure about 2 mm across.

A straightforward interpretation of these finds, in accordance with our earlier discussion of the cultural connections of a preference of particular additives, would conclude that hopped beer aimed at Dutch/German visitors was brewed in the earliest phase (*c.* 1480), and sweet gale beer aimed at Swedish/Danish/Norwegian visitors of west-coast origin in the later phase (*c.* 1612). However, in relation to one single individual case study such an interpretation appears rather naïve; the potential for error and coincidence is obvious. Therefore, our discussion concerning how ethnic patterns may be reflected in beer culture will focus on large-scale structural questions, and the case study be used to question and problematize those patterns.

The two major finds of brewing remains made on the same town plot in Nya Lödöse consist of traces of pure hopped beer and pure sweet gale beer, from the beginning and the end respectively of the town's history. It would be easy to suggest that originally the plot was inhabited by a Dutch/German household (which is supported by other find material such as Dutch/German ceramics), and some generations later by a Swedish/ Danish/Norwegian household of west-coast origin. However, the interpretation of the household as a tavern demands another perspective. The main aim of the brewing on this plot may have been to provide guests with beer to their specific tastes, and in that case to brew and keep a variety of beers in stock.

The use of additives revealed at Nya Lödöse provides a mirror image of the norm, both cases being somewhat contrary to expectation. Around 1480 we would perhaps have expected the sweet gale beer of local tradition to be more common, and hopped beer rather odd, on the west coast. Drinkers of hopped beer may at this time have been predominantly Dutch/German immigrants and people from eastern Sweden – perhaps the Stockholm area. In 1612 we would expect sweet gale beer to be rather unusual and hopped beer to be the prevalent type. Drinkers of sweet gale beer during this late period were probably for the most part people from the west coast with rather conservative tastes.

In other parts of the town submitted to archaeological study, hopped beer predominates, but there are also indications of mixed beers and hopped beer spiced with small amounts of sweet gale. The prevalence of hopped beer makes Nya Lödöse more similar to the contemporary German and Dutch towns, and the eastern parts of Sweden, and different from Danish towns on the (nowadays Swedish) mainland – like Halmstad – which were clinging conservatively to the sweet gale brewing tradition.[42] This raises the question of what was considered as the norm in Nya Lödöse. Was it the sweet gale beer favoured all along the west coast, or was it the hopped beer consumed mostly by the Germans, Dutch and the east coast Swedes? The finds discussed above could also be interpreted as evidence of a lack of "conflict" between the two kinds of beer and brewing methods; an indication that there was no conservatively-guarded norm in this multicultural town. Perhaps sweet gale beer and hopped beer could also be also seen as two different types of drink, appropriate for different occasions? We should also keep in mind that trading communities were able to develop levels of tolerance and flexibility that included creative responses to new food cultures and other customs.

CONCLUSIONS

During the medieval period beer culture in northern Europe was diverse, following specific regional patterns based on the use of hops or sweet gale as a main preservative/flavouring. This aspect of regional and local brewing traditions is not accounted for in the written sources (which merely focused on trade in hopped beer) but traceable and possible to reconstruct through the archaeobotanical record. At the beginning of the early modern period this pattern started to shift towards a preference for and predominance of hopped beer, largely due to successful lobbying and trade. However, the transition was sometimes slow, hampered by the conservative taste of the consumers and strong local traditions in household brewing. This was the case in many parts of Sweden where the sweet gale and mixed beer tradition survived throughout the early modern era and disappeared only with industrialization and the centralization of brewing in the 19th century.

The present study offers some new insights into the subject of this variation in beer culture in northern Europe during the period 1300–1500. The earlier, well-known gruit/sweet gale belt of Holland, north-eastern Germany and Denmark included also the west coast of Sweden and Norway, which operated in contrast to the hops-dominated area around the Baltic, including the region of former Livonia and Prussia, central Sweden, Poland and most of northern Germany. This pattern is often described as having developed during the 13th and 14th centuries, as a result of Hanseatic expansion. The preference for hopped beer is more or less regarded as an originally German/central European phenomenon which spread north during this time. Such a thesis is not fully supported by the archaeobotanical record, however, which rather suggests that the pattern is older, probably dating back to the 8th–9th centuries. Hops were present in many Viking Age settlements in this area, and are also a common find in towns predating the Hanse. Another previously unidentified pattern is the differentiation in beer culture between the central Swedish regions of Svealand and the south-eastern provinces of Götaland: in the former beer was almost exclusively brewed with hops, and in the latter mixtures of hops and sweet gale were used. This pattern seems to be reminiscent of older, pre-Christian traditions.

The strong links between the variations in local beer culture, and its connection to specific regions, makes it plausible to link beer culture to the question of identity and ethnicity. This link is also supported by written sources which confirm that people from different regions and of different ethnicities preferred different types of beer. However, if the link between beer type and ethnicity is easy and relatively clear on a larger, regional scale, a close interrogation of this phenomenon at a specific site – in our case the town of Nya Lödöse – immediately raises problems. This is partly due to the somewhat chaotic social structure of individual towns, where inhabitants and households occupying specific plots consisted of individuals from different social classes, and, sometimes, of different ethnicities, and where individuals and families were quite mobile, living on the specific plots for limited periods of time.

In the case study of Nya Lödöse, different brewery remains on a town plot have been identified and dated to *c.* 1480 and *c.* 1612. The plot contained an unusually large amount of pottery of German, Dutch and French origin, and a working hypothesis is that the site may thus be interpretable as the remains of a tavern. The archaeobotanical remains represent two different types of beer brewing: pure hopped beer in the earlier and pure sweet gale beer in the later phase. Hopped beer was the preferred drink among Dutch and German burgesses in their homelands, and would be the type of beer expected to have been brewed on a plot belonging to a person from this group. Sweet gale beer, on the other hand, was the predominant type on the west coast of the Swedish mainland (at this time belonging to Denmark) and in Norway, and perhaps also preferred in the Swedish west-coast countryside. The prevalent custom in Nya Lödöse was slightly different, with a preference for hopped beer together with some mixed beer-types – more like the situation in eastern Sweden. This may be interpretable in terms of the beer culture in Nya Lödöse being influenced either by eastern Sweden, or by the German/Dutch trader culture. This stands in contrast to the surrounding Danish/Norwegian areas of the west coast. The different beer types found on the plot could be undestood as representing the multi-ethnic environment of a tavern providing different beer types to guests of differing backgrounds and tastes.

The incidence of different beer types in Nya Lödöse confirms the picture of the town as a multi-ethnic environment. It may also be interpreted in terms of lack of conflict between the two kinds of beer drinker, and as implying that there was no rigid norm. Perhaps hopped beer and sweet gale beer could also be seen as two different types of drink, appropriate to different occasions, to accompany different dishes.

ACKNOWLEDGEMENT

This study was carried out within the project "Urban Diaspora – Diaspora Communities and Materiality in Early Modern Urban Centers", funded by the Danish Council for Independent Research.

NOTES

1 Jenkins 2004.
2 Drobin 1991; Nordberg 2004, 171–98.
3 von Hofsten 1960; Thunæus 1968; 1970; Sambrook 1996; Hornsey 2003; Unger 2004; 2011; Nelson 2005.
4 Hjelmkvist 1991, Behre 1999, Günter & Karg 2000; Heimdahl 2005; 2010b; Karg (ed.) 2007; Viklund 2007; 2011; Balic & Heimdahl 2015.
5 The sporadic use of the method in the last decades of the 20th century produced some evidence of hop and sweet gale use.
6 E.g. Von Hofsten 1960; Thunæus 1968; 1970.
7 Von Hofsten 1960, 29; Thunæus 1968, 71.
8 Behre 1999; Balic & Heimdahl 2015, 151-3.
9 Behre 1999, 39; Günter & Karg 2000.
10 Behre 1999, 38; Bäck & Heimdahl forthcoming.
11 Behre 1999; Alsleben 2007; Hjelle 2007; Karg 2007; Balic & Heimdahl 2015.
12 Latałowa et al. 2007, 58–9.
13 Sillasoo and Hiie 2007, 78–82.
14 Alsleben 2007, 27.
15 Karg 2007, 149.
16 Günter & Karg 2000, 9.
17 Günter & Karg 2000, 10–11.
18 This is according to both written sources: (von Hofsten 1960, 72; Thunæus 1968, 71) and archaeological evidence (Balic & Heimdahl 2015, 158).
19 Alsleben 2007, 22.
20 Lempiäinen 2007, 105–7.
21 von Hofsten 1960, 47–54.
22 von Hofsten 1960, 28.
23 Thunæus 1970.
24 Karlsson Strese & Tholin 2008.
25 Unger 2004, 78–81.
26 Thunaeus 1968, 164–5.
27 Unger 2004, 66–8.
28 Von Hofsten 1960, 29; Thunæus 1968, 71; Balic & Heimdahl 2015.
29 Unger 2004, 82.
30 Hjelle 2007, 169.
31 Latałowa et al. 2007, 58–9.
32 Sillasoo and Hiie 2007, 84.
33 Lempiäinen 2007, 105–7.
34 Grauers 1923; Almqvist 1929; Andersson 1973; Järpe 1986; Harlitz 2010.
35 Tønnesen 1985; Pettersson 2009, 53–60; Linaa 2012.
36 Thunæus 1968, 163.
37 http://www.stadennyalodose.se/ [accessed 29 August 2016].
38 Carlsson forthcoming.
39 Öbrink & Rosén forthcoming.
40 Heimdahl 2013b.
41 Heimdahl 2014a.
42 Heimdahl 2013b.

BIBLIOGRAPHY

Alering, A., Balić, I., Billström, L., Brorsson, T., Dutras Leivas, I., Heimdahl, J. Magnell, O., Ring C. & Romedahl, H. 2015. 'Växjö 10:14 och Domkyrkan 1. Arkeologisk undersökning 2013'. Statens Historiska museer, Arkeologiska uppdragsverksamheten. Rapport 2015:34.

Almquist, H. 1929. *Göteborgs historia: grundläggningen och de första hundra åren. Förra delen.* Vol. 1: *Från grundläggandet till enväldet (1619–1680)*. Skrifter utgivna till Göteborgs stads trehundraårsjubileum genom jubileumsutställningens publikationskommitté. Gothenburg: Göteborgs litografiska aktiebolag.

Alsleben, A. 2007. 'Food consumption in the Hanseatic towns of Germany', in Karg 2007, 13–37.

Andersson, H. 1973. *Nya Lödöse – Gamlestaden fem hundra år.* Gothenburg: Göteborg-Gamlestadens rotaryklubb.

Arfalk, K., Hedvall, R. & Lindeblad, K. 2009. 'Skänninge 3:3, Östergötland, Mjölby kommun, Skänninge stad'. UV rapport 2014:157. Linköping.

Åstrand, J. & Dutras I. L. 2013. 'Stortorget i Växjö Arkeologisk förundersökning inför ny utformning av torget 2013'. Smålands museum rapport 2013:5. Växjö.

Balic, I. & Heimdahl, J. 2015. 'Halmstads medeltida öltraditioner i nationellt och internationellt perspektiv', in Öbrink 2015, 143–84.

Bäck, M. & Heimdahl, J. forthcoming. 'Hur främmande var Birka i det regionala samhället?', in: Grönwall, R. (ed.), *Städernas uppkomst, seminarium vid Stockholms länsmuseum 2014*. Stockholms läns museum.

Bäckman, L., Drobin, U. & Berglie, P.-A. (eds) 1991. *Studier i religionshistoria tillägnade Åke Hultkrantz professor emeritus den 1 juli 1986*. Löberöd: Plus Ultra.

Behre, K.-E.1999. 'The history of beer additives in Europe – a review', *Vegetation History and Archaeobotany* 8: 35–48.

Bergman, A. & Söderlund, K. 2013. 'Gråbrödraklostret i Stockholm Arkeologiska och byggnadsarkeologiska undersökningar, stående byggnader och arkeologiska lämningar. Riddarholmen, Stockholm'. Stockholm stadsmuseum rapporterar 39. Stockholm.

Bergqvist, J. & Hedvall, R. 2014. 'Vistenagatan-Linköpingsgatan, RAÄ 5, Kv Radiatorn, Skänninge 2:1, Skänninge stad, Mjölby kommun, Östergötland'. Rapport.

Bjuggner, L. forthcoming. 'Senmedeltida odlingshorisonter, en stenläggning och nyare tids avfall'. Halmstad: Kulturmiljö Halland

Bjuggner, L. & Heimdahl, J. 2009. 'Odling och hus under historisk tid i kvarteret Broktorp, Halmstad. Arkeologisk förundersökning 2009'. Rapport. Halmstad: Kulturmiljö Halland.

Bramstång Plura, C., Carlsson, K., Rosén, C., Heimdahl, J., Vretemark, M. & Hjärthner Holdar, E. 2012. 'Arkeologisk undersökning. Nio tomter i Jönköping. Småland, Jönköpings stad, kvarteret Dovhjorten (Druvan), RAÄ 50'. UV rapport 2012:119.

Carlsson, E. forthcoming. 'Arkeologisk undersökning av stadslager i Västra Falun i Falu stad och kommun, Dalarna'. Dalarnas museum, Falun.

Carlsson, K. forthcoming. 'Pottery from Nya Lödöse in a diaspora perspective. The pottery in Nya lödöse – extent and delimination 2013 (2014)'. Report to Urban Diaspora – Diaspora Communities and Materiality in Early Modern Urban Centers.

Carlsson, K. & Rosén, C. 2013. 'En 1700-talstomt i Kungsbacka'. UV Rapport 2013:130. Stockholm.

Carlsson, M. & Runer J. 2012. 'Holländare, ryssar och tobak. Odling och bebyggelse inom kvarteret Ruddammen i Norrköping 1600-2010'. Särskild arkeologisk undersökning. Rapporter från Arkeologikonsult 2012: 2410. Stockholm.

Carlsson, M., Dyhlén-Täckman, I. & Nathanson C. 2008. 'Kvarteret Kvasten. Ett stadskvarters uppkomst vid 1600-talets mitt. Stockholms stad, Norrmalm, RAÄ 103'. Stockholm stadsmuseum. Arkeologisk rapport 2008:1.

Carlsson, R., Elfwendahl, M. & Perming, A. 1991. 'Bryggaren, ett kvarter i centrum. En medeltidsarkeologisk undersökning i Uppsala. Riksantikvarieämbetet UV 1991:1'. Stockholm.

Drobin, U. 1991. 'Mjödet och offersymboliken i fornnordisk religion', in Bäckman *et al.* 1991, 97–141.

Elfwendahl, M. 1990. 'Arkeologisk för- och slutundersökning. Uppland, Uppsala, Akademigatan'. UV Mitt rapport. Dnr 3223/90. Hägersten.

Ericsson, G. forthcoming. 'Kv Paradis 51, Lund. SU 2009'. Kulturhistoriska föreningen för södra Sverige. Lund.

Evanni, L., Hamilton, J., Linda Lindwall, L. & Runer, J. 2013. 'Gravfält och gårdstomt vid Äggelunda, Stockholms län; Uppland; Järfälla kommun; Järfälla socken; Veddesta 2:1; Järfälla 28:2 och 364:1'. UV Mitt, Riksantikvarieämbetet. Hägersten.

Gardelin, G. 2013. 'Kv. Saluhallen 1. Arkeologisk slutundersökning 2010'. Kulturens rapporter 6. Lund.

Grauers, S. (ed.) 1923. *Nya Lödöse tänkeböcker (1586–1621)*. Skrifter utgivna till Göteborgs stads trehundraårsjubileum 6. Gothenburg.

Guldåker, A. 2015. 'Adelgatan- Lund, fornlämning nr 73:1, Lunds kommun, Skåne. Arkeologisk förundersökning 2013 och 2015'. Kulturhistoriska föreningen för södra Sverige. Kulturmiljörapporter 2015:7. Lund.

Gullbrand, T. & Wennberg, T. forthcoming. 'Kv. Bastionen, Göteborg'. Gothenburg: Göteborgs stadsmuseum.

Günther, D. & Karg, S. 2000. 'Archäobotanische Funde von Gagel (*Myrica gale* L.) und Hopfen (*Humulus lupulus* L.) in Dänemark'. Nationalmuseets Naturvidenskabelige Undersögelser rapport 29. Copenhagen.

Gustavsson, J. 2013. 'Stadsgårdar i den medeltida stadens utkant, Östergötland, Skänninge, Kvarteret Fogden 4–6, Radiatorn 4, Magasinet samt Linköpingsgatan.' Rapport 2013:50.

Harlitz, E. 2010. *Urbana system och riksbildning i Skandinavien: en studie i Lödöses uppgång och fall ca 1050–1646*. Gothenburg: Institutionen för historiska studier.

Harnow, H. Cranstone, D., Bedford, P. & Høst-Madsen, L. (eds) 2012. *Across the North Sea: Later Historical Archaeology in Britain and Denmark, c. 1500–2000 AD*. Odense: University Press of Southern Denmark.

Heimdahl, J. 2005. *Urbanised Nature in the Past: Site Formation and Environmental Development in Two Swedish Towns AD 1200–1800*. PhD dissertation, University of Stockholm.

Heimdahl, J. 2007. 'Makroskopisk analys av jordprover från Södra Vallåkra bytomt', in Knarrström & Schmidt Sabo 2007, appendix 4.

Heimdahl, J. 2008. 'Kvasten 8, analys av botaniska makrofossil och sedimentinnehåll', in Carlsson *et al.* 2008, appendix.

Heimdahl, J., 2009a. 'Geoarkeologiska analyser av stratigrafi och växtmakrofossil från kvarteret Diplomaten, Jönköping', in Heimdahl & Vestbö Franzén 2009, 11–36.

Heimdahl, J., 2009b. 'Makroskopisk analys av jordprover från S:t Olofs konvent, Skänninge', in Konsmar & Menander 2009, appendix.

Heimdahl, J., 2009c. 'Makroskopisk analys av jordprover från Dyhagen, Skänninge', in Lindberg & Stibeus 2009, appendix 5a.

Heimdahl, J., 2009d. 'Makroskopisk analys Skänninge 3:3,Motalagatan', in Arfalk *et al.* 2009, appendix 6.

Heimdahl, J. 2009e. 'Makroskopisk analys av jordprover från tre arkeologiska undersökningar i Karlstad 2006', in Karlsson 2009, appendix.

Heimdahl, J. 2010a. 'Makroskopisk analys av jordprover och stratigrafi från kv. Saluhallen, Lund. Teknisk rapport', in Karlsson 2010, appendix.

Heimdahl, J. 2010b. 'Barbariska trädgårdsmästare. Nya perspektiv på hortikulturen i Sverige fram till 1200-talets slut', *Fornvännen* 105: 265–80.

Heimdahl, J. 2011a. 'Makroskopisk analys av jordprover från Guldsmedsgränd, Linköping Ög', in Karlsson 2011, 9–11.

Heimdahl, J. 2011b. 'Makroskopisk analys av jordprover från FU kv Mjölnaren, Norrköping', in Stibéus 2011, appendix 5.

Heimdahl, J. 2012a. 'Stratigrafisk och makroskopisk analys av kulturlager vid Västra kajen, Jönköping. Förundersökning 2011. Teknisk rapport', in Pettersson 2012, appendix 6.

Heimdahl, J. 2012b. 'Makroskopisk analys av jordprover och stratigrafi från kv Mästaren, Kalmar', in Tagesson & Nordström 2012, appendix.

Heimdahl, J. 2012c. 'Stratigrafisk och makroskopisk analys av kulturlager från kvarteret Fältskären, Enköping. Teknisk rapport', in Ölund & Kjellberg 2012, appendix.

Heimdahl, J. 2012d. 'Makroskopisk analys av kulturlager i kv Ruddammen, Norrköping. Teknisk rapport', in Carlsson & Runer 2012, 137–43.

Heimdahl, J. 2012e. 'Odling, växthantering och miljöutveckling i kvarteret Dovhjorten/Druvan, Jönköping Teknisk rapport av kvartärgeologiska och arkeobotaniska analyser', in Bramstång Plura *et al.* 2012, appendix.

Heimdahl, J. 2012f. 'Makroskopisk analys av kulturlager från Riddarholmen, Stockholm', in Wändesjö 2012, appendix.

Heimdahl, J. 2013a. 'Odling och växthantering i kv. Bokbindaren, Linköping. Teknisk rapport av kvartärgeologiska och arkeobotaniska analyser', in Tagesson 2013, appendix.

Heimdahl, J. 2013b. 'Kvartärgeologisk bedömning av kulturlager och makroskopisk analys av växtlämningar från Brogatan, Storgatan och Nygatan, Halmstad. Hallands länsmuseum', in Öbrink 2013, 73–92.

Heimdahl, J. 2013c. 'Kvartärgeologisk och makroskopisk analys av jordlager och jordprover från Kungsbacka, SU, Stortorget (Teknisk rapport)', in Carlsson & Rosén 2013, 73–84.

Heimdahl, J. 2013d. 'Makroskopisk analys av jordprover från kvarteret Ekorren, Nora', in Ramström 2013, appendix 6.

Heimdahl, J. 2013e. 'Makroskopisk analys av jord från Kvarteret Fogden, Skänninge 2009', in Gustavsson 2013, appendix.

Heimdahl, J. 2013f. 'Makroskopisk analys av jordprover, och kvartärgeologisk bedömning av odlingshorisonter från Äggelunda gårdstomt', in Evanni et al. 2013.

Heimdahl, J. 2013g. 'Makroskopisk analys av lager med köksavfall från Gråbrödraklostret, Riddarholmen Stockholm', in Bergman & Söderlund 2013, appendix.

Heimdahl, J. 2013h. 'Makroskopisk analys av jordprover från FU Slottsholmen i Västervik', in Palm & Einarsson 2013, appendix.

Heimdahl, J. 2013i. 'Makroskopisk analys av jordprover från RAÄ 170, Stortorget i Växjö, FU', in Åstrand & Dutras 2013, appendix 3.

Heimdahl, J. 2013j. 'Stratigrafisk och makroskopisk analys av kulturlager i kv Saluhallen, Lund. Teknisk rapport', in Gardelin 2013, appendix 1.

Heimdahl, J. 2014a. 'Makroskopisk analys av jordprover från SU, Askeby Kloster, Östergötland', in Lindeblad 2014, appendix 7.

Heimdahl, J. 2014b. 'Makroskopisk analys av jordprover från Fjärrvärmeschakt, Skänninge, FU 2009', in Konsmar 2014, appendix 4.

Heimdahl, J. 2014c. 'Makroskopisk analys av jordprover från Vistenagatan-Linköpingsgatan, Skänninge', in Bergqvist & Hedvall 2014, appendix 14a.

Heimdahl, J. 2014d. 'Odling och växthantering i kv Gesällen, Kalmar. Teknisk rapport av kvartärgeologiska och arkeobotaniska analyser', in Tagesson et al. 2014, appendix 2.

Heimdahl, J. 2015a. 'Makroskopisk analys av jordprover från Stigaren 1, Falun', in Sunding 2015, appendix.

Heimdahl, J. 2015b. 'Makroskopisk analys av jordprover från Ua 191 Trappan, Uddevalla', in Ytterberg 2015, appendix.

Heimdahl, J. 2015c. 'Makroskopisk analys av jordprover från VA-arbeten längst Adelgatan, Lund', in Guldåker 2015, appendix.

Heimdahl, J. 2015d. 'Kulturlagerstratigrafi och växtfossil från Kalmar slott – kvartärgeologiska och arkeobotaniska analyser', in Stibéus 2015, 199–204.

Heimdahl, J. forthcoming a, 'Makroskopisk analys av jordprover tagna vid arkeologisk undersökning av kvarteret Bastionen, Göteborg', in Gullbrand & Wennberg forthcoming, appendix.

Heimdahl, J. forthcoming b, 'Makroskopisk analys av jordprover från Västra Falun', in Carlsson forthcoming, appendix.

Heimdahl, J. forthcoming c, 'Kvartärgeologisk bedömning och makroskopisk analys av odlingshorisonter från Kv Drottning Kristina, Halmstad. Teknisk rapport', in Bjuggner forthcoming, appendix.

Heimdahl, J. forthcoming d, 'Makroskopisk analys av kulturlager i kv Paradiset, Lund', in Ericsson forthcoming, appendix.

Heimdahl, J. & Vestbö Franzén, Å. 2009. 'Tyska madens gröna rum'. Jönköpings läns museum. Arkeologisk rapport 2009:41. Jönköping.

Hjelle, K. L. 2007. 'Foreign trade and local production – plant remains from medieval times in Norway', in Karg 2007, 161–79.

Hjelmqvist, H. 1991. 'Några trädgårdsväxter från Lunds medeltid', *Svensk Botanisk Tidskrift* 85: 225–48.

Hofsten, N. von 1960. *Pors och andra humleersättningar och ölkryddor i äldre tider*. Uppsala: Gust. A. Academia Regiae.

Hornsey, I. 2003. *A History of Beer and Brewing*. Cambridge: Royal Society of Chemistry.

Järpe, A. 1986. *Nya Lödöse*. Medeltidsstaden 60. Stockholm: Riksantikvarieämbetet & Statens historiska museer.

Jenkins, R. 2004. *Social Identity*. London: Routledge.

Karg, S. 2007. 'Long term dietary traditions: Archaeobotanical records from Denmark dated to the Middle Ages and early modern times', in Karg 2007, 137–59.

Karg, S. (ed.) 2007. *Medieval Food Traditions in Northern Europe*. National Museum Studies in Archaeology & History 12. Copenhagen: National Museum of Denmark.

Karlsson, E. 2011. 'Fjärrkyla i Guldsmedsgränd. Arkeologisk förundersökning'. Östergötlands länsmuseum rapport 2011:17. Linköping.

Karlsson, M. 2009. 'Arkeologisk förundersökning längs Järnvägsgatan'. Värmlands museum rapport 2009:9. Karlstad.

Karlsson, M. 2010. 'Kv. Saluhallen 1, Lund – RAÄ 73:1, Lunds sn, Skåne. Kulturens rapporter 4'. Lund: Kulturen i Lund.

Karlsson Strese, E.-M. & Tollin, C. 2008. 'Humle – finns i öl av "fel" skäl', *Forskning och framsteg* 3: 30–5.

Klápště J. & Sommer, P. (eds) 2011. *Processing, Storage, Distribution of Food. Food in the Medieval Rural Environment*. Turnhout: Brepols.

Knarrström, A. & Schmidt Sabo, K. 2007. 'Södra Vallåkra bytomt Skåne, Helsingborgs kommun, Kvistofta socken, Södra Vallåkra 16:1, RAÄ 97'. UV Syd Daff Rapport 2007:1. Lund.

Konsmar, A. 2014. 'Från odlingsmark till stadsbebyggelse i Skänninge, Fjärrvärmedragning i gatu- och tomtmark, Östergötland, Mjjölby kommun, Skänninge socken, Linköpingsgatan, Tvärgränd och Krokgatan, RAÄ 5, medeltida stadslager'. Rapport 2014:67. Linköping.

Konsmar, A. & Menander, H. 2009. 'Kvarteret Brödraklostret, RAÄ 5 och 20, Kvarteret Brödraklostret 26, Skänninge 2:1, Skänninge stad, Mjölby kommun, Östergötland'. Rapport 2009:6. Linköping.

Larsson, E.-L. 1985. *Frukter och frön från det äldsta Göteborg – en botanisk makrofossilanalys av fyra 1600-1700-tals kvarter*. Enskilt arbete i Biologi. Botaniska institutionen. Gothenburg: Göteborgs universitet.

Latałowa, M., Badura M, Jarosińska J. & Święta J. 2007. 'Useful plants in medieval and post-medieval archaeobotanical material from the Hanseatic towns of Northern Poland (Kołobrzeg, Gdańsk and Elbąg)', in Karg, 2007, 39–72.

Lempiäinen, T. 2007. 'Archaeobotanical evidence of plants from the medieval period to early modern times in Finland', in Karg 2007, 97–118.

Linaa, J. 2012. 'In memory of merchants: The consumption and cultural meetings of a Dutch immigrant in early modern Elsinore', in Harnow *et al.* 2012, 91–104.

Lindberg, S. & Stibéus M. 2009. 'Dyhagen, RAÄ 5, Skänninge 2:1, 3:2, Skänninge stad, Mjölbykommun, Östergötland'. UV Öst rapport 2009:4. Linköping.

Lindeblad, K. 2014. 'Arkeologisk undersökning i cistercienserklostret i Askeby'. UV rapport 2014:64. Linköping.

Ljung, J.-Å. & Persson, B. 1989. 'Arkeologisk förundersökning Kvarteret Föreningen 18,

Nyköping, Södermanland'. Rapport UV Mitt. Hägersten.

Mogren, M. & Påhlsson, I. (eds) 1983. 'Svalan ett medeltida Uppsalakvarter'. Riksantikvarieämbetet rapport UV 1983:1. Stockholm.

Nelson, M. 2005. *The Barbarian's Beverage. A History of Beer in Ancient Europe*. London: Routledge.

Nordberg, A. 2004. 'Krigarna i Odins sal. Dödsföreställningar och krigarkult i fornnordisk religion'. PhD dissertation, University of Stockholm.

Nordström, A. & Heimdahl J. 2012. 'Arkeologisk förundersökning och särskild arkeologisk undersökning. Trädgårdsarkeologi i kv Lyckan, Östergötland, Norrköpings stad och kommun, kv Lyckan, RAÄ 96'. UV rapport 2012:180. Linköping.

Nordström, A. & Lindeblad, K. (eds) 2016. 'Båthus, stadsgårdar och stadsliv i Nyköping 650-1700'. Arkeologerna Statens historiska museer rapport 2016:77. Stockholm.

Öbrink, M. (ed.) 2013. 'Livet vid Storgatan under fyra sekler. Lämningar från tiden innan Halmstad till tiden efter stadsbranden'. Arkeologiska rapporter från Hallands länsmuseer 2013:1. Halmstad.

Öbrink, M. (ed.) 2015. *Halmstads äldsta historia. Vår by Broktorp*. Hallands länsmuseums skriftserie 11. Halmstad.

Öbrink, M. & Rosén, C. (eds) forthcoming. 'Rapport över arkeologisk undersökning av Göteborg 218, Nya Lödöse'.

Ölund, A. & Kjellberg J. 2012. 'Kvarteret Fältskären. Förundersökning av medeltida bebyggelse och hantverk i Enköping'. Upplandsmuseets rapporter 2012:01. Uppsala.

Palm, V. & Einarsson L. 2013. 'Slottsholmen, Arkeologisk förundersökning 2013, Slottsholmen 1 och Västervik 4:7, 4:28 och 3:5 i Västerviks stad, Kalmar län, Småland'. Kalmar läns museum arkeologisk rapport 2013:5. Kalmar.

Påhlsson, I. 1983. 'Växtlämningar i medeltida avlagringar från kvarteret Svalan, Uppsala', in Mogren & Påhlsson 1983, appendix.

Påhlsson, I. 1989. 'Makrofossilanalys av kulturlager från Föreningen 18, Nyköping', in Ljung & Persson 1989, 5–6.

Påhlsson, I. 1990. 'Makrofossilundersökning', in Elfwendahl 1990, appendix.

Påhlsson, I. 1991. 'Makrofossilanalys', in Carlsson *et al.* 1991, 199–206.

Pettersson, C. 2009. 'Den centrala periferin. Arkeologisk undersökning i kvarteret Diplomaten, faktori- och hantverksgårdar i Jönköping 1620–1790, RAÄ 50, Jönköpings stad'. Jönköpings läns museum arkeologisk rapport 2009:40. Jönköping.

Pettersson, C. 2012. 'Murar på stranden – bastion Carolus och sjömuren'. Jönköpings länsmuseum arkeologisk rapport 2012:17. Jönköping.

Ramström, A. 2013. 'Kvarteret Ekorren, Nora resecentrum Västmanland, Nora socken, Nora kommun, del av RAÄ 164:1'. Arkeologigruppen rapport 2013:04. Örebro.

Sambrook, P. 1996. *Country House Brewing in England 1500–1900*. London: The Hambleton Press.

Sillasoo, Ü. & Hiie, S. 2007. 'An archaeobotanical approach to investigation of food of the Hanseatic period in Estonia', in Karg 2007, 73–96.

Stibéus, M. 2011. 'Tidigmedeltida gravar och tidigmodern bebyggelse: RAÄ 96:1, kvarteret Laxen, Mjölnaren och Vårdtornet, Norrköpings stad och kommun, Östergötlands län'. UV rapport 2011:46. Linköping.

Stibéus, M. 2015. 'Kalmar slott – bebyggelse och fynd från 1100-1800-talen'. Statens historiska museet rapport 2015:54. Linköping.

Sunding, E. 2015. 'Arkeologisk förundersökning i Stigaren 1 av stadslager Falun 68:1 i Falu stad och kommun, Dalarna'. Dalarnas museum arkeologisk rapport 2015:4. Falun.

Swinnen, J. F. M. (ed.) 2011. *The Economics of Beer*. Oxford: Oxford University Press.

Tagesson, G. 2013. 'Särskild arkeologisk undersökning. Kvarteret Bokbindaren 28, Hemma hos fröken Löfgren – från 1600-talets kronotomter till 1700-talets hantverksgårdar, Östergötland, Linköpings stad och kommun, Kv Bokbindaren 28, RAÄ 153'. UV rapport 2013:31. Linköping.

Tagesson, G. & Nordström A. 2012. 'Särskild arkeologisk undersökning. Kvarteret Mästaren, Kalmar län, Kalmar stad, Kalmar domkyrkoförsamling, Kvarnholmen, Kv Mästaren 5-8, 21-22, 29, RAÄ 93'. Rapport 2012:104. Kalmar.

Tagesson, G., Konsmar, A., Bäck, M., Haggrén, G., Jeppsson, A., Dutra Leivas, I., Heimdahl, J., Lindström, D. & Vretemark, M. 2014. 'Kvarteret Gesällen 4 och 25 samt del av Kvarnholmen 2:2, Småland, Kalmar län, Kalmar stad och kommun, Kalmar domkyrkoförsamling, RAÄ 93'. Riksantikvarieämbetet UV rapport 2014:93. Linköping.

Thunæus, H. 1968. *Ölets historia i Sverige*. Vol. 1: *Från äldsta tider till 1600-talets slut*. Stockholm: Almqvist & Wiksell.

Thunæus, H. 1970. *Ölets historia i Sverige*. Vol. 2: *1700- och 1800-talen*. Stockholm: Almqvist & Wiksell.

Tønnesen, A. 1985. *Helsingør udenlandske borgere og indbyggere ca. 1550–1600*. Ringe: Forlaget Misteltenen.

Unger, R. 2004. *Beer in the Middle Ages and the Renaissance*. Philadelphia: University of Pennsylvania Press.

Unger, R. 2011. 'Beer production, profits, and public authorities in the Renaissance', in Swinnen 2011, 29–50.

Viklund, K. 2007. 'Sweden and the Hanse: Archaeobotanical aspects of changes in farming, gardening and dietary habits in medieval times in Sweden', in Karg 2007, 119–36.

Viklund, K. 2011. 'Beer brewing in medieval Sweden: Archaeobotanical and documentary evidence', in Klápště & Sommer 2011, 235–43.

Wändesjö, J. 2012. 'Gråmunkeholmen 3. Arkeologisk undersökning 2010 SR 1163. Riddarholmen, Stockholm'. Stockholm stadsmuseum rapporterar 16. Stockholm.

Ytterberg, N. (ed.) 2015. 'Hasselbacken. Arkeologiska undersökningar 2014–2015. Arkeologi i Uddevalla stad 3. Arkeologiska förundersökningar och slutundersökning, Uddevalla 191:1, Stadskärnan 1:173, Uddevalla socken, Uddevalla kommun'. Bohusläns museum rapport. Uddevalla.

5

Tactile Relations: Material Entanglement between Sweden and its Colonies

Jonas M. Nordin

This chapter deals with the exchange of material culture between Sweden and its colonies, focusing in particular on the colony of New Sweden (1638–55). It traces some of the Native American objects in Sweden, discusses their meaning and use in the new environment and places them in the context of collecting of exotic artefacts. An object-biographical approach underlines the complexity and relevance of things in a colonial situation. Both America and Sweden were influenced by the material culture of colonial contact; this material culture became part of a process that changed people and societies on both sides of the Atlantic.

By enforcing colonial institutions in the region, the colony of New Sweden left traces in America. New Sweden, however, had an impact on those who served in the colony, who corresponded with the old country and in some cases those who came back to Sweden. The returnees brought with them things: objects that served as physical reminders of their extraordinary experience. Some of these experiences seem to have been important and formative for the continued development of these people's lives. The former governor of New Sweden, Johan Printz, for instance, kept material objects from his time in the colony throughout his life, and so too did his daughter Armegot.[1] The pastor Johannes Campanius Holm, who served in the colony from 1643 to 1648, and who translated Luther's Catechism into Algonquin,[2] had his grave slab in Sweden inscribed in the Native American language. One may ask if these objects and material imprints were brought to the old country out of nostalgia, or whether other sentiments too were included: it is well recorded that Johan Printz disliked living in the colony, and the same probably went for Johannes Campanius Holm.[3] Yet Printz actually used objects he obtained from the native inhabitants in America and he kept them all of his life.

Certain aspects of these entangled histories of people and things related to the New Sweden colony will be discussed in this chapter, where I will examine the context of the collection of indigenous material culture from Lenapehoking and north-east America in mid-17th-century Sweden. As a parallel to this, I will also discuss the use of material culture traded by the Swedes to the Native Americans in the region of the colony. To these ends I will employ an object-biographical approach, together with an examination of the concurrent collecting of Sami material culture in Sweden.

The purpose of the chapter is to shed light on how the colonial reality in New Sweden and Sweden in the middle of the 17th century was contested and negotiated through material culture. This will be done by re-addressing the use of material culture in colonial praxis and by studying the multiple connections of objects as they linked and transformed not only the Americas but also Europe. The chapter furthermore acknowledges the multicultural situation of the early modern period in colonies and mother countries alike, in the context of a minor power like Sweden and its colonial ambitions. Contact meant the exchange of material things, in general through trade and gifts. Colonial encounters and praxis also entailed negotiating and using power in order to secure dominance, through trade, expansion and mission.[4]

A WORLD OF COLLECTING

In the early modern period, Europeans venturing across the oceans brought souvenirs, commodities and images of Africa, America and Asia to Europe. Through these objects, the continents and their exotic inhabitants and valuable resources were displayed, consumed and appropriated.[5] Foreign objects were used in a baroque staging of a perceived European supremacy displayed at European courts.[6] Scandinavian aristocrats and royalty were eager "consumers" of the New World but also devoted collectors, well exemplifying how collecting actually can be understood as a mode of consumption.

Naturalia and *artificialia* were brought from America via Amsterdam, London, Augsburg, Hamburg, Bremen and Copenhagen to the collections of people like Herman Francke in Germany, Ole Worm in Denmark, and the Wrangel family and the queen, later dowager queen, Hedwig Eleonora in Sweden.[7] Although the collecting of American objects in Europe expanded in the 17th century, it had a history stretching back to the 1492 contact.[8] Direct territorial access to America was not the only means of obtaining Native American material culture; it also spread through the networks of the Catholic Church and the Holy Roman Empire.[9] In the case of the Scandinavian countries, separated from the Catholic Church, the establishment of overseas colonies from 1620 (when Denmark founded the colony of Tranquebar in south-east India) onwards, brought radically enhanced access to coveted objects.

Concurrent to the New Sweden colony, the Swedish Crown had drastically augmented its involvement and aspirations in the arctic and subarctic regions by trying to obtain firmer control of the inner part of Lapland consisting of the historic and present region of Sápmi (i.e. the land of the Sami). Trade was concentrated at a few market-places, the Lutheran mission was intensified and religious persecution of the Sami was encouraged by the religious and political leaders of the realm.[10]

Extractive industries, including copper, iron and silver mining and subsequent refining of the ore, along with pearl fishing and mining of rock crystal, functioned as an important motor for colonial projects and attitudes towards the Sami and their land.[11] In *Colonialism in the Margins* (2006), Gunlög Fur has pointed out the similarities (and dissimilarities) between the overseas colony of New Sweden and the colonial processes in Sápmi. These similarities can also be traced in relations to material culture. Both the Danish and the Swedish courts were presented with gifts including *gievrie/goavddis*[12] (sacred ceremonial drums), and *seide/sieidi*[13] (sacred objects, often of stone, sent to them by local officials, most often against stark opposition from the Sami population).[14] In the royal collections in Copenhagen and in Stockholm the Sami drums and axes from the Americas were exhibited together.[15] Nordic collectors and scientists also took an active part in the translocation of Sami material culture, as in the case of the Swedish architect Nicodemus Tessin (the younger) who exchanged a Sami drum for a set of illustrations from Italy.[16] Objects from America and Sápmi created contacts between people on many levels.

The incorporation of America into European consciousness and European self-identity was enforced by a related colonial policy towards Sápmi. Not surprisingly, European colonial projects in Africa were intensified at the same time, as well. Here too, books were written, itineraries published and indigenous material culture collected. Employees of the Swedish Africa Company (1649–63), with trading posts on the Gold Coast, brought clothes, weapons and jewellery besides their imports of gold, ivory and sugar.[17]

This wide range of material culture can be viewed as a colonial transcript similar to those identified by Edward Said in late 18th- and early 19th-century novels.[18] The life lived on the English and other European estates of the colonial period was intertwined with that of the plantations in America which served as their economic base, and this connection was visible in architecture, literature and physical space as well as in material culture.[19] The lives lived in New Sweden, Sápmi, the Gold Coast and Sweden can be viewed contrapuntally to each other.

Sweden was part of the global world through the influx of commodities from distant parts of the world and the export of copper, iron and other commodities, but also through people's travels and contacts. Everyday goods such as tobacco and sugar, or exotic souvenirs – objects loaded with cultural meaning such as Inuit kayaks, South American hammocks or North American ball-headed clubs, pouches or pipes – made their way across the Atlantic.[20] As mentioned above, these objects were joined by Sami drums, *seidi/sieidi*, Sami spoons and stuffed (or live) reindeer.[21] These objects were part of a general fashion for consuming and collecting exotic objects that, on the one hand, helped to order the European aristocratic worldview – a European identity – and, on the other, to distinguish and visualize the 'other' – people without history and with no future other than satisfying the economic interests of Europe.[22]

Certain commodities imported from the new world lost their aura of exoticism and in the course of the 17th century became ordinary and widely accessible: tobacco and the custom of smoking may serve as an example of an indigenous practice which became widespread in Europe. Unlike such plantation crops and mass-produced commodities, objects made by indigenous people and brought to the centres of Europe were perceived differently and in a more ambivalent way, being used alongside familiar objects and displayed among extraordinary objects, but still singularized as rare and exotic when used and categorized.

The exchange of commodities between Europeans and Native Americans has generally been regarded as a reflection of reciprocal interest in desirable goods without a subsequent reciprocal change in identity and worldview. The European appetites for tobacco and beaver pelts, and the Native groups' demand for glass beads, copper kettles, cloth and weapons has been widely acknowledged.[23] Objects not for direct consumption, ending up at the princely courts of Europe and in the collections, are usually regarded as mere curiosities. When brought to Europe they were re-contextualized and used in the construction of the images of the non-European "Other" and the cosmopolitan "self".

Objects circulating in the early modern Atlantic world had individual, diversely evolving biographies. As they were exchanged, refashioned and altered, the meaning ascribed to them by their subsequent users changed as well. On its way from producers to buyers, Native American material culture was changed from being sacred symbols, gifts or emblems of power, to become commodities with new meanings added. These transformations, sometimes visible, sometimes not, meant hybridization of the objects and, subsequently, of people.[24]

When these commodities came into new contexts in Sweden, and other objects were made with material inspiration from New Sweden, such as the ball-headed club in Skokloster Castle or the phonetic writings on the grave slab of Johannes Campanius Holm, most of them became what Igor Kopytoff has labelled "singularized things". Through singularization the commodity is taken out of the market and becomes a "singular" and thus priceless object.[25] This process indicates that commodification can be a phase in the history of an object or a category of objects, as in the case of the material culture of New Sweden, where trade, which was an important driving force of the colony, resulted in much more than the mere exchange of copper or iron tools for furs and tobacco.[26]

The biographical chains – the lives of objects related to New Sweden – all seem to have undergone a process of changing meaning. The Native American objects acquired by the Printz family, the objects in museum collections in Scandinavia, in particular in Skokloster Castle, as well as the inscriptions on Holm's grave slab, are all tokens of material expressions of alteration and change. These material items were thus not unambiguous in New Sweden – or in any other colonial context – but went through a process that included being symbols, gifts, currency, commodities, and then singularized symbols again.

MATERIAL THINGS AND COLONIAL PRAXIS

Europeans wore beaver hats, added sugar to their tea and put tobacco in their pipes. The Americas came to be ever-present at the vernacular as well as luxury ends of European culture. The people living in the Swedish colony bought and brought objects from Sweden, the Netherlands, the English colonies, the American hinterland and other places. The colonists and residents in the colony were of African, Dutch, English, Finnish, German, Norwegian or Spanish descent, slaves, indentured servants, free or ennobled; but they all seemed to share an interest in and affection for things.[27] Contacts were made through things, and things enabled contact. This was all too evident to the Swedish colonists, who had a hard time providing trade goods for their Native American counterparts.[28]

Things were brought from Europe so as to enable a life in America and trade with the Native Americans. Among other goods, Swedes sold cloth, rifles, trade beads and mirrors from the Netherlands, and Swedish axes, copper kettles, knives and thimbles.[29] Copper in particular had an emblematic role in several Native American communities in the early 17th century, and the metal actually dominated the trade between several colonial settlements and indigenous communities, as in the well-known case of the Jamestown settlement and the Powhatan.[30] The trade in copper and brass kettles is one of the few things that can be regarded with relative certainty as an actual material trace of the Swedish colony among the Lenni Lenape, Nanticoke and Susquehannock nations.[31] Sweden was the world's leading producer of copper in the early modern period, and plenty of kettles are recorded as cargo on the ships sailing to America.[32] Over 300 kettles, for instance, were brought on the ship *Gyllene Hajen* ("Golden Shark") in 1646 alone.[33]

The Lenni Lenape wished to possess kettles not only as cooking vessels, but for the quality of the metal of which they were made. Copper was of great importance to many native societies in North America. Traded from the Great Lakes region or cold-hammered from exposed deposits in the eastern uplands, copper was powerful because it was rare. This can, at least partly, explain the great demand for it in North America.[34] Many kettles were transformed into other objects such as pendants, beads, pipes and arrowheads. Copper was used by many Native Americans on the east coast in the 17th century to decorate wooden or ceramic objects.[35] Kettles, thimbles or other objects were thus transformed into artefacts of use and significance in the native context. But plain fragments of kettles have also been found on archaeological sites. These might be traces of the multifaceted alteration: breaking the European material culture was just a part of the transformation; turning it into something else meant incorporating the object into a new context with a new meaning.[36]

The role of copper in the Americas changed however, during the first half of the 17th century and during the period of the New Sweden colony copper and brass objects, such as kettles, rapidly gained a stronger position in Native American household. The well-known town of the Susquehannock (who traded with the Swedes) known as the Strickler site in Pennsylvania, inhabited concurrently with the Swedish colony, has yielded a large number of complete European brass objects.[37]

Wampum – the shell beads of different colours made in the north-east Atlantic region – was likewise used in a wide variety of ways by both Europeans and Native North Americans. Wampum was used as decoration and had, among other things, a mnemonic function for the users, related to storytelling, diplomacy and communication. The beads were commonly misunderstood by the Europeans as the local currency, objects with a purely economic role. These different perceptions meant that already at an early stage, perhaps from the first contacts between Europeans and Native Americans, the beads were turned into an object of struggle and competition, functioning as a symbol as well as a means of payment between colonists and indigenous North Americans.[38] Per Lindeström, a fortification officer and surveyor who served in the colony, told of the use of wampum as a means of payment, but he also described some of the varied relations with the beads and their functions in communication, narrative and memory.[39] He also reported on the use of wampum by the Swedes in their position as middlemen in trade, but also for other purposes such as prestige or communication (Fig. 5.1). Governor Printz is said to have "had the savages make and thread up for him a suit of clothes with coat, trousers and sword belt entirely of their *own money*, which was very artistic, threaded and worked with all kinds of animals, which came to a few thousand florins".[40]

Printz also wrote to the Chancellor of the Realm, Count Per Brahe, that he was sending a string of beads to Queen Christina: "one of the foremost bands which the Indian chiefs use on their Kinteka [gathering] and greatest glory and is so highly esteemed among them as among us gold and silver".[41] In the same letter Printz mentioned that he

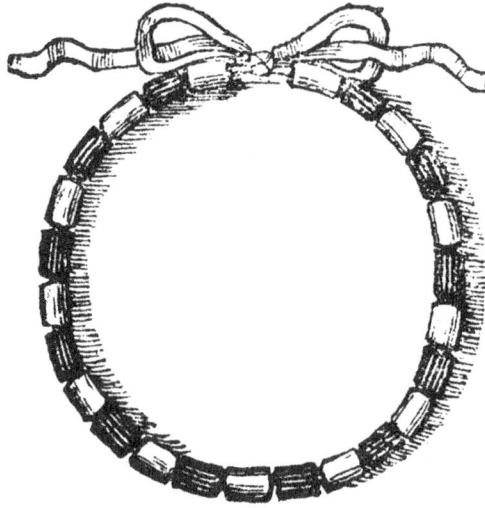

Fig. 5.1 Necklace of wampum from Thomas Campanius Holm's (grandson of Johannes) *Kort beskrifning om provincien Nya Swerige uti Amerika* ("Short description of the province of America"), 1988 [1702].

was sending a tobacco pipe made of stone by "the savages" to Queen Christina and a tobacco pipe of wood and an otter skin for a muff to Brahe. The whereabouts of these gifts are not known.

The wampum coat and trousers with belt to be worn by the governor of New Sweden is an example of the blending of several uses and meanings of material culture and their potential positions in manoeuvring social relations in the Delaware valley. The wampum costume was ordered, at least according to Lindeström, by Governor Printz and manufactured by Lenni Lenape out of materials loaded with various meanings in terms of indigenous identity and memory, colonial encounter, contact, commerce, and then delivered to and used by Printz.[42] The written accounts do not say in what way Printz used the costume: whether or not he used it in interaction with the Lenni Lenape, in front of his own people, or if he valued it as a treasure and stored it at Printzhof. The use of local material tradition, and certainly in this case a luxurious exemplar, might have given the governor access to the Native American communities, the coat thus serving as a form of mimicry. A closer look at American material culture or American influences brought to Sweden shows a similar pattern. The objects or influences were put in new contexts and singled out from their American background.

European commodities were traded for wampum and later traded for food, beaver pelts, tobacco, precious metals and other objects with the surrounding Lenni Lenape community. This material culture was not unambiguous, but an active part of an appropriation – beaver pelts were turned into hats, tobacco that was exchanged and smoked in indigenous ritual settings became an addiction for Europeans, copper kettles were turned into arrowheads, and so on. These transformations and reinterpretations subsequently added to the biographical chains of the objects.

THINGS IN THE OLD COUNTRY

Next to the altar in Frösthult parish church in the province of Uppland in central Sweden, lies a baroque grave slab with the inscription *Umar Sachiman Chinsika hacking haro ankarop machis chuki* ("Here lies a great sachem who died in old age") (Fig. 5.2).[43] These words in the Algonquin language of the Lenni Lenape commemorate Johannes Campanius Holm, who was stationed as a pastor in New Sweden from 1642 to 1648, and who died in Frösthult in 1683. Holm's grave is probably the only European early modern grave epitaph written in a Native American language. Over 300 years after his death the inscription is a stark reminder of the entangled life of Campanius Holm and his family.

In contrast to Holm's grave, other objects connected to New Sweden, such as the wampum belt of Johan Printz and the American pouches of his daughter Armegot, the things kept by Herman and Carl Gustaf Wrangel in Skokloster Castle, and the gifts received by Count Per Brahe and in the collections of Queen Christina, were kept in places with restricted access for the general public. These coveted material artefacts consisted of axes, clubs, headdresses, pipes, pouches and strings of wampum beads.[44] One of the axes is mentioned for the first time in 1686 as belonging to King Charles XI (1655–97).[45] It was kept in the royal armoury, but is now in the Ethnographical Museum in Stockholm (Fig. 5.3). The axe's helve is made of wood with wampum inlay, and it has an iron blade attached by thin leather straps. Although the helve has traces of use, the fitting of the head makes it unsuitable for practical use – either hunting or warfare.[46] The helve shows evident similarities to one of the ball-headed clubs related to the colony and kept at Skokloster (see below) and it is reasonable to assume that the "tomahawk" originally had a ball head and was transformed into an axe in Europe or

Fig. 5.2 The grave slab of Johannes Campanius Holm, Frösthult parish church, central Sweden (photograph: John Allinder 1922, courtesy of Upplandsmuseet).

Fig. 5.3 Axe or tomahawk in the Ethnographical Museum in Stockholm (Inv. no. 1889.04.4179). The axe was recorded as part of the collection belonging to Carl X Gustav (died 1660) in 1686 (photograph: Rose-Marie Westling, courtesy of the Ethnographical Museum, Stockholm).

at least in the hands of Europeans. The iron in the blade is of European – perhaps of Swedish production – and the helve of Native American origin. Sweden was a leading producer of iron in the 17th century and especially of high quality iron needed for axes, blades and hoes.[47] Oddly, an almost identical axe from the same period is kept in the Danish royal *kunstkammer* or museum in Copenhagen. This axe has the helve clad with both wampum and European glass beads; the blade, on the other hand, is not of iron but of stone of American origin.[48] Both axes thus emphasize their hybrid nature, by blending iron with wampum and glass with greenstone. Hybridization in this case also meant that practical objects were transformed into souvenirs and symbols.

Anthropomorphic clubs with ball-shaped heads in Copenhagen and Stockholm have been suggested to be 19th-century Swedish copies of the one in Skokloster.[49] Owning Native American objects was prestigious, and production of things associated with the New World was undertaken in Europe. Looking at the early modern collecting of perceived exotic objects and the existence of copies, traces of alterations and of usage suggest that these objects were seldom treated as collectibles in a modern sense, but rather as objects to be used.[50] Native American costumes, fake or real, were also used, alongside Sami clothing and other Sami material culture, at the festivities of Swedish aristocrats. Appropriation in the form of masquerading was meanwhile paired with the veritable kidnapping of individuals – Native Americans, Sami, Inuit and others – from regions perceived as primitive by the Europeans.[51]

In the royal armoury and in other state collections in Sweden there are also objects that might be related to the colony, but which probably arrived through the Swedish-speaking people who stayed on after its fall. A pair of leggings from the 17th or early 18th century is believed to come from the area of New Sweden (LSH inv. no. 20 643). Uppsala University has a calumet stone pipe from the former colony dating from the early 18th century.[52]

Objects which beyond doubt stem from the 17th century and almost certainly came from the New Sweden colony are the two clubs, three strings, and three red-dyed objects made to look like wolf-heads in Skokloster Castle (Fig. 5.4). One of the clubs has an inlay not only of wampum but also of copper, which may be of Swedish origin. The place of origin cannot be determined without a metallurgical analysis but, to an even greater extent than in the case of iron production, Sweden held a dominant position as world-leading producer of copper.[53] It would be a somewhat surprising connection for commodities produced in Sweden to travel so far and change their form in such a way, and still end up so close to their "birthplace". Tentatively, one part of the club's biography starts in a copper mine in Sweden, whence the sheets of copper were transported to Stockholm or the Netherlands, where kettles and other objects were made. Some of the kettles were then sent across the Atlantic to New Sweden and exchanged for fur or tobacco. Native North Americans who acquired the kettles then broke them up to refashion pieces of copper into familiar and more necessary objects. Bits of copper were used as inlay in a club, which was eventually sold or given to Swedes with whom they came back to Sweden. The putative biographical chain of this one object thus brings together two continents, different systems of values and cultural norms, and the work of many people.

Skokloster Castle is contemporary with the New Sweden colony. The castle was built by the count, admiral and Thirty Years' War general Carl Gustaf Wrangel and his wife

Fig. 5.4 An artificial wolf's head along with other objects from north-eastern America (Skokloster inv. no. 6906) (photograph courtesy of the Skokloster Museum).

Anna Margareta von Haugwitz, between 1654 and 1676. Skokloster is famous for its size, its well-kept exterior and interior, and for its collections of fine arts, furniture and collector's items from all over the world.[54] The death of Anna Margareta von Haugwitz in 1673 and of Carl Gustaf Wrangel in 1676, and the subsequent conversion of the property into an entailed estate, produced inventories in 1676 and 1710, giving thorough descriptions of the castle's possessions. Carl Gustaf Wrangel and Anna Margareta von Haugwitz had their eight objects from New Sweden displayed in the armoury (Fig. 5.5), as recorded in the inventory of 1710, which probably was based on the older inventory.[55] Here weapons from many parts of the world were kept, together with a kayak, a South American hammock and a preserved armadillo – the symbols of the Americas and the Arctic, alongside a Sami drum – the iconic emblem of Sápmi and the Sami people.

It is not recorded when and how these eight North American objects reached Skokloster, but it may have happened in various ways. Carl Gustaf Wrangel personally knew Johan Risingh, the last governor of New Sweden, just as he knew Per Lindeström and Per Brahe, according to dedicated books in his library and his correspondence. Carl Gustaf's father, Herman Wrangel, was also part of the committee signing the instructions for Johan Printz in 1642, together with Carl Gustaf's friend Per Brahe. In the 17th century, Sweden was geographically a vast country, but sparsely populated, and with a relatively small upper class; among the aristocracy and clergy people were bound to know each other.[56]

The castle at Skokloster was founded on the principles of the Renaissance: geometric harmony, classicism and science.[57] The four towers indicate the compass points and symbolize the four elements. The towers are adorned with armillary globes emphasizing the castle's cosmological as well as scientific position – it was built as a reflection of the harmony of the spheres mapped through the strenuous efforts of science. Inside the castle, Carl Gustaf Wrangel and Anna Margareta von Haugwitz had a vast collection of scientific instruments for measuring and optics, as well as several terrestrial globes, maps and travel books together with over twenty curiosity cabinets.[58]

On the walls of the dining halls, bedrooms and drawing rooms are paintings of exotic beasts, and the stucco ceilings are replete with the symbolism of the Renaissance world in the forms of classical myths, animals, wild men and representations of the four known continents. This is most evident in the great dining hall, where a dragon and its slayer are surrounded by depictions of the four continents in the shape of four lightly-clad women. Europe is represented by a woman holding a set of compasses surrounded by an antique ruin, arms and musical instruments. America, in another corner of the ceiling, is symbolized by a woman riding an armadillo together with a packet probably representing tobacco. Europe is presented as history, science, art and refinement, whereas America is depicted as an exotic resource, commodified nature ready for exploitation. The eight objects (inv. no. 6904, 6906–12) from New Sweden had a self-evident place in this context as physical tokens of the global world.

The Sami drum (inv. no. 13722), was probably brought to Skokloster Castle from another baroque palace, Salsta, after the death of Carl Gustaf Wrangel and Anna Margareta von Haugwitz, by the Brahe-Bielke family, and it is mentioned for the first time in 1793.[59] This sacred object can be viewed as a late comment on the vast collection of Wrangel and Haugwitz – they had everything except for this coveted object. There was

Fig. 5.5 The armoury of Anna Margareta von Haugwitz and Carl Gustaf Wrangel at Skokloster. The armoury has remained practically untouched since the death of Wrangel in 1676. Note the chest to the right where the north-eastern American objects are stored (photograph courtesy of the Skokloster Museum).

awareness of the Sami and Sápmi during Wrangel's and Haugwitz's time, but they had no physical object representing the landscape and its perceived exotic people. Johannes Schefferus's influential book *Lapponia* (1673), the first ethnographical and historical work on the Sami, formed part of the library, and images from its illustrations can be found recycled in furniture – for example, in one of the curiosity cabinets from the same time (inv. no. 3160). The inventory of 1710 includes several Sami objects belonging to the Brahe armoury. This collection was brought to the castle in the late 17th century.[60]

Skokloster Castle was created as a curiosity cabinet on an astonishing scale, a *theatrum mundi*, capturing the zeitgeist of the late Renaissance. The castle was constructed as the centre of an estate, but it was also a node in the newly-arisen global world. The proprietor drank cocoa, coffee and tea, smoked tobacco and collected items from South America, Asia, the North Atlantic and Sápmi in addition to the objects from Delaware basin area.[61] Skokloster as a "theatre of the world" was in part a stage where the whole colonial world was displayed – a colonial theatre.

The objects from the New Sweden area were incorporated into, in effect, a great *mappa mundi*, as a node pointing towards America. They became a part of the life of Skokloster, as a place where material things and their narratives connected New Sweden to the old country, and America to Europe. Johan Printz's manor of Gunillaberg, Fröst-hult parish church, Count Per Brahe's Visingsborg, the royal palace in Stockholm and many other places were sites where America and its hybridity kept on colouring society long after the Swedish colony was lost.

COLLECTED WORLDS – CONCLUDING REMARKS

The 17th-century Native American objects in Sweden are undoubtedly interesting and rather unique as regards age and preservation; they are, however, few in number. Although it is reasonable to suppose that the number of objects from the New Sweden colony was originally substantially larger, there were never many of them. But they are there, together with other traces of America such as the grave slab of Campanius Holm, or the descriptions of Per Lindeström. In Sweden these objects were reshaped, used and staged together with things from Sápmi, the Gold Coast and the past – America was included in a narrative of the world and the position of Swedes in that same world.[62]

In north-eastern America, at the Susquehannock town later known as Strickler in Lancaster County, Pennsylvania, which was contemporary with the New Sweden colony, an active incorporation of European material culture and architecture took place. Here kettles were not only transformed into other objects but seemingly used for their original purpose.[63] Further to the east, at the Tenakong Island, later known as Printzhof/ New Gothenburg, the Swedish colonists settled on a Lenni Lenape site, used their material culture and internalized parts of their experience.[64] Excavations conducted in the 1930s and 1980s at the Printzhof site reveal evidence of contact through the finds of a Native American smoking pipe and some chipped glass.[65] Although not dated, the traces of a wigwam were found adjacent to the Swedish manor, indicating close relations (historically, spatially or both) between the Swedish colonizers and the local population.

Sweden was a small-time player in colonial history. In comparison to the great museums of the European continent, material culture from the early contact between Europe and America there is scarce. But it exists, and most of it can be connected to the short-lived New Sweden colony. Indigenous Americans were entangled in material contacts with the Swedes, and the Swedes coveted not only furs and tobacco but also handcrafted objects. Back home, the collecting and incorporation of America coincided with the colonial endeavours in Sápmi. Royal, aristocratic and scientific collectors in Sweden had Sami objects and depictions alongside their American ones.

ACKNOWLEDGEMENTS

This text of this chapter forms part of the Collecting Sápmi project, financed by the Swedish Research Council (project no. 421-2013-1917). I would also like to express my gratitude to Audrey Horning for her constructive comments on an earlier draft.

NOTES

1 Göta hovrätts Arkiv Vadstena, File: E XIA:10, no. 916; RA Likvidationer, Försträckningar och leveranser serie B, vol. 221; Elfving 1986, 33.
2 Holm 1696 [1937].
3 Naum 2013.
4 Silliman 2005, 58–9
5 See studies in Feest 1989; Feest 1995; Kupperman 1995; Arnold 2006.
6 Mignolo 1995; Mauriès 2002; Yaya 2008.
7 Losman 1988; Mauriès 2002; Mordhorst 2009; Skogh 2013.
8 Columbus 1969; Russo 2008; Keating & Markey 2011.
9 Keating & Markey 2011.
10 Hansen & Olsen 2014, 239–49.
11 Nordin 2012; 2014; 2015.
12 South Sami/Lule Sami language.
13 South Sami/North Sami language.
14 See for instance Manker 1938; Rydving 1993; Snickare 2014; Nordin & Oajala 2015; Nordin & Ojala 2017.
15 Mordhorst 2009.
16 Snickare 2014, 65.
17 Jones 1994.
18 Said 1993.
19 Said 1993, 95–116; Johnson 2006.
20 Mordhorst 2009.
21 Berg 1954; Broberg 1982; Nordin 2017; Nordin & Ojala 2017.
22 See Wolf 1982; Sheller 2003.
23 Risingh 1988, 177; White 1991; Dolin 2010; Howey 2011.
24 See Thomas 1991; Keating & Markey 2011, 296.
25 Kopytoff 1986, 73–4.
26 See Appadurai 1986, 17.
27 Johnson 1911, 705; Carlsson 1995; Ekengren et al. 2013.
28 See for instance Norman 1988, 59–74.
29 Risingh 1988, 177; Johnson 1911, 242, 255.
30 Mallios & Emmet 2004; Horning 2009.
31 Immonen 2011.
32 Magnusson 2010, 124–31.
33 Johnson 1911, 255.
34 Mallios & Emmet 2004.
35 van Dongen 1995; Immonen 2011.
36 van Dongen 1995.
37 Kent 1984, 203–11, 348–53.
38 Otto 2010, 178.
39 Lindeström 1962, 129–38; Fur 2006, 147; Otto 2010.
40 My emphasis. Lindeström 1925, 222; Feest 1995, 339.
41 Printz, letter to Brahe, 14 July 1644, in Johnson 1930, 166.
42 Lindeström 1962, 128; Nordin 2013a.
43 My transcription. On the interpretation of the phonetic writings see Brunius 2007, 33 n. 3.
44 Becker 1990a; 1990b; Brunius 1990; 1995; 2007.
45 Brunius 1995; 2007; Snickare 2011.
46 Brunius 1995, 159.
47 Evans & Rydén 2007.
48 Due 1980, 31; Feest 1989, 53; Brunius 2007, 36.
49 Brunius 2007, 36.
50 Cf. Yaya 2008.
51 Vaughan, 2007; Nordin & Ojala 2017; Nordin 2017.
52 Brunius 2007, 39–40.
53 Becker 1990b, 23; Nordin 2013a.
54 Losman 1988; Bergström 2005; Nordin 2013b.
55 Brunius 2007, 34.
56 See for instance the diary of Lorenzo Magalotti from 1674 (1912) who gives an eye witness account of people of central Sweden and of the Swedish political system.
57 Herva & Nordin 2013, 214–15; Eriksdotter et al. 2015.
58 Losman & Sigurdsson 1975.
59 Manker 1938, 625.
60 Kylsberg 2006, 13.
61 Losman 1980, 179–82.
62 See e.g. Herva & Nordin 2015.
63 Futer 1959; Kent 1984.
64 Nordin 2013a.
65 Nordin 2013a, 214–15.

BIBLIOGRAPHY

Appadurai, A. 1986. 'Introduction: Commodities and the politics of value', in Appadurai 1986, 3–63.

Appadurai, A. (ed.) 1986. *The Social Life of Things: Commodities in Cultural Perspective.* Cambridge: Cambridge University Press.

Arnold, K. 2006. *Cabinets for the Curious: Looking Back at Early English Museums.* Aldershot: Ashgate.

Beaudry M. C. & Parno, T. G. (eds) 2013. *Archaeologies of Mobility and Movement.* New York: Springer.

Becker, M. J. 1990a. 'A wolf's head pouch: Lenape material culture in the collections of the Skokloster Museum, Sweden', *Archeomaterials* 4(1): 77–95.

Becker, M. J. 1990b. 'Two 17th-century clubs in the collections of the Skokloster Museum, Sweden', *Native American Studies* 4(1): 19–27.

Berg, E. W. (ed.) 2006. *A Glimpse of the World. Non-European in Skokloster Castle.* Skoklosterstudier 37. Skokloster: Skoklosters slott.

Berg, G. 1954. 'Lappland och Europa: Några anteckningar om renar som furstegåvor', in Strömbäck 1954, 221–44.

Bergström, C. (ed.) 2005. *Skoklosters slott under 350 år.* Stockholm: Byggförlaget.

Broberg, G. 1982. 'Lappkaravaner på villovägar: Antropologin och synen på samerna fram mot sekelskiftet 1900', *Lychnos* 1982: 27–86.

Brunius, T. 1988. *Efterskrift. Per Lindeströms Kort beskrivning om provinsen Nya Sverige uti Amerika.* Stockholm: Rediviva.

Brunius, S. 1990. 'North American Indian collections at the Folkens Museum-Etnografiska, Stockholm', *Native American Studies* 4(1): 29–34.

Brunius, S. 1995. 'Some comments on early Swedish collections from the northeast', in Hoffecker *et al.* 1995, 150–68.

Brunius, S. 2007. 'In the light of the New Sweden colony: Notes on Swedish pre-1800: ethnographic collections from northeastern North America', *Native American Studies* 21(2): 27–42.

Carlsson, S. 1995. 'The New Sweden colonists, 1628-1656: Their geographical and social background', in Hoffecker *et al.* 1995, 171–87.

Columbus, C. 1969. *The Four Voyages,* ed. J. M. Cohen. London: Penguin.

Dahlgren, S. & Norman, H. (eds) 1988. *The Rise and Fall of New Sweden: Governor Johan Risingh's Journal 1654-1655 in its Historical Context.* Stockholm: Almqvist & Wiksell International.

Dam-Mikkelsen & Lundbæk, T. (eds) 1980. *Ethnographic Objects in the Royal Danish Kunstkammer 1650–1800.* Copenhagen: Nationalmuseet.

Dolin, E. J. 2010. *Fur, Fortune and Empire: The Epic History of the Fur Trade in America.* New York: W. W. Norton & Company.

van Dongen, A. 1995. *One Man's Trash Is Another Man's Treasure: The Metamorphosis of the European Utensil in the New World.* Rotterdam: Museum Boymans-van Beuningen.

Due, B. 1980. 'America', in Dam-Mikkelsen & Lundbæk 1980, 18–40.

Ekengren, F. Naum, M. & Zagal-Mach Wolfe, U. I. 2013. 'Sweden in the Delaware Valley: Everyday life and material culture in New Sweden', in Naum & Nordin 2013, 169–87.

Elfving, F. 1986. *Kring Johan Björnsson Printz: Del 1, Familjen och ättlingarna.* Mölndal: Folke Elfving.

Eriksdotter, G., Nilsson, P & Nordin, J. M. 2015. 'A baroque landscape of earth, water and fire: The production of space at Skokloster, a Swedish estate of the seventeenth century', *Landscapes* 16(2): 126–44.

Evans, C. & Rydén, G. 2007. *Baltic Iron in the Atlantic World in the Eighteenth Century*. Leiden: Brill.

Feest, C. F. 1995. 'The collecting of American Indian artefacts in Europe, 1493–1750', in Kupperman 1995, 324–60.

Feest, C. F. (ed.) 1989. *Indians and Europe: An Interdisciplinary Collection of Essays*. Lincoln: University of Nebraska Press.

Forssberg A.-M. & Sennefelt, K. (eds) 2014. *Fråga föremålen: Handbok till historiska studier av materiell kultur*. Lund: Studentlitteratur.

Fur, G. 2006. *Colonialism in the Margins: Cultural Encounters in New Sweden and Lapland*. Leiden: Brill.

Futer, A. A. 1959. 'The Strickler site', in Witthoft & Kinsey III 1959, 136–47.

Göta hovrätts Arkiv File: E XIA:10, no. 916, Vadstena, Sweden.

Hall M. & Silliman, S. (eds) 2006. *Historical Archaeology*. Malden: Blackwell.

Hansen, L. I & Olsen, B. 2014. *Hunters in Transition: An Outline of Early Sami History*. Leiden: Brill.

Herva, V.-P., & Nordin, J. M. 2013. 'Classicism and knowing the world in early modern Sweden', in Watts 2013, 209–27.

Herva, V-P. & Nordin, J. M. 2015. 'Unearthing Atlantis and performing the past: Ancient things, alternative histories and the present past in the baroque world', *Journal of Social Archaeology* 15(1): 116–35.

Hoffecker, C. E., Waldron, R., Williams, L. E. & Benson, B. E. (eds) 1995. *New Sweden in America*. Newark: University of Delaware Press.

Holm, J. C. 1696 [1937]. *Lutheri Catechismus öfversatt på American-Virginiske Språket* och *Vocabularium Barbaro-Virgineorum*. Stockholm: Burchardi Trycker. Facsimile.

Holm, T. C. 1988 [1702]. *Kort beskrivning om provinsen Nya Sverige uti Amerika*. Stockholm: Rediviva.

Horning, A. 2009. 'Past, present and future: Exploring and restoring native perspectives on Roanoke and Chesapeake', in Sloan 2009, 131–42.

Howey, M. C. L. 2011. 'Colonial encounters, European kettles and the magic of mimesis in the late sixteenth and early seventeenth century indigenous northeast and Great Lakes', *International Journal of Historical Archaeology* 15(3): 329–57.

Immonen, V. 2011. 'Farming and brass kettles as forms of colonial encounter: New Sweden from an archaeological perspective', *Scandinavian Studies* 83(3): 366–86.

Johnson, A. 1911. *The Swedish Settlements on the Delaware: Their History and Relation to the Indians, Dutch and English 1638–1664*. Philadelphia: Swedish Colonial Society.

Johnson, A. 1930. *The Instructions for Johan Printz Governor of New Sweden*. Philadelphia: Swedish Colonial Society.

Johnson, M. 2006. 'The tide reversed: Prospects and potentials for a postcolonial archaeology of Europe', in Hall & Silliman 2006, 314–31.

Jones, A. 1994. 'A collection of African art in seventeenth-century Germany: Christoph Weickmann's *Kunst- und Naturkammer*', *African Art* 27(2): 28–43.

Kent, B. 1984, *Susquehanna's Indians*. Harrisburg: The Pennsylvania Historical and Museum Commission.

Keating, J. & Markey, L. 2011. '"Indian" objects in Medici and Austrian-Habsburg inventories: A case-study of the sixteenth-century term', *Journal of the History of Collections* 23(2): 283–300.

Kopytoff, I. 1986. 'The cultural biography of things: Commoditization as process', in Appadurai 1986, 64–91.

Kupperman, K. O. 1995. 'Scandinavian colonists confront the New World', in Hoffecker *et al.* 1995, 89-111.

Kupperman K. O. (ed.) 1995. *America in European Consciousness 1493–1750*. Chapel Hill: University of North Carolina Press.

Kylsberg, B. 2006. 'Introduction', in Berg 2006, 12–14.

Leone M. & Knauf, J. (eds) 2015. *Historical Archaeologies of Capitalism*. New York: Springer.

Lindeström, P. 1925. *Geographia Americae with An Account of the Delaware Indians: Based on Surveys and Notes Made in 1654–1656*. Philadelphia: Swedish Colonial Society.

Lindeström, P. 1962. *Resan till Nya Sverige: Geographia Americae*. Stockholm: Natur och Kultur.

Losman, A. 1980. *Carl Gustaf Wrangel och Europa: Studier i kulturförbindelser kring en 1600-tals magnat*. Stockholm: Almqvist & Wiksell International.

Losman, A. 1988. 'Skokloster: Europe and the world in a Swedish castle', in Losman *et al.* 1988, 85–103.

Losman, A., & Sigurdsson, I. 1975. *Äldre vetenskapliga instrument på Skokloster*. Skokloster-studier 10. Skokloster: Skokloster slott.

Losman, A., Lundström, A. & Revera M. (eds) 1988. *The Age of New Sweden*. Stockholm: Livrustkammaren.

Magalotti, L. 1912. *Sverige under år 1674: Från italienskan med 23 samtida bilder*, ed. C. M. Stenbock. Stockholm: Norstedt.

Magnusson, L. 2010. *Sveriges ekonomiska historia*. Stockholm: Norstedts.

Mallios, S., & Emmet, S. 2004. 'Demand, supply, and elasticity in the copper trade at early Jamestown', *The Journal of the Jamestown Rediscovery Center* 2004(2) http://apva.org/rediscovery/pdf/mallios_low.pdf [accessed 15 May 2012].

Manker, E. 1938. *Die lappische Zaubertrommel: eine ethnologische monographie*. Vol. 1: *Die Trommel als Denkmal materieller Kultur*. Stockholm: Thule.

Mauriès, P. 2002. *Cabinets of Curiosities*. London: Thames & Hudson.

Michaels, A. (ed.) 2010. *Ritual Dynamics and the Science of Ritual*. Wiesbaden: Harrasowitz.

Mignolo, W. 1995. *The Darker Side of the Renaissance: Literacy, Territoriality and Colonization*. Ann Arbor: The University of Michigan Press.

Mordhorst, C. 2009. *Genstands Fortællinger: Fra Museum Wormianum til de moderne museer*. Copenhagen: Museum Tusculanums forlag.

Naum, M. 2013. 'The malady of emigrants: Homesickness and longing in the colony of New Sweden (1638–1655)', in Beaudry & Parno 2013, 165–77.

Naum, M. & Nordin, J. M. (eds) 2013. *Scandinavian Colonialism and the Rise of Modernity: Small Time Agents in a Global Arena*. New York: Springer.

Naum, M. & Nordin, J. M. 2013. 'Situating Scandinavian colonialism', in Naum & Nordin 2013, 3–16.

Nordin, J. M. 2012. 'Embodied colonialism: The cultural meaning of silver in a Swedish colonial context of the 17th century', *Post-Medieval Archaeology* 46(1): 143–65.

Nordin, J. M. 2013a. 'There and back again – the material culture of New Sweden: Towards an archaeology of hybridity of 17th century colonialism', in Naum & Nordin 2013, 207–25.

Nordin, J. M. 2013b. 'The centre of the world: The material construction of Eurocentric domination and hybridity in a Scandinavian seventeenth-century context', *Journal of Material Culture* 18(2): 189–209.

Nordin, J. M. 2014. 'Materiella möten och globala nätverk', in Forssberg & Sennefelt 2014, 171–86.

Nordin, J. M. 2015. 'Metals of metabolism: The construction of industrial space and the commodification of early modern Sápmi', in Leone & Knauf 2015, 249–72.

Nordin, J. M. 2017. 'Center of Diversity: Sámi in Early Modern Stockholm in the Light of European Colonial Expansion. A Historical Archaeological Approach.' *International Journal of Historical Archaeology*. Published online July 2017. DOI 10.1007/s10761-017-0430-5.

Nordin, J. M. & Ojala, C-G. 2015. 'Collecting Sápmi: Early modern collecting of Sami material culture', *Nordisk Museologi* 2015(2): 114–22.

Nordin, J. M. & Ojala, C-G. 2017 'Collecting, connecting, constructing: Early modern commodification and globalization of Sámi material culture', in *Journal of Material Culture*. Published online November 2017. DOI: 10.1177/1359183517741663

Norman, H. 1988. 'The Swedish colonial venture in North America 1638–1655', in Dahlgren & Norman 1988, 45–126.

Otto, P. 2010. 'Wampum: The transfer and creation of rituals on the early American frontier', in Michaels 2010, 171–88.

RA Likvidationer, Försträckningar och leveranser serie B, vol. 221, Riksarkivet, Stockholm.

Risingh, J. 1988. 'Risingh's journal', in Dahlgren & Norman 1988, 127–87.

Russo, A. 2008. 'Cortés's objects and the idea of New Spain', *Journal of the History of Collections* 20(2): 229–52.

Rydving, H. 1993. *The End of Drum-Time: Religious Change among the Lule Saami, 1670s–1740s.* Acta Universitatis Upsaliensis, Historia religionum 12. Uppsala: University of Uppsala.

Said, E. 1993. *Culture and Imperialism.* London: Vintage.

Sheller, M. 2003. *Consuming the Caribbean: From Arawaks to Zombies.* London: Routledge.

Silliman, S. W. 2005. 'Culture contact of colonialism? Challenges in the archaeology of native North America', *American Antiquity* 70(1): 55–74.

Sloan, K. (ed.) 2009. *European Visions: American Voices.* London: British Museum.

Skogh, L. 2013. *Material Worlds: Queen Hedwig Eleonora as Collector and Patron of the Arts.* Stockhom: The Royal Swedish Academy of Sciences.

Snickare, M. 2011. 'The king's tomahawk: On the display of the other in seventeenth-century Sweden, and after', *Konsthistorisk Tidskrift* 80(2): 124–35.

Snickare, M. 2014. 'Kontroll, begär och kunskap: Den koloniala kampen om Goavddis', *RIG: Kulturhistorisk tidskrift* 97(2): 66–76.

Strömbäck, D. (ed.) 1954. *Scandinavica et Fenno-Ugrica: studier tillägnade Björn Collinder den 22 juli 1954.* Stockholm: Almqvist & Wiksell.

Thomas, N. 1991. *Entangled Objects: Exchange, Material Culture and Colonialism in the Pacific.* Cambridge, MA: Harvard University Press.

Vaughan, A.T. 2006, *Transatlantic Encounters: American Indians in Britain 1500–1776.* Cambridge: Cambridge University Press.

Watts, C. (ed.) 2014. *Relational Archaeologies.* London: Routledge.

White, R. 1991. *The Middle Ground: Indians, Empires and Republics in the Great Lakes Region, 1650-1815.* Cambridge: Cambridge University Press.

Witthoft, J. & Kinsey W. F. III (eds) 1959. *Susquehannock Miscellany.* Harrisburg: The Pennsylvania Historical and Museum Commission.

Wolf, E. R. 1982. *Europe and the People without History.* Berkeley: University of California Press.

Yaya, I. 2008. 'Wonders of America: The curiosity cabinet as a site of representation and knowledge', *Journal of the History of Collections* 20(2): 173–88.

II

Migration and Neighbourly Interactions

Introduction

MAGDALENA NAUM AND FREDRIK EKENGREN

Early modern Sweden was a multicultural kingdom. Within its 17th-century borders it included Finland (which was part of the realm since the Middle Ages) as well as Livonia, the German provinces of Bremen-Verden, Wismar and Pomerania, and old Danish regions of Halland, Scania and Blekinge, all acquired in war settlements. In the north, the lands of Sápmi (Lapland) were claimed and colonized with a new vigour at this time. The country also became home to various diasporas: groups of European immigrants who ventured to Scandinavia enticed by a possibility of social advancement, economic profit and a better life. It was furthermore a site of domestic resettlements, of which the most considerable was the movement of the so-called Forest Finns from eastern Finland to central and northern parts of Sweden proper. In many cases the Swedish government looked positively on migration or even sponsored the arrival of newcomers, who were regarded as a crucial ingredient in the ambitious plan to boost the economy and reputation of the country. Their injection of capital, market connections, skills and knowledge were rewarded with privileges, freedoms and various concessions. The expansion of the kingdom, relocations of its subjects and arrival of newcomers brought significant economic, technical and cultural changes. It created novel networks and connections which in turn posed new challenges, not least regarding how to respond to this multitude of cultures and customs, and how to accommodate members of different confessions in a sternly Lutheran kingdom. Even if the flow of people across the borders was not unique to early modern Sweden (but rather part of a contemporary global development of increased mobility, voluntary as well as forced), it nonetheless engendered and required localized responses.

This part of the book describes some of the individuals and groups that moved within the country's borders and who migrated to Sweden making it a temporary or permanent home. It focuses on their cultural strategies and interactions with the Swedish-speaking majority. Several chapters pay attention to borders and, noting their contested character, address questions of daily life in these charged areas, raising the issues of power, transgression and colonial expansion.

The relocation of the Forest Finns to the northern part of Sweden is the subject of Magnus Elwendahl's study. His chapter grapples with the questions of cultural conservatism and transformations within particular Finnish households and the group as a whole. Interrogating the stereotypes of Forest Finns as conservative, poor and radically different from the Swedish peasants, the author argues that while the families upheld certain customs they were also transforming their cultural practices, eagerly procuring, for example, imported and domestically-produced consumer goods such as ceramics. Adam Grimshaw and Christina Dalhede focus on German, Dutch and British (Scottish and English) urban immigrants. They illustrate how these cosmopolitan individuals, through competition, networking and collaboration across ethnic lines, carved spaces for themselves in Swedish towns. Through intermarriage and joint ventures these "culturally mixed Europeans", a term introduced by Christina Dalhede, were able to foster, capitalize upon and expand their connections and affluence, affecting in the process the culture of the towns they lived in.

Swedish trade was not the only enterprise that relied on foreign participation. Specialized manufactures, developing throughout the 17th century, involved immigrant professionals. A group of skilled textile workers who arrived in Jönköping from northern Germany is studied by Claes B. Pettersson, who reconstructs details of their life and work from archaeological remains. Similarly to other studies in this section, the author notices certain conservative tendencies among the immigrants, including foodways and domestic furnishing, as well as conflicts between the newcomers and the locals, most often revolving around cultural practices departing from Swedish legal and customary norms.

The expansion of the Swedish kingdom in the course of the 16th and 17th centuries made the country into the realm of many ethnic minorities. These included Karelians living in its easternmost territories, who were not only linguistically and culturally different from the Finnish majority but adhered to a different – Eastern Orthodox – faith. Although interactions between the two groups were sometimes shadowed by mistrust, violence and prejudice, Kimmo Katajala discusses more cordial instances of mixed marriages. Although these unions brought certain individuals together, they posed dilemmas to the strict Lutheran administration in Sweden (and to the Orthodox Church in Russian Karelia), and did not erase suspicions of the other in the local communities.

Still different relations developed in the northernmost parts of the kingdom. From the 16th century onwards Sápmi (Lapland) became a target of state policies that had a colonial hue. Their range – mapping of the landscape, searching for ores and exploitation of resources, mission, schooling and suppression of spiritual and communal practices – is described by Carl-Gösta Ojala, whose study deals also with responses to the Swedish policies in Sápmi, and their lingering legacies. Scholarship on the Swedish intervention in the region is divided on the issue of a definition of its character – whether or not it should be termed "colonial". Matti Enbuske argues, for example, that the special tax regulations introduced by the state were geared towards protecting Sami rights. This particularism reinforced the 'otherness' of the Sami and Sápmi but did not bespeak of colonial intentions.

The studies in this section present the complex ethnic and cultural landscape of early modern Sweden and discuss a mutually experienced otherness in the meetings and interactions between newcomers and locals. They illustrate the strategies of defining, maintaining and overcoming difference at a grassroots level as well as in the ideologies and policies of the state.

6

Marrying "the Other": Crossing Religious Boundaries in the Eastern Borderlands of the Kingdom of Sweden in the 17th Century

KIMMO KATAJALA

Marriages between people confessing different religious faiths are not a frequently studied topic among historians. This chapter focuses on mixed marriages in the Kexholm province in the easternmost borderland of the 17th-century Swedish realm. The province was settled by Karelian people who were Orthodox and by Finns who confessed the Lutheran faith. Although relations between these groups were strained, we have proof of several mixed marriages in the protocols of the local courts. The source material is unsystematic and scant; however, it can open a small window on the daily life of these mixed couples and on the local society in which they lived.

STUDYING EARLY MODERN MARRIAGES IN THE BORDERLANDS

Marriage practices among the common people, or peasantry, are a classic topic in cultural studies but have attracted much less attention from historians, especially when it comes to the pre-modern era. Since marriage was a legal institution, the approach adopted by historians has most often been a legal one.[1] This brief study focuses on marriages between people confessing different faiths in the eastern borderlands of 17th-century Sweden. The aim of the study is to throw light on the everyday lives of those early modern people who decided to marry a spouse of another religion. Despite laws, stipulations and common prejudices which did not favour mixed marriages, these people were ready to cross the borders between religions.

The territory concerned here is the province of Kexholm, which at that time covered an area west and north-west of Lake Ladoga that today lies on both sides of the Finnish–Russian border (Fig. 6.1). The provinces of Kexholm and Ingria were annexed to the Kingdom of Sweden under the peace treaty of 1617, but were greatly affected by the Great Northern War, which began in 1700, so that under the peace treaty of 1721 Kexholm was divided in half and its southern parts together with the whole province of Ingria were ceded to the Russian Empire while only the sparsely settled northern part of Kexholm was left in the possession of Sweden. The material available from the province of Kexholm in the Swedish period, 1617–1700, is nevertheless ideally suited to the study of the early modern borderlands.

Fig. 6.1 The province of Kexholm at the easternmost border of the 17th-century Swedish realm.

The province of Kexholm saw many changes in the course of the 17th century. The Russian system of government that had developed during the preceding century was replaced by a Swedish one, and at the local level, the crown bailiffs (*kronofogde*) and sheriffs (*länsman*) became responsible for collecting taxes and keeping order. The Swedish judiciary system and legislation, with district judges (*häradshöfdingar*) and regular district court sessions employing twelve local lay jurors (*nempdemän*), was introduced into the occupied provinces of Kexholm and Ingria and, of foremost importance, the Lutheran Church with its ministers and parishes spread to these areas that had formerly been inhabited by Karelian and Ingrian people belonging to the Russian Orthodox faith.[2]

Almost immediately after the treaty of 1617 Karelian and Ingrian people began to migrate away from these new Swedish provinces into Russia, and the abandoned houses, fields and meadows were taken over by Finns moving in from the province of Vyborg in the south-west and that of Savo in the west. During the Russo–Swedish War of 1656–8 the Karelian people of the province of Kexholm supported and joined the invading Russian troops and began to loot and kill their new Finnish neighbours, but when the Swedish armies gained the upper hand and were able to penetrate into the province again, the Karelians fled in hordes to the Russian side of the border in fear of revenge. The war was ended by the treaty of 1661, without any change in the position of the border between Sweden and Russia in Karelia.[3]

At the beginning of the 1660s there were many parishes in the province of Kexholm that were practically uninhabited. The Karelians had fled to Russia, many houses had been burned down and many people had been killed. Most of the abandoned farms were resettled in the course of the decade, however, as Karelian families returned from Russia to their homes. In the parishes of Libelits (Liperi) and Ilomantsi the Karelian inhabitants of the villages that owned the most fertile fields had stayed on their farms despite the hard times, and in the easternmost parishes of the province, Suistamo, Suojärvi and Salmi, Karelians even formed a majority of the population during the last decades of the 17th century. The migration of Finns into the province from the south-west and west was most pronounced during the 1660s and 1670s, and the situation during the last decades of the 17th century was that Lutheran Finns and Orthodox Karelians were living side by side on neighbouring farms and in neighbouring villages throughout most of the province of Kexholm. As a general rule we can say that the Finns were in the majority in the west and Karelian families in the east.

It can be assumed from previous studies that relations between these two groups were not very good. Their habits differed in matters of culture, religion, family life and even architecture,[4] and the cruelties and confrontations experienced during the war of the 1650s were not easily forgotten. Marriage over these religious and ethnic divides was not common, although we do know from several court cases that some inter-religious marrying did take place. There has been no previous systematic research into this topic, with only a few scattered examples mentioned in the literature.

What can we find out about these mixed marriages in the early modern eastern borderlands of the Kingdom of Sweden? What were the opinions and practices of the Lutheran and Orthodox churches in such cases? Were there any special patterns or habits involved in connection with these mixed marriages? What did the people concerned think about them? Meanwhile we must also ask whether there were any special features connected with the province's eastern border. Did people marry over the border? It is the aim of this chapter to try to answer these questions.

POOR SOURCES AND THE MICROHISTORICAL METHOD

It is not easy to study marriages between people who lived in the easternmost border-lands of the Kingdom of Sweden in the early modern period. The source material available is very scanty, as the available taxation registers do not give any information about this subject and churches did not yet keep registers of parishioners and their families. At the same time, most inhabitants of the region were illiterate and therefore they did not write letters or other documents which could shed light on the question. The only source materials from which we can extract some information are the rolls of the district court sessions.

Studying marriages across the religious divisions is in any case a somwewhat complex matter. Such marriages were mentioned incidentally in the court rolls in connection with other cases: when the court was resolving disputes over inheritance, for example, or trying cases of robbery, an illegitimate child or the killing of a peasant. There is no reason why these marriages should be mentioned in the court rolls at all systematically, and it was very seldom that such a marriage was in itself at issue. We can therefore only make sporadic observations about mixed marriages when using the court rolls as the source material. However, as we have no other source to turn to, these are the records we must fall back on.

Court sessions were held twice a year in each court district in the province of Kexholm, in winter and in autumn. Each jurisdictional district consisted of two or three parishes. The judge or his scribe would write an account of each court case in the minutes *in situ*, and these often messy records would be transcribed (reconstructed) later so that the resulting versions could be sent to the High Court for examination. It is usually only the transcribed versions of the 17th-century court rolls that have survived in the archives of the High Court in Turku, and in any case these archives were partially destroyed in the Great Fire of Turku in the 1820s, so that we now have access only to the rolls of the court sessions held in the province of Kexholm in the 1640s, 1670s, 1680s and 1690s.

Although the State Archives of Finland (now the National Archives) organized a project for the construction of a card index of the 17th-century court rolls in the 1960s, the work had only been partly completed before the project ended in the 1990s. The court rolls of the province of Kexholm were in fact the last to have been indexed with key words. The present study used this card index to find the relevant court cases from the rolls, using the key words "marriage between persons of different religions" (*avioliitto eri uskontokuntien välillä*). Experience has shown that the card index is not absolutely reliable, in that sometimes cases have not been indexed under the right key words. It is nevertheless generally assumed that the coverage of material accessed by card index and examined using the right key words will give reliable enough results for research purposes. The material was also supplemented with cases mentioned in the previous literature, and if one or two cases were missed because of the imperfection of the card index this can scarcely have affected the general conclusions.

The card index for the court rolls of the province of Kexholm identifies 15 court cases in which a marriage had taken place between a Lutheran Finn and an Orthodox Karelian, and a few other cases which are not mentioned in the card index can be traced from the available literature. Closer reading of the cases identified in the court rolls shows that these actually concerned only five married couples. The other cases dealt with relationships between Lutherans and members of the Orthodox Church, but not marriages specifically. But even so, the material taken from the court rolls and from the literature as a whole can give some information about the patterns of behaviour involved when people married across religious divisions. The relevant questions are: whether one party converted to the other's religion; whether there were differences between males and females in this respect; whether a person who converted changed his or her first name; whether a Lutheran or an Orthodox priest (or both) married these couples; and whether children were brought up in the father's or mother's religion.

The religion or ethnic origins of a person would not always be explicitly declared in court cases, and sometimes their religion had to be deduced from other available information. The most important and clearest clue to a person's ethnicity and the religion was the name. As the judges and scribes wrote the names of Finns in the court rolls in their Swedish forms (Antti – Anders, Pekka – Petter etc.) ethnicity can be recognized quite easily from the first name. In addition, the Finns living in eastern Finland have had family-based surnames for centuries (a practice that began in southern and western Finland only in the 19th and 20th centuries). Thus a Finn who lived in the province of Kexholm can often be recognized from his or her family name. The names of Karelian people usually differ markedly from Finnish ones (Maksima, Sava, Parfei etc.) but not always (e.g. the woman's name Mari), and sometimes Karelians had surnames very similar to the Finnish ones (e.g. Timonen). In these cases the ethnic group of the person had to be identified from the first name. In some instances deducing of the ethnic origins and religious group of a person from the name was a matter more of conjecture than of knowledge, but such unclear cases were rare.

The perspective chosen involves looking very closely at the everyday life and events concerned. The method resembles "close reading" or "thick description" as described in the works of the anthropologist Clifford Geertz and the microhistorians Carlo Ginzburg and Giovanni Levi in the 1980s and 1990s.[5] To put it simply, the source material must be carefully read through, classified according to content and contextualized with reference to the relevant literature. Trying to reach through to the patterns of thought and behaviour underlying the few remarks available on a given topic is an essential part of the analysis.

Such remarks about behaviour and patterns of thought in relation to our topic are often unintentional, as we shall see, and occur in the sources only in subordinate clauses. The crucial thing, however, with regard to this way of analysing the source material, is to work out why a mixed marriage, often in itself of no significance as far as the court case itself was concerned, was mentioned at all in the minutes. Why did the judge or scribe include it in the written record? These seemingly irrelevant words or clauses had a significance and meaning of their own for the judge, and, we can assume, also for the local community. We can thus hope to trace the attitudes and practices of past societies that would otherwise remain hidden from us. Adopting these guidelines, let us enter the easternmost borderlands of the 17th-century Kingdom of Sweden.

MIXED MARRIAGES AND THE LUTHERANS

As a result of the tumultuous events of the 16th and early 17th centuries, Swedish Lutheranism entered a purist phase in which the practising of religious creeds other than Lutheranism was strictly forbidden throughout the kingdom. As a result of the conflicts with Poland at the end of the 16th century and the Thirty Years' War, in which the Swedes fought on the side of the Evangelical movement, Roman Catholics were seen as the main opponents of Sweden. Ironically, at the very same time the king of Sweden acquired a considerable number of new subjects confessing the Orthodox and Catholic faiths with the annexation of Kexholm and Ingria in 1617 and Livonia in 1629.[6] At the same time, foreign officers from Scotland, England and Germany belonging to other Christian denominations were hired into the Swedish army, together with professional engineers for the mining industry recruited from Germany and France. This development made the question of mixed marriages a topical issue in the 17th century, and there is no doubt that there was a strong ideological movement at that time for the rejection of Christian affiliations other than the Lutheran, especially the Roman Catholic Church but also the Orthodox Church.[7]

In 1617 it was stated that the heirs of the royal family were not allowed to marry persons confessing any faith other than Lutheranism, so that, as Jyrki Knuutila puts it, the "*impedimentum mixtae religionis*" was a reality in Sweden in the 17th century. On the other hand, this applied only to the royal family,[8] and despite the learned religious debates, people in the newly-acquired provinces and borderlands lived their lives, practised their religion and sometimes married across religious boundaries. The Church Ordinance dating from the year 1571 does not say anything about mixed marriages, but article 8 of section 15 of the new Swedish Church Law of 1686 stated: "A strict warning should be expressed regarding marriages with adherents of foreign religions. They should not be totally forbidden, however, because of the hope of conversion to our religion…".[9] It seems that the new Church Law was taking due note of existing practices and that the new rule had been added to the Church Law in response to the need to define the attitude of the Church to mixed marriages between the Swedish women and the foreign officers and mining engineers working in Sweden, and also because of the mixed marriages occurring among ordinary people in the newly conquered provinces.

The next time the question of mixed marriages aroused visible legislative action was about a hundred years later, in the Swedish Diet of 1779. According to the Diet's statement, a mixed marriage should be performed according to the matrimonial customs of both religions, but in separate ceremonies. If the groom was a Lutheran the children should be raised in the Lutheran faith, but if the bride was a Lutheran the couple should agree together about the children's religion.[10] Although these stipulations were laid down much later than the period studied here, we can see in them indications as to the nature of marriage practices over religious boundaries in the 17th-century province of Kexholm.

In the early 1960s, Erkki Kuujo wrote in his classic work on the Karelian borderland of 17th-century Sweden, "Mixed marriages scarcely existed at all, because they would have resulted in many kinds of problem."[11] Scholars writing about the province of Kexholm have usually adopted this view,[12] but even so, they all agree that marriages did sometimes take place over religious boundaries, and Knuutila as well as Veijo Saloheimo and Pentti Laasonen present examples of court cases in which such mixed marriages are mentioned. According to Pentti Laasonen, cases which serve as examples of sexual intercourse between young people from different religions are quite common in the court rolls, from which it might be concluded that the common people of the province were emotionally prepared and willing to undertake mixed marriages.[13]

This was not necessarily the case, however. In autumn 1689, a Lutheran man and an Orthodox woman were questioned at the court on account of an extramarital liaison. They had been harvesting the crops in fields belonging to a local peasant in the month of August of that year, and, according to the man, he had got drunk after the work was done and the woman had enticed him to lie with her. He said that because the woman was of "the Russian religion" she could not prove that he had given any promise to marry her. Both parties announced in court that they did not want to marry. Consequently, the man was fined heavily for practising premarital sexual intercourse and both parties were ordered to confess their sins publicly in church.[14] We can see from the argument adopted by the man in this case that religion was such an obstacle to any intention to marry that it could be used as proof in court that no promise of any such engagement had been given. If a man promised to marry a woman and then abandoned her after lying with her, he would be severely punished.[15]

In one case a young Orthodox woman was tried in court because she had had an illegitimate child with a Lutheran man, a soldier. The man had promised to marry her, and they had even visited a Lutheran minister in order to be married, but he was not able to perform the ceremony because the soldier did not have any certificate that he was unmarried. According to the Church Ordinance of 1571, ministers were not allowed to marry people who were unknown to them unless they could present a certificate that they were free to marry.[16] The soldier moved to a remote posting with his regiment soon afterwards and his promise to marry the woman was never fulfilled. The woman was not punished for illegitimate sexual intercourse because the man had promised to marry her in front of witnesses. They were looked upon as engaged.[17] In this case, the promise was given to an Orthodox woman and the couple visited a Lutheran minister, but it is difficult to decide how serious the promise was, as the soldier would certainly have known that he would be transferred to another military post sooner or later.

In autumn 1691 a Karelian peasant, Pehko Gregorioff, was summoned to appear in court, having announced to the local clergy that he wanted to convert to the Lutheran faith because he was married to a Lutheran woman, Valborg Bengtsdotter. Pehko did not appear at the court session although the minister had summoned him to be there, and therefore he was fined three marks.[18] The minutes of the court do not state openly whether the marriage was solemnized with a Lutheran or Orthodox ceremony or both, but it is quite evident that the couple were married in a Lutheran church at least. The man's promise to convert to the Lutheran faith may have been a tactical ploy, for since the Church Law of 1686 stipulated that marriage with a foreigner was allowed because of the hope of that person's conversion to the Lutheranism, the minister may have insisted on this promise as a prerequisite for their marriage.

There is another case that supports the above reasoning. Erkki Kuujo describes how in the year 1700 the vicar of the small town of Sortavala beside Lake Ladoga enquired from the diocesan chapter, and the chapter in turn enquired from the national government, what should be done in the case of an Orthodox man who was betrothed to a Finnish woman whom he wished to marry. The man did not, however, express any inclination for converting to "our" religion, as the Lutheran minister, put it. Rather, he demanded that the girl should convert to the Orthodox faith. The government decided that such mixed marriages should be allowed and that decisions in such matters should be based on "customary usage" in the province.[19] In this case, clearly a promise to convert to Lutheranism had evidently been a condition for the marriage as far as the Lutheran minister was concerned.

When the Karelian peasant Teroska Matfeisson died in 1689, leaving a wife and two adult daughters, his widow married again after an interval of three years, this time a Lutheran Finn, Bengt Pålsson. The estate and property of the deceased had not yet been divided up, however, and the daughters began to claim their inheritance from their father through the local court. The court ordered the lay jurors to execute the partition of the property according to the law, and also ruled that the local Lutheran minister should be fined for joining the widow and Bengt in marriage before the matter of inheritance had been settled, although in fact the minister had already passed away.[20] Again nothing was said in this case about an Orthodox priest or wedding, and it seems that the marriage ceremony was conducted by the Lutheran minister alone.

We have too some court cases in which the parents of the accused or the victim in a crime are said to have been Lutheran and Orthodox. If we consider that these marriages must have taken place at least twenty years before their adult children appeared in the court rolls, these couples would have married around the 1650s or early 1660s, that is before, during or just after the Russo–Swedish War (1656–8) which severely inflamed relations between Finns and Karelians. It seems, however, that intermarrying was possible even in those years of high tension.

In autumn 1682 the victim in a complicated felony case was described in the minutes as follows: "the deceased had always been an evil and ill-disposed person who had attacked with words of abuse and violence not only his neighbours but often travellers on the road, too. His father had been a Russian and his mother a Finn, and he and his three sisters had been baptized by a Lutheran minister, but he had never been to church."[21] Here the writer of the minutes is trying to persuade the readers (the assessors of the High Court) to conclude that the deceased had been an evil person and had actually deserved his fate. The fact that the victim had been the fruit of a dubious mixed marriage and that although he and his sisters were baptized into the Lutheran Church they had never been to church seems to increase the wickedness of the deceased. This made his killing more acceptable and reduced the guilt of the Lutheran Finnish men accused of the act.

As Veijo Saloheimo has suggested, a mixed marriage could sometimes be a symptom of difficulties encountered by Orthodox people on the Swedish side of the border in finding a suitable spouse belonging to their own religious group. He gives as an example the case of Hodar Ossippasson from Pielisjärvi. Hodar is a Karelian name and he seems thus to have been Orthodox: in 1674 he took a woman from Repola on the Russian side of the border as his wife, but after only one and a half years she ran away and returned to her home parish. In 1678 Hodar applied for a divorce in order to be able to re-marry with a Finnish woman, Caisa Pussitar.[22]

THE MIXED MARRIAGE OF SARA AND PARFEI

Converting from the Orthodox faith was not a condition for marriage to a Lutheran spouse in the province of Kexholm, but sometimes this happened. One case of a mixed marriage between Sara Alhemia, a Lutheran, and Parfei Ifanov, who was Orthodox, came up several times in the court rolls and is worth closer examination. Parfei was born in the parish of Joukio in the province of Kexholm in the mid-1650s. After the death of his father he moved with his mother to the village of Impilahti in the parish of Suistamo, and it was there that he met a Lutheran woman, Sara Alhemia, who was the daughter of a district prosecutor (*Landsfiskalen*), Matthiae Alhemia.[23] The liaison was evidently not to the liking of the bride's father, because they were married at the house of Brita Andersdotter in Suistamo, in secret from Matthiae Alhemia.[24] It is not mentioned whether the clergyman who performed the ceremony was Lutheran or Orthodox, but in all probability he was Lutheran. From the description of his life that Parfei gave later in a court session we can take it that he had adopted the Lutheran faith before or soon after the wedding.[25]

The couple made such an exceptional case in the local community that they were mentioned in the court rolls on several occasions. For example, when the local court handled a case of a robbery in a church, it was mentioned, among other irrelevant matters, that Parfei and Sara had visited the parish of Liperi to meet a fortune teller.[26] This had evidently happened not long before their secret wedding. It seems that the decision to marry had not been an easy one to make. In a testimony made some years later Parfei described how he had talked (*öfwertalt*) Sara into marrying him.[27] Sara Alhemia also gave testimony at the trial involving a case of infanticide, when her position was described in the minutes as follows: "The Russian Parfei's wife, Sara Alhemia, from here in Impilahti, who is a daughter of the district prosecutor Matthia Alhemia and is Swedish and Finnish and of our religion…" (*Ryssens Parfeijs här i Imbilax hustru Sara Alhemia, som är Fiscalens Matthia Alhemij dotter, Swensk och Finsk och af wår Religion…*).[28]

The marriage of Sara Alhemia and Parfei Ifanov did not have a happy ending. According to Parfei's account, three children were born to them. Soon after the wedding, Parfei had travelled to the town of Vyborg and signed up as a horseman in the cavalry, which he probably could not have done without converting to Lutheranism. In winter he returned to his family, but in 1688 he signed up for the army again, now in Narva. There he served as a soldier for over two years, but then escaped from his regiment to return home to his wife, who in the meantime had been living with Parfei's elderly mother in Impilahti. There Parfei stayed for two years and worked in the fields and forests. Then he was captured as a fugitive and taken back to his regiment and court-martialled. He was sentenced to death but the king pardoned him and he had to run the gauntlet. After some months he escaped from his regiment again to join his family in Impilahti, knowing that as a "repeat fugitive" he could not avoid the death penalty if he was captured. He thus moved over the border on to the Russian side, leaving his wife and children in Impilahti to live with his elderly mother. Finally, Parfei joined a group of bandits on the Russian side of the border, which was quite a common phenomenon in border regions in early modern times.[29] They robbed and tortured several peasants on the Swedish side of the border and tried to blackmail the owner of the Impilahti manor. Occasionally, he would visit his wife and family in Impilahti. When he was finally captured in 1697 he was sentenced to death by a local court.[30]

The case of Parfei Ifanov is one of those rare ones in which a member of the Orthodox Church adopted, at least formally, the Lutheran faith. Marriage to a woman who was a Lutheran and the daughter of a member of the local gentry must have been the motive underlying this course of action. Although it may have been possible for a Lutheran peasant woman to adopt the Orthodox faith, this would surely have been impossible in practice for the daughter of the local district prosecutor. On the other hand, it can be surmised that converting to Lutheranism would perhaps have opened up new possibilities for earning a livelihood. It was perhaps easier for a member of the Lutheran Church to join the Swedish army, for example, than for an Orthodox person. These considerations may have carried some weight in Parfei's decision regarding his religion. Before marrying Sara Alhemia he had earned his living as a merchant travelling around the Karelian countryside; for some reason a military career proved most unsuitable for him and ended unhappily.

MIXED MARRIAGES AND THE ORTHODOX POPULATION

In the Orthodox tradition the marriage of an Orthodox person to a member of another Christian (heretic or schismatic) church was tolerated provided the children were raised in the Orthodox faith.[31] The practice in 17th-century Russian Karelia seems to have been otherwise, however. If a member of the Lutheran Church was to marry an Orthodox, especially on the Russian Karelian side of the border, he or she was first required to convert to Orthodoxy. There are several descriptions of such cases in the court rolls of the province of Kexholm.[32] In 17th-century Russia all marriages involving members of the Orthodox Church were ecclesiastical in nature, and in fact the state had no role in the marriages at all before the reform of the Russian Orthodox Church and its canons at the beginning of the 18th century, during the reign of Peter the Great.[33] Therefore, notwithstanding learned discussion of the canon law, the possibility of the bride and groom being of different religions was quite unacceptable in the 17th-century Russian Orthodox Church. It was taken for granted that religion was so crucial to the thinking of ordinary people that a real connection between the souls of spouses of different religions could be assumed impossible.[34]

In the 1720s, still during the reign of Peter the Great, the number of foreigners in Russia had increased, as the Czar had invited foreign officers and industrialists to the country. At the same time a considerable number of Swedish Lutheran prisoners of war had been taken and transported to Siberia. The need to solve the question of mixed marriages between these foreigners and local Orthodox women soon became acute. In June 1721, the synod of the Church published a decree which permitted mixed marriages between Swedish Lutheran prisoners of war and Orthodox women and laid down that it was no longer necessary for the Lutheran spouse to convert to Orthodoxy before the wedding. Nevertheless, the children of the couple had to be raised in the Orthodox faith.[35] According to Yury Shikalov, it was a common practice in the Russian White Sea district of Karelia in the 18th and 19th centuries for brides brought from Finland to retain their own faith if they so wished.[36]

As we have seen, in the province of Kexholm, on the western side of the border, spouses did not always convert to the same religion, and although the Swedish Church Law of 1686 (article 1, paragraph 2) ordered those who gave up "our right faith" to be exiled from the realm,[37] some Lutherans or Finns adopted the Orthodox faith if they married an Orthodox spouse. There is a description of a fratricide case in the court rolls for winter 1683 in which the brothers Levoska and Gauro Kordesson (Karelian and most probably Orthodox, judging from their first names and patronymic) had been drinking spirits brewed by their mother, whom the court minutes refer to first as Hodossia (a Karelian name) and then, more precisely, by the name Caisa Turuinen (a Finnish name). The evening ended in a quarrel between the two brothers over the drink, such that Levoska stabbed his elder brother Gauro to death with a knife.[38]

According to the minutes the mother of these two brothers had both a Karelian name and a Finnish name. It is evident here that she was a Finn and originally known as Caisa Turuinen. It seems likely that before marrying Korde (as seen from the sons' patronymic) she had converted to the Orthodox faith and taken a new, Karelian name, "Hodossia".

We have another example of name-changing in the court roll material. One of the accused in a murder case, a young man called Erik Kotilainen, told of his adventures when he had gone over the border into Russia to seek work, as many did at that time. On his way home he was, by his own account, captured by some Russian men, who had summoned an Orthodox priest and forced Erik to be baptized into the Russian religion. They had then called him by a Karelian name, "Teppana".[39] If a Lutheran Finn converted to the Orthodox faith, it seems that it was the custom to give that person a new Karelian name.

"Marriages in Russia were not based on mutual feelings and romantic sentiments, but were decided and established by tradition and the will of the parents of the parties to the marriage", writes Jelisei Heikkilä.[40] This may have been a general rule in Russia in early modern times, but it was the case on the Swedish side of the border, too. Not all marriages were planned by the parents, however, and in some instances only feelings can explain the choice of spouse. This was often the case when a Lutheran and Orthodox couple married each other, as can be seen, for instance, in some court cases involving escaped wives, usually the wife of a Lutheran Finn who had escaped from her husband, crossed the border to the Russian side and married again a man who was of the Orthodox faith.[41]

In spring 1683 a case of a wife who had escaped from her husband came up twice in the local courts, first in the parish of Pielisjärvi and then in Ilomantsi. From the names of the husband and the wife we can assume that they were both Finns and Lutherans. According to the witnesses at these court sessions, the husband had been very violent towards his wife and had tried to persuade her to confess to adultery, mistreating her and threatening to cut off her head and limbs with an axe. The wife had escaped to Ilomantsi, where she had begun to work as a maid in the house of a wealthy Karelian peasant, Maxima Toroskainen. Later she moved to the Russian side of the border with a Karelian man, Ortto Timonen.[42] Nothing was said in this case, however, about marriage between the Lutheran woman and the Orthodox man.

The border between Sweden and Russia was in practice open, which made escape possible not only for criminals but also for those who wanted to run away from undesirable circumstances in their marriage. In the cases described above two wives used this opportunity, and one at least married again in Russia. Such cases of escaped wives seem to have been quite common, usually coming up in the court rolls when the abandoned husband applied for a court investigation in order to sue for divorce and re-marry. The circumstances and grounds for divorce were examined by the local district court in each case and the pronouncement and results of the investigation would be sent to the Church's diocesan chapter. The chapter, under the direction of the bishop, would then decide on the divorce in accordance with the findings of the local court. We have found six cases in the court rolls of the province of Kexholm in which a spouse had gone over the border into Russian Karelia, and in at least one such case a Lutheran man had married a "Russian" woman on the Russian side of the border. In several cases where Finns had married Russian or Karelian brides or grooms on the Russian side it is mentioned that they were forced to convert to the Orthodox faith before marriage became possible.[43]

THE FATE OF A PROSELYTE

Both churches, Lutheran and Orthodox, were willing to accept proselytes from other churches but denied or severely condemned conversion from their faith to another. Although the churches were keen to have new members, prejudices against proselytes could be strong among the common people. We can shed some light on this issue by examining the court cases of Anna Jespersdotter Martikainen.[44] Anna's father had been a Lutheran Finn and her mother a Karelian (or "Russian" as the minutes state), Kylinä Ilyasdotter. All their seven children had been baptized according to their father's religion, that is into the Lutheran Church. In 1683, however, Anna was married to Oleksi Säkkinen, who was a member of the Orthodox Church (Russian religion). We can see from the name Oleksi that he was definitely Karelian and not Russian. As soon as Anna became pregnant she relinquished her "Finnish, or Lutheran faith", as the court minutes say, and turned to Orthodoxy. Her new Karelian relatives would not accept her as such, however, and when she was harvesting rye with the relatives of her husband one of them said to her, "There is a fence between the Finns and the Russians and now you are neither a Finn nor a Russian. When you come to the Russians they will push you away, and the Finns will do the same." On another occasion she was told, "When you come into the next world you will not be accepted as a Russian proselyte nor as a Swede, and so you will be left outside".[45]

When Anna Martikainen married an Orthodox man she was still a member of the Lutheran Church, but somehow her pregnancy became a turning point and she converted to the same faith as her husband. Changing one's religion was very problematic in a small local community. To be a proselyte could lead the individual into serious social conflicts and problems. In the case of Anna Martikainen she was eventually tried several times for witchcraft and was regarded as a witch by the community in which she lived.[46] Perhaps even the fact that her parents were of different religions strengthened local prejudices against her. Anna has multiple mentions in the court rolls: she was accused of using witchcraft to heal children and of cursing the neighbours, even by members of her own family. Being a proselyte and a child of parents of different religions seems to have caused her to be an outcast in the local community, and even in her own family.

CONCLUSIONS

In principle, both the Lutheran and Orthodox churches seem to have accepted mixed marriages, the Orthodox Church according to its principles of canon law and the Lutheran Church on practical grounds and in the hope that the spouse of a different faith would convert to Lutheranism. In practice, however, on the Russian side of the border, all those who wanted to marry an Orthodox partner or were forced to do so up to the 1720s were re-baptized into the Orthodox Church. It seems that in these cases the proselytes were given a new Orthodox name on both sides of the border. After the reforms of Peter the Great in Russia mixed marriages were allowed and the Lutheran spouse could retain his or her own religion.

On the Swedish side of the border conversion from Orthodoxy to Lutheranism was very random, but not impossible. Adopting the Orthodox faith seems to have been a more common phenomenon than converting to Lutheranism. We have found one case in the source material where a groom promised to adopt the Lutheran faith, but did not fulfil his promise, while in another case the groom really did convert, because it was impossible for the bride, being from the local gentry, to become Orthodox. It may be that in this case taking up the Lutheran faith was a means to open up possibilities for earning a livelihood in the Swedish army. On the other hand, we have also found instances of married couples of differing religions in the province of Kexholm.

According to the canons of both churches, wedding ceremonies in cases of mixed marriage should have been organized according to the traditions of both parties. The Swedish regulations from the 18th century prescribe two separate ceremonies, and the canon law of the Orthodox Church stipulates that if there is no Orthodox ceremony in the case of a mixed marriage the marriage cannot be seen as valid. In practice, however, there is no mention at all in the court protocols of the province of Kexholm of Orthodox priests taking part in the wedding ceremony for a mixed marriage; only Lutheran ministers are mentioned in this connection. This may be due, of course, to the nature of the available source: perhaps the judges in the local courts did not think it necessary to mention the Orthodox ceremonies that pertained to mixed marriages.

In principle, the Orthodox Church accepted mixed marriages only on condition that the children should be baptized into the Orthodox faith, while under the law established in the 1770s, the Swedish parliament accepted the rule that if the groom was Lutheran the children should be raised in the Lutheran faith, whereas if the bride was Lutheran, the pair should come to an agreement on the issue. The evidence obtained from the court rolls of the province of Kexholm suggests, however, that if one party to a marriage was Lutheran and the other Orthodox, the children were in all cases baptized into the Lutheran Church. In all these cases, however, the Lutheran beliefs of the concerned seem to have been of very superficial nature. It was only if the other spouse converted to Orthodoxy that the children were baptized into the Orthodox faith.

NOTES

1   See, for example, Nylander 1961; Mahkonen 1980; Knuutila 1990.
2   See Laasonen 2005, 64–5; Katajala 2008, 145–58.
3   See Lappalainen 1972.
4   Laasonen 2005, 121; Katajala 2006, 338–9.
5   Geertz 1973; Ginzburg 1980, 1993; Levi 1992.
6   See Katajala 2005, 227–32.
7   Knuutila 1990, 205.
8   Knuutila 1990, 205–6.
9   Thulin 1936, 43.
10 Mäntylä 1954, 31–2
11 Kuujo 1963, 195.
12 See Saloheimo 1976, 278–9; Laasonen 2005, 124.
13 Laasonen 2005, 124.
14 *The District Court of Kexholm*, 4.-9.11.1689, 184, gg8.
15 Knuutila 1990, 64.
16 Kjöllerström 1971, 119.
17 *The District Court of Kexholm*, 18.–21.3.1682, 330v–331, gg2.
18 *The District Court of Kexholm*, 24.–30.10.1691, 213v–214, gg10.
19 Kuujo 1963, 195.
20 *The District Court of Kexholm*, 9–15.3.1692, 58v–59, gg11.
21 *The District Court of Kexholm*, 16.–18.8.1682, 361–364, gg 2.
22 Saloheimo 1976, 278.
23 *The District Court of Kexholm*, 22.–28.9.1694, 102v–110v, gg13.
24 *The District Court of Kexholm*, 21–28.2.1687, 40, gg6.
25 *The District Court of Kexholm*, 22–28.9.1694, 102v–110v, gg13.
26 *The District Court of Kexholm*, 21–28.2.1687, 54v–61v, gg 6.
27 *The District Court of Kexholm*, 22–28.9.1694, 102v–110v, gg13.
28 *The District Court of Kexholm*, 29.2. –5.3.1692, 154v, gg11.
29 See Laasonen 2005, 123.
30 *The District Court of Kexholm*, 22–28.9.1694, 102v–110v, gg13.
31 Heikkilä 2015, 62–6.
32 See Katajala 2005, 214–5.
33 Heikkilä 2015, 9.
34 Meyendorf 1975, 56–7.
35 Heikkilä 2015, 93; Башкиров 2014.
36 Shikalov 2004, 277–8.
37 Thulin 1936, 5.
38 *The District Court of Kexholm*, 1–2.3.1683, 69–69v, gg2.
39 *The District Court of Kexholm*, 6–8.12.1681, 275, gg4.
40 Heikkilä 2015, 10.
41 See *The District Court of Kexholm*, 1–5.2.1697, 20v–21, gg16.
42 *The District Court of Kexholm*, 21–23.2.1683, 58v–59, gg2; 1–2.3.1683, 66–67, gg2.
43 Katajala 2005, 213–4.
44 See Katajala 2005, 55-8.
45 *The District Court of Kexholm*, 8–12.2.1692, 139–140v, gg11.
46 Katajala 2005, 181–2.

BIBLIOGRAPHY

Башкиров, В. 2014. *О смешанных браках*. http://azbyka.ru/dictionary/02/o_brakah_s_inovercami.shtml#s9 [accessed 27 October 2014].

Burke, P. (ed.) 1992. *New Perspectives on Historical Writing*. State College, PA: The Pennsylvania State University Press.

The District Court of Kexholm 1680–1700, vols gg2; gg4; gg6; gg8; gg10; gg11; gg13; gg16.

Engman, M. & Villstrand N. E. (eds) 2008. *Maktens mosaik: enhet, särart och självbild i det svenska riket*. Skrifter utgivna av Svenska litteratursällskapet i Finland 715. Helsinki: Svenska litteratursällskapet i Finland.

Geertz, C. 1973. *The Interpretation of Cultures: Selected Essays*. New York: Basic Books.

Ginzburg, C. 1980. *The Cheese and the Worms: The Cosmos of a Sixteenth-Century Miller*. Baltimore: Johns Hopkins University Press.

Ginzburg, C. 1993. 'Microhistory: Two or three things that I know about it', *Critical Inquiry* 20: 10–35.

Hämynen T., Partanen, J. & Shikalov, Y. (eds) 2004. *Family Life on the Northwestern Margins of Imperial Russia*. Studia Carelica Humanistica 19. Joensuu: Joensuu University Faculty of Humanities.

Heikkilä, J. 2015. 'Canonical development through dialogue: Marriage and divorce in the pre-conciliar period and in the All-Russian Church Council of 1917–1918'. PhD dissertation, University of Helsinki.

Hurd, M. (ed.) 2006. *Borderland Identities: Territory and Belonging in North, Central and East Europe*. Baltic and East European Studies 8. Eslöv: Gondolin.

Katajala, K. 2005. *Suurvallan rajalla: Ihmisiä Ruotsin ajan Karjalassa*. Historiallinen Arkisto 118. Helsinki: Suomalaisen Kirjallisuuden Seura.

Katajala, K. 2006. 'Early modern people(s) in the borderlands: Linguistic or religious definitions of "us" and "other"', in Hurd 2006, 331–53.

Katajala, K. 2008. 'Differentiering och unifiering: provinspolitiken vid det Svenska rikets östgräns ca 1617–1809', in Engman & Villstrand 2008, 141–64.

Kjöllerström, S. 1971. *Den svenska kyrkoordningen 1571, jämte studier kring tillkomst, innehåll och användning*. Lund: Håkan Ohlssons Förlag.

Knuutila, J. 1990. *Avioliitto oikeudellisena ja kirkollisena instituutiona Suomessa vuoteen 1629 (Matrimony as a Juridical and Ecclesiastical Institution in Finland up to 1629)*. Finska Kyrkohistoriska Samfundets handlingar 151. Helsinki: Suomen kirkkohistoriallinen seura.

Kuujo, E. 1963. *Raja-Karjala Ruotsin vallan aikana*. Helsinki: Kustannusosakeyhtiö Otava.

Laasonen, P. 2005. *Novgorodin imu: Miksi ortodoksit muuttivat Venäjälle Käkisalmen läänistä 1600-luvulla?* Historiallisia Tutkimuksia 222. Helsinki: Suomalaisen Kirjallisuuden Seura.

Lappalainen, J. T. 1972. *Kaarle X Kustaan Venäjän-sota v. 1656-1658 Suomen suunnalla: "räikkä, häikkä ja ruptuuri"*. Studia historica Jyväskyläensia 10. Jyväskylä.

Levi, G. 1992. 'On microhistory', in Burke 1992, 93–113.

Mahkonen, S. 1980. *Avioero. Tutkimus avioliittolain erosäännösten taustasta ja tarkoituksesta*. Suomalaisen lakimiesyhdistyksen julkaisuja A-sarja 149. Helsinki.

Mäntylä, R. A. 1954. *Eriuskolaiskysymys Suomessa 1809–1889*. Vol. 1: *1809–1871*. Annales Universitatis Turkuensis, Ser. B, 47. Turku: Turun yliopisto.

Meyendorff, J. 1975. *Marriage: An Orthodox Perspective*. New York: St. Vladimir's Seminary Press.

Nylander, I. 1961. *Studier rörande den svenska äktenskapsrättens historia*. Studia Juridica Stockholmiena 12. Stockholm: Acta Universitatis Stockholmiensis.

Saloheimo, V. 1976. *Pohjois-Karjalan historia, 2. 1617–1721*. Joensuun korkeakoulun julkaisuja, Sarja A, 6. Joensuu: Joensuun korkeakoulun.

Shikalov, Y. 2004. 'Marriages in the village of Uhta, Eastern Karelia, from the 1870s to 1905', in Hämynen *et al.* 2004, 261–83.

Thulin, G. 1936. *1686 års kyrkolag: utgiven av samfundet pro fide et christianismo – med inledning av Gabriel Thulin*. Stockholm: Svenska kyrkans diakonistyrelse.

7

Ideas from Abroad: German Weavers as Agents of Large-Scale Cloth Production and a Continental Lifestyle in 17th-Century Sweden

CLAES B. PETTERSSON

The Royal Chartered Textile Manufacture (Vantmakeriet) established in Jönköping in 1620 relied on the modes of production and skills of German weavers whose arrival significantly increased the town's population. Recent excavations have revealed a vivid picture of the material culture of this group with its marked preference for imported food and maintenance of its members' urban, continental lifestyle. But what can be said about the relationship between the German craftsmen and the Swedish population? In what ways were the locals adopting new lifestyles? What were the lasting results of this meeting between local and continental ways of life? This chapter addresses these questions.

Narratives of the encounter with the "Other" in early modern Sweden, its hinterland and newly-acquired overseas territories have in recent years often focused on colonialism and exploitation, and rightly so. This aspect has to a great extent been neglected, ignored or treated with indulgence in a country so much of whose self-image since World War II has been built around an idea of Sweden as a paragon of virtues, both human and political. The fact that Sweden too has a tainted colonial past, in many respects comparable to several other European countries, has been a salutary, albeit hard lesson to take in. The slave forts in western Africa, the New Sweden colony on the Delaware River, the silver mines in Sápmi and many other endeavours in the early modern period were all part of the same picture: the ambition of a relatively poor and sparsely-populated country on the northern fringes of Europe whose leaders wanted to play an active part on the political stage of the continent. And acquiring colonies was an important element in that scheme. The problem was that Sweden never had the muscle to compete with the great sea powers of the 17th century and consequently lost its short-lived possessions overseas. The internal colonization of Sápmi (Lapland) gave far better returns. And it still does to this very day, despite continuing infringement on the rights of the Sami people.[1] These are topics that beg discussion, both from a historical/archaeological point of view and as political matters of today.

However, there were also encounters in the 17th century where the 'Others' were far less vulnerable in the encounter with Sweden and its native inhabitants. One thing clearly realized by both the king and his council was that in order to achieve a rapid modernization of Sweden they had to import knowledge. Specialists in a vast number of fields were persuaded to make the journey north by promises of generous payments and privileges.[2] This chapter deals with one such group of coveted immigrants: a number of master craftsmen from northern Germany who were recruited in the early 1620s in order to create a modern textile manufactory in the Swedish fortress town of Jönköping.

To begin with, the impact of foreign influences on the local community must have been notable in many respects, since this new workforce was well paid and favoured by the authorities. They lived and worked in their own enclave in the city centre, a district called Tyska maden ("German meadow"), and they strove to retain their urban lifestyle and continental habits. The dwellings provided by the company for the German craftsmen may have been small, but recent excavations have yielded a vivid and some-what challenging picture of the material culture of this group, with its various imports and a marked preference for expensive and exotic food.[3] It was obviously possible to maintain a good lifestyle even in a provincial Swedish garrison town of the 17th century!

But what can be said about the relations between the German craftsmen and their Swedish neighbours? How did this group of immigrants and their families manage to co-exist with the locals? Did the native citizens adopt any new habits? And what parts of this new continental, urban lifestyle did they dislike? The cloth production site closed down in 1655 and few of the weavers stayed in Jönköping when the *Vantmakeriet*, The Royal Chartered Textile Manufacture, ceased its operations. So what were the lasting results of this meeting between local and continental lifestyles, between new methods and traditional crafts? These questions still await further research, but the archaeolog-ical evidence has given a first glimpse of how a town like Jönköping could become an essential meeting place for both people and ideas in 17th-century Sweden.

JÖNKÖPING, MANUFACTURES AND MODERNIZATION PROJECTS

In the first decades of the 17th century a thorough modernization of the then rural and undeveloped country of Sweden began. The administration became far more effective, the judicial system had its laws reformed and a number of new courts, among them the Göta Court of Appeal in Jönköping, were established in the realm. The monetary system was changed radically with the introduction of low-denomination copper coins, using a semi-precious metal that was available in large volumes from the mines in Falun. Town planning and fortification were areas where foreign know-how was used to achieve radical changes. Ideal cities following Simon Stevin's ideas were being built on the northern outskirts of Europe.[4] In the Swedish armed forces foreign soldiers served in all ranks, introducing modern knowledge of weapons, tactics and strategy. To create a modern navy, capable of taking on the Danish fleet, Dutch and later English shipwrights were employed.

In the civil community merchants, bankers and industrialists of foreign descent, like the wealthy Dutchman Louis De Geer, were welcomed into the country with generous privileges and extensive rights.[5] The positive results soon became evident, with a number of new mines, ironworks and different kinds of manufacture being established all around the vast Swedish territories. But not just the competence of the financiers was needed: skilled labourers were also in great demand. A famous example of this transfer of knowledge is the massive recruitment of Walloons, highly capable smiths and other craftsmen from the Low Countries/Flanders, to the new ironworks in central Sweden.[6] The migration of a number of equally competent weavers and textile workers to Jönköping in 1621 tells a similar, but less familiar story.

At the same time the natural resources of the kingdom were the subject of thorough research and mapping. Sweden was truly about to enter the early modern age, its "Age of Greatness", within the time-span of a few decades. The visions held by people in leading circles including Gustavus Adolphus and members of his council were indeed sufficiently radical, but the resources needed to meet the demands were inadequate. As a result many projects which began on a grand scale were left unfinished or adapted into less costly forms over the years. As we shall see, the town and castle of Jönköping is a good illustration of this deficiency.[7] But while recognizing the shortcomings, one still has to acknowledge the impact of the early modern modernization schemes on 17th-century Sweden. For after all, society as a whole was genuinely transformed, thereby creating structures and institutions that became very much parts of everyday life.

Let us begin with a contemporary view of the settings. The new town of Jönköping with its strategically important castle was a central link in the defences of southern Sweden during the first half of the 17th century (Fig. 7.1). With its manufactures and as the location of the main military magazines it also became vital for strategic production and for the store-keeping of the Swedish army. The illustration below (Fig. 7.2) is pure propaganda taken from *Suecia Antiqua et Hodierna* by Erik Dahlbergh, a volume presenting the ambitious young kingdom of Sweden to the continental reader: thus every motif was enlarged and exaggerated. Nevertheless, this prospectus for Jönköping gives us a good idea of the layout of the town with its castle, the law court and the large town church. The rest of the townscape consisted of squat timber buildings and cobbled courtyards, separated by narrow streets. Amidst it all were the buildings of two Royal Chartered manufactures, although these did not stand out from their close surroundings.

The town of Jönköping was being rebuilt in a new location after having been completely devastated during the Kalmar War in the summer of 1612 (Fig. 7.3).[8] The aim of the Crown was to create an impregnable unity of castle and town fortifications, an ideal fortress town after the Dutch fashion, surrounded by water and marshes. The project had a high national priority, as Jönköping was the key to one of the most strategically important locations in the realm. The junction of highways running east–west connecting the core areas of Västergötland and Östergötland, and south-west to the Danish coastal province of Halland, was vital to both commerce and warfare. Together with Elfsborg castle on the west coast and the fortress town of Kalmar by the Kalmar Strait in the south-east, Jönköping was to be one of the main strongholds protecting the vulnerable southern border against Danish attack. To achieve this on a site in most respects unsuited for building activities, massive landfilling had to be undertaken before the houses of the new blocks could be erected. An impressive logistic organization controlled the inflow of soil, timber, stone and other building materials used in the project. The estimation is that at least 15,000 to 20,000 wagonloads of earth had to be transported into the new city during the first ten years of its existence.

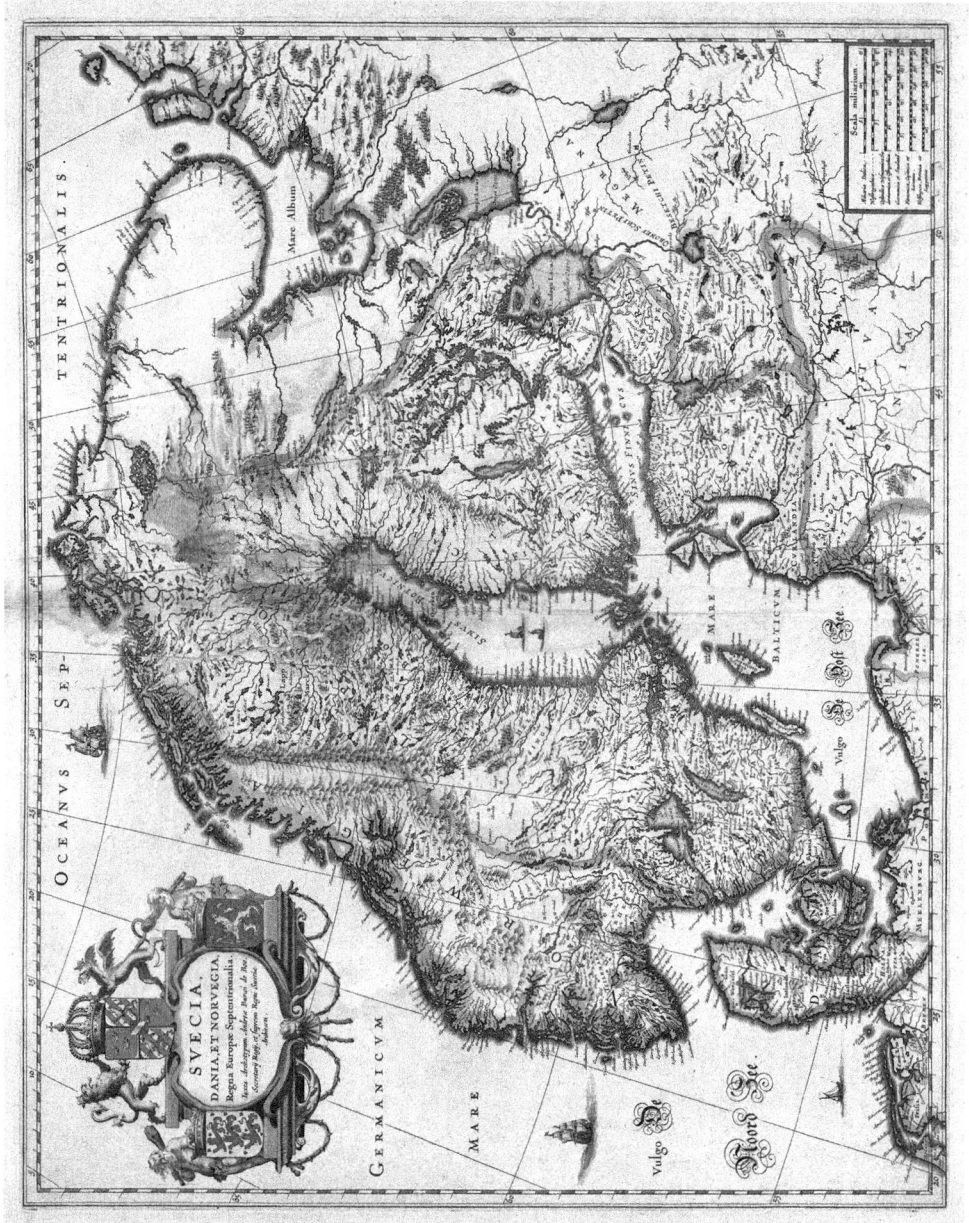

Fig. 7.1
Scandinavia in
1635, according to
the map *Svecia,
Dania et Norvegia,
Regna Europæ
Septentrionalia*
drawn by Andreas
Bureus. The
Swedish fortress
town of Jönköping
is at the southern
tip of the large,
crescent-shaped
Lake Vättern.

Fig. 7.2 Jönköping towards the end of the 17th century with the huge castle, the Göta Court of Appeal and Christine Church. Copperplate by Erik Dahlbergh for the work *Suecia Antiqua et Hodierna*, published in 1716.

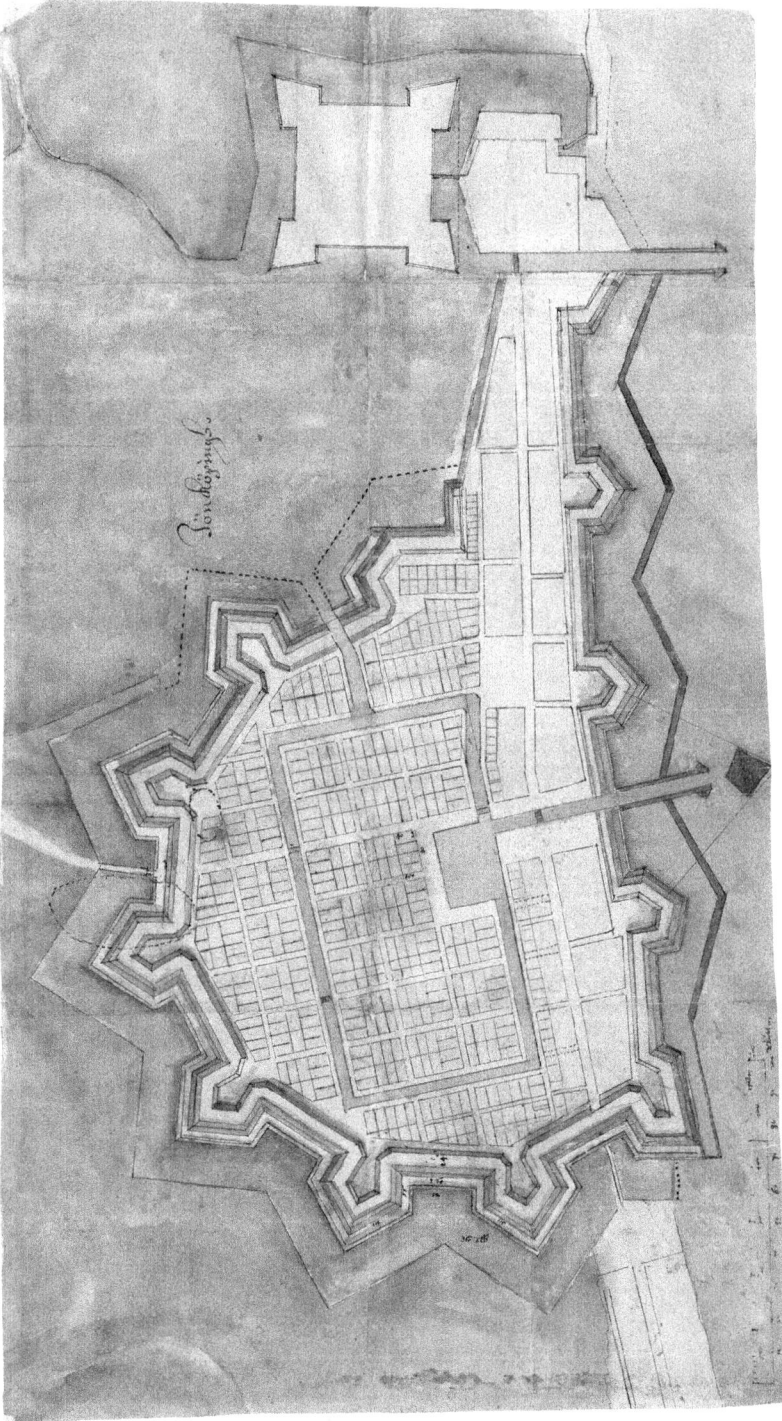

Fig. 7.3 The planned city fortress of Jönköping – the minor extension proposal (facing south). Draft by the Dutch master builder Hans Fleming, dated to 1619. Today kept in the Swedish War Archives as SFP Jönköping 15.

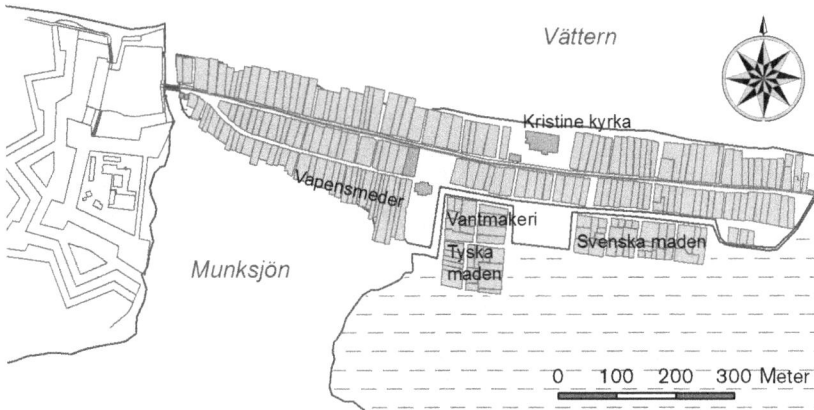

Fig. 7.4 Reconstruction of Jönköping in the mid-18th century based on C. M. Edelborgh's plot map from 1745 with the locations of the *Jönköpings Faktori* ("Vapensmeder") and the *Vantmakeriet* (drawing: Ann-Marie Nordman, Jönköping läns museum).

The Crown provided soldiers as a workforce and took an active part in both the financing and the preparations needed for the immense project. It included building an infrastructure for the manufacturing sites, among countless other things (Fig. 7.4). The first buildings at both manufactories, *Jönköpings Faktori* (arms and armour) and *Vantmakeriet* (textiles) were to a large extent the responsibility of the Crown.[9] On the arms factory site, barracks quite similar to those used by the army were erected on solid wooden foundations around the year 1620.[10] In the case of the *Vantmakeriet* textile production site, the authorities were aided by a group of wealthy local businessmen who had been given the assignment to run the operations after the initial breaking-in period.[11]

THE *VANTMAKERIET*

Both manufactories received their Royal Charter in 1620, although the preparations had already been going on for some time.[12] These two enterprises were of comparable importance to the Crown, but while the production of arms and armour built upon a long tradition in the region, large-scale manufacturing of textiles was something quite different. There had been efforts in this direction before 1620, mainly in the area west of Stockholm and around Kalmar in the south-east, but the output of textiles had been of a relatively limited volume.[13]

The *Vantmakeriet* in Jönköping was meant to be a greater enterprise and it represented quite a considerable investment. The aim was to produce cloth of different qualities for the army and the navy, to be used by soldiers and sailors as a part of their wages. Sweden was about to enter the Thirty Years' War so the thoroughgoing mobilization, or rather militarization, of the country and its resources had begun in earnest.[14] Another kind of product was to be finer textiles for decorating the official rooms in castles and churches, both for daily use and for special occasions. The production target for the first year was set at 24,000 metres of cloth, a completely unrealistic goal considering the fact that the manufactory was only beginning its operations.[15]

In the spring of 1621 the manufacturer Peter Struve travelled to Germany with the aim of hiring a number of competent textile workers and to buy high quality wool. In Rostock and Lübeck he recruited ten master craftsmen. They were to take part in what was meant to be the establishment of the first large-scale, modern cloth-making site in the realm. One reason for seeking expertise abroad was that this mode of production was hitherto almost untried in Sweden and that young men of local origin were supposed to learn the trade. This was something that the king himself pointed out in a letter of August 1620.[16]

In addition to hiring a skilled workforce and finding suitable apprentices, the board had a number of other problems to tackle, including complaints about the houses and workshops built by the Crown and the manufactories. The buildings were considered to be not properly finished and quite inadequate to requirements.[17] It was indeed a harsh beginning for the group of craftsmen who arrived in Jönköping after a long and tiring journey. All in all the contingent numbered about 150 people, including the master craftsmen, their families and a number of employees such as journeymen and apprentices.[18] Their arrival meant that the population of Jönköping increased by about 8% more or less overnight, since the total number of inhabitants at the time of the re-location of the city has been estimated at less than 2,000.

The Crown withdrew its financial support in 1623 and the *Vantmakeriet* manufactory was supposed to manage its own operation and financing thenceforth, although the company was in debt to the Crown and stayed so for years to come.[19] Still, the best years of its three decades of existence in terms of its productivity occurred during the late 1620s and 1630s under the well-qualified leadership of the merchant Peter Gudmundsson, who became the sole manufacturer in 1639.[20]

A significant feature of this new mode of production was its size; it required a number of facilities situated outside the core area of three blocks in the town. Mills and a stamp were built along the Dunkehalla river, an important source of water power in use since the Middle Ages.[21] South of the town, on two small "islands" in the vast marshes, a large windmill was built. It was a pumping mill used to lift fresh water into a system of dams used for bleaching linen.[22] Even though the most important product was cloth, various materials were processed at the *Vantmakeriet* factory, and other trades were introduced. Information collected from the rolls of the *Vantmakeriet* numbers the people employed at no fewer than 142 during its heyday in 1628, making it at that point a considerably larger workplace than the arms factory.[23]

Another important novelty was the introduction of the systematic breeding of sheep to get better raw materials: improved wool so that the demands of the *Vantmakeriet* weavers could be met. A number of large estates, called by the German name of *schäferi*, were created in the provinces of northern Småland and south-east Västergötland. The powerful manufacturer Peter Gudmundsson was one of the rich landowners who invested in these endeavours. On these estates rams imported from both Britain and Germany were used to improve the breed.[24] But these efforts seem to have been in vain, as complaints about insufficient quality of the locally-produced wool continued.

From an archaeological point of view it might be difficult to identify the remains of a textile production site. As opposed to the gunsmith's workshops in the arms factory with their easily identifiable forges, a weaver's or a tailor's workshop can be quite anonymous.[25] Some large, almost square timber buildings found in the earliest core area of the *Vantmakeriet* (the Dolken site) have been suggested as being designed for this purpose, the other houses on these plots being of a more ordinary appearance.[26] An interesting fact is that there seem to have been too few kitchens in the plots excavated in the southern part of the area (the Diplomaten site). Instead a number of large timber buildings have been interpreted as workshops and warehouses, indicating a well-thought-out organization and a division of functions within the factory itself.[27]

When it comes to the finds, the tools used by the craftsmen were often made of perishable materials and were of inconspicuous character. Needles, scissors and thimbles were parts of the inventory of every normal household of the 17th century. Still, the numbers in which these objects appear in an excavation, as well as their quality, are indicative of the production and the background of the craftsmen. Fortunately, it seems as if the skilled craftsmen employed in the *Vantmakeriet* relied on tools and equipment brought with them or imported from Germany, where high-quality brass utensils for textile production were made in towns like Nuremberg. A number of such small tools were found in the Diplomaten site together with buttons, crooks and metal threads of tin intended for decorations on more exclusive clothing (Fig 7.5).[28]

The Swedish production of cloth was never large enough to meet the demands of the armed forces. Imports from the continent were needed during the Thirty Years' War and over the entire period that the *Vantmakeriet* existed. High-quality wool came in from Rostock and other ports in Germany. Lead seals from different towns in northern Europe found among the remains of the workshops and warehouses illustrate the origins of these expensive imports.[29] For some time during the earliest years of the manufactory, the board even imported high-quality textiles and sold them to the Crown, pretending that the cloth was produced in Jönköping.[30] Their primary aim was to keep the lucrative contract providing cloth for the army and navy at any cost, while waiting for better times.

SPICES AND WATERMELONS – EVERYDAY LIFE OF THE CRAFTSMEN

When addressing the question of ethnicity and the interactions between different groups of inhabitants in the 17th-century town of Jönköping, the written evidence should be of great importance. However, as the *Vantmakeriet* manufacture kept its own rolls and registers, the remaining written sources are annoyingly incomplete. In connection with the Diplomaten excavation in 2007 a review of the available records and archives from the period from 1620 to 1650 was made, but useful information about the German workers in Tyska maden district was scarce.[31] Surviving maps, registers and archives show the blocks and other properties constituting the central manufacturing site and the outlying areas that were needed for the large-scale production of textiles.[32] Since the 1980s a number of plots filled with the remains of buildings have been excavated and identified as dwellings, workshops and storehouses.[33]

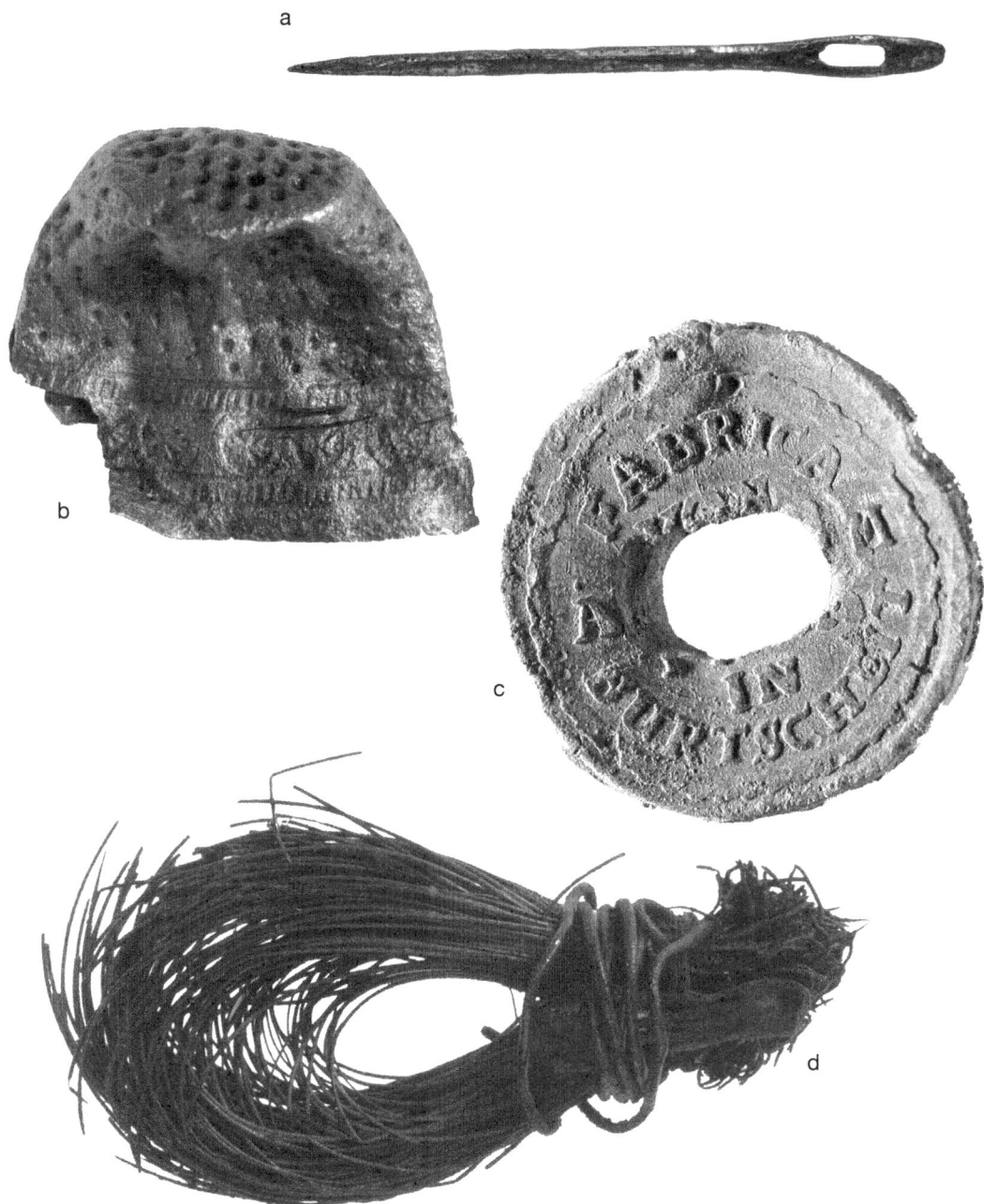

Fig. 7.5 The small tools of the cloth factory: (a) sewing needle made of brass; (b) brass thimble; (c) lead seal from the town of Burtscheid, near Aachen in Germany; (d) tin thread for decorative embroidery (photograph: Göran Sandstedt, Jönköpings läns museum).

But what about the actual people who lived and worked there? What traces of these individuals can be found on the archaeological sites? And is it really possible to identify any objects that can be defined as typically "German" – as possessions of the families that immigrated in 1621 or others that followed in their footsteps later on? Pottery is usually seen as one of the best indicators of exchange, being imported or, if locally produced, showing influences from abroad in form and decorative elements. On the *Vantmakeriet* sites there were remarkably few true imports from the period 1620–50, considering the size and volume of the excavations (Fig. 7.6a).[34] However, the ICP analyses undertaken on a small number of red earthenware sherds indicate that there may be more imported pottery hidden among the finds.[35] Some more expensive vessels such as tankards made in southern Germany or fine wine glasses might have been brought as personal belongings with a certain emotional value to their owners.[36] These fragile vessels might have been included among the limited amount of goods one could bring along when moving into Gustavus Adolphus's kingdom.

To some extent, archaeology can offer only chance encounters with the individuals who worked at the factory, their living conditions, habits and personal beliefs. The occasional portrait, the wedding ring with clasped hands, the little collar stud with a pink heart flanked by turtledoves and the padlocks of German origin are material mementoes, lost belongings offering fragmentary glimpses into their owners' lives (Fig. 7.6b, c).[37] But since so many of the records of the manufactory itself have been lost at some moment during the long period following its demise, we will never know the names and the full stories of the people who inhabited these plots in the early and mid-17th century.

An interesting and somewhat unexpected insight into the everyday life of the German group of inhabitants, the weavers, dyers and tailors of Tyska maden, comes, however, from the results of a comprehensive archaeobotanical analysis.[38] Contrary perhaps to expectation, there is plenty of tell-tale archaeological evidence of a good life from the *Vantmakeriet* site; of living conditions and of a taste for luxuries one would not expect to find in the "ordinary" craftsmen's households. It was possible for the German immigrants to maintain both their continental lifestyle and their food culture. Imported spices and fruits such as pepper, grapes, figs and citrus fruits appear in the soil samples from their seemingly humble dwellings (Fig. 7.6c).[39] One would expect this kind of luxury food to appear in connection with a 17th-century manor, used in dishes served to members of the nobility. But here they are, the remains of imports found on the floors, in the kitchens and in the refuse dumps of a working-class population. Other typical finds include stones from sour cherries, a common ingredient in traditional German cuisine. More problematic are the seeds from watermelons found in the cultural layers: these cannot be classified as imports, since melons were not suited for long-range transportation. Instead they must have been produced locally.[40] In the 17th century melons were grown in the greenhouses of Swedish manors with advice on how to handle the plants described in contemporary gardening handbooks.[41] The seeds found at *Vantmakeriet* could be interpreted as evidence of watermelons bought at the local market on rare occasions. They might, however, also have been gifts from a satisfied, high-ranking customer to a craftsman of foreign origin, known to appreciate exotic food.

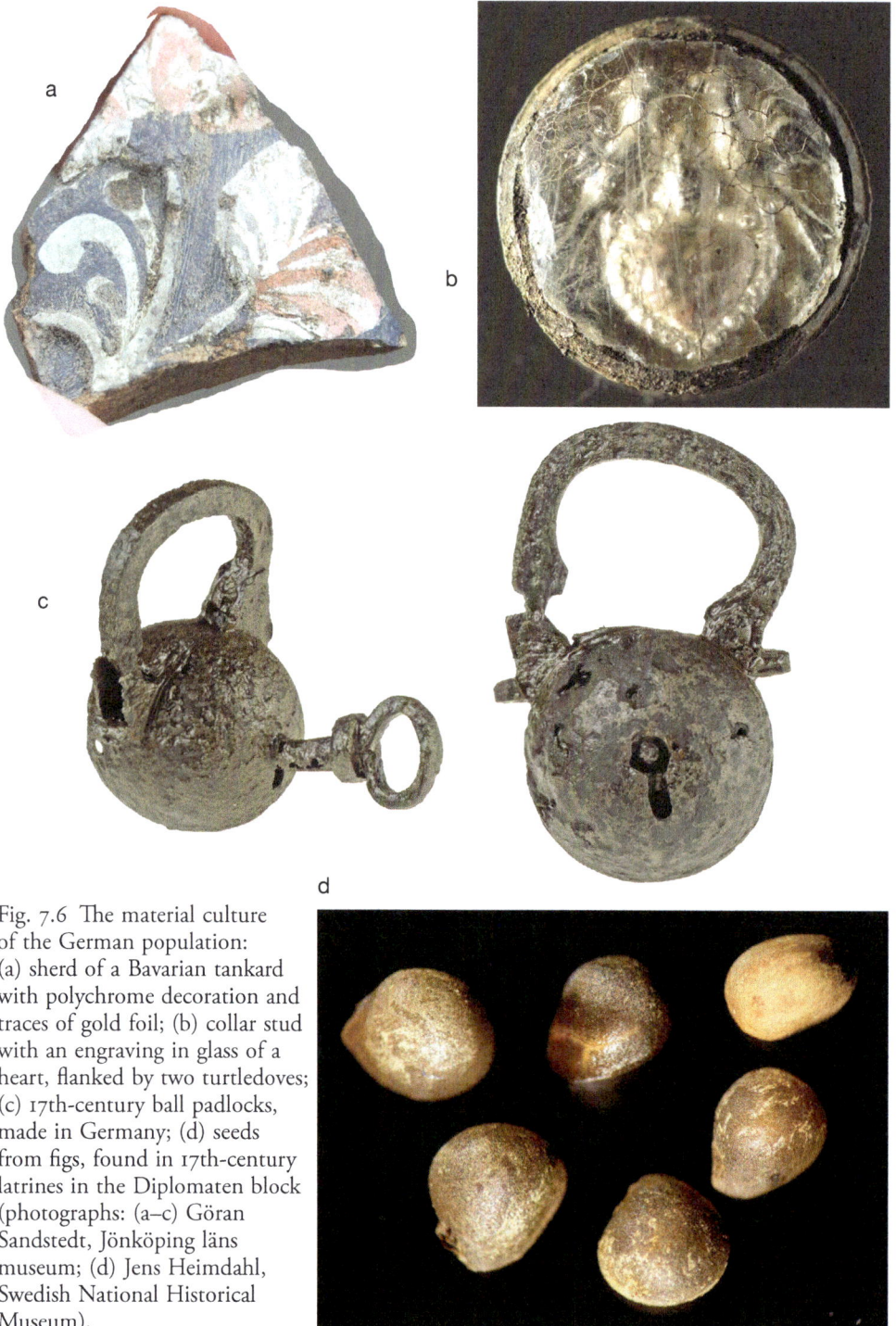

Fig. 7.6 The material culture of the German population: (a) sherd of a Bavarian tankard with polychrome decoration and traces of gold foil; (b) collar stud with an engraving in glass of a heart, flanked by two turtledoves; (c) 17th-century ball padlocks, made in Germany; (d) seeds from figs, found in 17th-century latrines in the Diplomaten block (photographs: (a–c) Göran Sandstedt, Jönköping läns museum; (d) Jens Heimdahl, Swedish National Historical Museum).

Refuse dumps – the source of our knowledge of the cuisine of the German population in Jönköping – are in themselves an indication of possible conflicts and complications arising between culturally and socially diverse populations of the town. The frictions arose around a question of how to handle refuse – or rather how not to handle it. While a large number of the Swedish burghers were also part-time farmers, having farm animals and a stake in the arable lands that belonged to the town, the Germans were simply craftsmen.[42] They were hired as specialists and were not expected – or allowed – to have too many side-line occupations. The *Vantmakeriet* manufactory consumed their time. Among the ordinary burghers, refuse (including latrine waste) must have been regarded as a valuable commodity, to be used as manure on their fields. In the archaeological excavations traces of handling of latrine waste are often found in the 17th-century levels, while the actual facilities are few.[43] What has been found represents matter spilled or dropped from barrels of latrine waste in the yards, alleys and streets. Waste management seems to have been fairly well organized, even in a 17th-century Swedish provincial town.

It is worth noticing that a number of byres and sheds for smaller domestic animals appear in the *Vantmakeriet* area.[44] The situation among the gunsmiths of the *Jönköpings Faktori* is different, as the presence of animals is less marked in the archaeological material from those plots.[45] It is difficult to compare these two districts, however, as regrettably no archaeobotanical analyses were made during the Apeln project in 2003–4 when four plots belonging to craftsmen employed by the arms factory were excavated. In the *Vantmakeriet* stables have been identified and stable gear together with other riding equipment has been found. This can hardly be seen as surprising, since the factory facilities were spread over a fairly large area and horses were needed as a means of transport.

Consequently, in a place like Jönköping where the compostable waste including latrine waste was supposed to end up as fertilizer on the arable land surrounding the town, the German district was different. There the refuse was not carted out. Instead it stayed in dumps at the back of the plots, quite possibly to the annoyance of the locals. Evidence from the 18th-century rolls of the court and magistrate bear witness to the kind of conflicts between neighbours that originated in the handling – or rather mishandling – of night soil within the narrow confines of an early modern town.[46] Unfortunately, the written sources for the previous period are not as eloquent, but it seems reasonable to assume that the situation was quite similar during the *Vantmakeriet* era. So how was a well-defined group of foreigners regarded within the small local community when they deviated from the behavioural norm with regard to such sensitive issues as the handling of rubbish and latrine waste? And, contrarily – what happened when a decidedly urban way of life was contrasted with the much more rural habits of the native burghers in a small Swedish town during a period of radical change in the community as a whole?

MEETING THE OTHER IN JÖNKÖPING

The German families lived in a well-defined area in the townscape: the two or three blocks that constituted what is still known as Tyska maden. This enclave was situated on what was then, in the 1620s, the southern outskirts of Jönköping. To the south were the marshes, Moratzet ("the Morass"), to the east the inner harbour. Their houses were built by the Crown or the company and belonged to the *Vantmakeriet*.[47] In contrast, the gunsmiths and other craftsmen employed by the arms manufactory lived in their own properties and, although there was a notable concentration along the street Smedjegatan, employees of *Jönköpings Faktori* lived all over town.[48] If this is to be regarded as a measure of integration, then the gunsmiths were a part of the community from the very beginning, while the German textile workers and their families were more of a group apart, at least at the start of their tenure in Jönköping.

This is not to say that the Germans who were engaged in the operations of the *Vantmakeriet* had to stay within its confines. Quite the contrary; as many of the facilities that belonged to the manufactory were situated in the districts around Jönköping the employees had to travel there on a daily basis or on particular occasions, depending on their roles in the production process. The presence of the stables and riding equipment mentioned above is a good indication of this mobility. Furthermore, if the mastercraftsmen were involved in the handling of the raw materials, trips to the sheep farms – *schäferierna* – might have been needed at intervals. If so, that meant journeys over considerable distances, as these farms were situated in the regions of northern Småland and south-eastern Västergötland.[49]

In daily life contact between the German families from Tyska maden and the locals must have been extensive, as neighbours met at the market, in the shops and in alehouses. There is no reason to believe that the majority of them lived anything but a quiet and peaceful life in this provincial Swedish town. Here the written sources let us down, however, as it is clearly stated in the census record of 1639 that "these craftsmen are not included among the burghers".[50] The rolls and archives from the period, potentially informative however fallible they might be, exclude this group of people entirely. The owners of the *Vantmakeriet* manufacture kept their own registers.

It is worth noticing that a town like Jönköping had a fairly international population in the first half of the 17th century. Skilled craftsmen, merchants and specialists such as pharmacists were often of foreign descent. The excavations in the Ansvaret block in 2008 included plots owned by the merchants Frank von Hövelen and Frantz Wernich, both Germans, and their neighbour, the Scotsman Petter Bursie. Another interesting resident was the barber Christian Oldenknecht, a former field surgeon who continued his trade in more peaceful surroundings.[51] As in other Swedish towns during the "Age of Greatness", the German language was something of a lingua franca in Jönköping.

Religious matters should not have posed much of a problem, as both the locals and the hired craftsmen were stern Protestants, or at least were supposed to be. In most Swedish towns that were important ports of trade or industrial centres during the 17th and 18th centuries there was a German church. In Jönköping, with a relatively small German congregation, a section was added to the makeshift timber church, erected in 1625. This building remained in use until the large Christine Church (Kristine kyrka, Fig. 7.4) was consecrated in 1673. But no German section was included in the new baroque stone edifice.[52] The Royal Chartered cloth factory had ceased its operations by then.

Over the years the *Vantmakeriet* factory evolved into an advanced textile production site where a number of different qualities of cloth were made.[53] This meant contacts with customers other than the Crown buyers, and possibilities for craftsmen like the tailor who lived on plot 208 on the Diplomaten site in the 1630s.[54] From the finds it might be concluded that a family of German origin lived in this house, and the exclusiveness of the materials used in the workshop shows that this tailor was no ordinary employee of the *Vantmakeriet*. It seems more likely that this was someone attracted to an environment where textiles were produced, but who had his customers among the upper echelons of the local community.

The most intense and lasting contacts between the German textile workers and the local population must have been through the young Swedish males who were accepted as apprentices and journeymen in the workshops of master craftsmen like Henrik von Collen, Lambrecht Eratus, Benedictus Stoltz, Johan Crantz, Hans von Rintelen and Hans Frank.[55] They learned the complicated trade by working together with their teachers and living in their households. Most of them came from Jönköping or the surrounding region, as the appeal from the authorities for recruits from other parts of southern Sweden appears to have had little effect.[56] But these lads learned a respected trade, and – what must have been equally important during the troubled times of the Thirty Years' War – like the workers in the arms manufacture they were exempt from military service.[57]

COPPER COINS, COUNTERFEIT MONEY AND LOST POSSESSIONS

The German minority was a group favoured by the authorities, and like the gunsmiths working for the arms factory, they were well paid. Master craftsmen were obviously able to make a living, not perhaps in real luxury but they were at least better off than most other contemporary craftsmen in Sweden. During the reign of Gustavus Adolphus (1611–32), at the same time that the manufactories in Jönköping were established, large numbers of low-value coins made of copper came into circulation in Sweden.[58] The mines in Falun provided a seemingly interminable supply of copper. In some respects this might be regarded as a parallel to the way in which silver from Potosí in Bolivia kept the Spanish Empire going: it is hard to imagine that the so-called "Swedish Age of Greatness" would have been possible without copper ore.

In the 1630s copper coins of low denomination were extensively minted, making them the most common coins found in excavated urban remains from the 17th century.[59] Consequently, large numbers of quarter, half and 1 *öre* coins have been found in the manufacturing sites in Jönköping. In fact, they appear in far larger numbers there than anywhere else in the town. Nor are these coins only found in or around the buildings where trade and commercial activities took place. They appear in all possible contexts; often given a secondary function.[60] On some occasions they were used as ritual offerings or as jettons on counting boards. The question is how practical these copper coins actually were for buying commodities in a town like Jönköping during the reign of Queen Christina (1632–54)? Was the local economy ready for large quantities of small change to come into circulation? Or were they regarded with mistrust, like the emergency coinage from the years of economic collapse in the reign of Charles XII, 80 years later[61]?

Then there are other numismatic finds from Jönköping, indicating that at least some people developed a get-rich-quick attitude that encompassed the use of counterfeit money. This was of course a dangerous pursuit, considering the severe punishments applied by the authorities against this type of offence; but by using fake coins of an alleged continental origin less familiar to the locals, the risk of being exposed was considerably reduced. One such counterfeit was found at the Diplomaten site in 2007 in the *Vantmakeriet* area. It was a silver coin that had been given a thin coating of tin and gold foil. There is also a fake thaler from the Holy Roman Empire that carries an interesting story. Made with a lead core coated in silver at an official Imperial mint, it was to be used in trade wars with the Ottoman Empire.[62] But somehow this particular counterfeit coin ended up in the Swedish fortress town of Jönköping. However, one could say that it did serve its purpose, because whether the counterfeit fooled a "heathen" Turk or a "heretic" Swede did not really matter, as both were seen as enemies of the Holy Roman Emperor. But what harm might be done to relations between the different groups of inhabitants in this small provincial town by a rumour that the German population in Jönköping were not to be trusted as they spread fake money?

Finally, among the archaeological finds from Jönköping there are also some traces of other, less fortunate visitors to the county of Småland. The Baltic provinces, the Estonia and Latvia of today, were among the richest and most developed areas of the Swedish realm during the "Age of Greatness". But with Russia as their neighbour to the east the border was always threatened. During the mid-1650s, when Sweden's armies were engaged in Poland and Lithuania, the forces of the Tsar invaded.[63] A small hoard containing coins and personal jewellery of Baltic origin, found in the remains of a store-house in the *Vantmakeriet* site, is of this very date.[64] It is telling and somewhat touching that these items were found in this part of town – the enclave of German-speaking craftsmen – because that language was also common among the urban populations in the Baltic provinces. The fugitives sought their kin.

WHAT REMAINS – THE LEGACY OF THE *VANTMAKERIET*

The *Vantmakeriet* textile manufactory managed to survive for just about 35 years. There were several reasons for its downfall. Firstly, it had never fulfilled the high hopes originally nurtured by the Crown and its group of owners. The promised goal of 40,000 ells (24,000 metres) of cloth to be delivered yearly, stipulated in the first contract, was never reached. Instead a normal average production varied between 5,000 and 10,000 ells yearly.[65] That represented only a small proportion of what was needed for the armed forces each year, though this input nevertheless remained important as long as the Thirty Years' War lasted. After the Westphalian Peace Treaty of 1648, however, prices for cloth and other textiles fell drastically. Imports became more readily available and international competition made things hard for the local Swedish manufacturers. On top of that, the quality of the raw materials, the wool from the large, newly-established sheep farms in the region, remained low despite attempts to improve the stock by breeding.[66]

Initially the intentions of both Crown and manufacturers had been to pass on the skills from the recruited foreign master craftsmen to a Swedish workforce.[67] These attempts had only been partially successful. And then came the severe floods of 1650, causing considerable damage to the low-lying areas of the *Vantmakeriet* manufacturing site. Eyewitnesses described the foul smell, the high water levels and how many people had left their inundated houses. Some even fled from the town, forced by the deluge to go elsewhere in order to make a living.[68]

The final blow came with the death of Peter Gudmundsson, the last and most powerful manufacturer, five years later. After his demise, the few textile craftsmen still left in town tried to carry on independently, but the days of the *Vantmakeriet* manufactory and large-scale production were over. An ambitious attempt to restart operations in the 1690s was to no avail.[69] Jönköping never became the textile centre of Sweden, the hub of modernity once hoped for by the Crown. Instead the Tyska maden area became a neighbourhood for ordinary craftsmen of mostly Swedish origin, as can be seen from the registers of property owners, dating from 1696. Few, if any, German names appear in these lists.[70]

A century later, in 1790, both the Tyska maden and the Svenska maden districts suffered from a devastating fire, reducing the buildings in 137 plots to ashes and cinder.[71] Recovery was slow and painful in many respects. While a number of large residences were erected along the main street in Jönköping by wealthy burghers, the inhabitants of the poorer districts had to make the best of the situation, using whatever they could afford. Skilled carpenters and commodities such as high-quality building materials had become expensive in the aftermath of the catastrophe.

In a number of the late 18th-century buildings investigated at the Diplomaten site in 2006–7 there were traces of work done in haste by unskilled labour: houses built on insufficient foundations, reuse of partly fire-damaged materials and thick layers of debris employed as landfill.[72] It is telling that these blocks figured in a report on poverty and poor housing conditions in Jönköping compiled in the 1930s. The situation then was described as appalling, probably among the worst of its kind in the country during the years of the Great Depression.[73] So the area that had once housed *Vantmakeriet* – a site of new techniques for large-scale production, a true hub of modernity – had instead become a slum district characterized by social unrest in an otherwise thriving industrial town. Consequently these same estates were earmarked for urban development in the 1960s and 1970s, when whole blocks were demolished and turned into parking lots.

In the end very little remained of the grand enterprise that once was *Vantmakeriet*, and of a group of people who moved from urban northern Germany to a small garrison town in Sweden – except, perhaps, for a certain taste for sweeteners used in the local cuisine, something not so common in other provincial Swedish towns of the 18th and 19th centuries.[74] But instead of the imported figs once favoured by the German weavers, now forest berries of local origin were used.

NOTES

1 Nordin 2014.
2 See Douhan 1985, 43–4.
3 Heimdahl & Vestbö Franzén 2009; Nordman & Pettersson 2009; Heimdahl 2014; Pettersson 2014.
4 Ahlberg 2012.
5 Magnusson 1996, 142.
6 Douhan 1985.
7 Ahlberg 2014; Pettersson forthcoming.

8 Björkman 1917, vol. 1, 444; Karlson 2010.
9 Rystad et al. 1965, 81.
10 Haltiner Nordström & Pettersson 2014, 65–8.
11 Kjellberg 1943, 123–5.
12 Haltiner Nordström & Pettersson 2014.
13 Kjellberg 1943, 70.
14 Magnusson 1996, 164.
15 Kjellberg 1943, 125.
16 Kjellberg 1943, 124.

17 Kjellberg 1943, 125.
18 Kjellberg 1943, 124.
19 Kjellberg 1943, 134.
20 Karlson 1996, 132.
21 Pettersson 2014, 166–7.
22 Vestbö Franzén 2009, 43.
23 Karlson 1996, 131.
24 Rystad *et al.* 1965, 93.
25 See Granberg 1984.
26 Tagesson 2014, 106–8.
27 Pettersson 2011a, 169.
28 Nordman & Pettersson 2009, 167–8.
29 Nordman & Pettersson 2009, 156–7.
30 Kjellberg 1943, 130.
31 Westerdahl 2009.
32 Ahlberg 2012; Pettersson 2014, 166–7.
33 Stibéus 2008; Nordman & Pettersson 2009.
34 Nordman & Pettersson 2009, 138–41.
35 Brorsson 2009.
36 See Nordman & Pettersson 2009, 145; Pettersson 2014, 172.
37 Nordman & Pettersson 2009, 152.
38 Heimdahl 2009.
39 Heimdahl 2009, 31–2; Pettersson 2014, 170.
40 Heimdahl 2009, 31.
41 Månsson 1642 with its appendix printed in 1643.
42 See Björklund 2010; Vestbö Franzén 2011.
43 Nordman & Pettersson 2009, 13–14; Haltiner Nordström & Pettersson 2014, 162.
44 Nordman & Pettersson 2009, 123.
45 Haltiner Nordström & Pettersson 2014, 162.
46 Per Ericsson, pers. comm. Based on Jönköpings läns folkrörelsearkiv 2004.
47 Rystad *et al.* 1965, 81.
48 Haltiner Nordström & Pettersson 2014, 61–2.
49 Kjellberg 1943, 128–9.
50 Björkman 1918, vol. 2, 210, my translation.
51 Stibéus 2012, 54.
52 Johanson & Johannsson 1940, 26.
53 Kjellberg 1943, 132.
54 Nordman & Pettersson 2009, 75, 119.
55 Rystad *et al.* 1965, 91.
56 Kjellberg 1943, 127.
57 Rystad *et al.* 1965, 87.
58 Magnusson 1996, 174–5.
59 Tonkin & Tonkin 2005, 3–4, 99; Menander 2003, 76; Nordman & Pettersson 2009, 155–6.
60 Nordman & Pettersson 2009, 156; Haltiner Nordström & Pettersson 2014, 157–60; Haltiner Nordström 2012, 51.
61 Royal Coin Cabinet "Nödmynt" http://www.myntkabinettet.se/fakta/foremalsfakta/nodmynt
62 Letter from Dr. Bernhard Prokisch, Schlossmuseum Linz, 6 April 2010; Pettersson 2011b, 106–7.
63 Sundberg 1998.
64 Pettersson *et al.* 2010.
65 Kjellberg 1943, 125, 136.
66 Kjellberg 1943, 128–9.
67 Kjellberg 1943, 127.
68 Björkman 1919, vol. 3, 331.
69 Kjellberg 1943, 137; Karlson 1996, 132.
70 Nordman & Pettersson 2009, 60; Westerdahl 2009.
71 Nordman & Pettersson 2009, 171; Pettersson & Jonsson 2014, 281–2.
72 Nordman & Pettersson 2009, 91–2.
73 Hyresgästernas riksförbund 1936; Ericsson 2013.
74 Heimdahl 2014, 332.

BIBLIOGRAPHY

Ahlberg, N. 2012. *Svensk stadsplanering: arvet från stormaktstiden, resurs i dagens stadsutveckling*. Stockholm: Forskningsrådet Formas.

Ahlberg, N. 2014. 'Jönköping och stormaktstidens stadsbyggande', in Nordman *et al.* 2014, 23–51.

Bäck, M. & Pettersson, C. 2011. 'Arbetets och boendets stratigrafi', *Suomen Keskiajan Arkeologian Seura SKAS* 2011(2): 24–41.

Björklund, A. 2010. *Historical Urban Agriculture: Food Production and Access to Land in Swedish Towns before 1900*. Stockholm Studies in Human Geography 20. Stockholm: Stockholm University.

Björkman, R. (ed.) 1917–20. *Jönköpings historia*, vols 1–4. Jönköping: Richards aktiebolags förlag.

Broberg, E. & Nilsson L. (eds) 2014. *City Fortresses in the Baltic Sea Region*. Stockholm: Sveriges militärhistoriska arv.

Brorsson, T. 2009. 'Lokalproducerad och importerad keramik: ICP-analys av 1600- och 1700-talskeramik från kv. Diplomaten, Jönköping, Småland'. KKS Rapport 35.

Cornell, P., Eliassen, F.-E., Ersgård, L. & Söhrman, I. (eds) forthcoming. *Urban Variation. Utopia, Planning and Practice*. The Early Modern Town 2. Gothenburg: Göteborgs universitet.

Douhan, B. 1985. *Arbete, kapital och migration: Valloninvandringen till Sverige under 1600-talet.* Studia historica Upsaliensia 140. Uppsala: Uppsala universitet.

Ericsson, M. 2013. '"Ut med er tattare, vi ska döda er!" Jönköpingskravallerna 1948 och det dubbla utanförskapet', in Holmlund & Sandén 2013, 320–37.

Fagerland, T. A. & Paasche, K. (eds) 2011. *1537 – Kontinuitet eller brudd?* Trondheim: Tapir.

Granberg, J. 1984. *Gården i den förindustriella staden: En studie i stadsbebyggelsens regionala variationer.* Stockholm: Nordiska museet.

Haltiner Nordström, S. 2012. 'Under Chinabiografen: Arkeologisk för- och slutundersökning inför nybyggnation inom kv. Abborren 6, inom RAÄ fornlämning 50, Jönköpings stad och kommun'. Jönköpings läns museum, archaeological report 2012:66.

Haltiner Nordström, S. & Pettersson, C. 2014. 'Vapensmedernas gårdar. Faktorismide och köpenskap vid Smedjegatan: bebyggelse 1620–1950. Arkeologisk slutundersökning 2003– 2004 i kv. Apeln och Arkadien. RAÄ 50, Jönköpings stad'. Jönköpings läns museum, archaeological report 2013:48.

Heimdahl, J. 2014. 'Det borgerliga livets kryddor', in Nordman *et al.* 2014, 327–91.

Heimdahl, J. & Vestbö Franzén, Å. 2009. 'Tyska Madens gröna rum: Specialstudier till den arkeologiska slutundersökningen år 2007 i kv. Diplomaten, RAÄ 50, Jönköpings stad'. Jönköpings läns museum, archaeological report 2009:41.

Holmlund, S. & Sandén, A. (eds) 2013. *Usla, elända och arma: Samhällets utsatta under 700 år.* Stockholm: Natur & Kultur.

Hur vi bo. Jönköpings bostadsfråga i siffrornas ljus. 1936. Rapport utgiven av Hyresgästernas riksförbund och Jönköpings hyresgästförening.

Johanson, E. O. & Johansson, G. 1940. *Jönköpings och Huskvarna kyrkor.* Sveriges kyrkor 48. Stockholm.

Karlson, B. E. 1996. *Bebyggelse i Jönköping 1612–1870: Produktion, rekreation.* Jönköping: Jönköpings läns museum.

Karlson, B. E. 2010. *Jönköping – den nya staden: bebyggelse och stadsplanering 1612–1870.* Jönköping: Jönköpings läns museum.

Karlsson, P. & Tagesson, G (eds) 2003. *I Tyskebacken: Hus, människor och industri i stormaktstidens Norrköping.* Arkeologiska undersökningar Skrifter 47. Stockholm: Riksantikvarieämbetet.

Kjellberg, S. T. 1943. *Ull och ylle: bidrag till den svenska yllemanufakturens historia.* Lund: H. Ohlssons boktryck.

Klingnéus, S. 1997. *Bönder blir vapensmeder: protoindustriell tillverkning i Närke under 1600- och 1700-talen.* Studia historica Upsaliensia 181. Uppsala: Uppsala universitet.

Linderson, H. 2008. 'Dendrokronologisk analys av byggnadsrester från kvarteret Diplomaten, Jönköping'. Nationella Laboratoriet för Vedanatomi och Dendrokronologi, report 2008:12.

Magnusson, L. 1996. *Sveriges ekonomiska historia.* Stockholm: Rabén Prisma.

Månsson, A. 1642. *En myckit nyttigh Örta-Book: Om the herlige örter som vthi thet höghberömde Konungarijket wårt käre Fädernesland Swerige åhrligen wäxa.* Stockholm: Ignatium Meurer.

Månsson, A. 1643. *Een Nyy Träägårdz-Book.* Stockholm: Ignatium Meurer.

Menander, H. 2003. 'Ingen bonde åhr och nu snart som icke skall dricka tobach', in Karlsson & Tagesson 2003, 74–83.

Nordin, J. M. 2014. 'Sveriges koloniala gruvprojekt har en lång historia', *Dagens ETC*, 14 October 2014.

Nordman, A.-M., Nordström, M. & Pettersson, C. (eds) 2014. *Stormaktsstaden Jönköping. 1614 och framåt.* Jönköping: Jönköpings läns museum.

Nordman, A.-M. & Pettersson, C. 2009. 'Den centrala periferin: Arkeologisk undersökning i kvarteret Diplomaten, faktori- och hantverksgårdar i Jönköping 1620–1790'. Jönköpings läns museum, archaeological report 2009:40.

Nordman, A.-M., Pettersson, C. & Heimdahl, J. 2011. 'På denna blöta grund – 2,5 meter stadsarkeologi i ett kärr', *Suomen keskiajan arkeologian seura SKAS* 2/2010: 11–23.

Pettersson, C. 2011a. 'Stormaktens byggstenar – Jönköpings kungliga faktori 1620–1721 i det arkeologiska materialet', in Fagerland & Paasche 2011, 151–81.

Pettersson, C. 2011b. 'Handelskrig? Falskt mynt i Jönköping', *Svensk numismatisk tidskrift* 2011(5): 106–7.

Pettersson, C. 2014. 'Jönköpings båda kungliga faktorier – en fråga om vapen och ylletyg', in Nordman, Nordström & Pettersson 2014, 153–75.

Pettersson, C. forthcoming. '"With Our Meagre Resources…". Jönköping: An Unfinished Fortified Town of the Seventeenth Century', in *Cornell et al.* forthcoming.

Pettersson, C., Heimdahl, J. & Pilav, S. 2010. 'Över Östersjön – baltiska spår i stormaktstidens Jönköping', *Fornvännen* 2010(2): 104–11.

Pettersson, C. & Nilsson I.-M. 2014. 'A tale of two cities: The troubled origins of city fortresses on both sides of a border', in Broberg & Nilsson 2014, 60–72.

Ridderberg, M. (ed.) 2010. *Minnen, människor, platser: Jönköpings stads historia.* Jönköping: Jönköpings läns museum.

Rystad, G., Sallnäs, B. & Wessman, L. 1965. *Jönköpings stads historia. Del 2, från stadens brand 1612 till kommunalreformen 1862.* Jönköping: Kulturnämnden.

Stibéus, M., 2008. 'Tyska maden i 1600-talets Jönköping'. Jönköpings läns museum, archaeological report, 2008:88.

Stibéus, M. 2012. 'Arkeologisk undersökning: Från vassbevuxen strandkant till handelsgårdar, Tre gårdar från 1600- och 1700-talen vid Munksjön, Småland, Jönköpings stad och kommun, kv. Ansvaret 5 och 6, RAÄ 50'. UV Rapport 2012:175.

Stibéus, M. (ed.) 2014. 'Fällberedarens gård, apotekarens trädgård och slaktarens kaj. Arkeologi i kv. Ansvaret, Jönköping'. Stockholm: Riksantikvarieämbetet.

Sundberg, U. 1998. *Svenska krig 1521–1814.* Stockholm: Hjalmarson & Högberg.

Tagesson, G. 2014. 'Tidigmoderna rum – gård, hus och rum i 1600- och 1700-talets Jönköping', in Stibéus 2014, 95–126.

Tonkin, A. & Tonkin, H. 2005. *Myntboken 2005: Sveriges sedlar och mynt ca 995–2005.* Ljungsbro.

Vestbö Franzén, Å. 2009. 'Diplomaten och kålgårdarna. En studie av markanvändningen i kålgårdsområdet mellan 1611 och 1850 utifrån det äldre kartmaterialet', in Heimdahl & Vestbö Franzén 2009, 37–54.

Vestbö Franzén, Å. 2011. 'Hur byarnas mark blev Bymarken de medeltida byarna som blev Jönköpings västra betesmark', *Gudmundsgillets Årsbok* 67: 73–89.

Westerdahl, D.-E. 2009. 'Det skriftliga källmaterialet. Appendix 5', in Nordman & Pettersson 2009, CD-ROM.

8

Foreign Merchants in Early Modern Sweden: A Case of Intermarriage, Trade and Migration

CHRISTINA DALHEDE

The family was very significant for foreign merchants settled in Sweden. These merchants and their families were not only active in commerce, but they acted as shareholders in ships, and played important roles in cultural spheres of society. They often chose to marry into foreign families. Intermarriage was to some degree motivated by the wish to expand geographical contact networks and international relations. It had great economic and social impact, allowing the merchants to foster trust and credibility, to avoid risk and cut business transaction costs. This chapter explores the national and international orientation of geographical contact networks established by foreign merchants living in Sweden and discusses their connections and cultural orientations.

For the foreign merchant settled in early modern Sweden, family networks were very significant. Family members and relatives were not only engaged with each other in commercial activities as, for example, creditors and shareholders in ships and companies, but they were also involved in sustaining and shaping social and cultural values, tastes and practices of burghership.

The foreign merchants who lived in Sweden often chose to marry outside of their own ethnic group and into other burgher families of foreign origin. Examples from Arboga, Stockholm and Gothenburg illustrate, for instance, intermarriages between German and Scottish as well as German and Dutch families. These unions were frequently dictated by pragmatic thinking and expectations of economic and social benefits. The decisions to relocate to Sweden and intermarry stemmed from the wish to boost capital, obtain monopolies and expand the area of business and the types, volumes and qualities of merchandise through access to new markets. Factors such as extending geographical contact networks and international relations, especially for families who could be described as *Misch-Europäer* – culturally mixed Europeans – had a great economic and social impact, too. These networks facilitated the formation of trust and credibility, which helped the merchants to avoid risk and cut business transaction costs. In the credit market, these factors were vital.

Migration, trading activities and partnership strategies of foreign merchants who settled in Sweden are the central focus of this chapter. Attention will be paid to the national and international orientations of their contact networks and the importance of family background and family origin in the ability to participate in, take advantage of and generate earnings from large-scale mercantile operations. The cultural orientation of the foreign merchants and their families in Sweden will also be considered.

MIGRATION, INTERMARRIAGE AND COMMERCIAL ACTIVITY

In the year 1674, a merchant named Robert Petre senior (Fig. 8.1) and three of his compatriots from Scotland sued Hans Andersson for defamation in the court in Arboga in Sweden. Robert Petre senior, Jacob Hunther, Robert Petre junior and Jacob Petre, all merchants, argued that the Scottish nation had been insulted by a Swede.[2] They told the court that epithets referring to Scottish thieves and crooks had been shouted at them by Hans Andersson. The court listened to the arguments from both sides; Andersson was found guilty and ordered by the court to pay compensation to the four Scots. Although the Scots had been living in Arboga for many years, this case illustrates a still-existing chasm between one section of the Swedish population and the Scottish families.

Fig. 8.1 The merchant and ironworks founder Robert Petre senior in Arboga. Detail from the Höijer epitaph in Arboga town church (photograph: Allan Dalhede).

In the same year, however, the magistrate and the burghers proposed Robert Petre senior as their candidate for the office of lord mayor in Arboga. Their recommendation was full of praise and admiration for Petre, who "has been living for many years in the city as a distinguished and praiseworthy inhabitant, and has always worked in praiseworthy occupations ... Almighty God has richly favoured Petre's house with good fortune, and he has always tried to accomplish what was good and *zirat* [beneficial] for the city."[3] This example and opinion of Petre, contrasting starkly with the angry slander of Andersson, gives us a picture of an immigrant as an accepted and valued member of Swedish society. The Petres, who lived in various towns in Sweden and supervised diverse business operations, were among the European merchant families deeply involved in international trade. They made a fortune dealing in merchandise such as metals, spices, wine and textiles.[4] They were also involved in the iron trade and in iron production, founding and owning ironworks in Hofors in Gästrikland.

The Petres were hardly alone in their pursuit of important social positions, their interest and ability to invest in versatile business operations and their success in generating earnings. What attracted them and other foreign merchant families to Sweden were the generous privileges, insignificant competition from the capital-poor domestic burghers and investment opportunties in the somewhat underdeveloped Swedish economy of the 16th and 17th centuries. Metals in particular – iron and copper – which were abundant in Sweden and which were staple commodities in the continental and global markets held a special attraction. They were the magnet for many, including the De Besche family who arrived from Antwerp in 1595 and who became actively involved in restructuring and reorganizing Swedish metal production. Willem De Besche was engaged in the production of copper coins, and together with Govert de Silentz built up the works in Avesta-Säter. The well-known banker, merchant and entrepreneur Louis De Geer was related to the De Besche family (through the marriage between De Geer's daughter and Willem de Besche's son) and the two managed several ironworks in the province of Uppland.

Marcus Danielsson Kock, later raised to nobility under the name of Cronström, was also involved in the production of copper coins, and was later involved in the brass industry. He had received a technical education in Liège and in northern Germany. The Kock family married into the German family of Momma from Aachen (ennobled as Reenstierna), with whom they shared an interest in the metal industry. During certain periods, Willem, Abraham and Jacob Momma, together with their relatives, had a virtual monopoly on brass production in Sweden. The Momma-Reenstierna brothers kept scrupulous records of their connections, dealings, trade and investments (ending in failure and bankruptcy) and their well-preserved archives therefore provide a wealth of information about these and other entrepreneurs and business operations in early modern Sweden.[5]

Other foreign merchant families who were involved in the Swedish ironworks were the Herweghs, the Sahlgrens, the Valcks, the von Mindens, the Thams, and the Rokes. The headquarters of their business operations were located in Gothenburg and they bought their goods for export principally in the counties of Värmland and Dalsland.[6] The German Amias (Amya) and Hertz (Hartz, Hertzen) families were closely connected with each other and were active both in Gothenburg and in the mining district of Bergslagen.[7]

Some of the members of the Leyel, the Radou, the Pemer, the van Gent, the Grill and the Petre merchant houses lived in Bergslagen, Arboga and Stockholm, and had similar interests in the mining districts. The Stockholm merchants Joachim Pötter and Hinrich Thun must be mentioned, too: raised to the nobility under the names of Lillienhoff and Rosenström they were involved in ironworks in Bergslagen. Such foreign merchant houses furthermore had family members placed in other locations in Sweden, where they took part in the chain of commerce, together with their relatives and friends. All of these families had a stake in long-distance maritime trade.

EARLY MODERN MARITIME TRADE – SOME EXAMPLES

In the 17th and 18th centuries the maritime trade in Sweden was concentrated in certain ports: the so-called "staple cities". Merchants, trading commissioners or agents of merchant houses who lived in these cities were allowed to carry on their trade directly with other merchant houses in Sweden and abroad.

Through the imposition of *Tull* (customs duties) and *Tolag* (additional customs duties) and taxation of cargo, Sweden developed a very secure means of collecting revenue to finance state and civic needs. The proceeds from *Stora Sjötullen* (Great Sea customs duties) went entirely to the state; while the *Tolag* served to bring a predetermined percentage of customs income into urban communities for public officials' salaries and to finance public infrastructure. The preserved records of the *Stora Sjötullen* are incomplete, but in certain cities, such as Gothenburg and Stockholm, the *Tolag* and other account books for the period from 1638 can be studied (Fig. 8.2).[8]

The *Tolag* journals from Gothenburg illustrate the paths of foreign trade to and from the city and offer a wealth of information about merchants involved in it, their business partners, networks and the scope of geographical connections.[9] It is also feasible to learn what branches of trade these merchants were active in and whether they preferred certain skippers and ships for the transportation of their goods. The names of the merchants and skippers are noted along with the destinations or arrival ports of their cargoes. Each skipper's home district is registered, as well as information about their vessels, such as name and cargo capacity.

These records are supplemented by other journals, registers and account books such as the so-called "boat book journals" covering the traffic of small boats, sailing between domestic ports, or the account journals of Lilla Edets Sluss (Lilla Edet lock) documenting traffic on the river Göta connecting Gothenburg with the mining, forest and agricultural districts of Värmland and Dalsland. The existence of these various records fortunately permits us to follow commerce right from its inland supply/production area, through Gothenburg, and on to foreign ports.[10]

The many merchant families who resided in Gothenburg moreover kept meticulous records of their businesses in the form of account books and business correspondence.[11] These records offer unique opportunities to complete the picture of particular trade interests of certain foreign merchant houses and merchant families. Among the preserved private merchant account books in Gothenburg are those of Sibrant Valck (1666–76), Johan Zander (1713–21) and the Ekman family (1729 to the present day). All these firms traded in a range of staples as well as continental and colonial goods,

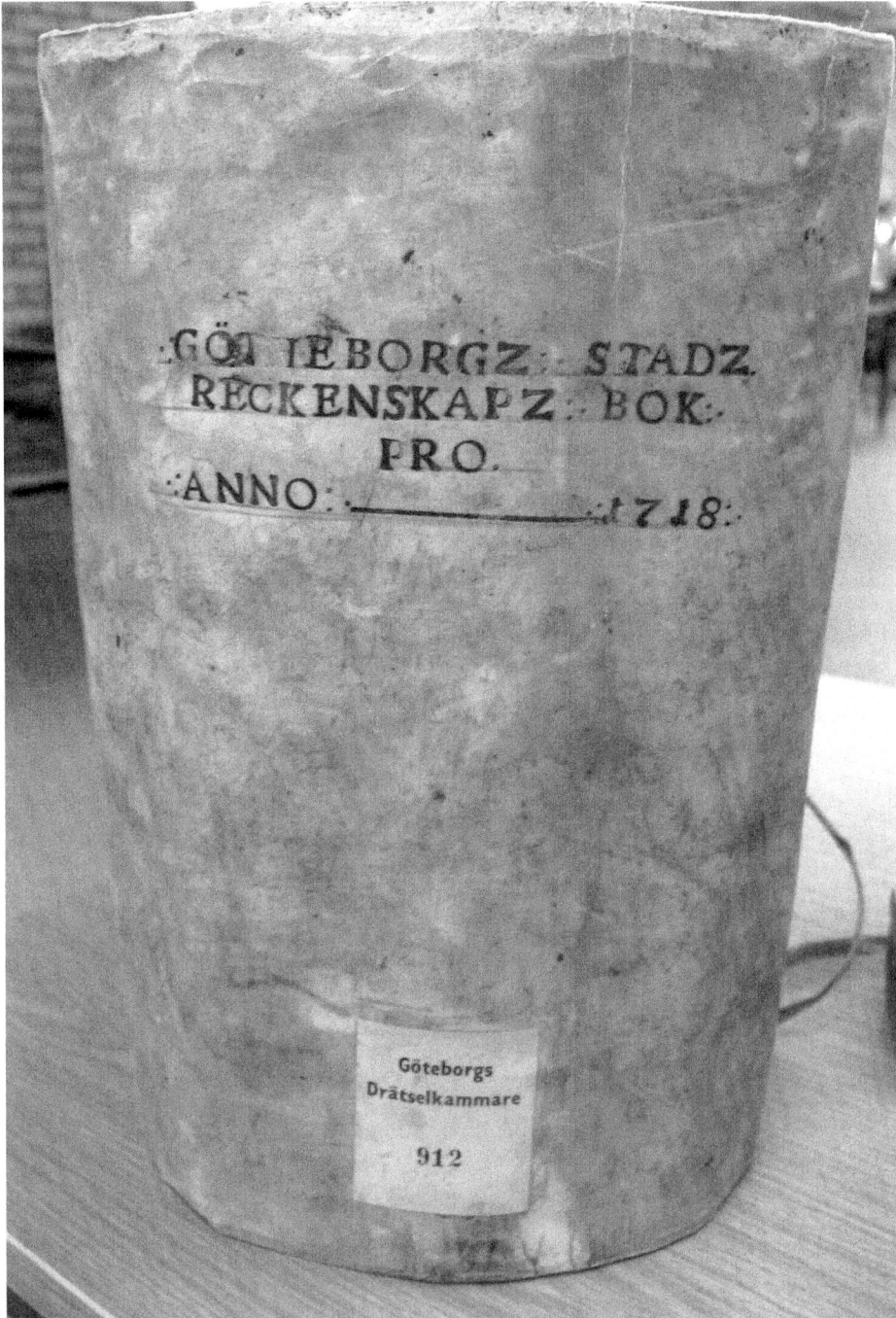

Fig. 8.2 The city of Gothenburg account book from 1718 (GLA, Drätselkammaren i Göteborg, Stadens räkenskaper, Huvudserien 1718, nr 912; photograph: Allan Dalhede).

within Sweden as well as abroad. Valck's maritime connections, noted in his account book, reached at least 71 ports in different countries all over Europe including Sweden, Norway, Denmark, Scotland, England, the Netherlands, the Spanish Netherlands (Belgium), France, Portugal, Spain, and German cities such as Hamburg, Lübeck and ports in the Baltic Sea region: Stettin, Konigsberg and Riga.[12] In the period 1666–76 covered by his journal, Sibrant Valck traded in the following goods:[13] raw metals and metal products (30.4% of total trade volume); timber and forest products (12.6%); fish and agricultural goods (23.9%); books and paper (0.1%); meat, game, skins, leather and pelts (0.2%); textiles and clothing (5.2%); furniture and artwork, jewellery, gold and silver wares (0.2%); and luxury articles, alcohol and wine vinegar (27.5%). Valck was thus orienting his trading around three main sectors of the Swedish economy.

TRACING THE FOREIGN MERCHANTS IN SWEDISH ARCHIVES

The relationships between the different merchant houses and families can be partially reconstructed through historical documents. The above mentioned customs and business records, the church and town records, such as personal probate inventories and tax records provide a wealth of information about the composition of the families and their relatives and business partners, properties owned, accumulated movable wealth and living standard as well as lists of merchandise dealt with by the individual merchants and their families.

Elsewhere I have argued for comprehensive use of the available source material in order to scrutinize the social, economic and cultural background of the early modern merchant houses and families.[14] I have also suggested the construction of a comparative merchant-family database, taking into consideration such factors as family background, geographical contact networks, international relations, trading goods, trading capital and credit markets.[15] The detailed reconstruction of family trees, backgrounds and connections is of fundamental interest and relevance for the understanding of business strategies, mercantile focus and traditions as well as the role of the merchants as intermediaries in promoting and spreading particular continental influences in Sweden and the Baltic Sea basin.

In order to highlight certain economic, social and cultural aspects of the merchant families with foreign background, in my previous work I focused on their role in Swedish towns and coastal regions. I asked to what extent these families acted as intermediaries and trend-setters of continental urban culture and what kind of influence they exercised on domestic culture and practices. In the context of Gothenburg I analysed the impact of the migration and extensive international networks of the immigrant burghers on the development of the 17th-century market, and posed a question as to whether it is possible to speak of an early modern European integration in Gothenburg.

To move the discussion on, I would like to introduce here the concept of "*Misch-Europäer*", which captures the complex family histories of the foreign merchant families living in early modern Sweden (and elsewhere), and which is essential to an understanding of the patterns of economic and social decisions made by these families.[16] The concept of *Misch-Europäer* ("Europeans of mixed ancestry") takes into consideration the intricate family histories of the merchants and their families (involving migration, changes of citizenship and marriages outside of an ethnic group) and looks beyond simple categorizations based on the migrants' places of birth or points of exit. The concept envisages a biographical approach, tracing the ancestry of the individual merchant, reconstructing family trees and connections and paying attention to the family's occupational specializations and traditions.

Historians and other researchers have not always recognized the complexity of family backgrounds and their impact upon economic and social choices, maintaining instead a somewhat simplistic understanding of individuals' identities as rooted in their places of residence or birth. Thinking in terms of such superficial labels as "nationality" skews understanding of early modern commercial activities and strategies, and can misrepresent the character of international commerce. The concept of *Misch-Europäer*, however, allows us a closer insight into the establishment of large family-run merchant houses, the background to international trade, the accumulation of capital, and mechanisms of collaboration and the creation of joint-venture enterprises, along with strategies for maximizing earnings and minimizing risks. It can also give us new perspectives on transmigration and contacts between European merchant colonies, mercantile centres and regions. Furthermore, the concept addresses cultural aspects of migration and intermarriage, and has the potential to enlighten discussion regarding conservatism and fluidity of culture in merchant and burgher circles, and the processes of construction of cultural and ethnic identities.

Nowadays we speak in terms of different categories of national belonging. A sense of territorial and cultural belonging was not foreign to early modern people, even though the idea of "nation states" was not yet current. Early modern merchants worked and acted within certain trade "nations", which obtained or tried to gain trading agreements and privileges for certain geographical markets and goods: for example the German trade nation in Venice ("Fondaco dei Tedeschi") uniting merchants from various towns, including Augsburg and Nuremberg, towns that also had privileges in Lyon.

It is quite possible that mixed ancestry gave certain merchants a chance to attain better deals and to avoid misunderstandings, and helped in navigating the channels of international trade. Merchant families' *Misch-Europäer* backgrounds also had a cultural impact on their new places of residence and inculcated certain mindsets – for example a willingness to marry outside of one's own ethnic group.

THREE CASE STUDIES OF TRANSMIGRATING *MISCH-EUROPÄER* IN SWEDEN

Many of the foreign merchants and entrepreneurs identified as Hamburgers, Lübeckers, Gothenburgers, Scots, Dutchmen, Germans and Walloons had complex family histories prior to their move to Sweden. Their mixed ancestry, migration and business collaborations often propelled their careers and incomes. After relocating to Sweden, these families continued the pattern of networking by maintaining existing collaborations and contacts and establishing new business and personal affiliations across ethnic boundaries. The selection of examples presented below illustrates the scope and orientation of the networks established by these individuals and families.

The Pemer Merchant Family

The young Nicolaus III Pemer came to Sweden in the 1630s. He was born and raised in a merchant family who maintained extensive trading operation from two locations: their native Augsburg in southern Germany and Antwerp in the Spanish Netherlands (Fig. 8.3).[17] They also had two *Gwölb* (vaults for trade and cargo) in the Fondaco dei Tedeschi in Venice and a factory in Hamburg.

The geographical radius centred on the Pemers' Antwerp branch, run by Nicolaus's uncles and grandparents, was wide and diverse, and included Seville in Spain, Lisbon in Portugal, Middelburg and Amsterdam in the Netherlands, Hamburg and Augsburg in the Holy Roman Empire and Stockholm in Sweden. In the 16th century the step-father of Nicolaus's mother, Ulrich Bader, and his companions and relatives the van Uffelns, left Antwerp and moved to safer Middelburg, Cologne, Leipzig and Hamburg. In Hamburg, Bader was the highest tax payer among the city's residents with foreign background and he became involved in the textile trade between Hamburg and Venice, while maintaining business connections with the great merchant houses in Augsburg.[18] The van Uffelns counted as the biggest money-lenders to the city of Leipzig. Through marriages the Baders and the van Uffelns became connected with the merchant families of de Greve, de Herthoge and de Haze. These families in turn had their own mercantile networks and connections, which included dealings with Louis De Geer in Sweden; as did two other relatives of the Baders and the van Uffelns – the Hoefnagels and van Sevendoncks, married into the Alewyns merchant family of Antwerp.

The Augsburg branch of the Pemers had equally wide business networks. They were involved in many branches of trade, but specialized in capital-intensive goods like fabrics (such as silk, velvet and broadcloth), salt and spices. In the second half of the 16th century the family married into and cooperated with another merchant family from Augsburg, the Cristells. Together they traded not only in Venice, Genoa, Milan, Verona, Bolzano, Brixen and Meran, but also with western, northern and eastern European cities and provinces such as Lyon and Paris in France, Bruges and Antwerp in the Spanish Netherlands, London, Cologne, Osnabruck and Frankfurt am Main, Hamburg, Leipzig, Brunswick, Meissen and Gdansk, Silesia and Sachsen. Through marriages and associations with families involved in the metal trade (for example the Böcklins, Höchstetters, Welsers, Jenischs, Stenglins, Hopfers, Zobels and Wittholtzs) the Pemer-Cristells merchant house expanded into that sphere of business too and was soon trading on the central stock markets for metal exchange in Leipzig, Frankfurt am Main, Hamburg and Bolzano.[19] Their versatile dealings and extensive networks allowed the Pemer-Cristells to accumulate considerable wealth: they paid the so-called *Reiche Steuer*, the highest possible capital tax in Augsburg, which their neighbours the Grills were not in a position to do. The Grills' initial rise to power and influence came only in the 17th century, and not in Augsburg (Fig. 8.4).[20]

The Pemers of Augsburg were active Protestants and in 1582 they co-founded the Collegium of St Anna, a Protestant boarding school for able young boys. Along with other prominent merchant families they continued to fund and supervise the school. In the late 1620s marked the beginnings of the Counter-Reformation in Augsburg, and many Protestant merchants regarded this as a threatening development for their Church, the Collegium and their own commercial operations. To protect and assure

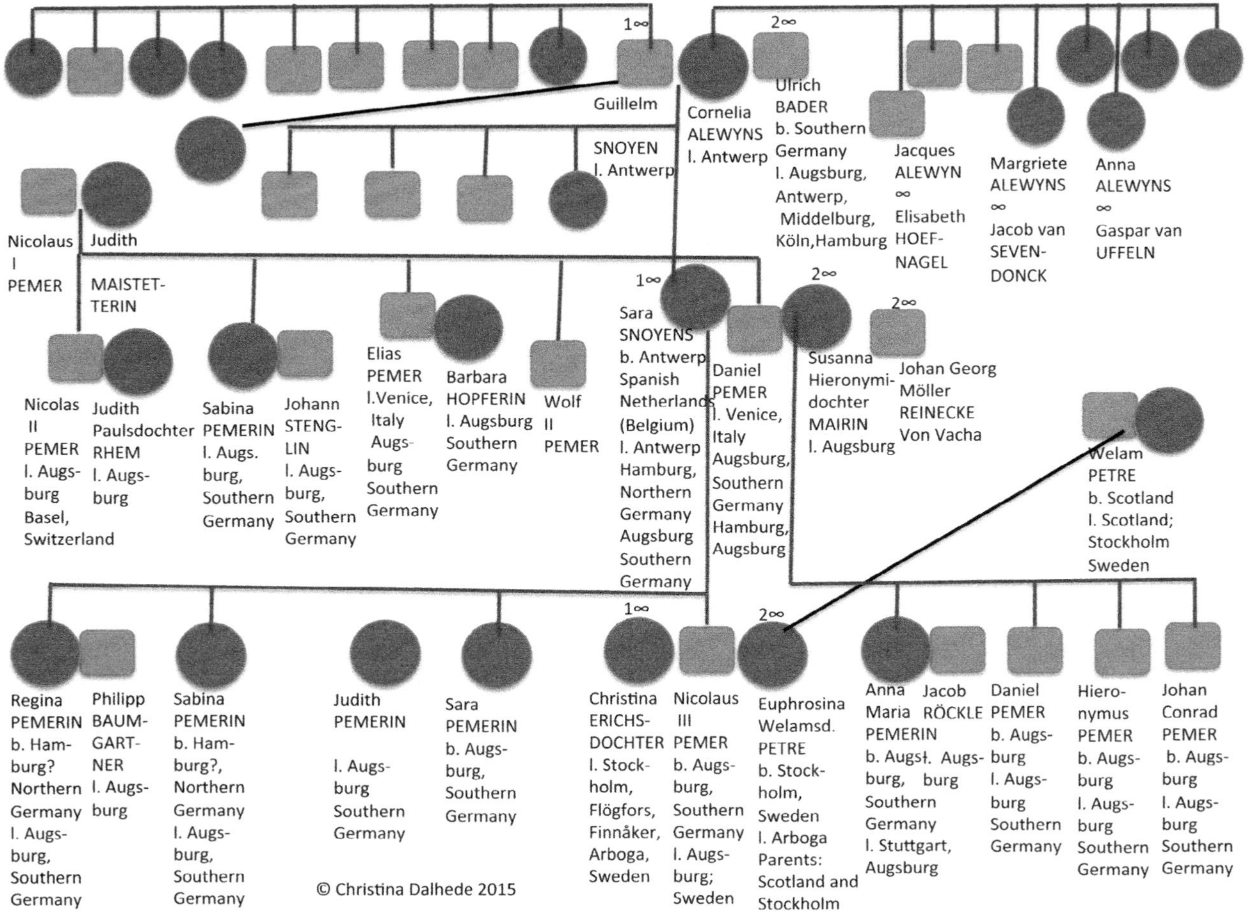

Anna ALEWYNS ∞ Gaspar van UFFELN

Margriete ALEWYNS ∞ Jacob van SEVEN-DONCK

Jacques ALEWYN ∞ Elisabeth HOEF-NAGEL l. Augsburg, Antwerp, Middelburg, Köln, Hamburg

Cornelia ALEWYNS l. Antwerp

Ulrich BADER b. Southern Germany

Guillelm SNOYEN l. Antwerp

2∞

Sara SNOYENS b. Antwerp Spanish Netherlands (Belgium) l. Antwerp Hamburg, Northern Germany Augsburg Southern Germany

1∞

Daniel PEMER l. Venice, Italy Augsburg, Southern Germany Hamburg, Augsburg

2∞

Susanna Hieronymidochter MAIRIN l. Augsburg

Johan Georg Möller REINECKE Von Vacha

Welam PETRE b. Scotland l. Scotland; Stockholm Sweden

Johan Conrad PEMER b. Augsburg l. Augsburg Southern Germany

Hieronymus PEMER b. Augsburg l. Augsburg Southern Germany

Daniel PEMER b. Augsburg l. Augsburg Southern Germany

Jacob RÖCKLE b. Augsburg, Southern Germany l. Stuttgart, Augsburg

Anna Maria PEMERIN b. Augsburg, Southern Germany

Nicolaus III PEMER b. Augsburg, Southern Germany l. Augsburg; Sweden

Euphrosina Welamsd. PETRE b. Stockholm, Sweden l. Arboga Parents: Scotland and Stockholm

2∞

Christina ERICHS-DOCHTER l. Stockholm, Flögfors, Finnåker, Arboga, Sweden

1∞

Nicolaus I PEMER

Judith MAISTET-TERIN

Nicolaus II PEMER l. Augsburg Basel, Switzerland

Judith Paulsdochter RHEM l. Augsburg

Sabina PEMERIN l. Augsburg, Southern Germany

Johann STENGLIN l. Augsburg, Southern Germany

Elias PEMER l. Venice, Italy Augsburg Southern Germany

Barbara HOPFERIN l. Augsburg Southern Germany

Wolf PEMER II

Regina PEMERIN b. Hamburg? Northern Germany l. Augsburg, Southern Germany

Philipp BAUMGARTNER l. Augsburg

Sabina PEMERIN b. Hamburg?, Northern Germany l. Augsburg, Southern Germany

Judith PEMERIN l. Augsburg Southern Germany

Sara PEMERIN b. Augsburg, Southern Germany

© Christina Dalhede 2015

Fig. 8.3 The *Misch-Europäer*: the Pemer merchant family in Augsburg and Antwerp (drawing: Christina Dalhede).

Fig. 8.4 Patrician houses at Maximilianstrasse 31–39 in Augsburg. From 1563 the Pemers owned the second house from the right (no. 37; Lit. A7 in Augsburg's *Grundbuch*), which had a copper roof and its own water closet. The Grills' address was Maximilianstrasse 33 (Lit. A5 in the *Grundbuch*). Members of the Pemer and the Grill families migrated to Sweden (photograph: Allan Dalhede).

the growth of their businesses and to avoid religious pressure the Pemers and their associates sent their children away from Augsburg, exploiting their relatives and business connections in order to do so.

Already in the 16th century Nicolaus I, the father of Nicolaus II, Daniel, Elias and Wolf II Pemer, made sure his sons were well prepared for their mercantile activities within and beyond the city: they studied at the University of Basel, and established connections with different firms in Europe and in the Fondaco dei Tedeschi in Venice. Daniel Pemer, the father of Nicolaus III, also prepared his son well to embark on his own mercantile career outside Augsburg.

After moving to Sweden in the 1630s, Nicolaus III Pemer started to work with the well-known De Geer merchant family in the mining district of Österby and in Stockholm.[21] Then, in the 1640s–50s, he was involved in the management of the big ironworks of Flögfors and Finnåker in the Swedish mining district of Bergslagen. At that time, the ironworks were rented from the Swedish Crown by Louis De Geer. In the 1650s Nicolaus III moved to Arboga where he continued his involvement in the iron trade exploiting his own and his family's wide connections. On his recommendation, his son-in-law, Jean Frumerie, took over the management of the ironworks in Finnåker. After Louis De Geer's death, the ironworks were sold by Nicolaus III to Gustaf Soop of Limingo, a *Riksråd* (member of the Royal Council) and Pemer's personal acquaintance. Iron products from Finnåker continued to be delivered to Arboga and to Pemer's relatives and partners in Stockholm, Gothenburg and other places in Sweden and abroad.

Nicolaus, his children and grandchildren married into many prominent families with mostly foreign backgrounds: the Scottish Petre family in Stockholm, the van Gents in Arboga, the Dreijlich family in Nora, the Schwardz family in Bergslagen and Arboga, the Schieurmanns in Falun, the Huberins in Stettin, and the Scottish Belfrage family in Karlstad. All these families were engaged in trade and manufacture, with a strong focus on metals. The Petre family in Arboga, Stockholm and Nora was trading in metals and textiles for example; the van Gent family owned ironworks and traded in military wares; and the Frumerie and the Dreijlich families had extensive connections in the mining district of Bergslagen. Nicolaus Pemer's eldest son, Nicolaus IV, married a daughter of the lord mayor Johan Dreijlich in Nora and was one of the founders of *Norra Bredsjö Hytta* (blast furnace). Jean Frumerie, who was married to Nicolaus Pemer's daughter and who followed Nicolaus Pemer as a manager of the ironworks in Finnåker, became later a part-owner of the ironworks in Wedevåg in the neighbourhood of Nora.[22] This shared interest in the industry and personal bonds provided trust and support, which helped these families to run and develop their operations.

In Sweden the Pemers, their relatives and associates continued their charitable work and commitment to the Protestant Church. Nicolaus's second daughter and her second husband, for example, donated expensive artefacts to the Arboga town church, such as two silver candlesticks, an antependium and a chasuble.[23] The Petre and the Höijer family donated the biggest brass chandelier in the same church. Members of the Pemer and Petre families were often noted in the church records as godparents in the baptisms of children from different families, who could belong to their relatives and friends as well as to business partners, employers, staff, clergymen, public officials and military officers of foreign or Swedish origin.

Arboga attracted not only the Pemers but a number of other families from southern Germany. Many of them followed Marcus Dieffstetter, who in the 1550s established the *Arboga Vapenfaktori* (arms factory).[24] Among the town burghers of south German origin was also the family of Leonhard Meyer, who migrated from Nuremberg to become involved in the copper trade in Sweden. The marriage and networking strategies of the Meyers show similarities to the practices of the Pemers.

With their multicultural family background and their experience growing up in the international merchant metropolis of Augsburg brimming with foreign merchants and goods, investment options and many cultural activities, the Pemers got a good start on their lives and careers. They could use their connections, capital and business engagements to link and expand their Augsburg trading networks by taking advantage of the investment and commercial opportunities available in Sweden, particularly in the sphere of ore extraction and metal industry.

The Grill Merchant Family

Another Augsburg family whose members sought opportunities and relocated to Sweden was the Grills. Since the early 16th century, the Grills had been living in Augsburg, marrying into German and other families.[25] In the late 16th century, Endres (Andreas) Grill was working as an innkeeper and wine merchant. He and his family were close neighbours of the Pemers in the main street, Maximilianstrasse, and they belonged to the same St. Anna's Lutheran church (Fig. 8.4). Grill's descendants worked within different branches of commerce and pre-industry, especially silver- and goldsmithery and mining, where they found recognition for their fine craftsmanship. Endres Grill's grandson Anthoni I and great-grandson Abraham Grill became famous across northern and central Europe for their filigree work. Many members of the Grill family married into goldsmith families in Augsburg, such as the Schierers, the Nathans, the Schweiglins, the Schandernells, the Kessborers and the Freys. Some of these families were related to the Pemer-Cristell family, too. Certain members of the Grills also migrated to Amsterdam where they married into Dutch and German families. Subsequently the first member of the Grills to arrive in Sweden found employment in branches of the metal trade and expanded beyond goldsmithery. Upon immigrating Anthoni Grill, for example, together with the De Rees and du Rietz families, was granted privileges in Lövåsens lead and silver works in 1655.[26] The Grills in Sweden married into the German Bremer merchant family in Stockholm, who owned a house at Stortorget (today known as the "Grillska Huset"). In the 18th century, the family grew in wealth and prominence thanks to well-calculated marriages, successful speculations and inheritances. They served as members, advisors and creditors of the Swedish court, and together with their continental relatives developed the Grill merchant house, moving commodities between Stockholm, Hamburg, Amsterdam and London. They also extended their involvement in the Swedish iron industry by becoming patrons of Österby ironworks, which they took over from the well-known De Geer family.[27] Parts of their wealth were invested in property – they owned several town houses in Stockholm and Uppsala and country estates in Godegård, Swindersvik, Österbybruk and Söderfors. Members of the Grill family were also involved in the Swedish East India Company (*Svenska Ostindiska Compagniet*, or *SOIC*) in Gothenburg, acting as supercargoes and directors of the Company.

Similarly to the Pemers, the skills and experience of the Grills and their international connections built prior to migration to Stockholm allowed them to secure lucrative positions and expand into other profitable ventures in Sweden. Throughout the 18th century, through marriages in the mercantile circles, investments and inheritances the family grew in wealth and prestige, maintaining and enlarging its connections with international merchant houses in Sweden and abroad.

The Foreign Merchant Families in Gothenburg

A considerable concentration of merchants with a continental background and connections lived in 17th- and 18th-century Gothenburg. The German Ehlers (Elers), Eilkinghs and Herweghs as well as the families of the Rokes, von Lengerkens, Dreÿers, Niebuhrs, Eggers, Engelkes and Felbiers, for example, belonged to the Hamburg-Lübeck colony in the city.[28] They all kept up continuing contacts with Hamburg and Lübeck through trade. The Engelkes married in Gothenburg into the German Möller-Kramer family and some of the above-mentioned families intermarried with each other (for example the Ehlers and the Eilkinghs), or formed marital bonds with other immigrant families. Sara Herwegh, for example, married into the Sahlgrens and became a female iron trader in Gothenburg.[29] Her eldest son Jacob engaged in the same business and her younger son Nicolaus was known as a wealthy benefactor, who donated funds to establish Sahlgrenska Hospital in Gothenburg and an orphanage outside it in Östad. As a teenager Nicolaus was sent to Amsterdam as an apprentice in the Tietzen & Schröder trading house. Upon return to Gothenburg he co-founded and acted as a director of the Swedish East India Company. The daughters in the Herwegh-Sahlgren family married into merchant families of multicultural backgrounds.

In the early 17th century Anthoni Schorer arrived in Sweden. His parents and other family members maintained an extensive trading network, which they personally supervised from their native Augsburg and the other major trading centres of Antwerp, Amsterdam and Hamburg. The Augsburg branch specialized in the silk and wool trade. The merchant family Haug, partners of Anthoni's family in Augsburg, was engaged in the mining industry and in the metal trade, dealing for example in Swedish copper. These families were also trading on the stock exchange in Lyon. The Schorer family belonged to the *Salzpartida* – a trading association – in Spain.[30]

Anthoni was born in Antwerp in the Spanish Netherlands, whence he moved to Amsterdam. He married twice, and went from Amsterdam to Archangelsk in 1610. His first wife was reportedly terrified about his voyage to Archangelsk and died instantly when she heard of his departure. He then married one Sara Hinckelboer from Hamburg and moved to Gothenburg, where he lived as a merchant. In the period 1622–33, together with other foreigners he received a privilege from the Swedish Crown granting the right to organize and control iron production in all mines and ironworks in the Östersysslet, the eastern part of the mining district in the county of Värmland.[31] Schorer and his companions, Jan and Jacob van Vosselen, Samuel Lott(er) and Godhart van Wachtendunck, also got permission to make iron cannon, which were then shipped to Europe via the harbour of Gothenburg. In March 1633, this business activity was taken over by Louis De Geer and the German Joachim Danckwart. The latter was engaged in trade and mining. Danckwart married at least three times and had about twenty children, of whom many lived in Norrköping and Nyköping (south of Stockholm) and in Bergslagen, owning and managing local ironworks.

Anthoni Schorer, his brother-in-law Willem van Castricum, and their associates Isaac Lot and Berent Jansz can be seen as exemplary entrepreneurs of their time. Their versatile business activities involved not only patronage of ironworks and weapons production and trade, but they also started a brandy distillery on the north side of the Göta river by Lindholmen (later moved to Gothenburg).[32] Schorer and the merchant family Amia were also involved in the copper trade and were active in bringing skilled foreign craftsmen to Gothenburg.

Members of Schorer's family married into the Antwerpian von Egmondt family, the German Lohmann family, the French Pinciers and the Danish Jürgensens. The Amias (Amyas) married into the Hertz (Hartz) family and into the German Tham family, thus becoming indirectly related to the von Savelands. All these families had a major stake in the Swedish mining and iron industry, which was shared with other members of the Hamburg-Lübeck colony in Gothenburg. Martin von Lengerken and Paul Rokes junior, for example, formed a joint-venture business specializing in the iron trade. The intermarriages between these families played out very well. Eilkingh was one of the early Gothenburg traders in Dalsland, at the time when Rokes founded the ironworks of Upperud in the province. Rokes was married to Jürgen von Lengerken's daughter, Marina, who had previously been married to the merchant Johan Eilking (d. 1659).[33] Martin von Lengerken, upon retirement, returned to his native Germany and in the early 1660s bought a farm in Minden, where he died. The merchant Johann von Minden was chosen as a guardian for von Lengerken's children. Thus in the city court on 30 June 1685 von Minden claimed the von Lengerken's inheritance on behalf of his underaged sons, Lorens and Gerhard.

Sibrant Valck, another Gothenburg resident with continental ancestry, had a different mercantile focus and web of connections. He was a wine merchant who in 1662 during a trip to Amsterdam married a local widow, named Maria Egbertsz Daelders.[34] Maria brought to the marriage her own circle of connections. Her first husband had been a native Antwerpian merchant, Henderick de Raet.[35] A sister of Maria Daelders married into the family of the Possemiers of Antwerp. Sibrant Valck's sister was married to the German Johan von Minden in Gothenburg. Valck and von Minden had a company together and were dealing in, among other things, timber, iron, salt, wine and alimentary goods. They were engaged in the sea trade and had several shares in vessels and ships sailing to and from Gothenburg. Their wives kept their own private account books, too. The trading radius of their merchant houses was wide, stretching between the Baltic Sea and the Spanish coast. Merchants from England and Scotland, Germany, France, Portugal and the Netherlands belonged to their commercial network.

These case studies show that very few of the newly-arriving foreign merchants in Gothenburg married into old Swedish families; and when this happened, the so-called "Swedish" family had a continental background, being second- or third-generation descendants of immigrants. Doubtless these marriage strategies served to preserve and strengthen the family's fortune, and cultivate continental culture, mercantile tradition and techniques.

REASONS FOR AND IMPACTS OF MIGRATION

Several important economic and social factors attracted immigration of continental merchants and entrepreneurs to Sweden. Expanding trading connections across the Baltic Sea, shipbuilding opportunities and the chance to tap into lucrative industries and gain monopolies or leases were perhaps of greatest significance. Metals, especially copper and iron, proved to be particularly strong magnets for foreign entrepreneurs, not least because the Crown offered generous conditions for investors with economic means and the necessary skills to operate ironworks and factories for which iron and copper were the major source materials (such as arms factories and brass foundries). Low competition and the ability to establish monopolies, such as that enjoyed by Schorer and his companions in the mining district of Värmland, or the similar monopolies granted to foreign entrepreneurs dealing in copper, tar and timber in Bergslagen and in

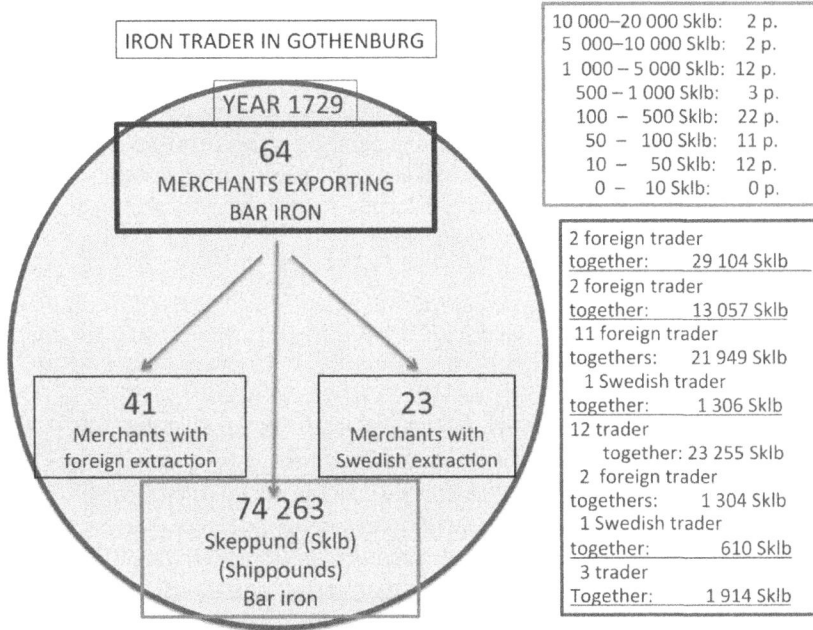

Fig. 8.5 Bar iron traders in Gothenburg in 1729: proportion of foreign to Swedish merchants, numbers of traders dealing in the largest quantities of bar iron (in Sklb = shippounds) and total of Sklb within the specified levels (1 Sklb = 136 kg in the staple cities). Source: GLA, Göteborgs Drätselkammare, Stadens räkenskaper, Huvudserien 1729 (drawing: Christina Dalhede).

western Sweden, contributed to the willingness to move and invest in the developing and profitable Swedish pre-industries. The effects of these policies and rush of foreign capital were already felt in the second half of the 17th century when metal trade became dominated by the companies and merchant houses founded by immigrant families. In Gothenburg, in the year 1729, almost two-thirds of bar iron traders were of foreign origin (and thus only a third were Swedes) (Fig. 8.5). The trade was highly concentrated: over 90% of the traded bar iron was in the hands of 19 merchants and merchant houses, while all but 3% of it was traded by 17 foreign merchants and merchant houses between the levels of 500 and 16,596 shippounds (1 shippound = 136 kg). The immigrants were also dealing in larger quantities of bar iron: they exported 65,414 of the total 67,330 shippounds traded within the specified levels over 500 shippounds (that is, 8,896,304 kg of the 9,156,880 kg traded).

Of significance too were privileges and freedoms that the ruling circles in Sweden were willing to grant to the immigrant merchants, including their exemption from a burdensome duty to lodge troops, and freedom to organize their own congregations. These freedoms were forcefully insisted upon in the immigrants' demands. The possibility of social advancement, political influence and ennoblement may have been an attractive "pull factor" as well.

A readiness to move in order to capitalize on economic opportunities and to contribute to the growth of familial enterprises was inculcated into merchants' upbringing and life-style. Perhaps it was especially strongly emphasized and embraced by the *Misch-Europäer* families, who could count on the support of relatives and exploit their cultural skills in different environments. The background and the connections of the family played a central role in 17th-century life and trade. Merchant families with mixed ancestry usually had more extensive networks, and thus more options to consider and take advantage of than those enjoyed by other families.

Migration was also looked upon as a way to save family businesses or to reinvent oneself. An interesting letter, left by German merchants and written during the period of difficulties and religious war experienced by 16th-century Antwerp in the Spanish Netherlands, provides valuable insight. It was addressed to the magistrate and asked for protection and time in order for the merchants to move their warehouses to other, safer places.[36] They then chose to move them to Middelburg, Cologne, Frankfurt, Hamburg and subsequently to Danzig. The move across the Baltic Sea proved a lifesaver for one merchant, Jacob Herwegh. He was thrown out of Lübeck, went to Lüneburg, and then arrived in Sweden "without a single thread on his body". In Sweden he became involved in the mining business and made a fortune, acquiring a considerable number of residential blocks and building sites.[37] The Herwegh family belonged to the Hamburg- Lübeck merchant colony in Gothenburg.

After relocating to Sweden the merchant families took care to reconstruct their household and home arrangements, transplanted and nurtured their continental traditions and practices and insisted on certain standards of education and spiritual care. They brought with them and continuously imported European literature, musical instruments, art, fine furniture, continental and colonial foodstuffs, clothes and textiles. Many of them had impressive private libraries. In Arboga, in the period 1652–1705, 13.4% of probate inventories left by craftsmen and merchants listed books. The literature showed great variety, with 475 titles in eight different languages.

The quantity of books and size of private libraries was even greater in Gothenburg. In the period 1663–1708, 42.5 percent of all preserved probate inventories recorded books, altogether 1,677 volumes in ten different languages. Merchant families tended to have more books, and were interested in different genres of literature than artisans, whose book collections focused on religious works. The libraries of the merchants included works on history, geography and travel. Merchant families of foreign origin, represented for example by Paul Rokes in Gothenburg and Hans Barckhusen in Arboga, had a wider selection of literature than other merchant families. Paul Rokes's library included specialized literature, such as *Probierbüchlein*, a technical handbook on assaying ores and metals, religious works, such as the Weimar Bible, Martin Moller's and Johan Michael Dillherr's postil, Joachim Lütkemann's *Epistel Postilla*, and non-religious literature on law, history and geography in German, Latin and Swedish. He even had a *Calendarium Gregorianum Perpetuum* (1583).

The Barckhusen family migrated to Arboga from Lübeck.[38] Just like his father, Hans Barckhusen was elected lord mayor in Arboga. He was an educated and well-travelled man and his cosmopolitanism was reflected in his book collection. His library consisted of at least 73 books (some inherited from his father), mostly of a non-religious character, written in German, Latin, Swedish, French and Dutch. The collection included works on law, history, geography, medicine and also fiction. One of Barckhusen's volumes was *Perspicillum Bellicum. Det ähr: Krigz-Perspektiv* written by a radical Bohemian thinker, Paul Felgenhauer, and translated to Swedish by Anders Kempe in 1664. Shortly after its translation the book was prohibited in Sweden and copies burnt.

Wealth, continental tastes and connections were also reflected in house furnishings and can be exemplified by the possessions of the Rokes. The family lived in a stone house on Gothenburg's main square (Stora Torget, today Gustaf Adolfs square).[39] The house consisted of two apartments and at least ten or eleven well-appointed rooms decorated with tapestries, diverse pieces of furniture, textiles such as *indiansk damast* and *indianiskt sängtäcke* – cotton and silk textiles imported from Asia – as well as Finnish, Dutch and other fabrics, and paintings (the family possessed 40 of these). They also owned musical instruments and a sizable library as well as multiple objects made of gold (104 *lod* or 1,385 kg), silver (2,440 *lod* or 32,452 kg), pearls (18 *lod* or 239 g) and precious stones (such as several diamond rings with a total of 21 stones).

The merchant families also lobbied for and financed the establishment of separate church congregations. Merchants migrating from southern Germany, for example, founded Lutheran churches based on the Augsburg Confession and established German schools, which upheld high standards of education. Schoolteachers were required to teach in the High German language (*Hochdeutsch*) and according to the Augsburg Confession. In Gothenburg and Norrköping the new inhabitants wished to have the power to choose their own clergymen and vicars.

To conclude: the desire to expand the area of business and the volume and quality of merchandise through entry into the new markets, as well as access to vital raw materials such as copper, iron, timber and tar, were all factors of central economic and social importance in encouraging the relocation of merchants in early modern times. Enlargement of the geographical scope of networks and international relationships had a great economic and social impact, and could help merchants to foster trust and creditability, which in turn enabled them to reduce risk and cut business transaction costs. For the credit market, these factors were crucial. Religion, infringements of rights and persecution, famine, wars and education can also be numbered among the possible social and economic factors motivating migration. The chance to reinvent oneself, start afresh after failed ventures, or advance one's own social position may have played a role as well.

COMMUNICATION BETWEEN FOREIGN MERCHANT FAMILIES IN SWEDEN AND ABROAD

Despite geographical distance, merchants residing in Sweden and their families living on the continent maintained communication with each other. News and messages were exchanged through official and private reports from the magistrate, clergymen and merchant agents, and by written and oral testimonies of travellers, visitors and consuls, skippers and supercargoes. Letters, however, remained the usual form of communication between merchants. Their delivery relied on couriers, skippers, consuls or the Swedish postal system, which was expanded in 1620 to include a line connecting Stockholm and Hamburg. Urgent matters were communicated through express letters signalled by a

tiny feather inserted into the seal (and thus called "feather letters"; Fig. 8.6). The feather
was not to be broken before the recipient held the letter in his or her hand.

Fig. 8.6 A rare feather letter of the 1750s from Värmland (source: Värmlandsarkiv,
Kyrkoräkenskaper, Frykeruds församling J I; photograph: Allan Dalhede).

Some of these business and private letters have been preserved, providing another
window on to merchant activities and daily business life. To the surviving correspondence belong, for example, letters of Nicolaus III Pemer written in Flögfors, Lindes-
berg, Finnåker and Arboga to De Geer's head office in Stockholm and to the office
in Norrköping.[40] The monthly letters contain information about the metal works:
anticipated production results, improvements proposed and introduced, market prices,
incoming and outgoing goods, drawn bills of exchange, condition of the workers and
other employees and agreements regarding transportation and delivery of foodstuffs.

There is also correspondence exchanged between Nicolaus, Nicolaus's son-in-law Peter
van Gent and his mother Barta van Gent, written from the Klockhammars bruk ironworks, and Elizabeth Pemer-van Gent's and Nicolaus Pemer's letters to the honourable
rent-master (*räntmästaren*) Börge Olofsson Cronberg in Stockholm, who was in charge
of the Swedish economy;[41] and letters exchanged between the members of the Walcke
family and written to their clients in Gothenburg and Hamburg in the 1790s.[42] The
Walcke business letters summarize business activities, the drawing of bills of exchange,
information about prices and the eventual difficulties of the venture.

It was foreign merchants who brought the technique of the bill of exchange – a cashless payment system – to Sweden. It constituted a very important type of business communication, securing payments in the credit market. It was crucial for merchants to be able to trust this payment system, and the firm or person paying the bill of exchange on their behalf.[43]

Newspapers, broadsheets, books and propaganda prints served as ways of exchanging information and communicating economic trends and political events between displaced members of the merchant families. The oldest newspaper in Sweden was founded in 1645, under the name *Ordinari Post Tijdender*. It was published once a week by the post-master in Stockholm and contained reprints from foreign newspapers, news supplied by domestic informants, correspondents and court agents living in the European metropolises, and information from the battlefields, along with war propaganda. Within Sweden the post trustee in different cities – often a merchant with good connections – had to deliver local news to the postmaster in Stockholm. This newspaper continued to be issued under different names (in the 1680s, for example it was published under the title *Mercurius*).[44]

Travel and family visits were another important way of socializing and maintaining close connections with each other. Events such as weddings, funerals and baptisms were important stages for gatherings of family, relatives and friends. These entailed coming together and reaffirming ties as well as forming new bonds, as for example in the case of baptisms of children. Acting as a godparent was associated with certain obligations to instruct and help the child through life. Such factors as trust, reliability, friendship or patronage were of great importance in the choice of godparents.

In the city of Gothenburg as well as in other Swedish centres with a substantial foreign presence, the merchants and burghers developed a system of representation in case a chosen godparent or witness in important ceremonies was unable to attend due to sickness, absence or travel. There are several examples of godparents from Hamburg being represented by someone else in Gothenburg, usually a member, friend or business partner of the family. Individuals of considerable position (a bishop or his wife, a member of the Pomeranian Governmental Council (*Regierungsrat*), a prominent merchant from Stockholm or elsewhere) who were present in the town at the time of baptism were also regarded as suitable godparents.

Family settings, geographical contact networks and international ties played a central role in early modern society and for migrating families.[45] So too did competence, loyalty, trust, credit and capital. The success or failure of immigrants in a new country, regardless of their occupation, depended on how and to what extent the individual, the family, the household and the company could shape trust around the family and their activities. Geographical contact networks, international connections, capital and credit were built on trust. Immigrants of *Misch-Europäer* extraction proved to be particularly resourceful in economic, social and cultural spheres of life in early modern Sweden – where they also maintained relations with the Swedish officials, clergymen, merchants and artisans.

NOTES

1 This chapter takes as the point of departure my research in Swedish and European archives, as well as my previous work. The concept of *"Misch-Europäer"* was first introduced in my PhD dissertation 'Oberdeutsche in Schweden' (University of Augsburg, 1993). See also n. 16.

2 Landsarkivet i Uppsala [ULA], Stadsarkivet i Arboga, Rådhusrätten, Protokoll 1674; Corin 1978, 473.

3 ULA, Stadsarkivet i Arboga, Rådhusrätten. Protokoll 1674; Dalhede 2009a, 142.

4 Stockholms Stadsarkiv [SSA], Stockholms Verifikationer.

5 Riksarkivet i Stockholm [RA], Enskilda arkiv, Momma-Reenstierna-Samlingen [MRS].

6 Landsarkivet i Göteborg [GLA], Göteborgs Drätselkammare, Stadens räkenskaper, Huvudserien. Tolagsjournaler, Båteböcker, Lilla Edets sluss Uppförslan. Nedförslan.

7 Dalhede 2001a, b, c.

8 Lind 1923; Dalhede 2001a, b, c; 2005b.

9 A database of about 40,000 noted cargo owners was made by Dalhede, using the *Tolag* journals in Gothenburg. See Dalhede 2001c, CD-ROM.

10 Häberlein-Jeggle 2010.

11 GLA, Enskilda arkiv. See also Dalhede & Andersson 2008.

12 Dalhede 2006a, 182–3.

13 Dalhede 2006, 62, 235–6.

14 Dalhede 2006c, 18–19.

15 Such a database is now under construction by the Preindustrial Research Group at the Department of Economy and Society/ Economic History, School of Business, Economics and Law, University of Gothenburg.

16 Dalhede 1993; 1998; 2006a, b; 2009a, b.

17 Wiberg (1874) and Pehrsson (1899) described Nicolaus Pemer (Bemer) as a Walloon. See Dalhede 1993 and 1998b, 342 for a different conclusion and family history.

18 On the Bader-van Uffelen firm in Antwerp and the Alewyns and Snoyens – relatives on Nicolaus Pemer's mother's side – see Dalhede 2005a, 197–222.

19 They were in some ways involved in the capital-intensive Hungarian ox trade and were able to take over important properties from members of the big butcher societies in Augsburg. Dalhede 1998, 1–2.

20 The *Reiche Steuer* was fixed to 500 Rhine florins at that time. The landlord and wine trader Endres Grill paid 2 florins and 45 *kreuzer*. However a city burgher could have wealth of up to 10 florins before he had to pay the capital tax. On personal estate one had to pay ½ per cent, on real estate ¼ per cent of the value of the properties. The Grills could have accumulated wealth of between 400 and 800 florins.

21 Dalhede 1993; 1998, 280–344.

22 The family's connections can be partially reconstructed from a probate inventory of Nicolaus's second daughter and her second husband written in Arboga in 1703. This childless couple divided their possessions among relatives and associates.

23 Dalhede 1988, 51–107; 1998, 132, 285, 315, 317, 449, 464–9, 476, 484.

24 Dalhede 1998, 285, 315, 317, 449, 464–9, 476, 484.

25 The origin of the Grill family is not quite certain. An Italian family origin, from Genoa, as well as a Dutch origin has been claimed. The family has been living in Augsburg for many generations. Dalhede 1998a, 1998b, 272–3, 578; 2009a, 35.

26 Dalhede 2009, 176.

27 Riksarkivet, Stockholm, Leufsta-arkiv. On the merchant houses Grill and Momma-Reenstierna and their activity as entrepreneurs in Sweden, see Samuelsson 1955 and Müller 1998.

28 Dalhede 2011.

29 The foreign bar iron export from Gothenburg was examined in Dalhede 2016, 65–76, 101–21, 186–93. In the period 1718–29, 20–21 female iron merchants exported 14,618 shippounds [Sklb] bar iron altogether, i.e. more than double the quantity of the 83 skippers combined. Dalhede 2016, 186–93. Around 6% of the merchants identified in Gothenburg were female. Dalhede 2012, 63–90, Tabell 1; Dalhede 2014, 269–306, Tabell 1, Tabell 3A–B.

30 Warnemünde 1956, 152–3. On the *Salzpartida*, see Ehrenberg 1896.

31 Dalhede 1998, 478.

32 Dalhede 2006a, 186–7, n. 21 specifies archival sources.

33 From her marriage with Johan Eilkingh, she had a son Hinrich Eilkingh junior; see GLA, Göteborgs Rådhusrätt och Magistrat tiden före 1900, 1662-08-25. Olga Dahls Privatarkiv,

Excerpter, von Lengerken.

34 Dalhede 2006a, 134.

35 Dalhede 2006a, 134–40.

36 Dalhede 1998, 298–9.

37 Olga Dahls Privatarkiv, Excerpter, Herwegh.

38 Dalhede 1991, 91–6.

39 Dalhede 2011, 88–96.

40 RA, Leufstaarkiv; Dalhede 1998.

41 RA, Enskilda arkiv, Börge Olofsson Cronbergs Samling.

42 On the Walcke family, see Andersson 2011, 120–1, 206, 208.

43 If anything went wrong the merchant had to act immediately by communicating a protest of the bill of exchange by the *notarius publicus*, in order to save his own payment and money.

44 Responsibility for the publishing of the newspaper was taken by the Royal Swedish Academy in 1791, and in 1821 by the still-existing *Post- och Inrikes Tidningar*. On cultural traffic and cultural transformation around the Baltic Sea, see Christensen 2003, 151–64; North 2011.

45 Dalhede 2009a, 8.

BIBLIOGRAPHY

Author's note: The bibliography contains both published and unpublished materials. For further clarification please contact the author.

Andersson, M. 2011. *Omvälvningarnas tid. Handelshuset Ekman i Göteborg på en europeisk kreditmarknad*. En tidig Europamarknad 4. Gothenburg: Preindustrial Research Group, Göteborgs universitet.

Christensen, S. T. 2003. 'Introduction', *Scandinavian Journal of History* 28(3–4): 151–64.

Corin, C.-F. 1978. *Arboga stads historia*. Vol. 2: *Från 1500-talets mitt till 1718*. Arboga: Arboga kommun.

Dalhede, C. 1988. 'En invandrarfamilj i andra generationen. Fallstudie av en bouppteckning', *Karolinska Förbundets Årsbok 1986*: 51–107.

Dalhede, C. 1991. *Den litterate borgaren. Punktstudier omkring handelsmän och deras litterära intressen utifrån bouppteckningar från perioden 1652–1825*. Gothenburg: Litteraturvetenskapliga institutionen, Göteborgs universitet.

Dalhede, C. 1993. *Zum europäischen Ochsenhandel: das Beispiel Augsburg 1560 and 1578*. St Katharinen: Scripta Mercaturae Verlag.

Dalhede, C. 1998. *Augsburg und Schweden in der Frühen Neuzeit. Europäische Beziehungen und soziale Verflechtungen. Studien zu Konfession, Handel und Bergbau, 1–2*. St. Katharinen: Scripta Mercaturae Verlag.

Dalhede, C. 2001a. *Handelsfamiljer på Stormaktstidens Europamarknad, 1. Resor och resande i internationella förbindelser och kulturella intressen. Augsburg, Antwerpen, Lübeck, Göteborg och Arboga*. Meddelanden från Ekonomisk-historiska institutionen, Handelshögskolan vid Göteborgs universitet 81. Partille: Warne förlag.

Dalhede, C. 2001b. *Handelsfamiljer på Stormaktstidens Europamarknad, 2. Resor och resande i internationella förbindelser och kulturella intressen. Augsburg, Antwerpen, Lübeck, Göteborg och Arboga*. Meddelanden från Ekonomisk-historiska institutionen, Handelshögskolan vid Göteborgs universitet 82. Partille: Warne förlag.

Dalhede, C. 2001c. *Handelsfamiljer på Stormaktstidens Europamarknad, 3. Resor och resande i internationella förbindelser och kulturella intressen. Augsburg, Antwerpen, Lübeck, Göteborg och Arboga* [CD-ROM]. Meddelanden från Ekonomisk-historiska institutionen, Handelshögskolan vid Göteborgs universitet 83. Partille: Warne förlag.

Dalhede, C. 2005a. '"Sara Baders" och Ulrich Bader på Stormaktstidens Europamarknad', *Släktforskarnas Årsbok 2005*: 197–222.

Dalhede, C. 2005b. *Tolagsjournaler under tidigmodern tid i Göteborg. Källmaterial och möjligheter. Projektrapporter Göteborg och Europa 1600–1800. Nr 1*. Rapport från Ekonomisk-historiska institutionen 17. Gothenburg: Ekonomisk-historiska institutionen, Handelshögskolan vid Göteborgs universitet.

Dalhede, C. 2006a. *Handelsfamiljer på Stormaktstidens Europamarknad, 4. Viner, kvinnor, kapital. En 1600-talshandel med potential. Fjärrhandelsfamiljerna Jeronimus Möller i Lübeck och Sibrant Valck i Göteborg.* Meddelanden från Ekonomisk-historiska institutionen 96, Göteborg. Partille: Warne förlag.

Dalhede, C. 2006b. *Handelsfamiljer på Stormaktstidens Europamarknad, 5. Varor & familjer, Lübeck & Göteborg* [CD-ROM]. Meddelanden från Ekonomisk-historiska institutionen 97, Göteborg. Partille: Warne förlag.

Dalhede, C. 2006c. 'Early modern merchant families. Foreign intermediaries in Swedish cities. The Gothenburg market in the 17th century'. Unpublished paper, 14th World Economic History Congress, Helsinki, 21–25 August 2006. [CD-ROM] http://www.helsinki.fi/iehc2006/papers1/Dalhede.pdf .

Dalhede, C. 2009a. *Invandrare som resurs. 1540–1820. Bland-européer och handelsfamiljer i Europa och Sverige. Kontakter, Krediter, Kultur.* En tidig Europamarknad 1. Gothenburg: Preindustrial Research Group, Göteborgs universitet.

Dalhede, C. 2009b. *Familjer, Förbindelser, Krediter, Kultur. 1540–1820.* En tidig Europamarknad 2 [DVD]. Gothenburg: Preindustrial Research Group, Göteborgs universitet.

Dalhede, C. 2011. 'Fjärrhandel på 1600-talets Europamarknad. Handelshus i Göteborg med engagemang i Värmland-Dalsland. Exemplen von Lengerken, Elers, Jürgensen, Eilkingh, Herwegh, Rokes', *Hembygden, Dalslands Hembygdsförbunds Årsbok* 2011: 49–124.

Dalhede, C. 2012, 'Kvinnliga handelshus – Handelsfamiljer med aktiva kvinnor 1638–1730', *Göteborg Förr och Nu. Göteborgs Hembygdsförbunds Skriftserie* 34: 63–90.

Dalhede, C. 2013. 'Eisen aus Göteborg. Beziehungsgeflechte schwedischer und norddeutscher Handelsfamilien im Frühneuzeitlichen westschwedischen Wirtschaftsraum', *Zeitschrift für Lübeckische Geschichte* 93: 121–65.

Dalhede, C. 2014. 'Preindustrial Flows and Contacts: Female Merchant Houses in Early Modern Times', in Denzel & Dalhede 2014, 269–306.

Dalhede, C. 2016. *Bundna Former, Fria Flöden. Handelshusens Göteborg före Svenska Ostindiska Compagniets tid. Europakontakter, Järn- och vinaktiviteter.* En tidig Europamarknad 5. Preindustrial Research Group, Göteborgs universitet.

Dalhede, C. & Andersson, M. 2008. *Tidigmoderna handelsböcker i svenska städer. Källmaterial och möjligheter.* Projektrapporter Göteborg och Europa 1600–1800. 2. Rapport från Ekonomisk-historiska institutionen, Handelshögskolan vid Göteborgs universitet 18. Gothenburg: Ekonomisk-historiska institutionen, Handelshögskolan vid Göteborgs universitet.

Denzel, M. A. & Dalhede, C. (eds) 2014, *Preindustrial Commercial History. Flows and Contacts between Cities in Scandinavia and North Western Europe.* En tidig Europamarknad 6. Gothenburg: Preindustrial Research Group, Göteborgs universitet/Beiträge zur Wirtschafts- und Sozialgeschichte (BWSG) 124. Stuttgart: Franz Steiner Verlag.

Ehrenberg, R. 1896. *Die Zeitalter der Fugger. Geld-, Kapital- und Kreditverkehr im 16. Jahrhundert.* 2 vols. Jena: Fischer.

Häberlein, M. & Jeggle, C. (eds) 2010. *Praktiken des Handels. Geschäfte und soziale Beziehungen europäischer Kaufleute in Mittelalter und früher Neuzeit.* Irseer Schriften N. F. Band 6. Konstanz: UVK-Verlag.

Landsarkivet i Uppsala [ULA], Stadsarkivet i Arboga, Rådhusrätten, Protokoll 1674.

Landsarkivet i Göteborg [GLA], Göteborgs Rådhusrätt och Magistrat tiden före 1900, 1662-08-25.

Landsarkivet i Göteborg [GLA], Göteborgs Drätselkammare, Stadens räkenskaper, Huvudserien, Båteböcker.

Landsarkivet i Göteborg [GLA], Göteborgs Drätselkammare, Stadens räkenskaper, Huvudserien, Lilla Edets sluss Uppförslan. Nedförslan.

Landsarkivet i Göteborg [GLA], Göteborgs Drätselkammare, Stadens räkenskaper, Huvudserien, Tolagsjournaler.

Landsarkivet i Göteborg [GLA], Enskilda arkiv.

Lind, I. 1923. *Göteborgs handel och sjöfart 1637–1920. Historisk-statistisk översikt.* Skrifter utgivna till Göteborgs stads trehundraårsjubileum genom jubileumsutställningens publikationskommitté 10. Gothenburg.

Müller, L. 1998. *The Merchant Houses of Stockholm, c. 1640–1800: A Comparative Study of Early-Modern Entrepreneurial Behaviour.* Studia historica Upsaliensia 188. Uppsala universitet.

North, M. 2011. *Geschichte der Ostsee. Handel und Kulturen.* Munich: Beck.

Olga Dahls Privatarkiv, Excerpter. http://www.gbgtomter.se [accessed 13 February 2015].

Pehrsson, P. 1899. *Ur Österby bruks och Vallonernas Krönika: Anteckningar till föreläsningar, hållna vid Österby 1898–1899.* Upplands Fornminnesförenings Årsskrift 20. Uppsala: Akademiska boktryckeriet Edv. Berling.

Riksarkivet i Stockholm [RA], Enskilda arkiv, Börge Olofsson Cronbergs Samling.

Riksarkivet i Stockholm [RA], Enskilda arkiv, Momma-Reenstierna-Samlingen [MRS].

Riksarkivet i Stockholm [RA], Leufsta-arkiv.

Samuelsson, K. 1955. *De stora köpmanshusen i Stockholm 1730–1815: en studie i den svenska handelskapitalismens historia.* Skrifter utg. av Ekonomisk-historiska institutet i Stockholm. Stockholm University.

Stockholms Stadsarkiv [SSA], Stockholms Verifikationer.

Värmlandsarkiv, Kyrkoräkenskaper, Frykeruds församling J1.

Warnemünde, C. 1956. 'Augsburger Handel in den letzten Jahrzehnten des 16. Jahrhunderts und dem beginnenden 17. Jahrhundert'. PhD dissertation, University of Freiburg.

Wiberg, C.-F. 1874. 'Louis De Geer et la colonie Wallone en Suède, au XVIIe siècle', *Bulletin de l'Institut Archéologique Liégois* 12: 438–82.

9

Aspects of "British" Migration to Sweden in the 17th Century

ADAM GRIMSHAW

While Scottish migration to Sweden has been extensively researched in recent years there has been little scholarship undertaken concerning migrants from other areas of Britain. This chapter therefore draws on established research on Scottish migration to Sweden in this period, as well as recent research focusing on the experience of English migrants. In comparing the experiences of the two, both continuities and differences will be examined, with the possibility of an extant "British" migrant community investigated. The chapter uses case studies ranging across the 17th century, focusing on areas in mainland Sweden as well as in Swedish Baltic possessions.

The contribution of foreigners to the development of Sweden during the 17th century has been firmly established for some time. The roles of Dutch and German migrants have been singled out in particular. However, an appreciation of the significance of Scottish immigration to Sweden in this period is much less widespread, and development of this has been largely left to the efforts of Scottish historians in recent times. Comprehension of the role played by the English has remained largely overlooked. Continuing the study of British migrants to Sweden during this period advances our understanding of migrant groups as a whole. By viewing the experience of the English and Scots we increase our knowledge of mobility during the period. This is achieved in two respects: in regard both to mobility through migration and mobility through social elevation. We also begin to touch upon ideas of interaction in several ways: how the British elements of Swedish migrant communities interacted with members of their host society, as well as with other foreign ethnicities and members of their own nation. Furthermore, the study of British migrants enriches our understanding of Sweden as a place of cultural diversity and a centre of impact of foreign activity.

This chapter outlines some of the key features in the historiography of British migration to Sweden in the 17th century. The discovery of unexploited archival material in Sweden, as well as the undertaking of a new research project focusing on Anglo-Swedish trade in this period, warrants an evaluation of the subject. The chapter therefore seeks to readdress previous conclusions, whilst querying how new material might add to present understandings.

Four separate localities have been given attention, according to the value and availability of archival sources as well as historiographical background. The first two areas considered are Stockholm and Gothenburg, which represent the portion of the study that deals with British migration to the Swedish mainland. The third area under consideration is Finland, with particular emphasis on Åbo. Finally, Sweden's Baltic possessions are represented by the inclusion of Narva. Sweden's control over port cities such as Elbing, Pillau, Memel and even those in the Trøndelag region, was transitory, and they are thus not considered in this study. German areas such as Bremen-Verden and Pomerania, although in Swedish hands for a longer period of time, are likewise left unconsidered.[1]

Case studies have been limited to English migrants in an attempt to redress the balance of knowledge of English migration in comparison to the wealth of existing work on the Scottish experience. Current research aims and the nature of available archival material have resulted in a focus on those English who were engaged in broadly mercantile activities. Military aspects of both Scottish and English migration have been sufficiently covered in previous works.[2]

The last decade has seen a determined effort to study British migration to continental Europe, with the publication of several collections of essays focusing upon the topic.[3] These cover a wide geographical and intellectual scope, bolstering understanding of the phenomenon in relation to the 17th century. At present, however, coverage of English migration in this period severely lags behind that of the Irish, and particularly the Scottish experience. In part, this can be attributed to the sheer dominance in numbers of Scots who migrated to the continent, as well as the impact they had on their host societies. It would also appear to reflect a preferred focus of historians of England, who have tended to concentrate their efforts elsewhere.

Awareness of Scottish migration to Scandinavia, in particular Sweden, has been reflected for quite some time. Early studies identified some of the individuals who migrated in the 17th century, but did little to link their experiences.[4] Further attempts to build on this research have also been undertaken by scholars based in Sweden.[5] Other Swedish scholars, meanwhile, have frequently come across Britons who migrated and traded with Sweden when researching quite separate subjects, such as town histories. This feature is particularly prominent in the case of Gothenburg.[6]

The aforementioned wider wave of British scholarship examining migration to continental Europe in general is perhaps most detailed in regard to Sweden in particular. Through a variety of publications, Alexia Grosjean and Steve Murdoch have provided the most comprehensive scholarship on the various facets of Scotland's relationship and interaction with Sweden to date.[7] Beyond commercial associations, diplomacy, and the military involvement of Britons in Swedish service, their research has sought to quantify and characterize Scottish migration and community-building in Sweden.[8]

These advances in our understanding were built on a foundation of archival material taken from both Britain and Scandinavia, and constitute the first research on British associations with Sweden to have adopted this approach. Grosjean and Murdoch have revealed how Scottish migrant communities in Sweden were still in contact with their homeland as well as with other communities across the Baltic and Scandinavia, such associations being particularly prominent in regard to commercial activity.[9] Among other important advances, their research was able to highlight how Scottish military service in Sweden was inherently connected to a migratory influx thereafter, and how this service and migration was in turn fostered through political cooperation.[10] According to surviving records, the influx first began during the first half of the 16th century and peaked during the early decades of the 17th.[11]

In line with what was said above, English migration to Sweden has received significantly less attention than its Scottish counterpart. Much of the scholarly focus on English interaction with Scandinavia and northern Europe in this period can be found in works devoted to trade, specifically relating to the English Eastland Company.[12] In contrast to the more recent findings of how embedded Scottish migrants in Sweden and the Baltic facilitated trade and interaction with their homeland, nothing has been said of the role of English migrants.[13] Much of the focus is upon how the English controlled trade from English ports. There has been little attribution of significance to those English traders who stayed in the region, let alone any attempt to identify and quantify their presence through consultation of archival material.

The present study deals with a variety of aspects of migration surrounding the question of interaction and integration. A historiographical treatment, along with selected case studies, draws out some of the key aspects for discussion. A primary area to consider is that of familial ties, such as marriage and guardianship of children, awareness of which can help to reveal, when attempting to trace commercial or civic alliances, what kinds of network and association were in place, as well as how families interacted with the various ethnicities inhabiting early modern Swedish towns. Further aspects to consider are the gaining of citizenship and social elevation, in as much as these reflect the willingness of particular groups of migrants to become part of the host society, and the advantages that were open to them, and provide achievement standards against which it is possible to determine the success of migrant group.

THE BRITISH IN STOCKHOLM

In recent years, Scottish migration to Stockholm has received significant attention which has shown how the Stockholm Scots were part of one of the oldest, most numerous and influential migrant communities in Sweden.[14] Indeed, one of the main benefits in migrating to Stockholm was the proximity to institutions of influence and the centre of the Swedish political power base. The civic and national bodies that Scots came to be a part of contained some of the wealthiest and most influential individuals in Sweden. Access to these institutions could (and often did) provide an important avenue for the rise in influence of the individual, but in a wider sense also increased the strength of the migrant community to which a person belonged.

While advantages of influence may not have been a palpable feature in determining a migrant's choice to settle in Stockholm, there were more obvious advantages. Not only was Stockholm the centre of government, it was also the most important commercial port for Swedish trade.[15] This factor drew many Scottish merchants to the area from as early as the 16th century, and over the course of the 17th.

The first Scottish migrants appeared in Stockholm in the first half of the 16th century, and by 1569 there were approximately 30 settled in the town.[16] As early as the 1570s Stockholm's *vågböcker* (weigh-books) note two unnamed Scots as being responsible for a combined 10% share of the town's overall trade.[17] By the latter quarter of the century there was a wave of Scottish merchants who had settled in the town and chose to take oaths of burgess-ship, demonstrating their commitment to a permanent life in Sweden.[18]

Scottish merchants were able to diversify their activities to trade in a variety of goods, from Swedish staples such as iron, copper, timber and tar,[19] to luxury goods such as tobacco: a possible indicator of their existing ties with the British Isles and accessibility to re-exports of colonial goods. Their tenacity in commerce, their web of contacts, and their willingness to take on the benefits of native Swedish trading status through oaths of burgess-ship, led to their success. These factors combined meant that during the period 1601–1707, over 150 identifiable Scottish merchants operated out of Stockholm with burgess status.[20]

Commercial diversification did not end in commodities traded. The Scottish merchants of Stockholm were also involved in the production of Swedish raw materials that were exported across Europe. Scottish families who had settled in Stockholm were able to use their wealth to invest significantly in Swedish production, in a manner akin to more frequently cited Dutch examples.[21] In the past, Swedish historians have been quick to laud the success and mastery of the Dutch in relation to the development of Swedish industry in this period, to the detriment, unfortunately, of an appreciation of the quiet success story of the Stockholm Scots. These immigrants combined knowledge and riches gained from years engaged in Swedish commerce, enabling them to manoeuvre into a position whereby they could gain a tighter hold through access to production. The defining factor was probably their access to foreign credit and capital, most likely from existing familial connections in the British Isles and in the Netherlands. As is well known, foreign capital had a stranglehold on Swedish production, and it was through these connections to foreign capital that native merchants were often outplayed when it came to gaining access to production.

Aside from the commercial edge of the Stockholm Scottish community, there was a significant element of Scottish ex-military personnel, who had served in Sweden and came to settle in Stockholm. By 1660, 47 Scotsmen, mostly comprising ex-soldiers, had been ennobled in Sweden and introduced into the *Riddarhus* (House of Nobility).[22] The 1634 *Riksråd* (Privy Council) had debated whether the sons of foreigners who had been ennobled also had the right to noble status. It was eventually decided that those Scots who were nobles in Britain would have to produce proof of their status. In contrast, the sons of those Scotsmen who had served Sweden and been ennobled in due course had the right to enter the *Riddarhus*.[23] This attitude indicates that in Sweden merit and service were highly valued. It also indicates another avenue available for foreigners to rise through the ranks of Swedish society, aside from the wealth and influence merchants accrued from their commercial endeavours.

It is unknown when the first English began to arrive in Stockholm. The earliest evidence of a possible English community is from 1573, when the Stockholm *tänkeböcker* (court records) note four English merchants as residing in the town.[24] There were also two possible Englishmen with the surname "Engelsman", who were hired as shipwrights amongst a larger body of Scottish shipwrights in the first decade of the 17th century.[25]

The established view is that the English did not begin to arrive in Stockholm in any significant numbers until the 1650s. It has been stated that a shift in commercial patterns brought the English to Stockholm, but there are conflicting opinions as to what caused this realignment.[26] A major aspect that came into play was Sweden's increasing control over its own exports. Previously Sweden had exported raw materials from Stockholm to ports such as Danzig (modern Gdańsk), where they were dressed and finished. Over the course of the 17th century, the southern Baltic middlemen were cut out of the process.[27] This factor is probably what began to draw increasing numbers of English merchants to Stockholm around the middle decades of the century.

The 1650s saw the first direct diplomatic relations between England and Sweden in over 50 years, and Bulstrode Whitelocke's negotiations in Stockholm in 1654 resulted in the Treaty of Whitehall in 1661.[28] Though increasing diplomatic contact certainly facilitated direct trade, there were two episodes in particular that gave the English an inroad into Stockholm. Both were associated with control over shipping, where the English profited from their neutral position in times of war to the detriment of the Dutch.[29] The first instance was in 1659 when the Dutch were allied with Denmark-Norway against Sweden. A similar situation arose during the Scanian War (1675-9) when the Dutch were once again allied against Sweden. This prevailing political situation served to cut out not only Swedish but more importantly Dutch shipping, at a time when the Dutch were the principal carriers of Swedish goods to the west. English freighters exploited the advantage of their neutral status, and assumed the role that the Dutch had formerly occupied.

With English shipping came English merchants. By 1675, the chief secretary to the English ambassador to Sweden, William Allestree, was able to state, "wee have a Factory of about 30 persons, some from London, but most from Hull and York. Here is also a considerable body of Scotch merchants."[30] Whether the "body" of Scottish merchants Allestree refers to were some of the burgesses already discussed, or whether they were itinerant traders based in Britain is currently unknown. It is possible to deduce from Allestree's confident proclamation, and his reference to the "factory" of merchants, that these men were probably a more permanent feature of the population of Stockholm, rather than traders who only intended to stay for the short trading season. Allestree's merchants and their later counterparts have received some scholarly attention.[31] However, the nationality and status of these merchants in scholarly works covering English trade has been misunderstood. Some Scottish merchants have wrongly been claimed as English, and there has been little attempt to determine what status these traders held in Sweden.[32]

Although the present understanding of English trade to Stockholm needs re-evaluation in itself, it also needs to undergo a switch in focus to view its impact on migration. In addition, there are unexploited archival sources to be consulted. The most lucrative are the court records of the *Svea hovrätt* (Svea Court of Appeal). At present over 190 people of British extraction have been identified in them for the period of 1615–80 alone, stretching over 500 potentially independent court cases. A considerable number of the individuals mentioned in these records are already-known migrants entered into the *SSNE* database.[33] However, there are a number of previously unknown Scottish and English names that warrant further investigation. Further sources to consult include the English Court of Chancery records which detail individual court cases. The cases themselves, though often not complete, provide a previously unknown glimpse into the business affairs, network of contacts and structure of trade involved in British-Swedish commerce.

As already noted, it is generally implied that English merchants did not make their way to Stockholm until the 1650s.[34] However, through consultation of new sources it has been possible to bring to light some details of an English merchant living in Stockholm in the early decades of the 17th century. John Coote, a London merchant, is first mentioned in the *Svea hovrätt* in 1614. His name also appears in 1619 and 1620, but by 1621 he was deceased, as a court case involving his widow is mentioned.[35] Having identified Coote, additional information has been uncovered in the Chancery records. This case demonstates that a merchant's identification in one source can facilitate the extraction of information pertaining to him from repositories elsewhere. Moreover, there are several interesting points to mention in relation to Coote's status as an English migrant in Sweden. Despite previous emphasis on English merchants acting as itinerant agents, who only stayed in Sweden for the short trading season over the spring and summer months, Coote's court cases stretch over a period of four years. It is possible that Coote stayed in Stockholm for a period of up to six years. However, further research needs to be undertaken to determine whether these court cases deal with separate issues or are parts of a longer, drawn out procedure.

The court case of 1614 sees Coote acting as representative for a Patrick Rutherford (Rudderfurt), where money matters are discussed in relation to trade with England.[36] Rutherford was a Scot and the case is representative of the cooperation and support that existed between the English and Scottish migrants in Stockholm.[37] It helps us to visualize how Britons interacted abroad, and provides an instance that goes some way to determining whether "Scottish" or "English" communities had a wholly "British" element to their character.

The Chancery records contain a case from the early 1620s on behalf of Coote's widow, Mary. The case involves Mary's supplications for her right to claim money from the widow of London merchant William Greene. The court case states that Coote was in Stockholm acting as an agent for Greene, who was selling goods directly to the king of Sweden.[38] Thus what may initially appear as relatively small discoveries in archival sources can go a long way towards answering questions surrounding the status, as well as the interaction, of English and Scottish migrants.

Having shown that English merchants were present far earlier than historiographical convention tells us, we may also enquire what commodities they were involved in trading. Regardless of who facilitated this trade, the increasing importance of the English market for Swedish exports and the larger share the English freighters had in the carrying trade for these goods, was reflected in the number of English merchants who settled in Stockholm in the latter decades of the century. Examination of the conflicts due to rival interests that developed between different groups, occasioned by the presence and actions of British traders in the city, provides significant insight into the status these individuals enjoyed, as well as the nature of their interaction with various communities in Stockholm.

The complaints of local merchants concerning non-naturalized Englishmen throughout the period can be traced primarily to two concerns. Firstly, those English residents in the town who had not taken citizenship were, as foreigners, exempt from local taxation. Secondly, the Stockholm merchants despised foreign attempts illegally to undercut their position by sourcing goods directly from production areas or non-staple ports in the region.[39]

The laws regarding the position of foreign traders in Swedish trade areas had long been established.[40] The problem of enforcement did not necessarily lie in a lack of desire or resources to police the issue. It lay rather in the increasing influence that the English market and its traders came to play in Sweden's export trade and subsequently in the financing of credit used to fuel production.

The conflict raged largely unabated from the beginning of the 1670s. It quickly spilled over into international politics, with successive English diplomatic missions to Sweden instructed to safeguard the traders' interests, demonstrating how important Swedish goods were to the English market.[41] Matters came to a head in 1696 when the Swedish government gave the English traders two options. One was to be allowed to stay provided they took Swedish citizenship and agreed to obey Swedish laws. The other was to leave Sweden at the end of the trading season. They would be allowed to return but would have to abide by Swedish trading regulations and limit their stay and business in Sweden to only eight weeks per year. Many of the English merchants elected to leave and large numbers of the "English" colony described by Allestree in 1675 were not to be seen again.

This little-known episode in relations between England and Sweden has received poor coverage from scholars. The conflict has been viewed through a diplomatic lens,[42] but has never been considered as part of the history of migration and interaction between the two countries. A reappraisal of the conflict is necessary, due to the discovery of additional archival sources, but especially so because of the more recent advances in our understanding of Scottish migration to Stockholm,[43] and also to Gothenburg.[44]

THE BRITISH IN GOTHENBURG

The British in Gothenburg have been given considerably more coverage than their counterparts in Stockholm. Historians such as Wilhelm Berg, Hugo Fröding and Helge Almquist introduced some of the better-known Scottish migrants who featured in the town's early history. However, no significant efforts were made to view these migrants as an identifiable group and thence pose questions therefrom.

Major inroads into the study of Scottish migration to Gothenburg were made with Grosjean's and Murdoch's research, mentioned above, into the various ties between Scotland and Sweden in this period. This research not only produced the most accurate study of the various facets of Scottish migration to the city and aspects of community-building once settled, but also provided the most significant quantification of the "British" migrant community as a whole.[45]

Where Stockholm held out the potential for a rise in social standing and influence through admission to a variety of government institutions, Gothenburg by contrast remained a developing town for a large part of the 17th century (Fig. 9.1). Its appeal to British migrants was mostly commercial. The town's founding charter allowed for a 15-year tax exemption on all trade, intended to induce foreign merchants with foreign capital, provided they settled and adopted burgess status.[46] The Swedish Crown was well aware of the potential influence of the Scots and their mercantile connections due to their presence in preceding settlements in the area. Accordingly they ensured Scottish political representation by allowing that community to fill two designated seats on the

Fig. 9.1 A plan of Gothenburg from 1655. The plan details the town's grid system, as well as its man-made and natural defences. The river is situated at the bottom of the picture. (*Gotho Burgum Urbs Praecera Emporium Celebre Portus Aptissimus Anno 1655*, Stads- och fästningsplaner, Göteborg 683; reproduced by courtesy of the Military Archives in Stockholm).

town council at all times.[47] Alongside the Scots, the native Swedes were represented by four seats, and the Germans and Dutch with three seats apiece. This composition shows that the Scots were part of a multicultural Swedish outpost from the very beginning.

Much of the research that has been undertaken on the Scottish community in Gothenburg was based on invaluable sources such as the German church records that detail baptisms, marriages and burials.[48] In addition, there are also extant burgess lists, which were published by Erland Långström,[49] as well as the town's surviving toll records. This foundation helped to bring about the advanced understanding of the Scottish community's social interactions, as well as its trading connections, that we have today.

Up until this point, Gothenburg's *domböcker* (various town court records) have remained underexploited as far as the study of British migration to Gothenburg is concerned.[50] The court records detail both the minutes of the town council's sessions and the progress of individual court cases. In addition, they divulge the composition of the town council, so that it is possible to view who occupied the seats over a period, and how the council changed over time. The ecords begin in 1635 and have yielded from then until 1657 over 800 instances of Britons being involved in court cases, although some refer to itinerant merchants, not migrants. Even at a brief glance the records reveal the various types of connection that British migrants maintained within the town. With more rigorous scrutiny it is possible to determine familial ties, and through commercial disputes it is also possible to trace what business associations existed.

At present it is difficult to determine whether any ethnic prejudice was directed towards either the Scottish or English elements of Gothenburg's migrant community. The court cases do however reveal that the subject matter of disputes was overwhelmingly business-related, and that there was a level of infighting in the community, as well as disputes with other migrant groups and Swedes alike.[51]

In addition to the discovery of additional archival sources, Olga Dahl's database, *Göteborgs tomtägare* (register of Gothenburg landowners) provides an almost exhaustive evaluation of the make-up of 17th-century Gothenburg.[52] The database is organized according to plots of land in relation to a mapped-grid system of the town. Over 60 individuals have currently been identified who are not currently represented in the *SSNE* database.

It is difficult to find any distinctive marriage pattern among the Scottish community. It seems Scots were just as likely to marry within their own ethnic community as they were with migrants of other nationalities, or even with native Swedes.[53] Scots were not oblivious to the potential benefits that union by marriage could afford, whether these benefits were for commercial or civic purposes, or purely for social elevation.[54]

A significant element among the Scottish mercantile migrants opted to take the oath of burgess-ship in Gothenburg, and duly became active traders as well as active members of the community. Although many of the surviving burgess lists are incomplete for some years, Grosjean and Murdoch also consulted the town's toll records to show a total of 50 Scots who became burgesses in the course of the century.[55]

In addition to their trading activities, and like their counterparts in Stockholm, many members of the Gothenburg Scottish community assumed civic positions in the town. As noted above, the town council provided two seats for members of the Scottish community, and in most sessions had at least one Scot present.[56] At certain points during the 17th century the Scots occupied the top, presidential, positions on the council, although they did not reach these heights until John Spalding became president of commerce in 1658.[57]

Unlike the case of the Stockholm Scots, there was less access to institutions of influence at a national level in Gothenburg. However, it was not impossible for those in the city to rise above the limits of the civic offices of the town itself. John Maclean appears to be the first Gothenburg Scot to have operated at a national level, when he attended the *Riksdag* on behalf of the town in 1649.[58] He was followed some years later by president John Spalding, who appeared in 1660 and 1664.[59] Representing the town at the *Riksdag* presented an important opportunity to not only court favour for one's career or business interests, but to air grievances or damage rivals in the town. Maclean and Spalding show how social elevation to the highest level, as well as ennoblement and entry into the *Riddarhus*, was possible for the Gothenburg Scots.

Civic opportunities were not limited to sitting on the town council. Henry Sinclair was a member of the burgess community and occupied the coveted position of chief toll officer in the town from 1627.[60] Nobody in a position of civic authority (including the toll officers) was restricted from participating in trade. By holding influence in local government, having a powerful credit base, forming a network of contacts across northern Europe, being part of a tight-knit community of merchants and furthermore obtaining a vital post such as customs officer, it is not hard to see how the Scottish mercantile community could have been very influential, if not the dominant element, in early Gothenburg.

English migrants to Gothenburg in this period appear fairly infrequently in the early literature. As is the case with Stockholm, the sources cannot always be trusted to state accurately whether a particular migrant was English or Scottish. The first survey to centre on the English experience was undertaken by John Ashton, and alluded to some of the key English migrants who were present in the town. However, there was little attempt to scrutinize them in terms of wider questions surrounding migration and community.[61] Ashton's study serves as a cornerstone insofar as it recognizes the significance of this community in regard to its place in the early history of the town. Grosjean and Murdoch were the first to attempt a quantitative estimate of the English who settled in Gothenburg.[62] So far there are 21 English residents listed as having been present in the town during the entire century, ten of whom possibly held burgess status.[63]

One of the first Englishmen we know of in Gothenburg was Anthony Knipe. His experience is fairly atypical when measured against the involvement of others. He thus serves to demonstrate what was possible, rather than what was commonplace. By using Knipe as an example, we can to answer a variety of questions concerning migration to Gothenburg, regarding matters such as familial ties, occupational roles and social advancement, as well as business associations and disputes.

Knipe first appears in 1631 in the marriage registers of the German church, when he married Maria Langer.[64] Langer is likely to have been the relation of an early Gothenburg burgess and councillor, Dutchman Peter Langer, or possibly a relative of *burggreven* (chief military officer/town mayor) Holsteiner Daniel Lange. From the outset it is thus revealed as possible for an English migrant marry outside his own ethnic group, or even the wider British community. Furthermore, Langer had two children from a previous relationship, two boys named Peter and Francis de Bloch. In addition to his two step-sons, Knipe had a daughter of his own with Langer, also named Maria. Knipe provides an excellent example, not only of how a British migrant could settle and raise a family, but of the extent to which it was possible to foster multi-ethnic families in Gothenburg.

From his initial appearance in the marriage register of 1631, Knipe rose to consider-able power in Gothenburg over the next few years. In 1635, under royal prerogative, he was placed on the town council.[65] It is difficult to determine within which ethnic group Knipe sat on the council. It would appear from the make-up of the council sessions that Knipe sat next to a Scotsman, John Young (Hans Jung). Although it was stated above that two seats on the council were reserved for Scotsmen, Knipe's presence suggests that the seats were more likely designated for men of British origin, despite *skotske* being the term applied to them.[66]

Knipe's appointment to the council came in connection with his involvement in the development of a Crown-backed monopoly company based in Gothenburg, which was geared toward the English market. The investors of the English Company of Gothen-burg successfully obtained support from the town council and then royal backing from Stockholm within a matter of a few months, and were established by 1635.[67] Merchants of any ethnic origin were permitted to enter provided they were merchant burgesses of the town. The investment lists for 1635 and 1636 include a variety of English, Scottish, Swedish and Dutch or German names. It was stipulated that a merchant of English origin must head the company, and Anthony Knipe was thereby appointed.[68] Although the company became insolvent by 1637, this venture serves as a prime example not only of how the English and Scottish elements of the migrant community interacted with one another commercially, but also of how this wider British venture interacted with other migrant groups as well as native Swedes. The stipulation that an Englishman was to head the enterprise highlights how the British merchants of the town still had connections with their homeland, and how these connections were prized enough to sanction the need for a company to control trade.

After the company failed, Knipe's career nevertheless went from strength to strength, and by 1639 he was sitting on the town council as president of commerce. Although Scots comprised the majority of the British in town, Knipe was the first Briton to become a president. His rise through the ranks points to the possibilities that were open not only to Scotsmen, but also to the English. It is unknown whether the presence of Scots in the town would have aided or have hindered Knipe's rise, as an Englishman. However, Knipe's wife Maria Langer appears to have been related to at least one of the influential Gothenburg civic elite. It is likely that these familial ties boosted Knipe's chances to elevate his social position, as well as his influence and power.

Familial ties may thus go some way to explaining his success, but Knipe must have also had some business acumen, and a variety of contacts, as well as talent as a commercial operator. By the time of his presidential appointment, he was associ-ated with the highest-ranking statesmen in the realm. His surviving correspondence reveals both the extent of his social elevation and the nature of his business dealings. A substantial body of correspondence exists between Knipe and Swedish chancellor Axel Oxenstierna. Most of it concerns commercial matters, but Knipe also regularly called on Oxenstierna to help remedy his problems in Gothenburg, demonstrating at some level a personal relationship.[69] Knipe's correspondence clarifies some of the ambiguity surrounding his commercial affairs: despite probable commercial connections back in London, his involvement in the Gothenburg English Company and his appointment as president of commerce, he is absent from the town's toll records.[70] It has since been revealed that he acted as an agent for the Swedish Crown, was personally answerable to Chancellor Oxenstierna, and imported a variety of goods from Britain and elsewhere.[71] Knipe provides an example of an English migrant playing a vital role in the functioning of the Swedish state.

Not only do Knipe's familial, civic and commercial ties exemplify the extent of his interaction and integration within the wider Gothenburg community, but a number of disputes he was involved in have come to light through the discovery and scrutiny of the town's court records. British migrants appear in the court records with alarming frequency, pointing either to the extent of their commercial dealings, or to their propensity for conflict. Even within this context, Knipe stands out as especially troublesome. The records show how he engaged in disputes with fellow Englishmen, Scotsmen, members of the wider migrant community and native Swedes, as well as with his fellow councillors.[72] Tracing associations such as this highlights the complicated and entangled relationships of British migrants in early Gothenburg.

Although we know Knipe became a burgess, the citizenship status of other English residents in the town remains unclear. Francis Sheldon, originating from Hull, was hired as a master shipbuilder to the Gothenburg *Masthugget* shipyard in the spring of 1659.[73] His shipbuilding activities and the difficulties he encountered with the established Dutch shipbuilders have been documented.[74] Sheldon also moved between Gothenburg and Stockholm before spending several years back in the British Isles, and was ultimately posted to Riga under Swedish service.[75]

Sheldon's experience therefore reveals how with employment in Swedish service, it was possible to relocate geographically to a variety of posts across the Swedish domains. Although his role as a shipbuilder has been previously explored, little is known of his citizenship status while in Sweden. Sheldon was a Crown-appointed employee of the Swedish realm, but it does not appear that he became a burgess in Gothenburg or elsewhere in Sweden. However, through consultation of English sources it is clear that, in addition to his artisan employment, Sheldon developed commercial connections, despite his omission from the town's toll records. Throughout 1668 and 1669, he was working as a commercial agent for the English Royal Navy (in Sweden), in close connection with timber magnate Sir William Warren who was based in London. For example, it appears that Sheldon was responsible for organizing the supply of timber and its shipment from Gothenburg.[76] Although many of Gothenburg's more influential British migrants adopted a plurality of civic and commercial roles, Francis Sheldon demonstrates how it was possible to spread financial interests over two occupations, and in multiple locations, while actually serving two Crowns at the same time. Furthermore, the Sheldon family stands as an example of an English dynasty of shipbuilders that established themselves in Sweden. Francis Sheldon's sons both became shipbuilders in Sweden and the family line there was maintained.[77]

The final English migrant to be considered here is Maccabeus Thornton, a merchant who was active in the later decades of the 17th century. Thornton's origins are unclear, but he had probably been active in the town for some time before he became a burgess of Gothenburg in 1685.[78] Thornton's trading activity exemplifies the Gothenburg English mercantile community's strong connections with the British Isles, but it was his activities within the town that demonstrate some particularly interesting features. He appears to have been an active member of the migrant community. In March 1683 merchant Lars Bratt requested to abstain from obligations of guardianship to Scotsman Robert Clerck's children on the grounds that he could not understand either Scots or English. It was decided by the town's court that someone who could understand these languages should be appointed. After a lengthy period of three years, Maccabeus Thornton stepped forward to act as legal guardian to the children.[79] The more specific details of the case are unknown, and it is therefore difficult to speculate why it took so long to appoint a new guardian, or whether the date merely marked the confirmation of an already-existing arrangement. Regardless, this episode reveals how English and Scottish migrants shared bonds of language and culture, whereby they were able to act as a support mechanism for one another.

Thornton was also active in the purchase of property in the town. Several accounts show that he was able to profit from his financially unstable or insolvent counterparts to purchase houses and land in the town centre.[80] Sources note that Thornton was one of the city's largest iron exporters, and the largest importer of coal.[81] It is therefore highly likely that much of his wealth was accrued through Swedish trade and he used this to support forays into the property market. How much of Thornton's success was built on access to foreign capital through associations with England is currently unknown, but it is probable that his English origins and the connections that came with it were highly beneficial.

Thornton died in 1698 and his widow inherited his estate and property in the town. She survived him by some 38 years, suggesting that there was a certain age discrepancy between them. Born Adelheit Valck, she was probably of German extraction, and provides a further, later example of how English migrants were continuing to mix with other ethnic groups in the city. After Adelheit's death their son Sigfried Thornton took over the estate, in 1736.[82]

THE BRITISH IN ÅBO AND NARVA

The majority of Finland's British migrants were Scottish and settled in the country's principal port town of Åbo. Brief attention has been paid to those Scots involved in commercial and civic positions in the city in various editions of the town's history.[83] However, little has been said about the existence of a Scottish community that supported these more prominent actors, let alone the role and status of this community.[84]

The most comprehensive information in English on Åbo's Scottish migrants can be found in *SSNE*, which reveal the presence of over 100 Scots over the course of the century. Due to the range of sources consulted, from university matriculation records to muster rolls, the majority of migrants who have appeared to date are university students, along with military men. As is the case with Gothenburg and Stockholm, Åbo's court records remain largely unexploited, and still require a full survey to document all instances of British contact. A definitive analysis of the various aspects of how

Åbo's Scottish community (commercial and civic as well as military and intellectual) interacted with one another, and its place within its wider host society, still remains to be undertaken. In addition, the Scottish community of Åbo awaits consideration within the wider fabric of British migration studies focused on northern Europe.

Currently the status of English migration to Åbo in comparison to other localities remains uncertain. It is highly likely that English vessels visited Åbo, but to what extent is currently unknown, as the town's shipping records have not survived. A considerable proportion of Finland's exports were sent to Stockholm, and this factor probably accounts for the negligible English presence in Åbo.

Although Narva was not the pre-eminent Baltic port under Swedish control, knowledge of British migration to and interaction with the town is greater than with regard to others in the region. Previous studies have revealed the existence of a number of English and Scottish traders who resided in the town over a number of years and undertook direct trade with England, using Narva as an important gateway to the Russian market.[85] Battles between the local burgess community and English merchants who were unwilling to become naturalized boiled over at a national level, involving the government in Stockholm.[86] English merchants resident in Narva appear to have enjoyed favourable relations with these decision-makers, allowing them to undercut the influence and authority of the town council.[87] It is likely that English merchants were favoured because of their access to credit and western goods, and their role in redirecting Russia's trade through Swedish areas. For these reasons, Narva appears to be the only Swedish port where English migrants were more dominant than their Scottish counterparts in both numbers and influence.

It is unlikely that revisiting Narva's court records will reveal an increase in the number of Englishmen known to have been present in the town, or indeed change our knowledge of commercial and political interaction. However, Narva's British community has been viewed through this lens only, and questions surrounding migration and integration still remain to be answered. Furthermore, Narva may well provide an interesting counterpoint to the experiences of British migrants on the mainland, in order to determine whether any differences can be identified through a case study of a Swedish province. It is therefore to be hoped that consultation of English archival sources will allow more questions to be answered regarding those British migrants who settled in Narva.

CONCLUSION

Over the past decade, our understanding of Scottish migration to Sweden has been advanced considerably, in respect both to our quantitative and our qualitative appreciation of the subject. Despite earlier knowledge of Scotland's migratory influx into Sweden during the 17th century, scholars had failed to tackle questions surrounding the interactions and integration of the Scottish community. The diversity, impact and enduring success of the Scottish migrants in Sweden can now finally be fully appreciated.

In contrast, understandings of English migration to and interaction with Sweden in this period is lagging behind. A new research project geared to viewing the English experience aims to investigate many of the aspects that have been explored in relation to the Scots. The present preliminary survey has revealed that this shift in attention is already reaping rewards. Combined with the discovery of archival material that is currently being exploited we can see that the English, though not as numerous as the Scots, were an active and important element in Swedish society, particularly in regard to their commercial activity and financial assets. Many questions remain to be answered on the English experience itself, but ongoing research is hoping at least to go some way towards determining the extent to which the English and Scottish migrants in Sweden were deemed, collectively, "British".

ACKNOWLEDGEMENTS

The article would not have been possible without the generosity and kind help of Dr Alexia Grosjean, Dr Mia Korpiola, Dr Adam Marks, Dr Claire McLoughlin, Dr Kathrin Zickermann, Dr Cynthia Fry, Professor Steve Murdoch, Professor Leos Müller, Olof Bortz, Charlotta Forss, Otso Kortekangas, Björn Nordgren, Panu Savolainen, Martin Skoog and Andrea Wesslén.

NOTES

1   German scholars are currently viewing British connections with these latter areas, and also focusing on aspects of migration: Zickermann 2005, 249–73; 2013.
2   Murdoch 2001; Grosjean 2003a, b; Marks 2012.
3   Grosjean & Murdoch 2005; O'Connor & Lyons 2006; Worthington 2010.
4   Fischer 1907.
5   Grage 1986; Behre 1990; Müller 1998; 2003; Svanberg & Tydén 2005.
6   Berg 1882; Fröding 1908, 1915; Almquist 1929; Dalhede 2001.
7   Grosjean 2003a, b; Grosjean & Murdoch 2005; Murdoch 2006; 2010.
8   Murdoch 2013.
9   Grosjean 2003a, 140, 159; Murdoch 2006, 207–48.
10 Grosjean 2003a, 4, 5.
11 Grosjean 2003a, 4–5, 13, 25, 37, 64–5.
12 Hinton 1959; Åström 1962, 1963.
13 Murdoch 2006, 207–48.
14 Grosjean 2003a, b; Murdoch, 2006; 2010.
15 Grosjean 2003a, 140.
16 Murdoch 2010, 34.
17 Grosjean 2003a, 140; Murdoch 2010, 34.
18 Grosjean 2003a, 140.
19 Murdoch 2010, 42.
20 Murdoch 2010, 42.
21 Murdoch 2006, 174–8, 184–93; Murdoch 2010, 42.
22 Grosjean 2003a, 148–9.
23 Grosjean 2003a, 153–4.
24 Grosjean 2003a, 140.
25 Grosjean 2003a, 122, 128.
26 Åström 1963, 29–46; Müller 2003, 61–3.
27 *SRP*, Vol. 8, 1640, 100, 11 July 1640.
28 *SP* 108/518, 21 October 1661, TNA.
29 Müller 2003, 63.
30 SP 95/9, ff. 238–42, 'The King of Swedens Havens', TNA.
31 Åström 1963, 133–46; Müller 2003.
32 Åström 1963, 123, 136, 141; Müller 2003, 69–71.
33 *The Scotland, Scandinavia and Northern European Biographical Database (SSNE)*, Grosjean & Murdoch 2004.
34 Åström 1963, 122; Müller, 2003, 62.
35 Court of Chancery, Greene vs. Coote, C2/JasI/ G9/7, TNA.
36 *SSNE* 6633.
37 *Svea hovrätt*, 1614, RA.
38 *Svea hovrätt*, 1621, RA.
39 Åström 1962, 59–64.
40 Kommission, Sveriges handelsordinantier, 4 December 1695, RA.
41 Åström 1962, 59–69.
42 Åström 1962.
43 Murdoch 2010.
44 Grosjean & Murdoch 2005.
45 Grosjean & Murdoch 2005.
46 Grosjean & Murdoch 2005, 192.
47 Grosjean & Murdoch 2005, 191.
48 Berg 1890–3.

49 Långström 1926.
50 *Göta hovrätt*, LAV.
51 The provision of seats awarded to Scottish nationals on the town council would suggest that they were not discriminated against in any official sense. Similarly, both Scots and English held high-ranking positions throughout the period.
52 Dahl 2004.
53 Grosjean & Murdoch 2005, 213–14.
54 Fagerlund 2000; Murdoch 2006, 27–38.
55 Grosjean & Murdoch 2005, 221–2.
56 Göteborgs domböcker, LAV.
57 *SSNE* 4467.
58 Grosjean & Murdoch 2014, 8.
59 Grosjean & Murdoch 2014, 8.
60 Murdoch 2006, 172, 214; Murdoch 2010; *SSNE* 4688.
61 Ashton 2003, 9–26.
62 Grosjean & Murdoch 2005, 223.
63 *SSNE*; Grosjean & Murdoch 2005, 223.
64 Berg 1890–3, 3.
65 Göteborgs domböcker, 1635, 10 September 1635, LAV.
66 Almquist 1929, 81; Grosjean & Murdoch 2005, 191.
67 *SRP*, Vol. 5, 1635, 132–4, 16 August 1635.
68 RR RA, 1635, Vol. 189, f. 750; Almquist 1929, 85–7, 236.
69 Oxenstierna samlingen, E636, Anthony Knipe to Axel Oxenstierna, undated, *c.* 1642, RA.
70 Dalhede 2001, vol. 3.
71 Oxenstierna samlingen, E636, Anthony Knipe to Axel Oxenstierna, 21 December 1640, RA.
72 Göteborgs domböcker, LAV, domböcker, 1642, 27 January and 3 March 1642.
73 Ashton 2003, 18; *SSNE* 2523.
74 Ashton 2003, 18; *SSNE* 2523.
75 Ashton 2003, 18; *SSNE* 2523.
76 *CSPD*, 1668–9, 185, 345.
77 *SSNE* 6650; *SSNE* 6651.
78 Långström 1926, 45; *SSNE* 6120.
79 Dahl 2004, 3.32.
80 Dahl 2004, 4.III, 5.23, 5.26, 5.35.
81 Dahl 2004, 5.26.
82 Dahl 2004, 5.59.
83 von Bornsdorff 1894–1904; Ranta, 1977.
84 Toropainen 2003.
85 Åström 1963, 124–33; Küng 2003.
86 Küng 2003, 88–9.
87 Küng 2003, 89.

BIBLIOGRAPHY

Almquist, H. 1929. *Göteborgs historia: grundläggningen och de första hundra* åren. Vol. 1: *Från grundläggningen till enväldet (1619–1680)*. Gothenburg: Göteborgs litografiska akteibolag.

Ashton, J. R. 2003. *Lives and Livelihoods in Little London: The Story of the British in Gothenburg 1621–2001*. Sävedalen: Warne förlag.

Åström, S. E. 1962. *From Stockholm to St Petersburg: Commercial Factors in the Political Relations between England and Sweden 1675–1700*. Studia historica 2. Helsinki: Finnish Historical Society.

Åström, S. E. 1963. *From Cloth to Iron: The Anglo-Baltic Trade in the Late Seventeenth Century*. Vol. 1: *The Growth, Structure and Organisation of the Trade*. Commentationes humanarum litterarum 33:1. Helsinki: Societas scientiarum Fennica.

Behre, G. 1990. 'Gothenburg in Stuart War Strategy, 1649–1760', in Simpson 1990, 107–18.

Berg, W. 1882. *Samlingar till Göteborgs historia*. Vol. 1: *Kulturhistoriska skildringar*. Stockholm: Beijers förlag.

Berg, W. 1890–3. *Samlingar till Göteborgs historia*. Vol. 3: *Christine kyrkas böcker för vigda, födda och döda*. Stockholm: Beijers förlag.

Bornsdorff, C. von 1894–1904. *Åbo stads historia under sjuttonde seklet*. 2 vols. Helsinki: Bestyrelsen för Åbo stads historiska museum.

Court of Chancery: Six Clerks Office. TNA.

CSPD (Calendar of State Papers), Domestic Series. TNA.

Dahl, O. 2004. *Göteborgs tomtägare*. http://www.gbgtomter.se [accessed 1 February 2014].

Dalhede, C. 2001. *Handelsfamiljer på stormaktstidens Europamarknad: resor och resander i inter-*

nationella förbindelser och kulturella. 3 vols. Partille: Warne förlag.

Fagerlund, S. 2000. 'Women and men as godparents in an early modern Swedish town', *The History of the Family* 5(3): 347–57.

Fischer, T. A. 1907. *The Scots in Sweden: Being a Contribution towards the History of the Scot Abroad*. Edinburgh: Schulze.

Fröding, H. 1908. *Berättelser ur Göteborgs historia*. Vol. 1: *Göteborgs äldsta historia*. Gothenburg: Wald. Zachrissons förlag.

Fröding, H. 1915. *Berättelser ur Göteborgs historia*. Vol. 2: *Under envåldstiden*. Gothenburg: Wald. Zachrissons förlag.

Göta hovrätt. Göteborgs renoverade domböcker. Advokatfiskalen Göteborg och Bohus län [0382503]. LAV.

Grage, E.-B. 1986. 'Scottish merchants in Gothenburg, 1621–1850', in Smout 1986, 112–27.

Grosjean, A. 2003a. *An Unofficial Alliance: Scotland and Sweden 1569–1654*. Leiden: Brill.

Grosjean, A. 2003b. 'A century of Scottish governorship in the Swedish empire, 1574–1700', in Murdoch & MacKillop 2003, 53–78.

Grosjean A. & Murdoch, S. 2004. *The Scotland, Scandinavia and Northern European Biographical Database (SSNE)*. http://www.st-andrews.ac.uk/history/ssne/index.php [accessed 1 February 2014].

Grosjean A. & Murdoch, S. 2005. 'The Scottish community in seventeenth century Gothenburg', in Grosjean & Murdoch 2005, 191–223.

Grosjean A. & Murdoch S. (eds) 2005. *Scottish Communities Abroad in the Early Modern Period*. Leiden: Brill.

Grosjean A. & Murdoch, S. 2014. 'Scottish involvement in the Swedish *Riksdag* of the seventeenth century: The period from Parliamentarianism to Absolutism, *c.* 1632–1700', *Parliaments, Estates and Representation* 34(1): 1–21.

Hinton, R. W. K. 1959. *The Eastland Company and the Commonweal in the Seventeenth Century*. Cambridge: Cambridge University Press.

Kommission angående främmande köpmäns handel och vistande i riket [310537]. RA.

Küng, E. 2003. 'English commercial activity in Narva during the second half of the seventeenth century', in Salmon & Barrow 2003, 77–108.

Långström, E. 1926. *Göteborg stads borgarelängd 1621–1864*. Skrifter utg. af Personhistoriska föreningen äldre Göteborgssläkter. Gothenburg: Utg.

Marks, A. 2012. 'England, the English and the Thirty Years' War'. PhD dissertation, University of St Andrews.

Murdoch, S. 2001. *Scotland and the Thirty Years' War: 1618–1648*. Leiden: Brill.

Murdoch, S. 2006. *Network North: Scottish Kin, Commercial and Covert Association in Northern Europe, 1603–1746*. Leiden: Brill.

Murdoch, S. 2010. 'Community, commodity and commerce: The Stockholm-Scots in the seventeenth century', in Worthington 2010, 31–66.

Murdoch, S. 2013. 'The Scots and early modern Scandinavia: A 21st century review. The eighth Hermann Pálsson lecture', *Northern Studies* 45: 27–45.

Murdoch S. & MacKillop, A. (eds) 2003. *Military Governors and Imperial Frontiers c. 1600–1800: A Study of Scotland and Empires*. Leiden: Brill.

Müller, L. 1998. *The Merchant Houses of Stockholm, c. 1640–1800: A Comparative Study of Early-Modern Entrepreneurial Behaviour*. Studia historica Upsaliensia 188. Uppsala: Uppsala universitet.

Müller, L. 2003. 'Britain and Sweden: The changing pattern of commodity exchange, 1650–1680', in Salmon & Barrow 2003, 61–76.

O'Connor, T. & Lyons, M. A (eds) 2006. *Irish Communities in Early Modern Europe*. Dublin:

Four Courts Press.

Oxenstiernska samlingen [720701]. II Oxenstierna af Södermore, 01 Axel Oxenstierna. RA.

Ranta, R. 1977. *Åbo stads historia 1600–1721.* 2 vols. Helsinki.

Riksregistraturet B [1112.1]. RR RA.

Salmon, P. & Barrow, T. (eds) 2003. *Britain and the Baltic: Studies in Commercial, Political and Cultural Relations 1500–2000.* Sunderland: University of Sunderland Press.

Secretaries of State, State Papers Foreign, Treaties: 108. TNA.

Simpson, G. G. (ed.) 1990. *Scotland and Scandinavia: 800–1800.* Edinburgh: John Donald.

Smout, T. C. (ed.) 1986. *Scotland and Europe 1200–1850.* Edinburgh: John Donald.

SP (State Papers Foreign) 95: Sweden. TNA.

Svanberg, I. & Tydén, M. 2005. *Tusen år av invandring: en svensk kulturhistoria.* Stockholm: Dialogos.

Svea hovrätt. Stockholm stads renoverade tänkebok. Advokatfiskalen Stockholms län [42042202]. RA.

SRP (Svenska Riksrådets Protokoll), 1878–1983. 20 vols. Handlingar rörande Sveriges historia, Tredje serien. RA.

Toropainen, V. P. 2003. 'Skottirotta ja ruotsin koira – turun ulkomaalainen porvaristo vuosina 1600–1660', *Genos* 4: 199–215.

Worthington, D. (ed.) 2010. *British and Irish Emigrants and Exiles in Europe, 1603–1688.* Leiden: Brill.

Zickermann, K. 2005. '"*Briteannia ist mein patria*": Scotsmen and the "British" community in Hamburg', in Grosjean & Murdoch 2005, 249–76.

Zickermann, K. 2013. *Across the German Sea: Early Modern Scottish Connections with the Wider Elbe-Weser Region.* Leiden: Brill.

10

Commodities, Consumption and Forest Finns in Central Sweden

MAGNUS ELFWENDAHL

The Forest Finns have been looked upon as a timeless, ingenious and resilient frontier people with an unchanging repertoire of cultural traits. Archaeological data are now not only providing us with general information on early modern Scandinavian mate-riality and cultural interactions, but also illustrate aspects of consumption, use and transformation of material culture in specific socio-cultural contexts. Using ceramic vessels as the focus for the study of consumption, this chapter considers Forest Finns households and the social practices associated with eating and drinking, and the mate-rial expressions of these practices.

The migration of individuals from the forested parts of Finland to forest areas in the central Scandinavia is one example among many of historical population movements (Fig. 10.1). The areas in present-day Sweden where the Finns settled became known, as they still are in many cases, as *Finnmarken* (the Finn land) or *Finnskogen* (the Finn forest). With reference to their particular agricultural technique, the settlers were later termed *svedjefinnar* (slash-and-burn Finns). Today the term *skogsfinnar* (Forest Finns) is used when referring to this group of people.

The Forest Finns were part of a steady flow of people who travelled between the Swedish kingdom's eastern and western parts between 1580 and 1650. Their move west-ward coincided with the Crown's ambition to increase its revenues and promotion of new settlements in sparsely populated forest areas. Features traditionally considered as underlying their ethnic identity are a common cultural background in eastern Finland, the use of the Finnish language, their agricultural practice and their mode of building houses, together with a livelihood and lifestyle characterized by mobility.[1]

The Finnish households gradually adopted a way of life in compliance with that of their Swedish-speaking neighbours. This transformation and its expression can be followed from the 19th century, but until recently has seemed inaccessible for earlier periods. By exploiting new archaeological data together with existing documentary sources, however, the recently completed project *Skogsfinsk arkeologi – identitet i det materiella* ("Archaeology of the Forest Finns – identity and materiality") has increased our understanding of the expression of a Forest Finn identity in material culture.

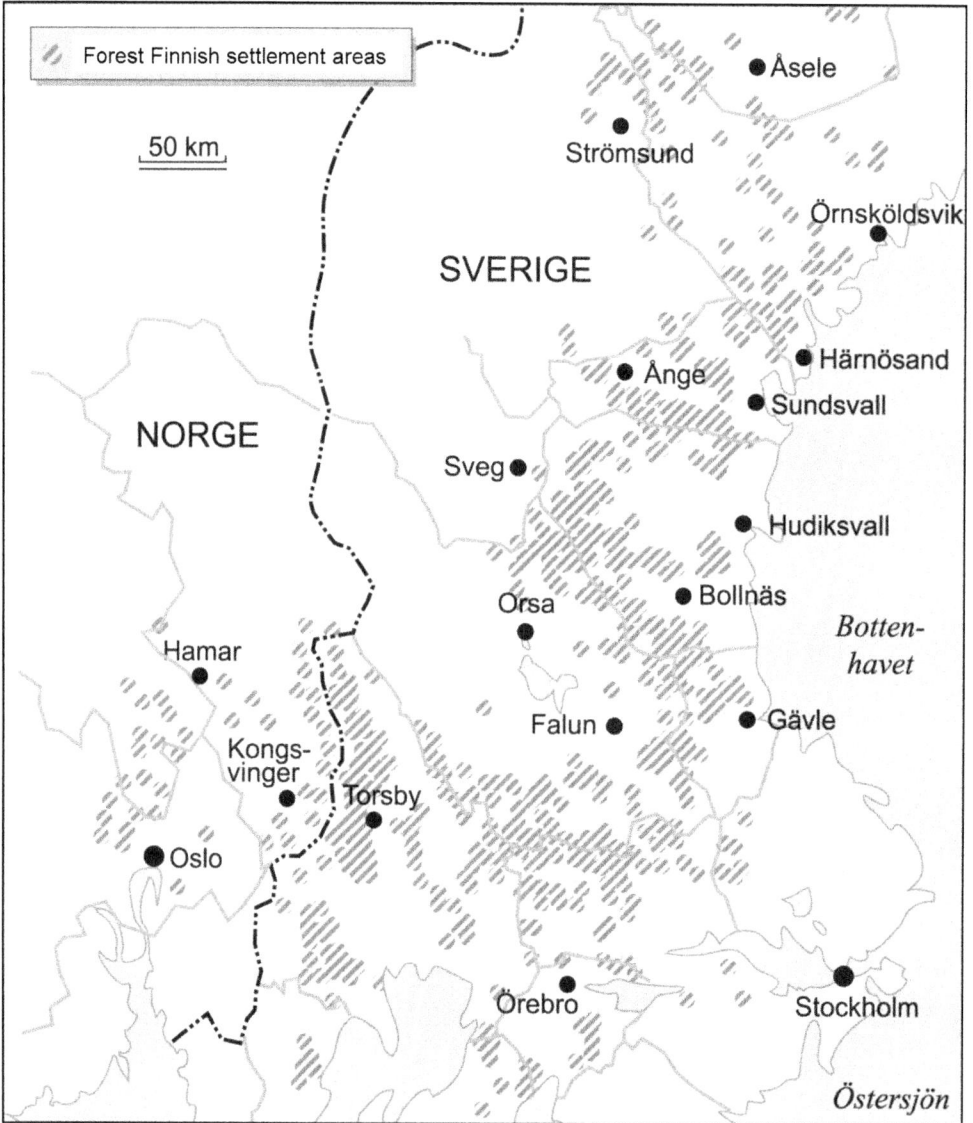

Fig. 10.1 Forest Finnish settlement areas in the late 16th and early 17th centuries (after Maud Wedin 2007, 104).

NEW PERSPECTIVES

The Forest Finns are regarded as a historical phenomenon: as an ethnic group they have no presence in present-day Sweden. However, among some individuals there is a growing consciousness of an ancestral relationship to the early modern settlers, and cultural affiliations are being cherished and encouraged in different ways. This development has also triggered an increasing interest in objects associated with the Forest Finns. Material items are recapturing people's imagination and are being ascribed a particular meaning, which is contributing to the emergence of ideas about Forest Finnish particularism and specific culture. When studied more closely, however, many of these conceptions can be exposed as stereotypes. In reality we have very little knowledge about the earliest Finnish settlers.

In studies of Forest Finns there has been a tendency to equate change with the assimilation of households to Swedish norms, and to equate continuity with a clinging to Finnish traditions. This imposed dichotomy has also been applied to description of the extent of the Forest Finnish settlements and their subsequent geographical decline. In the effort to identify specific architectural elements and to locate a point in time for changes in the agricultural practice of the settlers, the exploration of social change has been side-lined. It is apparent that any enquiry into consumption practices among Forest Finn households requires a radical rethinking. The Finns were not isolated from the rest of the world. Through travel and varying social and economic contacts they experienced contemporary changes in taste and fashion. They acquired domestic and personal objects not only to better handle various household tasks but also to enhance an imagined or actual personal and family identity.

Archaeology produces rich material evidence of consumption patterns across time and space, but to consider this simply as the flow of goods through the social world is to deprive it of an opportunity to explore the ways in which people socialize goods. Accepting consumption as a conceptual framework serves as a way of recognizing that goods assume meaning in a tension between structural and localized processes, and of embracing the agency of consumers.[2] By seeing artefacts as bearers of the ideas and values of their users, it is possible to understand how people use material culture in their daily life.

Abandoned farm sites, identified as belonging to Finnish households in the documentary sources of the early 17th century, are untapped sources of information. The refuse left behind offers us an opportunity to not only study objects used in the households, but also to access evidence of an everyday materiality not recorded in other sources. This chapter focuses on ceramics as one such category of everyday material culture. Acknowledging that ceramic vessels constitute suitable material for a study of consumption among 17th-century Forest Finn households (rather than merely providing chronological clues and serving as evidence of contact with others), these artefacts are regarded here as a source of information allowing a greater understanding of self-definition among the Forest Finns.

EARLIER RESEARCH

The archaeological study of groups of people defined by a common ethnicity connects with a nearly thirty-year-old research tradition within post-medieval archaeology. The project "Archaeology of the Forest Finns" could be looked upon as an attempt to revive this area of research.[3] Another field of scholarship within Swedish post-medieval archaeology in which the project can be located is the archaeology of the outlands,[4] which has focused on groups of people commonly considered as minorities or marginalized, neglected and overlooked.

Historians, human geographers, ethnologists, linguists, but above all many individuals in local historical societies have greatly contributed to our knowledge of the Forest Finns.[5] Considerable effort has been made to track settlements, buildings and place names, and to convert this information into descriptive reviews and comparative enquiries. Earlier research provides us with useful information about the Forest Finn way of life from the 19th century and later, but these data have also been used somewhat uncritically to describe daily life in a Forest Finn household during the 17th and 18th centuries.[6]

Fig. 10.2 *Under the Yoke* (Eero Järnefelt, 1893). The depicted toil and hardship of slash-and-burn agriculture has become a part of the Forest Finn myth. (Reproduced by courtesy of Ateneum Art Museum & The Central Art Archives, Helsinki, Finland).

Some specific features, or "ethnic markers", have been distinguished as being typical for the Forest Finn in a Swedish setting.[7] Among these are certain architectural elements, the spoken language, slash-and-burn agriculture and a few specific artefacts (Fig. 10.2). These markers have one thing in common – they are no longer a part of daily life. They exist only as historical sites, in museum collections or in archives, and sometimes in the stories of people with an interest in the revival of a long-gone culture.

Studies dealing with the Forest Finns have revolved around travel tales, ethnological records and documentary sources.[8] Before the project "Archaeology of the Forest Finns" there were very few archaeological studies dealing exclusively with the Forest Finns. An excavation carried out at the Forest Finn farm at Avundåsen in the province of Värmland has only been partially published, and whether a Forest Finn identity can be seen in this archaeological material is uncertain.[9]

The study of the Forest Finns is held up as a complex area of research.[10] It is presumed that it can provide us with the possibility of exploring issues associated with early modern Scandinavian materiality, colonialism and migration, as well as cultural interaction and the consequent dispersion, use and transformation of material culture. In a comparative analysis of Finnish colonists in Sweden and North America, Ekengren concludes that ethnicity is situational and should be studied contextually, which encourages archaeological research.[11]

THE APPROACH

What people eat and the way they eat and drink reflects their relations with the surrounding environment and relationships with other individuals. This serves to emphasize that enquiries into the social context of eating and drinking should also reflect upon economic and social structures.[12] Without a broader vision of society, and the forces that shape it, any discerning interpretation of past actions among Forest Finns seems very difficult to make. A comprehensive approach that exploits a wide-ranging interrogation of the past is required.

The 18th-century Swedish cookery writer Caijsa Warg (1703–69) is often quoted as having said "Take what you have…".[13] This was surely also one of the basic rules among the Forest Finn households even though such an approach probably also brought a certain monotony to the menu. Climate conditions enforced a subsistence husbandry characterized by slash-and-burn agriculture along with cattle husbandry, hunting and fishing. The collection, preparation and conservation of edible plants was typical of households in forest areas, whether Finnish or Swedish, and produced a subsistence economy that was more comprehensive and diversified than practices in intensively-farmed landscapes.

Official registers reveal that the Finnish settlers, soon after establishing themselves, had livestock in numbers that exceeded the Swedish farms in the same area, and milk-based products seem already to have been important during the 17th century (Fig. 10.3).[14] Milk runs like a silver thread through travellers' reports about the Forest Finns from the 18th century, and its prized value is expressed in sources mentioning the visitors being welcomed to the Finnish household with a tankard of milk.

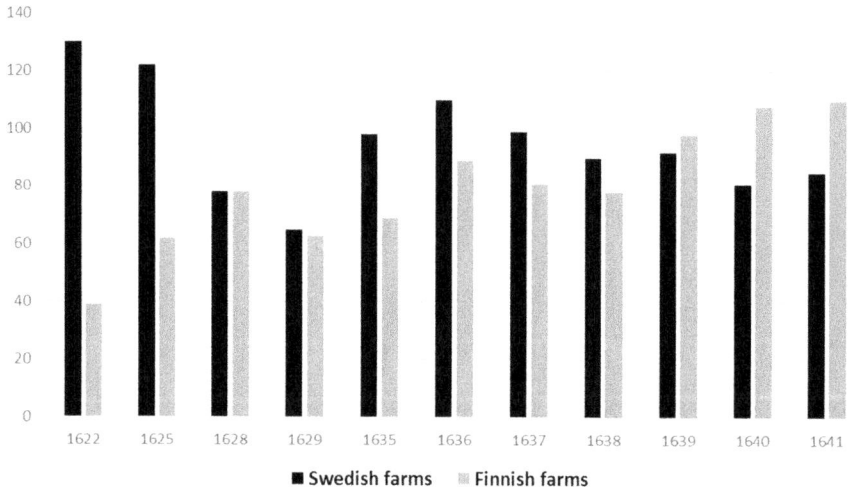

Fig. 10.3 Number of dairy cows among Finnish and Swedish farms in Hassela parish, Hälsingland (source: livestock register 1622–41; after Maud Wedin 2007, 151).

In 1736 the government officer Henric Kalmeter (1693–1750) visited northern Hälsingland in a search for valuable minerals. In his travel report he described food practices among the Forest Finn households in the area:

Fishing they do not neglect either. Pike they dry and sell, but whitefish and small whitefish and perch they ferment and fry on burning embers and eat. This fish smells terrible. When they don't have the opportunity to sell wildfowl, which they catch in great quantities, they cook and dry them in the oven. Milk is their main foodstuff.[15]

One person who provides us with a certain insight into later practices of cooking and dining is Carl Axel Gottlund (1796–1875). As a Finnish-speaking student at Uppsala University he carried out extensive travels to the Forest Finn settlement areas in central Sweden. Gottlund spoke to descendants of the Finnish settlers, and documented their traditions and daily way of life. Of special interest for our purposes are his notes from his trip to the provinces of Dalarna, Hälsingland and Värmland in 1817.[16]

Gottlund mentions that there certain dishes were still prepared that the Forest Finns regarded as typical of themselves as a group of people. Grain was the main cooking ingredient, and a distinctive feature of Forest Finn households was the preparation of large quantities of food at once. After the dishes were cooked they were consumed over a period of several days. *Motti* (Swedish *nävgröt*) was a type of porridge and the predominant dish during the summer season, when everyone was working outdoors and lengthy cooking was considered too time-consuming. Other dishes pointed out as typical of the Forest Finns were *hillo*, *peppo* and *reska*.[17] Gottlund also mentions cooking pots and cauldrons, saucers and bowls, plates and tankards in his notes. In the diary the vessels are often mentioned in situations describing their use.

Very few contemporary sources address eating and drinking in Forest Finn households during the 17th century,[18] a circumstance that requires us to turn to conclusions drawn from anthropological research on food and identity, to the effect that shared meals help to preserve and strengthen identities and community traditions among the members of ethnic groups.[19] This practice was observed, for example, among descendants of Scandinavian immigrants in America.[20] Several consecutive generations of Swedish-Americans still adhered to food traditions even although the families had stopped speaking their original mother tongue. A similar loyalty to traditional food and foodways may well also have existed among Forest Finns in Sweden.

It is suggested here that by linking information in written sources to new archaeological data it is possible to outline the use of ceramic vessels in Forest Finn households. As ceramic vessels are closely associated with storage of food and fluids, food preparation and its consumption, it is assumed that their presence in the archaeological record can also expand our understanding of culinary practice among the Forest Finns, and social and economic factors expressed in this habitual, virtually ritualized form of behaviour.

VESSEL PROPERTIES AND TYPES

Traditionally, large assemblages of pottery from excavations have been studied to determine quantity and quality of ceramic wares and thereby to assist in calibrating stratigraphic sequences in the archaeological record.[21] Integration of the remains of ceramic vessels within the social context of eating and drinking makes it necessary to employ another approach. In the present case the discussion will concentrate on the pottery, and will be based on an assumption that the availability of glass, metal and especially wooden vessels could have a dramatic effect on the repertoire of vessels associated with eating and drinking, and that particular cooking and dining traditions could have been associated with the use of particular vessels.

Pottery may seem at first sight insignificant and homogeneous, but when studied more closely it shows significant variation. Diversities in production techniques contribute to differences in appearance but also condition the vessels' porosity, heat-resistance and durability. These variations make particular vessels better suited for some purposes and useless for others. The bulk of the pottery from the excavated Forest Finn farms can be classified within familiar ceramic sub-groups, and thereby not only allows us to make assumptions about the vessels' provenance and dating, but also to draw conclusions about their special properties (Table 10.1).

Of the ceramic vessels once in use at the Finnish farms only sherds remained scattered at the different excavation sites. The circumstances make it necessary to identify these vessels from among all the pieces of pottery found. Ceramic vessels are produced in a variety of forms or shapes to comply with essentially practical requirements. To be able to compare information about vessel forms and shapes there is a need for a common terminology which also acknowledges that the basic vessel forms show great similarities over a large geographical area. A considerable number of sherds are without distinctive vessel features. These pieces are referred to as "fragments" (see Fig. 10.3 and Tables 10.1 and 10.2).

	Svartviken	Grannäs	Råsjö
Earthenware			
Rim	90	34	21
Body	582	133	42
Base	27	19	2
Handle	9	5	1
Fragment	504	73	1
Stoneware	-	-	-
Rim	2	-	-
Body	4	-	-
Base	-	-	-
Tin-glazed ware			
Rim	-	-	-
Body	8	-	-
Base	2	-	-
Fragment	1	1	-
Porcelain			
Rim	-	-	-
Body	1	-	-
Base	-	-	-
Flintware			
Rim	1	-	-
Body	-	-	-
Base	-	-	-

Table 10.1 The main ceramic vessel types registered at the sites studied (sherds/vessel parts).

THE SITES STUDIED

The three farms studied are identified as Finnish households in 17th-century historical sources (Fig. 10.4). They are small farms consisting of a dwelling-house and outbuildings situated around a farmyard and within an enclosed area located nearby to a lake and surrounded by extensive forests (see also the maps presented in Figs 10.5, 10.6 and 10.7).

Råsjö

Råsjö gammalgård ("The old Råsjö farm") is located in Borgsjö parish in the province of Medelpad (Fig. 10.5). It is situated on the south side of a small lake and surrounded by extensive forests. The earliest documentary evidence of a Finnish household is from 1620; pollen analysis suggests, however, that this area was farmed earlier, perhaps by Swedish-speaking farmers. The first buildings were located near the lake shore. Later new buildings were built on higher ground. In 1716 at the latest, one of the farm's main buildings was destroyed by fire. After that, the farm seems to have been relocated to the other side of the lake. The former location became outlying meadows and fields. The archaeological excavations revealed remains of three buildings, interpreted as a dwelling-house, a sauna and a building used for drying grain.[22]

During the 17th century slash-and-burn agriculture, hunting, fishing and forest foraging supplemented each other. The relative importance of the different branches of the household economy cannot be evaluated, but slash-and-burn and hunting seem to have been more important in the initial phase of

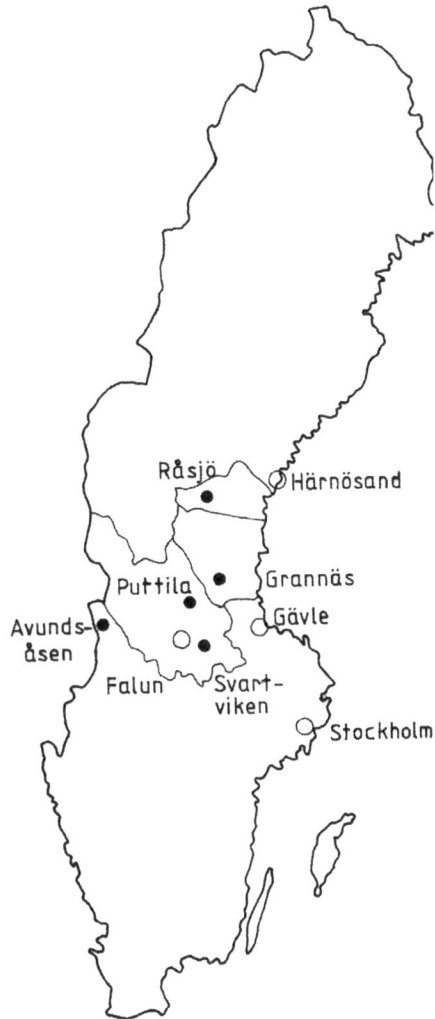

Fig. 10.4 Map of archaeological sites studied associated with Forest Finns (after Stig Welinder 2014, 31).

settlement than later. Looking at the bone material in household refuse, elk seems to have been a favoured target among the hunted game. The structural evidence of the preparation of food at Råsjö consists of a smoke oven and an open fireplace; food storage is reflected in the remains of two cellars at the house. The main body of the archaeological finds is related to food preparation and consumption, with pottery being the major artefact category recovered at the site. Other objects associated with cooking were pieces of vessels made of soapstone and an iron cauldron hanger.

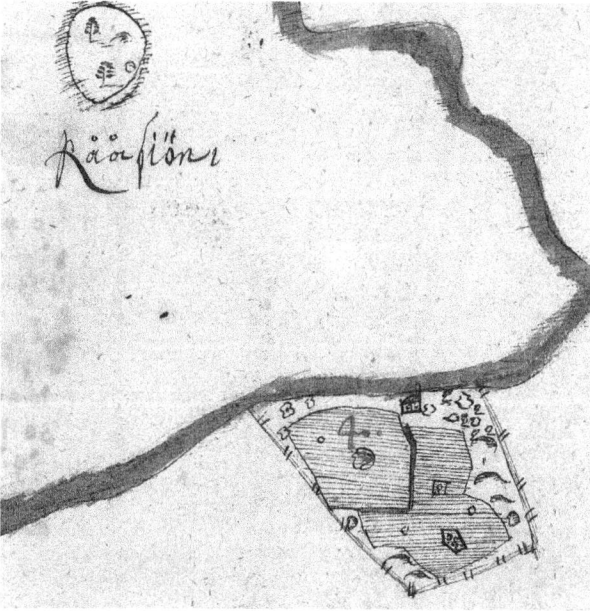

Fig. 10.5 Above: geometrical map of Råsjö from 1642; below: Råsjö and the surrounding landscape during the 1710s (after Stig Welinder 2014, 53; by courtesy of Lantmäteriet).

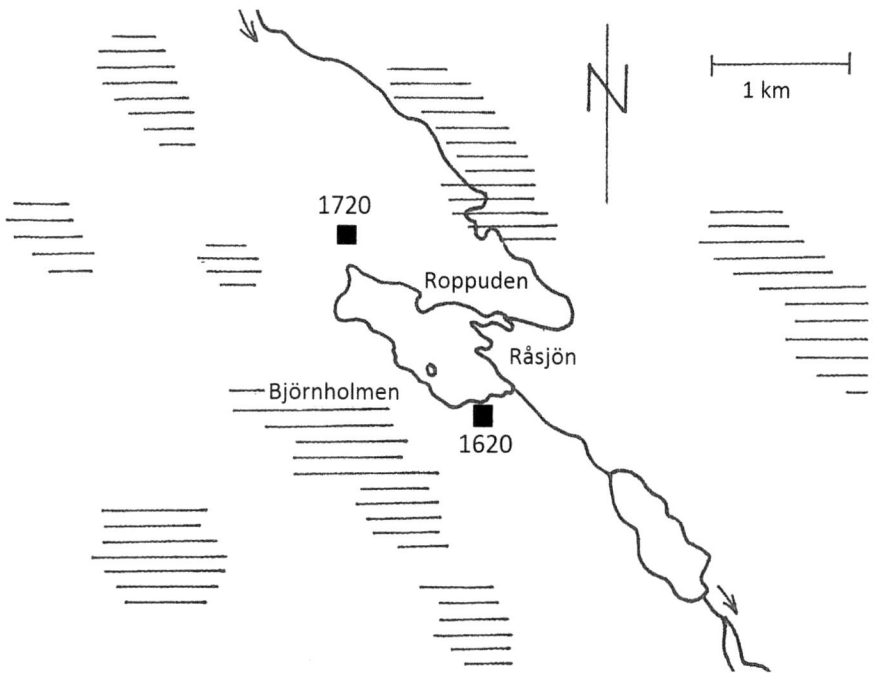

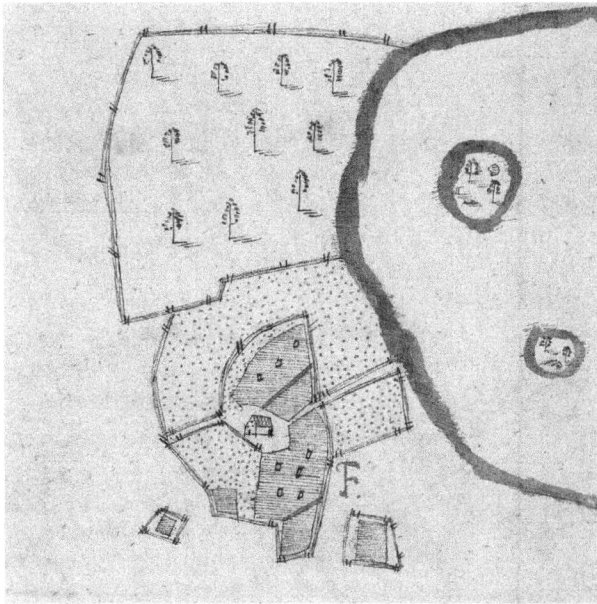

Grannäs

Grannäs is an abandoned Finn farm and a registered archaeological site in Alfta parish in the province of Hälsingland. The earliest documentary evidence is from 1613 when two Forest Finns, Mats and Knut Persson, received rights to land in this area (Fig. 10.6). Stock-raising appears to have been of greater importance in the earliest phase of settlement, and there is also documentary evidence from 1635 which shows that the two farms had 93 animals. The subsistence economy practised here seems to have resulted in some wealth, and

Fig. 10.6 Above: geometrical map of Grannäs from 1639. Note that the land surveyor placed the farm at the western end of the lake; below: Grannäs and the surrounding landscape during the 17th century, the excavated farm indicated by the upper square in the illustration (after Stig Welinder 2014, 96; by courtesy of Lantmäteriet).

enabled the families to acquire window glass, pottery, tobacco and English and Dutch tobacco pipes, and foodstuffs. There are indications of a rapid decline in the importance of slash-and-burn agriculture after the mid-17th century. Metalworking appears as a supplementary occupation in a later household.

The archaeological excavation uncovered remains of two successive buildings and a free-standing raised hearth.[23] The buildings were in use in the period 1610–1720 and the hearth between 1680 and 1720. Documentary evidence indicates that the site was abandoned before 1750. Cross-fitting pieces of pottery indicate that broken vessels were deposited in the farmyard. Structural evidence for the preparation of food at Grannäs includes the raised hearth and ovens. The ceramic vessels recovered at the site are associated with the storage and preparation of food. Of the three farms analysed here, Grannäs seems to have been the wealthiest. The presence of bought food among the household refuse has been interpreted as indicating a desire for a more varied diet.

Svartviken

This village is located in Stora Skedvi parish in the province of Dalarna. The earliest settlers built their farms on the south side of the lake Stora Lönn-vattnet (Fig. 10.7). Although documentary evidence is lacking, it is likely that the first Finns arrived here at the time when other Finnish families were establishing their households in the neighbouring surroundings. Two small farms surrounded by enclosed infields and belonging to Simon the Finn and Lars Hindricksson the Finn can be seen on a map from 1647, and documentary sources refer to Svartviken as a part of a *Finnmark* despite the fact that not all households seem to have been connected with the earlier arrival of the Finnish settlers.

The archaeological excavation revealed two building structures, interpreted as a dwelling-house and a stable.[24] Alongside the stable was a dunghill that was also

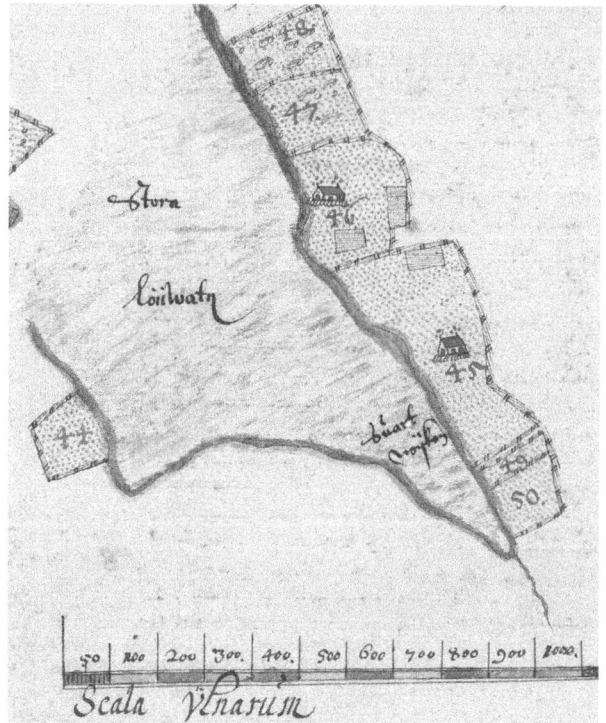

Fig. 10.7 Above: geometrical map of Svartviken from 1647 (nos 45 and 46 are farm buildings, no. 44 and 47–50 are shielings); opposite: Svartviken and the surrounding landscape (after Stig Welinder 2014, 139; by courtesy of Lantmäteriet).

Stora Lönnvattnet

500m

excavated. The excavated structures were dated to 1690–1820, and the household economy was interpreted as representative of a typical forest farm. Svartviken differs from the other farms studied in its high share of bones from older cattle among the household refuse, and the apparently lesser importance there of hunted game. Structural evidence for the preparation of food was a fireplace in the dwelling-house. Designated waste areas around the buildings were identified. The dunghill contained pottery, bones and other material associated with kitchen waste.

VESSELS FOR THE STORAGE, PREPARATION AND SERVING OF FOOD AND FLUIDS

Vessels exemplify the ways in which people store, prepare, present and eat food. But vessels can also carry ideas held in common by a group of people. The ceramic vessels examined cover a period of over 300 years and are from different Forest Finn farm sites (Tables 10.1 and 10.2; Fig. 10.8). To understand how differences in the assemblages connect to changes among the users, and how they relate to the production of and access to the ceramic vessels, it is necessary to bring together information from various sources. In the following discussion, archaeological and documentary evidence will be combined for a better understanding of a Forest Finn household and its use of ceramic vessels.

Jars
Subsistence husbandry makes it necessary to store food for shorter or longer periods in a way that preserves its original properties. Ceramic jars served this purpose and they could also have been used to transport food and meals from home to workplaces. Ceramic vessels were thought not to taint foodstuffs, and could be sealed. At Svartviken there are small stoneware jars of German origin. Lead-glazed earthenware storage jars,

	Rim	Base	Handle
Svartviken			
Bowl	31	7	6
Plate/shallow bowl	30	6	-
Bowl or plates	-	-	-
Saucer	6	-	-
Cup or mug	1	-	-
Jar	20	7	1
Unidentified	1	2	1
Grannäs			
Bowl	9	-	-
Plate/shallow bowl	10	-	-
Bowl or plates	-	13	-
Saucer	1	-	-
Jar		2	4
Cooking vessel	1	-	-
Jar/cooking vessel	3	-	-
Råsjö			
Bowl	7	-	-
Plate/shallow bowl	8	-	-
Cooking vessel	1		1
Unidentified	-	2	-

Table 10.2 Earthenware vessel types.

considered to be from local workshops, appear in Svartviken and Grannäs in both smaller and larger sizes.

Bottles
Bottles could be used to store or serve fluids. Those of stoneware offered protection against the harmful effects of sunlight and were not affected by sour fluids and food-stuffs. When mineral water from German spas became a commonly traded commodity in the 18th century the product was distributed in stoneware bottles.[25] Subsequently these could be reused for other fluids. Vessel parts belonging to German stoneware bottles from the 18th century appear at Svartviken. At both Svartviken and Grannäs there are vessel parts associated with lead-glazed earthenware costrels: flat, pear-shaped vessels used for carrying liquids, with two handle loops by which they could be attached to a belt and suspended from the waist.

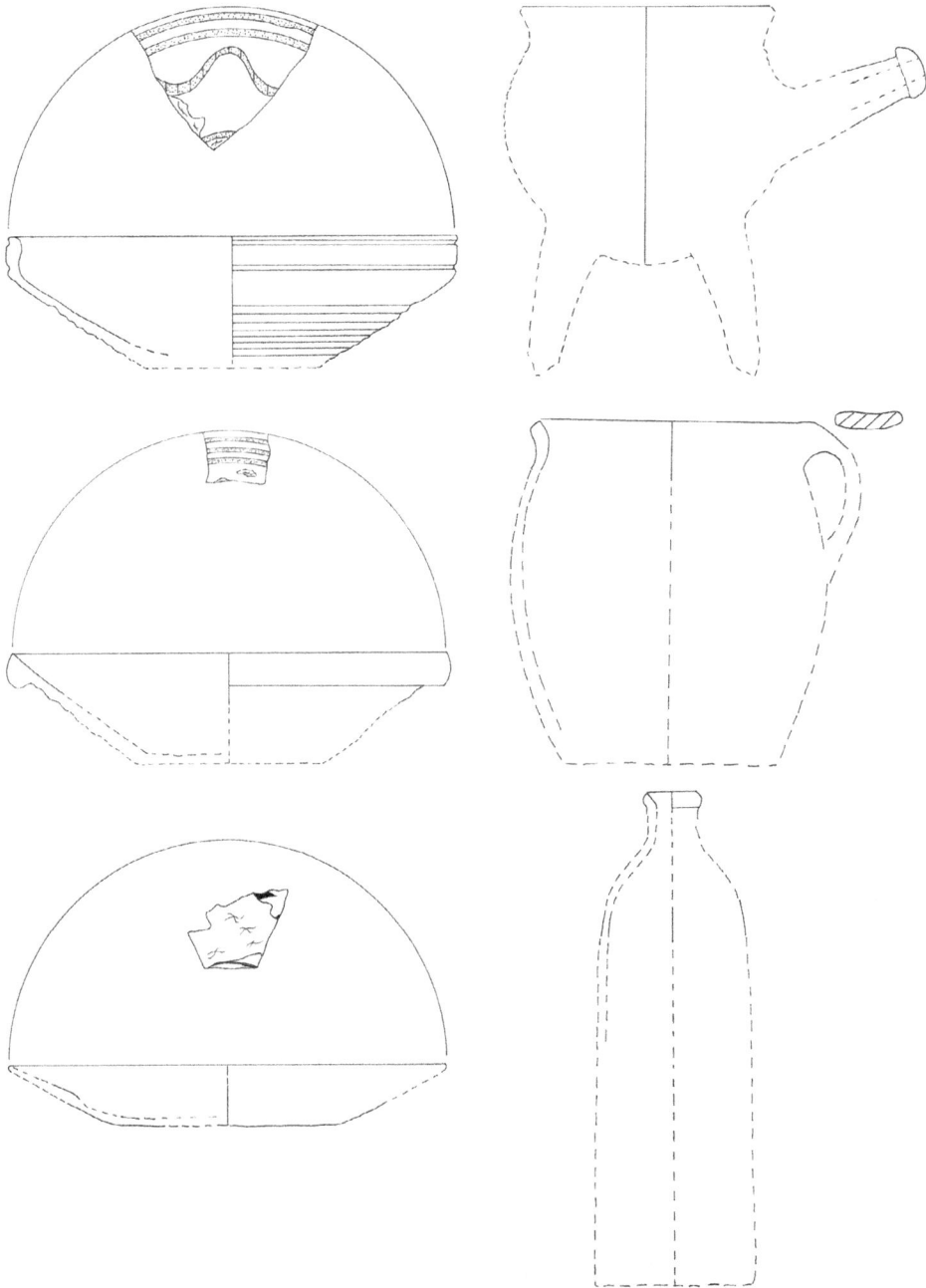

Fig. 10.8 Reconstructed vessels. Above left: bowl (earthenware, Grannäs); middle left: bowl (earthenware, Råsjö); below left: plate (tin-glazed, Svartviken); above right: cooking vessel (earthenware, Grannäs); middle right: jar (earthenware, Svartviken); below right: bottle (stoneware, Svartviken). Drawings by Magnus Elfwendahl, in Welinder 2014, 196).

Bowls, Plates, and Dishes

Bowls and dishes of earthenware predominate at the three excavated sites, and the clear majority of the products are from the local pottery workshops (Table 10.3). Decorated dishes and bowls show that households wished increasingly to demonstrate material well-being through the use and display of ornamented ceramics. Cheaper than their metal equivalents but more exclusive than everyday wooden vessels, the ceramic vessels made it possible to imitate the manners of those higher up the social scale. Plates and bowls were used not only for the serving of small dishes, but to impress others. For example, when Gottlund visited the Finnish farms at Fågelsjö in Hälsingland in the early 19th century he observed large shelves with porcelain and earthenware vessels in the kitchens. These farms, he said, showed a greater prosperity than any other places in Orsa Finnmark.[26]

	Cooking vessels (%)	Dishes/bowls (%)	Jars (%)	Dating
Svartviken		54	36	1690–1820
Grannäs, cabin	5	59	37	1610–1720
Grannäs, raised hearth house		94	6	1610–1720
Råsjö cabin		98	2	1630–1716
Råsjö, lake houses	80	20		1620–1630?

Table 10.3 Seriation based on the proportions of various vessel types from the sites studied.

Both tin-glazed tableware and lead-glazed earthenware may have been used in different ways, as plates and bowls from which an individual would eat meals, and as vessels for serving dishes. The smallest bowls could also have been used for drinking.

At the three sites the bowls differ considerably in size (rim diameter varied between 8 cm and 34 cm), but the great majority, 78% of recorded bowl rim fragments, had diameters in the range 12–20 cm. All bowls were decorated and at least some of them had handles to make their use easier. Large dishes and shallow earthenware bowls were also useful when serving various dishes. These vessels too vary in size (rim diameter 18–38 cm). A large majority (98%) of such vessels' rim diameters fall within the range 21–32 cm. These vessels were also ornamented in one way or another, mainly with an applied decoration in white clay contrasting with the red/orange/brown colour of the vessels' clay body.

Dairy subsistence was an important element of the household economy in the forest areas of central Sweden, especially in the early phases of the farms' histories. Even if milk was regarded as a staple it had to be treated before it was considered an adequate foodstuff.[27] Among the Forest Finn households this could involve allowing it to sour or converting it to different products with greater durability. Dishes of soured milk (Swedish *filbunke*) and cheese were a recurrent feature of Gottlund's travels in the Finnish settlement areas. On one occasion he mentions that yoghurt was transferred from a larger bowl to a smaller bowl in which it was whipped together with sweet cream and cranberries.[28] During his visits to the Finnish farms at Tandberg (in Orsa Finnmark) he states that the dinner consisted of soured milk and bread as on previous occasions.[29]

In the 19th century, soured milk was a characteristic ingredient in dishes consumed in central Sweden's farming districts. To make it, the fresh milk was sifted in larger vessels and stored in a milk shack. Of the greatest importance for this process was the selection of appropriate vessels that would not taint the milk and were easy to clean. Usually the bowls used for storing soured milk were made of wood, but there is also documentary evidence from the 19th century of ceramic vessels being employed. At all three excavated farm sites, bowls of different sizes were found, which could well have been used for soured milk.

In the mid-18th century Swedish manufacturers of tin-glazed wares started producing complete sets of tableware.[30] The undecorated wares were cheapest and produced in large numbers. Blue-painted tableware was rather more expensive. To compete with the tin-glazed vessels local workshops produced earthenware vessels covered with a white slip.[31] From Svartviken there is evidence of white tin-glazed plates with painted blue decoration. A fragmentary piece of blue-painted tin glaze at Grannäs shows that these vessels also were in use there. Lead-glazed decorated earthenware plates with a white slip appear among the vessels at Svartviken.

A few sherds indicate that shallow dishes or bowls from the workshops along the rivers Weser and Werra were used. These vessels form a distinct ceramic category familiar throughout north-western Europe, and date to the late 16th and early 17th centuries.[32] The appearance of these wares in Grannäs demonstrates that the household there was using sophisticated and decorative ceramic vessels soon after the settlement was established and before tableware of such quality became easily accessible through the emergence of local pottery workshops in the nearby towns.

Cooking Vessels

Documentary and archaeological evidence demonstrate that from the late 16th century increasing numbers of pottery workshops were being set up, indicating a growing demand for ceramic vessels among Swedish households.[33] Tripod earthenware cooking vessels with hollow handles (pipkins) are one of the main types made at the workshops until the 18th century. These vessels can be considered specialized cooking vessels, as they allowed greater control over the process of cooking and heating food. Earthenware and lead-glazed cooking vessels are present at Grannäs and Råsjö. However, the small numbers of these vessels suggest that the Forest Finn households did not make much use of pipkins and probably preferred large metal cooking pots.

Drinking Vessels

Coffee and tea were exotic drinks brought to Sweden from Asia and from European colonies in the Caribbean. When the Swedish East India Company began its trade with China during the 1730s, the drinking of tea gained in popularity together with the fashion for specialized tea-ware and associated accessories.[34] By the beginning of the 19th century, coffee too had spread to households in the rural areas. Responding to these new fashions, from the late 18th century onward Swedish manufacturers of vessels in flintware were supplying consumers with both white and hand-painted ceramics for serving both tea and coffee.[35]

Cups and saucers, presumably connected with the drinking of coffee and tea, do not seem to have been strange to the Forest Finn households. Collected pottery fragments hint that tea was served at Svartviken during the late 18th, and coffee from the early 19th century. Coffee plates in flintware can be interpreted as an indication of the custom of drinking coffee from small plates. The fact that vessels associated with the drinking of coffee and tea are missing from Grannäs and Råsjö can be explained by the fact that these settlements had already been abandoned at the beginning of the 18th century.

The analysis of pottery from the sites studied thus demonstrates an interesting consumption pattern among the families who lived on the farms, indicating that these Forest Finn households were acquiring imported and locally-made ceramic vessels and putting them to a variety of uses – for food storage, preparation, serving and consumption and possibly as decorative elements. The ceramics analysed reflect similarities in cultural and culinary traditions and temporal variations in the use of the vessels at different sites.

TOWARDS A COMMON EUROPEAN CULTURE

Towards the end of the Middle Ages there was an explosion of new ceramic forms and technological advances in Europe. Mass production, capitalistic entrepreneurs and the establishment of far-reaching trade networks were some of the factors that have been associated with this development.[36] Competitive pricing of ceramics and changes in people's consumption patterns are noted as further significant features of the process. We are dealing with a time when an increasing number of objects merged into a common European material culture, and were used to structure and influence emotional responses in social relations.[37]

From the early 17th century onwards, Sweden was in close contact with the European continent more widely. The Thirty Years' War (1618–48) led to it becoming a major political and military power and experiencing not only territorial gains but also a long period of economic growth and an increasing interest in continental spiritual and material culture. The 17th century is also marked by an open attitude towards foreign labour with more experience in business, specialized crafts and skills than were possessed by contemporaries at home. These continental connections contributed to the spread of European trends through various levels of society.

During this period there was a growing public demand for different types of ceramic vessel, paralleled by increasing availability of vessels in a variety of materials.[38] Through an increasing differentiation in vessel materials, social similarities and differences were becoming more clearly articulated. It is in this context that we should understand the increasing number of small-scale pottery workshops in Swedish towns. The proliferation of ceramic vessels mirrors household demand for new kitchen- and tableware.

APPROACHING A FOREST FINNISH MATERIALITY

Arriving in central Sweden, the settlers from central Finland found spruce forests on fertile soils; during the early phases of their settlement, large-scale slash-and-burn cultivation of rye was of crucial significance for the economy and sustenance of the migrating families. This particular method of agriculture gave the group its name and defined their settlement areas as the *Finnmarken.*

There is archaeological evidence of the slash-and-burn technique and cultivation of rye at all three sites discussed above, but precise dating of the longevity of these practices is not possible.[39] Nor is it possible to judge to what extent the farms abandoned slash-and-burn in response to the official banning of this practice in the mid-17th century.[40] However, analysing the three farms it is possible to observe certain changes over time, from a life that resembled the traditional picture of the Forest Finn household to that of an ordinary forest farm. The prominent role of a combination of slash-and-burn cultivation, livestock husbandry and hunting exemplified by 17th-century Råsjö was replaced by an economy dominated by livestock rearing and relatively small-scale arable farming, as represented by 19th-century Svartviken. Despite these general changes, the material analysed indicates a consistent interest in purchasing consumer goods, such as pottery, and possible persistence of culinary traditions.

A high degree of self-sufficiency – an ability to produce food and necessary tools – was an important component in rural communities' everyday life. Ceramic vessels were a category of things which households did not make themselves. Forest Finn households were not only producers but also consumers. In a world of intensely practical things made at home, the ceramic vessel was an object that was bought.

The archaeological finds of pottery discussed here are concrete proof of the Forest Finn households acquiring and using a variety of ceramic vessels in different situations. To understand what could have persuaded the households to acquire certain vessels, it is necessary to disregard previously expressed views regarding the Forest Finns. The daily life of the Forest Finn settler is often described as lonely, isolated and laborious;[41] it is to be questioned whether this assumption can apply to all Forest Finns during the 17th century.

The Forest Finn household was in some cases the place both of production and consumption. Influenced by others, the Finns were acquiring a desire for things that were different from or superior to those made at home and for practical daily purposes. The wooden vessels in the Forest Finn household offered limited possibilities for individual expression. The acceptance of new things in the household can be interpreted as representing developing tastes and a growing interest in fashions and the expression social ambitions; it can be seen in terms of socially- and culturally-determined strategies regarding non-economic choices made in everyday life.

Contemporary Swedish society was hierarchically ordered and this was reflected too in actions at the level of the household.[42] It was accepted that useful items be exchanged for other commodities, but greed was strongly condemned. The norm implied that a household should be well balanced in relation to its social position. Ceramic vessels indicate that already during the 17th century some of the Forest Finns were acquiring new objects and picking up on new social trends. They demonstrate that Forest Finn households at Råsjön and Grannäs, not long after the farms were established, spent time and money on things that were not produced in the household. Its members seem to have been aware of European consumer trends; it is hard to gauge, however, what connections, what social and commercial contacts, existed with market-places in Sweden where this pottery was sold.

CONCLUSIONS

Consumption is an important factor to take into account when analysing past households, and offers many new avenues of exploration. By linking to new archaeological data it has been possible to outline the Forest Finn households' use of ceramic vessels and to identify the social actions of individual households. In this case pottery stands out as a promising starting point in studies on the materiality of the Forest Finns, but also on cultural interactions and the consequent distribution, use and transformation of material culture.

For some Forest Finn households, migration was not merely a march from the forests of the eastern part of the Swedish kingdom. It was also a journey from an existence within the confines of a subsistence economy to a life with greater potential for engaging in a wider consumer economy. The Finns can be regarded as pioneers, or colonizers, in the sparsely populated forest areas of central Sweden. We do not know what things they had with them when they arrived in Sweden, but we can see that they were both interested in and could afford to purchase selected consumer goods.

Excavations have provided us with new data exposing certain features of Forest Finn material culture and its dynamic and continuous change. The Finnish households, if not fully integrated with the surrounding society, lived in co-existence with it, as is evident from things they bought and sold. To adopt new material practices is an open and free choice – but a choice the Forest Finn households made through engagement with others.

ACKNOWLEDGEMENT

I would like to take this opportunity to express my gratitude to Stig Welinder for inviting me to collaborate with him on the project "The Archaeology of the Forest Finns".

NOTES

1   Takiainen 1990; Wedin 2007, 122; Ekengren
    2013, 149; Welinder 2014, 19.
2   Mullins 2011.
3   Welinder 2014.
4   Svensson 1998a; Svensson 1998b.
5   See references in Tarkianen 1990; Bladh 1995;
    Wedin 2007; Söder 2008; Welinder 2014.
6   Welinder 2014.
7   Tarkiainen 1990, 133; Wedin 2007, 137;
    Ekengren 2013, 149; Welinder 2014, 20.
8   Wedin 2007, 17.
9   Welinder 2014, 28.
10 Ekengren 2013, 147.
11 Ekengren 2013.
12 Pilcher 2012.
13 Swahn 1996.
14 Wedin 2007, 150.
15 Kalmeter quoted in Wedin 2007, 201.
16 Gottlund 1984.
17 Gottlund 1984, 200.
18 Wedin 2007, 201.
19 Pilcher 2012.
20 Bringéus 1988, 14.
21 Elfwendahl 1999, 30.

22 George 2004; 2005; 2006; 2007; Welinder
    2014, 68.
23 Welinder 2014, 105.
24 Welinder 2014, 151.
25 Gaimster 1997.
26 Gottlund 1984, 182.
27 Ränk 1987.
28 Gottlund 1984, 99.
29 Gottlund 1984, 191.
30 Dahlbäck Lutteman 1980.
31 Elfwendahl 1996.
32 Hurst et al.1986, 242–3; Stephan 1987.
33 Elfwendahl 1999, 76.
34 Wirgin 1998, 226–7.
35 Dahlbäck Lutteman 1980, 131–2.
36 Courtney 1997.
37 Welinder 2003; Andersson & Welinder 2010;
    Ekengren 2013.
38 Elfwendahl 1999, 133–4.
39 Welinder 2014, 187.
40 Welinder 2014, 189.
41 Welinder 2014.
42 Runefelt 2001.

BIBLIOGRAPHY

Andersson, J. & Welinder, S. 2010. 'Glasrutor i en skogsgård', in Hansson et al. 2010, 179–88.

Bladh, G. 1995. Finnskogens landskap och människor under fyra sekler: en studie av natur och samhälle i förändring. Karlstad: Högskolan i Karlstad.

Bringéus, N.-A. 1988. Mat och måltid; studier i svensk matkultur. Stockholm: Carlsson.

Courtney, P. 1997. 'Ceramics and the history of consumption: pitfalls and prospects', Medieval Ceramics 21: 95–108.

Dahlbäck Lutteman, H. 1980. Svenskt porslin: Fajans, porslin och flintgods 1700–1900. Västerås: ICA bokförlag.

Ekengren, F. 2013. 'Materialities on the move: Identity and material culture among the Forest Finns in 17th century Sweden and America', in Naum & Nordin 2013, 147–65.

Elfwendahl, M. 1996. 'Postmedieval pottery in Sweden: Some notes on local red earthenwares', Lund Archaeological Review 1: 21–34.

Elfwendahl, M. 1999. Från skärva till kärl: ett bidrag till vardagslivets historia i Uppsala, Lund Studies in Medieval Archaeology 22. Stockholm: Almqvist & Wiksell International.

Gaimster, D. R. M. 1997. German Stoneware 1200–1900: Archaeology and Cultural History. London: British Museum Press.

George, O. 2004. 'Arkeologisk forskningsundersökning av en skogsfinsk gård, RAÄ 165'. Rapport 2004:1. Härnösand: Länsmuseet Västernorrland.

George, O. 2005. 'Arkeologisk undersökning av en skogsfinsk gård vid Råsjön från 1600-1700-tal'. Rapport 2005: 11. Härnösand: Länsmuseet Västernorrland.

George, O. 2006. 'Arkeologisk undersökning av rösugn och huslämning på den skogsfinska gården vid Råsjön'. Rapport 2006: 1. Härnösand: Länsmuseet Västernorrland.

George, O. 2007. 'Arkeologisk undersökning av en huslämning på den skogsfinska gården RAÄ 165 vid Råsjön, Borgsjö socken'. Rapport 2007: 9. Härnösand: Länsmuseet Västernorrland.

Gottlund, C.-A. 1984 [1931]. *Dagbok öfver dess Resor på Finnskogarne år 1817*. Falun: Dalarnas museum.

Hansson, M., Kock, J. & Vellev, J. (eds) 2010. *Renæssanceglas i Norden: Symposium, Malmö museum, 27–28. januar 2010*. Højberg: Förlaget Hikuin.

Hurst, J. G., Neal, D. S. & van Beuningen, H. J. E. (eds) 1986. *Rotterdam Papers: A Contribution to Medieval Archaeology*. Vol. 6: *Pottery Produced and Traded in North-west Europe 1350–1650*. Rotterdam.

Mullins, P. 2011. 'The Archaeology of Consumption', *The Annual Review of Anthropology* 40: 133–44.

Naum, M. & Nordin, J. M. (eds) 2013. *Scandinavian Colonialism and the Rise of Modernity: Small Time Agents in a Global Arena*. New York: Springer.

Pilcher, J. M. (ed.) 2012. *The Oxford Handbook of Food History*. New York: Oxford University Press.

Runefelt, L. 2001. *Hushållningens dygder: affektlära, hushållningslära och ekonomiskt tänkande under svensk stormaktstid*. Stockholm Studies in Economic History 34. Stockholm: Almqvist & Wiksell International.

Söder, T. 2008. 'Värmlandsfinska genom 300 år', *Nordisk Tidskrift* 4: 359–68.

Stephan, H.-G. 1987. *Die bemalte Irdenware der Renaissance in Mitteleuropa: Ausstralungen und Verbindungen der Produktionszentren im gesamteuropäischen Rahmen*. Munich: Deutscher Kunstverlag.

Svensson, E. 1998a. 'Expanding the household', *Lund Archaeological Review* 4: 85–100.

Svensson, E. 1998b. *Människor i utmark*. Lund Studies in Medieval Archaeology 21. Stockholm: Almqvist & Wiksell International.

Swahn J.-Ö. 1996. 'Warg, Anna Christina', *Nationalencyklopedin* 19, 251.

Tarkiainen, K. 1990. *Finnarnas historia i Sverige*. Vol. 1: *Inflyttarna från Finland under det gemensamma rikets tid*. Nordiska museets handlingar 109. Stockholm: Nordiska museet.

Ränk, G. 1987. *Från mjölk till ost: drag ur den äldre mjölkhushållningen i Sverige*. Nordiska museets handlingar 66. Stockholm: Nordiska museet.

Wedin, M. 2007. *Den skogsfinska kolonisationen i Norrland*. Falun: Finnbygdens förlag.

Welinder, S, 2003. *Skogsfinnarna i den svenska maktstaten: Lokalhistoria, etnicitet och landskap*. http://www.finnskogsmuseet.se/Skogsfinnar_v2004.pdf [accessed 28 July 2015].

Welinder, S. (ed.) 2014. *Skogsfinsk arkeologi: etnicitet i det materiella*. Falun: Finnbygdens förlag.

Wirgin, J. 1998. *Från Kina till Europa: kinesiska konstföremål från de ostindiska kompaniernas tid*. Östasiatiska museets utställningskatalog 53. Stockholm: Östasiatiska museet.

Encountering "the Other" in the North – Colonial Histories in Early Modern Northern Sweden

---

CARL-GÖSTA OJALA

This chapter explores Swedish colonial and missionary projects in Sápmi (in present-day northern Sweden) in the 17th century, with a special focus on encounters with the indigenous Sami population, and the consequences for relationships between "Swedish" and "Sami" identity, culture and history today. Early modern colonial history in northern Sweden is in general afforded little recognition in Sweden. However, it is a history of great importance to many people today, with connections to present-day conflicts over land and cultural rights. Early modern views on the Sami have had a great impact on later representations of Sami identity, culture and religion. There is a need to analyse critically this history of "Us" and "Them" in the north. How can archaeology contribute to a more complex understanding of the colonial histories and encounters in Sápmi and northern Sweden in the early modern period?

The aim of this chapter is to discuss aspects of the early modern colonial histories and encounters in present-day northern Sweden, with special focus on the Sami populations in the north. The colonial history of northern Sweden is a contested and in many ways controversial field of study, with connections to present-day conflicts over land and cultural rights. This history is also connected with the understanding of the relationships between "Swedish" and "Sami" history and identity, and in recent decades also with debates on the use of the concept of indigeneity in Sweden.[1] There is a great need further to examine Swedish colonial policies and practices in Sápmi, and the responses of the indigenous Sami population, as well as the larger ideological and political contexts of Swedish colonial expansion in the north. It is important to recognize and engage with the question of how archaeology can contribute to a more complex understanding of colonial histories and encounters in Sápmi in the early modern period.

Archaeologists and other scholars interested in exploring the early modern colonial history of Sápmi and northern Sweden, and its consequences and importance today, face many challenges concerning the connections between past and present, and the power relations involved in historical archaeology and the field of Sami archaeology. There are also many important issues concerning the roles and responsibilities of archaeology and archaeologists in Sápmi: for instance, in relation to current controversies concerning Sami indigenous land and cultural rights, which need to be considered and discussed by archaeologists working within this field.

SAMI ARCHAEOLOGY IN SWEDEN

The Sami – the people indigenous to northern Norway, Sweden and Finland and the Kola Peninsula in the Russian Federation – have been the object of particular interest, indeed fascination, for several hundred years, as being "exotic" and different. Previously the Sami were called "Lapps", which is today considered a derogatory term (but the old ethnonym is still used in the geographical term "Lapland"). The Sami core settlement and cultural area, today known as Sápmi, stretches across the national borders in northern Fennoscandia and covers a large area with great variation in topography and landscapes. The Sami are not a homogeneous group (their diversity in traditional subsistence strategies is reflected in the naming of Sami sub-groups, such as the mountain Sami, forest Sami, sea Sami and fishing Sami communities); nor is Sápmi a homogeneous region, as can be illustrated by its linguistic diversity, with ten different Sami languages.[2] Sápmi is not an officially recognized and defined region, but can be seen as an expression of the revitalization of Sami identity and culture, and the ethno-political struggle for Sami empowerment and self-determination. The very notion of Sápmi, and the construction and meaning of its borders in the past and the present, have been and still are contested issues in Swedish society.[3]

In Sweden, throughout most of the history of archaeology, Sami (pre)history has been marginalized and conceptualized as "the Other" in relation to national narratives, and viewed in opposition to ideas of Swedish identity and history.[4] Images of Sami culture and history have often been rather homogenizing and static, often strongly influenced by the ethnographic and historical source material from the 17th and 18th centuries, ignoring much variation and dynamics in time and space. It is only in recent years that historians and archaeologists have begun seriously to study diversity, transformations and change in Sami history. The general level of knowledge of Sami culture and history among the public in Sweden today is very low, and too often very little about the Sami is taught in Swedish schools or universities (including archaeology courses).

Sami archaeology has been considered a controversial field of archaeological study in Sweden, with many political implications.[5] In the South Sami area (covering approximately the area of the provinces of Jämtland and Härjedalen in Sweden and the neighbouring regions in Norway (Fig. 11.1)), Sami history writing has been especially contentious. Archaeologists have debated how to interpret archaeological remains from the Iron Age and the Middle Ages in this region – often as belonging either to early Scandinavian or Sami groups; but also the possibilities and limits of ethnic interpretations of archaeological material. In recent decades, archaeologists have taken part as expert witnesses in several court cases in which the traditional rights of Sami villages to reindeer grazing lands have been questioned. Part of the background to these conflicts over land rights stems from ideas formulated in the late 19th century, to the effect that the South Sami were newcomers to this region (that the Sami people had immigrated to Scandinavia from somewhere in the east rather late in prehistory, and gradually spread further to the south, reaching today's South Sami area only in the 17th century) – a perspective which has been heavily criticized by archaeologists in recent decades, not least on the basis of new archaeological discoveries in the region.[6] In this context of contested Sami history and heritage, several research projects have been conducted

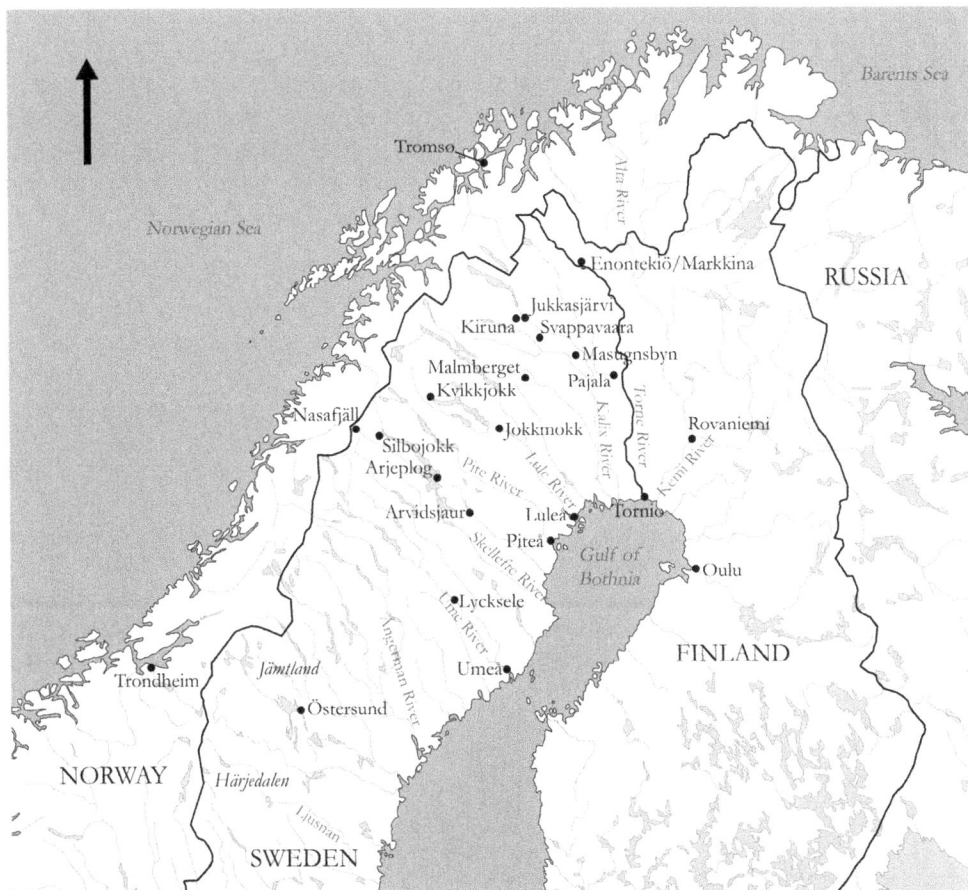

Fig. 11.1 Map of northern Fennoscandia, with some of the sites mentioned in the text (drawing: Carl-Gösta and Karin Ojala).

in collaboration between archaeologists, local populations and Sami tradition bearers, especially documentation and survey projects, with the aim of giving voice to unwritten South Sami history.[7] These approaches might serve as inspiration for the development of future collaborative community-based research in the field of historical archaeology, in Sápmi and elsewhere.

Traditional archaeology and cultural heritage management have, in recent decades, been challenged by Sami ethno-political and cultural revitalization movements striving for greater Sami political self-determination. Citing the international indigenous peoples' movement and international law and human rights, Sami groups have claimed greater responsibility for and control over the future management of Sami cultural heritage in Sweden, including requests for the repatriation of its significant elements: the most controversial and debated topic in recent years has concerned demands for the repatriation and reburial of Sami human remains which were to a large extent collected in the late 19th and early 20th centuries in the course of anatomical and later racial biological research, and which today are kept at museums and institutions in the Nordic countries.[8]

In recent years, another controversial issue – with relevance to the study of early modern histories in Sápmi – has concerned the boom in mining activities in the Sami areas in northern Sweden. Plans for the construction of new mines and the re-opening of old ones have put much pressure on reindeer herding and other forms of land use, leading to protests from Sami groups and environmentalists. The establishment of new mines with associated infrastructure adds to earlier large-scale exploitations of land and water resources in Sápmi, such as the exploitation of lakes and river systems for hydro-electrical power,[9] an extensive forestry industry, the development of tourism and military activities, and the construction of wind-farms,[10] roads and other infrastructure. In the anti-mining protests, the question of Sami land rights and the role of indigeneity in Sweden are central – and history becomes important. For the protesters, however, colonialism is not only about the past – but also about the present.[11]

EARLY MODERN COLONIAL PROJECTS IN SÁPMI

From the 16th century onwards, the Sami areas in the north became increasingly interesting to the Swedish kingdom. In 1607, King Carl IX (1550–1611) was crowned "King of the Lapps", a title which was used for the first time in Sweden-Finland (Finland was part of the Swedish kingdom until the war with Russia in 1808–9).[12] The Swedish Crown attempted to strengthen and expand its territorial control over Sápmi (aiming to extend its authority to the Arctic Sea to the north), in competition with its neighbouring states, Denmark-Norway and Russia. Beginning in the early 17th century, several colonial projects were initiated, with the purpose of tying the Sami population closer to the Swedish state and Church, and with the aim of exploring and appropriating the natural riches of the region. The colonial policies of the Swedish Crown included control over trade and the establishment of market-places, the exploitation of natural resources, and also the establishment of churches and missionary projects with the aim of christianizing the Sami population and erasing any remaining non-Christian Sami religious beliefs and practices.

During the Middle Ages, Swedish colonial expansion in the north started with the establishment of churches and parishes along the coast of the Gulf of Bothnia from the 14th century onwards.[13] The earliest towns in the northern part of the Gulf of Bothnia – Piteå, Luleå, Tornio and Oulu – were founded in the early 17th century, as part of a greater wave of urbanization, and regulation of trade, in Sweden-Finland. In many cases, these new towns replaced harbours and market-places that had existed on the Gulf of Bothnia since the Middle Ages, for instance in Tornio, and which specialized in large-scale trade in furs, dried and salted fish and other commodities. The medieval market-places were located by the river mouths, providing good communications with the inland Sami regions whence much of the merchandise originated.[14]

From the early 17th century, market and church locations were established by the Swedish Crown in the Sami areas, and state control over the economic, cultural and religious life of Sami communities was strengthened by various policies and decrees. The first market and church sites in the inland regions of northern Sweden were established in

Jokkmokk, Arvidsjaur, Lycksele and Enontekiö (in present-day Finland) by order of King Carl IX, with the aim of regulating and controlling trade and taxation, but also in order to facilitate missionary activities among the Sami (Fig. 11.2).[15] The early modern markets and churches in Sápmi can be seen as nodes in the colonial landscape, where trade, taxation and legal and religious affairs were concentrated during certain periods of the year. During these periods, the Sami population of the region was obliged to be present at the market centre. These places of course also became important gathering places for the Sami communities, and spaces for social interaction within the Sami groups.

Some limited archaeological investigations have been conducted at various early modern market sites (for example, in Lycksele,[16] Arvidsjaur,[17] Jokkmokk[18] and Enontekiö[19]). However, there is great potential for more comprehensive and systematic archaeological exploration of these sites, and discussion of them in a wider context of modernization and urbanization in Sweden-Finland. There has been extensive debate among archaeologists regarding earlier (pre-17th century) Sami settlement patterns and social organization,[20] and the possible existence of earlier central gathering places in the Sami cultural landscape.[21] Archaeologists have discussed the transformations of Sami sacred landscapes and sacrificial sites before and during the early modern period, in pursuance of an interest in Sami religious beliefs and practices and the relationships between Sami indigenous religion and Christianity.[22] Early modern material culture and trade and exchange between Sami groups and other groups have also been explored.[23]

Fig. 11.2 The church in Jukkasjärvi, near Kiruna, founded during the missionary campaigns among the Sami in the 17th century. The oldest part of the church building dates to the early 17th century (photograph: Carl-Gösta Ojala, June 2015).

However, there are still many blanks in our knowledge of Sami cultural landscapes and colonial sites in the early modern period: still more research is needed.

The early modern Swedish state also promoted new settlements in the Sami areas through various decrees, such as the *Lappmarksplakat* in 1673 and 1695, which granted freedom from taxation for a certain period and exemption from military service to new settlers willing to take up farming in Lapland. Taxation of the Sami was also reformed in the 17th century, becoming more extensive and burdensome, with a shifting focus from furs to reindeer meat and dried fish, which had a great impact on the economic and social organization of Sami communities. These decrees mark the beginning of a long history of state involvement in local identity politics through the categorization of people into different groups with different rights and responsibilities, separating reindeer herding Sami from non-reindeer herding Sami, for instance, and leading to the loss of Sami land rights at the end of the 19th century.[24] The school education of the Sami was another central feature of the colonization of the bodies and minds of the inhabitants of Sápmi. This process began early with the founding of the Skyttean school for Sami youths in Lycksele in the county of Västerbotten in 1632. In 1723, a state decree followed to establish residential schools for Sami youths in each of the parishes in Lapland.[25] The Swedish colonial educational programs for Sami youths continued well into the 20th century, the segregated and discriminatory nomad school system in the early 20th century being a particularly dark episode.[26]

EXPLOITATION OF NATURAL RESOURCES AND INDUSTRIALIZATION

At the same time, programmes for the exploitation of natural resources in the Sami areas, such as silver and copper, were initiated. In 1634, silver ore was discovered in the mountain areas in the Pite Lappmark district on the border with Norway. The discovery led to the opening of the Nasafjäll mines already in the following year (Fig. 11.3). The silver ore from Nasafjäll was transported down to the silver works at Silbojokk, established by Lake Sädvvájávrre, north-west of Arjeplog in the county of Norrbotten.[27] The Silbojokk works site, with residential and industrial buildings, was excavated in 1983–4, because of the damming of the lake for hydro-electrical exploitation.[28] In recent years, because of heavy erosion from the dammed lake, a large number of graves from the early modern churchyard (which was not discovered during the excavations in the 1980s) have been destroyed. In order to document the remaining graves, the Norrbotten County Museum has conducted rescue excavations at the churchyard, and about 30 graves have been investigated.[29] Silver ore was also found later in the 17th century, in Kedkevaare and Alkavaare near Kvikkjokk, north-west of Jokkmokk in Norrbotten, and another silver works was established in Kvikkjokk,[30] a site which was partly excavated in the early 1970s.[31] These discoveries of silver in the north were connected with great expectations of new riches for the Swedish Crown, and northern Sweden was referred to as a "Swedish America".[32] However, these hopes were not quite fulfilled – not yet.

In the Torne River Valley, iron ore was discovered in 1642 in Masugnsbyn, near the village of Junosuando, and mining of the deposits began a few years later. In the 1650s, mining of copper ore was initiated in Svappavaara, which is located south-east of the

Fig. 11.3 A view of the cemetery at Nasafjäll silver mine, located at about 1,000 metres above sea level, where silver was first discovered in the 1630s (photograph: Carl-Gösta Ojala, August 2015).

present-day town of Kiruna. In order to refine the iron and copper, a copper and iron works was established in Kengis by the Torne river, near the present-day town of Pajala, in the 1640s.[33] In this case, the mines and works were run on private capital, first by burghers from the town of Tornio, and later also by the Dutch investors Abraham and Jacob Momma (ennobled in Sweden under the name Reenstierna, "Reindeer star").

These early industrial projects employed local Sami and Finnish people, Swedish inhabitants of the Bothnian coastal regions, and workers from the southern and central parts of Sweden as well as from the European continent – making the industrial sites multicultural contact zones. The metal works and the mines can be viewed as colonial contact zones or arenas, where different groups of people met and interacted, and where different kinds of relationship, identity, material culture and power relations were played out, negotiated and transformed.

Local Sami inhabitants were pressed or forced to work for the mines and works, especially for transportation, which in many cases had to be by reindeer and sleighs. The remote location of these sites, and great difficulties in arranging the necessary transportation to and from them due to the lack of roads, continued to be serious obstacles.[34] The knowledge and skills of the local Sami population were necessary for the successful running of the mining enterprises. There are several known instances when local Sami populations protested against forced labour and bad treatment. Some Sami individuals also escaped from the areas near the mining and works complexes, in many cases to

Norway, in order to avoid having to work there, and these escapes were considered a serious problem.[35] Since the mining enterprises needed the local Sami and their reindeer, the Sami population had some resources to defend itself and, at least in some instances, avoid the worst of abuse and harsh punishments.

The archaeological material from the excavated silver works in Silbojokk and Kvikkjokk indicates some of the networks within which they operated, and gives some insights into relations between different groups of people at the sites. Finds include objects related to industrial production and everyday life at the site, but also imported goods: for instance, clay tobacco pipes and faience, and several Sami objects, such as copper pendants, antler spoons and other antler and bone objects. During the Silbojokk excavations in the 1980s, a drum hammer (which was used with Sami ceremonial drums in various rituals) was discovered, apparently inside a heap of dung at the works site.[36] What history might lie behind this artefact? Was it thrown away by one of the missionaries in Silbojokk, or was it hidden by someone, or discarded by some newly-converted Sami employed at the silver works? In the scarce excavated Sami settlement sites dating to the early modern period (which are most often identified by the remains of hearths), one of the most common finds is imported clay tobacco pipes – another example of the movement of objects and the adoption of new habits during this period.[37]

These early industrial projects were the start of a long history of extractive industries in Sápmi and northern Sweden, leading up to the development of large mining complexes, and the establishment of adjacent mining towns, in Malmberget and Kiruna in Norrbotten (the Kiruna mine is today the world's largest underground iron ore mine), the building of roads and railways, the expansion of the forestry industry and the large-scale exploitation of river systems for hydro-electrical power, with huge consequences for local people and local subsistence. The Sami communities lost more and more land to various industrial and infrastructural projects. In the 19th century, once again, northern Sweden was represented as a source of hidden riches of natural resources, and northern Sweden was portrayed as "the land of the future" or as Sweden's America – now with enormous profits for private companies and the Swedish state.[38] In this narrative of progress and modernization, there was little, or no, space for the Sami people.

MISSIONARY ACTIVITIES AND THE CHRISTIANIZATION PROCESS

Although there had been contacts and interaction between non-Christian Sami groups and Christian Scandinavian groups throughout the Middle Ages, and some limited missionary activities among sections of the Sami population had taken place during that period, more thorough and systematic missionary campaigns directed towards the Sami in present-day northern Sweden were not initiated until the 17th and 18th centuries.[39] It was highly embarrassing for the Kingdom of Sweden, aspiring to the role of a Protestant great power in northern Europe, to have "heathens" living within its borders. The state activities of regulating and controlling trade and taxation in the Sami areas, and the exploitation of mineral resources, were closely interconnected with ambitions to christianize the heathen Sami. The mining projects discussed above also provided an opportunity to intensify the conversion of the local Sami populations. Earlier attempts to create new parishes in the Sami areas by Carl IX, at the beginning of the 17th century, had encountered opposition from the clergy in the old coastal parishes. In 1640, however, as a result of the discoveries of silver at Nasafjäll, the Swedish government decided to establish four parishes with churches in the Pite Lappmark, in Arvidsjaur, Arjeplog, Silbojokk and Nasafjäll.[40]

The missionary programmes and forced conversion imposed and carried out by the Swedish state and the Swedish Church entailed a serious attack on indigenous Sami religious beliefs and practices. As mentioned above, churches and parishes were established in the Sami areas, the Sami population being forced to attend church services and to perform Christian rituals. Indigenous Sami religious rituals – including the use of ceremonial drums – were forbidden, with the threat of harsh punishment, even capital punishment. Many sacrificial sites were destroyed, along with confiscated Sami drums and other sacred objects such as *sieidi*-stones (sacred stones) or sacred wooden objects. Still today, for many of those concerned, it is a traumatic and difficult history. This period of forced conversion and interference in the religious life of Sami groups in the 17th and 18th centuries also, in many ways, "set a standard" for later state policies, regulations and interventions in the lives of Sami people.

However, the Sami were not just passive victims in the process of the Lutheran mission and the christianization process. The historian of religion Håkan Rydving has discussed Sami responses to the missionary campaigns, and different Sami strategies for coping with, resisting, escaping, embracing and/or adapting to the insistent new demands for religious uniformity from the Swedish Church and Crown. In the religious encounters in the early modern period, Sami persons could adopt a variety of more, or less, active positions, with more, or less, positive attitudes with regard to the indigenous religion and the new one. Because of the intense pressure, including threats and violence from the clergy and authorities, Sami indigenous religion to some extent "went underground", and certain traditions and rituals were kept alive and transferred to new generations in secrecy.[41]

In the early modern written source material, a number of Sami individuals offer glimpses of Sami perspectives on the religious encounters, such as Erik Eskilsson, who in the 1680s defended the indigenous religion in front of the clergyman Per Noraeus, who was stationed in Silbojokk. On a later occasion, when Noraeus had destroyed several wooden sacred objects and confiscated his drum, Eskilsson attacked the clergyman and took the drum back from him. Another, and tragic, case concerned the 60-year-old Sami man Lars Nilsson in Pite Lappmark who was sentenced to death and executed, in Arjeplog in 1693, because he had used his drum in order to try to bring his grandson to life after he had drowned. He had a good knowledge of the Christian faith, but in the court he explained that he had experienced the old Sami gods as being more helpful than the Christian god.[42] There are however very few accounts in the source material regarding how the Christian mission was experienced by Sami individuals – and those that exist have all been recorded by clergymen, missionaries or government officials. Here, historical archaeological investigations – combining different kinds of sources – might contribute new perspectives to the discussion of Sami responses and actions in the colonial and missionary processes.

During the 17th century a number of individuals of Sami descent participated in Swedish society as members of the "upper" or "learned" classes. For instance, there were several students with a Sami background at Uppsala University at this period. Moreover several clergymen in the Swedish Church were Sami or had Sami parents or grandparents.[43] Johan Graan (d. 1679), ennobled in 1645, and from 1653 appointed governor of the province of Västerbotten (covering the northernmost part of Sweden), was of Sami descent. Graan was a central actor in discussions of state policies concerning the colonization of the Sami lands in the 17th century and the exploitation of natural resources in Sápmi. For instance, he argued that the Sami areas should be surveyed and mapped and that a comprehensive register of all Sami lands should be established, in order to better control the land and people and promote farming and new settlers in the Sami areas. He also put forward the idea of parallel settlement, according to which there would be enough space for both reindeer herding and farming in the Sami areas, as these economies would supposedly not compete over the same ecological niches. In several instances, Graan also acted to protect Sami groups from excessive abuse in connection with the mining enterprises.[44] The participation of Sami individuals in Swedish state and Church affairs in the early modern period has not attracted much attention in earlier research, perhaps because it did not match 19th- and early 20th-century views of the Sami as a primitive and passive people.[45]

DESCRIBING, COLLECTING AND DEFINING THE SAMI

The far north has attracted much interest in the European imagination throughout the centuries, as a place of wilderness, darkness and evil, or as a place of happiness and virtuous noble savages.[46] Olaus Magnus (1490–1557), the last Swedish Catholic archbishop and the author of *Historia de gentibus septentrionalibus* ("History of the Northern Peoples"), first published in 1555, described the Sami in writing as well as by pictures. His descriptions of them were ambivalent, combining negative and positive judgements, condemning their heathen practices but admiring their natural virtues.[47]

During the 17th century, the earliest more comprehensive written descriptions of the Sami, their culture and religion, were compiled by missionaries and clergymen from the Swedish Church. These texts contained information on, for instance, landscapes and natural resources, hunting, fishing, reindeer husbandry, handicrafts, food, trade, marriage, inheritance, childbirth, burial ceremonies, religion, rituals and language, and theories of the origins of the Sami people.[48] The Swedish chancellor Magnus Gabriel de la Gardie requested written reports from the clergymen working in the Sami areas, to be used by the Uppsala professor Johannes Schefferus (1621–79) in his monograph on the Sami and their lands, *Lapponia*, which was first published in Latin in 1673 in Frankfurt am Main and quickly translated into several European languages (the first edition in English, with the title *The History of Lapland*, appeared in 1674).[49] The first Swedish translation was published only in 1956, which is a quite remarkable fact. Catholic propaganda and rumours in European countries that Sweden had used Sami sorcerers in their military campaigns in Europe during the Thirty Years' War were among the underlying reasons for ordering the compilation of the monograph.[50] *Lapponia* became widely read in Europe and had considerable influence on subsequent Swedish as well as international views and representations of the Sami and their culture, religious practices and ways of life (Fig. 11.4).

Fig. 11.4 An early modern depiction of the "heathen" Sami, worshipping a sieidi-stone (sacred stone) surrounded by sacrificial antlers. From Lapponia by Johannes Schefferus (1956 [1673], 140).

The monograph by Schefferus, as well as the commissioned reports by missionaries and clergymen – for example by Samuel Rheen (1897 [1671]), Johannes Tornæus (1900 [1672]), and Nicolaus Lundius (1905 [1670s]), himself of Sami descent – provide very valuable source material which has been widely used by scholars, not least historians of religion. However, it is important to approach these sources with caution, with a source-critical approach, considering that these texts were written by missionaries and clergymen whose overall aim was to christianize the Sami population and eradicate any traces of the old Sami religion. The written accounts are also limited in temporal and geographical scope (they cover only certain periods and regions of Sápmi). Furthermore, all are written by men, and reflect to a large extent Sami men's religious practices, ignoring much of the female Sami religious sphere.

In the attempts to define, delimit and understand the Sami as "the Other", one central debate in the 17th century concerned the perceived origins of the Sami people and their relationship to neighbouring peoples. Because of the contrast between the Swedish and Norwegian languages and those of the Sami, the latter were already considered as distinctly different from Swedes and Norwegians. However, the Sami languages belong to the Finno-Ugric language family, so the question of how the Sami and the Finns were related was much debated.[51] Johannes Schefferus argued that the Sami were descended from the Finns. He believed that the Sami had been forced to leave their homelands in Finland and migrate further north to their present settlement area because of external pressure from other population groups. Schefferus argued against other scholars who considered that the Sami stemmed from the Russians or the Tatars. He explained the differences between the languages, ways of life and physical appearance of the Sami and the Finns in terms of adaptation to new circumstances and physical environments.[52] Throughout the centuries, the issue of defining their origins has been one of the most common themes of scholarly interest regarding the Sami. A great number of theories have been proposed by writers and scholars in different disciplines, such as linguistics, history, archaeology, ethnography, physical anthropology and, lately, genetics.[53] Sami origins have often been portrayed as something unknown and mysterious, as a riddle to be solved: a way of thinking about "the Other", that is, with roots in the early modern period.

Parallel to the colonial projects of exploring, controlling and exploiting the Sami areas, a fascination with Sami material culture developed among collectors in Sweden as well as in other European countries. This fascination was, to a large extent, connected with an interest in "heathen" Sami rituals, sacrificial practices and alleged sorcery – elements which were central to the early modern construction of the Sami as "the Other".

Already in the 16th century, reindeer were used as gifts from Swedish and Danish royalty to noble and royal families in Europe, sometimes with accompanying Sami to take care of the reindeer and add an extra exotic dimension to the gift.[54] As a continuation of the early modern interest in the "otherness" and exoticism of the Sami, several groups of Sami travelled with reindeer as part of living exhibitions in various European countries during the 19th century.[55] The motif of the reindeer and the *ackja* (Sami sleigh), introduced by Olaus Magnus in the 16th century and further spread by Schefferus's *Lapponia*, was reproduced innumerable times in drawings, paintings and museum exhibitions – becoming an emblematic, and problematic, image of "Saminess".[56]

Sami ceremonial drums, which were confiscated by agents of the Swedish Crown and the Swedish Church (but also by Danish-Norwegian missionaries across the border) as part of their campaigns against Sami non-Christian religious beliefs and practices, were especially sought-after by collectors.[57] The drums were very much at the centre of the religious encounters and confrontations of the 17th and 18th centuries. In many ways, the drums were symbols of Sami resistance against assaults on their indigenous religion. At the same time, the drums were, for the missionaries and authorities, symbols of Sami sorcery and worship of the forces of evil.[58] Many drums were burnt by missionaries (though it is difficult to estimate from the available sources how many were destroyed), along with the destruction of other sacred objects and sacrificial sites.

In their collecting of Sami religious objects, the collectors exhibited an ambivalence typical of colonial encounters: on the one hand feelings of attraction and desire, and on the other repulsion and a will to destroy.[59] Johannes Schefferus, the author of *Lapponia*, created his own museum in Uppsala (in a building which still stands in central Uppsala near the cathedral), where he assembled mineral samples from Sápmi, Sami drums, sieidi-stones and other Sami objects. His museum can be considered one of the earliest in Sweden. After his death some of these objects became part of the collections of the College of Antiquities (*Antikvitetskollegium*), which had been founded in the 1660s. The collections of the College of Antiquities subsequently formed the basis of the State Historical Museum in Stockholm.[60] Thus, the coveting and collecting of Sami objects, especially religious ones, played a significant part in the history of the creation of the earliest museums in Sweden.

Some of the Sami drums that escaped destruction can today be found in museum collections in several European countries. The surviving drums have become powerful symbols of Sami culture and identity, and of the time before the colonization and christianization of Sápmi (sometimes called the "Drum Time"). In some respects, the drums can still be seen as symbols of Sami resistance, and they have been in focus in debates on repatriation and the future management of Sami cultural heritage in Sweden.[61]

CONCLUSION: COLONIAL ENCOUNTERS IN SÁPMI

This chapter has discussed some aspects of colonial histories and encounters in Sápmi in what is now northern Sweden, primarily in the 17th century. The exploitation of natural resources, missionary activity and the regulation of trade and taxation were all closely interrelated. As exemplified above, images and views of the Sami as "the Other" – exotic, different and defined by their perceived origins – which were established in the early modern period have had great influence in later times, and in some respects still today. Current conflicts over land rights, including disputes over the exploitation of natural resources, as in the case of mining, and discussions on Sami indigenous cultural rights, including repatriation and reburial claims, mark out the field of tension in which the study of the early modern period in Sápmi takes place. However, there are still many blank spots in our knowledge and understanding of this period, not least concerning Sami involvement, and the changes and transformations that took place within Sami communities, in these colonial processes.

In order better to understand the colonial histories of the north, it is important to examine the early modern colonial projects in Sápmi within a broader, global perspective. A few researchers only have discussed the connections between Scandinavian early modern expansion in Sápmi and Scandinavian colonial projects in other parts of the world (such as the Swedish colony New Sweden in North America in 1638–55) or European colonial ideologies and projects in general.[62] In much of Swedish historiography, early modern Swedish expansion in Sápmi has not been considered in terms of European colonial ideologies and practices, but rather as a form of "internal colonization", within the "pre-definedly" Swedish territory, leading to a view of Swedish policies in Sápmi as essentially different from colonial expansion elsewhere.[63] Swedish and Scandinavian colonialism in general – in other parts of the world – has also often been viewed as milder and kinder than that of other colonial powers.[64] However, as the historian Gunlög Fur argues,

> More than 100 years of Swedish historical scholarship offer plenty of evidence that Sweden fully participated in European expansion and shared in all its bolstering arguments. But what differentiates Sweden from, for example, Britain and France is that there was no decolonising moment, during which Sweden had to rethink its position [...] This also led to a lack of interest in the ways in which Swedish rulers, subjects and citizens continued to serve and benefit from colonisation, through trade and various forms of exploration and exploitation.[65]

Fur's assertion can be considered relevant also to the early modern history of Sápmi, and pinpoints the need to re-examine and rethink the colonial histories and identities of the north. In this re-examination and rethinking, historical archaeological approaches, informed by developments in the international fields of indigenous archaeology[66] and postcolonial scholarship,[67] can play an important role. There is a great potential for future studies, drawing on various kinds of source – written sources, archaeological material, maps and depictions, oral histories and landscape perspectives – to contribute to more nuanced and complex images of early modern encounters and identities in the north.

The early modern colonial process in northern Sweden was complex, dynamic and multidimensional. One great challenge that researchers face when discussing this history is how to avoid reproducing old ways of conceptualizing and representing the Sami as a static and homogeneous entity.[68] Although it is important to recognize that the Sami were active agents in the processes under discussion, and that the relationship between different population groups was not necessarily the same in the 17th century as in the 19th and 20th centuries, one should not forget the asymmetrical power relations between the Swedish government and authorities and local Sami populations. The complexities include too possible internal tensions and conflicts between different Sami groups and individuals – between socio-economic groups as well as generations in relation to the industrialization and christianization processes. This theme has been little discussed in previous research on northern early modern history.

This chapter has focused on the part of Sápmi which lies within the borders of present-day Sweden. These northern borders were, to a large extent, established during the early modern period, and it is important to remember that Sápmi stretches across today's national boundaries in the north, with traditional migration routes and language areas, for instance, crossing the borders. It is important, therefore, that a Sami history should not be delimited by these colonial boundaries.

Thus, in this field of tension between past and present, archaeologists face many challenges. It is important to develop certain critical perspectives with regard to the study of colonial encounters in early modern Sápmi: whose history is told, and from what angle? What are the aims of these engagements with history and identity? What is the relevance of the past in the present? What are the roles and responsibilities of archaeologists in this context? These are some of the issues that face archaeologists and other scholars working in this conflicted area in the north.

There is great need for more research on the early modern colonial histories in Sápmi, and the involvement of Sami and other groups in the colonial projects, with the potential to contribute fresh perspectives. In turn, the recognition and examination of colonial relations, encounters and identities in the northern areas might contribute to a deeper understanding of the early modern history of the Swedish kingdom, and its colonial ambitions, as well as the relationships between what are today considered "Sami" and "Swedish" history and identity.

ACKNOWLEDGEMENTS

This article was written as part of the research projects "Arctic Origins – Archaeology and the Search for the Origins of the Northern Peoples in the East and the West" (project no. 421–2010–1583) and "A Colonial Arena – Landscape, People and Globalization in Inland Northern Sweden in the Early Modern Period" (project no. 2013–1475), both funded by the Swedish Research Council.

NOTES

1 See e.g. Ojala 2009; 2014; Hagström Yamamoto 2010.
2 Lehtola 2004, 11.
3 See further Ojala 2009, 71–4.
4 See further discussions in Ojala 2009.
5 Wallerström 2006 and contributions in Lundström 2007.
6 Zachrisson 2007; Ojala 2009, 141–64.
7 See further Ljungdahl & Norberg 2012; Norberg & Winka 2014.
8 Harlin 2008; Ojala 2009; Ojala 2014; Ojala 2016.
9 See Össbo 2014; Ojala & Nordin 2015.
10 See Lawrence 2014.
11 See e.g. contributions in Gärdebo et al. 2014.
12 Cramér & Ryd 2012, 49.
13 For more about the medieval colonization process in northern Sweden, see e.g. Wallerström 1995.
14 Herva et al. 2012.
15 Bergling 1964, 160–7; see also Göthe 1929; Granqvist 2004.
16 For an overview of excavations and a presentation of find material from Lycksele, see Rydström 2009.
17 Liedgren 1997 on excavations and archaeological finds from the market site at Arvidsjaur.
18 E.g. Grundström 1930 on discoveries of graves from the old churchyard in Jokkmokk.
19 See contributions in Harlin & Lehtola 2007.
20 E.g. Mulk 1994; Hedman 2003; Bergman et al. 2013; Hansen & Olsen 2014.
21 On the theory of the so-called Sámi winter villages, see Tanner 1929. For more critical perspectives on this theory, see Aronsson 2009; Eidlitz Kuoljok 2011.
22 E.g. Fossum 2006; Mulk & Bayliss-Smith 2006; Äikäs & Salmi 2013; Äikäs 2015.
23 See e.g. Nurmi 2009; Immonen 2013.
24 See e.g. Arell 1977; Lundmark 2008; Lundmark & Rumar 2008; Cramér & Ryd 2012.

25 Lindmark 2013.
26 Lundmark 2008, 166–74; Huuva & Blind 2016.
27 Bromé 1923; Awebro et al. 1989; Nordin 2015.
28 See Awebro et al. 1989.
29 Lindgren et al. 2007; Lindgren 2015.
30 Awebro 1983.
31 Bäärnhielm 1976.
32 Cf. Bromé 1923, 64–5; Bäärnhielm 1976; Nordin 2012.
33 See Awebro 1993; Nordin & Ojala 2017.
34 Hoppe 1945, 96–101.
35 See further Lundmark 2008, 42–9.
36 Bäärnhielm 1976; Roslund 1989, 119–32.
37 Hedman 2003, 188.
38 Sörlin 1988; cf. also Hagström Yamamoto 2010, 57–61.
39 Rydving 1995; 2010a; Lindmark 2006; Bäckman 2013; Lundmark 2016.
40 Awebro 1986, 10–16.
41 Rydving 1995; see also Lindmark 2006.
42 Awebro 1986, 26–31; see further Rydving 1995.
43 Rydving 2010b; Rasmussen 2016.
44 Göthe 1929; Nordlander 1938.
45 Rydving 2010b.
46 Naum 2016; Davidson 2005.
47 Olaus Magnus 1976 [1555]; Balzamo 2015, 109–26.
48 Ruong 1983; Naum 2016.
49 Schefferus 1956 [1673]; Schefferus 1971 [1674].
50 See further Rydving 2006.
51 Pulkkinen 2000.
52 Schefferus 1956 [1673], 79–91.
53 See further Ojala 2009, 115–41; Hansen & Olsen 2014, 9–38.
54 Berg 1954.
55 Broberg 1982; Baglo 2011.
56 Nodermann-Hedqvist & Manker 1971; Lindin & Svanberg 1990; Mathisen Opdahl 2014.
57 Manker 1938; Manker 1950; Kroik 2007; Christoffersson 2010.
58 Rydving 1995; Rydving 2010a.
59 Snickare 2014.

60 Arne 1931.
61 See e.g. Den samiska trumman ... 2000;
   Harlin 2008; Ojala 2009, 228–64.
62 See Fur 2006; Fur 2013; Naum & Nordin 2013.
63 Lindmark 2013, 132–3.

64 Naum & Nordin 2013.
65 Fur 2013, 24.
66 See e.g. Bruchac et al. 2010; Nicholas 2011.
67 Liebmann & Rizvi 2010; Lydon & Rizvi 2012.
68 See further Ojala 2009.

BIBLIOGRAPHY

Arell, N. 1977. *Rennomadismen i Torne lappmark: Markanvändning under kolonisationsepoken i fr.a. Enontekis socken*. Kungl. Skytteanska samfundets handlingar 17. Umeå: Umeå universitet.

Arne, T. J. 1931. 'Antikvitetskollegiets och Antikvitetsarkivets samlingar', *Fornvännen* 26: 48–93.

Aronsson, K.-Å. 2009. 'Saami societies and the siida: Reflections from an archaeological perspective', in Äikäs 2009, 58–67.

Awebro, K. 1983. *Luleå Silververk: Ett norrländskt silververks historia*. Luleå: Norrbottens museum.

Awebro, K. 1986. *Kyrklig verksamhet i Silbojokk*. Stockholm: Institutet för Lappmarksforskning.

Awebro, K. 1993. 'Kring bruksrörelsen i Tornedalen', in Hederyd & Alamäki 1993, 361–80.

Awebro, K., Björkenstam, N., Norrman, J., Petersson, S., Roslund, Y., Sten, S. & Wallquist, E. 1989. *Silvret från Nasafjäll: Arkeologi vid Silbojokk*. Stockholm: Riksantikvarieämbetet.

Äikäs, T. (ed.) 2009. *Máttut – Máddagat: The Roots of Saami Ethnicities, Societies and Spaces/Places*. Publications of Giellagas Institute 12. Oulu: Oulu universitet.

Äikäs, T. 2015. *From Boulders to Fells: Sacred Places in the Sami Ritual Landscape*. Monographs of the Archaeological Society of Finland 5. Helsinki: Archaeological Society of Finland.

Äikäs, T. & Salmi, A.-K. 2013. '"The sieidi is a better altar/the noaidi drum's a purer church bell": Long-term changes and syncretism at Sami offering sites', *World Archaeology* 45(1): 64–82.

Baglo, C. 2011. 'På ville veger? Levende utstillinger av samer i Europa og Amerika'. PhD dissertation, University of Tromsø.

Balzamo, E. 2015. *Den osynlige ärkebiskopen: Essäer om Olaus Magnus*. Stockholm: Atlantis.

Bäärnhielm, G. 1976. *I Norrland hava vi ett Indien: Gruvdrift och kolonisation i Lappmarken under 1600-talet*. Stockholm: Ordfront.

Bäckman, L. 2013. *Studier i samisk religion: Samlade artiklar*. Religionshistoriska jubileumsserien 1. Stockholm: Stockholms universitet.

Beaudry, M. C. & Parno, T. G. (eds) 2013. *Archaeologies of Mobility and Movement*. New York: Springer.

Berättelser om samerna i 1600-talets Sverige. 1983. Skytteanska samfundets samlingar 27. Umeå: Skytteanska Samfundet.

Berg, G. 1954. 'Lappland och Europa: några anteckningar om renar som furstegåvor', in Strömbäck 1954, 221–44.

Bergling, R. 1964. *Kyrkstaden i övre Norrland: Kyrkliga, merkantila och judiciella funktioner under 1600- och 1700-talen*. Kungl. Skytteanska samfundets handlingar 3. Umeå: Skytteanska Samfundet.

Bergman, I., Zackrisson, O. & Liedgren, L. 2013. 'From hunting to herding: Land use, ecosystem processes, and social transformation among Sami AD 800–1500', *Arctic Anthropology* 50(2): 25–39.

Broberg, G. 1982. 'Lappkaravaner på villovägar: Antropologin och synen på samerna fram mot sekelskiftet 1900', *Lychnos* 1981–2: 27–86.

Bromé, J. 1923. *Nasafjäll: Ett norrländskt silververks historia*. Stockholm: Nordiska bokhandeln.

Bruchac, M. M., Hart, S. M. & Wobst, H. M. (eds) 2010. *Indigenous Archaeologies: A Reader on*

Decolonization. Walnut Creek, CA: Left Coast Press.

Christoffersson, R. 2010. *Med tre röster och tusende bilder: om den samiska trumman*. Religionshistoriska forskningsrapporter från Uppsala 20. Uppsala: Uppsala universitet.

Cramér, T. & Ryd, L. 2012. *Tusen år i Lappmarken: Juridik, skatter, handel och storpolitik*. Skellefteå: Ord & visor.

Davidson, P. 2005. *The Idea of North*. London: Reaktion Books.

Den samiska trumman i historisk tid och nutid: Rapport från seminarium vid Ájtte, Svenskt Fjäll- och Samemuseum 15–16 juni 1999. 2000. Duoddaris 16. Jokkmokk: Ájtte.

Eidlitz Kuoljok, K. 2011. *Den samiska sitan och vinterbyarna: En utmaning*. Dissertations and Documents in Cultural Anthropology 10. Uppsala: Uppsala universitet.

Fossum, B. 2006. *Förfädernas land: En arkeologisk studie av rituella lämningar i Sápmi, 300 f.Kr.–1600 e.Kr.* Studia archaeologica Universitatis Umensis 22. Umeå: Umeå universitet.

Fur, G. 2006. *Colonialism in the Margins: Cultural Encounters in New Sweden and Lapland*. Leiden: Brill.

Fur, G. 2013, 'Colonialism and Swedish history: Unthinkable connections?', in Naum & Nordin 2013, 17–36.

Gärdebo, J., Öhman, M.-B. & Maruyama, H. (eds) 2014. *Re: Mindings – Co-Constituting Indigenous/Academic/Artistic Knowledges*. Uppsala Multiethnic Papers 55. Uppsala: Uppsala universitet.

Göthe, G. 1929. *Om Umeå Lappmarks svenska kolonisation: Från mitten av 1500-talet till omkr. 1750*. Stockholm: Almqvist & Wiksell.

Granqvist, K. 2004. 'Samerna, staten och rätten i Torne lappmark under 1600-talet: Makt, diskurs och representation'. PhD disseratation, Universtiy of Umeå.

Grundström, H. 1930. 'Ett gammalt gravfält i Jokkmokk', *Norrbotten* 9: 135–40.

Hagström Yamamoto, S. 2010. *I gränslandet mellan svenskt och samiskt: Identitetsdiskurser och förhistorien i Norrland från 1870-tal till 2000-tal*. Occasional Papers in Archaeology 52. Uppsala: Uppsala universitet.

Hansen, L.-I. & Olsen, B. 2014. *Hunters in Transition: An Outline of Early Sami History*. Leiden: Brill.

Harlin, E.-K. 2008. *Recalling Ancestral Voices – Repatriation of Sami Cultural Heritage: Projektets Interreg IIIA Slutrapport*. Inari: Siida

Harlin, E.-K. & Lehtola, V.-P. (eds) 2007. *Peurakuopista kirkkokenttiin: Saamelaisalueen 10 000 vuotta arkeologin näkökulmasta, Arkeologiseminaari Inarissa 29.9.–2.10.2005*. Publications of the Giellagas Institute 9. Oulu: Oulu universitet.

Hederyd, O. & Alamäki, Y. (eds) 1993. *Tornedalens historia. Vol. 2: Från 1600-talet till 1809*. Haparanda: Tornedalskommunernas historiebokskommitté.

Hedman, S.-D. 2003. *Boplatser och offerplatser: Ekonomisk strategi och boplatsmönster bland skogssamer 700–1600 AD*. Studia archaeologica Universitatis Umensis 17. Umeå: Umeå universitet.

Herva, V.-P., Ylimaunu, T. & Symonds, J. 2012. 'The urban landscape and iconography of early modern Tornio', *Fennoscandia archaeologica* 29: 73–91.

Holm, N. G. (ed.) 2000. *Ethnography is a Heavy Rite: Studies of Comparative Religion in Honor of Juha Pentikäninen*. Religionsvetenskapliga skrifter 47. Åbo: Åbo Akademi.

Hoppe, G. 1945. *Vägarna inom Norrbottens län: Studier över den trafikgeografiska utvecklingen från 1500-talet till våra dagar*. Geographica: Skrifter från Uppsala universitets geografiska institution 16. Uppsala: Uppsala universitet.

Huuva, K. & Blind, E. 2016. *"När jag var åtta år lämnade jag mitt hem och jag har ännu inte kommit tillbaka": Minnen från samernas skolgång*. Stockholm: Verbum.

Ikäheimo, J., Salmi, A.-K. & Äikäs, T. (eds) 2014. *Sounds like Theory. XII Nordic Theoretical Archaeology Group Meeting in Oulu 25–28.4.2012*. Monographs of the Archaeological Society of Finland 2. Helsinki: Archaeological Society of Finland.

Immonen, V. 2013. 'Intercontinental flows of desire: Brass kettles in Lapland and in the colony of New Sweden', in Beaudry & Parno 2013, 17–30.

Kroik Virdi, Å. 2007. *Hellre mista sitt huvud än lämna sin trumma*. Hönö: Boska.

Lawrence, R. 2014. 'Internal colonisation and indigenous resource sovereignty: Wind power developments on traditional Saami lands', *Environment and Planning D: Society and Space* 32: 1036–53.

Lehtola, V.-P. 2004. *The Sami People: Traditions in Transition*. Fairbanks: University of Alaska Press.

Liebmann, M. & Rizvi, U. Z. (eds) 2010. *Archaeology and the Postcolonial Critique*. Lanham, MD: AltaMira Press.

Liedgren, L. 1997. 'Den gamla kyrk- och marknadsplatsen i Arvidsjaur, Pite lappmark – en mötesplats med medeltida anor', *Norrbotten* 1997: 36–53.

Lindgren, Å. 2015. 'Silbojokk 2015: arkeologisk räddningsundersökning av kyrka och kyrkogård inom Raä Arjeplog 368:1, Arjeplogs KRÖLM, Arjeplogs kommun, Lapplands landskap, Norrbottens län'. Archaeological report. Luleå: Norrbottens museum.

Lindgren, Å., Östlund, O., Sundberg, S. & Backman, L. 2007. 'Rapport arkeologisk undersökning 2005, Silbojokk, Raä 368, Arjeplog socken, Norrbottens län, Lappland'. Archaeological report. Luleå: Norrbottens museum.

Lindin, L. & Svanberg, I. 1990. 'Ren dragande en ackja', *Västerbotten* 1990(2): 110–19.

Lindmark, D. 2006. *En lappdrängs omvändelse: Svenskar i möte med samer och deras religion på 1600- och 1700-talen*. Skrifter från Centrum för samisk forskning, Umeå, 5. Umeå: Umeå universitet.

Lindmark, D. 2013. 'Colonial encounter in early modern Sápmi', in Naum & Nordin 2013, 131–46.

Lindmark, D. & Sundström, O. (eds) 2016. *De historiska relationerna mellan Svenska kyrkan och samerna*. Skellefteå: Artos & Norma.

Ljungdahl, E. & Norberg, E. (eds) 2012. *Ett steg till på vägen: Resultat och reflexioner kring ett dokumentationsprojekt på sydsamiskt område under åren 2008–2011*. Östersund: Gaaltije.

Lundius, N. 1905 [1670s], 'Descriptio Lapponiæ', *Bidrag till kännedom om de svenska landsmålen ock svenskt folkliv* 17(5): 3–41. Stockholm: J. A. Lundell.

Lundmark, B. 2016. 'Medeltida vittnesbörd om samerna och den katolska kyrkan', in Lindmark & Sundström 2016, 221–40.

Lundmark, L. 2008. *Stulet land: Svensk makt på samisk mark*. Stockholm: Ordfront.

Lundmark, L. & Rumar, L. 2008. *Mark och rätt i Sameland*. Rättshistoriska skrifter, Serie 3, 10. Stockholm: Stockholms universitet.

Lundström, I. (ed) 2007. *Historisk rätt? Kultur, politik och juridik i norr*. Stockholm: Riksantikvarieämbetet.

Lydon, J. & Rizvi, U. Z. (eds) 2012. *Handbook of Postcolonial Archaeology*. Walnut Creek, CA: Left Coast Press.

Manker, E. 1938. *Die lappische Zaubertrommel: eine ethnologische Monographie*. Vol. 1: *Die Trommel als Denkmal materieller Kultur*. Stockholm: Thule

Manker, E. 1950. *Die lappische Zaubertrommel: eine ethnologische Monographie*. Vol. 2: *Die Trommel als Urkunde geistigen Lebens*. Stockholm: Thule.

Mathisen Opdahl, S. 2014. 'Etnisitetens estetikk: Visuelle fortellinger og forhandlinger i samiske museumsutstillinger'. PhD dissertation, University of Oslo.

Mulk, I.-M. 1994. *Sirkas: Ett samiskt fångstsamhälle i förändring Kr.f.–1600 e.Kr*. Studia archaeologica Universitatis Umensis 6. Umeå: Umeå universitet.

Mulk, I.-M. & Bayliss-Smith, T. 2006. *Rock Art and Sami Sacred Geography in Badjelánnda,*

Laponia, Sweden: Sailing Boats, Antropomorphs and Reindeer. Kungl. Skytteanska samfundets handlingar 58. Umeå: Skytteanska Samfundet.

Mundal, E. & Rydving, H. (eds) 2010. *Samer som "de andra", samer om "de andra": Identitet och etnicitet i nordiska kulturmöten*. Sami Dutkan 6. Umeå: Umeå universitet.

Naum, M. 2016. 'Between Utopia and Dystopia: Colonial ambivalence and early modern perception of Sápmi', *Itinerario* 40(3): 489–521.

Naum, M. & Nordin, J. M. 2013. 'Introduction: Situating Scandinavian colonialism', in Naum & Nordin 2013, 3–16.

Naum, M. & Nordin, J. M. (eds) 2013. *Scandinavian Colonialism and the Rise of Modernity: Small Time Agents in a Global Arena*. New York: Springer.

Nicholas, G. (ed.) 2011. *Being and Becoming Indigenous Archaeologists*. Walnut Creek, CA: Left Coast Press.

Nodermann-Hedqvist, M. & Manker, E. 1971. 'En lapp, kiörandes en oppstoppad rehn: kommentar till en kunglig representationsgåva', *Livrustkammaren* 12(7–8): 193–214.

Norberg, E. & Winka, U. S. (eds) 2014. *Sydsamer – landskap och historia: Ett dokumentationsprojekt på sydsamiskt område under åren 2012–2014*. Östersund: Gaaltije.

Nordin, J. M. 2012. 'Embodied colonialism: The cultural meaning of silver in a Swedish colonial context in the seventeenth century', *Journal of Post-Medieval Archaeology* 46(1): 143–65.

Nordin, J. M. & Ojala, C.-G. 2017. 'Copper Worlds: A historical archaeology of Abraham and Jakob Momma-Reenstierna and their industrial enterprise in the Torne River Valley, c. 1650–1680', *Acta Borealia* 34(2): 103–33.

Nordlander, J. 1938. *Johan Graan: Landshövding i Västerbotten 1653–1679*. Stockholm: Thule.

Nurmi, R. 2009. 'The others among us? Saami artefacts in a 17th century urban context in the town of Tornio, Finland', in Äikäs 2009, 68–87.

Ojala, C.-G. 2009. *Sami Prehistories: The Politics of Archaeology and Identity in Northernmost Europe*. Occasional Papers in Archaeology 47. Uppsala: Uppsala universitet.

Ojala, C.-G. 2014. 'East and west, north and south in Sápmi: Networks and boundaries in Sami archaeology in Sweden', in Ikäheimo et al. 2014, 173–85.

Ojala, C.-G. 2016. 'Svenska kyrkan och samiska mänskliga kvarlevor', in Lindmark & Sundström 2016, 983–1018.

Ojala, C.-G. & Nordin, J. M. 2015. 'Mining Sápmi: Colonial histories, Sámi archaeology, and the exploitation of natural resources in northern Sweden', *Arctic Anthropology* 52(2): 6–21.

Olaus Magnus 1976 [1555]. *Historia om de nordiska folken*. Stockholm: Gidlund.

Össbo, Å. 2014. *Nya vatten, dunkla speglingar: Industriell kolonialism genom svensk vattenkraftutbyggnad i renskötselområdet 1910–1968*. Skrifter från Centrum för samisk forskning 19. Umeå: Umeå universitet.

Pulkkinen, R. 2000. 'Giants, dwarfs or Lapps? A discussion of the origins of the Sami people and the first inhabitants of Scandinavia and Lapland in the 17th to 19th centuries', in Holm 2000, 216–30.

Rasmussen, S. 2016. 'Samiske prester i den svenske kirka i tidlig nytid', in Lindmark & Sundström 2016, 283–314.

Rheen, S. 1897 [1671]. 'En kortt Relation om Lapparnes Lefwarne och Sedher, wijd-Skiepellsser, sampt i många Stycken Grofwe wildfarellsser', *Bidrag till kännedom om de svenska landsmålen ock svenskt folkliv* 17(1): 3–68. Stockholm: J. A. Lundell.

Roslund, Y. 1989. 'Den arkeologiska undersökningen', in Awebro et al. 1989, 71–132.

Ruong, I. 1983. 'Efterskrift: Vad kan vi i dag utläsa ur 1600-talsprästernas relationer?', in *Berättelser om samerna i 1600-talets Sverige* 1983, 1–8.

Rydström, G. 2009. 'Det äldsta Lycksele – Öhn, Rapport över genomgång och bearbetning av fyndmaterial från undersökningar åren 1949–2001, Raä 343, Gammplatsen, Lycksele socken,

Lappland'. Skogsmuseet rapport 8. Archaeological report. Lycksele: Skogsmuseet.

Rydving, H. 1995. *The End of Drum-Time: Religious Change among the Lule Saami, 1670s–1740s.* 2nd edn. Acta Universitatis Upsaliensis – Historia Religionum 12. Uppsala: Uppsala universitet.

Rydving, H. 2006. 'Gustav II Adolf och samerna', *Saga och Sed – Kungl. Gustav Adolfs Akademiens Årsbok* 2006: 15–27.

Rydving, H. 2010a. *Tracing Sami Traditions: In Search of the Indigenous Religion among the Western Sami during the 17th and 18th Centuries.* Oslo: Institute for Comparative Research in Human Culture.

Rydving, H. 2010b. 'Samiska överhetspersoner i Sverige-Finland under 1600-talet', in Mundal & Rydving 2010, 259–65.

Schefferus, J. 1956 [1673]. *Lappland.* Translated by Henrik Sundin. Uppsala: Almqvist & Wiksell.

Schefferus, J. 1971 [1674]. *The History of Lapland wherein are shewed the original, manners, habits, marriages, conjurations, &c. of that people.* [Oxford]: At the Theater in Oxford.

Snickare, M. 2014. 'Kontroll, begär och kunskap: Den koloniala kampen om Goavddis', *RIG* 97(2): 65–77.

Sörlin, S. 1988. *Framtidslandet: Debatten om Norrland och naturresurserna under det industriella genombrottet.* Stockholm: Carlsson.

Strömbäck D. (ed.) 1954. *Scandinavica et Fenno-Ugrica: Studier tillägnade Björn Collinder den 22 juli 1954.* Stockholm: Almqvist & Wiksell.

Tanner, V. 1929. *Antropogeografiska studier inom Petsamo-området, 1, Skolt-lapparna.* Fennia 49(4). Helsinki: Societas geographica Fenniae.

Tornæus, J. 1900 [1672]. 'Berättelse om Lapmarcherna och Deras Tillstånd', *Bidrag till kännedom om de svenska landsmålen ock svenskt folkliv* 17(3): 9–64. Stockholm: J. A. Lundell.

Wallerström, T. 1995. *Norrbotten, Sverige och medeltiden: Problem kring makt och bosättning i en europeisk periferi 1–2.* Lund Studies in Medieval Archaeology 15. Lund: Lunds universitet.

Wallerström, T. 2006. *Vilka var först? En nordskandinavisk konflikt som historisk-arkeologiskt dilemma.* Stockholm: Riksantikvarieämbetet.

Zachrisson, I. 2007. 'Arkeologi inför rätta: Sydsamernas äldre historia', in Lundström 2007, 137–57.

12

Lapland's Taxation as a Reflection of "Otherness" in the Swedish Realm in the 17th and 18th Centuries: Colonialism, or a Priority Right of the Sami People?

Matti Enbuske

Taxation has been a mechanism for the wielding of power in relation to control over land areas throughout history. As late as the 17th and 18th centuries, Lapland comprised its own special region in the Swedish Empire, where the Crown sought through taxation to consolidate "otherness" – the Sami culture – into a fixed part of the empire. The focus of this chapter is upon the question of whether the government sought to colonize Lapland by means of dictates related to taxation, or whether the aim of Lapland's tax system was to protect the rights of the people living there. Examination of the tax system permits an understanding of how the government sought to find an administrative solution that best suited a population group which differed from the mainstream culture. However, the system also had negative consequences for the Sami people.

Throughout history, taxation has been crucially linked to the wielding of power. Taxation has never been an independent, unconnected or solely local phenomenon, but rather a top-down mechanism for controlling the economy and exercising authority. In Sweden, as late as the 17th and 18th centuries, Lapland clearly constituted a special region in which it was not possible to practise large-scale agriculture. However, the Crown sought to consolidate otherness – Sami culture – as an integral part of the realm. This unification was a reflection of intellectual values, since the government understood Lapland's special economic and livelihood-related circumstances and the taxation could not be the same in Lapland as in other parts of the Swedish Empire.

In this chapter I examine the special characteristics of Lapland's system of taxation and the significance these had from the standpoint of "otherness" and diversity. The focus is on whether in the 17th and 18th centuries the Swedish Crown – the central power – sought to pursue a colonialist agenda in Lapland by means of its regulations with regard to taxation, or whether Lapland's system of taxation was intended rather to protect the traditional rights of the population there. What did Lapland's taxation and Lappish "tax-land" – whereby earnings from hunting and fishing but not the quality and extent of the terrain were taken into account – mean from the standpoint of "otherness" and diversity?

TAXATION AND LAPLAND'S "OTHERNESS"

Since the Middle Ages, taxes had been collected from Lapland's inhabitants in the form of products of their livelihoods. In medieval Sweden, taxes became an annual burden imposed on settled farms and their fields, meadows, pastures and fishing waters. Because Lapland was part of the realm of Sweden, the Swedish tax system also had an impact there, though in the 13th century the Crown had relinquished tax collection as a privilege to the "birkarls" (*birkarlar*), settlers who had the exclusive right to trade with the Sami.[1]

There were no farms in Lapland as there were elsewhere in Sweden, so taxation had to be adapted to the region's special circumstances.[2] In principle, all taxpayers in a *sijdda* (village-like Sami community) paid an equal sum to the Crown through the birkarls: *den fastställde stadgeskatten* ("fixed permanent tax").[3] The means of payment – taxable products – could not be standardized, as the yield of natural products could vary greatly from year to year.[4] For hundreds of years, tax contributions were therefore in the form of a standardized per capita amount. During Gustav Vasa's reign in the mid-16th century, however, Sweden's strengthened central government reformed the realm's taxation system. Taxes were raised significantly. Reform was also implemented in Lapland, where tax collection was transferred in 1553 from the birkarls to bailiffs of the Crown. The change hardly had any practical significance for the inhabitants of Sami villages; but the loss of the right to collect taxes was a severe financial setback for the birkarls.[5]

Taxation in Lapland in the 17th century remained based on each "Lapp's" – as the Sami inhabitants of Lapland were called – personal liability to pay. The taxable yield of livelihoods came from the lands and waters, which were the usufruct of tax-paying Sami. Contrary to the taxation system applied to peasants, the amount of tax paid in Lapland still did not depend on the quantity of products obtained from usufruct land each year – from hunting and fishing; rather, the tax payable was a set sum specified beforehand for each contributor – that is, the head of each family.

Overall, taxation of Lapland's inhabitants was implemented from the Middle Ages to the 17th century in a manner suited to local circumstances. It can reasonably be claimed that up to the 17th century the Swedish Crown understood Lapland's "otherness" at a practical level. The Sami were given a special status in relation to the rest of the realm. Their free status was also emphasized by the vagueness of boundaries in the northern part of the realm: they were able to migrate freely between their hunting grounds, the fells and the sea coast. This also made it possible to practise reindeer husbandry, which grew robustly in the 16th century, and in the 17th, large-scale reindeer farming became a very widespread means of livelihood.

The basis of the Sami *sijdda* was the old Sami families of the village community, but it operated in a different manner from the typical traditional peasant village. The families lived on their usufruct lands permanently, and moved on their land according to the yearly rhythm of their livelihoods. The role of the Sami village, or winter-village, as a physical location, was minor from a communal perspective: the annual winter meeting there was mainly important for trade, taxation and for attending to the general affairs of the community.

During the existence of the Swedish Empire, the central government tried to unify the provincial systems under a national administration, which would also include Lapland.

In part the unification was expressed in the *Lappsmarksplakaten* of 1673 and 1695, which aimed to facilitate Swedish settlement in Lapland. Only after 1673 was it possible to establish farms there. The settlement programme drawn up by the Västerbotten county governor Gabriel Gyllengrip during the 1730s and 1740s became a milestone in the history of land colonization in Lapland. The governor's aim was to attract new settlers to the territory, to reform Sami ways of life, from nomadism to permanent settlement, and to emphasize the responsibilities of agriculture – proper farming practices – among pioneering settlers. The principles formulated by Gyllengrip also constituted the framework of the third settler proclamation, issued in 1749.

THE INSTITUTION OF "TAX-LAND"

King Carl IX tried to introduce a new form of taxation in 1602 but this reform was unsuccessful. Changes in taxation began to take place in the second half of the 17th century. The Crown's officials began to define family land inherited by taxpaying inhabitants of Sami villages by applying the concept of "tax-land" (*skatteland*). The earliest recorded use of the term *skatteland* is from 1658, in Åsele in Lapland. Sami were warned at the rural court sessions in Åsele about the consequences of three years of back taxes – they would lose their tax-land.[6] The idea of tax-land did not have negative consequences for the local communities: for example, the *sijdda*'s role was not reduced and taxation was not harsher than before. From the viewpoint of cameral jurisprudence, payment of taxes was understood to give Sami the right to use certain land and water areas for their livelihoods; part of their yield was taken as payment to the Crown in a form of Lappish tax. Thus the concept of "Lappish tax-land" (*lappskatteland*) arose.[7]

The reason for this change in the mid-17th century was to make it possible for the Crown's officials to administer more efficiently, by means of the new tax-land concept, land use and legal order in Sami villages. The concept paralleled the land tax system, and related decrees applied elsewhere in the realm. The Lappish tax-land was comparable to the peasant tax system, but with a unique application. It should be noted that in the 1620s the Swedish Crown had tightened its control over peasant farms. This was especially apparent with regard to taxation, where the concept of "tax-abandonment", for example, was adopted in specifying the status of farms. The Crown saw a need to apply the same kinds of procedure to the usufruct lands of the Sami as to peasants' farms, including regulations relating to cases of inability to pay taxes and abandonment of land.[8]

In a broader context, the 17th-century state intervention and extension of legal rules and customs of the realm to Lapland would also be easy to see in parallel to, for example, the establishment of the colony of New Sweden in Delaware, and to Sweden's expansionist power politics in general.[9] Indeed, the extension of the tax-land institution to Lapland can be represented as direct intervention by the Swedish Crown – a colonialist act in Lapland by which the inhabitants of Sami villages could be subordinated to the Crown[10] and Lapland could be subjugated as a productive part of the realm of Sweden. In reality, however, the Lappish tax-land system can be regarded as a positive phenomenon for inhabitants of Sami villages who lived on family lands, and in the light of later developments, also as a successful initiative.

In 1922 Swedish researcher Åke Holmbäck incorporated the "Lappish tax-land institution" (*Lappskattelandsinstitutet*) into the title of his study: he basically understood it to
be an ancient internal system of the Sami villages.[11] Contrary to Holmbäck's assumption,
however, Lappish tax-land was not an institution spontaneously developed by the Sami,
even though tax-lands were comprised of the traditional usufruct lands of families in
Sami villages. Lappish tax-land started to develop in the 17th century as a result of a
reform shaped by the ideas of a governor of Västerbotten county, Johan Graan (1653–79),
himself of Sami origin. The new tax system created a link between the Crown and the
Sami – the Crown administration was able to use the tax-land institution to administer
the usufruct lands of the Sami in an organized manner, depicted in Figure 12.1 below.

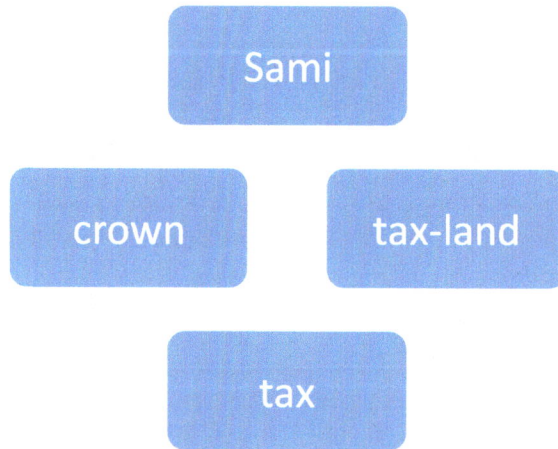

Fig. 12.1 Organization of the 17th-century Sami tax system (drawing: Matti Enbuske).

From the standpoint of historical development, Lappish tax-land had great significance, as this intermediary link made it possible for taxed land within Sami villages
to remain under the control of families united within the *sijdda* and finally to become
directly part of the farm's land under the pioneer farm system in the 18th century.[12] It
should be noted that from the perspective of modern taxation legislation, individual
Sami people's control of Lappish tax-land fulfilled the characteristics of ownership at
that time. In that sense too Lappish tax-land was comparable to the peasant farm
system.[13]

Sweden's central authority sought to come up with an administrative solution best
suited to a population group that differed from the dominant culture in the 17th and
18th centuries. Indeed, the Lappish tax-land system had some very positive effects for
members of Sami villages. Family lands remained under Sami control. The Lappish
tax-lands also acquired a legally-protected status which, especially under the pressure of
pioneer settlement in the 18th century, guaranteed the Sami the possibility to control
their own usufruct land. The possessor of Lappish tax-land had a farmer's rights but no
farmer's encumbrances such as requirements to clear the land and to practise agriculture,
or an obligation to build a farm. Another significant benefit was the preservation of

certain privileges of Lapland, such as exemption from military service.[14] Thus the system *reinforced* "otherness".

LAPPISH TAX-LAND FROM THE STANDPOINT OF ETHNIC DIVERSITY

From the viewpoint of ethnic diversity it can be said that as a result of the tax system, Lapland was preserved as a unique part of the realm of Sweden, and the Sami retained a privileged status compared with other population groups. On the other hand, in intellectual and religious terms, the Swedish Crown applied a purposeful unification policy in Lapland from the 17th century onwards. There was no room for otherness in religion.[15] This was a question of ideological and "intellectual colonialism".[16]

A significant change had occurred in Lapland in 1673, when the Crown issued a proclamation of settlement that enabled the establishment of the first farms – pioneer farms – in the territory. The question arose of how these pioneer farms in Lapland should be taxed. At first taxes were determined in the same way as Lappish tax. This was not in practice problematic at the end of the 17th century, since the pioneer farms were in any case exempt from tax for a number of years.

A change was introduced in Lapland's taxation system in 1695, whereupon Sami villages began to be taxed at a fixed village-specific rate. At the same time King Carl XI issued a new proclamation to promote settlement in Lapland. The change was connected to broader administrative reforms in the realm of Sweden, the most significant being the "Great Reduction" – returning noble fiefs to the Crown – decreed by Carl XI. In the reform of 1695, one common tax was levied upon each Sami village, which the inhabitants of the village paid collectively. The change was not significant, as each taxpaying member of the village had to pay the same fixed sum as before. In other words, the common tax sum paid by the village was calculated on the basis of the contributions due previously from individual taxpayers, and the tax burden neither increased nor decreased. Lappish tax-lands also remained the usufruct lands of individual taxpayers. Pioneer settlers in Sami villages were included in this collective village tax.[17]

According to some researchers, the tax reassessment of 1695 indicates that Sami villages owned all the land in the village collectively.[18] This view is historically unsustainable. The Sami *village* was not the object of taxation – it functioned as an administrative unit comprised of individual taxpayers. Correspondingly, the collective tax of the Sami village was determined by the number of taxpayers, not the territorial size of the unit. The Sami village was comparable to the parish in peasant-farm regions. The Lappish tax-lands of the Sami formed properties comparable to farms, and the payer of Lappish tax had a possessory relationship similar to that of peasants elsewhere in the Swedish realm. Like parishes, Sami villages also contained tracts of common land (*allmänningar*).[19]

However, the Lappish tax-land institution broke down among reindeer-herding nomads in the 18th century, as was clearly apparent in Jokkmokk, for example, with regard to the many disagreements over land use.[20] Large-scale reindeer husbandry required ever larger areas of grazing land, and the grounds inside Sami villages were not large enough for the continuously increasing number of reindeer.

The taxation of those who practised reindeer husbandry as their main occupation came to be based on the number of their reindeer, not the land area utilized in pursuing their livelihood. Reindeer husbandry was not connected to the farm system, but the Sami large-scale reindeer husbandry was given a special ethnic "Lapp" status in the 18th century: it became regarded the only acceptable "Lappish" livelihood, for the Crown wanted to protect reindeer husbandry in the fell regions.[21] It should be noted that reindeer husbandry was also allowed on farms, though only as a side-occupation. However, livelihood and taxation decrees of the mid-1700s (third settler proclamation in Lapland in 1749 and the taxation ruling of 1760) led to reindeer nomadism gradually becoming the dominant form of Sami culture, indeed so much so that being Sami was understood as being nomadic.[22] The image of a diversified Sami culture was transformed into homogenized stereotype. This had significance in the 20th century, when forest Sami culture, for example, was thought to have disappeared entirely.

THE CULMINATION OF SETTLEMENT DEVELOPMENT

Examining the history of Lapland's settlement as a long-term, overall development, the most significant change can be identified as taking place in the mid-1700s. The principal measures involved were the third settler proclamation of 1749 and the related Lapland taxation ruling of 1760. Lapland's administration was thereby linked into the nation-wide system which adopted an ideology of utility and included also a strong ecclesiastical influence, within a context of Enlightenment thinking. Indeed, the policy of the Swedish Crown in Lapland in the mid-1700s reflected a utilitarian notion current at the time, in accordance with which physiocratism – an emphasis upon the centrality of agriculture – became the starting point for development plans. The development of Lapland in the 18th century was guided by four elements:[23]

1. the idea of economic benefit, which underlay Lapland's pioneer settlement (including Sami as pioneer settlers);

2. nation-wide economic development, which stressed productive livelihoods in Lapland (agriculture, mines, utilization of forests);

3. "civilization" and education in line with mainstream culture;

4. Lutheran mission, erasure of traditional beliefs and practices and establishment of parishes in Lapland.

In line with this development, after the 1760s the inhabitants of Lapland's forest Sami villages, in particular, were required to change their status to that of pioneer settlers, and at the same time their traditional Lappish tax-lands were reclassified as pioneer farm lands. As a result of the 1760 tax reform, the Sami began to pay taxes on their tax-lands that resembled those levied according to the system applied to farms, based upon the farm's yield and the dimensions of its areas of land and water.[24]

CONCLUSIONS

In all, Swedish systems of taxation in the 17th and 18th centuries reflected the existence of "otherness" within the realm. The central power understood this, but at an intellectual level such otherness represented a threat to authority: the population had to be made uniform. Thus, Lapland's otherness was a two-pronged phenomenon. On one hand it was economically beneficial for the central power to preserve Lapland's special status, but on the other, the Sami population's diversity was ideologically detrimental to the central power.

Regardless of the central power's actions, the special characteristics of Lapland's system of taxation upheld otherness – cultural and also ethnic diversity. In examining the tax system we are able to perceive how the government in the 17th and 18th centuries sought to find an administrative solution that best suited a population group which differed from the dominant culture. From this point of view taxation was a priority right of the Sami people.

The Swedish central government tried to unify provincial systems under a national administration, which would also include Lapland. A clear turning point was experienced in the mid-17th century, when the government began to apply an administrative model comparable to that applied to farmland use to the private family lands of Sami villages. This development produced the settler proclamations of 1673, 1695 and 1749, as a result of which pioneer settlers who joined the farm system found themselves at an advantage compared to those practising the Sami livelihoods of hunting, fishing and reindeer husbandry. The change provoked a movement of Sami from the Lappish tax-lands into the sphere of the new farm system.

Even if the Crown's taxation policy served to protect individual Sami, both judicially and administratively, it also had negative consequences. Taxation might be termed a bureaucratic "key" of the government to the administration of land use in Sami villages. The Crown also reserved to itself the right to resolve disputes involving the tax-lands of the Sami, as well as to deal with questions of ownership and usage rights. The Crown's strengthening of its administrative grip on Sami land from the 17th century onwards can be interpreted, on the local level, in a negative light. The reclassification of the Lappish tax lands into pioneer farmlands put pressure on the Sami families to become agricultural farmers. The Crown also forced many inhabitants of Lapland to labour in the local mines and to transport ores and other commodities by reindeer. When the burdens increased, many of the reindeer herders moved to Norway. Another negative consequence of the taxation system was alterations to the livelihood of the mountain Sami and of people living in areas where agriculture was subordinate to the occupation of reindeer herding.

In the 19th century, the Sami were further constrained by the dominant culture and the influence of racial theory and racial bias, in what may be termed an "ideological colonialism". The government became the dominant player in the shaping of Lapland's circumstances in the 19th century, when administrative institutions became more powerful, individual regions' economic dependence on the government grew, travel conditions improved and the national education system made ever deeper inroads into the education of Sami children. The expectation was that ethnic diversity would inevitably disappear. These pressures were magnified by the strengthening of a nationalistic ideology in Sweden and Finland, according to which a unified, progressive people was seen as the ideal condition for the nation state.

NOTES

1 Hannerberg 1981, 457–61.
2 Kvist 1990, 264–5.
3 See Fellman 1915, 29–31.
4 Dovring 1951, 135; Jonsson 1971, 23–4, 42–8.
5 Enbuske 2008, 251–2.
6 Holmbäck 1922, 26; Hiltunen 2007, 127.
7 Enbuske 2013, 42–3.
8 Enbuske 2008, 263–4.
9 Ilmonen 1988; Fur 2006.
10 Hiltunen 2007, 127–30.
11 Holmbäck 1922, 26–9; also Arell 1977, 66–9 and Päiviö 2001, 21–6.
12 Enbuske 2008, 263; Arell 1979.
13 The question of owners of the land in Lapland has been investigated by many scholars: see for instance Korpijaakko-Labba 1994; Lundmark 2008; Joona 2006; Enbuske 2008.
14 Enbuske 2008, 263.
15 Kylli 2009, 158–9.
16 For a definition, see Tuominen 2010, 336–7; Lehtola 2012, 17.
17 Enbuske 2008, 259–62.
18 Especially Korpijaakko-Labba 1994.
19 Enbuske 2008, 188; also Prawitz 1967, 17–18.
20 Hultblad 1968; Korpijaakko-Labba 2000, 126.
21 Enbuske 2008, 211.
22 Enbuske 2013, 48–9.
23 Enbuske 2008, 192–4.
24 Enbuske 2008, 271–5.

BIBLIOGRAPHY

Arell, N. 1977. *Rennomadismen i Torne lappmark: markanvändning under koloni-sationsepoken i fr.a. Enontekis socken*. Geografiska institutionen, Meddelande 24. Umeå: Skytteanska Samfundet.

Arell, N. 1979. *Kolonisationen i Lappmarken: några näringsgeografiska aspekter*. Stockholm: Esselte studium.

Åkerman, S. & K. Lundholm (eds) 1990. *Älvdal i norr: Människor och resurser i Luledalen 1300–1800*. Acta Universitatis Umensis, Umeå Studies in the Humanities 91. Umeå: Umeå universitet.

Dovring, F. 1951. *De stående skatterna på jord 1400–1600*. Skrifter utg. av Kungl. Humanistiska Vetenskapssamfundet i Lund 49. Lund: Gleerup.

Elenius, L. (ed.) 2009. *Fredens konsekvenser: samhällsförändringar i norr efter 1809*. Studier i norra Europas historia 7. Luleå: Luleå tekniska universitet.

Enbuske, M. 2008. *Vanhan Lapin valtamailla. Asutus ja maankäyttö Kemin Lapin ja Enontekiön alueella 1500-luvulta 1900-luvun alkuun*. Bibliotheca Historica 113. Helsinki: Suomalaisen Kirjallisuuden Seura.

Enbuske, M. 2013. 'Saamelaiset Lapin uudisasuttajina', in Sarivaara *et al.* 2013, 33–53.

Fellman, I. 1915. 'Inledning', in Fellman 1915, 1–33.

Fellman, I. (ed.) 1915. *Handlingar och uppsatser angående Finska Lappmarken och Lapparne*, vol. 4. Helsinki: Finska litteratursällskapets tryckeri.

Fur, G. 2006. *Colonialism in the Margins: Cultural Encounters in New Sweden and Lapland*. Leiden: Brill.

Grinder-Hansen, P. (ed.) 1996. *Margrete 1: Nordens Frue og Husbond: Kalmarunionen 600 år: essays og udstillingskatalog*. Copenhagen: Nationalmuseet.

Hannerberg, D. 1981. 'Markland', *Kulturhistorisk lexikon för Nordisk medeltid från vikingatid till reformationstid.* Vol. 11: *Luft–Motståndsrätt.* 2nd edn. Copenhagen: Rosenkilde og Bagger.

Hiltunen, M. 2007. *Norjan ja Norlannin välissä: Enontekiö 1550–1808: asukkaat, elinkeinot ja maanhallinta.* Scripta historica 32. Oulu: Oulun historiaseura.

Holmbäck, Å. 1922. *Om Lappskattelandsinstitutet och dess historiska utveckling.* Statens offentliga utredningar 1922:16. Uppsala: Socialdepartementet.

Hultblad, F. 1968. *Övergång från nomadism till agrar bosättning i Jokkmokks socken.* Acta Lapponica 14. Stockholm: Almqvist & Wiksell.

Ilmonen, S. 1988. *Delawaren suomalaiset.* Hämeenlinna: Karisto Oy.

Jonsson, I. 1971. *Jordskatt och kameral organisation i Norrland under äldre tid.* Meddelande 7, Geografiska institutionen. Umeå: Umeå universitet.

Joona, J. 2006. *Entisiin Tornion ja Kemin Lapinmaihin kuuluneiden alueiden maa- ja vesioikeuksista.* Juridica Lapponica 32. Rovaniemi.

Korpijaakko-Labba, K. 1994. *Om samernas rättsliga ställning i Sverige-Finland: En rättshistorisk utredning av markanvändnings förhållanden och -rättigheter i Västerbottens lappmark före mitten av 1700-talet.* Helsinki: Juristförbundets förl.

Korpijaakko-Labba, K. 2000. *Saamelaisten oikeusasemasta Suomessa: kehityksen pääpiirteet Ruotsin vallan lopulta itsenäisyyden ajan alkuun.* Dieđut 1999:1. Rovaniemi: Sami Instituhtta.

Kvist, R. 1990. 'Beskattningen av samerna i Sverige 1695–1860', in Åkerman & Lundholm 1990, 264–305.

Kylli, R. 2009. '1809 års gräns och dess inverkan på samerna', in Elenius 2009, 157–65.

Lehtola, V.-P. 2012. *Saamelaiset suomalaiset: kohtaamisia 1896–1953.* Helsinki: Suomalaisen Kirjallisuuden Seura.

Lundmark, L. 2008. *Stulet land. Svensk makt på samisk mark.* Stockholm: Ordfront.

Päiviö, N.-J. 2001. *Lappskattelandens rättsliga utveckling i Sverige: en utredning om lappskattelandens och de samiska rättigheternas utveckling från mitten av 1600-talet till 1886-års renbeteslag.* Dieđut 2001:3. Guovdageaidnu: Sami Instituhtta.

Prawitz, G. 1967. *Samernas skattefjäll III. Samernas domstolinslaga den 22 september 1967. Lappskattelanden I.* Utredning av Gunnar Prawitz Den 14 August 1967. Stockholm: Svenska samernas riksförbund.

Rantala, H. & S. Ollitervo (eds) 2010. *Kulttuurihistoriallinen katse.* Cultural History – Kulttuurihistoria 8. Turku: Turun yliopisto.

Sarivaara, E., Määttä, K. & S. Uusiautti (eds) 2013. *Kuka on saamelainen ja mitä on saamelaisuus: identiteetin juurilla.* Rovaniemi: Lapin yliopistokustannus.

Tuominen, M. 2010. 'Missä maanpiiri päättyy? Pohjoisen kulttuurihistorian paikat ja haasteet', in Rantala & Ollitervo 2010, 309–37.

III

Overseas Travel

Introduction

Magdalena Naum and Fredrik Ekengren

The final chapters of the book discuss otherness experienced as a result of personal encounters with the outside world. The case studies from diverse geographical locations – North and South America, Spain, North Africa and China – illuminate the complex processes of defining, interacting with, and coming to an understanding of unfamiliar places and peoples, and grappling with linguistic and cultural barriers.

Encounters with foreign peoples, landscapes and cultures were most commonly brought about by travel. These meetings spurred comparisons and judgements of the other against oneself, confirming and questioning existing stereotypes and adding to the body of knowledge about the inhabitants of exotic parts of the world. Opportunities to travel beyond both the realm and the European continent became more numerous in early modern Sweden. In the 17th century Sweden expanded its international commerce and joined other European nations in the pursuit of profitable colonial trade. Individual seamen and adventurers joined foreign and later domestic trading companies, whose ships took them to Africa and Asia, bringing them face to face with the inhabitants of these continents. Narratives of these encounters – from mid-17th century account of Japan by Olof Erickson and descriptions of South Africa, the Middle East, India and South-east Asia by Nils Matsson Kiöping to numerous 18th-century reports of China written by the employees of the Swedish East India Company – bespoke vast differences and diversity of peoples and cultures and fed the imaginations of the readers back home.

In the 17th century, the politically and territorially ambitious Kingdom of Sweden started to formulate a plan for colonial expansion, following examples of other European nations. In 1624 the king authorized the foundation of the Swedish South Company. Its broadly-defined goals included trade, colonization and missionary work in Asia, Africa, America and the still hypothetical *Terra Magellanica* (Australia). A concrete result of this ambitious endeavour was the colony of New Sweden established along the Delaware river in north-eastern America.

Besides long-distance travel and colonial endeavours, envoys and embassies created important settings for the encounter with and observation of foreign peoples and cultures. One exotic destination for Swedish emissaries was the Ottoman court in Constantinople. Although geographically closer than Africa or the Far East, the city was no less colourful and "outlandish", and it supplied a wealth of stories and depictions of eastern customs, Islam and civil life, as well as life at the royal court. The Swedish emissaries became a fixture in the city from the early 18th century onwards, and were also stationed in the North African states which were the regencies of the Ottoman Empire.

These travels to conduct trade, to see the antipodes, to colonize and to mediate political agreements were supplemented in the 18th century by journeys in the name of science. Elevated by Linnaeus as an essential aspect of scientific progress, the object of such explorations was to describe the flora and fauna of the world, put the known and unknown natural realm into manageable categories and systems, and study their properties from a utilitarian point of view. These seemingly innocent aims were in fact well incorporated into the colonial agenda of appropriating the other and advancing national claims to land and resources. Linnaeus's students were diligent scholars and travellers whose pursuit of knowledge took them to all the continents. While collecting, classifying and studying plants, animals and minerals they also pondered variation in the human world, and compiled ethnographic accounts of the "natives" they encountered.

The studies in this section of the book elaborate upon these diverse circumstances of meeting the other and illustrate the variety of responses these meetings inspired. Lisa Hellman studies the interactions between Swedish East India Company supercargoes, representatives of other European companies, and Chinese merchants and administrators. She pays particular attention to the development of trans-cultural trust, which required a complex process of understanding the other's cultural norms, downplaying existing differences and elaborating a common language and practice for the sake of commercial benefits. Magdalena Naum analyses the many facets of otherness experienced by Swedish settlers in the multicultural landscape of colonial America. She studies how categories of "other" were produced, maintained and erased in the colony, noting ambivalence to be an enduring condition of colonial settings. Fredrik Ekengren stresses an important cultural aspect of the colony: its geographical space was continuously shared and cohabited, and its landscape co-produced, by Native Americans and Swedes, a fact that is often obscured by methodological biases in archaeological research. Joachim Östlund analyses the historical and ethnographic narratives of Carl Reftelius, a Swedish consul in Algiers, whose appointment terminated a century-long era of privateering and kidnappings of Swedish (and other) ships in the Mediterranean. Enslavements of seamen were widely-publicized events, which evoked varying responses from the Swedish public, from patriotic and restrained comments in newspapers and royal decrees to strong views on the brutality and wickedness of the 'Turks' in prayer books. In the narratives of Reftelius the judgement became more ambivalent and nuanced, combining praise for the learning and culture of the Caliphate with contempt for Islam. Travels and experienced difference of Linnaean scholars, in particular Pehr Löfling, are discussed by Kenneth Nyberg. During his short career Löfling had to navigate and grapple with new social, cultural and intellectual contexts that confronted him with the challenges of diversity. He was a Swedish Protestant living in Catholic Spain, a Linnaean in an intellectual environment adhering to Tournefort, an educated and cosmopolitan European in colonial rural Venezuela. Together the chapters presented here illustrate the wide geographical scope of early modern Swedish travel and range of attitudes towards the world which was encountered.

13

"How It Would Be to Walk on the New World with Feet from the Old": Facing Otherness in Colonial America

MAGDALENA NAUM

To prospective emigrants and to the newcomers in New Sweden, America appeared as a strange and ambiguous place – wild and dangerous yet beautiful and bountiful. The settlers tried to overcome the "otherness" they encountered, of the landscape, people and culture, through the strategies of domestication and "translation". However, the many aspects of otherness faced in colonial America affected the everyday behaviour of the Swedish-speaking population. These contradictory forces were reflected in material culture and material decisions of the colonists. Drawing upon historical and archaeo- logical sources, this chapter explores these complex engagements with old traditions and new cultural elements in the multicultural settings of New Sweden.

IMAGINING AMERICA

In the early decades of the 17th century, when the idea of the Swedish colony of New Sweden was conceived and realized, America had a vague place in popular conscious- ness. Knowledge of the new continent was rather limited, and early Swedish images of it were influenced by tales told by foreign travellers and sailors, by pictorial representations in prints and maps, and by news and reports published in foreign and domestic news- papers and broadsheets. These diverse accounts mixed fact with fiction and presented the continent as a confusing place.[1]

America was often judged to be the materialization of a biblical paradise, a land of plenty promising quick and substantial profits.[2] Such a version of the continent was presented by Willem Usselincx in his 1624 negotiations with Gustavus Adolphus to establish a Swedish colonial trading company, and promoted by Johan Risingh, New Sweden's last governor. The potential of the New World and benefits of a colonial venture were painted with broad strokes as an answer to the aspirations of the ambitious Swedish kingdom. Usselincx and Risingh argued, for example, that the New World and trans-oceanic connections were the major source of wealth of the Dutch Republic and Spain, and Sweden should follow the colonial path to enhance its economy, political status and culture.[3] The perception of America as a seemingly boundless source for quenching European appetites and desires was also fuelled by reports of the legendary riches of the Spanish treasure fleet that occasionally appeared in *Ordinari Post Tijdender* ("Regular Mail Times"), founded in 1645.

However, there was no shortage of contradictory and disillusioning opinions, describing the trans-Atlantic journey as a precarious endeavour and portraying the New World as a dangerous and barren place. According to these reports, America was a place of unpredictable weather, scorching summers and unbearably cold winters, incurable diseases, and various unfamiliar nuisances.[4] What made it even worse was the supposed barbarity, cruelty and cannibalism of its natives. It was a land-mass far removed not only physically but also culturally from Europe. The novelty and unfamiliarity of the continent and the dangers of the trans-oceanic crossing were too much to bear for some of the early English and French colonists who gave these testimonies, and whose stories may have reached Sweden in the form of both written and oral accounts.

Along with these testimonies, a number of popular tales circulating through Europe depicted America in a grotesque and exaggerated manner. It was a land of bizarre marvels, roamed by monstrous and curious creatures – dog-headed beings, headless blemmyes, cannibals, giants and pygmies – races that were believed to inhabit the margins of the world.[5] It was also a place of wonder, a location of the mythical Fountain of Youth, City of Gold and Paradise. In these widespread stories, America served as a backdrop on which to project popular desires, fantasies and fears, and was fitted into already familiar discourses of exotic, marvellous and monstrous margins deriving from Antiquity and popularized in the Middle Ages.[6]

America, then, represented a great unknown and the ultimate "other". This uncertainty and incongruity made it difficult initially to attract prospective emigrants willing to relocate to New Sweden and led to its styling as an appropriate destination for adventurers as well as petty criminals and unwanted elements of society.[7] Those who boarded the ships bound for New Sweden, either by force or willingly, must have anxiously wondered "how it would be to walk on the New World with feet from the Old" – a rhetorical question posed by a Swedish pastor, Erik Björk, who arrived in America in 1697.[8]

ENCOUNTERING THE OTHER IN AMERICA

The first physical encounters with the new continent simultaneously confirmed and denied preconceived notions. It inspired a mixture of wonder and disdain. "It is a remarkably beautiful country, with all the glories which a human being on earth ever at any time may wish," wrote governor Printz to chancellor Oxenstierna.[9] "Such a fertile country that the pen is too weak to describe, praise and [sufficiently] extol; yes indeed, on account of its fertility it may well be called a land flowing with milk and honey"; "[It] can be compared to Canaan. In my opinion a more beautiful land cannot be found. The earth gives abundantly, through God's blessing, what has been sown and planted in it," seconded Per Lindeström, who visited the colony in 1654–5,[10] and pastor Andreas Rudman in his 1697 report back to Sweden.[11]

The splendid fertility and exotic abundance of the country was not without its perils. Lack of knowledge about indigenous flora and fauna led to lethal encounters with poisonous plants and animals.[12] In summer, boggy areas along the Delaware river were infested with mosquitoes, causing outbreaks of malaria.[13] Fevers, agues and new diseases periodically decimated the communities. But the greatest curiosity, anxiety and fear were caused by encounters with the indigenous inhabitants of the country.[14] If the natural landscape of America was the desirable "other" that was generally understood and appreciated as bountiful, beautiful and better than European homelands, then the Native Americans were for the most part portrayed as a despicable "other" – bestial, idolatrous and primitive.

Perception and description of the Native Americans displayed a spectrum of opinion. Roughly contemporary to each other, pastor Anders Sandel and a portrait-painter Gustav Hesselius had a very low opinion of the Lenape – a group living in the vicinity of the Swedish settlements. Sandel called them *"barbarorum barbarissimi"* – the most barbarous of barbarians – because of their supposed cruelty towards their enemies and prisoners and their cultural practices at odds with Christian sensitivities.[15] Shortly after his arrival in America, Gustav Hesselius confessed his disdain for the Native Americans in a 1714 letter to his mother:

> Concerning the Indians, it is a savage and terrifying folk. They are naked both menfolk and womenfolk, and have only a little loincloth on, they mark their faces and bodies with many kinds of colors as red, blue and black. (…) They grease their bodies and head with bearfat and hang broken tobacco pipes in their ears, some hang rabbit tails and other devilments, and they think they are totally beautiful. (…) The king is no better that the others, all go naked and live worse than swine. I have also been in their village where they live some miles from here. They build their houses of bark and wish to please us; give us food and drink but God save us from their food. Some time they eat man meat when they kill each other.[16]

The majority of descriptions and attitudes, however, showed considerably more ambivalence and oscillated between astonishment and distaste, fascination and dismay, admiration and critique. Such incongruity featured in the first detailed description of the Lenape, authored by Per Lindeström, a fortification engineer who arrived in the colony in 1654 (Fig. 13.1). Lindeström was an inquisitive and acute observer. During his travels across the colony he met with several Lenape chiefs, visited some of the Lenape settlements and gained a rudimentary understanding of their language. Lindeström praised their intelligence, heroism, strength, industriousness and patience. He was impressed by their hospitality, loyalty and skills, and especially by their medicinal knowledge. But he also judged them to be mischievous, mistrustful, bestial and thievish, "more inclined towards bad than towards good".[17] His impressions were similar to the notes made by the governor Printz (1642–53) in his letters and reports to Sweden. He too envied Native American health, stamina and strength, features that the exhausted, starved and disease-stricken settlers lacked, and he admired their skills and artistry, but he mistrusted them and was appalled by their cultural practices, supposed barbarity and perceived vindictiveness.

This ambivalence and the simultaneous attraction and repulsion the European observers felt towards the indigenous people is identified in postcolonial scholarship as a common occurrence in colonial settings. It stemmed from the concurrent realization

Fig. 13.1 A drawing of a Lenape family made by Per Lindeström and published in Campanius Holm's *Kort beskrifning om provincien Nya Swerige uit America* (1702).

of similarity and difference between oneself and the other; from the projection of one's own desired virtues and abhorred vices on to the other, and interrogation of one's own experience of the other against a background of deeply-rooted preconceptions.[18] Such ambivalence also revealed troubled juxtapositions in the colonizers' attitudes: on the one hand their wish for their colonial subjects to become like Europeans, and on the other the need for the colonized to remain different. Finding and accentuating difference and signs of supposed inferiority were rhetorically essential in justifying European claims in the colonies.[19]

In the context of New Sweden, this problematic stance was not only reflected in the rhetoric and particular styling of ethnographic observations. It also affected daily decisions and interactions between the Swedes and the Lenape. The confrontation between the preconceptions about "the other" and the realities of everyday life engendered certain paradoxes and hypocritical attitudes stemming at least partially from a failure to admit commonalities with regard to seeing the world in relational terms, and to assign Lenape practices to the same categories as vernacular folklore. Travel diaries and reports offer countless examples of the colonists' double standards, particularly as regards attitudes towards indigenous knowledge and spiritual practices.[20] Nearly all Swedish accounts from colonial America acknowledged the superiority of the indigenous understanding of nature, especially Lenape knowledge of edible, healing and poisonous plants, and their expertise in treating different ailments. When their own cures failed, the settlers sought and obtained medical help from the Lenape even if some treatments involved shamanistic practices, which in other contexts were scorned as idolatrous, barbaric and devilish.

A good illustration of this duplicity is provided by comparing the observations of Per Lindeström made in 1654–5 with an interview of one Nils Gustafsson conducted by Per Kalm in 1749.[21] Gustafsson, a senior representative of the second generation of Swedes, served as a source of detailed information about different aspects of Native American daily life. He told Kalm how in his younger days the settlers and the Lenape lived very close, learned from each other and grew to appreciate one another even though both sides lacked a complete grasp of culturally acceptable behaviours and occasionally fell into conflict by crossing a line. When the interview moved to the subject of religion, Gustafsson was full of disapproval for the perceived ignorance and heathen beliefs of the Lenape. Once, he said, he was sharing a path in conversation with a Lenape when their walk was interrupted by the appearance of a snake on the road. When Nils reached for a stick the Indian begged him not to kill it. Hurting the animal was against the spiritual sensitivities of the Lenape. Gustafsson ignored the pleas of his companion and killed the snake, saying "because thou believest in it, I think myself obliged to kill it".[22] Gustafsson and other "old Swedes" admitted, however, their reliance on Native American preventive and healing practices involving engagement with the spiritual world and Lenape folklore.[23] Lindeström, for example, noted how Swedish women learnt from the Lenape to use rattle snake skin to ease the pains of childbirth, observing that "when they tie it around their bodies they have an immediate and easy delivery."[24]

Such colonial paradoxes and duplicity are visible throughout the history of New Sweden, and continued to shape and define colonial society. The lofty rhetoric of European civility, authority and paternalism in which the colonial programme of New

Sweden (and other colonies) was wrapped often evoked the unattainable when it came
to confrontation with the realities on the ground. Governors, time after time, had to
acknowledge, not without anxiety, the upper hand or at least considerable influence
the indigenous people held in the political game along the Delaware. This reversal of
positions was also notable with regard to the rhetoric of the Indian as a child. Speeches
of Lenape leaders and correspondence sent from the colony indicate that it was the
colonists who felt and acted in an inexperienced, child-like fashion, requiring guidance
and direction from the Lenape, who offered to take the Swedes "by the hand", lead
them into the country and provide protection against enemies.[25] The notion of supposed
European civility as opposed to indigenous barbarity was turned on its head as well:
Lindeström and many others commented on the incompatibility between their preconceptions and their experience, and were humbled by the honesty and generosity of the
Lenape. Many observed the harmony, respect and absence of crime in the indigenous
communities and noted the corrupting influence of the colonists. The notion of the
"noble savage" also became a rhetorical tool in missionary narratives, used to pinpoint
the moral weaknesses of the colonists and to shift the blame for failures to convert the
Native Americans.[26]

Daily interactions between the Swedes and the Lenape, traces of which are captured
in archaeological and historical material, revealed certain discrepancies between rhetorical assumptions about the Native Americans and the realities in practice; between
public utterance and actual engagement. They indicated co-dependencies: efforts to
overcome perceived or real differences and discover similarities – the necessity to establish common ground despite mistrust – as well as creative incorporations and mimicry
of each other's cultural expressions and practices: in effect, the creation of what Richard
White has termed a "middle ground".[27] This situation was not permanent and is most
easily observed in the 17th century and perhaps in the early decades of the 18th.[28]
Within this general characterization however, individual attitudes and actions could fall
between clear extremes. Some individuals, like James (Jonas) Steelman, owned Native
American slaves.[29] Others formed firm friendships and business partnerships, as was the
case for Peter and Lasse Cock and Israel Helm, who were well acquainted with several
Lenape sachems (paramount chiefs) and served as messengers and interpreters between
them and the English; of Olof Stille who was well-liked and often visited by the Lenape;
and of Peter Yocum (Joachimsson), who shared his home in Kingsessing with a Native
American boy and his business partner Polycarpus Rose.[30] Sometimes, however, such
mutual respect and friendships were overshadowed by self-interest. Peter Yocum, for
example, was accused of illegally selling brandy to Indians to persuade them to trade
with him and to outwit the competition, even though he must have been well aware
of the problems strong alcohol caused as well as indigenous pleas to forbid its sale.[31]

The Native Americans were not the only culturally different people that the colonists
met and interacted with in America, although these encounters and cohabitation had a
particular weight and discursive meaning. New Sweden and the colonies that replaced it
in the late 17th century were multicultural endeavours and the settlers included Swedish,
Finnish and German-speaking citizens of the Kingdom of Sweden; the Dutch, the
English and Africans. With the exception of Africans, these other groups of colonial
residents were considered as fairly familiar and "predictable", sharing with the Swedish

colonists a certain cultural commonality and understanding rooted in European, Christian sensibilities. Nevertheless, the proximity of the English and Dutch communities, and the complex relationships with them of dependency, diplomacy and competition sparked mutual observation of cultural/ethnic difference and judgements regarding national character. Such observations and assumptions are very clear in the travel narratives of, for example, Peter Sluyter and Jaspar Dankers, who journeyed between Massachusetts and Delaware in 1679–80, and in the diaries and letters of the Swedish governors and pastors who served the Swedish Lutheran congregations throughout the late 17th and the 18th century.[32] Despite differences, however, close cohabitation and neighbourly contacts led to intermarriage across ethnic boundaries, changes of religious affiliation and reworkings of identity which grew in significance among the third and later generations of Swedes.

Enslaved Africans were present in the colony from the 1640s, when governor Prinz arrived with his Angolan slave Anthony. The number of slaves increased during the Dutch tenure along the Delaware river. In a region that was unsuitable for and lacked large monoculture plantations, relatively few Swedish families had a need for or could afford to purchase slaves (only eight out of 87 inventories dated between the 1690s and 1730s list them); those that did were wealthy freemen of the Wicacoa congregation, who employed the enslaved workforce as house servants and plantation workers. One of the first freemen to acquire Africans was Jacob Svensson: in the summer of 1661 he purchased one William Braun, a runaway slave from Virginia, who after finding temporary refuge among the Native Americans was sold to Svensson.[33] By the end of the 17th century, the family of Sven Gunnarsson of Wicacoa counted as the largest slave-owners – his children Sven, Olle and Katarina between them owned six Africans.[34]

Issues of slavery merit relatively scant attention in Swedish writings from the colony. Most radical in his opinion of the system and the African slaves was pastor Erik Björk. He described the Africans as ignorant, stubborn and stupid, and he justified their harsh treatment by the slave-owners.[35] Other pastors pleaded for humane treatment of enslaved people and preached on the owners' moral obligation to baptize their servants and teach them about Christianity. Anders Sandel (1702) pointed out that "it is a great problem for a master's responsibility before God if he does not have his slaves baptized as Christians, for, according to the English law, a slave is freed from his slavery seven years after his conversion".[36] Despite the recognized moral dubiousness of slavery some pastors, even upon their own deaths, failed to free their enslaved servants.[37]

DOMESTICATING THE LANDSCAPE

The newness and otherness of the landscape signified its "unhomeliness". Whether admired or feared, the landscape of America appeared utterly foreign. To become a replica of the old Sweden, as the colonial company and the Royal Council had envisioned it, the newly-purchased land needed to be domesticated. Rising to the task with diligence and tireless effort governors Johan Printz (1643–52) and Johan Risingh (1654–5) directed a wholesale process of turning the colony into a familiar and orderly space. This began with the setting of boundaries marked with national emblems, clearing the land and inscribing the landscape with familiar-sounding names (Fig. 13.2). Places known by

Fig. 13.2 Domesticating America: Swedish settlements along the Delaware River in 1654–5: detail from a map drawn by Per Lindeström published in Campanius Holm's *Kort beskrifning om provincien Nya Swerige uit America* (1702).

the local Lenape as Hopokehocking, Chamassung, Mecoponacka and Tenakong were renamed as Christina, Finland, Upland and Nya Göteborg.[38] Renamed, the colonial landscape was further transformed by diverse projects: churches, water mills, forts, docks and plantations dotted New Sweden's countryside.[39]

Equally crucial to the process of domestication were the more mundane endeavours of clearing the land and establishing farms undertaken by the settlers themselves. Turning foreign and unpredictable surroundings into a recognizable and comfortable environment was achieved through the material means of house-building and home-making, appropriating the landscape for agriculture and connecting the farmsteads by a network of pathways and neighbourly ties. When choosing sites suitable for plantation, freeholders tried to find places that would offer possibilities comparable to those in their old homelands, and were drawn to areas with promise of a versatile economy, enabling agriculture, husbandry, fishing and hunting. Archaeological material and historical documents indicate that the architecture and layout of farms resembled the rural settings of Sweden.[40] Inventories and wills that started to be written down in the last decades of the 17th century indicate that the colonists' cottages with sleeping lofts[41] were partially furnished with objects brought from Sweden. These objects constituted tangible links and mnemonic and emotional devices for reconnecting oneself with the past.[42] They were thus an important element in the process of emplacement.

Ceremonies and material acts of claiming the land, the establishment of visible boundaries and domestication projects had political objectives. They served to manifest colonial claims, to project visions of civility and order and to produce loyal citizens, actors who properly belong to a situated community of Swedish subjects. This manipulation of landscape also had more mundane goals and affected homemaking, enrooting, creating communities and ties to places. Material decisions, the wholesale process of transforming the landscape and creation of neighbourly networks were of great importance to the colonists. Displacement subjected them to a loss of the confidence and ease with which they were accustomed to conduct their daily lives and forced them to sever intimate ties with well-known landscapes. Cultural norms and traditions that were upheld in the colony helped to counter the resulting feelings of alienation, and fuelled "homing desires": hopes that what was declared to be a new home would eventually feel genuinely like home.[43] Engagement in familiar material practices and the ability to reconstruct patterns of everyday routines contributed to the process of emplacement.[44] This place-making and production of locality and community was meant to keep at bay the sense of anxiety and instability inherent in displacement and to create a sense of familiarity and continuity.[45] It turned what was previously alien and meaningless space into recognizable and meaningful places. This process, however, had radically different consequences for the native Lenape. For them, the intensive appropriation and reordering of the landscape by the colonists resulted in dispossession and at least partial alienation of the landscape.

The processes of homemaking and defining a community continued after the fall of the colony in 1655. The end of Swedish colonial rule did not produce large-scale return migration. In fact, the majority of the settlers stayed in America, and until the establishment of Pennsylvania in 1681 they constituted the largest European group in this part of America. A majority of the Swedish families lived in dispersed farms along the Delaware river between New Castle and southern outskirts of Philadelphia, but despite the lack of towns and larger villages the settlements were close enough to each other to create and maintain the tightly-woven fabric of communal relationships. A sense of belonging and common identity was fuelled by shared experiences and practices, language and adherence to Lutheranism.[46] The Dutch and later English colonial governments saw and described their Swedish-speaking subjects as a relatively coherent "Swedish Nation".[47] Similar traits of conservative adherence to cultural norms and practices were later noticed by the clergymen serving the Swedish congregations. Pastor Andreas Rudman, shortly after his arrival in Pennsylvania in 1697, described his congregation as follows:

> The [Swedish] people live far scattered, yet all along the water (…). Round about them, and partly in between them, English people live, which language they know, as well as the Indian and Dutch [languages], and on top of that their mother tongue as clear as it was ever spoken in Sweden, but they break [i.e. accent] somewhat on the Östgöta and Västgöta ending (…). All the houses are timbered in the Swedish manner. The women cook food according to the Swedish custom and brew fine and pleasant tasting drinks.[48]

On occasion, the grip of the homeland, a real or imagined sense of connection with Sweden and a sense of the injustice of the Dutch and English administrators prompted acts of open disobedience and political mobilization. The most serious incident happened in 1669 when 42 Swedes and Finns (about a quarter of the adult male Swedish-speaking population) were charged and heavily fined for participation in a conspiracy to overthrow the English government along the Delaware. The whole affair, known as "the Long Finn rebellion" was instigated by the enigmatic figure John Binckson, alias Coningsmarke, alias Matheus Hencks, alias Marcus Jacobson.[49] Appealing to an apparently deep-seated allegiance to Sweden and a sense of connection with the old homeland, as well as an animosity towards the English government, he enticed the Swedes into rebellion, claiming that the Swedish king was about to regain the colony and restore New Sweden. The English governor of the colony perceived this action as a serious threat, as the Swedish population was reasonably numerous, and tried Binckson and the rebels for treason. The instigator was publicly whipped, branded and sold into slavery in Barbados, while his confederates were fined according to their suspected involvement.[50] Six years later, Swedish and Finnish settlers were involved in another insurgency, this time over their labour contribution to the construction and maintenance of the dykes in New Castle.[51] The troubles caused by this "plebeian faction" caused William Tom, sheriff of New Castle, to utter in frustration that "the Sweeds and Fynnes being such a sort of people (…) must be Kept under else they will rebell and of that nation these here are the worse sort".[52]

These mutinies of the second half of the 17th century, and later efforts to establish a regular Swedish Lutheran mission in America, can serve as illustrations of the "engagement of even the most obscure colonists with a transatlantic world of connections both real and imagined".[53] These actions and sensibilities in common of the "Swedish Nation" can be taken as signifying identification with the European homeland and distinction from other groups with which it co-existed in the colonial landscape. The way in which the society and culture of the 17th-century American colonies were continuously shaped by their European roots can be seen as an expression of how deeply the Old World lived on in the hearts and minds of those in America.[54]

INCORPORATING THE "OTHER"

The process of homemaking went beyond a simple matter of transplanting familiar and tested cultural solutions. Their new environments challenged the settlers constantly to elaborate new practices, learn and adopt from others with whom they shared the colonial space, and rework their self-image.[55] Indeed, as pointed out by Robert Blair St. George[56] and by John Smolenski,[57] life in America entailed negotiated processes of "becoming" rather than "being" colonial. It involved continuous and protracted adjustments and negotiations between conflicting value systems, gender roles, perceptions of the surrounding world, ways of organizing work and household; between definitions of same and other, civility and savagery, propriety and transgression. The realities of New Sweden and later Pennsylvania – its increasingly multicultural character, ideologies and policies colouring daily decisions and attitudes, and economic currents connecting local and global markets – affected the daily lives of the Swedish settlers. They lived in a rapidly changing world, in which trans-Atlantic connections and colonial inequalities and entanglements were virtually tangible, and materialized in the form of consumption patterns, practices and household arrangements. In this world, new objects and ideas made their way into daily routines and found their place next to carefully-guarded customs of the old country.

Interactions and close co-existence with the Lenape and the Dutch and English settlers stimulated cultural borrowings and elaboration of new practices (but not the necessarily abandonment of prejudices). Early on, indigenous knowledge, material culture and solutions to problems had an important impact on the settlers' lives. The most visible and long-lasting transformations were in the sphere of diet. The initial inability of the settlers to produce enough food caused them to rely upon supplies sold by the Lenape, which consisted of plants and meat partly unfamiliar to the Swedes, including maize, beans, pumpkins, squashes, watermelons, game meat, native fowl and fish. With these new staples, a range of recipes and cooking techniques followed. *Sapan* – a stew of maize and meat – maize mush, ash-cooked turtles and grasshoppers, roast venison, cakes made of crushed maize and beans, boiled *hopniss* (groundnut) and *katniss* (broadleaf arrowhead) became popular dishes in colonial households.[58] Colonists were also keen buyers of Lenape-made straw mats, baskets, wooden dishes, boxes and pails; they learned to use calabashes as storage vessels, to employ indigenous trapping and hunting techniques, and in time acquired at least a basic understanding of the Lenape language.[59] The irregularity of shipments from Sweden and the high prices of European commodities offered by the English and Dutch merchants led to the pragmatic adoption of home-made hide and leather clothes and use of furs and hides instead of woollen blankets and bedcovers. Close cohabitation, dependency and frequent interaction between the Lenape and the Swedes had fairly profound consequences on the settlers' culture. Indeed, Per Kalm, after conducting interviews with the oldest residents of the colony, consulting early records and observing the colonists living in the frontier areas, noted a deep impact of the manners and "turn of thinking" of the Native Americans on the Swedes and other colonists:

> The Swedes themselves are accused, that they were already half Indians, when the English arrived in the year 1682. And we still see that the French, English, Germans, Dutch, and other Europeans, who have lived for several years together in distant provinces, near and among the Indians, grow so like them, in their behaviour and thoughts, that they can only be distinguished by the difference of their colour.[60]

At times, then, close co-existence and dependency turned the settlers into caricatures of "the other", signalling yet another discrepancy between colonial ideology, which presupposed a complete sway of European culture over the indigenous, and the realities on the ground, which proved to be more complex and based on a mutual give-and-take practised by all inhabiting the colonial landscape.

The material everyday world of the Swedish families also resembled that of other European settlers. Some of continental commodities – valuable and commonplace objects – found their way into the travel chests and trunks taken by prospective settlers to America. During the period of New Sweden, the essentials and more exclusive European and colonial commodities, such as metal tools, ceramics, tobacco pipes, cloth, clothing, silk and dress accessories, were shipped directly from Sweden or offered by travelling English and Dutch merchants, but their availability and affordability varied.[61] With the Dutch and English takeover in the second half of the 17th century, bringing an influx of people, economic development and establishment of stable and regular connections across the Atlantic, access to consumer goods became easier, and the influence of English and an emerging Euro-American fashion more visible. Objects listed by Swedish families in late 17th- and early 18th-century inventories and found archaeologically, besides fairly standard chests, trunks, beds, tools and pewter dishes, included more expensive pieces of furniture such as chests of drawers and chairs, silver objects, candlesticks, mirrors, books, imported ceramics (such as delftware and stoneware), glassware and decorative fabrics made of homespun linen and imported wool.

Of this mingling of cultural traditions and the material aspect of the constantly-evolving colonial culture, illustrated by archaeological material and analyses of wills and inventories left by the Swedish families, a good example is the Mårtonson family, whose progenitors, Mårten Mårtenson and his wife migrated to America in 1654 from the Finnish-speaking area of Sweden. They acquired properties along the Darby Creek in a place known as Calcoon Hook and in neighbouring Ammansland, areas which at that time constituted hubs of Scandinavian settlement. In 1698 (the date carved on the fireplace lintel) a log cabin was erected on the property along the Darby Creek. Built with white cedar logs with double notch corners, the approximately 4 m by 6 m dwelling featured a fireplace in the corner and a staircase leading to a second floor.[62] This was one of the houses mentioned by Mårten Mårtenson junior in an inventory made shortly after his death in 1718. In the middle of the 18th century, Jonas Mårtonsson (Morton) built a new house on the property, to serve either as a station for his ferry operation across the Darby Creek or, perhaps more likely, as a dwelling for his daughter and son-in-law. Unlike the older house, which showed clear technological references to Scandinavian building traditions, the newer house freely blended Scandinavian and Anglo-American solutions. It was still a log cabin, but was built of oak, a material preferred by the English. It also incorporated Anglo-American roof framing and a large fireplace located along the wall.[63]

Material culture collected in deposits dated to the late 17th and the first half of the 18th century represent an eclectic collection of locally-made redware pottery, imported German Westerwald stoneware, Dutch delftware and a considerable assortment of English ceramics that include white salt-glazed stoneware, tin-glazed tableware, Staffordshire slipware plates and mugs, Manganese Mottled mugs, and Whieldon and Jackfield-type ware (Fig. 13.3). Besides the pottery, the generations of the Mårtonssons left behind a large number of broken pipes that came mainly from the workshops of Robert Tippett and John or James Abbott of Bristol, single examples of Venetian trading beads, shards of rum bottles, snuff and other substances as well as tools and personal accessories of anonymous origins.[64] Early 18th-century inventories of the Mårtonssons complete the picture of the family's consumption habits and taste. They include items such as religious books in Swedish and English, fashionable black walnut furniture, pewter dishes, glass bottles, tablecloths and blankets, as well as sacks of rye – a grain that was popular in Swedish and Finnish households.[65]

Fig 13.3 The Morton homestead: reconstruction of the cabin built at the end of the 17th century (right room), middle of the 18th century (left room), and a stone hallway added at a later time. Examples of European pottery and pipes found in the deposits dated to the late 17th–early 18th century (photographs: Magdalena Naum).

A similar blending of material cultures can be noted in the case of the household of Måns Jonasson (Mounce Jones). Until 1704, Måns and his family lived in Aronameck/ Kingsessing, south of Philadelphia, on a property previously owned by his father. He is credited with building a log house that survived on the property until the second half of the 18th century and was depicted in a 1758 drawing of the house of John Bartram, the then owner of the plantation.[66] From the drawing one can deduce that the house was built of notched logs and had the traditional corner stove. In the early 1700s, Måns moved to the new and predominantly Swedish community of Manatawny/ Morlatton (Douglassville) on the Schuylkill, where he built a simple two-storey stone house equipped with a large fireplace in an English style, along one of the kitchen walls. Måns engaged in trade with the local groups of Native Americans (his inventory included a "box [of] Indian goods"), occasionally hosted them in his house and mediated between the sachems and government in Philadelphia.[67] This close co-existence was also reflected in household objects mentioned in his inventory: baskets and mats made by indigenous artisans, and a barrel and a trough for *sapan* (maize mush). Other material possessions mentioned in his inventory or found during ongoing excavations include Swedish religious books, furniture, pewter dishes and earthenware including tin-glazed tableware, English stoneware and kaolin pipes.[68]

This mixture of ideas and objects in the Mårtonsson and the Jonasson households embodies trans-Atlantic colonial connections, consumption patterns, tastes and fashions that emerged from multicultural meetings and co-existence. The eclectic and changing material world and increasingly complex colonial landscape of America brought challenge to ideas of belonging and the construction of identity, in which a gradually mythologized homeland lost its bearing as a sole reference point.

CONCLUSIONS: FACING OTHERNESS IN NEW SWEDEN

After posing the question of "how it would be to walk on the New World with the feet from the Old" and disembarking from the ship that had carried him over the Atlantic, pastor Erik Björk discovered a landscape different from his native Västmanland. He encountered a bewildering plethora of new smells, sounds and images, and a multi-ethnic group of people divided by beliefs, goals and visions but brought together by colonial schemes and desires. Faced with this otherness and newness Björk, like many others before him, proceeded to defend himself against it while at the same time embracing certain aspects of it.[69] A defence and coping mechanisms were found in embodied practices and traditions. These proved to be important guiding elements in the processes of homemaking, in seeing oneself (and being seen by others) as a member of a particular ethnic group, in defining the borders of community and in materializing imagined and real affiliations with the European homelands. But the New World made visible imprints on the colonists and temporary visitors. It prompted self-discovery and self-definition; it created a setting for confrontation with existing assumptions, for reviewing and enacting colonial ideologies and for an uncomfortable discovery of the arbitrary character of one's own knowledge and culture. It also had a visible and lasting impact on the material world and cultural expression. Close co-existence and interactions invited cultural blending, borrowings and appropriations: representations of the dynamic, entangled and complex character of colonial landscapes.

Facing the multifaceted otherness of this new world produced ambiguous responses. On the one hand, the colonists aimed at erasing and conquering the strangeness of America. They did this through complex processes of domestication, which employed well-rehearsed and embodied skills, traditions and knowledge in order to transform the landscape into a space resembling old homelands. On the other hand, they consciously and unconsciously embraced the novelty of their surroundings, incorporating new knowledge, practices, material culture and folklore into existing traditions. The effect was a two-way transformation: as America became colonized and claimed as home, it too "colonized" and altered the settlers, upsetting their traditional ways of doing and thinking.[70]

NOTES

1 Lindeström 1925; Campanius Holm 1702.
2 Campanius Holm 1702.
3 Jameson 1887; Rising 1959 [1655].
4 Kupperman 1984; Moogk 1989.
5 Ramey 2008.
6 Studies in Kupperman 1995; Greenblatt 1998; Ramey 2008.
7 *Handlingar* 1848, 210–12; Ekengren *et al.* 2013, 172.
8 Metcalf 1988, 203.
9 Printz to Oxenstierna, April 14, 1643.
10 Lindeström 1925, 172–3.
11 Rudman and Björk to Johan Thelin, 29 October 1697, 64.
12 E.g., Kalm 1773, 60–4, 139–40.
13 Lindeström 1925, 157.
14 Jacobsson 1922; Lindeström 1925; Fur 2006.
15 Blomfelt 1988, 81–2.
16 Fleisher & Arnborg 1989, 7–9.
17 Lindeström 1925, 191–2, 233–5, 239–41.
18 Greenblatt 1991.
19 Young 1995, 161; Bhabha 2003, 85–92.
20 Lindeström 1925; Fur 2006.
21 Kalm 1773, 394–407.
22 Kalm 1773, 402.
23 Kalm 1773, 161.
24 Lindeström 1925, 186.
25 Rising 1988; Metcalf 1988, 58–9; Fur 2006, 124.
26 Jacobsson 1922, 308–10; Blomfelt, 1988, 81–2; Fur 2006, 193–5.
27 White 1991; 2006.
28 Merrell 2000.
29 *Inventory of James Steelman 1734*.
30 Campanius Holm 1834, 81; *Minutes of the Provincial Council of Pennsylvania* 1, 1838, 358, 398; Gehring 1977.
31 Duncan Hirsch 2004, 75; *Minutes of the Provincial Council of Pennsylvania* 1, 1838, 398.
32 Dankers & Sluyter 1867; Stebbins Craig & Williams 2006.
33 Gehring 1981, 309.
34 *Inventory of Wolly Swanson 1692*; *Inventory of Swan Swanson 1696*; *Inventory of Katharine Benktson 1710*.
35 Jacobsson 1922, 283–4.
36 Metcalf 1988, 57.

37 Acrelius 1874, 287, 295; Burr 1890, 285; *Will and Inventory of Andrew Rudman 1708*.
38 Acrelius 1874; Lindeström 1925.
39 Printz 1959 [1647].
40 Ekengren *et al.* 2013, 174–7; Naum 2016.
41 Some of these cottages can be interpreted as traditional *enkelstuga* (one-room house) and *parstuga* (two-room house) on the basis of probate inventories – the former, for example, from the inventory of Johan Andersson Stålkofta; the latter from the inventory of Anders Svensson Bonde.
42 E.g. Belk 1992; Digby 2006; studies in Svašek 2012; Naum 2013.
43 See Brah 1996, 193, 197.
44 Brah 1996.
45 Casey 2001; Turton 2005; Naum, 2016.
46 Fur *et al.* 2016, 4–6.
47 E.g. Dankers & Sluyter 1867, 175, 177.
48 Rudman to Prof. Jacob Arhhenius, 29 October, 1697.
49 Gehring 1977, 6–10; Haefeli 2006.
50 Haefeli 2006, 162–5.
51 Gehring, 1977, 92–3.
52 Gehring 1977, 93.
53 Haefeli 2006, 139.
54 Cressy 1987, 191–212; Warner 2000; Haefeli 2006, 139.
55 Calloway 1998.
56 St. George 2000.
57 Smolenski 2010.
58 Kalm 1773, 385–90; Fur 2006, 154–5.
59 Kalm 1773, 49; Jacobsson 1922.
60 Kalm 1773, 336.
61 Lindeström 1925, 226; Johnson 1930.
62 Frens & Fens 1989.
63 Frens & Frens 1989.
64 Frens & Frens 1989.
65 *Inventory of John Morton 27.02.1724*; *Inventory of Mathias Morton 21.12.1736*.
66 Jacobs 2001, 12–13.
67 *Minutes of the Provincial Council of Pennsylvania* 2, 1838, 569–70.
68 *Inventory of Mouns Jones 3.05.1727*.
69 Burr 1890.
70 See e.g. Calloway 1998.

BIBLIOGRAPHY

Acrelius, I. 1874. *A History of New Sweden: or, The Settlement on the Delaware River*. Philadelphia: Historical Society of Pennsylvania.

Beaudry, M. & Parno, T. (eds) 2013. *Archaeologies of Mobility and Movement*. New York: Springer.

Belk, R. W. 1992. 'Moving possessions: An analysis based on personal documents from the 1847–1869 Mormon migration', *Journal of Consumer Research* 19(3): 339–61.

Bhabha, H. 2003. *The Location of Culture*. London: Routledge.

Blomfelt, F. (ed.) 1988. *Andreas Sandels dagbok 1701–1743*. Uppsala: Erene.

Brah, A. 1996. *Cartographies of Diaspora: Contesting Identities*. London: Routledge.

Burr, H. 1890. *The Records of Holy Trinity (Old Swedes) Church, Wilmington, Delaware from 1697 to 1773*. Wilmington: Historical Society of Delaware.

Calloway, C. 1998. *New Worlds for All: Indians, Europeans, and the Remaking of Early America*. Baltimore: The Johns Hopkins University Press.

Campanius Holm, T. 1702. *Kort beskrifning om provincien Nya Swerige uti America, som nu förtjden af the engelske kallas Pensylvania. Af lärde och trowärdige mäns skrifter och berättelser ihopaletad och sammanskrefwen, samt med åthskillige figurer utzirad af Thomas Campanius Holm*. Stockholm: J. H. Werner.

Campanius Holm, T. 1834. *Description of the Province of New Sweden. Now Called, by the English, Pennsylvania, in America. Compiled from the relations and writings of persons worthy of credit, and adorned with maps and plates*. Translated from the Swedish, for the Historical Society of Pennsylvania, with notes, by Peter S. Du Ponceau. Philadelphia: M'Carty & Davis.

Casey, E. S. 2001. 'Between geography and philosophy: What does it mean to be in the place-world?', *Annals of the Association of American Geographers* 91(4): 683–93.

Cressy, D. 1987. *Coming Over: Migration and Communication between England and New England in the Seventeenth Century*. Cambridge: Cambridge University Press.

Dahlgren, S. & Norman, H. (eds) 1988. *The Rise and Fall of New Sweden: Governor Johan Risingh's journal 1654–1655 in its Historical Context*. Uppsala: Uppsala universitet.

Dankers, J. & Sluyter, P. 1867. *Journal of a Voyage to New York and a Tour in Several of American Colonies, 1679–80*. Brooklyn: Long Island Historical Society.

Digby, S. 2006. 'The casket of magic: Home and identity from salvaged objects', *Home Cultures* 3(2): 169–90.

Duncan Hirsch, A. 2004. 'Indian, metis and Euro-American women on multiple frontiers', in Pencak & Richter 2004, 63–84.

Ekengren, F., Naum, M. & Zagal-Mach Wolfe, U. I. 2013. 'Sweden in the Delaware Valley: Everyday life and material culture in New Sweden', in Naum & Nordin 2013, 169–87.

Fleischer, R. E. & Anborg, C. K. 1989. '"With God's blessing on both land and sea": Gustavus Hesselius describes the New World to the Old in a letter from Philadelphia in 1714', *American Art Journal* 21(3): 4–17.

Frens, D. & Frens, S. 1989. 'The Morton homestead: A historic structure report'. Unpublished report prepared for the Pennsylvania Historical and Museum Commission.

Fur, G. 2006. *Colonialism in the Margins: Cultural Encounters in New Sweden and Lapland*. Leiden: Brill.

Fur, G., Naum, M. & Nordin, J. M. 2016. 'Intersecting worlds: New Sweden's transatlantic entanglements', *Journal of Transnational American Studies* 7(1): 1–22.

Gehring, C. (ed.) 1977. *New York Historical Manuscripts*. Vols 20–21: *Delaware Papers (English Period) 1664–1682*. Baltimore: Genealogical Publishing Co.

Gehring, C. (ed.) 1981. *New York Historical Manuscripts*. Vols 18–19: *Delaware Papers (Dutch Period) 1655–1644*. Baltimore: Genealogical Publishing Co.

Greenblatt, S. 1991. *Marvelous Possessions: The Wonder of the New World*. Chicago: Chicago University Press.

Gustin, I., Hansson, M., Roslund, M. & Wienberg. J. (eds) *Mellan slott och slagg. Vänbok till Anders Ödman*. Lund Studies in Historical Archaeology 17. Lund: Lunds universitet.

Haefeli, E. 2006. 'The revolt of the Long Swede: Transatlantic hopes and fears on the Delaware, 1669', *Pennsylvania Magazine of History and Biography* 80(2): 137–80.

Handlingar rörande Skandinaviens Historia 29. 1848. Stockholm: Kungliga Samfundet för utgivande av handskrifter rörande Skandinaviens historia.

Inventory of James Steelman 1734. Gloucester County Archives, New Jersey.

Inventory of John Morton 27.02.1724. Chester County Archives, Pennsylvania.

Inventory of Katharine Benktson 1710. Philadelphia City Archives, Pennsylvania.

Inventory of Mathias Morton 21.12.1736. Chester County Archives, Pennsylvania.

Inventory of Mouns Jones 3.05.1727. Philadelphia City Archives, Pennsylvania.

Inventory of Swan Swanson 1696. Philadelphia City Archives, Pennsylvania.

Inventory of Wolly Swanson 1692. Philadelphia City Archives, Pennsylvania.

Jacobs, J. A. 2001. *John Bartram House & Garden, House, 54th Street & Lindbergh Boulevard, Philadelphia, Philadelphia County, PA, HALS No. PA-1*. Historic American Landscapes Survey, Washington, D.C.: Library of Congress.

Jacobsson, N. 1922. *Svenskar och Indianer: studier i svenskarnas insats i den tidigare protestanska missionens historia*. Stockholm: Svenska kyrkans diakonistyrelses bokförlag.

Jameson, J. F. 1887. *Willem Usselinx, Founder of the Dutch and Swedish West India Companies*. New York: G. P. Putnam's Sons.

Johnson, A. 1930. *The Instruction for Johan Printz, Governor of New Sweden: The First Constitution or Supreme Law of the States of Pennsylvania and Delaware*. Philadelphia: The Swedish Colonial Society.

Kalm, P. 1773. *Travels into North America*, vol. 1. London: Lowndes.

Kupperman, K. O. 1984. 'Fear of hot climates in the Anglo-American colonial experience', *The William and Mary Quarterly* 41(2): 213–40.

Kupperman, K. O. (ed.) 1995. *America in European Consciousness, 1493–1750*. Williamsburg: University of North Carolina Press.

Lindeström, P. 1925. *Geographia Americae with An Account of the Delaware Indians*. Philadelphia: The Swedish Colonial Society.

Merrell, J. 2000. *Into the American Woods: Negotiators on the Pennsylvania Frontier*. New York: Norton.

Metcalf, M. 1988. 'Letters from the Delaware, 1. The Rev. Erik Björck, March 22, 1698', *Swedish-American Historical Quarterly* 39(1): 195–214.

Minutes of the Provincial Council of Pennsylvania: From the Organization to the Termination of Proprietary Government, vol. 1. 1838. Philadelphia: State of Pennsylvania.

Minutes of the Provincial Council of Pennsylvania: From the Organization to the Termination of Proprietary Government, vol. 2. 1838. Philadelphia: State of Pennsylvania.

Moogk, P. 1989. 'Reluctant exiles: Emigrants from France in Canada before 1760', *The William and Mary Quarterly* 46(3): 463–505.

Myers, A. C. (ed.) 1959. *Narratives of Early Pennsylvania, West New Jersey and Delaware 1630–1707*. Original Narratives of Early American History 12. New York: Barnes & Noble.

Naum, M. 2013. 'The malady of emigrants: Homesickness and longing in the colony of New Sweden (1638–1655)', in Beaudry & Parno 2013, 165–77.

Naum, M. 2016. 'Displacement and emplacement in New Sweden and colonial Middle Atlantic (1638–1750)', in Gustin *et al.* 2016, 177–82.

Naum, M & Nordin J. M. (eds) 2013. *Scandinavian Colonialism and the Rise of Modernity: Small*

Time Agents in a Global Area. Contributions to Global Historical Archaeology 37. New York: Springer.

Pencak, W. & Richter, D. K. (eds) 2004. *Friends and Enemies in Penn's Woods: Indians, Colonialists, and the Racial Construction of Pennsylvania*. University Park: Pennsylvania State University Press.

Printz, J. 1959 [1647]. 'Report of Governor Johan Printz, 1647', in Myers 1959, 117–29.

Printz, J. 1930. Letter 'Printz to Oxenstierna, April 14, 1643', in Johnson 1930, 152–4.

Ramey, L. 2008. 'Monstrous alterity in early modern travel accounts: Lessons from the ambiguous medieval discourse on humanness', *L'Esprit Créateur* 48(1): 81–95.

Rising, J. 1959 [1655] 'Report of Governor Johan Rising, 1655', in Myers 1959, 156–65.

Rising, J. 1988. 'A short narrative concerning the journey to New Sweden in America', in Dahlgren & Norman 1988, 131–244.

Rudman A. 1697. 'Letter to Prof. Jacob Arhhenius', 29 October, in Stebbins Craig & Williams 2006, 65–71.

Rudman, A. & Björk, E. 1697. 'Letter to Johan Thelin', 29 October, in Stebbins Craig & Williams 2006, 61–5.

Smolenski, J. 2010. *Friends and Strangers: The Making of a Creole Culture in Colonial Pennsylvania*. Philadelphia: University of Pennsylvania Press.

St. George, R. B. 2000. 'Introduction', in St. George 2000, 1–29.

St. George, R. B. (ed.) 2000. *Possible Pasts: Becoming Colonial in Early America*. Ithaca: Cornell University Press.

Stebbins Craig, P. & Williams, K.-E. (eds) 2006. *Colonial Records of the Swedish Churches in Pennsylvania*. Vol. 2: *The Rudman Years 1697–1702*. Philadelphia: Swedish Colonial Society.

Svašek, M. (ed.) 2012. *Moving Subjects, Moving Objects: Transnationalism, Cultural Production and Emotions*. New York: Berghahn Books.

Turton, D. 2005. 'The meaning of place in a world of movement: Lessons from long-term field research in Southern Ethiopia', *Journal of Refugee Studies* 18(3): 258–80.

Warner, M. 2000. 'What's colonial about colonial America', in St. George 2000, 49–70.

White, R. 1991. *The Middle Ground: Indians, Empires, and Republics in the Great Lakes Region, 1650–1815*. Cambridge: Cambridge University Press.

White, R. 2006. 'Creative misunderstandings and new understandings', *The William and Mary Quarterly* 63(1): 9–14.

Will and Inventory of Andrew Rudman 1708. Philadelphia City Archives, Pennsylvania.

Young, R. 1995. *Colonial Desire: Hybridity in Theory, Culture and Race*. London: Routledge.

14

Inscribing Indigeneity in the Colonial Landscape of New Sweden, 1638–1655

FREDRIK EKENGREN

In the narrative of New Sweden, the indigenous inhabitants are often styled as "the others", sharing only an ephemeral presence alongside the Swedish colonists. Similarly, the interpretations of landscape and settlement patterns are often rooted in ideas of European hegemony. This chapter asks what would happen if we instead acknowledge this region as socially constructed, and inscribe the Native American population in the landscape and the history of New Sweden, using both archaeological and literary sources. Mapping both Native American and Swedish sites, this chapter discusses the issue of cohabitation and shared space in the Lower Delaware valley.

A LANDSCAPE BETWEEN NATURE AND CULTURE – A LANDSCAPE BETWEEN PREHISTORY AND HISTORY

The encounter between the settlers of New Sweden and the indigenous population in 17th-century America has for a long time produced a somewhat contradictory image. On the one hand, Swedish historical accounts appropriated the widespread European notion of the American landscape as virgin, pristine and bountiful, full of riches and potential resources, but virtually devoid of culture or civilization. It was characterized, in writing as well as in visual representations, as a natural landscape rather than a cultural one, thus legitimizing and manifesting territorial annexation.[1] This notion has been appropriated into academic research as well,[2] whereby maps of colonial America carefully outline the territorial extent and claims of New Sweden in relation to the other colonial powers, but rarely include the Native American communities who shared the political landscape.[3] Accordingly, an interpretative model is perpetuated based on European hegemony, where the Swedes are envisioned as pioneers who transplanted all the institutions and material traditions of home on to the wilderness,[4] while the Native Americans are relegated to the borderlands or margins of colonial landscapes (physical as well as mental) and given the role of "the others" in the narrative of New Sweden. On the other hand, we have several 17th-century Swedish sources that acknowledge the Native Americans as rightful owners of the land and emphasize the close relationship and dependency between the Swedes and their indigenous neighbours, though their physical presence in the landscape is noted or implied rather than detailed. These accounts are in turn often highlighted by the few, primarily historical, studies that have sought to inscribe indigeneity into the colony of New Sweden.[5] However in archaeological studies, the relationship between Swedes and Natives remains largely unexplored,[6] with the Natives appearing to share only an ephemeral presence with the Europeans in the mid-17th century Lower Delaware valley.

A partial reason why so much historical and archaeological research on New Sweden is still coloured by the colonial gaze is the inexact nature of the written sources on the indigenous communities in the area, making it difficult to ascertain their presence in the landscape. Another reason is the limited attention traditionally paid to the study of Native peoples by historical archaeologists working on early colonial America, which in turn largely has to do with the fact that most research and fieldwork on early 17th-century Native American sites falls within the field of prehistoric archaeology. Consequently, we are dealing with two separate discourses that maintain an artificial separation between indigenous and non-indigenous as well as counteract their contemporaneousness.[7] This segregation still very much affects research on the colony of New Sweden, and has complicated any attempts at an analysis of the multicultural aspects of post-contact space.

What happens then, if we acknowledge the Delaware valley in the 17th century as socially constructed, and inscribe the Native American population in the landscape and the history of New Sweden, using both archaeological and literary sources? This chapter will attempt to collapse the above-mentioned segregation by outlining an inclusive spatial history of New Sweden. Understanding space is vital, since space is one of the material modalities through which past cultural relations were negotiated. Drawing inspiration from studies focusing on the shared, transcultural, pluralistic, or middle ground nature of colonial space,[8] it will explore overlapping and co-existing ways of using and understanding the landscape by combining evidence of both indigenous and non-indigenous communities. Thus it will try to bring together those worlds whose edges melted and merged[9] and created the colonial arena of New Sweden. The strength of this approach lies in seeing the Native Americans as interlocutors in the constitution and negotiation of colonial identity, space and power – in treating them as participants in the colonial discourse.

MAPPING INDIGENOUS SPACE

When the *Kalmar Nyckel* and *Fogel Grip* sailed up the Delaware river in 1638 and proclaimed the colony of New Sweden, the Swedes entered a landscape already inscribed with identities, both indigenous and colonial. A sense of this is gained from looking at one of the earliest maps of the area, based on fortification engineer Peter Lindeström's surveys of the colony in 1654–5 (Fig. 14.1). Besides the Swedish place names, several of the areas, rivers and streams on the map bear Native American names, often referring to the various indigenous communities or groups living in their vicinity. While the map was designed as a representation of the Swedish colonial domain, it also shows us a landscape already conceptualized by its indigenous population, invested with ideas of utility, power and ownership and thus given names, borders, and functional divisions. The map also confirms how important these identifications were for the Swedes' understanding of the region. In this landscape, the Swedes entered as "the others"; they

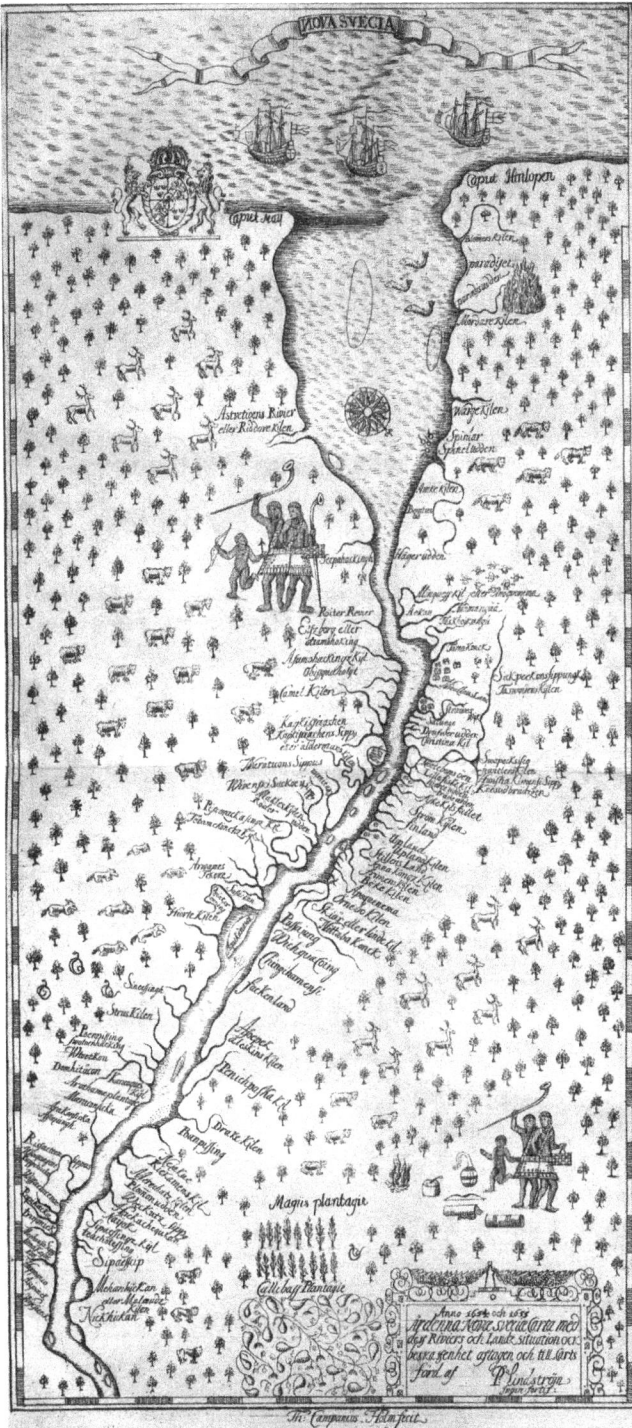

Fig. 14.1 Map of *Nova Sveciae* mixing Native American place names with Swedish ones. The map reads from south at Delaware Bay (top) to north at modern-day Trenton (bottom). This copy of Peter Lindeström's survey of the colony in 1654–5 was made by Thomas Campanius Holm and published in 1696 in Johannes Campanius's *Lutheri Catechismus*, öfwersatt *på American-Virginiske språket* (reproduced here by courtesy of Lund University Library) and 1702 in T. Campanius Holm's *Kort beskrifning om provincien Nya Swerige uti America*.

bought Native American land, settled on old Native American camps and villages, learnt where resources could be found, walked along well-trodden trails, and paddled the rivers and streams.

Reconstructing this landscape of the early and mid-17th-century Lower Delaware valley demands a careful analysis of various sources, ranging from historical accounts to maps and archaeological material. The present study has limited its scope to include only sources approximately contemporary to the New Sweden colony, that is, those dating to the period from the mid-1630s up until the late 1650s. This is done for two reasons. First of all, the aim of the study is to focus on the cultural landscape of that first period of contact and settlement. Second, it is done in order to avoid the mistake of using sources from the late 17th century onwards to study the Swedish colony and its relationship with the indigenous communities and in the process disregard the social, political and territorial changes this area underwent under Dutch and English rule, as well as due to later inter-Native conflicts.[10] The historical sources used include letters, reports and travel accounts, as well as maps of Swedish, Dutch and English origin.[11] All of these make references to the cultural geography along the Delaware and its tributaries, and identify and locate the various indigenous groups and communities as well as the colonial acquisitions and settlements of the region. The picture gained from these sources is then reinforced and expanded by archaeological investigations, primarily of Native sites. Although it is unlikely that all groups, communities and settlements identified in the material were exactly contemporary with each other, or represented permanent inclusions in the landscape, the overall picture nevertheless provides us with the necessary sense of the indigenous conformation of the region in relation to the colonial Swedish presence.

From the late 1630s to the late 1650s, various indigenous groups inhabited and used the landscape in the Lower Delaware river valley and Delaware Bay, from the Falls at modern-day Trenton (NJ) all the way down to Cape May and Cape Henlopen, and extending along the tributaries into the interiors of modern-day Pennsylvania, Delaware and New Jersey (Fig. 14.2 a–c). The western coast of Delaware Bay, particularly the area around Cape Henlopen, was settled by a tribal group referred to as the *Sickoneysincks*.[12] Their primary settlement, which was visited by the Swedes in 1654,[13] was located along the Horn Kill, in today's Lewes in Sussex County (DE). Inland, further south-west on the Delmarva peninsula in the area around the Nanticoke river, one of the major tributaries of Chesapeake Bay, lived the *Kuscarawaoks*, later known as the *Nanticokes*. At the north-western end of the peninsula, around the Sassafras river, lived another tribe, called the *Tockwoghs*. Both these tribes belonged to the Algonquian linguistic family, and were first encountered by Captain John Smith in 1608 and mentioned in his journals.[14] They were later included on the Visscher map from *c*. 1655.[15]

The interior of modern Pennsylvania was inhabited by the Iroquoian-speaking *Minquas* (i.e. the *Andaste*, commonly referred to as the *Susquehannock*) and the Algonquian-speaking *Sauwanoos* (i.e. the *Shawnee*), while the western shores of the Lower Delaware river were dominated by a tribe whom the Swedish colonists referred to as the *Renappi*, or simply "our Indians": the Algonquian-speaking *Lenape*.[16] Native people on the New Jersey side of the Delaware, generally considered to belong to the Lenape,[17] were sub-divided by numerous tribal or community names in the 17th-century sources:

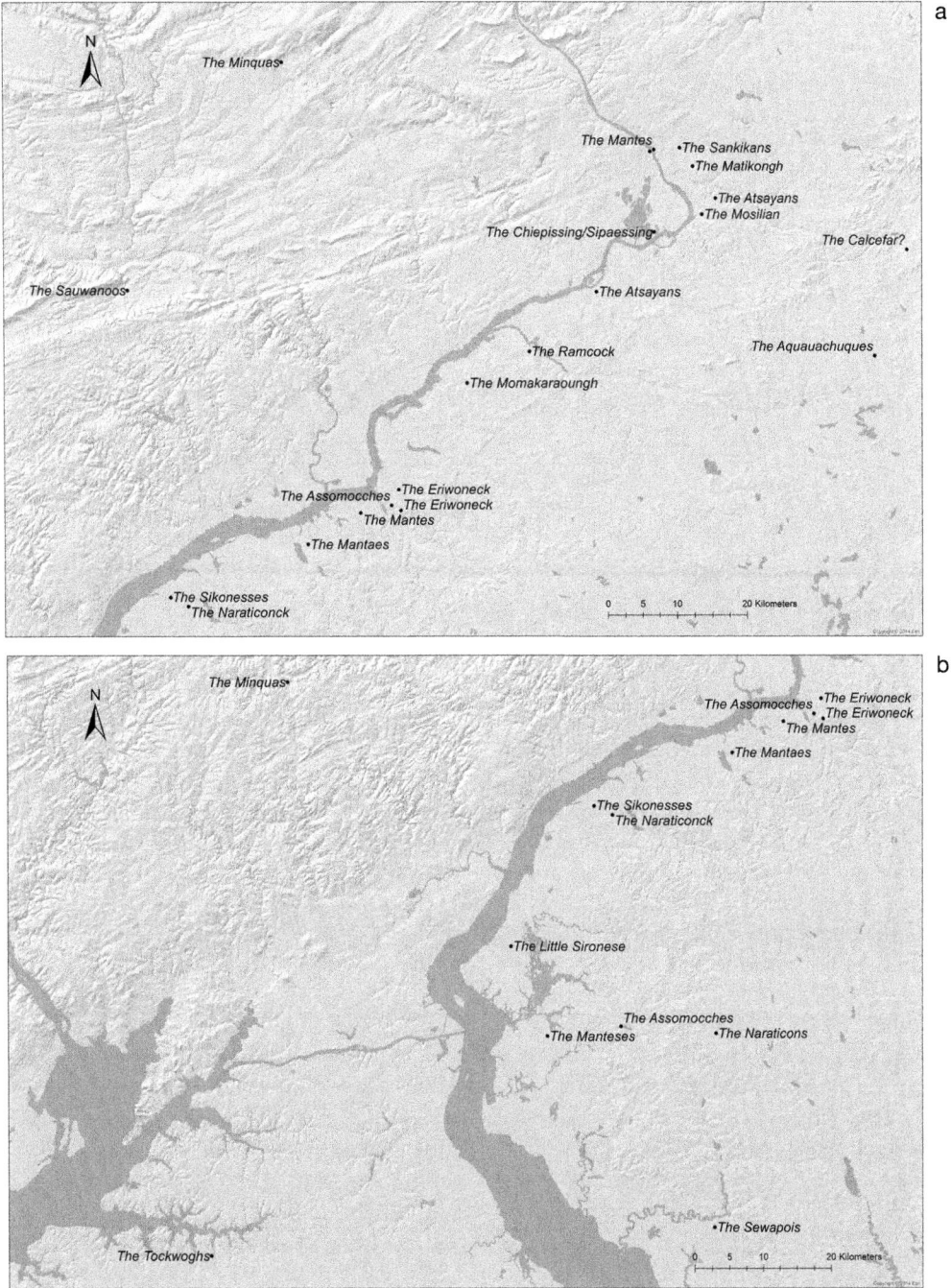

Fig. 14.2 a–c (above and overleaf) Maps showing the approximate locations of Native American tribal groups in the Lower Delaware valley and the Delaware Bay area c. 1635–55, based on contemporary accounts and maps (drawing: Fredrik Ekengren using ArcGIS® software by Esri).

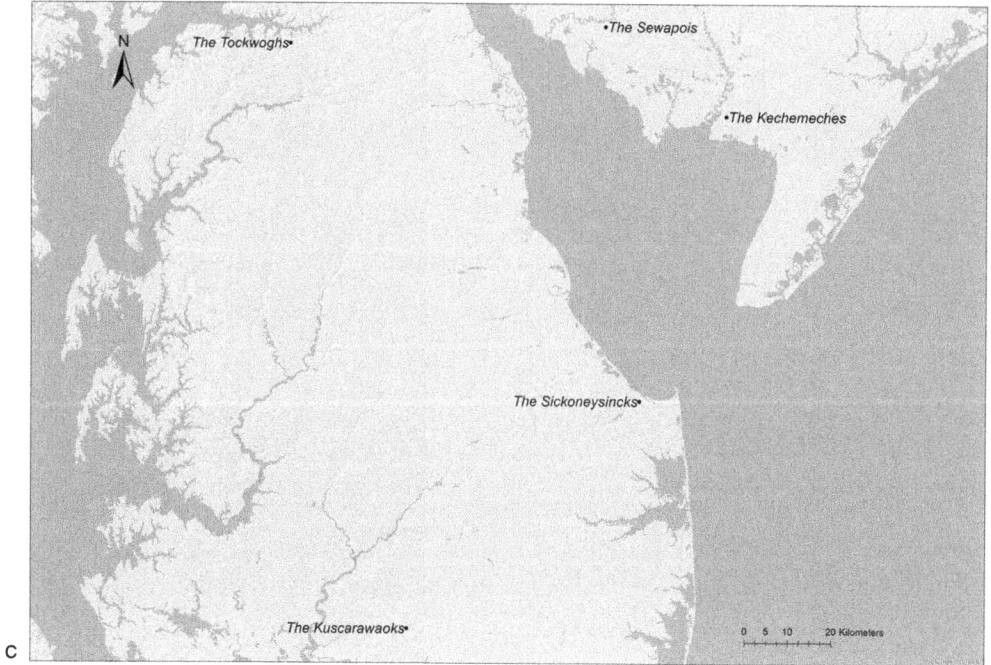

the *Aquauachuques*, the *Assomocches*, the *Atsayans*, the *Calcefar*, the *Eriwoneck*, the *Keche-meches*, the *Little Sironese*, the *Mantes*, the *Matikongh*, the *Momakaraoungh*, the *Mosilian*, the *Naraticonck*, the *Ramcock*, the *Sankikans*, the *Sewapois*, and the *Sikonesses*. In several cases, the name of the same tribal group appears at different locations depending on the source (Fig. 14.2 a–c). The *Mantes* are a typical example of this. Lindeström located them on both sides of the Falls of the Delaware, although he indicates that their primary settlement area was along the Assunpink creek in the vicinity of today's Trenton on the New Jersey side.[18] On his map, however, he had christened modern Mantua Creek in Gloucester County (NJ) *Manteskijl*, which incidentally is the same area in which Ving-boons's map located the *Mantaes*.[19] Similarly, the Dutch navigator David Pieterszoon De Vries located the *Mantes* in the areas drained by Mantua Creek and Big Timber Creek in his account from 1633.[20] Lastly, the letter of the Englishman Robert Evelyn from 1634, which is the earliest of our sources, located the *Manteses* along the present Salem river in Salem County (NJ).[21] These conflicting observations most likely reflect the mobility of Lenape groups in the 1630s to 1650s, indicating perhaps that the *Mantes* lived along the Salem river and Mantua and Big Timber creeks in the 1630s and 1640s, and in 1650s, when Lindeström made his observations, had settled further north by the Falls of the Delaware.[22] The same mobility may be reflected in the case of groups like the *Assomocches*, *Atsayans*, the *Naraticons*, and the *Sironese/Sikonesses/Sickoneysincks*.

    Looking at the spatial distribution of Lenape settlements, based on the historical accounts alone, we may divide the Lower Delaware valley into 13 areas, consisting of one or more indigenous settlements or plantations often located close to, or clus-tered around, the river's many tributaries (Fig. 14.3 a–b). The first consisted of two

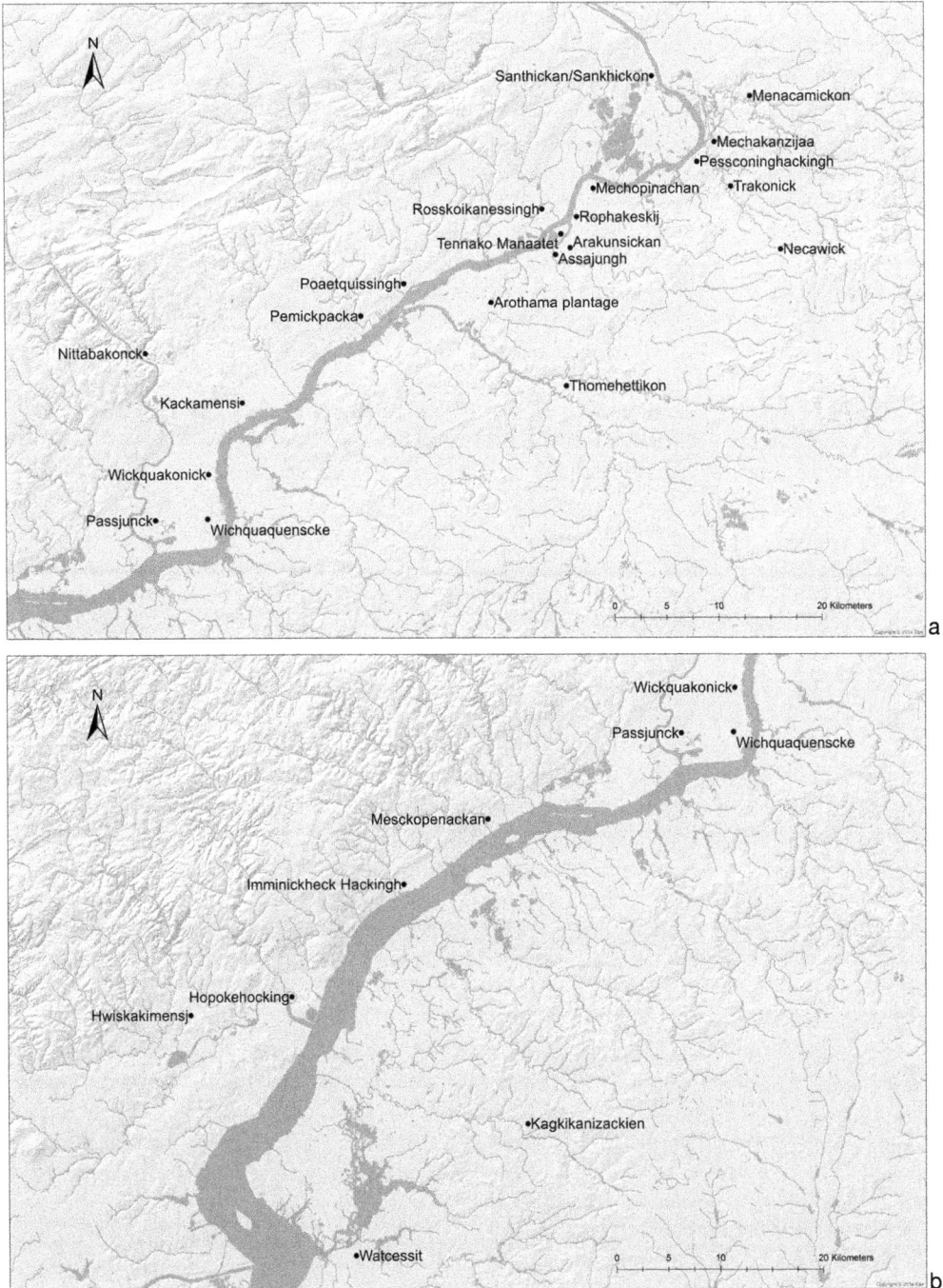

Fig. 14.3 a–b Maps showing the approximate locations of Native American settlements in the Lower Delaware valley, c. 1635–55, based on contemporary accounts and maps (drawing: Fredrik Ekengren using ArcGIS® software by Esri).

settlements, *Hopokehocking* and *Hwiskakimensj*, located on the western side of the Delaware. *Hopokehocking*, the site later known as being the location of the Swedish Fort Christina, was situated at the confluence of Brandywine Creek and the Christina river, while Lindeström's map located *Hwiskakimensj* north of the Christina river and Mill Creek, approximately in the vicinity today's Newport, Delaware.[23] Further up the Delaware, by the mouths of the Naaman and Chester creeks in today's north-eastern New Castle County (DE) and Delaware County (PA) respectively, were the settlements and plantations of *Imminickheck Hackingh* and *Mesckopenackan*.[24] The third settlement area on the western side of the river, at the confluence of the Schuylkill river and the Delaware, appears also to have been the largest, namely the Greater Passjunk, occasionally characterized in the historical accounts as one of the most important areas of the Lenape. Lindeström described it as follows:

> This is occupied in greatest force by the most intelligent savages of several nations of savages, who own the River and dwell here. There they have their dwellings side by side one another, wherefore also this land is thereby being cleared and cultivated with great power.[25]

This area, which is today covered by the city of Philadelphia, included the settlements of *Passjunck* at the mouth of the Schuylkill, *Wichquaquenscke* at the mouth of the now hidden Hollander Creek, *Wickquakonick*, which would later be called Wicaco, on the bank of the Delaware in the northern part of today's South Philadelphia, and *Nittab-akonck* at the confluence of the Schuylkill and Wissahickon Creek.[26] The fourth settlement area, north-east along the Delaware, was located along the now hidden Gunner's Run in today's neighbourhoods of Fishtown, Kensington and Port Richmond in Philadelphia, opposite Petty Island. It was called *Kackamension* on Lindeström's map, but late 17th-century sources know it as *Shackamaxon*; the Lenape village where the infamous Shackamaxon Treaty was drawn up between the Lenape and William Penn.[27] Further north-east, at the mouths of the Pennypack and Poquessing creeks, was an area consisting of the settlements of *Pemickpacka* and *Poaetquissingh*.[28] Beyond, along Mill Creek in the northern end of today's Bristol (PA), was another area consisting of a settlement and plantation called *Rosskoikanessingh*.[29] The last settlement area on the western bank of the Delaware, *Santhickan*,[30] was found around the bend of the river in the area of Biles and Moon islands.[31]

If we turn to the east side of the Lower Delaware, and look for the indigenous settlement areas in modern New Jersey, we first encounter the settlement of *Menacamickon* inland along the Crosswicks creek, in today's Mercer County. At the mouth of the same creek, as well as at the mouth of Blacks Creek and extending along its course in modern Burlington County, we find the settlements and plantations of *Mechakanzijaa*, *Pessconinghackingh*, *Trakonick*, and *Necawick*. To the south-east, from the bend of the Delaware at Florence, down to the mouth of the Assiscunk creek, including Burlington Island, we find a group of settlements and plantations consisting of *Mechopinachan*, *Rophakeskij*, *Arakunsickan*, *Assajungh*, and *Tennako Manaatet*.[32] On the land between the Assiscunk and Rancocas creeks in Burlington County, Lindeström located the *Arothama plantation*,[33] and further south along the Rancocas, at the fork of the creek's north and south branches, lay according to him an area called *Domhitticon*,[34] most likely identical to the indigenous settlement called *Thomehettikon* by Thomas Campanius Holm.[35]

The last two known settlement areas on the New Jersey side of the Delaware were located some distance away, along the Salem river: *Kagkikanizackien* near today's Woodstown, and *Watcessit* at the mouth of the river near today's Salem, both in Salem County. Incidentally, *Watcessit* is described as the principal village of the *Manteses*, and its name is the same word as *Wootsessungsing*, *Oydsessing* and *Oijtsessingh* which are in turn the various renderings of the name given to the land where the Swedish Fort Nya Elfsborg was built in 1643.[36]

The size and nature of the settlements listed above are difficult to assess. Some of the English translations of the Swedish sources refer to them as "towns", although the original Swedish texts rather refer to them as "places" (*platser*), "settlements" (*boställen*) or "plantations" (*plantager*).[37] There is likewise in the historical research a tendency to refer to all of them as villages, indicating large and permanent clusters of dwellings. However, at the same time Campanius Holm wrote,

> The American Indians have no towns or fixed places of habitation; they mostly wander about from one place to another; and generally, go to those places where they think they are most likely to find the means of support. In spring and summer, they choose the banks of rivers, where they find plenty of fish; but in winter, they go up into the country, where they find abundance of venison.[38]

This has led other scholars to classify the known Lenape settlements along the Delaware as summer stations, indicating their seasonal nature,[39] which in turn has given rise to a general notion of an almost ephemeral Native presence in an otherwise European colonial landscape at this time. However, if we include the archaeological material at hand we may balance these two positions, and offer a more nuanced picture of the region.

There is no question that the riverside landscape in the Lower Delaware valley had already been transformed by human activity when the Swedes settled there. This study has been able to identify a total of 20 sites in the area, all with dates falling within the operative time frame: the late 1630s to the late 1650s (Table 14.1, see p. 273). This number most likely only represents a small percentage of the original Lenape settlements in the region.[40] The maps in Fig. 14.4 a–e show their distribution in relation to the historically-known sites. Some of them, like the Abbott Farm complex (including the burials from Rowan Farm), Lenhardt-Lahaway, and Salisbury (including Goose Island), as well as the cemetery collection from the Indian Burial Ground, probably represent quite substantial, recurrent or sedentary settlements or villages, exhibiting features such as storage and rubbish pits, burials, a high density of artefactual material, and occasionally the remains of shelters.[41] Others, such as the Chain Shop (part of the Douglas Gut complex), Sandhickey, Marcel Haines, Farnum Park, Nicolosi, Ware, Julian Powerline and Churchmans Marsh, as well as Printzhof, appear to be the remains of smaller recurrent camps for hunting or trade, most likely used by smaller social units on a seasonal basis.[42] The remaining sites, 122 Mongomery, Burlington Island, Caleb Pusey House, Pennsbury Manor, and Remer, exhibit material that falls within the relevant time frame, but are of unknown character due to a lack of contextual information.

a

b

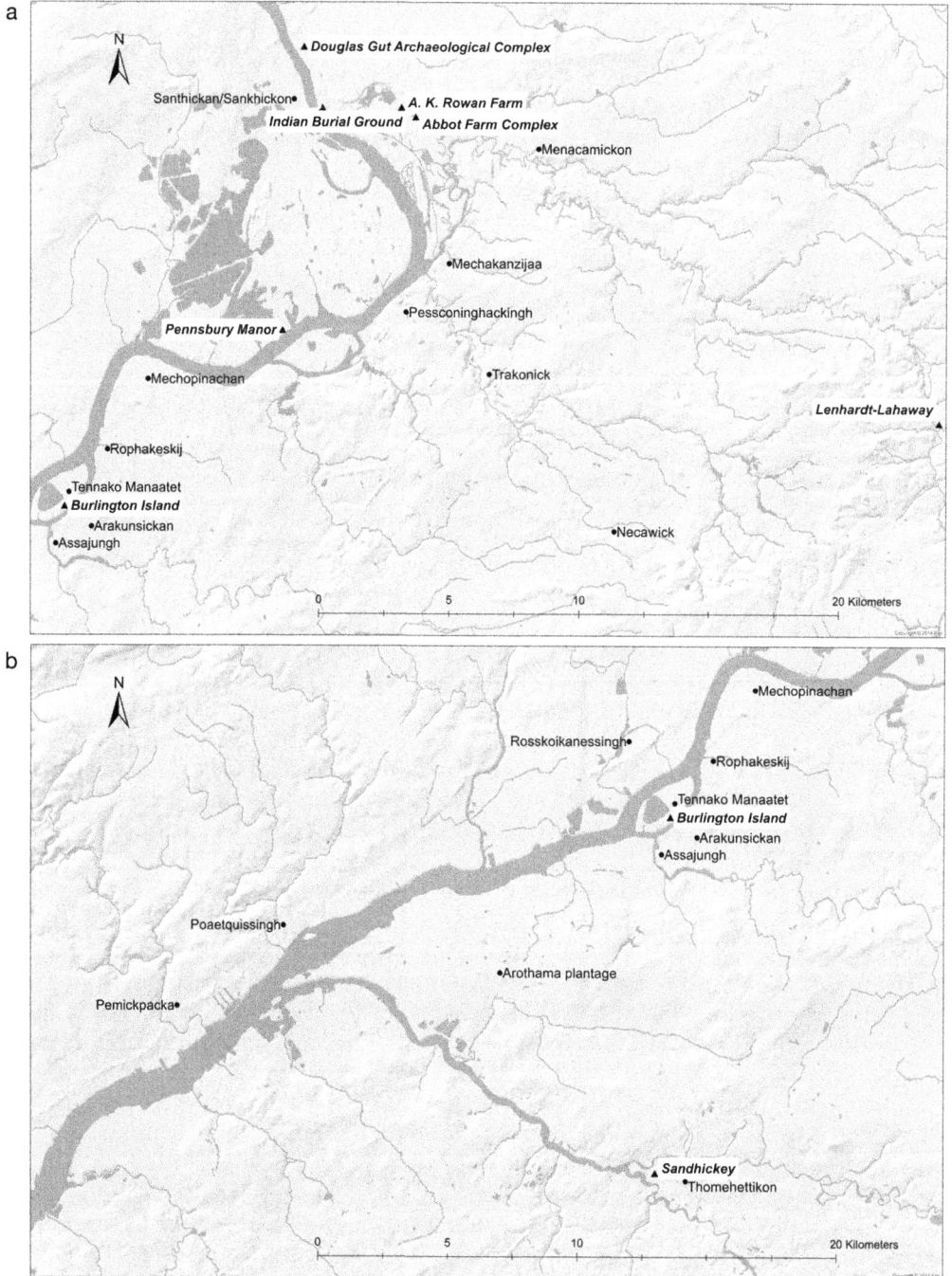

Fig. 14.4 a–e (above, and following pages) Maps combining archaeologically identified Native American sites (▲) dating between the mid-1630s and the late 1650s, with the approximate locations of Native American settlements referenced in contemporary historical accounts and maps (drawing: Fredrik Ekengren using ArcGIS® software by Esri).

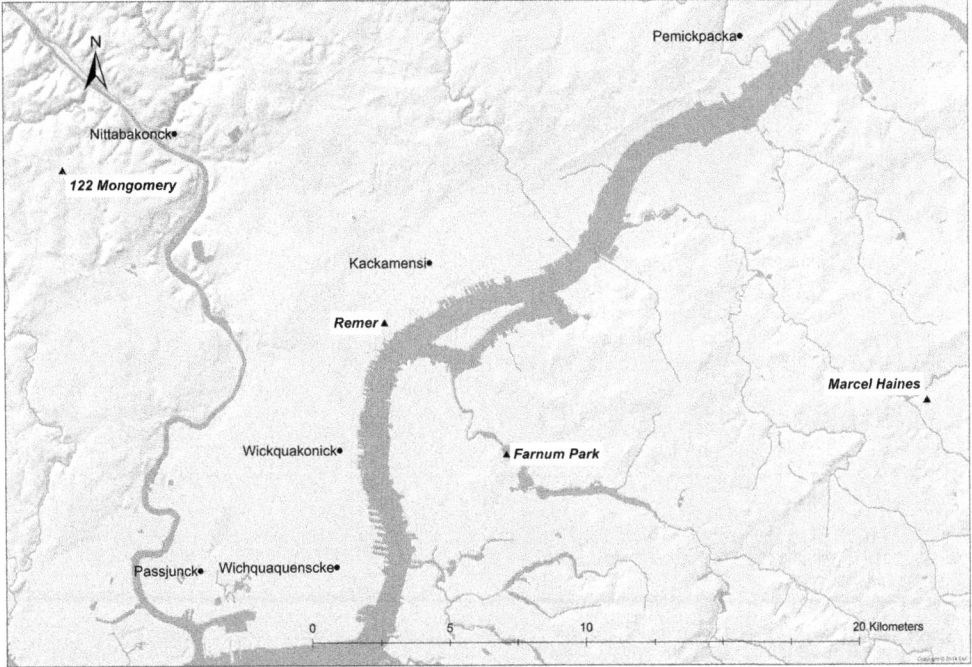

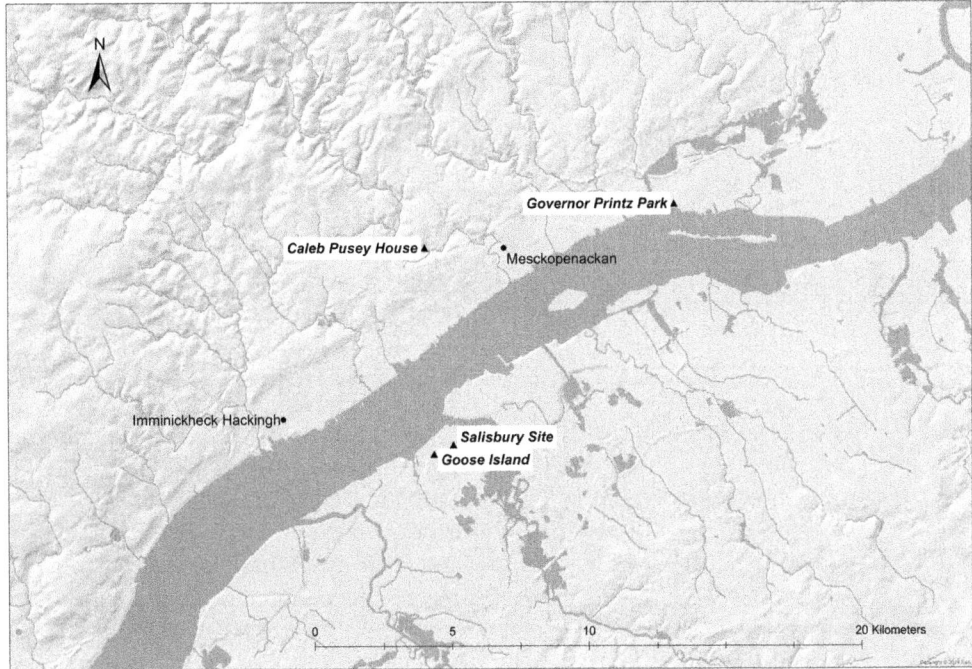

e
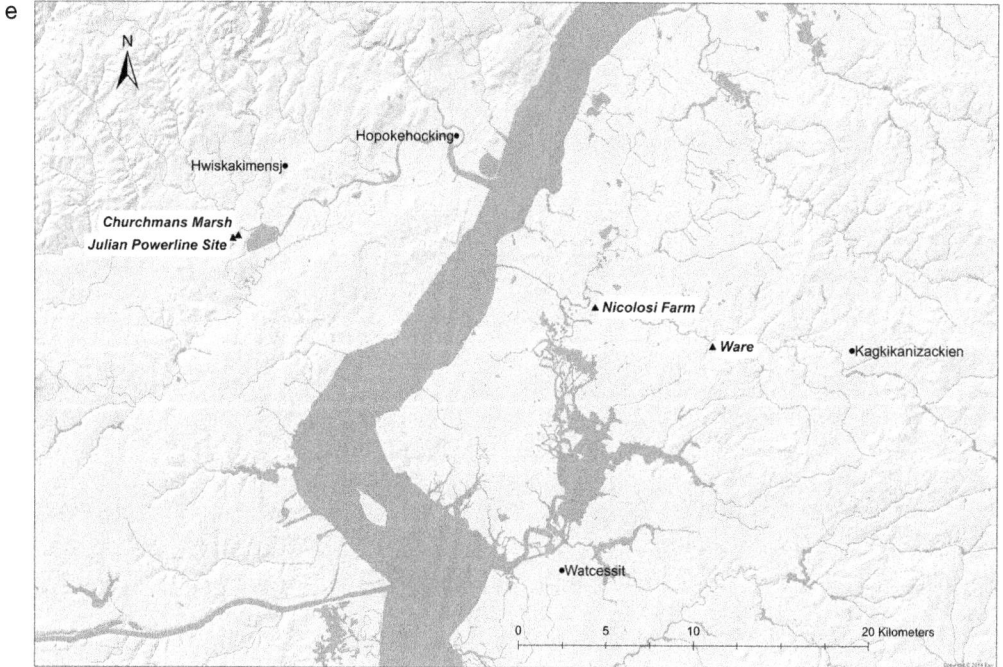

What can be said for the majority of the sites noted above is that they show continuity far back in time, before European contact, from at least the Late Woodland period and often from periods earlier than that.[43] Thus, indigenous use and conceptualization of the landscape and these places, even the smaller non-permanent camps, had deep roots.

In some cases, the sites may even be associated or identified with some of the historically-known settlements. The Julian Powerline site as well as Churchmans Marsh along Mill Creek may have been associated with *Hwiskakimensj*, while Caleb Pusey House may have been the same as the *Mesckopenackan* settlement along Chester Creek. The Remer site may represent archaeological evidence for the *Kackamensi* settlement, and the collection of artefacts from Burlington Island may be identified as the *Tennako Manaatet* settlement. The most striking match between archaeology and the historical sources, however, may be the Sandhickey site, located at the confluence of the northern and southern branches of Rancocas Creek, which is most likely identical to the *Thomehettikon* settlement mentioned by Campanius Holm and visible as *Domhitticon* on Lindeström's map.[44] Furthermore, several of the historically-known settlement areas are now further expanded by the addition of the archaeological sites. *Menacamickon* along the Crosswicks Creek is joined by a number of sites around the well-known Abbot Farm complex, while the Nicolosi Farm and the Ware site join the *Kagkikanizackien* settlement along the Salem river.

Table 14.1 (opposite) Archaeologically identified Native American sites dating from the late 1630s to the late 1650s.

Site	County	State	Date	Type	References
122 Mongomery (36-MG-219)	Montgomery	PA	1600–1650; 1650–1700	Unknown	Stewart 2014; CRGIS
Abbott Farm Complex (28-ME-1)	Mercer	NJ	1650–1750	Village (settlement + burials)	Cross 1956; Grumet 1995; Pagoulatos 2007; Hunter et al 2009; Stewart 2014
Burlington Island	Burlington	NJ	1630–1730	Unknown (collection)	Veit & Bello 1999
Caleb Pusey House (36-DE-4)	Delaware	PA	1600–1650; 1650–1700	Unknown	Stewart 2014; CRGIS
Churchmans Marsh (7NC-E-60)	New Castle	DE	1600–1660	Transient camp	Custer et al. 1998; Stewart 2014
Chain Shop Site (Douglas Gut Complex 28-ME-273)	Mercer	NJ	1620–1650	Transient camp	Pagoulatos 2007; Hunter Research 2011; Stewart 2014
Farnum Park	Camden	NJ	1620–1720	Transient camp	Pagoulatos 2007; Stewart 2014
Governor Printz Park & Printzhof Site (36-DE-3)	Delaware	PA	1643–1655	Transient camp	Becker 1993a; Grumet 1995; Stewart 2014
Goose Island	Gloucester	NJ	1650–1750	Village (settlement + burials)	Cross 1941; Stewart 2014
Indian Burial Ground	Mercer	NJ	1640–1675	Village cemetery (cemetery collection)	Veit & Bello 2001; Pagoulatos 2007; Stewart 2014
Julian Powerline Site (7NC-E-42)	New Castle	DE	1630–1740	Transient camp	Custer 1982; Custer & Watson 1985; Pietak 1995
Lenhardt-Lahaway	Burlington	NJ	1625–1710	Village (settlement + burials)	Cross 1941; Grumet 1995; Pietak 1995; Pagoulatos 2007; Stewart 2014
Marcel Haines	Burlington	NJ	1620–1720	Transient camp	Pagoulatos 2007; Stewart 2014
Nicolosi Farm	Salem	NJ	1620–1720	Transient camp	Pagoulatos 2007; Stewart 2014
Pennsbury Manor (36-BU-19)	Bucks	PA	1650–1700	Unknown	Stewart 2014; CRGIS
Remer (36-PH-159)	Philadelphia City	PA	1600–1650; 1650–1700	Unknown	CRGIS
Rowan Farm (Abbot Farm Complex 28-ME-1)	Mercer	NJ	1650–1750	Village cemetery (cemetery collection)	Veit & Bello 2001; Pagoulatos 2007; Stewart 2014
Salisbury	Gloucester	NJ	1635–1750	Village (settlement + burials)	Grumet 1995; Pietak 1995; Sansevere 2009
Sandhickey	Burlington	NJ	1620–1720	Transient camp	Pagoulatos 2007; Stewart 2014
Ware (28-SA-3)	Salem	NJ	1620–1720	Transient camp	McCann 1950; Pietak 1995; Morris et al 1996; Pagoulatos 2007; Stewart 2014

COHABITATION IN NEW SWEDEN

The overall picture gained from this mapping of historically- and archaeologically-known Native sites is of a culturally embedded and fairly densely populated landscape, characterized by a few central, sedentary habitations interspersed by smaller settlements of a more transient nature.[45] It was this landscape the Swedish colonists navigated when they arrived in 1638 (Fig. 14.5 a–e).[46] The Swedes were, however, not the first Europeans to settle along the Lower Delaware. Already in 1623 the Dutch had erected Fort Nassau at the mouths of the Big Timber and Little Timber creeks, which would stand until 1651, and in 1633 they built a blockhouse at the confluence of the Schuylkill river and Mingo Creek, which was demolished by the Swedes in the 1640s.

This Dutch familiarity with the Delaware river and their Lenape neighbours was instrumental for the founding of the Swedish colony. That is why Peter Minuit, the former director of the New Netherland colony and the co-founder of New Sweden, bought land at the confluence of the Minquas Kill and the Brandywine Creek from a group of Lenape and Susquehannocks in order to erect Fort Christina.[47] By doing so, he knowingly intersected one of the important trade routes to the Susquehannock in the Pennsylvania interior. Through the Minquas Kill the Swedes gained access to the Lenape territories westward, and through the Brandywine they could access the Great Minquas Path, the 17th-century trade route that spanned Susquehannock territory and connected the Delaware and Susquehanna rivers. Its entry point lay at the confluence of the Schuylkill and the Delaware, opposite the Dutch Fort Nassau, which was one of the reasons the Swedes also established forts and settlements near the Schuylkill as well as the Darby and Cobbs creeks.[48] Likewise, the Swedes built a trading post at "Zanchikan" (the same as *Santhickan* mentioned above) by the Falls of the Delaware in 1640s, at today's Trenton,[49] while Fort Nya Elfsborg allowed them not only to control the traffic up the Delaware but also facilitated contact with the Lenape living along the Salem river and Alloway Creek in south-western New Jersey. But these political and economic strategies not only intersected the already established networks between the various Native American groups (particularly between the Lenape and the Susquehannock) and between the Native Americans and other Europeans, such as the Dutch. It also placed the Swedes in the midst of Native American life, since they did not just buy land that belonged to the Lenape but actually became tenants in areas that to some extent still functioned as Lenape settlements, at least seasonally. Fort Christina was located on the site of *Hopokehocking*, mentioned above, which was one of the seasonal camps along the Delaware,[50] the Upland and Printztorp settlements were located in the vicinity of the *Mesckopenackan* settlement,[51] and the trading post at Zanchikan shared the area of the Moon and Biles islands with a settlement of the same name. Perhaps Fort Nya Elfsborg should also be added to the list, since it was located at *Watcessit*,[52] the principal settlement of the Mantes along Salem river.

The reason why the Swedes should be viewed as tenants rather than masters of this landscape is demonstrated in the Swedish sources themselves, as well as in the Lenape attitude towards land sales. Both the instructions to governor Printz and Lindeström's account of his visit in the colony, as well as the description by Campanius Holm, acknowledged the Lenape as the "rightful owners" of the land.[53] This recognition should partly be understood in the light of Swedish competition with the Dutch, in so far as

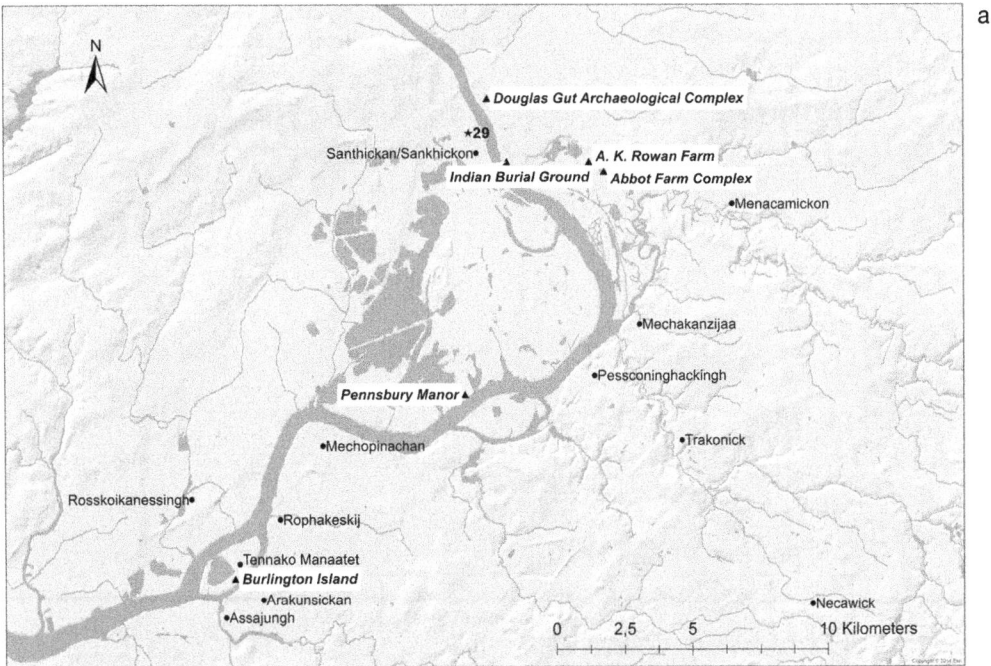

Fig. 14.5 a–e (above and following pages) Maps combining the approximate locations of sites belonging to the New Sweden colony (nos. 1–31), as well as Dutch sites (a–e), with historically and archaeologically identified Native American settlements. *New Sweden sites*: **1.** Fort Trefaldigheten (1654–5); **2.** Niew Claerlandh (1654/1655); **3.** Strandviken settlement (1654); **4.** Översidolandet settlement (1654); **5.** Sidoland settlement (1654); **6.** Christina settlement (1638 & 1641); **7.** Fort Christina (1638–55); **8.** Timber Island settlement (1654); **9.** Finland settlement (1641 & 1643); **10.** Printztorp settlement (1643); **11.** Blockhouse Upland/Mecoponacka (1643); **12.** Upland settlement (1641 & 1643); **13.** Tequirassy settlement (1643); **14.** Fort Nya Göteborg & Printzhof (1643–55); **15.** Tenakonk/Tinicum settlement (1643); **16.** Ammansland settlement (1654); **17.** Minqua's Island settlement (1644); **18.** Province Island settlement (1643); **19.** Blockhouse Province Island (1643–7); **20.** Fort Nya Kårsholm (1647–53) built on the site of a short-lived English blockhouse (1642); **21.** Blockhouse Nya Wasa (1645–7); **22.** Kingsessing/Wasa settlement (1644); **23.** Printz's/Old Swedes Mill (1645); **24.** Blockhouse Mölndal (1645–51); **25.** Mölndal settlement (1645); **26.** Torne/Aronameck settlement (1647); **27.** Blockhouse Torne (1647–55); **28.** The blockhouse in front of Dutch Fort Beversreede (1648–?); **29.** Zanchikan/Santhickan trading post (1640s); **30.** Varkens Kill settlement. English blockhouse and settlement under Swedish authority (1641–3); **31.** Fort Nya Elfsborg (1643–51). *Dutch sites*: **a.** Sandhook settlement (1651); **b.** Fort Casimir (1651–4); **c.** Blockhouse at the Schuylkill (1633–43/1647?); **d.** Fort Beversreede (1648–51); **e.** Fort Nassau (1623–51) (drawing: Fredrik Ekengren using ArcGIS® software by Esri).

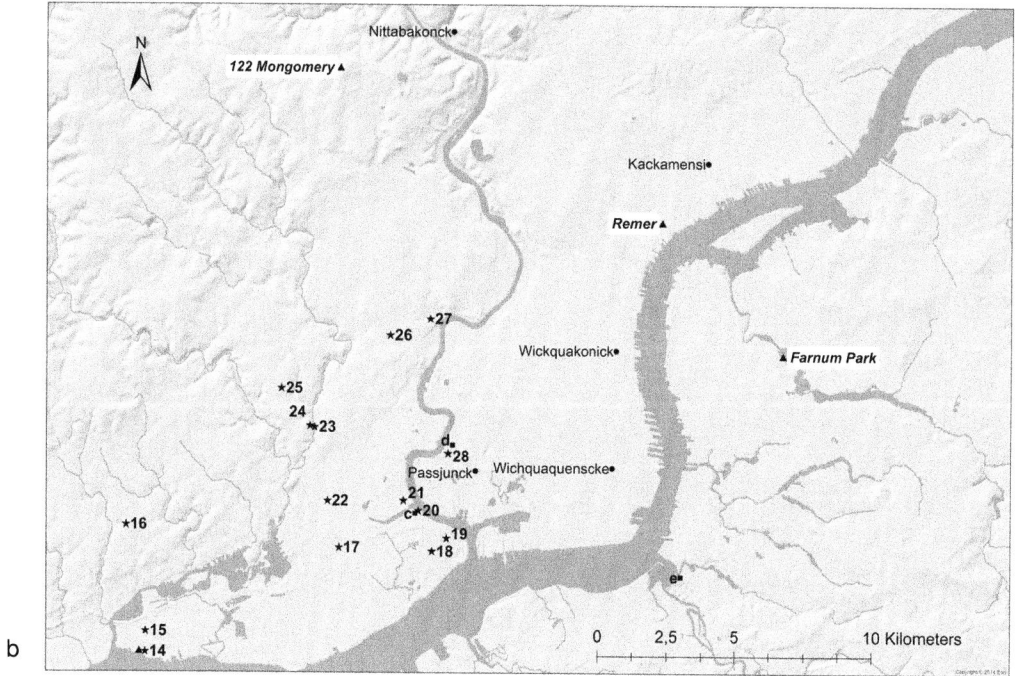

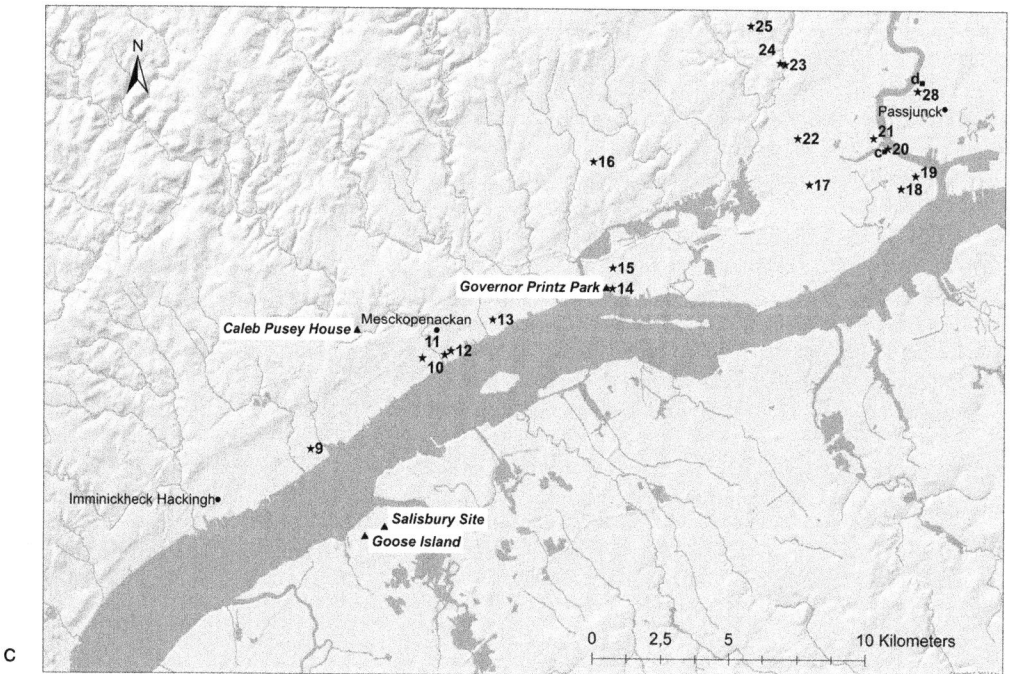

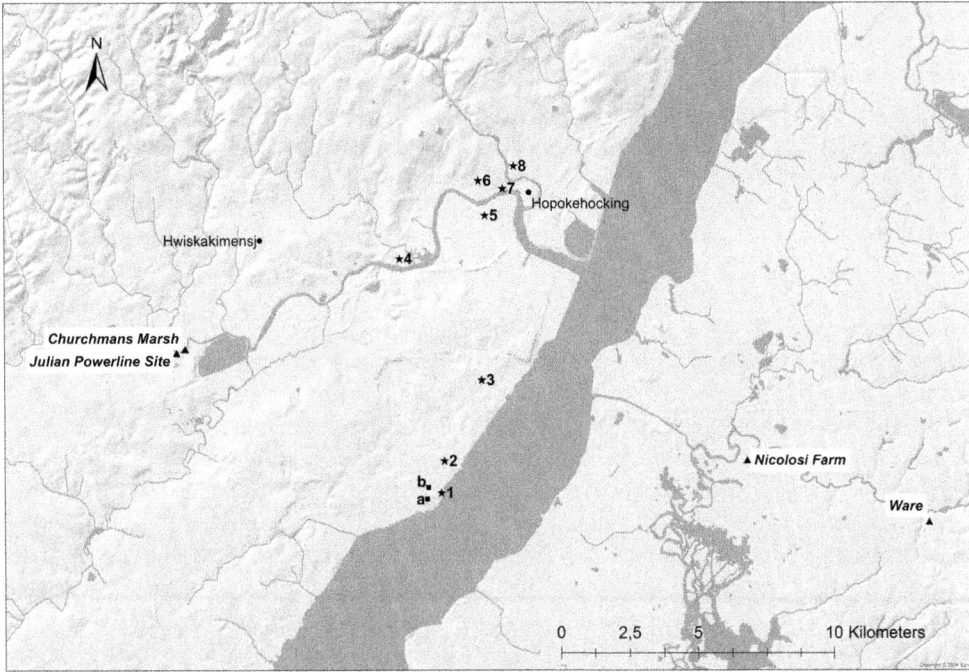

d

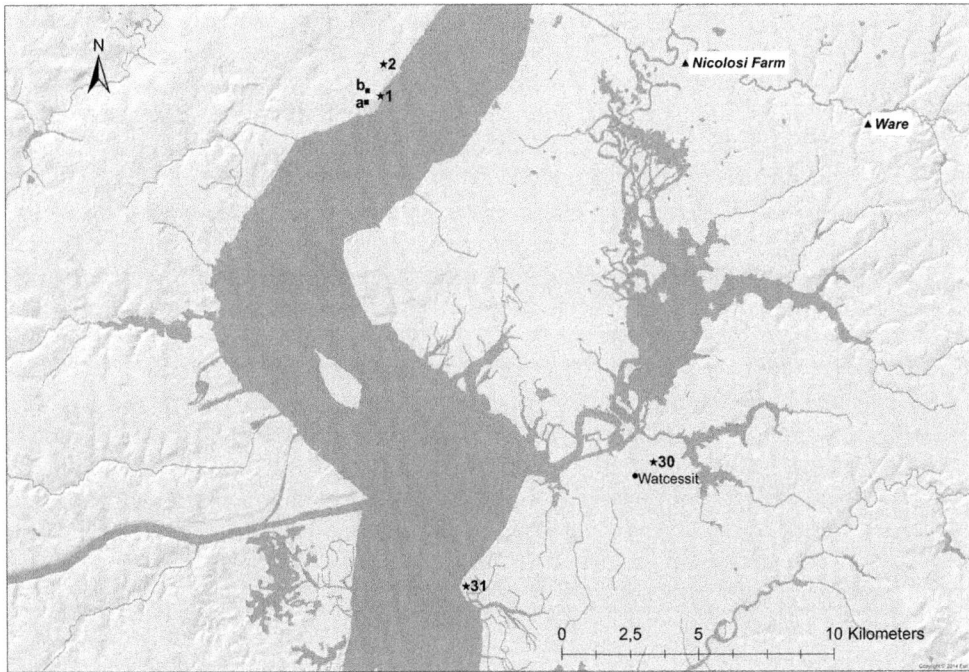

e

emphasizing Native ownership and the lawful acquisition of their land was a way to contest the Dutch claim to the Delaware.[54] But such statements also asserted the Lenape presence among the Swedish settlements as common and expected.

The Lenape view of ownership differed markedly from the European, forcing the Swedes continually to renew their acquisitions. The Lenape communities did not consider land purchases as closed deals involving the *transferral* of rights, but rather as the formation of social relationships which entailed the *sharing* of a specific territory and its resources – an agreement of cohabitation.[55] At the centre of this agreement stood the reciprocal exchange of gifts, which facilitated the Lenape inclusion of the Swedes within their territory. The Swedish settlements and forts were welcomed on Lenape territory in return for annual gifts and promises of access to European trade,[56] and the Lenape did not hesitate to turn to the Swedes' competitors in the Delaware valley, the Dutch, when the Swedes fail to live up to their side of the agreement. This appears to be the most common cause behind the documented conflicts between Swedes and the Lenape in the mid-17th century.[57] The Lenape considered themselves independent from the foreign nations: "they let it be understood that they are a free people, subject to no one", and acted accordingly.[58]

Regardless of the legal validity of the land transactions, the fact remains that the Swedes entered into formal agreements to share the indigenous landscape encompassing the majority of the Lower Delaware valley, including the Delaware Bay area. Therefore, the large-scale relocation of indigenous populations so often associated with colonial occupation is not observable in the material from New Sweden. It is not until the late 17th century, with the influx of new settlers, the founding of new Euro-American communities and the subsequent shifting western frontier, that we witness a widespread displacement of the Native American communities in the Lower Delaware valley.[59] Until then, large sedentary Lenape settlements still existed within the reaches of New Sweden. In the case of the Salisbury/Goose Island Native complex at the mouth of Raccoon Creek, this was directly opposite and visible from the colonial Finland settlement on the other side of the Delaware, which would naturally shape the daily experiences of their inhabitants. Beyond these villages, the colonial landscape was dotted with settlements of a more transient nature, with people or groups of people moving between them. Overall, this shows the danger of excluding the Native presence from geopolitical maps of the colony, since it fails to capture its cultural diversity and perpetuates an image of Swedish hegemony in the Lower Delaware valley in the mid-17th century.

We may now begin to question how separate these communities, Lenape and Swedish, really were. Looking at the maps in Fig. 14.5 a–e, we may identify at least six areas where cohabitation, perhaps even a shared community, of Lenape and Swedish groups can be argued for. Granted, it is not possible to confirm absolutely their contemporaneousness, on account of the nature of the archaeological and historical evidence; however the sites all fall within the time frame of the late 1630s to late 1650s, and would have overlapped for at least a portion of that time. These areas include:

1. *Hopokehocking* together with Fort Christina, the Christina settlement, the Timber Island settlement, and the Sidolandet settlement;

2. *Mesckopenackan* and the Caleb Pusey House site, together with the Printztorp settlement and Upland settlement, as well as the Tequirassy settlement;

3. the Governor Printz Park site, together with Fort Nya Göteborg and Printzhof, as well as the Tenakonk settlement;

4. the settlements around the mouth of the Schuylkill river, particularly *Passjunck*, together with the Province Island settlement and its blockhouse and the Kingsessing/Wasa settlement and its blockhouse, Fort Nya Kårsholm, as well as the blockhouse erected in front of the Dutch Fort Beversreede on the eastern shore of the Schuylkill;

5. *Santhickan*, together with the Swedish trading post on the site;

6. lastly, *Watcessit*, together with the Swedish-controlled English settlement and blockhouse in the area, possibly also with the addition of Fort Nya Elfsborg.

The Governor Printz Park and Printzhof site (36-DE-3) deserves special attention in this context, since it is the only site where an archaeological case could be made for a contemporaneous and intersecting Native and Swedish habitation. The site was excavated in 1937, 1976, 1985, 1986 and 1990, and revealed pre-contact material (including burials) indicating the site had been a sedentary Native American settlement, at least before European contact. The material dating to subsequent periods came to a large degree from disturbed layers, and included indigenous pottery, debitage, worked bottle glass and gun flints. Some features contained a mixture of Native American and European material, such as pipes dating to the period 1640–50, placing it within the time frame of the New Sweden colony. The pipes were of Dutch manufacture, including a funnel-angled Edward Bird trade pipe modelled after indigenous stone pipes, one of which was also found on the site (Fig. 14.6). The most striking feature, however, was the remains of what is generally considered to be Printzhof, the private residence of the Swedish governor Johan Printz originally erected in 1643 as part of Fort Nya Göteborg and then rebuilt after a fire in the winter of 1644–5. In layers formed possibly in the process of rebuilding the residence the excavators found a Native stone adze and the fragment of a large trade-bead manufactured in 17th-century Amsterdam or Venice, along with other European material such as iron spikes and nails, sherds of glazed pottery, tobacco pipes, fragments of glass vessels, and bricks. Next to the Printzhof structure were also found the postmolds of two *wigwams*: the domed, circular type of shelter used by the indigenous groups in the area. Taken together, the material points toward a site that functioned as the private residence for the Swedish governor as well as being contemporarily Native American camp, perhaps hosting the pipe ceremonies whereby the social and economic relationships between Natives and Swedes were reaffirmed.[60] Similar heterogeneity appears to have characterized the other forts in the colony as well, such as Fort Christina, which prompted admonitions from English visitors who were alarmed by the free movement of Native Americans among the Swedes.[61] Consequently, we might say that the Swedish settlements were *added* to the ranges of the Lenape, representing an indigenous territorial inclusion or extension rather than a deterritorialization.[62]

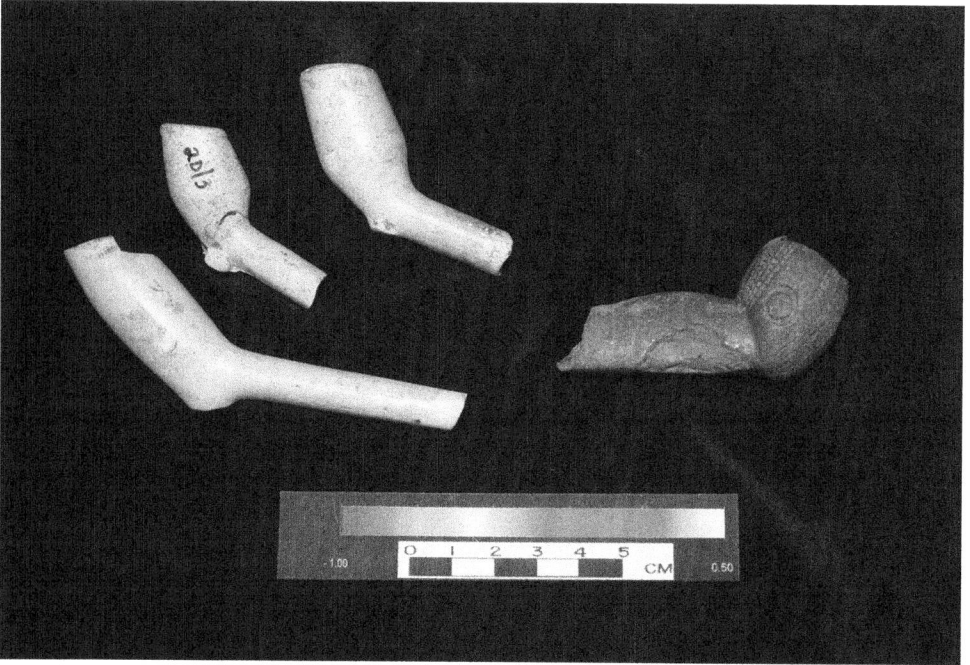

Fig. 14.6 Smoking pipes from Governor Printz Park and the Printzhof site (36-DE-3): on the left, three Dutch clay pipes, including a funnel-angled Edward Bird trade pipe (bottom left), modelled after Native American pipes; on the right, an Native American stone pipe (reproduced by courtesy of the State Museum of Pennsylvania, Pennsylvania Historical and Museum Commission).

While the Governor Printz Park and Printzhof is the only excavated site that through archaeology, in combination with historical sources, can be linked to both Native Americans and Swedish settlers, the other identified Lenape sites exhibit a similar mixture of indigenous and European material culture. However, the amount of European objects on the indigenous settlements in the region is meagre compared to the wealth of material on Susquehannock sites along the Susquehanna river in the interior of modern Pennsylvania. This dearth does not imply a lack of interaction between Europeans and Lenape, but rather reflects the distribution of trade relations. Access to the fur trade with the Susquehannock, who were one of the great trading powers in the American interior, was the reason why the Swedes settled close to the Christina, Brandywine and Schuylkill rivers. By building forts, blockhouses and settlements in strategic locations in relation to the Great Minquas Path they managed to cut off the supply of western peltry from the Dutch. This trade, where European goods were exchanged for furs, took place either directly with the Susquehannock who journeyed to the Delaware and its tributaries, or indirectly with the Lenape as brokers.[63] In 1655, the Swedish governor Risingh wrote that goods were given on credit to the Lenape, who traded them for Susquehannock peltry that they then sold for higher profits to the Dutch in New Amsterdam, much to the annoyance of the Swedes.[64] Thus, European goods were channelled through indigenous networks to markets that did not necessarily lie along the Lower Delaware. This would naturally affect the quantity of European objects found on Lenape sites in the region, and explain why the written sources refer to a wide array of objects being traded by the Swedes to the Lenape, while the archaeological sites reveal only a fraction of these materials.

What we do see on the sites excavated in the Lower Delaware valley, however, despite the scantiness of the material, is how European objects were integrated into Native American material and technological practices, as well as creating new ones.[65] The presence of kaolin pipes indicates that European fashions and indigenous smoking practices became entangled,[66] while gunflints on the sites are evidence of how traditional practices of hunting and warfare were modified through the use of European guns.[67] European flints, which arrived on the Delaware as ballast on board ships, were used to manufacture lithic tools,[68] while other objects, such as beads, bracelets and arrowheads made out of sheet copper, demonstrate not only the material transformation of European objects (most likely kettles) but also indirectly the use of European tools such as scissors and metal snips.[69] Furthermore, the number of glass beads found, either as stray finds or together with indigenous ornaments in the context of graves,[70] indicates that European objects became part of an indigenous expression of identity.

By affording the Swedes land to settle, the Lenape gained access to European goods, but were also drawn into cross-cultural dependencies with the Swedes. The material and cultural transformations that are visible in the archaeology would have required this entanglement with the Swedes in order to be sustained. Likewise, the Swedes were drawn into dependencies with the Lenape, and not only regarding access to land. For instance, the Swedes' reliance for survival on Lenape cash-crop farming of maize, and their subsequent adoption of maize cultivation as well as other changes in diet and cooking, would have tied the Swedes even closer to Lenape culture.[71] Consequently, both Swedes and Lenape, were "forced to meet their needs on the middle ground".[72]

CONCLUSIONS

The fur trade, and the access and closeness to Native American communities it necessitated, moulded the pattern of settlement along the Delaware. By mapping both historically- and archaeologically-known sites, and identifying areas of cohabitation and shared community, the biography of the landscape emerges: a cultural landscape, rather than a natural one, and a palimpsest of inscribed identities, where Native influences on the Swedish settlers were considerable. But the Swedes and the Lenape were not only neighbours; they moved in the same landscape and dwelled in the same places, at least temporarily. Swedish sites such as Printzhof in Fort Nya Göteborg, as well as the Lenape settlements, were thus places where material culture and practices were interpreted and transformed, blurring the distinctions between indigenous and non-indigenous. The landscape may therefore be understood as both "middle ground", to employ Richard White's metaphor describing places of cultural accommodation and hybridization, and "Native ground", to cite Kathleen DuVal's conceptualization of areas where Native

Americans dictated the form and content of interactions with the Europeans, and kept their independence by incorporating the colonists into indigenous networks and practices.[73] The close relationship between the Swedes and the Lenape, often emphasized in scholarly texts, should naturally be viewed in light of the Lower Delaware valley as shared space. Famous Swedish intermediaries, go-betweens and interpreters like Peter Cock (1610–87), Lasse Cock (1646–99), Israel Helm (1630–1701), Olof Stille (1610–84) and Peter Yocum (1653–1701), were formed by this landscape, and had thus learnt to navigate the merging edges of Swedish and Native communities.[74]

Rather than contrasting the two groups, Swedish and Native, and focusing solely on the distinction between indigenous and European objects (or "trade items"), a focus on shared history and shared space permits us to speak of a colonial world encompassing the entangled and hybrid. This certainly does not mean that there existed no inequalities of power.[75] But to view the Lower Delaware valley in the early 17th century from a perspective of Swedish or European hegemony would be misleading, and would deny the fact that the European settlements were part of a larger Native American landscape. For the Swedes, cooperation with the indigenous population was consequently vital. The same was true for the Lenape, who in this period display neither submission nor resistance to the Swedish presence. Thus, to gain a fuller understanding of New Sweden we must look at both the colonizer and the colonized, and grasp how they together conceptualized space and shaped the foundation for cultural production in the Lower Delaware landscape.

ACKNOWLEDGEMENTS

I wish to thank Jay Custer (University of Delaware), Jack Cresson (Archaeological Society of New Jersey), Craig Lukezic (Delaware Division of Historical and Cultural Affairs), Wade Catts (John Milner Associates, Inc.), as well as Janet Johnson and the staff at the Section of Archaeology at the Pennsylvania Historical & Museum Commission, for their kind assistance in my preparation of this chapter.

NOTES

1   See also Barr 2011, 6–7.

2   See also White 1991, 50–1.

3   One exception, although in large parts incomplete, is the map in Fur 2006, 133.

4   E.g. Heite 1991, 8; See also Barr 2011, 8.

5   Most notably Fur 2006; 2009 and Soderlund 2015.

6   However, see Immonen 2011 and Ekengren *et al.* 2013.

7   See critique by e.g. Lightfoot 1995; Rubertone 2000; Silliman 2010; Stewart 2014.

8   White 1991; Pratt 1992; Harrison 2004; Mrozowski *et al.* 2007; Silliman 2010; Schwartz & Green 2013; Vitelli 2013; Harrison 2014.

9   White 1991, 50.

10 E.g. Merrell 1999; Merritt 2003; Schutt 2007.

11 The sources include the letter of Englishman Robert Evelyn from 1634, first published in 1641 and then in 1648 – see Scull 1881, 95–9 and C. A. Weslager's 1954 interpretation of Evelyn's account; the *Instructions for Peter Minuit* drafted by Samuel Blommaert in 1637 – see Johnson 1911a, 109, 114 and the translation by Weslager & Dunlap 1961, 169–81; Dutch navigator David Pieterszoon De Vries's *Korte historiael ende journaels aenteyckeninge*, published in 1655 and translated in Jameson 1909 and Myers 1959, particularly the journal entries dated 1638–43; the reports and letters by Swedish governor Johan Printz dating to

the period 1644–56, translated and published
by Johnson 1930; the court records of New
Sweden dating to the period 1643–4, translated
and published by Johnson 1930; the report of
Dutch colonial official Andries Hudde dated
1648, translated and published in Johnson
1930; the report by Swedish governor Johan
Risingh dated 1654, translated and published
in Meyers 1959 and Dahlgren & Norman
1988; the *Geographia Americae* by Swedish
fortification engineer Peter Lindeström,
completed in 1691 but based on his visit in
New Sweden 1654–5, translated and published
in Johnson 1925; the *Kort Beskrifning om
Provincien Nya Swerige uti America* issued by
Swedish publisher Thomas Campanius Holm
in 1702 and based partly on notes made by
his grandfather, John Campanius, who served
as a priest in the colony between 1643 and
1648; the map *Nova Belgica et Anglia Nova*
by Willem Janszoon Blaeu, dated 1635 – see
Burden 1996, #247; the map *Caerte vande
Svydt Rivier in Niew Nederland* by Johannes
Vingboons, dated to 1639 by Snyder (1973) and
available at the Library of Congress (http://
www.loc.gov/item/2003623407/); the map
*Novi Belgii Novaeque Angliae nec non partis
Virginiae tabula*, first published by Joannes
Jansson in 1651 and reproduced by Nicolaes
Visscher *c.* 1655 – see Burden 1996, #315,
available at the Library of Congress (http://
www.loc.gov/item/97683561/); and finally the
maps *Nova Suecia, Eller the Swenskas Revier in
India Occidentali* and *Karta med beskrifning
öfver Nova Suecia i Virginia Florida i Amerika
upprättade 1654 och 1655*, both compiled by
Peter Lindeström alongside the *Geographia
Americae*, and reproduced and edited in
Campanius 1696, Campanius Holm 1702,
Acrelius 1874 [1759] and Johnson 1925 (maps A
and B).

12 Also referred to by names such as *Sironesack,
Sikonesses*, or the *Great Sironese*: see Weslager
2008, 33–4. In this study I primarily use the
spellings found in the Swedish sources.

13 Dahlgren & Norman 1988, 187.

14 Smith 1907 [1624], 125–6.

15 Burden 1996, #315.

16 E.g. Lindeström in Johnson 1925, 204 and
Rising in Myers 1959, 156.

17 Occasionally referred to by scholars as *Jersey
Indians, Jerseys* or the *Lenopi* to distinguish
them from the Lenape in south-eastern
Pennsylvania, e.g. Becker 1986 & 2008.

18 Johnson 1925, 167.

19 Vingboons 1639; Lindeström's map A in
Johnson 1925.

20 Myers 1959, 18–20.

21 Weslager 1954, 4–7.

22 Weslager 1954, 7.

23 Lindeström's map A, in Johnson 1925; Becker
1986, 98; 1993b, 324.

24 Lindeström's map A, in Johnson 1925.

25 Johnson 1925, 170.

26 Johnson 1925, 169–71; Lindeström's map A, in
Johnson 1925; Campanius Holm 1702, 36–7.

27 Lindeström's map A, in Johnson 1925;
Donehoo 1928, 185–6.

28 Johnson 1925, 169–71; Lindeström's map A, in
Johnson 1925; Campanius Holm 1702, 36–7.

29 Lindeström's map A, in Johnson 1925.

30 Also referred to as *Sankhickon* or *Zanchikan*.

31 Lindeström's map A, in Johnson 1925;
Campanius Holm 1702, 77–8.

32 Lindeström's map A, in Johnson 1925;
Campanius Holm 1702, 77–8.

33 Lindeström's map A, in Johnson 1925.

34 Lindeström's map A, in Johnson 1925.

35 Campanius Holm 1702, 77.

36 E.g. Lindeström's map A in Johnson 1925;
Weslager 1954, 7. In this area, ten or fifteen
miles from the mouth of Alloway Creek,
Johnson (1925) also locates *Asamo Hacking*,
which he interprets as a possible indigenous
settlement or plantation based on information
in Lindeström's map A. This is however
also the name given to the area of Fort Nya
Elfsborg, so perhaps it is more likely to be a
reference to a geographical area larger than a
settlement.

37 See Campanius Holm 1702, 36 and 1834, 46.

38 Campanius Holm 1834, 123.

39 E.g. Becker 1989, 119; 1995, 122–3; 1999, 45;
2011a, 67–8.

40 For the sake of chronological precision, this
study has deliberately excluded sites with broad
and general dates such as *Late Woodland Period*
(*c.* 900–1550), *Contact Period* (*c.* 1500–1763) or
Historic Period (*c.* 1600–). It must furthermore
be noted that the sites included are dated
primarily by diagnostic artefacts of European
manufacture, which creates an unfortunate
but unavoidable bias. In general, the only
thing that separates Historic Period sites from
Late Woodland is the inclusion of European
objects. It is thus quite possible that many of
the Native American sites of Late Woodland
date without European objects are actually

contemporary with the European sites. For the latest listing of known Native American sites dated to the Historic Period (*c.* 1600–) in the Delaware river basin and environs, see Stewart 2014.

41 See Stewart *et al.* 1986, 71.

42 See also Stewart *et al.* 1986, 72; Stewart 2014, 23.

43 See Stewart 2014, 22.

44 Campanius Holm 1702, 77; Lindeström's map A in Johnson 1925.

45 See also Stewart *et al.* 1986, 70–8.

46 E.g. Campanius Holm 1702; Acrelius 1874 [1769]; Johnson 1911a–b; 1925; 1930; Dahlgren & Norman 1988.

47 See *Affidavit of four men from the Key of Calmar, 1638* in Myers 1959, 86–9.

48 Wallace 1971.

49 Johnson 1930, 222.

50 Johnson 1911a, 182; Becker 1993b, 324.

51 Possibly identified archaeologically through the Caleb Pusey House site (36-DE-4).

52 Called *Wootsessungsing, Oydsessing*, and *Oijtsessingh* in some of the written sources, cf. Lindeström's map A in Johnson 1925 and the Campanius Holm's copy from 1696 and 1702 (see Fig. 14.1).

53 Campanius Holm 1702, 28; 1834, 38; Johnson 1925, 170; 1930, 68.

54 E.g. O'Callaghan 1858, 241; Fur 2006, 117–18.

55 E.g. Shutt 2007, 31–40.

56 See Lindeström in Johnson 1925, 130; Fur 2006, 160–7.

57 E.g. Printz's reports from 1644 and 1647 in Johnson 1930, 116–17, 132; the report of Risingh

from 1655 in Myers 1959, 157; Campanius Holm 1702, 173–9; see also Fur 2006, 160.

58 Printz's letter to Oxenstierna of April 14, 1643, in Johnson 1930, 153.

59 E.g. Merrell 1999; Merritt 2003; Schutt 2007.

60 Johnson 1938; Becker 1987; MAAR Associates, Inc. & Frens and Frens 1991; Stebbins Craig 1992; Becker 1993a; 2011b; Furlow & Lukezic 2012, 38.

61 Risingh's journal in Dahlgren & Norman 1988, 173.

62 See also Barr 2011, 19.

63 See also Jennings 1968; Stewart 2014, 15–20.

64 The report of Risingh from 1655 in Myers 1959, 157, 159.

65 See also Erhardt 2005; Schwartz & Green 2013, 542–3.

66 E.g. the Abbott Farm complex, Burlington Island, the Chain Shop site, Churchmans Marsh, Indian Burial Ground, Julian Powerline site, Lenhardt-Lahaway, and Salisbury.

67 E.g. the Abbott Farm complex and Churchmans Marsh.

68 E.g. Churchmans Marsh.

69 E.g. the Abbott Farm complex, Indian Burial Ground, Lennhardt-Lahaway, and the Ware site; cf. Anselmi n.d., 24–5; 2008, 168–70.

70 E.g. the Abbott Farm complex, Burlington Island, the Chain Shop site, Indian Burial Ground, and Lenhardt-Lahaway.

71 Becker 1995; 1999; Fur 154–5.

72 Schwartz & Green 2013, 543.

73 White 1991; DuVal 2007; cf. Schwartz & Green 2013.

74 See Naum, this volume.

75 Harrison 2014, 50.

BIBLIOGRAPHY

Acrelius, I. 1874 [1769]. *A History of New Sweden or the Settlements on the River Delaware*. Memoirs of the Historical Society of Pennsylvania 11. Philadelphia: The Historical Society of Pennsylvania.

Anselmi, L. M. n.d. 'Comparing Northern Iroquoian use of European-introduced copper-based metals in the Early and Middle Contact Periods'. Ms. at the Pennsylvania Historical and Museum Commission, Harrisburg.

Anselmi, L. M. 2008. *Native Peoples Use of Copper-Based Metals in NE North America: Contact Period Interactions*. Saarbrücken: Verlag Dr. Müller.

Barr, J. 2011. 'Geographies of power: Mapping Indian borders in the "borderlands" of the early southwest', *The William and Mary Quarterly* 68(1): 5–46.

Becker, M. J. 1986. 'Cultural diversity in the Lower Delaware River Valley, 1550–1750: An ethnohistorical perspective', in Custer 1986, 90–101.

Becker, M. J. 1987. 'A report on the 1986 excavations at the Printzhof Site (36DE3): Operation 13'. Ms. at the Pennsylvania Historical and Museum Commission, Harrisburg.

Becker, M. J. 1989. 'Lenape population at the time of European contact: Estimating Native numbers in the Lower Delaware valley', *Proceedings of the American Philosophical Society* 133(2): 112–22.

Becker, M. J. 1993a. 'Lenape shelters: Possible examples from the Contact Period', *Pennsylvania Archaeologist* 63(2): 64–76.

Becker, M. J. 1993b. 'A New Jersey haven for some acculturated Lenape of Pennsylvania during the Indian Wars of the 1760s', *Pennsylvania History* 60(3): 322–44.

Becker, M. J. 1995. 'Lenape maize sales to the Swedish colonists: Cultural stability during the early colonial period', in Hoffecker *et al.* 1995, 121–36.

Becker, M. J. 1999. 'Cash cropping by Lenape foragers: Preliminary notes on Native maize sales to Swedish colonists and cultural stability during the early colonial period', *Bulletin of the Archaeological Society of New Jersey* 54: 45–68.

Becker, M. J. 2008. 'Lenopi; or, What's in a name? Interpreting the evidence for cultures and cultural boundaries in the Lower Delaware valley', *Bulletin of the Archaeological Society of New Jersey* 63: 11–32.

Becker, M. J. 2011a. 'Lenape culture history: The transition of 1660 and its implications for the archaeology of the final phase of the Late Woodland period', *Journal of Middle Atlantic Archaeology* 27: 53–72.

Becker, M. J. 2011b. 'The Printzhof (36DE3): A Swedish colonial site that was the first European center of government in present Pennsylvania', *Bulletin of the. Archaeological Society of Delaware* 43: 1–34.

Burden, P. 1996. *The Mapping of North America: A List of Printed Maps 1511–1670*. Rickmansworth, Herts.: Raleigh Publications.

Campanius, J. J. 1696. *Lutheri Catechismus, öfwersatt på American-Virginiske språket*. Stockholm: tryckt vhti thet af Kongl. Maytz. privileg. Burchardi tryckeri, af J. J. Genath, f.

Campanius Holm, T. 1702. *Kort beskrifning om provincien Nya Swerige uti America, som nu förtjden af the engelske kallas Pensylvania. Af lärde och trowärdige mäns skrifter och berättelser ihopaletad och sammanskrefwen, samt med åthskillige figurer utzirad af Thomas Campanius Holm*. Stockholm: J. H. Werner.

Campanius Holm, T. 1834. *Description of the Province of New Sweden. Now Called, by the English, Pennsylvania, in America. Compiled from the relations and writings of persons worthy of credit, and adorned with maps and plates*. Translated from the Swedish, for the Historical Society of Pennsylvania, with notes, by Peter S. Du Ponceau. Philadelphia: M'Carty & Davis.

CRGIS (Pennsylvania's *Cultural Resources Geographic Information System*). Map-based inventory of historical and archaeological sites and surveys stored in the files of the Bureau for Historic Preservation (BHP). https://www.dot7.state.pa.us/CRGIS/ [accessed 3 February 2015].

Cross, D. 1941. *Archaeology of New Jersey*, vol. 1. Trenton, NJ: The Archaeological Society of New Jersey and the New Jersey State Museum.

Cross, D. 1956. *Archaeology of New Jersey*. Vol. 2: *The Abbott Farm*. Trenton, NJ: The Archaeological Society of New Jersey and the New Jersey State Museum.

Custer, J. F. 1982. 'The prehistoric archaeology of the Churchmans Marsh vicinity: An introductory analysis', *Bulletin of the Archaeological Society of Delaware* 13: 1–44.

Custer, J. F. (ed.) 1986. *Late Woodland Cultures of the Middle Atlantic Region*. Newark: University of Delaware Press.

Custer, J. F. & Watson, S. 1985. 'Archaeological investigations at 7NCE42: A Contact Period site in New Castle County, Delaware', *Journal of Middle Atlantic Archaeology* 1: 97–116.

Custer, J. F., Doms, K., Allegretti, A. & Walker, K. 1998. 'Preliminary report on excavations at

7NCE60, New Castle County, Delaware', *Bulletin of the Archaeological Society of Delaware* 35: 1–27.

Dahlgren, S. & Norman, H. 1988. *The Rise and Fall of New Sweden: Governor Johan Risingh's Journal 1654–1655 in its Historical Context.* Acta Bibliothecae R. Universitatis Upsaliensis 27. Stockholm: Almqvist & Wiksell International.

Donehoo, G. P. 1928. *A History of the Indian Villages and Place Names in Pennsylvania with Numerous Historical Notes and References.* Harrisburg: The Telegraph Press.

DuVal, K. 2007. *The Native Ground: Indians and Colonists in the Heart of the Continent.* Early American Studies. Philadelphia: University of Pennsylvania Press.

Ekengren, F., Naum, M & Zagal-Mach Wolfe, U. I. 2013. 'Sweden in the Delaware Valley: Everyday life and material culture in New Sweden', in Naum & Nordin 2013, 169–87.

Erhardt, K. L. 2005. *European Metals in Native Hands: Rethinking the Dynamics of Technological Change 1640–1683.* Tuscaloosa: The University of Alabama Press.

Ferris, N., Harrison, R. & Wilcox, M. (eds). 2014. *Rethinking Colonial Pasts through Archaeology.* Oxford: Oxford University Press.

Fur, G. 2006. *Colonialism in the Margins: Cultural Encounters in New Sweden and Lapland.* Leiden & Boston: Brill.

Fur, G. 2009. *A Nation of Women: Gender and Colonial Encounters among the Delaware Indians.* Early American Studies. Philadelphia: University of Pennsylvania Press.

Furlow, D. A. & Lukezic C. 2012. 'Tracing the archaeological footprints of the Dutch and Swedes in the seventeenth-century Delaware River Valley', *de Halve Maen* 85(2): 33–9.

Grumet, R. S. 1995. *Historic Contact: Indian People and Colonists in Today's Northeastern United States in the Sixteenth through Eighteenth Centuries.* Norman: University of Oklahoma Press.

Harrison, R. 2004. *Shared Landscapes: Archaeologies of Attachment and the Pastoral Industry in New South Wales.* Studies in the Cultural Construction of Open Space 3. Sydney: University of New South Wales Press.

Harrison, R. 2014. 'Shared histories: Rethinking "colonized" and "colonizer" in the archaeology of colonialism', in Ferris *et al.* 2014, 37–56.

Heite, E. F. 1991. *Phase I and Phase II Cultural Resource Surveys at Wagamon's Pond Dam, Milton, Broadkill Hundred, Sussex County, Delaware.* Delaware Department of Transportation Archaeology Series 88. Camden DE: Heite Consulting.

Hoffecker, C. E., Waldron, R., Williams, L. E. & Benson, B. E. 1995. *New Sweden in America.* Newark: University of Delaware Press.

Hunter, R., Tvaryanas, D., Byers, D. & Stewart, R. M. 2009. *The Abbott Farm National Historic Landmark Interpretative Plan.* Cultural Resource Technical Document, Hamilton Township, Mercer County, Bordentown Township and the City of Bordentown, Burlington County, New Jersey. Trenton, NJ: Hunter Research Inc. Historical Resource Consultants.

Hunter Research 2011. *Archaeological Data Recovery. Excavations and Monitoring, New Jersey Route 29, City of Trenton, Mercer County, New Jersey.* Vol. 2: *Lambert/Douglas Plantation and Rosey Hill Mansion Site.* Trenton, NJ: Hunter Research Inc. Historical Resource Consultants.

Immonen, V. 2011. 'Farming and brass kettles as forms of colonial encounter: New Sweden from an archaeological perspective', *Scandinavian Studies* 83(3): 365–86.

Jameson, J. F. (ed.) 1909. *Narratives of New Netherland 1609–1664: Original Narratives of Early American history.* New York: Charles Scribner's Sons.

Jennings, F. 1968. 'Glory, death, and transfiguration: The Susquehannock Indians in the seventeenth century', *Proceedings of the American Philosophical Society* 112(1): 15–53.

Johnson, A. 1911a. *The Swedish Settlements on the Delaware: Their History and Relation to the Indians, Dutch and English 1638–1664. With an Account of the South, the New Sweden, and the American Companies, and the Efforts of Sweden to Regain the Colony,* vol. 1. New York:

University of Pennsylvania.

Johnson, A. 1911b. *The Swedish Settlements on the Delaware: Their History and Relation to the Indians, Dutch and English 1638–1664. With an Account of the South, the New Sweden, and the American Companies, and the Efforts of Sweden to Regain the Colony*, vol. 2. New York: University of Pennsylvania.

Johnson, A. 1925. *Geographia Americae with an Account of the Delaware Indians Based on Surveys and Notes Made in 1654–1656 by Peter Lindeström. Translated from the original manuscript with notes, introduction and an appendix of Indian geographical names with their meanings by Amandus Johnson*. Philadelphia: Swedish Colonial Society.

Johnson, A. 1930. *The Instructions for Johan Printz, Governor of New Sweden*. Philadelphia: Swedish Colonial Society.

Johnson, A. 1938. 'Stenarna tala', *Allsvensk samling* 25(5–6): 12–13, 81–7.

Lightfoot, K. G. 1995. 'Culture contact studies: Redefining the relationship between prehistoric and historical archaeology', *American Antiquity* 60(2): 199–217.

MAAR Associates, Inc. & Frens and Frens, 1991. *Historical Documentation and Archaeological Investigation Conducted at Governor Printz Park, Essington, Delaware County, Pennsylvania*. Unpublished report, The Pennsylvania Historical and Museum Commission, Harrisburg.

McCann, C. 1950. 'The Ware site, Salem County, New Jersey', *American Antiquity* 15(4): 315–21.

Merrell, J. 1999. *Into the American Woods: Negotiators on the Pennsylvania Frontier*. New York: W. W. Norton & Company.

Merritt, J. T. 2003. *At the Crossroads: Indians and Empires on a Mid-Atlantic Frontier, 1700–1763*. Chapel Hill: The University of North Carolina Press.

Morris, G. J., Reed, W. F., Karageanes, C. & DiGiugno, G. 1996. 'The Ware site ceramics: A proposed chronological sequence', *Bulletin of the Archaeological Society of New Jersey* 51: 17–34.

Mrozowski, S. A., Hayes, K. H. & Hancock, A. P. 2007. 'The archaeology of Sylvester Manor', *Northeast Historical Archaeology*. 36(1): 1–15.

Myers, A. C. (ed.) 1959. *Narratives of Early Pennsylvania, West New Jersey and Delaware 1630–1707*. Original Narratives of Early American History 12. New York: Barnes & Noble.

Naum, M. & Nordin, J. M. (eds) 2013. *Scandinavian Colonialism and the Rise of Modernity: Small Time Agents in a Global Arena*. Contributions to Global Historical Archaeology 37. New York: Springer.

O'Callaghan, E. B. (ed.) 1858. *Documents Relative to the Colonial History of the State of New York, Produced by Holland, England and France*, vol. 2. Albany: Weed, Parsons and Company.

Pagoulatos, P. 2007. 'Native American Contact Period settlement patterns of New Jersey', *Bulletin of the New Jersey Archaeological Society* 62: 23–40.

Pietak, L. M. 1995. 'Trading with strangers: Delaware and Munsee strategies for integrating European trade goods'. PhD thesis, University of Virginia.

Pratt, M. L. 1992. *Imperial Eyes: Travel Writing and Transculturation*. London: Routledge.

Rubertone, P. E. 2000. 'The historical archaeology of Native Americans', *Annual Review of Anthropology* 29: 425–46.

Sansevere, K. 2009. 'Interpreting forgotten colonial material at the Salisbury site', in *Crossroads: An Undergraduate Research Journal of the Monmouth University Honors School, 2009*, 177–267.

Schutt, A. C. 2007. *Peoples of the River Valleys: The Odyssey of the Delaware Indians*. Early American Studies. Philadelphia: University of Pennsylvania Press.

Schwartz, S. & Green, W. 2013. 'Middle Ground or Native Ground? Material culture at Iowaville', *Ethnohistory* 60(4): 537–65.

Scull, G. D. (ed.) 1881. *The Evelyns in America: Compiled from Family Papers and other Sources*.

Oxford: Parker and Co.

Silliman, S. 2010. 'Indigenous traces in colonial spaces: Archaeologies of ambiguity, origin, and practice', *Journal of Social Archaeology* 10(1): 28–58.

Smith, J. 1907 [1624]. *The generall historie of Virginia, New England and the Summer Isles, together with the true travels, adventures and observations, and a sea grammar*, vol. 1. Glasgow: James MacLehose and Sons.

Snyder, J. P. 1973. *The Mapping of New Jersey: The Men and the Art*. New Brunswick, NJ: Rutgers University Press.

Soderlund, J. R. 2015. *Lenape Country: Delaware Valley Society before William Penn*. Early American Studies. Philadelphia: University of Pennsylvania Press.

Stebbins Craig, P. 1992. 'Errata & addenda: Historic documentation and archaeological investigations conducted at Governor Printz Park, Essington, Delaware County, Pennsylvania'. Ms. at the Pennsylvania Historical and Museum Commission, Harrisburg.

Stewart, R. M. 2014. 'Native American archaeology of the Historic Period in the Delaware Valley', in Veit & Orr 2014, 1–48.

Stewart, R., Hummer, C. & Custer, J. F. 1986. 'Late Woodland cultures of the Middle and Lower Delaware river valley and the Upper Delmarva peninsula', in Custer 1986, 58–89.

Veit, R. & Bello, C. A. 1999. 'A unique and valuable historical Indian collection', *Journal of Middle Atlantic Archaeology* 15: 95–123.

Veit, R. & Bello, C. A. 2001. 'Tokens of their love: Interpreting Native American grave goods from Pennsylvania, New Jersey, and New York', *Archaeology of Eastern North America* 29: 47–64.

Veit, R. & Orr, D. 2014. *Historical Archaeology of the Delaware Valley, 1600–1850*. Knoxville: The University of Tennessee Press.

Vingboons, J. 1639. *Caerte vande Svydt Rivier in Niew Nederland*. http://www.loc.gov/item/2003623407/ [accessed 6 April 2015].

Visscher, N. 1656. *Novi Belgii Novaeque Angliae nec non partis Virginiae tabula multis in locis emendate*. http://www.loc.gov/item/97683561/ [accessed 6 April 2015].

Vitelli, G. 2013. 'Living side by side: Approaching coexistence through narrative', *Historical Archaeology* 47(1): 80–9.

Wallace, P. A. W. 1971. *Indian Paths of Pennsylvania*. Harrisburg: Pennsylvania Historical and Museum Commission.

Weslager, C. A. 1954. 'Robert Evelyn's Indian tribes and place-names of New Albion', *Bulletin of the Archaeological Society of New Jersey* 9: 1–14.

Weslager, C. A. 2008. *The Delaware Indians: A History*. New Brunswick, NJ: Rutgers University Press.

Weslager, C. A. & Dunlap, A. R. 1961. *Dutch Explorers, Traders and Settlers in the Delaware Valley 1609–1664*. Philadelphia: University of Pennsylvania Press.

White, R. 1991. *The Middle Ground: Indians, Empires, and Republics in the Great Lakes Region, 1650–1815*. Cambridge: Cambridge University Press.

15

Men You Can Trust? Intercultural Trust and Masculinity in the Eyes of Swedes in 18th-Century Canton

LISA HELLMAN

This chapter uses the idea of trust to study intercultural interaction in 18th-century Canton. Focusing on the employees of the Swedish East India Company, it highlights the multitude of groups active in the foreign quarters, and the need for cultural adaptation there. Establishing trust entailed using certain language strategies and spaces to present oneself and evaluate others – practices intertwined with the construction of masculinity. In the trade environment of Canton, trust and distrust existed parallel to each other; there was neither complete cooperation nor competition. These realities afford a multifaceted image of the intercultural everyday life of 18th-century Swedish traders.

Eighteenth-century Canton was a key hub in the global trade network, and yet, all commercial contact was restricted to the small foreign quarters. In a place only a few kilometres long and wide, a multitude of traders from different places had to negotiate norms and learn local practices: in short, they had to make trade work. For most of the long 18th century, international trade worked quite well there: Chinese goods were exported to Europe, and silver flowed into the Qing Empire.

Smooth trade operations rely upon trust, and Canton was no exception in this regard. Foreigners and Chinese alike had to be able to rely on debts being paid, cargo being delivered and deadlines being met. In the words of the historian David Sunderland, trust can be defined as "an expectation, expressed in action and disappointed or fulfilled, that a partner will honour his implicit or explicit obligations."[1] Through the lens of trust, we can study the social environment of the foreign quarters of Canton, and even map some of the power hierarchies that emerged.

The aim of this chapter is to analyse how trust was established, negotiated and lost in the foreign quarters of 18th-century Canton. Firstly, attention is paid to the individuals between whom trust could be established, and secondly to the logistics of the process – the spaces, practices and strategies – used in negotiating and upholding trust. To establish trust with someone it was essential to present oneself in a specific way, while at the same time evaluating the person with whom one interacted. Establishing oneself as trustworthy was intertwined with the construction of gender, nationality, and class.[2]

Finally, this chapter examines how both discourses and practices were used to establish intercultural trust.

The spotlight is first turned on the groups between which trust could be established. There was a multitude of groups living in the foreign quarters of Canton: European and non-European traders, Chinese merchants, workers and officials. While some of the trade was in private hands throughout the century, most foreigners residing in or visiting the city were employed by European chartered companies, one of which was the Swedish East India Company (1731–1813).[3] Despite the multicultural nature of this environment, historical studies on the East India companies have traditionally focussed on single enterprises, placing the research firmly within the tradition of national history. Existing research on the Swedish East India Company is no exception.[4] Such studies run the risk of misrepresenting local interaction and not paying enough attention to its multinational nature.[5] The Swedish traders were neither the largest nor the most powerful group there. Rather, as employees of a small and militarily weak company, the Swedish traders had particularly good reasons to quickly establish smooth cooperation with their Chinese counterparts, as well as with the other foreign traders.

Focussing on a small and relatively unknown company, in this case the Swedish East India Company, makes it easier to stress the multi-party nature of contacts; indeed, the very fact that they did not represent the dominant party makes the employees of the Swedish company suitable as a case study. To avoid a one-sided view of this complex world, however, some material from other foreign groups has been included in this study. Consequently, correspondence, account books and travel writings from the employees of the Swedish East India Company are combined with Dutch and British logbooks and North American travel writings. The aim is not to establish a definitive version of an event, but to let the various sources constitute different pieces of the jigsaw puzzle that is 18th-century Canton.

The term "Swede" is used in the sense of an employee of the Swedish East India Company, regardless of his birthplace. The high-ranking employees during the first decades were often Scotsmen, and there were always employees from several other countries in the Swedish East India Company.[6] The company was a multinational work place, and the self-perceived nationality of its employees far from evident. Nor were the "Chinese" a homogeneous group. The term here denotes inhabitants of the vast multi-ethnic Qing Empire. The term "foreigner" is used for non-Chinese traders instead of "European" or "Westerner", words that ill describe the complexity of the foreign trade community. There were indeed many Europeans; the foreign quarters of Canton housed French, English, Dutch, Danish and Swedish traders, both associated with chartered companies and as private traders. Spanish and Portuguese traders had been in Macao for centuries. Eventually, in 1784, American traders entered the scene. The term "Westerner" or "European" includes all these individuals, but it excludes, for example, Armenians, who worked closely with the Swedes, as well as the Jewish, Parsee and Muslim traders.[7]

The parties between whom trust needed to be formed were not a given. Foreign traders and Chinese officials and merchants teamed up according to what configurations were seen as the most advantageous at the time. For example, Armenian and Swedish traders could be in joint conflict with the Dutch company, the Swedish and French company could cooperate against the English, and several companies could together form a team to resolve a conflict with the officials.[8] This chapter focuses on the trust established for and by the Swedish traders, with Chinese merchants as well as with other foreigners.

SPACES FOR THE FORMATION OF TRUST

There are, of course, many kinds of trust: for example institutional trust, or trust in a particular person. Trust can be established between individuals, or within and between groups such as families.[9] Much of the trust described in the sources from Canton developed between individuals, rather than between entire groups of particular ethnicities or nationalities. That individuals and not groups were the key brokers for relationships of trust can be gleaned from the reaction to changes in the number of merchants licensed to trade with the Europeans – for example the loud complaints raised when changes were introduced in the selection of Chinese trade partners in Canton in 1775. The foreign traders wanted to be able freely to choose whom to trade with, guarded this right fiercely, and did not see the Chinese merchants as a homogeneous bloc in terms of their trustworthiness.[10] For example, the Chinese merchant Poankequa was on good terms with the Swedes. He was their main trading partner for years. In Swedish letters written in the 1760s and 1770s, Poankequa recurrently sent and received personal greetings.[11] As the Dutch noted in 1762: "He [Poankequa] has always preferred to deal with the Swedes and the Danes, mainly because the former usually dance to his piping, and upon their arrival they hand over most of their cash money to him."[12]

This kind of trust in a particular merchant was transferred within the company. In one letter exchanged between the Swedish supercargoes (the officers responsible for trade) Jean Abraham Grill and Jacob Hahr, the financial credibility of the Chinese merchants was discussed: "Among the debtors I consider Ponqua the worst, and it should be possible to dismiss him next year, Samqua is a slow payer, and it was a good thing that I do not have too much with him," writes Hahr. Sometimes a clear distinction is made between skill and trustworthiness: in the same letter Hahr states that, "The embroiderer Soychang, is surely the best of them all, but one cannot entrust him with the slightest amount of cash."[13] The same kind of evaluation was common in the Dutch and English companies. In their summary of the year 1739 English supercargoes wrote, "We divided our affairs between Texia, Leunqua, Chinqua, old Leuqua and Hunqua, and all these Gentlemen have served us extremely well particularly the two first."[14] Chinese merchants evaluated the foreigners in a similar way. The *hoppo*, the customs supervisor, probably recorded all goods and payments for all company and private traders in his account books. These books were balanced every year, and the information therein was transferred between merchants.[15]

Around 1740 a system of trade had been established, which was formalized in 1760. The Chinese kept a tight leash on the trade, controlling with whom the foreign traders could trade, and where they were allowed to live.[16] The establishment and endurance of the system enabled trust formation, even if the degree to which the rules were enforced and adhered to varied over time. Its continuity has sometimes been taken, even in modern research, as a sign of the rigid "tyranny" of the Chinese. The controlling institutions have been construed as an example of the severity of Chinese rules, and of xenophobic distrust. Robert Hermansson, who has written on the Swedish company, describes it as being "hounded by Chinese customs", and the system as one of "Oriental whims".[17] Rather, however, the consistent and predictable behaviour of Canton merchants and officials in Canton, and the stability of the rules may well have simplified the encounter, and diminished the need for on-the-spot improvisation. Some employees of the Swedish company, particularly during its first decade, had been in the service of other East India companies. There they had learnt the ropes, before joining the Swedish company.[18] Since the trade structure remained similar, their experiences were useful and directly applicable. From a Swedish perspective, the predictability of the system can, at least partially, explain why trade in Canton worked so well, so quickly (Fig. 15.1).

On the Pearl River, beyond the confines of the foreign quarters, the French and the Danish rented their own islands. There, the foreigners were allowed to move freely. From the mid-18th century, these islands became the only spaces where foreign funerals were permitted.[19] Sharing a graveyard created a strong sense of community, and participation in funerals constituted one opportunity to demonstrate it.[20] When a supercargo was being buried, all of the other nations' supercargoes, and the Chinese merchants, used to be present. A Swedish supercargo wrote in 1768 that "Tomorrow morning the deceased English Supercargo H. Horner will be buried on the French island, when as usual the foreign nations and his own will honour him."[21] There are also examples of foreign supercargoes attending Chinese funerals, showing their respects.[22] Being present at these occasions was a way to demonstrate connection, and the funerals thereby constituted a space for the formation of trust.

When navigating Canton, foreigners relied on locals functioning as go-betweens. During the greater part of the 18th century, every company ship was connected to one Chinese merchant in particular, called a "security merchant". He was responsible to officials for the behaviour of the foreigners on "his" ship, and in exchange was granted the priority right to provide them with the largest share of the ship's cargo.[23] This was a relationship of mutual dependency: the foreigners could not be disruptive, and the security merchant had to provide good merchandise at fair prices. Other go-betweens were the "compradors" (the men who provided the factories with daily supplies), the pilots and the interpreters. In several ways the foreign traders were dependent on these intermediaries. To navigate the tricky Pearl River delta leading up to Canton, they had to hire (or even, for some desperate captains, kidnap) a Chinese pilot.[24] Once they had arrived safely at Canton, they depended on the comprador to get supplies. Several Swedish traders mention the importance of the pilot and the comprador.[25] However, go-betweens were often suspected of disloyalty by both sides. The skills and the trustworthiness of interpreters were questioned outright, and the compradors and pilots were also doubted. One Swedish captain was so exasperated with an interpreter that, when settling the accounts, he wrote: "to my knowledge, I owe the linguist nothing but half a dozen slaps."[26] Trust in the go-betweens was far from absolute.

Fig. 15.1 "Image of Whampoa", Carl Gustav Ekeberg 1773, 98.

STRATEGIES FOR ESTABLISHING TRUST

One way in which the Swedish traders could establish trust in Canton was through sharing modes of communication, such as using a certain language.[27] However, from the mid-18th century it was forbidden for foreigners to learn Chinese, and strict rules applied to Chinese who learned European languages.[28] As mentioned above, the officials provided interpreters, but dependence upon them was not absolute. From the early 18th century, Pidgin English became well established in Canton. Dictionaries were sold to Chinese merchants that compiled useful terms in the "language of the red-haired foreigners", as they would call this pidgin dialect, which mixed English with Portuguese, Malay and Patúa (the creole language of Macao) – and even included Scandinavian terms.[29] This pidgin was more than a linguistic curiosity: it was a language specific to Canton and common to many groups – including Chinese merchants, but excluding officials. To speak Pidgin English was to acknowledge that one's conversation partners belonged to the same environment, perhaps even the same community. It was always spoken by more than one trade group, underlining the limitations, for historians, of a single national perspective on the social relations of Canton.

A common language could establish trust, as could language strategies, whether transmitted directly or translated. A popular trust-formation practice in this particular environment was secrecy.[30] Sharing a secret implied an intimacy. The sociologist Erving Goffman stressed the importance of secret-sharing and keeping for the formation of a common group – a team.[31] This intimacy and access to privileged information was not only a strategy in the relationship between the Swedish traders and the Chinese merchants, but can be found in the English ledgers as well. For example, when one of the Chinese merchants, Poankequa, told the English of an upcoming change in the trade conditions, he requested "that this information may be made known but [that is, only] to the gentlemen to whom it is addressed."[32]

Calling information a "secret" was a common trope. It signified the value of the news, and the trustworthiness of the transmitter. The value lay not so much in the information itself, as in the bond created by excluding others from it. In practice, interpreters were present whenever final contracts were drawn up. Throughout the 18th century there was only a handful official interpreters (no more than five), meaning that they all worked for all companies and private traders. That guaranteed that local officials knew most of what was going on. Furthermore, there was a constant exchange of news between and amongst foreign traders and Chinese merchants, meaning that very few secrets were kept.[33] Rather, there was a continuous flow of secrets, misinformation, and news between the trade groups.

Additionally, secrets were shared at dinners held in the factory houses. All companies regularly held dinners in their factories to which they invited supercargoes from some or all other companies. Sometimes foreign traders invited Chinese merchants, sometimes they were invited by them. The chartered companies thereafter invited each other with a certain regularity, and these dinners were a constant factor in the social life in Canton throughout the 18th and the early 19th centuries. In this situation, the foreign traders revealed as little as possible about their own affairs, but gossiped heartily about third parties who were absent.[34] This is what Goffman calls a "free secret": information that does not affect the one who is sharing it in a significant way, but forms a bond of trust with whoever is included in the secret.[35]

According to David Sunderland, dinner was an important social event for the fostering of trust – he describes it as the most important assembly in social life.[36] For these reasons it was not taken lightly when an invitation to attend dinner was declined. When an English friend of the supercargo Grill did not accept his invitation to dine, Grill wrote an offended letter, comparing the rudeness of the Englishman with the politeness of their French friend, who had accepted Grill's gesture: "if your inclination had been to sup at our Factory M Dumont knew too much what true politeness was, not to let M. Hahr [the messenger] off from a common invitation on so particular an occasion."[37] In order for such trust-formation strategies to work, everyone needed to play the game.

Another strategy for trust formation was to join the Freemasons' lodge. Sunderland underlines in his research how important masonic lodges were as spheres for trust forma-tion in early modern Europe, and Goffman takes masonic ties to have been a quick and direct way to establish trust with someone who otherwise would remain a stranger.[38] The earliest masonic activity in Canton was initiated by a Swedish ship's lodge, and from the 1760s the masons held regular meetings. They always made a point of including other nationalities as well, notably many Scotsmen, but also French, Dutch, English and Danish supercargoes. In the lodge, the Swedes created an international space for the fostering of trust, in a form they recognized from Europe. This space, however, was not open to everyone. In contrast to dinners or funerals, the Chinese were excluded, as were the Armenians, Jews and Parsees.[39]

Trust played a role in the relationship between the local factory and the board of directors at home: a relationship in which the foreign trader acted as a go-between. There was a constant tension between establishing oneself as someone who cooperated well with the locals, and simultaneously someone who was loyal to the company.[40] Being trustworthy in both worlds at the same time required some verbal acrobatics. One person who handled this well was the Swedish supercargo Johan Peter Bladh. He complained in the 1770s about other supercargoes badmouthing him to the Chinese merchants, and considered it the ultimate sign of their disloyalty to the company, since being estranged from the Chinese merchants would make it impossible for him to trade. In a personal letter back to Sweden, however, he claimed that he had excellent relations with several Chinese merchants, and that his friends could confidently entrust him with their business in Canton.[41] The same tension between keeping the trust of the central administration and that of the locals constituted a problem for the Canton merchants. Chinese officials were suspicious of those who were too close to the foreign traders. In the 1830s this mistrust had grown to the extent that when a Chinese commissioner was discussing the corruption of the Chinese merchants with a Mr King, an English jour-nalist, "Once he laughed outright when Mr King, on being asked which of the Chinese guild-merchants was the most honest, found himself unable to name one."[42]

The many groups staying in Canton thus shared social spaces, such as funerals, dinners and the masonic lodge; but these spaces were never all-inclusive. While they offered a community for some men, they excluded men of the lower classes, men of certain ethnicities and, of course, women. Moreover, while the men in the foreign quarters used a common language and common language strategies to establish trust, no strategy functioned instantly, or continuously. Trust was not effortlessly maintained once established, but had constantly to be negotiated and re-established.

THE MYTH OF SPECIAL FRIENDSHIP

In Canton during the long 18th century, all foreigners traded under the same conditions. These circumstances put the militarily weak Swedish East India Company in a relatively advantageous but not a unique position. Nevertheless, in publications on the Swedish company and on Swedish–Chinese historical relations, one recurrently finds arguments for a special friendship between the Chinese and Swedes.[43] In one of the first works on the Swedish East India Company, Eskil Olán suggested that one reason behind the regularity of the company's operations in China was the good relationship between the royal family in Sweden and the emperor in China.[44] However, there were no official diplomatic relations between Sweden and China at this time, nor is there any reliable evidence in the sources for the claim that the Swedes must have enjoyed disproportionately greater favour with the Chinese than other nations. Indeed, turning to studies of other companies, the same historical claim can be found for relations between the Chinese and the Dutch, the Danish and the American traders.[45] "A relationship of particular friendship" has been claimed in particular for the Chinese–American affiliations.[46] Describing the relationship between one American trader and a Chinese merchant, Francis Ross Carpenter writes, "So close was the relationship between the two that there was never a written contract between them. Their word to each other was enough".[47]

To proclaim trust and access to special favours was part of the social game for both Chinese merchants and foreign traders. Many traders stressed their good relations with the Chinese, and some went so far as to say that they had better relations with them than did other nations – for example the Swede Johan Brelin.[48] Studying the choice of wording in the records of the Swedish, Dutch and English East India Companies, one could argue that all nations at some point considered themselves the most favoured nation in Canton.[49] This made for an excellent strategy, of posing as a successful international trader. The problem arises when such claims in the source material are reproduced as facts. As late as 2007, the Swedish historian Christina Granroth was writing that "in Asia it seems that Swedes indeed received a warmer welcome than other European traders";[50] and such claims of a historical friendship between China and Sweden have been revived still more recently, with regard to both political relations and trade.[51] There is, however, no clear indication that the employees of one company were in fact treated significantly better than others. This suggests that the Chinese were adept at convincing everyone they traded with that they were in favour – a useful strategy indeed. There were probably individual traders who by networking, skill and wit managed to establish a better position than others. But this was not on account of them being from a particular nation. A study of trust can thus demonstrate the importance of looking at more than one trade group when studying multi-ethnic environments.

ADAPTING ONE'S CULTURE

The traders were not just attempting to present themselves as trustworthy persons, but as trustworthy *men*. Donna Haraway, a scholar of the history of science and gender, has shown the connection between trust formation and gender construction. Since the Canton foreign quarters were dominated by men, the recognition and liking of their male peers became crucial for the traders. David Sunderland even categorizes this as a special kind of "masculine trust". He takes the masonic circle as a particular site for construction of type of bond, since "Freemason rituals celebrated the virtues of manliness, generating masculine trust". But gender construction alone does not explain the relationship between the Swedes and the Chinese traders. The Chinese merchants could never be part of the homosocial masonic circle, for example. Haraway argues that ideas of "the Other", and relations with it, are crucial for understanding power relations and the construction of masculinity.[52] That is, in the encounter between Swedish and Chinese traders and merchants, masculinity construction and nationality were intertwined with their attempts at establishing intercultural trust.

This is where descriptions of Chinese men come into play. Many Swedish travel narratives noted that the Chinese were loyal and subordinate, which might be an argument for reliability.[53] However, this description was of a strictly intra-Chinese hierarchy, in terms of class and family relationships. It is questionable if it applied to a commercial setting; the foreign traders were not the superiors of the Chinese, and both parties were well aware of that fact. The Chinese merchants were almost invariably described as greedy and untrustworthy, and indefatigable when it came to the pursuit of profit.[54] Olof Torén, a priest on a Swedish ship, claimed that "they could have a look as sweet as sugar, if they thereby hoped to gain something".[55] The Swedish supercargo Christian Henric Braad added that "It is hard to say what virtues they have, since profit and money control all of their senses."[56] Furthermore, their widespread corruption was mentioned, and looked down upon.[57]

However, the descriptions given were not entirely negative. The Chinese were said to be expeditious and hardworking.[58] The supercargo Braad wrote, "One cannot find that they have the kind of spirit that is manifested in all sorts of ludicrous behaviour and extensive and unnecessary talk in a certain European nation; for they do not speak very much, but you find that with them reflection is all the greater."[59] In short, the view taken of Chinese men was a complex one. While they were sometimes described as cruel, they were not seen as uncivilized.[60] Had they been considered so, adaptation would not have been the strategy chosen in regard to them. The formation of trust was thus similar to that embarked upon when meeting unknown traders in Europe.

The foreign traders had to adapt to a multinational environment that they did not dominate. Consequently, they had to present themselves as trustworthy in a way that was comprehensible across cultural boundaries. The sociologist Raewyn Connell, who has studied global gender construction by looking at men working in modern multinational corporations, suggests that a particular kind of masculinity is needed, made and manifested in a life at the crossroads of global trade networks led by these men. She argues that the most successful individuals develop "adapting masculinities", a gendered behaviour that does not aim to impose one's own culture on a foreign environment, but that blends different local and global behavioural norms that fit the particular international setting.[61] The East India companies have been compared to today's multinational corporations, with a similar global workforce.[62] From the late 1750s, Swedish traders began to stay in Canton for long periods of years, allowing them to acquire a good idea of how local society worked and forcing them to develop "adapting masculinity". Establishing oneself was not a matter of "throwing one's weight around", but rather of smoothly fitting in with a multitude of groups. At the beginning of the 19th century, increasing numbers of foreign travellers came to Canton, and adaptive behaviour then seems to have given way to a more confrontational style, and conspicuously Anglo-Saxon culture.[63]

Swedish traders left traces of the discourse and ideas of how to best adapt to the Canton environment in their travel narratives: in part their writings can be read as crude manuals of proper behaviour. The writers discussed how the Chinese bowed, and how they served tea, quite aware of the need to take part in this social ritual.[64] One supercargo stated that, "In company the Chinese are very polite, as some argue, but their many compliments would, for all those who are not used to them from birth, be utterly unbearable."[65] The supercargo Braad agreed: "they are committed to the performance more circumlocutory expressions of politeness, than almost any other nation".[66] The reasons for these discussions of politeness, and how to best interact, might have been quite practical (Fig. 15.2).

Social interaction seems to have been something of a tightrope-walk. While the Chinese were seen as polite in general, they were presented as excessively proud. Many Swedish writers discussed how to best relate to this Chinese self-perception. Braad, again, claimed that the Chinese had the "ridiculous arrogance [to claim] that no refined nation other than theirs exists on this earth".[67] The authors generally recommended not to contradict such claims, but to focus on how to please the Chinese: "Since the Chinese are very self-loving, they also infinitely appreciate when their customs, institutions and other characteristics are praised by the Europeans."[68] This pride is not presented as being a reason to provoke distrust, but only as an additional factor to consider and adapt to in the course of interaction. The Swedes seem to have keenly observed the social norms of Canton, and tried to a certain extent to adhere to them, in order to be trusted.

When talking about trust, one must distinguish between the officials and the Canton merchants. In practice, officials did their best to be flexible when communicating both respect and authority – within their boundaries. But such adaptation is most clearly visible in the behaviour of the merchants, who for example could procure European-style chairs and cutlery for European and North American traders when they were visiting.[69] This difference is not surprising: the officials were in Canton for just a few years, and they had less and less direct contact with the foreigners, especially during the second half of the 18th century. Their official image of foreigners, as it appears in a description of the various ethnic groups in Canton and Macao presented to Emperor Qianlong in the mid-18th century, does not single out any nation as favoured or more trustworthy.[70] In the descriptions of foreigners in this region such as the *Aomen Jilue*, however, the trustworthiness of all foreigners was called into question. In the 1751 edition of the book it is noted that foreigners had a different way of thinking, and that they were by nature crafty and arrogant.[71] In a decree regarding a court case in Macao in 1748, foreigners

Fig. 15.2 "Depiction of Chinese men", Carl Johan Gethe 1746–9, 92.

in general are said to be cruel and savage and are accused of being overly proud (the same as is said about the Chinese in Swedish sources).[72] In contrast, Chinese merchant families who lived in Canton for generations had frequent and close contact with the foreigners. They could certainly tell the different groups apart, and endeavoured to form personal relations with the foreign traders.

TRUST AND DISTRUST IN DAILY PRACTICES

In research on the Swedish East India Company, transactions in Canton are often treated as a straightforward exchange of cargo for money.[73] As can be seen in the logbooks, however, the prices and conditions for trade were negotiated for months in nearly daily meetings with Chinese merchants, illustrating the complex nature of these economic exchanges.[74]

Even in cases when a deal was mostly settled, its finalization was not certain. The English described how, having obtained a better offer, they "immediately acquainted Suequa that we entirely relinquished his Contract; comfortable that we had told him the very instant."[75] The trade was a constant game involving traders and merchants from all nations, trying to outbid and outwit each other. Even in the final stage, when packing the goods, traders could run into problems. Captain Carl Rappe noted in his journal, "We wanted to pack tea at Ketqua's tomorrow, but he replied that he had fulfilled his part of the Co-hong contract, and thus had no more tea for us, finally after many objections he promised to pack yet another time."[76] The bargaining process was not over until the final number and cost of the barges for transport to the ship had been settled: that is, during the ship's last days in Canton.[77]

Most companies traded with several merchants at once, which required balancing their favours with various parties, while not losing the trust they had earned. As it is phrased in the Dutch records, "Thus we should be intent on means and way to keep him [a Chinese merchant] serving our interests without damaging the trust and affection which the three others [Chinese merchants] feel for us. However, this will be hard to maintain and quite a trick to work out."[78] The Chinese merchants had to maintain the same balancing act in order to be regarded as trustworthy throughout the trade season – judgements could be swift and negative opinions quickly transferred to other parties. A diary from the British company noted in the 1730s that "Powqua to whom we sold our Putchuck delaying from time to time [sic] to come to an accord on some frivolous pretence or another, lest he should disappoint us at the last we thought proper to write to the supercargoes of the *Walpole* and *Princess of Wales*, and of the *Normanlou*, to stop so much as may be due to him from either of them".[79]

Examples of distrust in Canton are as numerous as those of trust, but especially common was a frustration over business deals. In 1763, the Dutch found it near impossible to settle on a price for tea, since the Chinese merchants daily provided contradictory information about what other companies paid. One Dutch supercargo wrote, "How can one actually find out what the English are paying, when the merchants give us examples daily of how they can lie without any shame."[80] Foreign and Chinese merchants showed their distrust openly, and information was rarely taken at face value.

Distrust was in some sense highly conventional, and was not seen as something unique to the intercultural encounter in Canton. In fact, the first inspection of a ship for forbidden commodities took place before it had even left Sweden.[81] The Chinese officials too would inspect the ship, a practice that has been construed as an example of their ultra-strict regulations, rigid control and absolute distrust. But a Swedish trader wrote that the search in China was not particularly thorough in comparison to the similar practice in Sweden, and that the Chinese only seemed to come for the drinks.[82] The Swedish ship's clerk Israel Reinius wrote a long list of all the things a trader in Canton must consider, much of it involving personally checking packing, the quality of goods and methods of payment.[83] All of these precautions were security measures commonplace in international trade.[84] There was a widespread acceptance in both western Europe and China – in rhetoric, even if not borne out in practice – that merchants could not be perfectly honest.[85] Bargaining, even bending the truth to a certain degree, was an expected part of the culture of trade.

Indeed, the further one examines social relations in the China trade, the less binary the concept of trust appears to be: trust and distrust do not exclude each other. Human beings can compartmentalize their opinions of the other people's various facets in professional and personal relationships. As the management scholars Lewicki, McAllister and Bies put it, "Just as it is possible to experience attraction and dis-attraction, to like and dislike, and to love and hate, it may be possible to both trust and distrust."[86] Thus, trust and distrust had a parallel existence in 18th-century Canton. While the foreign traders doubted the Chinese merchants' statements about prices, they did not fear for their safety when in their company. In short, it is possible to move away from a binary view of early modern intercultural interactions as being relations either of cooperation or of conflict.

CONCLUSION

Investigation of the establishment, negotiation and loss of trust informs us about the social world of Canton, how it was structured, and which strategies were needed to navigate it. The need for trust, and the struggle to establish it, illuminates the social side of local commercial transactions.

Studying the employees of the Swedish East India Company shows how trust was a matter of relations between individuals, or small groups, rather than between nations. Indeed, there is little basis for any claim of a special trust existing between entire nations. Trust gained by individuals could be transferred within the company and to fellow traders. The establishment of trustworthy relationship was an on-going process involving a number of practices, such as use of language strategies, socializing during dinners and important events and membership in the masonic lodge. Furthermore, this intercultural trust demanded a certain degree of cultural understanding and accommodation, and gave rise to adaptation, rather than forceful assertiveness. The relationship between European traders and Chinese merchants was never one either of total trust or of total distrust. Trust was established, transferred, negotiated and lost in a constant game of relations, a game that involved not only the Swedish traders and the Chinese merchants but other foreign groups in Canton and the Chinese officials as well. Trust and distrust overlapped and existed parallel to each other and were related to a gendered construction of self that was not unique to the foreign quarters of Canton. This non-binary view of trust offers us an opportunity to move beyond interpretation of intercultural contacts in terms of either cooperation or conflict. Adopting a social-historical perspective, it can be shown that feelings of trust and distrust could exist at the same time, and still allow for the smooth operation of trade.

NOTES

1   Sunderland 2007, 1.
2   Goffman 1978, 1.
3   For an overview of the Swedish East India
    Company, see Kjellberg 1974; Koninckx 1980.
4   Olán 1923; Kjellberg 1974; Frängsmyr 1990;
    Johansson 1992.
5   This is discussed further in Van Dyke 2011,
    xiii–xx.
6   Kjellberg 1974, 22.
7   Van Dyke & Smith 2003; Van Dyke & Smith
    2004; Guo 2005.
8   Examples of interaction with officials are
    given in Fu 1966, 192, 222, 254. For shifting
    allegiances, see Lindahl 1784.
9   Sunderland 2007, 6.
10 Diary 1775.
11 Grill to Michael Grubb, 8 January 1767. This
    and all the following quotations by Swedish
    traders have been translated from Swedish by
    the author.
12 Van Dyke & Vialle 2006, 12.
13 Hahr to Grill, November 1768.
14 Diary 1739–1740, 38; other examples include
    Van Dyke & Vialle 2006, 8; Letter Book
    1777–1778, 1.
15 Van Dyke 2011, 25.
16 Cheong 1997.
17 Hermansson 2003, 91.
18 Nováky 2006, 52–75.
19 Osbeck 1969, 188.
20 On the importance of funerals, see Ward 2009,
    255.
21 Grill to Lehman, 5 August 1768.
22 Van Dyke 2005.
23 Van Dyke 2005, 11.
24 On kidnapping, see Van Dyke 2005, 37.
25 Osbeck 1969, 113–14; Reinius 1939, 169; Braad
    1748–9, 50–1.
26 Grill to Palladini, 27 November, 1767.
27 Sunderland 2007, 7; Goffman 1978, 176.
28 Si 2009.
29 Bolton 2003, 166–95.
30 Grill to Palladini, 27 November 1767; Van
    Dyke & Vialle 2006, 104; Benyowsky 1790, 135;
    Rappe 1760–2, 77.
31 Goffman 1978, 141.
32 Letter Book 1777–1778, 8–9.
33 Van Dyke 2005, 79.
34 Rappe 1760–2, 19; Campbell 1996, 94; Osbeck
    1969, 169; Torén 1961, 204; Van Dyke &
    Vialle 2006, 100; Reinius 1939, 204; Hayne

1797–1828, 119–28. For more on these dinners,
    see Ching 2012.
35 Goffman 1978, 143.
36 Sunderland 2007, 28.
37 Grill to Fitzhough, 20 December 1768.
38 Sunderland 2007, 58; Goffman 1978, 192.
39 Frimureri i Kanton och Macao.
40 Carlos & Hejeebu 2007, 141–9.
41 Lunelund, 2008, 25–7.
42 Waley 1960, 51.
43 For an example, see Johansson 1992,
    'Introduction'; The tendency is criticized
    in Cassel 2010. The problematic use of the
    Swedish company for arguing this claim has
    been stressed in Lundahl 2010, 91–7.
44 Olán 1923, 161.
45 For the Dutch, see Parmentier 1996; for the
    Americans, see e.g. Carpenter 1976; Wei 2009;
    for the Danes, e.g. Brødsgaard & Kirkebæk
    2000; Bramsen & Lin 2000.
46 Goldstein 1978, 5.
47 Carpenter 1976, 36.
48 Brelin 1973, 55.
49 See examples in Van Dyke & Vialle 2008, 95;
    Diary 1735–1737.
50 Granroth 2007, 152.
51 Lundahl 2010.
52 Haraway 1997, 28–30; Sunderland 2007, 43–58.
53 Lindahl 1784.
54 Torén 1961, 101–10; Reinius 1939, 206; Hayne
    1797–1828, 121–2.
55 Torén 1961, 92.
56 Braad 1748–9, 106–9.
57 Torén 1961, 110.
58 Braad 1748–9, 107.
59 Braad 1748–9, 108.
60 Torén 1961, 110–11; Osbeck 1969, 172; Reinius
    1939, 206. For a discussion of the Swedish view
    of Chinese masculinity, see Hellman 2014.
61 Connell 2004.
62 Carlos & Hejeebu 2007, 141–9.
63 This culture is described in Ride & Ride 1996,
    50–3.
64 Braad 1748–9, 114.
65 Von Stockenström n.d., 7–8.
66 Braad 1748–9, 112.
67 Braad 1748–9, 109.
68 Von Stockenström 1767–9, 25.
69 The flexibility of the officials is discussed in
    Hevia 1995. The merchants' flexibility can be
    seen in Hickey 1749–75, 223–4; Campbell 1996,
    95.

70 Xin 1995.
71 Yin & Zhang 1992, 238.
72 Fu 1966, 186–8.
73 Frängsmyr 1990; Kjellberg 1974.
74 *Brevkopiebok för skeppet Hoppet; Journal 1776–1777; Journal 1765–1767.*
75 *Diary 1749–1751,* 48.
76 Rappe 1760–2, 27.
77 *Diary 1749–1751,* 4.

78 Van Dyke & Vialle 2006, 48–9.
79 *Diary 1735–1737,* 63.
80 Van Dyke & Vialle 2008, 43.
81 Von Stockenström 1767–9, 1–48.
82 Von Stockenström 1767–9, 42.
83 Reinius 1939, 223–34.
84 Ogborn 2007, 50.
85 Lufrano 1997; Grassby 1995.
86 Lewicki *et al.* 1998, 458.

BIBLIOGRAPHY

Benyowsky, M. A. 1790. *Memoirs and Travels of Mauritius Augustus, Count de Benyowsky.* London: G. G. J. and J. Robinson.

Bolton, K. 2003. *Chinese Englishness: A Sociolinguistic History.* Cambridge: Cambridge University Press.

Braad, C. H. 1748–9. *Berättelse om resan med skeppet Hoppet under Capitaine Fr. Pettersons Commando 1748–1749.* Manuscript Collection, X 389, UUB.

Bramsen, C. B. & Lin, H. 2000. *Peace and Friendship: Denmark's Official Relations with China 1674–2000.* Copenhagen: Nordic Institute of Asian Studies.

Brelin, J. 1973. *En äfventyrlig resa til och ifrån Ost-Indien, Södra America och en del af Europa Åren 1755, 56 och 57.* Stockholm: Rediviva.

Brevkopiebok för skeppet Hoppet. Svenska Ostindiska Kompaniets arkiv, H 22:1, GUB.

Brødsgaard, K. E. & Kirkebæk M. 2000. *China and Denmark: Relations since 1674.* Copenhagen: Nordic Institute of Asian Studies.

Campbell, C. 1996. *A Passage to China: Colin Campbell's Diary of the First Swedish East India Company Expedition to Canton, 1732–33.* Gothenburg: Kungliga Vetenskaps- och vitter-hets-samhället.

Carlos, A. M. & Hejeebu, S. 2007. 'Specific information and the English chartered companies', in Müller & Ojala 2007, 139–68.

Carpenter, F. R. 1976. *The Old China Trade: Americans in Canton, 1784–1843.* New York: Coward, McCann & Geoghegan.

Cassel, P. 2010. 'Traktaten som aldrig var och fördraget som nästan inte blev. De svensk-norsk-kinesiska förbindelserna 1847–1909', *Historisk tidsskrift* 103(3): 437–66.

Cheong, W. E. 1997. *Hong Merchants of Canton: Chinese Merchants in Sino–Western Trade (1684–1798).* Richmond, Surrey: Curzon.

Ching, M.-B. 2012. 'Chopsticks or cutlery? How Canton Hong merchants entertained foreign guests in the eighteenth and nineteenth centuries', in Johnson 2012, 99–116.

Connell, R. 2004. 'Globalization, imperialism, and masculinities', in Kimmel & Hearn 2004, 71–90.

Diary 1735–1737, for Richmond, China factory records, G/12/40. East India Company Archive, British Library.

Diary 1739–1740, for Augusta, China factory records, G/12/47. East India Company Archive, British Library.

Diary 1749–1751, for Duke of Cumberland, China factory records, G/12/54. East India Company Archive, British Library.

Diary 1775, China factory records, G/12/58. East India Company Archive, British Library.

Ekeberg, C. G. 1773. *Capitaine Carl Gustav Ekebergs Ostindiska resa åren 1770 och 1771: beskrefven uti bref til Kongl. Svenska Vet. Academiens Secreterare.* Stockholm: Henr. Fougt.

Frimureri i Kanton och Macao. Logen St. Elisabeth, Räkningar. Godegårdsarkivet, Nordic Museum Archive.

Frängsmyr, T. 1990. *Ostindiska kompaniet: Människorna, äventyret och den ekonomiska drömmen*. 2nd edn. Höganäs: Wiken.

Fu, L.-S. 1966. *A Documentary Chronicle of Sino–Western Relations (1644–1820)*, vol. 1. Tucson: The Association for Asian Studies.

Gethe, C. J. 1746–9. 'Dagbok hållen på resan till Ost Indien begynt den 18 octobr: 1746 och slutad den 20 juni 1749'. Manuscript collection, National Library of Sweden.

Goffman, E. 1978. *The Presentation of Self in Everyday Life*. Harmondsworth: Penguin.

Goldstein, J. 1978. *Philadelphia and the China Trade, 1682–1846: Commercial, Cultural, and Attitudinal Effects*. University Park: Pennsylvania State University Press.

Granroth, C. 2007. 'Flora's apostles in the East Indies: Natural history, Carl Linnaeus and Swedish travel to Asia in the 18th century', *Review of Culture* 21: 137–56.

Grassby, R. 1995. *The Business Community of Seventeenth-Century England*. Cambridge: Cambridge University Press.

Grill, J. A.1767. 'Letter to Michael Grubb', 8 January. Godegårdsarkivet, Utgående brev, Nordic Museum Archive.

Grill, J. A. 1767. 'Letter to Palladini', 27 November. Godegårdsarkivet, Utgående brev, Nordic Museum Archive.

Grill, J. A. 1768. 'Letter to Lehman', 5 August. Godegårdsarkivet, Utgående brev, Brevkopiebok 1768–1770. Nordic Museum Archive.

Grill, J. A. 1768. 'Letter to Fitzhough', 20 December. Godegårdsarkivet, Utgående brev, Nordic Museum Archive.

Guo, D. 郭德焱 2005. 清代廣州的巴斯商人 *Qingdai Guangzhou de Basi shangren [Parsee Merchants in Canton during the Qing Period]*. Beijing: Zhonghua Shuju.

Hahr, J. 1768. 'Letter to J. A. Grill', [?] November. Godegårdsarkivet, Inkomna skrivelser. Nordic Museum Archive.

Haraway, D. J. 1997. *Modest_Witness@Second_Millennium. FemaleMan©_Meets_OncoMouse™: Feminism and Technoscience*. New York: Routledge.

Hayne, H. 1797–1828. *Diaries of Henry Hayne 1797–1828*, vol 1. Perkins Library, Reel 19, Duke University Archive.

Hellman, L. 2014. 'Using China at home: Knowledge production and gender in the Swedish East India Company, 1730–1800', *Itinerario* 38(1): 35–55.

Hermansson, R. 2003. *Det stora svenska äventyret: Boken om Svenska Ostindiska Compagniet*. Gothenburg: Breakwater Publishing.

Hevia, J. L. 1995. *Cherishing Men from Afar: Qing Guest Ritual and the Macartney Embassy of 1793*. Durham, NC: Duke University Press.

Hickey, W. 1749–75. *Memoirs of William Hickey*. Vol. 1: *1749–1775*. 17th edn. London: Hurst and Blackett.

Holgersson, H., Thörn H., Wahlström, M. & Thörn, C. (eds) 2010. *Göteborg utforskat: Studier av en stad i förändring*. Gothenburg: Glänta Produktion.

Johansson, B. (ed.) 1992. *The Golden Age of China Trade: Essays on the East India Companies' Trade with China in the 18th Century and the Swedish East Indiaman 'Götheborg'*. Hong Kong: Viking Hong Kong.

Johnson, K. (ed.) 2012. *Narratives of Free Trade: The Commercial Cultures of Early US–China Relations*. Hong Kong: Hong Kong University Press.

Journal 1765–1767 för skeppet Stockholms Slott. Manuscript Collection, L 184 Fol, UUB.

Journal 1776–1777 för skeppet Adolph Fredrich. Svenska Ostindiska Kompaniets arkiv, GUB.

Kimmel, M. S. & Hearn, J. R. (eds) 2004. *Handbook of Studies on Men and Masculinities*.

Thousand Oaks: Sage.

Kjellberg, S. T. 1974. *Svenska Ostindiska Compagnierna 1731–1813: Kryddor, Te, Porslin, Siden.* Malmö: Allhem.

Koninckx, C. 1980. *The First and Second Charters of the Swedish East India Company (1731–1766): A Contribution to the Maritime, Economic and Social History of North-Western Europe in its Relations with the Far East.* Kortrijk: Van Ghemmert.

Letter Book 1777–1778, China factory records, G/12/62. East India Company Archive, British Library.

Lewicki, R. J., McAllister, D, J. & Bies , R. J. 1998. 'Trust and distrust: New relationships and realities', *The Academy of Management Review.* 23(3): 438–58.

Lindahl, O. 1784. *Ett superkargkrig i Kanton 1784.* Manuscript Collection, M 285, National Library of Sweden.

Lufrano, R. J. 1997. *Honorable Merchants Commerce and Self-Cultivation in Late Imperial China.* Honolulu: University of Hawai'i Press.

Lunelund, B. 2008. *Peter Johan Bladh och Svenska Ostindiska Compagniet ären 1766–84.* Helsinki: Svenska Litteratursällskapet i Finland.

Lundahl, M. 2010, 'Den enfaldiga Götheborgaren', in Holgersson *et al.* 2010, 91–7.

Müller, L. & Ojala J. (eds) 2007. *Information Flows: New Approaches in the Historical Study of Business Information.* Helsinki: Suomalaisen Kirjallisuuden Seura.

Nováky, G. 2006. 'Swedish naval personnel in the merchant marine and in foreign naval service in the eighteenth century', *Forum Navale* 62: 52–75.

Ogborn, M. 2007. *Indian Ink: Script and Print in the Making of the English East India Company.* Chicago: University of Chicago Press.

Olán, E. 1923. *Ostindiska Compagniets saga: Historien om Sveriges märkligaste handelsföretag.* Gothenburg: Wettergren & Kerber.

Osbeck, P. 1969. *Dagbok öfver en ostindisk resa åren 1750, 1751, 1752.* Stockholm: Rediviva.

Parmentier, J. 1996. *Tea Time in Flanders: The Maritime Trade between the Southern Netherlands and China in the 18th Century.* Ghent: Ludion Press.

Rappe, C. 1760–2. *Dagbok för skeppet Rycksens Ständer på resa till Surat och Canton 1760–1762.* Manuscript Collection, M 288, National Library of Sweden.

Reinius, I. 1939. *Journal hållen på resan till Canton I China* [...]. Helsinki: Svenska litteratursällskapet i Finland.

Ride, L. & Ride, M. 1996. *An East India Company Cemetery: Protestant Burials in Macao.* Hong Kong: Hong Kong University Press.

Si, J. 2009. 'Breaking through the "jargon" barrier: Early 19th century missionaries' response on communication conflicts in China', *Frontiers of History in China* 4(3): 340–57.

Sunderland, D. 2007. *Social Capital, Trust and the Industrial Revolution 1780–1880.* London: Routledge.

Torén, O. 1961. *En ostindisk resa.* Stockholm: Tiden.

Van Dyke, P. A. 2005. *The Canton Trade: Life and Enterprise on the China Coast, 1700–1845.* Hong Kong: Hong Kong University Press.

Van Dyke, P. A. 2011. *Merchants of Canton and Macao : Politics and Strategies in Eighteenth-Century Chinese Trade.* Hong Kong: Hong Kong University Press.

Van Dyke, P. A. & Smith, C. T. 2003. 'Armenian footprints in Macao', *Review of Culture* 8: 20–39.

Van Dyke, P. A. & Smith, C. T. 2004. 'Muslims in the Pearl River delta, 1700 to 1930', *Review of Culture* 10: 6–15.

Van Dyke, P. A. & Vialle, C. 2006. *The Canton–Macao Dagregisters, 1762.* Macau: Instituto Cultural do Governo da R.A.E. de Macau.

Van Dyke, P. A. & Vialle, C. 2008. *The Canton–Macao Dagregisters, 1763*. Macau: Instituto Cultural do Governo da R.A.E. de Macau.

Von Stockenström, E. n.d. *Kort beskrifning öfver kejsaredömet China*. Manuscript Collection, Is 46, National Library of Sweden.

Von Stockenström, E. 1767–9. *Dagboksanteckningar under en resa till Ostindien 1767–1769*. Manuscript Collection, M 270, National Library of Sweden.

Waley, A. 1960. *The Opium War through Chinese Eyes*. 2nd edn. London: Unwin Brothers.

Ward, K. 2009. *Networks of Empire: Forced Migration in the Dutch East India Company*. Cambridge: Cambridge University Press.

Wei, G. 2009. 'The American presence in Macao: Some Chinese perceptions of the U.S.', *Review of Culture* 29: 7–16.

Xin, X. 1995. 'Macao and the Tributaries Scroll of the Qianlong Emperor', *Review of Culture* 23, 25–55.

Yin, G. 印光任 & Zhang, R. 張汝霖1992. Zhao, C. 赵春晨, (ed.), 澳門紀略 *Aomen Jilue*. Macau: 澳門文化司署 Aomen Wenhua Sishu.

16

The Barbary Coast and Ottoman Slavery in the Swedish Early Modern Imagination

JOACHIM ÖSTLUND

Between 1650 and 1770 around 1,000 Swedish subjects involved in long-distance trade in the Mediterranean were captured by Muslim corsairs operating from North Africa. European–North African conflicts were commented on in Swedish newspapers, associated with alms collections for ransom and noted in academic literature. This chapter analyses attitudes towards the Barbary Coast and towards Ottoman slavery in different genres. It argues that information on North Africa was widespread in early modern Sweden and that the discourse on North Africa and Ottoman slavery was multifaceted, both confirming and challenging European stereotypes of the "Orient".

Throughout the 17th and until the beginning of the 19th century, Sweden's most controversial contact with Islamic cultures was with the so-called Barbary powers: Tripoli, Tunis and Algiers, all regencies of the Ottoman Empire and Morocco. Between 1650 and 1770 approximately 1,000 Swedish subjects were captured by corsairs roaming the waters of the Mediterranean and the Atlantic. The large majority of the captives were civilians serving in the merchant fleet, and many of them ended up on slave markets in North Africa. Captivity in North Africa could mean a life spent chained to an oar, working in harbours, in private households or as servants in palaces. Compared to other Europeans, Swedish subjects represented only a small fraction of those held in North African captivity. The majority of captives were Spanish, but there were also French, Dutch, German, Portuguese and other Scandinavians. Approximately half of the captured Swedes made it back home. Captivity and potential death for those working in the merchant fleet was the price of the state enterprise to import salt directly from southern Europe – a commodity of vital importance for preserving food during the winter in Sweden.

The Ottoman Empire had long been "the Other" in the eyes of Europe, and vice versa. But between the two there was also a fascinating exchange of ideas and commodities, and personal encounters between individuals such as merchants, travellers, diplomats, consuls, soldiers and captives. Those who returned could tell stories about the other, narratives that often blended fact and fiction and fed the European imagination of "the Turk" and slavery on the Barbary Coast, as will be discussed in this chapter.

European–North African encounters have become a vibrant field of research.[1] Relevant in this case is the question of what attitudes, images and debates emerged as the result of the Swedish–North Africa encounters. When it comes to the question of "orientalism", the historian Linda Colley has argued for the existence of a multi-faced British discourse on Islam and North Africa, mostly because places like Tangier, Salé, Tunis and Algiers were markedly cosmopolitan.[2] One of the most extensive studies of European attitudes towards North Africa is that authored by the historian Ann Thomson. In her *Barbary and Enlightenment: European Attitudes towards the Maghreb in the 18th Century* (1987) she argues that Enlightenment perceptions of North Africa did not neatly fit into existing classification schemes for non-European societies. For example, the region was viewed neither as a seat of an ancient and respected civilization, as India and China were conceptualized, nor as a land of "primitive savages", as the New World was presented. And, despite its Roman heritage, North Africa was not seen as part of the European (Christian) world, nor was it viewed as truly African.[3] To date, few studies have scrutinized Scandinavian or Swedish perceptions of the region. This essay contributes to the field by analysing Swedish discourse on North Africa and Ottoman slavery.[4]

In the following discussion, three different genres of text belonging to different societal spheres are considered: newspapers, alms collections and one influential academic book. Special attention is given to the academic work written by Carl Reftelius, the Swedish consular secretary in Algiers (1732–3). His book, *Historisk och politisk beskrifning, öfwer riket och staden Algier* [*A Historical and Political Description of the Kingdom and the City Algiers*], was published in two volumes in 1737 and 1739. It has been almost totally forgotten by Swedish historians, just as the historical contacts between Sweden and North Africa have been overlooked (Fig. 16.1).[5]

SAILING SOUTH FOR SALT

The expansion of Swedish seaborne trade started in the middle of the 17th century when Swedish economic policies were formulated around new interests: the need for cheap salt and the development of markets for Swedish staple commodities in southern Europe. Rising salt prices in Setubal and Lisbon pushed Swedish merchants into the Mediterranean, a region characterized by warfare and a struggle for control between the two dominant powers of the region, Spain and the Ottoman Empire. During the 17th century, the conflict expressed itself in coastal raids, semi-official privateering and piracy. Constantinople's control over its North African vassals declined and the Barbary Coast became a centre of corsairing ventures. On the Christian side, Malta and Livorno played similar roles.[6]

The merchant enterprise in the Mediterranean soon resulted in losses of Swedish ships and crews to North African corsair raids. These losses were recorded in the archival sources as early as 1646, when one Jonas Timmerman was ransomed in Algiers.[7] The first preserved letter from a group of captives in Algiers was written in 1662 and addressed to the counsellor of state Magnus Gabriel De la Gardie.[8] The losses were considered by the government to be serious, and a first attempt to negotiate peace with the most powerful North African state, Algiers, was proposed in 1667. The agreement, however, never materialized, mainly for political reasons: groups within the Swedish state feared that a peace treaty between Sweden and Algiers would cause irritation among other European powers.[9]

Fig. 16.1 Algiers viewed from the sea. The picture shows a powerful city protected by thick walls and a fortified harbour. Illustration by Carl Erik Bergquist (1711–81) in Reftelius 1739, 232.

Sweden's attempts to sign peace treaties and ransom its subjects were beset by major problems until the early 18th century. Lack of information about the captives, the insufficient skills of the negotiators, the North African rulers' interest in releasing prisoners in exchange for money, the Swedish government's reluctance to pay the amounts required – all these factors meant that many captives were never freed from slavery. Rough calculations indicate that approximately 1,000 Swedes were captured by the corsairs. Estimates of their numbers are problematic, however, because many Swedish sailors from the Baltic region were captured when they were serving under foreign flags.

By the end of the Great Northern War in 1721, secure trading and the economy had become of the utmost importance for the bankrupt Swedish state. The protection of shipping in southern Europe and the Mediterranean became a high priority task and in 1724 the Swedish Convoy Office (*Konvojkommissariatet*) was founded. During the middle of the 18th century the time was ripe for Swedish peace treaties. The process began with a treaty with Algiers in 1729, and was followed up by agreements with Tunis in 1736, Tripoli in 1746 and finally with Morocco in 1763.[10] When this treaty with Morocco was concluded, the event ended a one hundred-year period of conflict and co-existence that inspired a significant amount of commentary in different genres of text. While letters from captives and peace treaties were normally read by only a rather limited audience, the stories of captivity and slavery in North Africa reported in newspapers and through alms collections reached a much wider group of people.

THE BARBARY COAST IN NEWSPAPERS

For 17th-century readers of the Swedish newspaper *Posttidningarna* ("Post Times") information about piratical activities by Barbary corsairs in the Mediterranean was regular news. *Posttidningarna* was published weekly and the information was gathered from diplomats and agents and also translated from foreign newspapers. Even if the readers of *Posttidningarna* consisted mainly of groups within the elite, such as the nobility and burghers in the bigger towns, the information found its way to larger audiences. Newspapers were available on market squares, and the stories on their pages were carried further by reports and rumours.[11]

The large majority of reports concerning corsairing ventures were presented in the form of war despatches. On 25 September 1656, for example, the newspaper reported on sea battles between "Turkish pirates" and the Venetians, and, a few years later, on 1 July 1663, on Barbary corsair raids against Dutch merchant ships.[12] The same year, reports from Vienna told of a sea battle against the Turks with hundreds of ships engaged on each side, and of the release of over 4,000 Christians from captivity as a result of European victory.[13] Corsair raids on French ships were often mentioned.[14] Some news were in the form of spy reports or warnings. They tell of rearmament and the planning of corsair raids.[15] In 1682 the amount of news related to the conflict with the North African corsairs peaked because of the intensified struggle between Algiers, France and England. The English demanded peace with Algiers and "the release of all slaves" in exchange for the freedom of 500 Turks. This offer was countered by an Algerian demand for 10,000 barrels of powder, 10,000 cannon-balls and 1,000 slaves from the English. The newspaper reported that the negotiation failed in this instance.

The above example shows how *Posttidningarna* explains conflict between Europe and North Africa as a matter of diplomacy and economic tensions. Conflicts in the region are often portrayed as a consequence of breaches of the treaties between European powers and the Ottoman regencies of North Africa. The corsairs in North Africa are thereby assigned a political agenda rather than ideological motives for their raids against European ships. Reports also indicate that both parties involved in the conflict enslaved their enemies.[16] Europeans too – the French and the English – are described as aggressors: they declare war and are not willing to release captured Turks.[17] Even so, the reports are not free from moral judgements of the conflict. The corsairs are described as bloodthirsty and brutal barbarians.[18] But the "othering" of the Turk is nevertheless comparable with the contemporaneous othering of Danes. Because of the conflicts between Sweden and Denmark during the 17th and early 18th centuries, the Danes are described as "worse than Turks" when it comes to the killing of innocents, which in turn shows a biased understanding of the word "Turk".[19]

Information about Swedish confrontations in the Mediterranean is uncommon. One report tells of a Swedish victory at sea against corsairs from Tunis, and another, reported in the issue for 19 September 1682, tells of a successful ransoming affair including Swedes. The ransoming affair is presented in a neutral form, simply stating that the Swedish agent Carl Cantersteen had joined up with the Dutch and that both Swedish and Dutch subjects had been successfully ransomed from slavery and had left "Barbary" on a Swedish warship.[20] Later that year a Swedish victory against corsairs from Tunis was presented in a very patriotic way. The despatch came from Lisbon and described the heroic fight by Captain Myrman on the ship *Engelen* ("Angel") from the Swedish town of Uddevala. Myrman was fighting against overwhelming odds but his ship forced two Turkish vessels to a costly defeat, spreading the rumours that the "Swedes didn't fight like humans, but more like devils".[21] Captain Myrman is portrayed as an example whom other captains and sailors in the merchant fleet should learn from and follow. Swedish losses against the corsairs are never mentioned in the newspaper, clearly indicating that the news reproduced in *Posttidningarna* is selective, reporting only the positive with regard to the Swedish merchant fleet. Nevertheless, it should be noted that the aggression in the Mediterranean is framed not in terms of a religious discourse, as a struggle between Christendom and Islam, but rather as a maritime conflict fuelled by power ambitions and disagreement over the terms of treaties.

NORTH AFRICA IN ALMS COLLECTIONS

Nationwide alms collections organized by the Church and state were an effective way to spread information about North Africa, Islam and slavery. These texts reached a wider group of people than newspapers and unlike the *Posttidningarna* they informed readers about losses of Swedish subjects in corsair raids and about slavery in North Africa. In Sweden and elsewhere in Europe, the collection of alms was an important source of funding for ransoming captured individuals. The methods of collecting money, ransoming the hostages and celebrating regained freedom differed to some extent between Protestant and Catholic countries. The Protestant countries, whose subjects were a minority among those kidnapped by the corsairs, had no special ransoming orders like the Mercedarians and Trinitarians that existed in the Catholic countries in southern Europe. There moreover the return of ransomed slaves was an occasion for public celebrations and parades of the returnees through the countryside. In the Protestant countries, the return of captives was not widely marked in the same manner.[22] In Sweden the responsibility to collect money and to ransom the captives was shared between the state and the Church. In 1724 the new Convoy Office (*Konvojkommissariatet*) became responsible for the funding of ransoms.

The problem of kidnappings by corsairs and of Swedes suffering "a difficult thraldom" on the Barbary Coast was first acknowledged as a serious national issue in the 1671 proclamation of the Queen Regent Hedwig Eleonora (Fig. 16.2). In this document, the Queen urged all subjects to give alms towards releasing the captives, and explained this act as a moral obligation, a sign of Christian compassion and love of one's neighbour.[23] This initiative was seen as an act of benevolence from the king towards its subjects, recognition of a right to be ransomed and to be free again. What is striking in this and other proclamations, however, is the moderate tone in the portrayal of the Turks when presenting and explaining the losses. Even if concepts like "pirates", "enemies" or "Barbary slavery" are used in arguments to motivate ransoms, the corsairs are never described as bloodthirsty or in religious terms, as "Muhammedans". The restrained wording becomes apparent when compared with the negative view of the Turks in prayer books, as well as the royal announcements of special prayer days to be held in Sweden during the second half of the 17th century. In both latter genres, the Turks were portrayed as the arch-enemy of Christendom, cruel and bloodthirsty, especially during the time when the Ottoman Empire had invaded the Balkans and was besieging Vienna.[24] Apparently the state had no interest in producing too negative and fearful an image of the Turk when explaining the dangers of trade in the Mediterranean. It would have been counterproductive to do so if such a portrayal deterred sailors from joining in this enterprise. Instead, the authorities focused on celebrating the sailors for their service to the king and country.

During the 17th century a number of royal collections for ransom were announced nationwide, both for individuals and for larger groups of captives. In 1682, the king pleaded to his subjects to aid one Debora Berg, who had lost her son Fredrik to "Algerian pirates in Barbary". The king argued that it was an act of Christian compassion to aid the poor mother and her son, who had sailed with the good intention of becoming a better sailor.[25] In other proclamations the same type of argument is repeated, stressing Christian empathy towards the poor victim who had accidently been captured by corsairs at sea and then enslaved on the Barbary Coast.[26] In parallel with the fundraising announced by state authorities, a number of private and local collections were also organized.[27] In 1724 it was decided that collections should be held nationwide four times a year to fulfil the need previously met by ransoming funds. One can thus conclude that for very many people in Sweden by this time Barbary slavery was not a strange and exotic tale, and was understood as a result of accidents at sea whose unfortunate victims – loyal subjects of the Crown – were in need of support from the home country.

The Swedish ransom system underwent a gradual institutionalization. When the Great Northern War (in which a Russian-led alliance challenged Sweden's hegemony

Wij CARL medh Gudz Nåde/ Sweriges/ Göthes och Wändes Konung och Arff-Förste/ Stoor-Förste til Finland/ Hertig vthi Skåne/ Estland/ Lijffland/Carelen/Brehmen/Vehrden/Stettin-Pommeren/Cassuben och Wend en/ Förste til Rügen/ Herre öfwer Ingermanland och Wißmar ; Så ock Pfaltz-Grefwe widh Rhein i Beyern/ til Gülich Cleve och Bergen Hertigh/ etc. Göre witterligit/ at Wij fast ogärna förnimme / huru som en deel aff Wåre Undersåtare/ så wäl vthi förledne Krijgztijder/ som i synnerheet widh the til Spanien och Medelhafwet anstälte Seglationer/ skole fångne och til Turckijet i en swår Träldom förde och försålde wara / hwilket theras vsle och beträngde wilkohr Wij medh Konungzligh mildheet ansedt/ ock förthy på medel och vthwägar hafwe warit betänckte / hwar igenom the samme åter löösgiöras ock vthi förra Frijheet sättias måge ; Och såsom thetta är ett godt och Christeligit Wärck/ thet vthan twifwel alle rättsinnige skole willia befordra / til at ther medh wijsa ett skåligt Medhlijdande emoot then Nödhlijdande/ så hafwe Wij för godt eractat then-

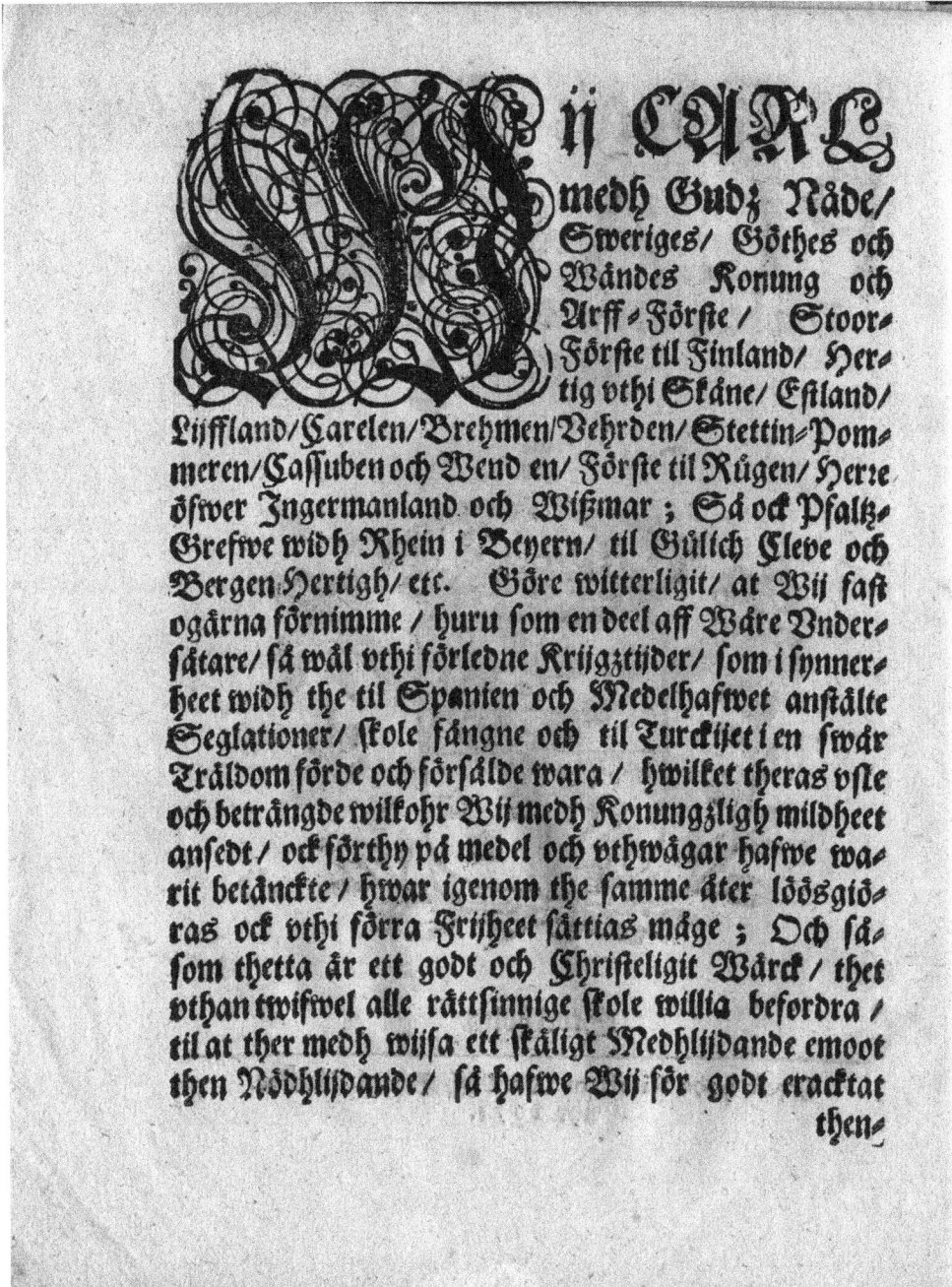

Fig. 16.2 An announcement of a national collection of ransom for Swedish sailors "suffering slavery" in Barbary, issued by Queen Regent Hedwig Eleonora in 1671.

in the Baltic region) ended in 1721, Swedish seaborne trade with southern Europe increased, and alongside convoys and insurance policies, peace treaties with the North African states become the most important factor in increasing security. When, as noted above, the Swedish government set up the Convoy Office (*Konvojkommissariatet*) in 1724, it was tasked with managing convoys to southern Europe, annual collections for captives' ransoms, tributes to the rulers in North Africa and the wages of Swedish consuls there. When Sweden signed a peace treaty with Algiers in 1729, the other states along the North African coast soon followed. With the conclusion of peace treaties, Swedish consuls were stationed in the region and their published personal experiences drastically changed the view of North Africa in Sweden.

BARBARY ALGIERS IN ETHNOGRAPHIC WRITING

During the late 17th century, the first books describing North Africa were published in Sweden. The publications on the region represented different genres and included dissertations, adventure stories and captivity narratives.[28] One of the best examples representing academic discourse is a book written by the Swedish consular secretary Carl Reftelius, active in Algiers in 1732–3, and published in Stockholm in two volumes in 1737 and 1739. The book titled *Historisk och politisk beskrifning, öfwer riket och staden Algier* (A Historical and Political Description of the Kingdom and the City Algiers) represents the first in-depth Scandinavian study on Algiers.

According to Ann Thomson, the 18th-century European genre of scientific literature covering North Africa tended towards similarity of content, regardless of the authors' personal cultural affiliations. In many cases translations were made with added comments and smaller changes. This was the case with *Historie van Barbaryen En de zelfs Zee-Roovers* compiled by the Dutch author Simon de Vries, based on a translation of the more famous work written by the Catholic priest Pierre Dan in 1634. Other examples are the works by the French consul Laugier de Tassy, published in 1725, translated into English by Joseph Morgan, and the work by the Englishman Thomas Shaw published in 1738 and soon translated to French. There were also personal contacts between authors like Peyssonnel, La Condamine and Thomas Shaw. Books travelled quickly across borders to be read, translated and reviewed in accordance with the interest of each author and audience.[29]

Many of the European titles were also available in Sweden before Carl Reftelius published his study. Among the references he mentions in his work were books by the leading authors, such as Dan, D'Aranda, La Faye, Laugier de Tassy, D'Arvieux, Morgan, Pitts and Frisch. Reftelius writes that he has been inspired by these studies, but also criticized some of the assumptions they made, especially those of Laugier de Tassy, and also added some observations of his own from his stay in Algiers.[30] In others words, Reftelius did exactly what a number of authors had done before him.

Reftelius's description of Algiers is in many ways a tale of contrasts between what is considered as barbarous and as civilized. He both repeated and challenged rumours and stereotypes of Algiers, on the basis of his own observations. He describes Algiers as a city known for its riches, its piracy towards Christendom and its "tyrannical ways towards Christian slaves", even if he admits that many stories of captivity and maltreatment were exaggerated.[31] He depicted the people as "brutal and barbaric", but at the same time characterized by internal "order and justice".[32]

The civilized character of the city is exemplified in a description by Reftelius of the schools in Algiers. The lectures were open to everyone and, according to Reftelius, the shared participation in and openness of these schools had much in common "with our baker-shops, with the exception that they are open on to the street making it possible for those passing by to take part of the teaching of the youngsters".[33] Reftelius also included stories of friendly meetings between Algerians and Swedes in the city. The most notable was the moment when the peace treaty between Sweden and Algiers was celebrated in 1729. Joint parties with Algerian state officials and Swedes were held on a Swedish ship in the harbour and the peace was celebrated with a toast and the firing of Algerian guns. As described by Reftelius, "This was a time in Algiers that probably never will reappear: For Swedes and Turks lived there like brothers, kissing and hugging on the streets and promised each other mutual friendship and love."[34]

The question of civilization and the lack of it is a recurring theme in the book. For example, Reftelius asserted that in the Algerian city of Tremensen there lived a number of "poor Arabs, Moors and Jews, but even so more civilized and honest then the Algerians".[35] Africans were also mentioned: some of them lived like "wild animals", while others dwelled in the cities like other "civilized peoples".[36] The concept of civilization advanced by Reftelius was not related to a certain group of people or particular culture, but instead to what he saw as the positive characteristics of human beings: lifestyles and ways in which a society managed to uphold justice, law and order. However, when it came to religion and to the treatment of women, a much more negative view was presented. For example, Reftelius suggested that the Algerians appeared loyal to their religion when it came to making gestures, but in reality, he felt, they were slaves to gold. Greed, laziness and cruelty were defining characteristics in the author's eyes. Other vices highlighted by Reftelius were lewdness and sodomy, supposedly practised in secret baths. Reftelius also argued that women in Algiers were imprisoned in a society dominated by men, and that they were only perceived as useful in fulfilling sexual and reproductive roles. He reported that women were not allowed to participate in religious services and they were not buried together with their husbands. Reiterating typical orientalist stereotypes, Reftelius explained the custom of women covering their faces and not being allowed to leave their homes unaccompanied as motivated by the jealousy of their own husbands and as a protection mechanism against the lusts of other men.[37]

The analytical character of Reftelius's work is apparent in his discussion of different reasons behind negative attitudes towards Christians in Algiers and in his proposals to change existing preconceptions. He listed upbringing and habituation to the sight of enslaved Europeans as one of the reasons behind adverse stereotyping. Since many homes in Algiers owned Christian slaves, young people were raised to view Christians as enemies and servants. Travel, according to Reftelius, played a significant role in altering such views. Those Algerians who travelled widely, those who visited Mecca, and had been to Christian countries freely or as slaves, came to treat Christians "very well", according to Reftelius.[38]

Reftelius also attributed unfavourable images of the Europeans to the on-going conflict in the Mediterranean, which was portrayed locally as an Algerian struggle for survival against the greedy Europeans:

> Especially they despise the Spaniards, the Portuguese and the Maltese [...] since they are the ones who have taken the land illegally from their ancestors, persecute them in many ways, and bring nothing other than mayhem, rampaging and doom, and never try to bring peace with them.[39]

But political reasons and European expansionism are not the only reasons for the conflict and animosity, according to Reftelius. Shifting focus, he also places blame for corsair raids and for the enslavement of Christians on Islam: the Muslims were blinded by "the false prophet Mohammed's teachings".[40] Reftelius presented Christianity as superior to Islam, citing in particular the tradition of monogamy. While he acknowledged some moral lessons from the Koran, he otherwise dismissed it as a collection of fables, silly parallels, tautologies and absurdities.[41]

Notwithstanding the limits of Reftelius's understanding, his writings make it clear how perceptions of Algiers were debated and understandings transformed. Compared to the stories published in newspapers and propagated in alms collections, the writings of individuals who visited the region, such as consuls, could map, define, and debate the character of the region and its people upon a basis of first-hand experience. Reftelius and other European authors writing on societal and cultural topics related to North Africa compared and measured their observations against the equivalent processes and occurrences in Europe. In other words, compared to texts in newspapers and associated with alms collections, Reftelius's study placed its readers in a dialogue with not only one, but two cultures, which are analysed and measured against each other. This process is well exemplified in his account of the ceremony when meeting the Dey of Algiers:[42]

> Many argue that visits to the Dey in Algiers are made with the same awe, respect and servility that are shown to emperors and kings in Europe. But nothing is more wrong: in front of him everyone speaks with him like a friend and equal.[43]

Reftelius developed his argument by suggesting that the courts in Algiers were more equal and rational than those in Europe, as exemplified by the customs of presenting the cases and visiting the office: one did not talk to the Dey with a long and graceful speech and flattery, but instead presented a proposal in sincerity and in truth.[44] The tradition of kissing the hand of the Dey was explained as an expression of friendship, compared to the "ceremonies and oddities at the courts of the Christians". When the Dey allowed a visitor to kiss his hand it was a gesture of welcome; not offering the hand indicated the unworthiness of the guest, who was still nevertheless allowed to present their case.

In other words, Reftelius's work should also be valued for its contribution to comment on contemporary political questions, such as the character of European monarchy. His observations can be seen in the context of the aftermath of the downfall of Caroline absolutism in Sweden in 1719, which resulted in a changed view of citizenship, as expressed in the constitution of 1720 that converted Sweden into the most limited of monarchies in Europe. All power was vested in the people as represented by the parliament – the Riksdag. This change allowed, for example, Voltaire to declare Sweden to be "the freest land in the world". Rousseau called the constitution "an example of the perfect", and Gabriel Bonnot de Mably called it "a masterpiece of modern legislation".[45] When Reftelius argued that political authority in Algiers was more equal and rational than royal ceremonies in Europe, this was also a political statement relevant to Sweden, where around 30 years later, in 1772, the political landscape changed again when a bloodless *coup d'état* carried out by King Gustav III reinstalled absolute monarchy.

The practice of slavery was also thoroughly debated by Reftelius. About 100 out of the total 697 pages of his two volumes are dedicated to Ottoman slavery, which makes his work the earliest and most detailed description of the topic in Swedish. It was evident from his book that the life of slaves in Algiers took many different forms. He noted that some slaves moved freely around the city as peddlers of various goods, while the rulers of Algiers allowed slaves to run taverns and restaurants. As these estab-lishments sold alcohol and as "the Turks" were prohibited from consuming or dealing in this commodity, Christian slaves filled this niche market and even had the right to become owners of taverns if they possessed the financial wherewithal. Reftelius noted that taverns were located by the prisons and were frequented by soldiers and "brutes", who spent their time drinking and smoking. According to Reftelius, the prisons in Algiers, three in number, were "a hell for Christians": the rooms in the prison were very crowded and dirty, people lived with no moral standards and the guards were cruel.[46]

A description of a slave auction in North Africa was usually included in books on the region written by European authors. This is also the case with Reftelius's account.[47] He wrote that after a successful corsair raid the Dey of Algiers regarded all of the captives as slaves. The differences between the captives' fates were then determined by their social status, nationality and training. Captives with special skills were integrated into society and worked as skippers, mates, surgeons and carpenters, while those without desirable skills were sold.[48]

There are similarities between Reftelius's description of a slave auction and those of D'Arvieux and Dan, as considered further below.[49] Reftelius's own visit to a slave auction in Algiers made a profound impression on him:

> The suffering I still can remember, but only with great difficulty describe with a pen; the defamation, hardness, contempt, fear and terror that these unhappy humans had to experience during the auction: I have seen their bodies shake like aspen leaves because of their lack of knowledge of the country and their own destiny, and often because they picture for themselves more difficulties than what actually will be the case.[50]

Slave markets were commonly evoked in stories that did not exclusively focus on the fear and suffering of the Christians. When captives from all over Europe were brought to the markets they exhibited different attitudes that were interpreted by the onlookers as signs of national character and even afforded humorous comments. Reftelius quoted one such story, borrowed from D'Arvieux and Morgan. It was a tale of a proud Spaniard who considered that the price offered for him on the slave auction was too low: "he asked the man who was going to buy him if he considered him a donkey, to value a man of his position for the price he offered".[51]

Reftelius estimated the number of enslaved Christians in Algiers to be around 9,000. He speculated however, that the overall number was higher since many of them lived outside the city. Among the captives he listed Swedes, Danes, Englishmen, Dutch, Poles, Spaniards and Maltese. Reftelius concluded that despite the peace treaties and the system of ransoming most slaves died in Algiers. He questioned the possibilities of slave resistance or revolt, as the captives were scattered in different locations, feared punishment, lacked weapons and were divided by national disagreements.[52]

Reftelius listed three types of slave in Algiers: the poor who sold themselves into slavery; the so-called "rogues" who were enslaved as a punishment for a crime committed, and finally seamen and others who were kidnapped while at sea. [53] He described a system whereby large slaveholders rented out slaves for a variety of purposes, including service to corsairs and as household servants (Fig. 16.3). [54] Enslaved persons of high rank, such as captains, officers, priests and doctors, often became public or state slaves and were treated better than others in consideration of the potentially high ransoms they might attract. Individuals with specialist skills of use in Algiers were often appreciated for their practical knowledge and unwillingly released by their owners. Lowest in rank were the

Fig. 16.3 Two slaves and an Algerian woman riding a donkey protected by a *rekkabie*, a square rack covered by fine cloth. The woman is on her way to her country house, while the father travels on horseback (outside the picture): a comment on the life of house slaves by Reftelius. Illustration by Jean Eric Rehn (1717–93) in Reftelius 1737, 168.

slaves who were placed in the prisons (*bagnos*), marked, according to Reftelius, with a small iron ring around their leg.[55]

Reftelius's description of slavery in Algiers included a moral consideration of the practice and questioning of slavery as an institution. He concluded that slavery is wrong and immoral, as he saw it as contradicting the teachings of the "Church fathers" and specifically the notion that humans are the crown of God's creation. To sell human beings into slavery was to equate them to animals, a crime against God, in the estimation of Reftelius. He further considered slavery as a special form of theft: when the corsairs took captives they robbed individuals of "their natural freedom"; he thus demonstrated the influence of philosophical notions of natural rights. At the same time, Reftelius perceived slavery as a social contract, a relationship in which both the master and the slave had to fulfil designated roles. He thus opined that a slave who did not behave as expected should rightly be punished. Enslaved people should work to make their situation better while masters should in turn treat slaves fairly.[56]

Reftelius's discussion of Ottoman slavery presented arguments of different tone and intent. His discussion did not only focus upon Algiers; he also addressed European perspectives on Ottoman slavery and on slavery within Europe. As Ann Thomson has shown, 18th-century European scientific literature on North Africa questioned the European image of slavery under Islam. One of the reasons for this questioning was ideological: for thinkers within the Enlightenment movement, positive views of Islam were used as a strategy to criticize Christendom in general and especially the (Catholic) Church.[57] Reftelius joined these critics by presenting Islam as a tolerant counterpart to Christian Europe. He argued, for example, that contemporary galley slaves in Christian Europe – captured subjects of Ottoman Empire – faced much worse conditions than galley slaves in Algiers.[58] The same went for the custom of bearing chains by the enslaved: this practice was judged as much worse in Christendom. When slaves in Algiers were in chains it was as a punishment for transgression of the rules, for which the slaves were to be "ashamed" according to the author. More generally, he observed that in Algiers almost all slaves walked as "freely" as free individuals in Europe.[59]

Reftelius thus questioned the European image of slavery in Algiers, and noted his surprise at what he considered to be fabricated stories told by ransomed slaves or slaves in Algiers trying to convince European audience that they bore heavy iron chains. In his estimation, chains were a well-deserved punishment for misbehaviour.[60] His Protestant bias emerges too in his description of enslaved Europeans who were in the service of the Dey or in private households as not so "unhappy in their slavery as a number of monk-stories or stories told by ransomed slaves at home claim".[61] The "monk-stories" Reftelius referred to were those produced by the Catholic ransoming orders active in North Africa, and therefore suspicious from a Protestant perspective.

Many slaves lived well, according to Reftelius, and their lives resembled in many ways the situation of household servants in Sweden. He considered that it was very common in Algiers to see "old and grey-haired slaves carry young girls on their arm and young boys riding on their shoulders".[62] In some cases slave-owners maintained mail contact with their former slaves after their release, and in his opinion household slaves in Algiers were important members of the family.[63] Reftelius questioned stories that claimed Algerians endeavoured to convert Christians to Islam, insofar as he believed that the conversion of slaves would put their owners at risk of losing ransoms from Europeans who focused on Christians.[64] Furthermore, Islamic law did not allow forced conversions.[65] Reftelius reported meeting some Swedes in Algiers who had converted to Islam, but their conversion did not change their status as slaves.[66] He observed that Christians in Algiers, free or enslaved, were permitted to worship according to their own religion, but could not criticize Islam; nor could practitioners of foreign religions be members of the ruling elite.[67]

In summary, Reftelius expressed both strongly positive and negative evaluations of Algerian society and culture, characterizing it as both barbaric and civilized. By including Europe in his arguments, he signals his own Enlightenment positioning in terms of his focus upon moral universalism.[68] When Reftelius wrote that European slavery was worse than slavery in Algiers, he shared values expressed by other Enlightenment authors writing on North Africa.[69] He also criticized Catholic ransoming orders and also Christian slaves for allegedly exaggerating their suffering. At the same time, Christianity was presented as superior to Islam and the treatment of women as being better in Europe. Reftelius and others employed the situation in Algiers as a tool to both criticize and praise Europe. Overall, Reftelius's Swedish work on Algiers reproduced and reflected the main arguments present in contemporary European discourse on slavery in Ottoman North Africa.

CONCLUSIONS

Awareness of North Africa and the dangers of sailing to the Mediterranean were not exclusive to Swedish sailors and merchants active in long-distance trade with southern Europe. Thanks to newspapers and nationwide alms collections organized by the Church, the region also became known to people who were not directly involved in maritime enterprise. The images and attitudes generated by Swedish contacts with the Muslim world in the Mediterranean were, to some extent, shaped by economic interests defined by the state and merchant culture. After all, the purpose for the Swedish maritime presence in the Mediterranean was to import salt – a commodity of vital importance for preserving food during the winter in Sweden. Even if stereotypes like "bloodthirsty Turkish pirates" are used in newspapers, the logic of the conflict was presented as being driven by political and economic competition rather than as a clash between good and evil, or between Muslim and Christian civilizations. Both sides were blamed for enslaving their enemies and ignoring agreements made in peace treaties. An economic and maritime framing also conditioned the arguments employed in alms collections that eschewed over-explicit descriptions of "a Turkish arch-enemy" in the Mediterranean. Sailors were celebrated for their service to king and country, and subjects at home were rendered as patriots for contributing to ransom funds.

During the middle of the 18th century, writers such as consuls and academics introduced a more complex understanding of North Africa and the corsairs. Carl Reftelius's book on Algiers, published in Swedish in 1737 and 1739, is a good example of this new understanding. Reftelius's work reproduced European discourse on Ottoman Algiers, confirming some orientalist stereotypes whilst criticizing others. Ottoman slavery was described as a complex system with a variety of social roles, based upon a social contract between master and slave. Because of the ransom system, slaves were reportedly well treated, even if the payment of ransoms was uncommon. Like other Enlightenment authors, Reftelius criticized European misinterpretations of slavery in Algiers, and argued that slavery was worse in Europe. Notwithstanding the vulnerability of Sweden to North African privateering for a period of over a hundred years, the academic attitude towards the Ottoman regencies was thus not entirely negative. The intellectual impact of Enlightenment philosophy was clearly reflected in texts and books on North Africa in Sweden during the 18th century.

NOTES

1 For example: Friedman 1983; Belhamissi 1988; Bono 1993; Baepler, 1999; Matar, 2001; 2005; Vitkus 2001; Colley 2002; van Krieken 2002; Davis 2003; Torres Martínez 2004; Barrio Gozalo 2006; Weiss 2011; Ressel 2012; Sears 2012.

2 Colley 2002, 107–9; Fontenay 2008; Dávid & Fodor 2007.

3 Thomson 1987, 4–5. For a more critical view on European descriptions of North Africa, see Benhayoun 2006.

4 The purpose of the essay is to analyse the language of slavery in Sweden, not to discuss whether captured Swedes should be defined as slaves or as captives. Inspiration comes from Epstein 2001.

5 This essay is developed from the results presented in Östlund 2014.

6 Östlund 2014; Müller 2004; Krëuger 1856.

7 'Spanien'; see also *Tyske Kancelli; Resident Henrik Willumsens*.

8 Hansson *et al.* 1662.

9 Östlund 2014, 104–7.

10 Östlund 2014, 104–7.

11 Holmberg *et al.* 2000, 83–5.

12 *Posttidningarna*, 25.9 1656; 11.8 1663.

13 *Posttidningarna*, 21.8 1656.

14 *Posttidningarna*, 24.1 1682; 26.6 1683; 5.2 1684.

15 *Posttidningarna*, 20.6 1682; 17.6 1686.

16 *Posttidningarna*, 6.10 1685.

17 *Posttidningarna*, 31.5 1686.

18 *Posttidningarna*, 28.4 1685.

19 Forsberg 2007, 18.

20 *Posttidningarna*, 19.9 1682.

21 *Posttidningarna*, 26.9 1682.

22 Colley 2002; Matar 2006; Weiss 2011.

23 [Hedwig Eleonora] 1671.

24 Östlund 2007, 53–4; [Hedwig Eleonora] *Kongl. Maj: ts* [...] 1664; Anon. *Tacksäyelse-Skrifft* [...]

1683; 1685; 1692; Anon. *Allmän Tacksäyelse* [...] 1691. See also Dryselio1694.

25 [Charles XI] 1682.

26 [Charles XI] 1690; Swedberg 1707.

27 Östlund, 2014, 147.

28 Helding 1699; Retzelius 1700; Thelaus 1716; Neuhoff 1737; Landcrona 1740; Berg 1757.

29 Thomson 1987, 4–5.

30 Reftelius 1737, 16; D'Arvieux 1735; La Motte 1736; Laugier de Tassy 1750; Dan 1649; Morgan 2008 [1729–31].

31 Reftelius 1739, 1.

32 Reftelius 1739, 426–7.

33 Reftelius 1739, 261–2.

34 Reftelius 1739, 628. All citations from Reftelius are translations by the author.

35 Reftelius 1737, 109.

36 Reftelius 1737, 117.

37 Reftelius 1737, 168–9.

38 Reftelius 1737, 158.

39 Reftelius 1737, 158.

40 Reftelius 1739, 454.

41 Reftelius 1737, 188.

42 'Dey' was a title of the governor.

43 Reftelius 1739, 579.

44 Reftelius 1739, 585.

45 Roberts 1995, 91.

46 Reftelius 1739, 260–79.

47 Reftelius 1739, 454–5.

48 Reftelius 1739, 455.

49 See D'Arvieux 1735, 267 and Dan 1649, 392.

50 Reftelius 1739, 454–5.

51 D'Arvieux 1735, 267–8. See also Morgan 2008 [1729–31], 270–1.

52 Reftelius 1737, 177.

53 Reftelius 1737, 175.

54 Reftelius 1737, 180.

55 Reftelius 1739, 464.

56 Reftelius 1739, 485–6. The view of slavery as a

social contract was also advanced by Samuel Pufendorf: see Östlund 2014, 29.

57 Thomson 1987, 24–8. A comparative and critical perspective upon slavery in Algiers had already been introduced during the middle of the 17th century by the German Johann Frischs (Frischs 1666). Swedish authors before Reftelius also criticized exaggerated accounts of slavery in Algiers: see e.g. Thelaus 1716; Östlund 2014, 250, 265.

58 Reftelius 1737, 175.

59 Reftelius 1739, 465.

60 Reftelius 1739, 464–5.

61 Reftelius 1739, 457.

62 Reftelius 1737, 170.

63 Reftelius 1739, 470, 472.

64 Reftelius 1737, 180–1.

65 Reftelius 1737, 183.

66 Reftelius 1737, 184.

67 Reftelius 1737, 221.

68 On the topic of Enlightenment and universalism, see Israel 2001.

69 Thomson 1987, 38.

BIBLIOGRAPHY

Anon. 1683. *Tacksäyelse-Skrifft öfwer den Keysserl. Residence-Staden Wiens Förlåssning och dhe Christnas erhåldne Seger emoth Turcken* [...]. Stockholm: Wankijff.

Anon. 1685. *Tacksäyelse-Skrift Öfwer Den Turkiske Belägringens Uphäfwande för Staden Braan* [...]. Stockholm: Wankijff.

Anon. 1689. *Tacksäyelse-Skrift Öfwer De Keyserliges erhåldne Seger emoot Arf-Fienden Turcken* [...]. Stockholm: Wankijff.

Anon. 1691. *Allmän Tacksäyelse Öfwer De Keyserliges, den 9/19 Augusti Åhr 1691 Uti Ungern emillan Peter Waradein och Salankemen erhållne märckelige Seger emot Arf-Fienden Turcken* [...]. Stockholm: Wankijff.

Anon. 1692. *Tacksäyelse-skrifft ofwer den nampnkunnige och faste stadens, Store Waradins, eröfring uti Ungern: upläsen uti församlingarne öfwer hela Swerige och desz underliggiande länder och härskaper åhr 1692 uti Junij och Augusti månader.* Linköping: Kempe.

Baepler, P. M. 1999. *White Slaves, African Masters: An Anthology of American Barbary Captivity Narratives.* Chicago: University of Chicago Press.

Barrio Gozalo, M. 2006. *Esclavos y cautivos: Conflicto entre la cristiandad y el islam en el siglo XVIII.* Valladolid: Junta de Castilla y León.

Belhamissi, M. 1988. *Les captifs algériens et l'Europe chrétienne (1518–1830).* Algiers: ENAL.

Berg, M. 1757. *Beskrifning öfwer barbariska slafweriet uti kejsardömet Fez och Marocco i korthet författad af Marcus Berg, som tillika med många andra christna det samma utstådt tvenne år och siu dagar, och derifrån blifwit utlöst tillika med åtta stycken andra swenska den 30 augusti 1756.* Stockholm: Lor. Ludv. Grefing.

Benhayoun, J. E. 2006. *Narration, Navigation and Colonialism: A Critical Account of Seventeenth- and Eighteenth-Century English Narratives of Adventure and Captivity.* Brussels: Peter Lang.

Bono, S. 1993. *Corsari nel Mediterraneo: Cristiani e musulmani fra guerra, schiavitù e commercio.* Milan: Mondadori.

[Charles XI]. 1682. 'Debora Berg collection for her son, 4.3 1682'. RR RA.

[Charles XI]. 1690. 'Collection for Håkan Falk 15.2 1690'. RR RA.

Colley, L. 2002. *Captives, Britain, Empire and the World, 1600–1850.* New York: Pantheon.

Dan, P. 1649. *Histoire de Barbarie, et de ses Corsaires. Des royavmes, et des villes d'Alger, de Tvnis, de Salé, [et] de Tripoly. Divisée en six livres. Ov il est traitté de levr govvernement, de leurs moeurs, de leurs cruautez, de leurs brigandages, de leurs sortileges, [et] de plusieurs autres particularitez remarquables. Ensemble des grandes miseres et des crvels tourmens qu'endurent les Chrestiens captifs parmy ces infidels.* Paris: P. Rocolet.

D'Arvieux, L. 1735. *Memoires du chevalier D'Arvieux, envoyé extraordinaire du roy [...] contenant ses voyages à Constantinople, dans l'Asie, la Palestine, l'Egypte, & la Barbarie [...] Par le R. P. Jean-Baptiste Labat, de l'ordre des freres precheurs. A Paris chez Charles-Jean-Baptiste Delespine* [...] M.DCC.XXXV. Paris: C.-J.-B. Delespine.

Davis, R. C. 2003. *Christian Slaves, Muslim Masters. White Slavery in the Mediterranean, the Barbary Coast and Italy, 1500–1800.* Basingstoke: Palgrave Macmillan

Dávid, G. & Fodor, P. (eds) 2007. *Ransom Slavery along the Ottoman Borders (Early Fifteenth – Early Eighteenth Centuries).* Leiden: Brill.

Dryselio, E. 1694. *Luna Turcica eller Turkeske måne, anwijsandes lika som uti a spegel det mahometiske wanskelige regementet, fördelter uti fyra qwarter eller böcker* [...], Jönköping: Petter Hultman.

Epstein, S. A. 2001. *Speaking of Slavery: Color, Ethnicity and Human Bondage in Italy (Conjunctions of Religion and Power in the Medieval Past).* Ithaca: Cornell University Press.

Fontenay, M. 2008. 'Esclaves et/ou captifs: préciser les concepts', In Kaiser 2008, 15–24.

Forsberg, A. M. 2007. 'Glada budskap eller inga. Posttidningarna under skånska kriget', *Presshistorisk årsbok 2007*: 7–25.

Friedman, Ellen G. 1983. *Spanish Captives in North Africa in the Early Modern Age.* Madison: University of Wisconsin Press.

Frischs, J. 1666. *Der Schauplatz Barbarischer Schlavery.* Altona: Victor de Löw.

Hansson, E. *et al.* 1662. 'Brev från Alger 20.11 1662' [Letter from Algiers], Diplomatica Turcica, bihang algerica vol. 15, RA.

[Hedwig Eleonora]. 1664. *Kongl. May: ts PLACAT, Om tree Allmenne Solenne Tacksäyelse- Faste och Bönedagar/ som uthi innewarande Åhr/ öfwer heele Swerige/ och dess underliggiande Provincier, jemwäl Storfurstendömet Finland/ sampt Lijff- och Ingermanland/ hållas och fijras skole. Datum Stockholm den 19. Martij, Anno 1664.* Stockholm: L.S Rådet.

[Hedwig Eleonora]. 1671. *Kongl: mayst:ts placat, om hielp til the fångnas i Turckiet återlösn.* Stockholm: Wankijff.

Helding, J. 1699. *Dissertatio Academica Mauritaniam Seu Regna Fes – Maroccanum Et Algier, Succinte delineans Qvam Ex Consensu Ampliss:ae Facul:tis Philos:ae In Reg. Acad. Upsal. Praeside Viro Celeberrimo, M. Haraldo Wallerio, Geom. Prof. Reg & Ord. Ad Publicum Examen modeste defert Johannes Heldingh. Holm. In Aud. Gust. Maj. Anno 1699, die 15 (alt. 21) Febr.horis Ante merid. Folitis.* Uppsala: Impressa literis Wankifvianis.

Holmberg, C.-G., Oscarsson, I. & Torbacke, J. (eds). 2000. *Den svenska pressens historia. 1, I begynnelsen (tiden före 1830).* Stockholm: Ekerlid.

Israel, J. 2001. *Radical Enlightenment: Philosophy and the Making of Modernity, 1650–1750.* Oxford: Oxford University Press.

Kaiser, W. (ed.) 2008. *Le Commerce des captifs: Les Intermédiaires dans l'échange et le rachat des prisonniers en Méditerranée, XVe-XVIIIe siècle,* Rome: École française de Rome.

Krëuger, J. H. 1856. *Sveriges förhållanden till Barbaresk Staterna i Afrika,* vol. 1. Stockholm: P. A. Norstedt.

Krieken, G. van 2002. *Corsairs et marchands. Les Relations entre Alger et les Pays-Bas 1604–1830.* Paris: Bouchène.

La Motte, P. de. 1736. *Several voyages to Barbary. Containing an historical and geographical account of the country. [...] With a journal of the late siege and surrender of Oran. To which are added. The maps of Barbary [...] by Captain Henry Boyde. [...].* 2nd edn. London: printed for Olive Payne, Joseph Duke and Samuel Baker.

Landcrona, G. 1740. *Gustav Landcronas, en swensk adels-mans märkwärdige lefwerne och fahrliga resa, tå han som en sanfärdig Robinson sig med en döpt turkinna, vti tolf åhrs tid på en obebodd ö underligen vppehållit, och eljest the förskräckeligaste olyckor: med ståndachtighet lidit och öfwerwunnit, til thes han ändteligen helt oförmodeligen til rätt lycksalighet kommit. Efter hans eget något otydeligit concept med förbättrad skrif-art på tyska språket til offenteligen tryck befordrat. Af : C.F.v.M. Och nu sedermera på thet swenska språket öfwersatt af E.H. Stockholm, tryckt hos Lorentz L: Grefing.* Åhr *1740.* Stockholm: Lorentz L. Grefing.

Laugier de Tassy, J. P. 1750 [translated by E. Morgan]. *A Compleat History of the Piratical States of Barbary, viz. Algiers, Tunis, Tripoli and Morocco. Containing the origin, revolutions, and present state of these kingdoms, their forces, revenues, policy, and commerce. Illustrated with a plan of Algiers, and a map of Barbary.* London: Printed for R. Griffiths.

Matar, N. I. 2001. 'English accounts of captivity in North Africa and the Middle East, 1577–1625', *Renaissance Quarterly* 54(2): 553–72.

Matar, N. I. 2005. *Britain and Barbary, 1589–1689.* Gainesville: University Press of Florida.

Morgan, J. 2008 [1729–31]. *Complete History of Algiers – To Which Is Prefixed, An Epitome Of The General History Of Barbary, From The Earliest Times – Interspersed With Many Curious Remarks And Passages, Not Touched On By Any Writer Whatever.* La Miranda, CA: Davidson Press.

Müller, L. 2004. *Consuls, Corsairs, and Commerce: The Swedish Consular Service and Long-Distance Shipping.* Uppsala: Uppsala universitet.

Neuhoff, T. von. 1737. *Tilförlåtelig efterrättelse angående baron Theodor von Neuhoff, hwarutinnan denna herrns härkomst, födelse, fädernesland, och första ungdoms förrätningar, en kort berättelse om des resor, fångenskap uti Algier, resa til Tunis, och änteligen: des ankomst på öen Korsika, korteligen finnas beskrefne. Utaf franskan öfwersatt. 1737.* Gothenburg.

Östlund, J. 2007. *Lyckolandet: maktens legitimering i officiell retorik från stormaktstid till demokratins genombrott.* Lund: Sekel.

Östlund, J. 2014. *Saltets pris: Svenska slavar i Nordafrika 1650–1770.* Lund: Nordic Academic Press.

Posttidningarna, 21.8 1656–17.6.1686. Centrala Filmarkivet 468:2, Post och inrikes tidningar 1663–1679. LUB.

Reftelius, C. 1737. *Historisk och Ppolitisk Beskrifning, Öfwer riket och staden Alger, ifrån år 1516 til och med år 1732*, vol. 1. Stockholm: Peter Jör. Nyström.

Reftelius, C. 1739. *Historisk och Politisk Beskrifning Öfwer Riket och Staden Algier*, vol. 2. Stockholm: Peter Jör. Nyström.

Resident Henrik Willumsens Gesandtskabsarkiv, legg I. Korrespondance ang. fangers løskøbelse 1642–1652. RADK.

Ressel, M. 2012. *Zwischen Sklavenkassen Und Turkenpassen: Nordeuropa Und Die Barbaresken in Der Fruhen Neuzeit.* Leiden: Brill.

Retzelius, O. 1700. *De pactis cum barbaris dissertatio, qvam […] præside […] Dn. Johanne Reftelio […] pro gradu, ad examen publicum in Aud: Gust: Maj: d. XX. Octob: Ann. MDCC. modeste defert Sae. Rae. Mtis. alumnus Olaus Retzelius Ostro-Gothus.* Uppsala: Uppsala universitet.

Roberts, M. 1995. *Sverige under frihetstiden 1719–1772.* Stockholm: Prisma.

Sears, C. E. 2012. *American Slaves and African Masters: Algiers and the Western Sahara, 1776–1820.* New York: Palgrave Macmillan.

'Spanien'. arkivnr 301, TKUA.

Swedberg, J. 1707. 'Letter to the deans in Skara diocese', 20 Dec. 1707. UUB.

Thelaus, M. 1716. *Dissertatio gradualis de piratica, quam […] sub præsidio viri amplissimi & celeberrimi, mag Fabiani Törner […] Ad publicum examen modeste defert Magnus Thelaus Helsingus. In audit. Gustav. maj. die 14. Maji anni MDCCXVI. horis pomeridianis.* Uppsala: Uppsala universitet.

Thomson, A. 1987. *Barbary and Enlightenment. European Attitudes towards the Maghreb in the 18th Century.* Leiden: Brill.

Torres Martínez, J. A. 2004. *Prisioneros de los infieles: vida y rescate de los cautivos cristianos en el Mediterráneo musulmán (siglos XVI–XVII).* Barcelona: Bellaterra.

Tyske Kancelli, Udenrigske afdeling, Gesandtskabsarkiver, 1642–1652. RADK.

Vitkus, J. D (ed.) 2001. *Piracy, Slavery, and Redemption. Barbary Captivity Narratives from Early Modern England.* New York: Columbia University Press.

Weiss, G. L. 2011. *Captives and Corsairs: France and Slavery in the Early Modern Mediterranean.* Stanford: Stanford University Press.

17

A World of Distinctions:
Pehr Löfling and the Meaning of Difference

KENNETH NYBERG

Pehr Löfling (1729–56) was a Swedish botanist who studied with Carl Linnaeus in Uppsala and worked in Spain and South America. In the course of his short life he had to navigate a remarkable sequence of new social, cultural and intellectual contexts that confronted him with the challenges of diversity. Meanwhile, as a Linnaean naturalist, making distinctions and producing difference became his preeminent task. Using the example of Pehr Löfling, this chapter explores the many ways in which Linnaeans encountered and defined racial, ethnic/national, biological, social, linguistic, religious and intellectual dimensions of otherness.

In January 1729, the wife of a bookkeeper at the Tolvfors ironworks in northern Sweden gave birth to a son. Barbro Strandman came from a family of clergymen, so it is not surprising that she and her husband Erik Löfling planned for their boy, Pehr, to train for the priesthood when he came of age. The chances were that if he had done so, he would have been able to live out his life in relative comfort as a minister of some rural Swedish parish. But this was not to be. Instead, Pehr Löfling became a botanist in the service of the king of Spain, travelled to the province of New Andalusia in what is today Venezuela, and died at 27 years of age from a tropical fever. At that time he was the leading naturalist in a major expedition tasked with settling a long-standing border dispute between Spanish and Portuguese colonies.[1]

Löfling was one of the so-called "apostles" of the Swedish botanist Carl Linnaeus, a group of 17 or 18 young men who travelled beyond Europe between 1746 and 1799 in order to collect and describe plants, animals and other specimens of natural history. These travels engendered many encounters with "the other" in different contexts around the world, and like few other Swedes at the time the students of Linnaeus were confronted with their own notions of identity and belonging in a multitude of ways. As a group, they were also responsible for a significant share of original Swedish printed travel accounts of non-European regions in the latter half of the 18th century.[2]

Altogether, their writings represent a remarkably rich body of sources on Swedish encounters with "the other" and identity formation during this time. What makes them especially interesting in this regard is that the whole basis of the Linnaean enterprise consisted of producing distinctions out of empirical diversity. What distinctions did they make in their encounters with "the other", and how did they make them?[3]

What follows here is a contribution to this field of investigation divided into two parts. The first, more general, is an attempt to situate the Linnaean "apostles" in their historical and historiographical context and discuss a few major aspects of the world of distinctions one encounters in their writings. The second, more specific, is a brief survey of identity formation and the meaning of difference in the preserved correspondence of Pehr Löfling, spanning from 1749 to his death in 1756. Löfling can be regarded as both a fairly typical Linnaean traveller and, in some respects, rather unusual. What were his encounters with "the other(s)" and his outlook on the world through which he moved? How did he categorize what he experienced during his travels, and with whom did he identify as he did so? How did those distinctions and classifications change, if at all, in the course of his journey?

SITUATING THE LINNAEAN TRAVELLERS

For a long time, the history of "Linnaeus's apostles" was told from a distinctly Swedish and Eurocentric perspective. One of its main themes was the prestige that Linnaean natural history enjoyed in a European context and its importance to Sweden at a time when military defeats had reduced the country from a great power to a minor nation on the periphery of the continent. At times, international scientific exploration has also been considered as morally superior to the direct and overtly violent forms of colonialism in which many other European countries became implicated.[4]

More recently, however, it has become increasingly obvious that it is not possible to distinguish between "science" and "colonialism" as clearly separate and different endeavours. For while natural history did not really bring the rewards to Swedish agriculture, manufactures and medicine that Linnaeus had promised (explicitly or implicitly), it did come to have a lasting global impact as an ever more valuable instrument for colonial exploration and exploitation by great powers such as Spain, Britain, France and Russia. This development coincided with a shift of the centre of gravity of Linnaean science from Uppsala to cities like Paris and, most of all, London, where it enabled processes of knowledge collection and accumulation that were crucial for the evolution of colonialism and imperialism on a truly global scale.[5]

As part of a more general reorientation of the history of science over the last few decades, the literature on this entanglement of natural history, especially botany, with colonialism and processes of globalization has grown rapidly over the last ten to fifteen years. For reasons beyond the scope of this study such currents have only just begun to affect scholarship on the Swedish Linnaeans, including the travelling students. Examples exist, however, and some of these relate explicitly to the specific issues we are interested in here: cultural encounters and identity formation.

One of the most influential voices on the colonial dimension of Linnaean natural history and the images of "the other" belongs to Mary Louise Pratt. In *Imperial Eyes* (1992, new edn 2008), she described some of Linnaeus's main works, especially *Systema naturæ* (1735), as fundamental to the epistemology underpinning European expansion and modernity itself.[6] Pratt argued that the "herborizer" that now "began to appear everywhere" might have seemed like a "benign, decidedly literate figure," but he was in fact an essential part of the whole machinery of empire.[7] Her analysis has, in turn, become a starting point for much subsequent scholarship on the deep connections between natural history (Linnaean or not) and western colonialism, as well as European encounters with and views of "the other" more generally.

Scholarly discussion regarding "encounters" and "the other" has often revolved around the dichotomy of European vs. non-European peoples in the early modern and later eras, in many cases as it manifested itself in the unequal relationship between metropolitan centres and colonial peripheries. While the emphasis on this kind of perspective is understandable, it has also tended to exclude other (types of) encounters and more complex interpretations of the identity formation associated with them. As Pratt herself pointed out, Linnaean systematics was "not only a European discourse about non-European worlds [...] but an urban discourse about non-urban worlds, and a lettered, bourgeois discourse about non-lettered, peasant worlds. The systems of nature were projected within European borders as well as beyond them".[8] Today, many would argue that this interpretation is also too rigid, emphasizing as it does the capacity of "systems of nature" to exercise dominance over the "others", whether European or not. A more nuanced understanding of identity and cultural encounters has emerged, where the sense of belonging is less monolithic and more fluid, changing over time and adapting to new contexts. The "contact zones", as Pratt called the spaces of colonial encounters, were not marked by the simple, one-way exercise of power, but rather by the mutual, dynamic negotiation of identities among all those involved in the exchange.[9] Such an interpretation does not mean that relationships of power were equal – in many cases they were indeed tremendously unequal – but rather that unequivocal European hegemony was perhaps less common than has sometimes been assumed or suggested.

On a more general level, as human beings we rarely have only one set of motives; on the contrary, at any given time there are many different factors – complementary and contradictory – influencing how we act and think. In one sense, therefore, while "the other" is often used to denote encounters between people as representatives of the groups they belong to, it is strictly speaking only applicable to individuals in individual encounters – and even then it is to some extent an oversimplification since individual identities also change.[10] They are diverse, incoherent and fluid, being grounded in many different levels and dimensions of belonging: family, local, regional, national, religious, cultural, social, to name a few.

This means that for Swedes and other Europeans in the early modern era, there were many (types of) "others"; as several contributions to the recent edited volume *Scandinavian Colonialism* (Naum & Nordin 2013) emphasize, then as today identity was multifaceted, fluid and contextually defined and negotiated. This was true also for the Linnaean travellers, who identified themselves and others with a whole range of attributes. Not least important, many of them indeed seem to have felt a strong sense of belonging as "Linnaeans" (although the specific word was not used), an identity that in turn was composed of several signifiers, including but not limited to being "urban, lettered, [and] male".[11]

Approaching these travellers, then, we need to see them on the one hand as individuals, on the other as a group that acted within local and global, constantly changing contexts. In some respects they had a common background of similar experiences and training, but their life journeys took place at different times and along different routes.

In their travels there were also certain patterns that tended to change as the decades passed. For instance, during the first few years most of the "apostles" were in actual fact sent out by Linnaeus himself on journeys that were planned and funded from Sweden, in the process mobilizing the resources of the Royal Swedish Academy of Sciences, the Swedish East India Company, universities and government agencies. From the late 1750s onwards, however, the initiative gradually moved elsewhere as the travels to an increasing degree became associated with European projects for colonial exploration and expansion in Asia, Africa and the Americas.

While this shift is clear in hindsight, and natural history would become deeply intertwined with colonialism in the late 18th century onwards, it was only later that European powers would achieve anything even close to hegemony on a global scale. As Lisbet Koerner has pointed out, by the middle of the 18th century no one could realistically envision such a future and many Europeans still looked to China, for instance, as a civilization equal or superior to Europe.[12] This fact is important to bear in mind when interpreting Linnaean travellers' encounters with and understanding of "the other", regardless of what we know today about the later development of European imperialism and how naturalists – Linnaeus's students and others – contributed to making that development possible.

It is not least in this context that Pehr Löfling is particularly interesting as an example of a Linnaean encountering the world. Many of his fellow "apostles" availed themselves of the infrastructure of the East India trade, Swedish and other, to visit the Cape, India, Java, China, and Japan. Löfling, however, was the first among them to enter into the direct service of a colonial empire, the Spanish, which at this time also happened to be, by far, the largest such empire anywhere. In some ways, therefore, he was an early example that foreshadowed how Linnaean travel would evolve over the next few decades, as the connection between natural history and colonial expansion grew ever deeper and more intricate.

Even this seemingly well-established and extensive colonial domain, however, was often rather fragile, and in many parts of Latin America Spanish forces could only maintain control over coastal areas of varying depth and thin stretches of territory along the main rivers. This was certainly true in what is today Venezuela, where the Spanish had a shallow and tenuous grasp upon the interior. In fact, it was only as a result of the very Orinoco expedition (1754–61) in which Löfling took part that a string of settlements was founded along the Orinoco which, as they grew into towns and cities over the coming decades, would finally secure Spanish control of the area.[13] In that sense, Löfling became involved in not only a colonial, but an actively colonizing enterprise, of which science-based resource mobilization was an essential aspect. Other Linnaean "apostles" would follow, embarking on journeys organized by emerging or existing colonial empires: Johan Peter Falck in Siberia (Russia), Daniel Solander and Anders Sparrman in the Pacific and Indian Oceans (Britain), and Carl Peter Thunberg in southern Africa, Ceylon, Java, and Japan (Netherlands), to mention only the best-known examples.

Earlier scholarship, marked by a view of science as a largely autonomous domain rather than as a set of practices inseparable from the social context in which it is situated, tended to see these travellers as taking advantage of colonial and commercial infrastructure to further their scientific ends. While it may be true that the Linnaeans used colonial institutions for their own purposes, it is however equally accurate to say that colonial institutions used them for theirs. That seemingly trivial observation represents a fundamental change of perspective that is at the heart of much recent work on natural history and colonialism, and should be applied also to the study of Linnaeus's "apostles".

A WORLD OF DISTINCTIONS

The Linnaeans' sense of being Europeans was certainly important in interactions with non-Europeans, as might be expected, but it was clearly not the only identity that mattered to them. They were also Swedes in relation to other European "nations", men in relation to women – there were many female naturalists, some of whom travelled extensively, but the "apostles" were all male – Lutherans when encountering Catholics and Buddhists, and Linnaeans when confronted with scientists adhering to competing traditions of natural history. Today, we might consider such affiliations to be less significant, but perhaps we would be wrong in doing so; if nothing else it is important to understand how they affected the travellers' sense of European identity, since all of these loyalties influenced each other in complicated ways.

For instance, the kind of Orientalism that Edward Said exposed and criticized has left few traces in 18th century Swedish travel accounts of China, several of which were authored by Linnaean naturalists. They certainly contained stereotypes, but these were quite specific and based on earlier European travelogues from China rather than from other parts of "the Orient" – a concept that is barely used in the writings of Swedish travellers at this time. There was an interplay between nationalism, nascent racial stereotypes and religious identities, where the "otherness" of the Chinese depended more on their not being Protestants (or even Christians at all) than on being "Easterners". While the distinction between Europeans and non-Europeans did figure prominently, a Swedish identity defined in relation to other European "nations" and the divide between Protestants and Catholics were both also important. Explicitly "racial" distinctions, however, were rare or non-existent in these accounts.[14]

This is interesting since, at around the same time in the middle of the 18th century, Linnaeus had begun to develop a classification of humans into groups that resembled "races".[15] These ideas were instrumental in the development of now discredited racial research in the 19th century, which in turn became an important justification for not only colonialism and slavery but also the racist ideologies that culminated with the large-scale extermination of Jews and other "undesirables" in Nazi-era Europe. It should be stressed that Linnaeus could hardly have foreseen this outcome, but even so some of his students – especially Anders Sparrman, to whom we shall soon return below – very early saw the dangers of distinguishing different "varieties" of human beings in the way Linnaeus did, and of the latter's lack of interest in the ethical consequences.[16]

Again, however, in this respect as in others there were great individual variations between the Linnaean travellers. Sparrman represented one extreme end of the spectrum, becoming a vocal opponent of slavery from the 1780s onward and often being credited with having influenced the movement that eventually led Britain to abolish the slave trade in 1807.[17] Others, like Pehr Kalm who went to North America in the late 1740s or Carl Peter Thunberg who visited southern Africa, Ceylon, Java, and Japan during the 1770s, perhaps followed Linnaeus more closely; apparently they were solely concerned with their scientific work and how it might contribute to Swedish prosperity and European science (or vice versa), while its repercussions for non-European peoples through its association with existing and emerging colonial empires were of less interest.

Kalm, for example, may have appreciated the indigenous Americans and their culture, but he thought that their marginalization was, in Laura Hollsten's words, "inevitable and even desirable" since they were an obstacle to the efficient exploitation of the natural resources of the British colonies in America.[18] For him, and for Thunberg, the organization of colonies was primarily an economic issue. Accordingly, when Thunberg a few decades later criticized the administration of the Dutch East India Company in the Cape, it was not for their inhuman treatment of Africans but for their failure to develop the commercial and legal infrastructure that was necessary for the colony to grow and prosper.[19]

In the case of Thunberg, however, the attitude towards indigenous people went beyond simple indifference. Many scholars have pointed out that he was not only very derogatory towards indigenous populations in Africa and in Java – whose enslavement he seemed to have accepted or even thought of as natural – but these negative judgments were also associated with a (proto-)racial anthropology influenced by that of Linnaeus. Here we see perhaps a precursor of the kind of Eurocentric and racist evolutionism that would become a staple in 19th-century Europe. If anything, such conjecture is given added weight by the fact that the one instance where Thunberg exhibited some traces of cultural relativism or respect for "other" civilizations was in his account of Japan, which would remain something of a special case throughout the culminating phase of European racism and Eurocentrism in the decades around 1900.[20]

That Thunberg's contemporary Anders Sparrman has often been portrayed as his absolute opposite in this regard is perhaps testament to the fact that there were few obvious patterns in how the apostles' views of "the other" changed over time. Sparrman was not only close in age to Thunberg, but among all of Linnaeus's students this pair had the most extensive and varied travel experience, which entailed encounters with Europeans as well as non-European peoples in different parts of the world. In Sparrman's case that meant a journey to China in the mid-1760s (setting out when he was only 17), a sojourn in southern Africa interrupted for a few years by his participation in Cook's second circumnavigation (with the bulk of the time spent in the Pacific) in the 1770s, and a brief visit to western Africa in the late 1780s (Fig. 17.1).

Sparrman's unflattering accounts of Dutch colonists in the Cape and their treatment of Africans were not unique, as inter-European rivalries and national pride would often manifest themselves through such passages in travelogues; if anything, the theme of other, "bad" European colonizers as opposed to the "good" colonialism of one's own nation was a common trope.[21] What made Sparrman unusual among the Linnaeans was his unambiguous and sustained critique of slavery in theory and practice. Freedom, he argued, was an inalienable right for every human being, against which slavery was a crime.[22] He also explicitly linked the continuing existence of slavery to the demand for labour in the silver mines of Spanish America, whose output in turn was used to pay for Chinese tea, silk, and porcelain.[23] Such discussions of

Fig. 17.1 Portrait of a Pacific islander in Anders Sparrman's account of his travels in southern Africa and as a member of James Cook's second circumnavigation in the early 1770s, *Resa Till Goda Hopps-Udden, Södra Pol-kretsen och Omkring Jordklotet* [...], vol. 1 (1783). The peoples and societies of the South Pacific played an important role in European debates about how to understand and explain human diversity in the last decades of the 18th century, debates in which Sparrman took an active part (photograph by Kenneth Nyberg of a copy in the Gothenburg University Library, reproduced by permission).

humanitarian issues seen in a broader, global context were very rare in the writings of other Linnaean travellers.

In recent years, it has often been this particular aspect of Sparrman's life and work – his seemingly unusual cultural relativism – which has attracted scholarly attention. Unlike many of his fellow travellers, he was capable of seeing himself as "others" saw him and he understood, for instance, how indigenous people at the Cape could find him and other Europeans ridiculous and laughable, rather than the other way around.[24] With that in mind it is perhaps surprising that Mary Louise Pratt, in her critical analysis of the impact of Linnaean systematics, gave Anders Sparrman an especially prominent role, arguing that his depiction of indigenous people in southern Africa deprived them of agency and was more Eurocentric than those of earlier travellers like Peter Kolb.[25]

As Swedish journalist and author Lasse Berg has commented, however, while she might be right in principle she "could hardly have chosen two less suitable objects for comparison" than Kolb and Sparrman. The former often used simple hearsay, while Sparrman engaged in direct conversation with people of different backgrounds and ethnicity and gave voice to their perspectives. According to Berg, very few of Sparrman's many predecessors in the area "demonstrate his level of empathy for native people or his desire to understand how they reason".[26] That assessment also seems to be supported by other scholars who have studied Sparrman's work more closely.[27]

It is important, however, not to exaggerate Sparrman's relativism or its character. In an early speech at the Royal Swedish Academy of Sciences, for example, Sparrman emphasized that "Caffres and Hottentots" lacked the capacity for creating complex societies or "higher" cultures because of their primitive lifeways. There were clearly elements here of an evolutionism that, as in the case of Thunberg mentioned above, is reminiscent of a later time and place.[28] The crucial difference is that Sparrman's opinion was not linked to any notion of races, or the belief that some groups of people were doomed to subjugation or even extinction due to their presupposed inferiority. Instead, he argued for the development of "primitive" societies and explicitly rejected the idea that there were fixed levels of development determined by fundamental biological – that is, racial – differences.[29]

In many ways, then, Sparrman represented what is today considered to be, for better or worse, a typical late-Enlightenment view of humans and the world. On the one hand it emphasized the essential equality of all human beings; on the other it assumed that modern, rational and scientific European civilization was an absolute and universal standard against which all other cultures could, and should, be measured. It is in such a light that Pratt's critique of Sparrman begins to make some sense. As Sörlin and Fagerstedt have pointed out, there was in fact considerable ambivalence in Sparrman's position, since to some extent he did contribute to upholding a colonial order.[30]

This refers, among other things, to his involvement in an ill-fated Swedish colonization project in western Africa, where Sparrman's (but perhaps not all his collaborators') goal was to establish a haven for liberated African slaves. The enterprise failed before it had really begun, but in its conception it carried overtones of both Utopian aspirations and European civilizing missions. It was also deeply incongruous in some fundamental ways, since the whole project depended on the colony's participation in global commercial exchanges that were linked (directly or indirectly) to the slave trade.[31]

It is precisely these kinds of ambiguity and contradiction that make Anders Sparrman such an interesting case when discussing early modern Swedish encounters with "the other", and that is why I have given him so much attention here. For the remainder of this chapter I will focus even more narrowly on another individual, Pehr Löfling, who complicates our assumptions about how 18th-century Swedes understood and related to "others" in quite a different way. He was not as widely travelled as Sparrman or Thunberg and did not live nearly as long, but he was one of the first Linnaeans to be employed directly in the service of a European colonial empire. On his way there he spent several years in its capital, Madrid, where a substantial collection of his papers are now preserved. Like few others, therefore, Löfling can be used to study social, cultural, national or "racial" identities and how they were interrelated in practice, in a single Linnaean life.

PEHR LÖFLING AND THE LINNAEAN CIRCLE

What did Linnaean natural history mean to Pehr Löfling? Was it merely a method or a system, or did it also provide an ideology and an outlook on life? Was it a way to make a living, of building a career, or rather a community that provided life with meaning? As we shall see it was probably a little of all of these, but at some point Löfling must have made a deliberate choice, rejecting the path to the priesthood that was the main route to a social position for most young men of his background at the time, in favour of pursuing natural history with an emphasis on botany.

It was a decision accompanied by rather bleak career prospects due to the scarcity of available posts, and we know that later, in Madrid, Löfling worked tirelessly and very purposefully to lay the foundations for a future academic career in anticipation of his return to Sweden. There is little to nothing in contemporary, independent sources that tells us why or how he was attracted to botany during his early years at Uppsala University, but his arrival there in 1743 must have been something of an encounter with "the other" in various ways. He had studied before, but now he had left the rural setting where he had grown up and found himself in a leading centre of Swedish learning and education. The Linnaean circle, in particular, was a dynamic intellectual environment that attracted many talented young men. Linnaeus was, if nothing else, an inspiring teacher who had an eye for finding talent among his hundreds of students.

In the case of Löfling the discovery of his abilities apparently took a while, but in the summer of 1748 he was given the chance to show Linnaeus his promise as a botanist, which established a more personal and rapidly evolving connection between the two. Soon Linnaeus appointed Löfling to be his son's tutor and his own private secretary, living with the family in their house in the Uppsala botanical garden. Among other duties, Löfling wrote out much of the manuscript to the *Philosophia botanica* (1751), one of his teacher's major works, as dictated by the author.[32] Considering this close relationship, it is not surprising that Löfling became one of the pupils who identified themselves most strongly with the whole Linnaean enterprise. While I have argued elsewhere that Linnaeus's own perspective on the "apostles" and their travels has often been accepted too uncritically, Löfling is one of the few early students who seem to have internalized this outlook and made it their own.[33]

This is apparent already in a letter that he wrote in 1750 to Fredric Hasselquist, another student of Linnaeus, who in the late 1740s had left for the eastern Mediterranean to study the plants and animals of the Holy Land. Here, Löfling repeatedly referred to the honour of being a Linnaean "apostle" like Hasselquist, a term that Linnaeus probably used frequently in teaching and informal settings around this time, but rarely if ever in print; it is also very uncommon in the writings of the travelling students. In his letter, Löfling professed his wish to one day be worthy to follow Hasselquist's example and become an "apostle" himself.[34]

We might dismiss these turns of phrase as mere rhetoric or flattering courtesies, but they also show the kind of discourse that Löfling thought would be appropriate and effective in a letter from one student of Linnaeus to another. In his mind, clearly, there existed such a thing as a community of Linnaean natural historians, bound together by their training, common objectives and loyalty to the endeavour of classifying every living thing on earth according to their teacher's principles.[35]

It is also interesting to see how Löfling related this endeavour to a both broader and more specific community: that of the botanists. Broader, since it included many who did not accept the Linnaean system, and narrower, since botany was only one part, however important, of natural history, Linnaean or otherwise. Here, too, one can trace an influence from his master in the way Löfling often framed botanists as a distinct, clearly-defined group that he identified strongly with. This can be seen in a letter similar to the one just quoted but written from Madrid in 1752. Now Löfling was courting Pehr Kalm, who had recently returned from his voyage to North America, for a share of his rich collections of plant material by appealing to him as "the first Botanicus I have [ever] seen and respect".[36] Similarly, while still in Uppsala in the autumn of 1750, he had complained to another fellow student that Linnaeus had forced him to move out of his house in order to prepare for his exams in philosophy and theology, meaning he had to "leave all the Botanists" with whom he had spent so much time over the last two years.[37]

That Löfling quite early saw himself as a botanist and identified with the Linnaean enterprise does not mean that he lacked a mind of his own or the ability to question his teacher's decisions in scientific matters. But it does mean that these identities were important to him, and as they became closely interwoven with other allegiances – personal, national and religious – in the new settings in which he soon found himself, they would sometimes be the predominant factor in shaping his encounters with and perception of "the other". Only a few months after "leaving the botanists", Löfling was selected for the assignment that would bring him to Spain and South America.

A SWEDE AT THE SPANISH COURT

In late 1750 the Spanish government approved, and agreed to fund, a proposal by Linnaeus that one of his students should travel to Spain to investigate its flora for a few years. Linnaeus named Löfling for the task, and when the latter arrived in the Portuguese coastal city of Porto in July 1751 the dominant impression he conveyed to his teacher as well as his parents was that he was now in "a land, where all is alien to me": the climate, the people, and the culture.[38]

In this new environment, nationality became a relevant and at times important distinction in Löfling's writings. In spaces such as Porto, where people of different backgrounds mixed, he would often mention the nationality of those he interacted with, such as the "Swedish Sea Captain" with whom he sent home plants from Lisbon or the "French Mathematician" Louis Godin who accompanied him on his way from Lisbon to Madrid.[39] When he planned a journey from Porto to Setubal he arranged to go with a Captain Gädda, "for I am safest among Swedish Folk, and Mr. Grill admonished me, not to willingly go on the small Portuguese Caravels, being more dangerous and exposed to the piracy of the Turks."[40]

Soon, of course, the Spanish became the predominant "other" nationality in his life and in his letters. Writing to Linnaeus within weeks of his arrival in Madrid, Löfling included a special section called "Res privatæ" where he discussed the leading Spanish botanists in some detail. Some were rather hostile to him, but several of the most prominent ones were friendly despite adhering to Tournefort's rather than Linnaeus's system in botany. Already at this early stage Löfling looked forward to the opportunity to travel to America, both to see "curious things, and to avoid the eyes of the Spaniards, who do not readily like the sight of foreigners having success."[41] Two weeks later, Löfling again mentioned the great "envy" or hostility towards foreigners in Madrid, and that he felt uncertain about whom he could trust. He also worried that if he ever did get to America it might be difficult to keep writing to Linnaeus, "for there the Jealousy of their lands is infinitely greater still".[42]

These first reports established a recurring theme in Löfling's correspondence during the two years he spent in Madrid: the tensions between the national interests of Spain and Sweden on the one hand, and scientific cosmopolitanism on the other. For the Spanish botanists, there were several reasons to be wary or sceptical of Löfling: he was both a foreigner and a Linnaean. For the botanists perhaps the latter was the more significant factor, while the former may have been more important for officials and politicians whose outlook was that of the Spanish Empire. At least, this is the impression we get from Löfling himself, who seems to have been deeply convinced of the necessity of not provoking the Spanish. He therefore developed strategies to appease and build trust with them from the very start, referring repeatedly to such considerations in his letters back home. He also asked his correspondents not to print any letters without his explicit consent, nor let it be known that he was sending collected specimens to Linnaeus and others in Sweden.[43]

Löfling appears to have been successful in these efforts; his relationship with the Spanish botanists evolved considerably during his years in Madrid, from the first few months of great caution and apprehension to the last of mutual appreciation and in some cases even affection. Despite all his attempts to be accommodating, however, there were times when he clearly felt alienated and very much painted the Spanish as the collective "other" in harsh and unforgiving language. In one such instance he explained that by working hard to adapt and fit in, he had gained trust and friendship so that "the majority love me highly. [But the] general behaviour of the Spaniards I can hardly describe. That they are proud, despising of foreigners, indolent and whoring, are their most common traits."[44]

In the same letter to his friend Pehr Bjerchén, Löfling complained that in order to keep Spanish "envy" in check he was forced to study more of Tournefort's and Vaillant's classification systems than he would have wished.[45] A few months earlier he had written to another former fellow student, Georg Svahn, then in Paris, that while he himself was a Linnaean, "since my arrival here I have intensely studied T[ournefort's system] so that no Spaniard can trump me there. So I understand both [systems], and know the flaws of both."[46] Passages such as these reveal how the perception of "otherness" of the Spanish largely sprang out of his identity as a Linnaean rather than as a Swede – although, as we have seen, that also mattered. For Löfling, Linnaean natural history was more than just a set of principles to observe and classify plants; it was a system of beliefs that permeated his outlook on the world and his encounters with the people inhabiting it (Fig. 17.2).

While botanical discussions and the relationship to Tournefortian natural history dominated Löfling's correspondence with Linnaeus, letters to his parents were mainly occupied with issues of religion. This topic dominated what little space he devoted in all of his writings to describing Spanish culture and society, and aside from scientific loyalties it was primarily religious differences that defined the Spanish – and the Portuguese – as "other" in Löfling's eyes. One of the first things he told his father upon arriving in the Iberian peninsula in 1751 was that Porto's streets were filled by priests, monks, and frequent processions with relics and icons that wound their way from one richly-decorated church to another.[47] Around half a year later, a general exoticism had given way to concern about feeling "exposed to the Spaniards' attacks in Religious matters. I defend myself as well I can, but I fear then to make them into enemies, since for no reason they could leave me in the hands of the Inquisition."[48]

Although the issue was primarily brought up in letters to family and friends, after a few months in Madrid Löfling even told Linnaeus that religion was his most difficult challenge, since "they [the Spanish] much love these disputes" and as a religious people were eager to try to convert him to their own faith. Mostly it was the priests he had to be careful with, for ordinary people had little knowledge of theology and few of them had any clear notion about the differences between Catholics and Protestants. The majority thought Christian and Catholic to be synonyms, so if you were not Catholic you were not Christian. Since they equated the two, Löfling argued that he did not actually transgress against "conscience or either religion" by telling those he met that he was Catholic.[49]

Interestingly and perhaps not coincidentally, there was a parallel here to how Löfling discussed differences of scientific epistemology. Reporting on the state of pharmacology in Spain in a letter in May 1752 to the leading Swedish physician Abraham Bäck, he wrote ironically that Hippocratic medicine was still much esteemed in Spain. He also claimed that the "philosophy" there was still largely based on Aristotle, and since he himself was not very familiar with Aristotelianism the Spanish even doubted that he had studied philosophy at all. He added, "Praise God that it [Aristotelianism] has expired in our seats of learning, where reason has founded a sound Philosophy." It often happened, he noted, that "Philosoph. and Metaphysicum aristotelia were confounded in the same manner as commonly Christian and Catholic."[50]

Fig. 17.2 Bust of Carl Linnaeus from 1859 in the Real Jardín Botánico in Madrid. On its base the name of his student Pehr Löfling (1729–56) is surrounded by those of contemporary Spanish botanists, who for a long time largely favoured Joseph Pitton de Tournefort's system of classification over that of Linnaeus. While Löfling in some respects identified strongly with his Spanish colleagues as fellow scientists, they also represented "the other" to him in terms of nationality, religion, and – perhaps most importantly – epistemological affiliation (photograph: Kenneth Nyberg).

BOTANIST TO THE CATHOLIC KING

Despite Löfling's recurring sense of alienation in Spain and his occasionally derogatory portrayal of its people, he was now closely affiliated with the Spanish Empire. Indeed, Linnaeus addressed several letters to him as "Botanist to the King of Spain",[51] a title Löfling used himself when drafting a letter to the Swiss botanist Albrecht von Haller.[52] This position and Löfling's association with the Spanish Crown became even more pronounced when he was transplanted, as it were, from Madrid to the colonial environment of New Andalusia in present-day Venezuela.

There, he was still a Swede among Spaniards and a Protestant among Catholics, but new layers of identity were added since he was now also a European scientist in a colonial context. The distinction between European (whether defined as "white", "Christian", or "Spanish") and non-European (whether "Indian", "black" or "indigenous") suddenly came to the fore, but Löfling himself never discussed in detail any purely racial classifications of human races of the type that his teacher Linnaeus was developing at this time. In contrast to Thunberg some 20 years later he tended to discuss non-European peoples quite matter-of-factly rather than belittling them, but unlike Sparrman he also did not seem to be particularly interested in the injustice of their treatment at the hands of European colonists.

It was in July 1753 that Löfling began informing his family, friends and patrons, including Linnaeus, that the long-rumoured expedition to America had now been decided upon and that he would join it as chief naturalist, commanding two assistants and two draughtsmen. Addressing Abraham Bäck, he intimated that it would be "a more extensive voyage than I had imagined up to now [...] in a large and fine company of Spanish Gentlemen, Mathematici and Engineers". This turn of phrase about his travel companions, repeated again and again in letters over the coming months, is interesting since it shows that while nationality was still an aspect of identity that mattered, the strong sense of otherness that Löfling had sometimes felt toward "the Spaniards" was now subsiding.[53]

In the preface to Löfling's posthumously published *Iter Hispanicum* (1758), Linnaeus primarily describes the Orinoco expedition as a scientific endeavour, while in reality it was a military operation entrusted to a group of naval officers with connections to, and the resources of, commercial Basque companies trading with Venezuela.[54] This context was more apparent in Löfling's own letters, but in general it is striking how little attention these political and military aspects were given in his and Linnaeus's writings. In fact, what he became deeply involved in was an active, on-going colonizing effort aimed at indigenous populations as well as other Europeans. The expedition had several objectives that were all designed to reinforce Spanish control of the area: settling the border with Portuguese Brazil, countering Dutch incursions in Guiana, and gathering information about local natural resources in order to exploit them more efficiently for the Spanish Crown.

One week after landing, Löfling composed his first letter to Linnaeus from Cumana, the capital of New Andalusia province (which, as he noted, was often simply called Cumana province). The letter was mostly preoccupied with scientific descriptions and Löfling expressed his hopes of making new discoveries in "this unknown part of

America, where no Naturalist has yet trodden".[55] The same day he wrote to his parents about the joy of being able to address them from "this new world" after a successful journey. Giving an account of the Atlantic crossing, he returned once again to the topic of religion, where pressure was now apparently easing in his new surroundings; despite having discussed such issues with the archbishop of Santo Domingo, who travelled on his ship, he told his parents that "on the point of Religion I have been spared, and have also constantly sought to avoid occasions, to awaken such questions."[56]

Six months later, Löfling wrote the only two other letters from Venezuela that are known to have survived (drafts of two more are preserved in RJB II.2.1). Again his letter to Linnaeus was quite brief and conveyed almost no information about the context in which he now worked, except a note about the hot climate affecting his ability to get things done.[57] One day earlier, however, he had once more written to his parents and given a brief description of both the land and the people in "America". Again he mentioned the heat that made it difficult to stay outdoors for most of the day, and then he added, "The land itself is otherwise quite wonderful, always green, always flowering, fair soil, but the forests towards the sea with thorny bushes entirely full." He also talked about the "white people" and the "lesser and black people", describing the former as extraordinarily lazy; it was considered much below their dignity to work with their hands, "whether Spanish or born here in the country."[58]

Löfling then launched into a more detailed account of the various groups of people living in the area, presumably Cumana and its surroundings. There are some discrepancies between the original letter in the Linnean Society of London and the copy in the Royal Swedish Academy of Sciences in Stockholm, but they are minor and the following is based mainly on the original. An approximate translation of what seems to be the finally intended version of the text reads:

> The people consist of 4 classes: 1. Whites, descending from Europeans. 2. Blacks that in Sweden are called Moors, who have come here from Africa as bondservants, but have increased much and a part of them are free, and no longer serfs. 3. Mulattoes, who are a mix of white father and black mother and have several degrees, for the 4th generation makes them almost whiter than the Spaniards themselves. These [the Mulattoes] are either serfs or free. The serfs are sold like other goods for 3 or 400 Riksdaler each and these do all the work that needs doing. [− − − 4.] the Native Indians, and lawful children of the land, of whom some use clothes and some do not […].[59]

In the copy of this letter at the Swedish Academy of Sciences, the wording about the indigenous people is different and partly without equivalent in the original, which is worth quoting:

> the 5th [sic] class is the ancient inhabitants of the land, and native Indians, who before the arrival of the Europeans owned the country. They live in great misery, so that a big part do not use clothes but settle with a patch to cover the natural private parts. These are partly still heathen.[60]

It is interesting to see exactly which labels Löfling used here, and how they were used. "White" and "black" might suggest racial categories of the type that Linnaeus had begun to develop, although (as pointed out earlier) in Linnaean travellers' accounts of China, for instance, skin colour rarely figured at all. Here, however, Löfling was less influenced by his teacher's ideas than by the elaborate system of racial classifications used in the Spanish and Portuguese colonies in South America. This is clear from the appearance of "Mulattoes", a category that would not fit well in the rigid schema of fixed and racially based "varieties" that Linnaeus was working on. Yet Löfling's perspective had not entirely become that of the Spanish colonizers, as is evident from his pointed remark about the Indians as "lawful children of the land".

CONCLUSION

Who were "the others" to Pehr Löfling? As I have tried to show, the answer to that question is neither simple nor stable over time. Löfling classified and described people he met using ethnic, national and (perhaps) racial categories, but the process of "othering" he engaged in was often entangled with other identifications, most of all perhaps with his sense of being a Linnaean botanist surrounded by Tournefortians. How the negative qualities of the latter came to characterize also "Spaniards" as a group is a telling example of how difficult it can sometimes be to know where one mark of distinction ends and where another begins. Such ambiguities illustrate the complexity of identity as well as inequalities of power.

The overall argument I have been trying to make here is to emphasize the range of positions, rather than crude and monolithic views of "the other". What is analytically interesting, if we want to understand cultural encounters and their role in processes of identity formation, is these more complicated patterns and changing relationships between different loyalties and senses of belonging. This will necessarily entail moving, as much as possible, beyond simplistic characterizations and generalizations.

As a final point, this should also apply to the encounter with "the other" that we as scholars experience when engaging with the past. In a sense, what we are doing to the historical sources is what their authors did to "the others" they described. We are conveying an impression of them and of their views that may be more or less well-founded, more or less generalized and simplified. What we often criticize, explicitly or not, in people of the past is the tendency to see identity as singular, static and essential in nature; the very least we can do, then, is not to make the same mistake ourselves. Ultimately, we face the same cognitive challenge of diversity as the indigenous peoples of Spanish America or the travelling students of Linnaeus. It is a challenge that forces us to search for patterns in the past while recognizing complexity, and to acknowledge existing power relations without forgetting that all human beings possess their own agency.

ACKNOWLEDGMENTS

This chapter was written as part of a research project funded by the Riksbankens Jubileumsfond. I also wish to acknowledge the support of the Department of Historical

Studies at the University of Gothenburg, and the generous assistance of the staff at the Archives of the Real Jardín Botánico in Madrid, in particular M. Pilar de San Pío Aladrén and Yara Mostazo Fernández.

Some passages in the first three sections of this chapter are based on material previously published in Nyberg 2008, 2010 and 2012. Parts of the first and last sections also draw on my keynote address at the conference "Encountering the 'Other' – Understanding Oneself", Lund University, 8 November 2013, now available at http://kennethnyberg. org/2013/11/11/text-you-and-i-we-and-they/ (accessed 7 November 2014).

NOTES

1 Rydén 1965; Lucena Giraldo 1998; Nyberg 2008.
2 Lindroth 1978, 239-42; Sörlin & Fagerstedt 2004; *The Linnaeus Apostles* 2006–2012; Nyberg 2009.
3 That question has been touched upon in many studies and there are some more general previous discussions, but so far only a small part of the rich material that the Linnaeans left behind has been used. See, e.g., Broberg 1975; Holmberg 1988, 40; Pratt [1992] 2008; Sörlin & Fagerstedt 2004; Nyman 2013.
4 Fries 1903, 2:86; Selander 1960, 20–1; Sörlin 2000, 60–5; Hodacs & Nyberg 2007, 20–1.
5 Koerner 1999; Sörlin 2000; Stewart 2003; Müller-Wille 2007; Lafuente & Valverde 2007; Bleichmar 2011.
6 Pratt 2008, 24–37; see also Fur 2009, 48; Nyman 2013.
7 Pratt 2008, 26.
8 Pratt 2008, 34.
9 Pratt 2008, 8; Nordin 2013, 210; Symonds 2013, 315; Nyman 2013, 9-15; Skuncke 2014.
10 Horning 2013, 303.
11 Pratt 2008, 37. It should be mentioned that from a gender perspective there was an interesting tension within Linnaean natural history. Pratt has pointed out that on the one hand it had a markedly patriarchal character, with Linnaeus as a father figure in Uppsala and the students, his loyal sons, who travelled the world on his behalf. (As already suggested, in many individual cases Linnaeus was not really the initiator or organizer of his "apostles'" journeys, but that is a different issue and beside the point here.) On the other hand the figure or the ideal of the naturalist was androgynous, decidedly non-combatant and thus not masculine in the same way as the exploring "heroes" of the 19th and 20th centuries. While

gender aspects will not be the main category of analysis here, Pratt's observation is important and much clearly remains to be done in the study of such aspects of Linnaean natural history. See Pratt 2008, 55; see also Schiebinger 1996 and Skuncke 2014, 29.
12 Koerner 1999, 100.
13 Lucena Giraldo 1993, 287–90; Lucena Giraldo 1998.
14 Nyberg 2001, 55–93.
15 Broberg 1975, esp. 206; see Pratt 2008, 32–7 and Skuncke 2014, 35, 72.
16 Sörlin & Fagerstedt 2004, 116.
17 Ogden 2012.
18 Hollsten 2010, 246; see also Fur 2009.
19 Skuncke 2014, 74.
20 Broberg 1993, 78; Sörlin & Fagerstedt 2004, 191; Skuncke 2014, 72–6, 98–9, 285.
21 See Fur 2013, 27–8.
22 Sparrman 1783, 81–2, 213–14; see also Broberg 1993, 75–6.
23 Sparrman 1791, 22–3.
24 Berg 1997, 93.
25 Pratt 2008, 48–57.
26 Berg 1997, 101–5.
27 Broberg 1993, 75–6; Sörlin & Fagerstedt 2004, 152–83, and Nyberg 2012, 25–7.
28 Sparrman 1778, 21.
29 Sparrman 1778, 18.
30 Sörlin & Fagerstedt 2004, 163.
31 Ambjörnsson 1976; Broberg 1993, 79–82; Sörlin & Fagerstedt 2004, 173–6.
32 Linnaeus 1758.
33 Hodacs & Nyberg 2007, 140; Nyberg 2009, 9–10.
34 Löfling to Hasselquist, 11 December 1750, UUB W 836; cf. Hodacs & Nyberg 2007, 142–3.
35 See Koerner 1999, 114.
36 Löfling to Kalm, 15 May 1752, RJB II.2.1.
37 Löfling to Lidbeck, 4 September 1750, LUB

Brevsamling.

38 Löfling to his parents, 31 July 1751, KVA BBS;
    see also Löfling to Linnaeus, 31 July 1751, LSL
    LC.

39 Löfling to Lidbeck, 28 September 1751, LUB
    Brevsamling; see also Löfling to his father, same
    date, KVA BBS.

40 Löfling to Linnaeus, 7 August 1751, LSL LC.

41 Löfling to Linnaeus, 15 November 1751, LSL
    LC.

42 Löfling to Linnaeus, 28 November 1751, LSL
    LC.

43 Löfling to Salvius, [?] July 1751; to Linnaeus, 14
    February 1752; and to Wahlbom, 10 July 1752,
    RJB II.2.1.

44 Löfling to Bjerchén, 8 January 1753, KVA BBS.

45 Löfling to Bjerchén, 8 January 1753, KVA BBS.

46 Löfling to Georg Svahn, 18 September 1752,
    RJB II.2.1.

47 Löfling to Erik Löfling, 7 August 1751, KVA
    BBS; see also Löfling to Erik Löfling, 8 January
    1753, KVA BBS.

48 Löfling to his parents, undated but probably
    December 1751 or January 1752, KVA BBS.

49 Löfling to Linnaeus, 27 December 1751, LSL
    LC.

50 Löfling to Bäck, 15 May 1752, HB MS 27:67.

51 E.g., RJB II.1.6.6 and II.1.6.8.

52 RJB II.2.4.

53 Löfling to Bäck, 30 July 1753, HB MS 27:70;
    cf. Löfling to Wargentin, 1 October 1753, HB
    MS 27:71, and to Erik Löfling, 2 July 1753, RJB
    II.2.1, and 30 January 1754, KVA BBS.

54 Linnaeus 1758, unpag.; Lucena Giraldo 1993,
    105.

55 Löfling to Linnaeus, 18 April 1754, LSL LC.

56 Löfling to his parents, 18 April 1754, KVA BBS.

57 Löfling to Linnaeus, 20 October 1754, LSL LC.

58 Löfling to his parents, 19 October 1754, LSL
    LC; copy dated 29 October 1754 in KVA BBS.

59 Löfling to his parents, 19 October 1754, LSL
    LC.

60 Löfling to his parents 29 October 1754, KVA
    BBS.

BIBLIOGRAPHY

Ambjörnsson, R. 1976. '"Guds Republique": En utopi från 1789', *Lychnos* 1975–6: 1–57.

Berg, L. 1997. *När Sverige upptäckte Afrika*. Stockholm: Rabén Prisma.

Bleichmar, D. 2011. 'The geography of observation: Distance and visibility in eighteenth-century botanical travel', in Daston & Lunbeck 2011, 373–95.

Broberg, G. 1975. Homo sapiens *L: Studier i Carl von Linnés naturuppfattning och människolära.* Stockholm: Almqvist & Wiksell.

Broberg, G. 1993. 'Världens ändpunkt och vändpunkt – Thunberg vid Kap', in Nordenstam 1993, 57–85.

Broberg, G., Dunér, D. & Moberg, R. (eds) 2012. *Anders Sparrman: Linnean, världsresenär, fattigläkare.* Uppsala: Svenska Linnésällskapet.

Daston, L. & Lunbeck, E. (eds) 2011. *Histories of Scientific Observation.* Chicago: Chicago University Press.

Fries, T. M. 1903. *Linné: Lefnadsteckning.* 2 vols. Stockholm: Fahlcrantz.

Fur, G. 2009. 'Andreas Hesselius, Pehr Kalm och synen på indianer', in Fur & Engsbråten 2009, 42–63.

Fur, G. 2013. 'Colonialism and Swedish history: Unthinkable connections?', in Naum & Nordin 2013, 17–36.

Fur, G. & Engsbråten, E. (eds) 2009. *Svenska möten: Hemma och på resa.* Reports from Växjö University, Humanities 18. Växjö: Linnéuniversitetet.

Hodacs, H. & Nyberg, K. 2007. *Naturalhistoria på resande fot: Om att forska, undervisa och göra karriär i 1700-talets Sverige.* Lund: Nordic Academic Press.

Hollsten, L. 2010. 'Per Kalms skildring av resan till England och Amerika 1747–1751 som global miljöhistoria', in Müller *et al.* 2010, 231–53.

Holmberg, Å. 1988. *Världen bortom västerlandet: Svensk syn på fjärran länder och folk från 1700-talet till första världskriget.* Acta Regiae Societatis Scientiarum et Litterarum Gothoburgensis,

Humaniora 28. Gothenburg: Göteborgs universitet.

Horning, A. 2013. 'Insinuations: Framing a new understanding of colonialism', in Naum & Nordin 2013, 297–305.

Jardine, N., Secord, J. A. & Spary, E. C. (eds) 1996. *Cultures of Natural History*. Cambridge: Cambridge University Press.

Koerner, L. 1999. *Linnaeus: Nature and Nation*. Cambridge, MA: Harvard University Press.

Lafuente, A. & Valverde, N. 2007. 'Linnaean botany and Spanish imperial biopolitics', in Schiebinger & Swan 2007, 134–47.

Lindroth, S. 1978. *Svensk lärdomshistoria*. Vol. 3: *Frihetstiden*. Stockholm: Norstedts.

Linnaeus, C. 1735. *Systema naturæ, sive regna tria naturæ systematice proposita per classes, ordines, genera, & species*. Leiden.

Linnaeus, C. 1758. 'Företal', in Löfling 1758, unpaginated [9–22].

The Linnaeus Apostles. 8 vols. 2006–2012. Whitby: IK Foundation.

Lucena Giraldo, M. 1993. *Laboratorio tropical: La expedición de límites al Orinoco, 1750–1767*. Caracas: Monte Avila Editores Latinoamericana.

Lucena Giraldo, M. 1998. 'El Dorado geométrico. La expedición de límites al Orinoco, 1754–1761', in San Pío Aladrén 1998, 23–40.

Löfling, P, n.d. [December 1751 or January 1752]. Letter to his parents. KVA BBS.

Löfling, P. 1750. Letter to Lidbeck, 4 September. LUB Brevsamling.

Löfling, P. 1750. Letter to Hasselquist, 11 December. UUB, W 836.

Löfling, P. 1751. Letter to Salvius, [?] July 1751. RJB, Div.II, Fondo 'Expedición de Límites al Orinoco. Pehr Löfling' (1743–1766), 2.1.

Löfling, P. 1751. Letter to his parents, 31 July. KVA BBS.

Löfling, P. 1751. Letter to Linnaeus, 31 July. LSL LC.

Löfling, P. 1751. Letter to Linnaeus, 7 August. LSL LC.

Löfling, P. 1751. Letter to Erik Löfling, 7 August. KVA BBS.

Löfling, P. 1751. Letter to his father, 28 September. KVA BBS.

Löfling, P. 1751. Letter to Lidbeck, 28 September. LUB Brevsamling.

Löfling, P. 1751. Letter to Linnaeus, 15 November. LSL LC.

Löfling, P. 1751. Letter to Linnaeus, 28 November. LSL LC.

Löfling, P. 1751. Letter to Linnaeus, 27 December. LSL LC

Löfling, P. 1752. Letter to Linnaeus, 14 February. RJB, Div.II, Fondo 'Expedición de Límites al Orinoco. Pehr Löfling' (1743–1766), 2.1.

Löfling, P. 1752. Letter to Bäck, 15 May. HB MS 27:67.

Löfling, P. 1752. Letter to Kalm, 15 May. RJB, Div.II, Fondo 'Expedición de Límites al Orinoco. Pehr Löfling' (1743–1766), 2.1.

Löfling, P. 1752. Letter to Wahlbom, 10 July. RJB, Div.II, Fondo 'Expedición de Límites al Orinoco. Pehr Löfling' (1743–1766), 2.1.

Löfling, P. 1752. Letter to Georg Svahn, 18 September. RJB, Div.II, Fondo 'Expedición de Límites al Orinoco. Pehr Löfling' (1743–1766), 2.1.

Löfling, P. 1753. Letter to Bjerchén, 8 January. KVA BBS.

Löfling, P. 1753. Letter to Erik Löfling, 8 January. KVA BBS.

Löfling, P. 1753. Letter to Erik Löfling, 2 July. RJB, Div.II, Fondo 'Expedición de Límites al Orinoco. Pehr Löfling' (1743–1766), 2.1.

Löfling, P. 1753. Letter to Bäck, 30 July. HB MS 27:70.

Löfling, P. 1753. Letter to Wargentin, 1 October. HB MS 27:71.

Löfling, P. 1754. Letter to Erik Löfling, 30 January. KVA BBS.

Löfling, P. 1754. Letter to his parents, 18 April. KVA BBS.

Löfling, P. 1754. Letter to Linnaeus, 18 April. LSL LC.

Löfling, P. 1754. Letter to Linnaeus, 19 October. LSL LC.

Löfling, P. 1754. Letter to Linnaeus, 20 October. LSL LC.

Löfling, P. 1754. Letter to his parents, 29 October. KVA BBS.

Löfling, P. 1758. *Iter Hispanicum, eller Resa til spanska länderna uti Europa och America, förrättad ifrån år 1751 til år 1756* [...]. Ed. Carl Linnaeus. Stockholm: Lars Salvius.

MacLeod, R. (ed.) 2000. *Nature and Empire: Science and the Colonial Enterprise*. Chicago: Chicago University Press.

Müller, L., Rydén, G. & Weiss, H. (eds) 2010. *Global historia från periferin: Norden 1600–1850*. Lund: Studentlitteratur.

Müller-Wille, S. 2007. 'Walnuts at Hudson Bay, coral reefs in Gotland: The colonialism of Linnaean botany', in Schiebinger & Swan 2007, 34–48.

Naum, M. & Nordin, J. M. (eds) 2013. *Scandinavian Colonialism and the Rise of Modernity: Small Time Agents in a Global Arena*. New York: Springer.

Nordenstam, B. (ed.) 1993. *Carl Peter Thunberg: Linnean, resenär, naturforskare 1743–1828*. Stockholm: Atlantis.

Nordin, J. M. 2013. 'There and back again: A study of travelling material culture in New and Old Sweden', in Naum & Nordin 2013, 209–27.

Nyberg, K. 2001. *Bilder av Mittens rike: Kontinuitet och förändring i svenska resenärers Kinaskildringar 1749–1912*. Avhandlingar från Historiska institutionen i Göteborg 28. Gothenburg: Göteborgs universitet.

Nyberg, K. 2008. *Pehr Löflings Letter-Book in the Archives of the Real Jardín Botánico in Madrid: A Catalogue*. Skrifter från Historiska institutionen i Göteborg 12. Gothenburg: Göteborgs universitet.

Nyberg, K. 2009. 'Linnaeus' apostles, scientific travel and the East India trade', *Zoologica Scripta* 38, Suppl. 1: 7–16.

Nyberg, K. 2010. 'Om ordnandet av global kunskap – Linné och hans apostlar', in Müller *et al.* 2010, 209–30.

Nyberg, K. 2012. 'Anders Sparrman – konturer av en livshistoria', in Broberg *et al.* 2012, 13–34.

Nyman, M. 2013. *Resandets gränser: Svenska resenärers skildringar av Ryssland under 1700-talet*. Södertörn doctoral dissertations **77**. Huddinge: Södertörn University.

Ogden, D. T. 2012. 'Anders Sparrman and the abolition of the British slave trade', in Broberg *et al.* 2012, 141–56.

Porter, R. (ed.) 2003. *The Cambridge History of Science*. Vol. 4: *Eighteenth-Century Science*. Cambridge: Cambridge University Press.

Pratt, M. L. [1992] 2008. *Imperial Eyes: Travel Writing and Transculturation*. London: Routledge.

Rydén, S. 1965. *Pehr Löfling: En linnélärjunge i Spanien och Venezuela 1751–1756*. Bidrag till Kungl. Svenska Vetenskapsakademiens historia 6. Stockholm: Almqvist & Wiksell.

San Pío Aladrén, M. P. (ed.) 1998. *La comisión naturalista de Löfling en la Expedición de Límites al Orinoco*. Madrid: Real Jardín Botánico.

Schiebinger, L. 1996. 'Gender and natural history', in Jardine *et al.* 1996, 163–77.

Schiebinger, L. & Swan, C. (eds) 2007. *Colonial Botany: Science, Commerce, and Politics in the Early Modern World*. Philadelphia: University of Pennsylvania Press.

Selander, S. 1960. *Linnélärjungar i främmande länder: Essayer*. Stockholm: Bonnier.

Skuncke, M.-C. 2014. *Carl Peter Thunberg – Botanist and Physician: Career-Building across the Oceans in the Eighteenth Century*. Uppsala: Swedish Collegium for Advanced Study.

Sparrman, A. 1778. *Tal, Om Den tilväxt och nytta, som Vetenskaperne i allmänhet, särdeles Natural-Historien, redan vunnit och ytterligare kunna vinna, genom undersökningar i Söder-hafvet* [...]. Stockholm: Johan Georg Lange.

Sparrman, A. 1783. *Resa Till Goda Hopps-Udden, Södra Pol-kretsen och Omkring Jordklotet, Samt till Hottentott- och Caffer-Landen, Åren 1772–76*, vol. 1. Stockholm: Carl Deleen.

Sparrman, A. 1791. *Åminnelse-Tal Öfver Framledne Capitainen vid Kongl. Amiralitetet Samt Riddaren af Kongl. Wasa Orden Herr Carl Gust. Ekeberg* […]. Stockholm: Johan A. Carlbohm.

Stewart, L. 2003. 'Global pillage: Science, commerce, and empire', in Porter 2003, 825–44.

Symonds, J. 2013. 'Colonial encounters of the Nordic kind', in Naum & Nordin 2013, 307–19.

Sörlin, S. 2000. 'Ordering the world for Europe: Science as intelligence and information as seen from the northern periphery', in MacLeod 2000, 51–69.

Sörlin, S. & Fagerstedt, O. 2004. *Linné och hans apostlar*. Stockholm: Natur och Kultur.

IV

Conclusions

18

Encountering Some Others and Not Others

LU ANN DE CUNZO

In the prequel to this volume, *Scandinavian Colonialism and the Rise of Modernity*,[1] the authors introduced provincial colonials like myself to exciting new scholarship reconsidering the place and consequences of Sweden's and Denmark's colonial projects in northern Scandinavia, Greenland and Iceland, North America, the Caribbean and Africa. This volume revisits and expands our view of these colonial encounters in Finland, among the Sami in northern Scandinavia, and in North America. We also learn about early modern Sweden's other exploratory and mercantile ventures outside the kingdom – in South America, China and North Africa. Perhaps most important for Anglophone archaeologists and historians of the modern world, this volume illuminates the complicated diversity and arena of contested encounters that was 17th-century Sweden.

Editors Magdalena Naum and Fredrik Ekengren argue that during this period Sweden did not remain on the margins of Europe. Rather the nation and its peoples became collaborators in the creation of modern Europe. Sweden encompassed Finland, Livonia, the German provinces and Danish regions acquired in war settlements, as well as the Sami homeland in the north, Sápmi. In the opening chapter, Per Cornell and Christina Rosén contend that we must begin by distinguishing between "other" (that defined as different in particular settings) and "Other" (alterity, the unknown) in 17th-century Sweden. Home to various European immigrants, ethnic minorities, peasants and noblemen, merchants and administrators, soldiers, sailors, farmers, and craftspeople, urban and rural communities, distinctive regions, Lutherans and Orthodox and others, 17th-century Sweden is difficult to describe. The roles and powers of the state, nobility, and Church varied considerably across the century.

Cornell and Rosén examine the more than 12,000 cadastral maps drafted between 1630 and 1655, inscribing details of farms and settlements that form one measure and document of change, of othering and of the Other in Sweden. The maps themselves "othered" the landscape, severing the connection between it and the people living on it, making it unfamiliar and unknown. They also represented new, *other* landscape practices (such as enclosure) and Other settlement forms that scholars have too easily conflated into hamlet, village, and town. Starting in the Swedish homeland, Cornell and Rosén rightly maintain, and challenging what we thought we knew and the categories our predecessors developed to classify and analyses places, people and objects, is critically important to "encountering" early modern Sweden and Swedish colonialism anew.

As Sweden increasingly engaged with the wider world, Swedes at home and abroad confronted new people, ideas, and commodities that reshaped their world. From maps like the intriguing cadastral specimens Cornell and Rosén scrutinized, church records, merchants' accounts, court cases, imported spices, burned forests, ceramic pipkins, letters, buildings and city plans, sweet gale and hopped beer, newspapers, probate inventories, fur bedding and silk dress accessories, wampum, brass kettles, tax records, *puukko* knives, reindeer bones, and drums, the authors expose a range of experience, from the intimacies of marriage to the physical and cultural distances consciously constructed by travellers transforming "Others" into "others". These encounters occurred, firstly, across the country's borders; secondly, through immigration into Sweden; and thirdly and fourthly through interrelated processes of global exploration and trade, and of colonization.

ACROSS THE BORDER AND BORDER CROSSINGS

Christina Dalhede's work on intermarriage among German, Scottish and Dutch mercantile families in Sweden, Adam Grimshaw's comparative analysis of Scottish and English immigrants to Sweden, Claes Pettersson's portrait of a community of German weavers in a Swedish town, Magnus Elfwendahl's fresh look at the Forest Finns who travelled across the Swedish kingdom in the course of the 17th century, and Kimmo Katajala's study of Lutheran Finn and Orthodox Karelian intermarriage across the eastern borderland of Sweden and Russia together depict a complicated landscape of encounter. They highlight both continuities and disparities of experience, fashioned from a wide array of circumstances and choices.

Swedish, Dutch, German, Scottish and English merchant families across Europe embraced opportunities to expand their networks and international relations through intermarriage, creating a *Misch-Europäer* (mixed European) mercantile elite (Dalhede, Grimshaw) distinguished by multifaceted identities. Imposing national labels on these families misrepresents the nature of early modern international commerce and of these families' experiences. Members simultaneously retained regional identities and established ethnic enclaves under national identities through othering processes that Americanists have modelled, and continuously remodelled, for generations.

It is illuminating to think of the *Misch-Europäer* as embodying a process that had enormous economic and social impact: that enabled merchants to access foreign capital and build monopolies, expand their geographic reach and thereby access to raw materials, new merchandise, and the markets in which to exchange these, while minimizing risk and business costs. Port tax and private mercantile accounts document the astonishing impact of this process. For example, records of one merchant reveal his trading connections to 71 ports throughout Europe. Intermarriage and migration were fundamental to this iterative process, as were the accrual and deployment of material, social, cultural and political capital. Dalhede explains how *Misch-Europäer* merchant families cultivated a specific continental culture of mercantilism, bringing to their new homes abroad European literature, art, music, decorative arts, clothing and foodways. Grimshaw reports that, at least for Scottish and other British immigrant merchants, political service formed another important component of the process.

Elfwendahl engages in a similar intellectual analysis of the othering of the Forest Finns, who moved back and forth across Sweden through the late 16th and 17th centuries, encouraged by the Crown's ambition to increase revenues and promote new settlement in the nation's extensive and sparsely-populated forests. Traditionally, their slash-and-burn subsistence forest agriculture and mobile subsistence lifestyle have defined Forest Finn otherness, reinforced by Finnish cultural practices and language. Archaeological evidence has challenged this stereotype of timeless migratory populations. Elfwendahl and his colleagues contest the imagined isolation of Forest Finns and their inability to understand and incorporate anything new and "modern" into their lifeways. Like other mythic, subordinating histories of underrepresented others, this one denied Forest Finns agency and dynamism. Encounters with the material record of the Finns is yielding new understandings of how cultural interaction contributed to the appropriation of new and stylish objects, and an economic shift to livestock raising and limited agriculture.

In contrast, Pettersson demonstrates that German textile workers enticed to Jönköping in 1620 maintained a physically, culturally and socially bounded and distinctive community, despite extensive daily interactions with the town's diverse citizenry. The textile workers numbered among several specialist immigrant groups attracted to support the King and Council's efforts to rapidly modernize the Swedish economy, and their skills were highly valued. Archaeologists have discovered, unexpectedly, that even the "ordinary" craftsmen among them consumed imported amenities and costly foodstuffs. These German sojourners were effectively "othering" Swedish material life, privileging their continental culture. Like the immigrant merchant families living abroad, they were "ethnic" others; unlike them, however, these German craftspeople could not, even had they wished to, create a *Misch-Europäer* identity and community in the single generation that their industrial enterprise abroad survived.

Lutheran Finns and Orthodox Karelians in Sweden's eastern borderland with Russia similarly maintained a cultural and religious border. The disruptive political, economic, legal, and religious change characteristic of unstable border zones led to heightened anxiety over group identity and autonomy. Katajala shows that by the last decades of the 17th century Finns and Karelians were living side by side, yet sustained, and perhaps elaborated and highlighted, their cultural, religious, familial and even architectural differences. Nonetheless, men and women sought to marry across religious denominations. Through close reading of the documentary record, Katajala has discerned the complexity and contested nature of the approval process, and how successful both communities were at limiting intermarriage. In the volatile, opportunistic, fluid space of this borderland, Lutheran Finns and Orthodox Karelians chose retrenchment, social enclosure and "othering" to negotiate what they perceived as a threatening rather than propitious situation.

GLOBAL EXPLORATION AND TRADE

While Germans, Scots, Dutch, Finns and others were crossing borders into Sweden, Swedes crossed the same borders heading in the other direction. Among them were explorers, and perhaps the best known are the so-called "apostles" of Swedish botanist Carl Linnaeus, who travelled the world collecting and describing plants and animals in the latter 18th century. Their travels occasioned many encounters with Others, and their writings comprise a significant share of Swedish travel accounts beyond Europe's borders. Kenneth Nyberg introduces us to Pehr Löfling. In his short life, which ended at the age of 27 on an expedition to Venezuela, Löfling reflected on his own identity as he categorized the people he met. His letters from Spanish America offer wonderful insight into his notions of identity and belonging. Gender, nationality and "continentality", religion and occupation emerge as most meaningful to him, even as race is revealed as the primary feature of differentiation he applies in categorizing others. In essence Löfling appropriated a simplification of the Spanish colonial *casta* system that had its origins in Old–New World encounters two and a half centuries before he ventured beyond Sweden's shores.

Four authors delve into the ways global trade in raw materials and commodities shaped early modern Sweden: Göran Tagesson analyses its impact on Sweden's urban infrastructure, specifically in Kalmar; Jens Heimdahl interrogates beer, a commodity deeply entangled with European regional identities; and Lisa Hellman and Joachim Östlund examine Swedes and the "Orient".

Seventeenth-century urban policy, planning and construction in Sweden served the Crown and Council's modernizing ambition in many important ways. International harbour towns such as Kalmar were the portals through which new people, goods and ideas penetrated the nation's borders. They enhanced the nation's infrastructure for global trade and as a consequence became spaces dense with the disruptive threats of the Other. Tagesson describes Kalmar as a sort of reified, "Lutheranized" place that introduced Renaissance-inspired cultural sophistication into the northern European borderlands. The new plan for the town "mentally and structurally divided [it] into [two] part[s, …] as an idealized structure mirroring a hierarchical society […] in equilibrium". Its divisions, with their architectural and landscape homogeneity, thus imposed a naturalized order on the built environment that worked to discipline the destabilizing capacity of difference.

Jens Heimdahl turns our attention to that archaeological favourite, beer. Like, and yet unlike today, brewing traditions and preferences varied between geographical regions and social groups. Heimdahl enquires into the transformations in meaning that beer underwent in northern Europe in the centuries following its secularization. His study of imports into and exports from Nya Lödöse on Sweden's western coast reveal that in this era before corporate branding, beer types showed deeply-rooted regional patterns. Swedes maintained a strong preference for beer traditionally flavoured with sweet gale, more than a century after their continental counterparts in northern Europe developed a taste for hopped beer. This was not attributable to unavailability. In this period, Sweden conducted extensive trade with Europe, and as we shall see, China and the Ottoman Empire.

Östlund and Hellman's work explores the ways the "Orient" has long been the Other in the eyes of Europe and vice versa, encounters contained and constrained within brokered places like Canton and Kalmar, and the ships that moved goods, people, and ideas between them. Hellman details the complexity of these liminal ports of global trade for understanding early modern Sweden and its place in the world. Focusing on Canton through the lens of the Swedish East India Company, she begins with the crucial point that many of the officials were Scotsmen, and that indeed the company was a multinational place of work in which nationality was a fraught and far from evident identity. Neither were the "Chinese" traders a homogeneous group. Her question, then, is how trading *worked* in this contest for positions of power in negotiating value and "winning" the goods. How, and who, could one come to trust in this world of fluid alliances and battles of wits? Her research suggested that a particular intercultural trope of "masculinity" emerged, through which trust and thus trade were enabled between individuals and small groups, whatever national trading company they represented. Attending funerals, hosting dinners, joining the Freemasons' lodge, conversing in Pidgin English and exchanging secrets crafted a shared masculine identity and behaviours that sufficiently masked and/or transcended their internal othernesses.

While traders in Canton shared bottles of wine and planned their next moves, corsairs roaming the Atlantic and Mediterranean disrupted trade. Between 1650 and 1770 they captured and enslaved approximately 1,000 Swedish subjects sailing with the merchant fleet. Most passed through North African slave markets, and about half ultimately returned home. For the others, captivity meant hard work on board ships, in port harbours, and in private service – the price that the Swedish state paid to import directly food-preserving salt. The resulting encounters between merchants, diplomats, soldiers and captives, Östlund contends, yielded a multi-dimensional discourse on North Africa and Ottoman slavery in newspapers, alms appeals and books that simultaneously confirmed and challenged European stereotypes of the "Orient".

COLONIZATION

In their concluding commentaries on *Scandinavian Colonialism and the Rise of Modernity*, Audrey Horning and James Symonds[2] respectively characterize colonialism as "insinuations" into and "entanglements" wrought upon everyday life. The archaeology of everyday life illuminates warfare, enslavement, diaspora, social marginalization, institutional oversight and other forms of chronic colonial interference.[3] Colonialism matters, Horning and Symonds concur, because its legacies remain unresolved and still pervade our lives today. Our task, they affirm, is to disrupt the dichotomies of self and other that reified in the context of colonizer and colonized, and to query agency from different perspectives. We build our current understanding of the colonial process on historical contingency and collaboration, mutable and negotiated identities, syncretism and hybridity. Seven authors enrich our appreciation of the complexity and humanity of these processes in New Sweden and Sápmi: Magdalena Naum, Jonas Nordin, Fredrik Ekengren, Matti Enbuske, Anna-Kaisa Salmi, Annemari Tranberg and Risto Nurmi, and Carl-Gösta Ojala.

Magdalena Naum and Jonas Nordin write of Swedes' ambivalence toward America coupled with the ambiguity of objects in this (and other) colonial places. Naum evokes the experiences and emotions of Swedish colonists arriving in America with European imaginings of a splendid and wild utopia. Deadly encounters with indigenous flora and "primitive Indians" fuelled new imaginings and projections of their experiences and preconceptions on to the Other. Ambivalence remained, rooted in their simultaneous desire for the colonized to become like them and need for them to remain different. Not unlike global traders in Canton, Swedes and Lenape forged a co-dependency on a common ground negotiated through creative and sometimes consciously misinterpreted mimicry. Naum develops the important point that this process "colonized" not only the Lenape but also the Swedes, disrupting their traditional ways. Although they worked to domesticate the alien spaces of what their sovereign and mercantile elite named New Sweden and to fashion meaningful and familiar landscapes, taskscapes, and homes, the places remained other than Sweden.

Ekengren turns his gaze directly on the Lenape, the native inhabitants whose landscapes the Europeans' actions de-familiarized and thereby othered. His is an "archaeology of shared histories, [...] an archaeology of *becoming* in which categories of colonized and colonizer must necessarily be troubled and treated with suspicion".[4] Surveying mostly "prehistoric" archaeological evidence as well as "historical" letters, reports, travel accounts and maps by European actors between 1638 and 1655, Ekengren mapped Lenape and Swedish sites. Analysis of the settlement pattern revealed six locales of shared residence and potential community. Like Naum, Ekengren interprets these hybrid Lenape-Swedish landscapes as what Richard White first described less literally as "middle ground".[5] In the mid-17th century, the analogy of islands of middle ground in a sea of native ground seems apt, with the principal contests for the Lenape still in the future.

Half a world away, the Swedish Crown was engaging another indigenous Other, the Sami people in the north of the realm. Ojala asks how archaeology can contribute to a more complex understanding of colonial histories and encounters in Sápmi. Enbuske examines economies of land value and use. He argues that the Swedish Crown was deeply invested in sustaining Sami otherness, recognized Sami people's unique status, and protected their migratory lifestyle through tax structures. The unit of taxation shifted from individual family heads to family land, then Sami villages, and ultimately reindeer and farms. Economically the system increasingly favoured a Sami "other ground", literally and figuratively, of reindeer herding, and an "improved agricultural ground" for Swedish immigrants practising farming, distinctions that survived as stereotypes well into the 20th century.

Salmi, Tranberg and Nurmi also highlight the incompatibility of Sami identity and traditional way of life with Sweden's nation-building agenda. They approach the question through the lenses of urban planning and foodways in Tornio, Finland, a port town the Swedish Crown founded in 1621 to control regional trade. In the later 17th and 18th centuries, the town was home to a typically colonial array of diverse Finnish, Scandinavian, Russian, and Sami "others". Urban space was structured on a grid plan and plots were enclosed after the European fashion in a process parallel to that described by Tagesson for Kalmar. Domestic material culture and food became increasingly hybridized. Modern European table knives met traditional Finnish, multi-purpose *puukko* knives, richly endowed with symbolism and power. Table knives joined, rather than replaced, *puukko* in the social performance of identity and value in this cosmopolitan outpost at the head of the Gulf of Bothnia.

Sami sacred ceremonial drums, *sieidi*-stones, wooden objects and other emblems of Sami otherness, including human remains, were purposely both destroyed and appropriated during colonial acculturation efforts. Some reside in European national museums, given to heads of state as symbols of Sweden's imperial diplomacy. Today, they represent cultural identity, rights, and empowerment for Sami people, and their repatriation is demanded. Ojala's interest in a more "complex" understanding of Sápmi and its indigenous inhabitants is not merely academic. Sápmi's history is one of fluid, strategically defined, and contested borders deeply implicated in current controversies over Sami land claims and self-determination. He reminds archaeologists of the need for vigilance and reflection on our responsibilities to the people whose pasts we study.

RETURN TO OTHERNESS

"Otherness" is that fundamental category of social interaction involving two or more groups with different assumptions and structures of meaning through which they make sense of life and function within their world.[6] The Other "reminds us that we have a choice: (a) to try to understand and accommodate our experience of strangeness, or (b) to repudiate it by projecting it exclusively onto outsiders". Confrontations with otherness subvert established categories, disrupt cultures and destabilize the shared order.[7] It is in the struggle to transform the Other – the unknown – into the other – the different but known – that change takes place.[8] The scope and scale of early modern encounters with Others made negotiating otherness a particularly pervasive structural feature of the era.

In the early modern era, a host of images, artefacts, and narratives of a "natural and social cosmos wholly unlike theirs" assaulted mid-17th-century Europeans.[9] Especially in colonial contexts, otherness was often imagined as a cultural binary comprised of European and Indigenous. Classical, Christian, and aristocratic ideological traditions contributed to Western thinking that native peoples were something other than fully human, objectifiable for use, transformation, or destruction as European superiors desired.[10] This view reified the dichotomy in simplistic ways that ignored the complexities of identity and the personal nuances of interaction.[11] Group identities, recorded by chance during the first few decades of European colonial interaction, tended to "become rigid categorizations of race, language, and 'Other', both retroactively for the deep archaeological past [...] and through subsequent centuries of colonial impact."[12] In essence this imaginary of otherness preserved the "imperialism of the Same", and still does today.[13]

Material objects contribute to propagating this "imperialism" when directly translated as proxies for behaviour and group identity. Archaeologists translate assemblages into sociocultural qualities that merely reproduce these essentialized tropes, especially those of European and Indigenous. Doing so denies people the "ability to be something more, less, or other than the categories" our cultural historical narratives impose.[14]

This volume's authors counter this impetus through detailed attention to the forms, components, manifestations and workings of othering in early modern Scandinavia and the increasingly global context in which the region's people participated. Their analyses all incorporate four central elements: identity and group formation, forms of cultural expression, contexts of encounter, and interpretive concepts. Sophisticated approaches to identity have ensured that complex intersections of national, ethnic, geographic, occupational, economic, social, religious, gendered, racialized, legal and political priorities, motivations and world views are interrogated. Multiple cultural forms and media are scrutinized. In the built environment, these include land use and landscapes, settlement forms, architecture, livestock and crops. In the home and on the body, possessions such as furnishings, art and dress are queried. Behaviours, rituals, ceremonies, performances and labour practices receive attention. Language, narratives, aesthetics and taste are deconstructed. All are analysed in the context of the purposes, nature, material settings, institutional structures and unintended consequences of encounters between strangers. Concepts of distancing, distinction, hybridity, syncretism, power, appropriation and mimicry provoke and inspire interpretation.

... AND NOT OTHERS

In concluding, let us return to one of Ojala's questions: Whose history is told, and from what perspective? And, by extension, whose is not? One of the first Swedish historical archaeologies I read was Anna Lihammer's *The Forgotten Ones: Small Narratives and Modern Landscapes*.[15] Lihammer contributes compelling "small narratives" about impoverished people in Sweden's "slumlands" and about "demonized groups" like travellers, refugees, the landless and hidden, institutionalized people.

In this volume, we have met immigrants to Sweden from across Europe, a community of Lutheran Finns and Orthodox Karelians, Swedish scientific explorers, traders in Canton, captives in North Africa, colonists in New Sweden, and indigenous Lenape and Sami people. Arguably, not all of them experienced exclusion or marginalization like the subjects of Lihammer's narratives, but they did influence the shape of early modern Sweden and its place in Scandinavia and the larger world. And of course, in a single volume, we cannot expect to meet everyone. Nevertheless, there were some others present in these narratives who appear in outline, or perhaps in shadow, and not as three-dimensional characters, as actors, as individuals.

Consider family. In this volume's narratives of encounter, some authors situate families at the centre of the story, some reference family, and others implicate family. Dalhede and Grimshaw, for example, analyse the development of pan-European merchant and manufacturing family businesses. In these narratives, families emerge as a site of intimately negotiated and mediated cross-cultural encounters. They are also portrayed as clearly patriarchal and patrilineal. Daughters and widows emerge as objects of exchange who *were* married (the passive voice specifically indicating others' agency, not their own) to create alliances among families and expand dynasties. Serial monogamy among widows "doubled" the connections and assets the next husband acquired. And this practice had further multiplying effects over generations. Indeed, both authors argue, marriage substantially broadened these families' base of capital and connections. Kinship rituals such as weddings and baptisms reinforced these connections across generations. Less clear is how men *and* women worked actively to broker the cross-cultural engagement essential to creating the cultural *Misch-Europäer*.

These chapters and others raise further questions about gendered and familial relationships, roles, responsibilities and identities in the early modern period. Scandinavian patronymic naming practices, residence practices, rituals and the use of fictive kin all warrant further consideration. Which communities were patrilocal? What happened when men and women with different traditions of postmarital residence intermarried?

How did these and other patterns change across generations? How were children enculturated into familial culture? How did they resist or transgress family traditions? How did families "other"? How did families incorporate others? What objects embodied and inscribed generational and gendered family connections and identities?

I measure the success of a volume by the questions it provokes in readers, and the new research these questions prompt. The work of these authors has raised provocative and challenging questions, and contributed substantive foundations on which to build in new directions. They model postcolonial approaches to European homelands and colonies that account for the complex dances entangling Europeans and the indigenous in the modernization project without reducing the former to the empowered privileged and the latter to the victimized other.

NOTES

1 Naum & Nordin 2013.
2 Horning 2013; Symonds 2013.
3 Ferris *et al.* 2014, 12.
4 Harrison 2014, 51.
5 White 1991.
6 Rozbicki & Ndege 2012, 1–2.
7 Kearney 2003, 4; Rozbicki 2012, 207.
8 Isherwood & Harris 2013, 164.
9 Mandalios 2000, 92–3.
10 Mandalios 2000, 106.
11 Beaudoin 2014, 314.
12 Ferris *et al.* 2014, 4.
13 E. Levinas's term, cited in Bergo 2011.
14 Ferris *et al.* 2014, 1.
15 Lihammer 2011.

BIBLIOGRAPHY

Beaudoin, M. 2014. 'The process of hybridization among the Labrador Metis', in Ferris *et al.* 2014, 315–32.

Bergo, B. 2011. 'Emmanuel Levinas', in Zalta 2011, http://plato.stanford.edu/entries/levinas/ [accessed 11 May 2016].

Ferris, N., Harrison, R. & Beaudoin, M. 2014. 'Introduction: Rethinking colonial pasts through the archaeologies of the colonized', in Ferris *et al.* 2014, 1–34.

Ferris, N., Harrison, R. & Wilcox, M. (eds) 2014. *Rethinking Colonial Pasts through Archaeology*. Oxford: Oxford University Press.

Harrison, R. 2014. 'Shared histories: Rethinking "colonized" and "colonizer" in the archaeology of colonialism', in Ferris *et al.* 2014, 37–56.

Horning, A. 2013. 'Insinuations: Framing a new understanding of colonialism', in Naum & Nordin 2013, 297–305.

Isherwood, L. & Harris, D. 2013. *Radical Otherness: Sociological and Theological Approaches*. Bristol, CT: Acumen.

Kearney, R. 2003. *Strangers, Gods and Monsters: Interpreting Otherness*. New York: Routledge.

Lihammer, A. 2011. *The Forgotten Ones: Small Narratives and Modern Landscapes*. Stockholm: Museum of National Antiquities.

Mandalios, J. 2000. 'Being and cultural difference: (Mis)Understanding otherness in early modernity', *Thesis Eleven* 62: 91–108.

Naum, M. & Nordin, J. M. (eds) 2013. *Scandinavian Colonialism and the Rise of Modernity: Small Time Agents in a Global Arena*. New York: Springer.

Rozbicki, M. 2012. 'Cross-cultural history: Toward an interdisciplinary theory', in Rozbicki &

Ndege 2012, 207–19.

Rozbicki, M. & Ndege, G. (eds) 2012. *Cross-Cultural History and the Domestication of Otherness*. New York: Palgrave MacMillan.

Rozbicki, M. & Ndege, G. 2012. 'Introduction', in Rozbicki & Ndege 2012, 1–12.

Symonds, J. 2013. 'Colonial encounters of the Nordic kind', in Naum & Nordin 2013, 307–19.

White, R. 1991. *The Middle Ground: Indians, Empires and Republics in the Great Lakes Region, 1650–1815*. Cambridge: Cambridge University Press.

Zalta, E. (ed.) 2011, *Stanford Encyclopaedia of Philosophy*, Fall 2011 edn, http://plato.stanford.edu/ [accessed 11 May 2016.]

INDEX